"DELIVERY IS POWER"

WRITTEN BY

SHAZADI BAIG

Unlock the pleasure of reading and attain intellectual growth!

BRIEF INTRODUCTION:

DELIVERY IS POWER:

Islam captivates many people. This religion emphasizes personal and communal morality and respect for the divine. Contentment comes from genuine belief and faith. The truth reveals its tenacity to those who seek it.Analyzing beliefs' impact on openness to change affects faith concepts, ideologies, receptivity, and contrasts in instinctual effects.

Those who follow Islam are familiar with its beliefs and practices. It may be burdensome for some to commit. The commitment to Islam and its regulations is a privilege for some. Time is a constraint for others. Worshiping Allah is a global phenomenon.

I used my finest brushes to paint this arena. I'm confident the strokes will be appreciated. No rules, limitations, or obstacles to my writing or dreams. Take a moment to listen, read and learn what I am about to share.

The human body is more spacious than gadgets. Islam values refraining from making assumptions about others' feelings or words. Allah hears the heart's silence, loudness, and pleas. The assumptions about others' thoughts are noteworthy. Assumption is incomprehensible rhetoric.

Understanding truth distinguishes us from noisy blamers. Only Allah judges, human judgments can be based on assumptions. Guessing or assuming is not Islam because you cannot guess what is on my next page.

The Golden Age of Islam and the Ottoman Empire is a revered period in Muslim history. Negative scenarios result from overthinking, while a positive mind brings fulfillment in life. My thoughts are shared as Allah permits. I am not accountable for your reaction to my journey.

My book is a tribute to Islam. We owe our allegiance to Allah in our pursuit of truth. Closed doors hinder truth due to errors and doubts. My references include Hadiths, the Quran, text, and observations. I analyze the contrasting aspects of Western society, Islam, and Christianity with a focus on the Abrahamic faith of Islam. Cultural adaptation contrasts diverse cultures and Islamic beliefs. Islam does not follow trends, it progresses.

My comparison of Islam and Abrahamic faiths is not extensive, but it sufficiently shows the nuanced differences. Differences endure in reflection and solitude. Despite contrasting views of Christianity and Islam in a diverse society, friendships remain unaffected.

The contrast is neither negative nor positive, but life's challenges are crucial for understanding Islam. Contrast between society's portrayal and reality. This venue aims to educate the masses, inspired by Muslims for decades. I analyze the influence of diverse societies on Abrahamic faiths and showcase Islam's development. Societal evolution cannot ignore Islam's truth.

Arabic was chosen by Allah for revealing the Quran. Humanity's contribution lies in comprehending life's concepts and stories. The Quran is best grasped through language proficiency. But every language has a power of learning and delivery. Islam's truth flows from the heart, no sketch necessary.

Religious votive images and passions are enjoyable. Exploring distant lands deepens comprehension. Observing, learning, and teaching are priorities in the Islamic faith. Everything aligns perfectly. Your path is determined by your root search. Destiny controls everything. Allah's plan includes all creatures.

Alhamdullilah "praise be to God"...

TABLE OF CONTENTS

CHAPTER 1

UNDERSTANDING ISLAM IS THE STARTING POINT

(Bismillahir Rahmanir Raheem).In the name of Allah, Most Gracious, Most Compassionate.

Allah's mercy knows no bounds, for He is the All-Merciful. He is the Lord of all good and the Worlds. Allah is unparalleled and His blessings are limitless. Sleep, food, and human traits are absent in him. His mercy knows no bounds and His power is unrivaled. He is the all-seeing Creator, the source of eternal blessings. Allah is the only God.

He owns time and doesn't calculate life or hours like humans. Effective time users see abundance, while those who waste it feel scarcity. This application is open to all, irrespective of their emphasis on material possessions for success. Those feeling time slipping away need Allah to extend their timings.

It is necessary for Muslims to take the initiative to clarify the true teachings of Islam. When faced with baseless negativity against Islam, a Muslim would bravely confront and challenge it. By speaking the truth and amplifying voices of truth, we can make a significant impact. Social media platforms persist in being a detrimental source for anti-Islamic narratives. The portrayal of Islam as corrupt and deceitful on the shores of misinformation is not only a nuisance but also a source of havoc and a distortion of the truth.

Given the current circumstances, it is crucial to present Islam accurately and without misleading connotations. Islam strives to transmit the truth in a manner that is respectful and free from any form of negativity towards any faith or person. Living in this world without raising one's voice against those who manipulate the truth using social media platforms would render the existence of a Muslim meaningless. Islam, being a self-sustaining belief system, does not require protection, but lies are in need of correction.

The belief in one God, specifically Allah, is not only the beginning but also the ultimate culmination of faith. The unyielding belief of Muslims is that Islam will be the final chapter as this world reaches its end. In every era, the truth stands firm, fortified by substantiating evidence rather than empty rhetoric. The principles of Islam include humanity, kindness, and the voice of truth. Despite the echoes of the call to Muslim prayer resonating worldwide, determined Muslims uphold and express their faith, refusing to let it be overshadowed by false misrepresentations.

Allocating a grant to enable the exploration of Allah's mercy and the teachings of his Prophets is a compassionate provision of refuge. The ability to contrast differences is both a grant and mercy. It is a privilege to grasp and comprehend concepts. It is quite fascinating to note that there are certain individuals who possess the unique capability of actively listening, whereas others are blessed with the exceptional gift of sight. It is important to note that there are individuals who possess the ability to speak verbally, but encounter difficulties in effectively expressing their thoughts and emotions.

The ability to present oneself with simple smiles and truthful ways has the power to captivate those who are in search of something and ultimately bring them contentment. When a believer is in the company of another believer, they experience the positive energy and momentum that comes with it. We can witness the mercy of Allah in this, as His words hold more value than any precious metals. In an increasingly declining market for lifestyles, there is a specific aim to perceive precious metals or materials. Through the coexistence of two believers, the stillness of the heart seeks to convey a sense of inner peace. In a battle of opinions, one believer who stands firm is equivalent to a thousand disbelievers.

In this world, there exists a diverse range of individuals, including both believers and disbelievers. It is widely recognized and appreciated by the majority that maintaining a clear distinction between ethics and moral codes for both business and personal life is of utmost importance. Friendships are not influenced by the spiritual context, and humans develop affection for one another as long as they adhere to the fundamental moral principles of care and understanding.

The ability to recognize and empathize with the emotions of others is a characteristic that humans highly value. The collective efforts of many individuals to support each other are commendable, yet the detrimental impact of greed, arrogance, and a tendency for chaos cannot be overlooked. Any use of force is rendered unnecessary due to the presence of truth in Islam. There are numerous unanswered events that leave us with lingering questions deep within our subconscious.

There is no alternative but to follow the revealed truth. This application applies to daily life, and the voice seeking the Creator is within everyone. Finding truth is tough for those living in doubt and succumbing to peer pressure. It's for the bold seekers who confront their inner spirit and truth. Facing fears and accepting reality takes courage and strength. The truth sets us free and aligns us with our purpose. Some silence it, feeling its heaviness, while others welcome and crave to know more.

This truth can bring peace and contentment to anyone who pursues it. With understanding and acceptance, one can find true joy and fulfillment in life. All life's highs can become lows, and vice versa. This is the bitter truth that keeps finding solace to find peace within. Accepting this truth can be difficult, but ultimately, it can lead to a more meaningful life.

The heart yearns for a sense of tranquility and fulfillment, just as the soul experienced peace prior to its arrival on this Earth. It is in search of the same belief that brings about peace and contentment from within.

To attain the desire and inner peace found in Allah through "dhikr", engaging in discussions about Allah with a believer, and experiencing happiness in the face of adversity is a universal longing shared by every human being. The pursuit of happiness drives humans towards the flashbacks. Islam stresses the importance of raising children in the most appropriate way because it recognizes the significance of this.

When an individual is in pursuit of happiness, they often traverse the familiar path of reminiscing about memories that have provided them with a sense of solace and contentment. In order to prioritize their inner soul and happiness, the same individual retreats from any path that does not support these aspects of their life. Within the context of our spicy society, it is common to encounter both noise and nuisance. In the realm of human nature, people have a tendency to gravitate towards the beginnings that provide them with a feeling of contentment.

The act of finding a path after getting lost is preferable to the alternative of losing everything. Islam is not just a religion, but also a profound way of life that brings solace and enlightenment to its followers. Similarly, a believer in Islam is not merely a person of faith, but someone who has found a deep connection with their spirituality. The path to true happiness lies in aligning oneself with the inner soul's desires and following the teachings of Islam.

2

The distinction in today's society lies because those who discovered true contentment in the era of the prophet Muhammad made a conscious decision to avoid returning to the same challenging situations they had previously escaped. Their words did not convey fondness for the days of ignorance in the "Jahiliyyah" era. It is related to a state of ignorance. In contrast, they moved forward with a completely different approach instead. In place of stating their opinions outright, they opted to show that their true beliefs were clear through their observation of the shift.

The comments that conveyed distress regarding a life that does not align with Allah's approval were swiftly suppressed and eventually faded into oblivion. Today's society serves as a stark reminder of the actions and mistakes that were not pleasing to Allah in the past. It is a prudent decision to let go of things unless they can bring about positive change and make up for them.

The act of repentance is common among numerous individuals, including present-day believers, who acknowledge their transgressions and seek Allah's forgiveness. The memory of mistakes, when transformed into repentance, becomes a vivid reminder rather than a burden. Time is in conflict with time. Those seeking truth and contentment often find that constant reminders are in their favor. The reason why some people lack confidence is because they are constantly envious of others. Those individuals who have a strong foundation cannot be influenced or affected by the negativity of haters and enviers. Many lives have the potential to be transformed by the act of holding their ground.

LIES DON'T ABANDON THE TRUTH.

The world's reality and the human soul ultimately strive to find balance. The rewards of strength and courage await those who persevere and stand firm. Standing up for the truth can be challenging for those who seek society's approval and acceptance. The result makes it all worthwhile for those who boldly speak the truth, even when faced with lies. It's never too late to embrace your true self and fight for what is right. To make a lasting impact.

Regardless of the specific religion that individuals developed, it was commonly inherited from their parents, even if it happened to be paganism. They placed great importance on both educating and instilling faith in their children. Over the course of time, certain individuals have the capacity to convert challenges into resounding victories. The extensive documentation of these victories has been ensured by Allah and, undoubtedly, by the world that will inherit their legacy.

Those who decide to join the enemy and undergo a change in their attitudes are standing on uncertain ground. The believer does not conform to the shallow discourse of others, maintaining their own attitude. The unceasing exploration for truth and the perpetual analysis of this truth, considering pressing questions and an inherent curiosity about Islam, become essential in order to reconcile any disparities that may arise.

When comprehension of Islam transforms into a state of comprehensibility, and society's perception shifts, it is our duty to articulate the mirage of light rather than decadence. Just like a thunderbolt accompanied by rain, the revelation of truth concealed by light has the power to rejuvenate the earth, giving rise to the growth of trees and habitation. Muslims do not need to protect Islam's faith. The faith of Islam is under the ownership of Allah. The ultimate authority over the finality of this faith lies with Allah.

In this corrupt and unpalatable market, where the climate is harsh, the expression can oscillate between cold and warm in coherence. When we express gratitude and understanding, we create a space where contrasts can be openly discussed and acknowledged as opportunities.

The individuals residing in Western cultures and adhering to antiquated ideologies is a diverse mix of cultures and learning. Combining the principles of Islam with the expectations and pressures of society can be a significant hurdle, akin to overcoming a series of week-long challenges. Defending the truth is essential when it comes to achieving a harmonious equilibrium between solitude, isolation, reflection, detachment, and derailment. The coherence and truth within humanity are both influenced and strengthened by the presence of these elements.

By practicing their faith, Muslims have the opportunity to demonstrate an extraordinary model of an alternative lifestyle that challenges the prevailing cultural norms. This can provide a valuable and enriching opportunity for individuals to come together, learn from one another, and gain a deeper appreciation for the diverse range of cultures, faiths, and belief systems.

Ultimately, the ultimate outcome of this can be the establishment of a society that is characterized by peace and understanding. The contrasting expressions of truth and ideologies, with their significant impact, fail to redirect the course of humanity's mutual relations as individuals. The integrating of pseudo-culture into our society, a diverse and inclusive environment that encourages the exploration and comparison of the Abrahamic faiths became necessary. There are some people who are acquainted with the achievements and knowledge of Muslims, but for many, these accomplishments and expertise are completely foreign.

Allah has endorsed Islam as the only true faith, and the Quran remains the untouchable and unaltered book. While statements may be bold, truth is fearless. Lies have a way of stalling, but the truth is always swift and decisive. The plasma of truth reveals itself in a seamless manner, devoid of any turbulent waves that might impede the smooth delivery of the message and prevent it from reaching the intended recipient.

Growing up in a Muslim household while residing in Western countries provides individuals with a distinctive outlook on life. Although the world may seem unchanged on the surface, the rise of alternative ideologies that challenge traditional values and principles has resulted in a decline in ethical behavior. While they may be perceived as innovative, ideas that endorse chaos are experiencing a surge in global popularity.

The worth of cultures and beliefs that differ from those of the outside world is often questioned by many individuals. The consequence of this is a lack of connection between the modern Westernized and adapted society and those who still adhere to ancient traditions. Islam is often blamed for the decline of society, but interestingly, they actually embraced the vibrant traditions of the pre-Islamic pagan era.

The evolving society is dedicated to bridging the gaps that were left behind by the previous generation, as it recognizes the importance of unity and progress. However, it is important to acknowledge that the ethical codes of numerous nations do not align with the fast-paced and interconnected nature of this modern world. Moreover, traditional Western society is still grappling with the difficulties of adapting to the harmful consequences of this deceitful modern society.

Amidst the rapid and chaotic developments of the Western world, the uniqueness and individuality of a home are ultimately determined by its inhabitants. Throughout history, certain ancient societies have demonstrated an unwavering commitment to their ethical codes, while others have unfortunately succumbed to lesser ideologies and regressive modes of thinking, which Islam firmly rejects. Outside forces have the ability to sway individuals who are weaker, leading to a situation where some individuals gain faith while others lose it.

On the other hand, individuals who have the qualities of strength and resilience are capable of successfully navigating any ship they may come across. Despite their best efforts, it is possible that someone may not find Allah's truth within the environment they were raised in. Nevertheless, there are certain individuals who have been raised with a strong Islamic faith and are able to demonstrate remarkable resilience and adaptability in navigating the challenges posed by a society that is shrouded in veils and governed by outdated ideologies.

The majority of individuals tend to seek peace and gravitate towards what is familiar, however, there are those who actively pursue new experiences and willingly let go of the old. The existence of prophets serves as tangible evidence that this faith can manifest itself in surprising locations and degrees. Those who are blessed with beauty should ensure that ugliness does not take its place.

In the quest for comparative study and understanding the essence of humanity, it is essential to recognize that the usefulness of criteria and thoughts lies in their ability to enhance our inner pursuits and our understanding of others. The majority of people who waste time are often dedicated to pondering the lives of others while neglecting their own surroundings. The things that are encompassed in this are not only life failures, but also the temptations of Satan. Time is the most valuable commodity in life. It's important to remember that your faith is a personal journey and should be prioritized and worked on.

A meaningful life requires finding the right equilibrium between understanding others and focusing on your faith. The pursuit of truth and reality opens up endless possibilities. If Allah grants permission for it to take place. Who is Allah? God is denoted by this word in Arabic. Understanding the literal description is crucial for readers to comprehend Muslims' perspective on their faith.

SWT is an abbreviation for Allah Subhanahu Wa Ta'ala, which signifies our praise and devotion to the most merciful Allah SWT, and it is exclusive to Allah, not God (SWT). The Arabic name Subhanahu Wa Ta'ala means "the most glorified, the highest," and it is used exclusively for Allah. In Islam, Allah is the name used to describe the higher power, also known as the Creator, as the term God can be ambiguous. Greek Gods and goddesses are among the deities known as gods. Allah is singular, and Islam is distinct.

Allah's name symbolizes his qualities. The nature he possesses is reflected in each of his names. In times of distress, the worshiper can address him as Al Basir: the all-seeing. Allah records all of those names. Ar Rahman: Al Wahid: the singular one. The Hadiths have been compiled by Muslims for better understanding. Allah can be invoked through 99 distinct names, each with a significant meaning.

Quran: Surah Ta Ha 20:14 "Surely I am Allah, there is no god but I; therefore, worship Me and keep up prayer for My remembrance."

Muslims show respect and allegiance by adding Sallallahu Alayhi Wa Salem (SAWS) when addressing Prophet Muhammad. Muslims equally respect all Prophets mentioned by name in the Quran. Muslims incorporate PBUH peace be upon him as a sign of respect when referring to the Prophets of Allah. These abbreviations signify respect. The same principles are followed by Muslims.

Islamic mandate includes respect as a core component. You can't transfer these abbreviations. The foundations of Islam are integrity, trust, moral values, ethics, and modesty.

Faith is the symbolic value of life that a man hold's heart. Following Islam involves tracing the truth fairly and diligently. The message of Allah has consistently been the same for both humanity and the jinns throughout history. The only one deserving of worship is Allah. Every prophet conveyed an identical message to humanity.

The Quran's use of "We" when Allah addresses himself may raise questions or surprise readers. The Quran states that Allah is the sole entity deserving of worship. "We" make a coherent statement in Quranic passages as Allah addresses and delivers. The doctrine of Trinitarianism is not followed in Islam. Muslims cannot accept or establish a Trinity through the word "We" in delivery. There is only one God, and that is Allah. Arabic possesses an unmatched elegance and style compared to any other language. "Nahnu" is the word we use to show respect when glorifying Allah.

In ancient times, monarchs employed the term "We" when speaking publicly. "We" is commonly used by politicians in various cultures for their addresses. Islam is concluded by a closing statement in the Quran. Allah created a faith that emerged through life. Consistency is present in all prophetic prophecies. What is your definition of Islam? Muslims follow the monotheistic religion of Islam, believing in one God, Allah, and Abrahamic Prophets. The last messenger is Prophet Muhammad. A Muslim is someone who follows Islam and submits to Allah's commands and will. Prophet Muhammad is accepted as the last and final prophet of Abrahamic faiths and Islam.

Islam holds the distinction of being the oldest faith among many. Adam and Eve held this faith. Monotheism. Every prophet sent by Allah shares this faith. It could be argued that Islam came later, and the Quran served as the last testament. Muslims acknowledge Islam as the oldest religion. The protocol of Allah has not changed. Despite the fluctuation of other religions, Islam, as a monotheistic faith, cannot disappear. The general belief is that Adam and Eve worshiped Allah. Allah was worshiped by Abraham, the father of all Prophets. Muslims worship only Allah; clarity is essential for understanding the unchanging trail of belief since creation.

It existed at the world's creation and will exist on Judgment Day. The Islamic world and belief system offer limitless opportunities for those who seek to share, but are limited for those bound by social trends. In Islam, it is mandatory to show respect to all Prophets of the Abrahamic faith and the Creator, Allah.

The Bible does not contain the word Trinity. Tortellini, the writer, not Jesus, was the one who introduced it. The Quran mentions the Trinity as a form of opposition.

Muslims do not accept dignitaries or any polytheistic concepts. Islam believes in the existence of a single God. In Islamic concepts, the three did not merge into one, and the one did not divide into three. By comparing Abrahamic faiths, we can examine theological differences and variations in faith acceptance. The worship of Muslims revolves around a single God. By eliminating doubts, we can differentiate all concepts.

Bible: Luke 24:19."About Jesus of Nazareth," they replied. "He was a prophet, powerful in word and deed before God and all the people.

The adoption of auricular confession as a sacrament and the establishment of the doctrine of the Trinity were indeed controversial decisions made during the council of Nicea in 325 CE. Emperor Constantine, who had recently converted to Christianity and sought to unify the empire under one religion, played a significant role in shaping the outcomes of the council. The inclusion of auricular confession allowed the church to exert control over the spiritual lives of believers, as priests were given the power to absolve sins and grant forgiveness.

This practice, however, raised concerns about privacy and the misuse of personal information. The doctrine of the Trinity, which declared the three-in-one nature of God, was a departure from the monotheistic teachings of Jesus, who emphasized the worship of one God. The council's decision to adopt this doctrine was influenced by theological debates and political considerations, rather than a direct derivation of Jesus' teachings. Nonetheless, the doctrine of the Trinity became a foundational belief in Christianity and shaped the understanding of God for centuries to come.

It is important to note that the concept of one human taking away the sins of another is a central belief in Christianity. According to Christian doctrine, Jesus Christ, as the Son of God, willingly sacrificed himself on the cross to redeem humanity from its sins. This act of atonement is seen as a unique and divine act that only Jesus, as both fully human and fully God, could accomplish. Confession, as practiced in Christian traditions, involves the act of confessing one's sins to a priest for Catholics. This practice is based on the belief that priests have been given the authority by God to forgive sins on behalf of the Church.

In contrast, Islamic tradition places a greater emphasis on confessing sins directly to Allah. Muslims believe that Allah is all-knowing and forgiving, and that sincere repentance and seeking forgiveness directly from Allah is sufficient. Confessions to other individuals are not encouraged, unless it is to seek guidance or assistance in rectifying one's actions. The influence of religious authorities in shaping societal norms and controlling the masses is a complex issue. While historical figures like Constantine used Christianity as a means of exerting control, it is important to recognize that religion can also provide moral guidance and a sense of community for believers.

Regarding the promotion of celibacy, some Christian denominations, such as Catholicism, have historically upheld the practice. However, monotheistic faiths do not indoctrinate celibacy. In fact, many religious figures in monotheistic traditions, including Abraham, were married and had families. It is crucial to approach discussions about religion and its impact on society with nuance and respect for differing beliefs and interpretations. While there have been instances of exploitation and abuse within religious institutions, it is unfair to generalize and condemn an entire faith based on the actions of a few individuals. It is important to separate the teachings and core principles of a religion from the actions of its followers.

Regardless, it is important to make it clear that humanity is entering a highly charged phase where Islam does not necessitate a metamorphosis, but instead invites understanding.

An example is the story of the wolf:

The wounded wolf doesn't ask other wolves for assistance. Instead, he conceals himself in either a cave or high up in the mountains until he can recover. This instinctual behavior showcases how animals protect themselves when injured. It emphasizes the significance of self-care and resilience.The wolf gains strength as its wounds heal. Life lessons are learned by the wolf through wounds it experiences. His strength and wisdom grow, allowing him to confidently tackle larger challenges. His resilience grows with every hardship he conquers.

Life is filled with joys and letdowns, both anticipated and unforeseen. Unlike Christianity, Islam views pain and pleasure as a confession solely to Allah or a believer who can provide assistance. In

Islam, pain and suffering are viewed as a means of spiritual purification and strengthening faith in Allah. Muslims are advised to maintain patience and gratitude in the face of adversity.

They are taught to depend on Allah for emotional and spiritual support during tough times. Confessions to disbelievers will never bring peace to practicing Muslims due to their contrasting mindsets. Humanity will always assist one another, regardless of faith. Only Allah decides a Muslim's intricate life paths and answers.

A reliable Muslim who can provide guidance without engaging in gossip or spreading rumors. Muslims are not allowed to participate in frivolous rhetoric that could harm their faith.To gain strength and value your own decisions, it is imperative to have knowledge, education, and understanding of theology. Just like the wolf telling the truth is strength not weakness.

Constantine, the Roman Emperor, played a significant role in the development of theology in Christendom. In the 4th century, he called for the Council of Nicaea, which aimed to address theological disputes and establish a unified belief system within Christianity. During this council, the concept of the Trinity was introduced and eventually adopted as the orthodox belief of the Christian faith. However, this decision was not without opposition.

Arius of Alexandria vehemently opposed the idea of the Trinity, arguing for a more unitarian view of God. Despite his resistance, the majority of the council voted in favor of the Trinitarian doctrine.The introduction of the Trinity brought about significant changes in Christian theology and worship practices. People began to perceive God as a triune being, consisting of the Father, Son, and Holy Spirit. This shift in understanding led to alterations in the interpretation of biblical texts, as the concept of the Trinity was applied to various passages. These modifications, however, were not widely known to the general public, who accepted them wholeheartedly without awareness of their historical origins in Constantinople, Turkey.

The theological changes introduced by Constantine and the Council of Nicaea sparked ongoing battles and disagreements within Christianity. One of the major conflicts emerged between Protestants and Catholics. Some individuals fought to preserve the traditional forms of worship, including the veneration of deities and statues, which were deeply ingrained in Catholicism.

On the other hand, others embraced a more simplified form of worship without statues, aligning themselves with the Trinitarian belief introduced by Constantine.It is important to note that Constantine's actions during this time have been regarded as deceitful by some historians. They argue that he manipulated the people to accept the Trinity, leading to centuries of confusion and division within Christianity. Nevertheless, the impact of these theological changes cannot be denied, as they shaped the course of Christian history.

Throughout the years, Turkey's lands have witnessed numerous battles and victories, often intertwined with religious conflicts. The region holds a rich historical background, and understanding this history is crucial in making informed decisions about personal religious beliefs and practices. Factual knowledge about the origins of theological doctrines can aid individuals in making choices about their worship, enabling them to navigate the ongoing battles and controversies that persist within the Christian faith. Additionally, recognizing the role of Satan in sowing discord and confusion is important in maintaining a steadfast and informed faith.

Bible: King James Version: Exodus 20:Thou shalt not make unto thee any graven image or any likeness of anything that is in heaven above, or that is in the Earth beneath, or that is in the water under the Earth:

Analyzing changes in the Bible becomes easier by understanding their origins, which are not influenced by Jesus. Only the creator holds forgiveness, but humanity holds hope in Allah. Believers can only hope for forgiveness and repentance, but Allah holds all finality. The introduction of rebirth in Christendom has taken place, as those with rebellious pasts get rebaptized and seek forgiveness and call themselves reborn. Every faith seeks forgiveness but naming it born again falls out of monotheism as monotheistic beliefs have no reincarnation, not even the same human evolving with new rebirth. The revelation of this doctrine exposes its clear non-compliance with monotheistic faith guidelines. Jesus referred to Allah as Allah Ha, the only God. Jews rejected all of it and are waiting for a Messiah from the lineage of David, including their rejection of Jesus.

The theological differences between Islamic concepts and the Torah or the Bible result in dramatically different stories. The dogmas in other scripts have undergone a complete shift. The Quran is stationary. According to Islamic belief, Jesus will remain a prophet and the Messiah, not attaining divinity, while spreading the same message. Changing Allah's protocol is impossible. Jesus preached the same message as the other Prophets: worship one God, Allah. Ascribing divinity to human Prophets or adding partners to Allah is considered blasphemous shirk by Muslims.

According to the Abrahamic faith, Islam considers this sin as the only one that is unforgivable. This might come across as harsh to some due to its clarity. Lies disrupt human existence when humans remain ignorant, while truth is devoid of violence. In the Abrahamic faith, laws seek to soften hearts through truthfulness.

Quran: Surah Nisa:4;116 Indeed, Allah does not forgive association with Him, but He forgives what is less than that for whom He wills. And he who associates others with Allah has certainly gone far astray.

For Muslims and Islam, attaching anything to Allah is a grave sin. He is the Creator, the owner of both worlds present and the here-after. Far beyond a human to attach his divinity to any human. If a person dies without repenting, Allah will not forgive this sin. Regulations and rules are clear. It is not a matter of force but of information and clarity for those who believe if one follows the theme of the belief system and explanation. Islam clarifies Jesus as a separate identity. Muslims did not regard him as co-equal or as a partner with Allah.

Allah sends miracles through prophecies and continues showing his miracles in this world. One of his miracles was the birth of Jesus without a father to a virgin mother, Mary. No miracle is too big for the creator. But the human mind has weak concepts that don't fathom his majesty for those who don't believe. Jews rejected Jesus' birth as a prophet.

Later, Christians made God his father. Muslims regarded him as a miracle who came about as a Messiah. Only as a prophet, no miracle is too big for Allah. Similarly to Christians, Muslims believe Jesus is the Messiah but also do not grant him any divinity or coexistence with Allah. Islam affirms that there is only one God, and Jesus is his servant and Messiah.

Bible:7:21:27. Jesus says something quite astounding: many people call him Lord, but he doesn't know them and calls them workers of Iniquity.

Jesus did not refer to himself as a Christian or introduce the name Christianity. This name only propagated after his ascension to Allah.

Bible: Acts 11;26. And in Antioch, the disciples were first called Christians.

As the Quran is clear in its delivery, it tolerates no reforms or negligence of human hands, and it will not alter it to suit the fashions of humankind. Most people do not understand what the Abrahamic faith is, so these distinctions clarify it for them. Abrahamic faith means monotheism, as Abraham was a monotheist. Anyone who cannot meet this standard is devoid of Abrahamic faith. Prophets also occupy a prominent place in these books sent by Allah. The stories and presentations differ dramatically from the Quran.

The purpose of contrasting beliefs is not to create hostility but to explain the differences and origins of belief systems. They have altered stories many times in certain doctrines. Muslims, therefore, can only pay attention to stories consistent with the Quran. The distinctions provide clarity for those who don't understand what the Abrahamic faith is. Though humanity has progressed in understanding, many still cannot comprehend Allah's messages. Islam was the faith of all Prophets.

We will continue to understand Islamic submission to Allah. Submission to God was a message of all Prophets. Islam was the religion of Adam and Eve. They were the first Muslims. Humanity may wonder how it can be. The answer is simple. The two first humans created by Allah submitted to the will and command of Allah, proving they were Muslims. They worshiped one God; Islam is monotheistic. Islam was born with humanity.

The pre-Aryans of Eastern India are traditionally and historically known as the first religions. Muslims are clear about the episode of faith that stems from Adam and Eve. This faith Known as Islam, its beliefs have remained unchanged since its inception. Thus, the faith of Adam and Eve began with submission to Allah, which later strengthened and emerged in Islam.

Why did Allah not reveal the faith at the beginning of creation and call the faith of the first creation Islam? Throughout the ages, Allah's commands have not changed or become imbalanced; humanity has always been required to obey him alone. The rules of Islam haven't changed, but the name of Islam came later through Muhammad, the last prophet. Islam was the faith of all Prophets.

Allah's timing is beyond questioning by humanity. He is the Creator, knowledgeable of both the seen and unseen. The Quranic explanation of monotheism aligns with the faith of Adam and Eve, making Islam the faith of the first creation. The Quran, which is the closing statement of monotheism, came into existence through Prophet Muhammad, the last prophet.

Abraham was committed to the same faith. No books were sent by Allah during that period; belief in monotheism was the only option for a faithful heart, regardless of the absence of written texts. The absence of books for Adam, Eve, and Abraham may raise questions about Allah's intentions. The answer is uncomplicated.

Humanity's times and capacities for receiving and understanding have been set by Allah. The biblical books were sent by Allah through the chosen Prophets of that era. With Prophet Muhammad's departure, Allah did not disclose any more books, establishing the Quran as the last testament of the Abrahamic faith. In various stages, Allah revealed the Quran to humanity. The Quran and Islam are followed by Muslims. Allah is supreme in all things. Muslims adhere to this belief system.

Success for a Muslim is not material success. Inner peace, which results from serving Allah, measures it. Allah blesses such humans with plenty of favors. The academic achievement and all worldly measures with their belief in Allah and submission to Him. This is a genuine success. The Creator feeds all his creatures, believers and disbelievers alike. It is Allah's mercy for humanity, but disobedience to Allah has a price, as it has for generations and throughout history.

In history and the present, humans have consistently disobeyed Allah for many centuries. Material success is not synonymous with obedience to Allah. It is the success of a believer that differs from the success of a disbeliever, and the heart of a disbeliever does not possess the same contentment.

Worship of others than Allah does not mean Allah will not provide worldly gains. It's the inner peace that nothing can buy except obedience to Allah. Pagan worship continued to grow, with new Gods and Goddesses created and worshiped, colorful celebrations, and human sacrifices. You name it; they wreaked plenty of havoc in this colorful society of disobedience to Allah. The pagan worshipers held a polytheistic belief. Majorities gave supremacy to some Gods. They assigned tasks to each God according to their preferences, and they worshiped statues as Gods.

The emergence of Islam abolished all polytheism and brought humanity back to the faith of Adam and Eve. It also brought clarity and a name to this faith called Islam through the chosen last prophet of monotheism, Muhammad. He called the Prophets of the Abrahamic faith brothers of the same faith as Abraham was a staunch monotheist. The same Prophets appear in all the Abrahamic faiths. If a faith falls into the category of Abraham, any additions fall short of monotheistic belief. And added deities are no longer on the pendulum of Abrahamic faith.

The one who follows the Abrahamic faith is a monotheist, not a polytheist. As the earth's water dried up and hearts dried up, Islam was born as earth-borne flowers nourished by water and faith-filled the heart of the Arabian Peninsula. Allah has delivered books and revelations through different Prophets according to mindsets.

Quran: Surah Al Dhariyat 51:56 I did not create humans and Jinns except to worship me.

The arrogant err in disobedience. Islam strives to learn and worship one God (Allah). A lousy company is a proxy for ill health. An unsatisfactory lifestyle. There is a frightening display of incompetence, inferiority, and premeditated insults to believers, to those who choose a different path.

Satan has retaliated beyond repair. He realizes the truth only after he has lured his own. His company does not meet his or her needs. He is grudging and unfulfilled. It is apparent to him that his landing leaves him unsatisfied. The outcast between Satan and his partisans.

Allah has given humanity limited knowledge. The reprieve Allah granted Satan also has limitations. Gratitude can sometimes be high. Sometimes the tide is low. Those who waver in faith are sadly misguided by doubts from no other than the accursed Satan. Allah leads believers into the company of believers. Will Allah guide those who disbelieve after believing in Him?

Quran: Surah Imran 63 But if they turn away, Allah is aware of the corrupters.

A Muslim who follows Islam knows right from wrong. Making mistakes is not a reason for leaving Islam. Instead, it opens up the possibility of repentance to rid oneself of injurious companions. Humanity is born knowing Allah, according to Islam. Every child is born a Muslim. Each soul knows Allah is his Creator.

Allah established these bounties thousands of years before souls arrived on earth. His purpose in life is to worship Allah. He was allegiant to Allah even before entering his mother's womb. It is the parents or guardians of the child who direct or misdirect his guidance and beliefs. Few were privileged to be brought up as Muslims by the will of Allah.

Some of them converted to his faith Islam after being raised in another faith. It can only happen if Allah invites them to his faith. Some raised in the faith of Islam don't appreciate beauty. It is the voice or delivery of one who touches the heart of the other. This makes the change and renewal of the faith of birth necessary to worship Allah.

Allah plants the seed in the hearts of those who seek Him. It is He who directs them to goodness and guides them directly. Or sometimes Allah sends a *'khareen,'* a friend who keeps advocating the same path. This is a genuine friend. Many will lose the road along the way; others will reach the heights.

Worship of Allah is an allowance for a sound heart. Being exposed to Islam as a child at a young age is of the utmost importance. Converts are like children who have had their souls cleaned when they accept Islam. He invites anyone he wishes to join his faith.

Stalling faith after seeking it has detrimental effects and causes souls to become confused. Islam emphasizes the expansion of knowledge and learning, along with the association of believers. Muslims who revert to Islam or who grow up in a Muslim environment are eligible to apply with the permission of the highest authority.

For some requests, Allah answers immediately, while for others, he answers at his discretion. Allah hears and understands every sound and whisper. The moment a believer raises his hands. It reaches the Creator. Humanity's connection with the master is diabolical on the master of the universe, and this connection can occur without appointments or secretaries.

When a human's prayer comes to pass by the will of Allah, some turn away in disrespect and arrogance. As he stood by for the better part, he eventually forgot that he had turned to Allah when he was struggling. Such humans are unfortunate. He sometimes sacrifices his beliefs for those who do not believe in Allah.

As some humans experience unexpected rewards after the trials of life, they become closer to Allah. It replenishes one with more when he maintains a grateful attitude. Core values and beliefs strengthen. No disbeliever can influence the emergence of solidarity that comes with trials for a believer. There are no offspring, parents, friends, or relatives in the likes of Allah's divine power, and no one can claim their place.

Allah and Islam hold the highest authority. No one can stand between Allah and a believer. Islam is submission to the will of Allah. The followers of Islam aim to submit to "His" will. They derive the root word Islam from submission and surrender. A convert to Islam may find himself or herself at a crossroads with a non-Muslim family.

Transformation of the environment requires an exit. Muslims who accepted Islam with the Prophet Muhammad left contaminated waters for fresh waters and a fresh start in learning and commitment. Muddy waters would not satisfy someone who drank clear water. Throughout his life, Allah exposed humanity to many unexpected and expected currents of life. A few currents can break for some years. And some currents can savor every moment. There is no way to predict the course of life.

Islam is the belief in monotheism and submission to Allah's will instead of our own. A plateau of understanding and comprehension lies between a firm belief that slowly rises and a shaky foundation that sinks beneath. Islam is a religion that requires understanding and comprehension to follow. Those who are capable are not susceptible to external peer pressure. There is nothing excessive about a Muslim who prays five times a day. Islam mandates the (Salat) ritual prayer five times a day at specific times. The sublime truth of its existence is without cracks.

Quran: Surah Muminun 23;115. Did you then think that we had created you without purpose and that we would never return you to us?"

Allah designed a purpose for every surviving being. Allah invented nobody without a reason. They left instructions on how to operate the robot for the operator. Allah did not leave a human without instructions on how to survive.

Life unfolds and folds at the most unexpected times. Allah has written the rules and laws of destiny. Despite advances in technology, the excuse of inadvertence is no longer valid. Human nature dictates that we worship Allah in subtle ways or through our inner voices. By deterring humans from following the straight and misdirecting them to the narrow path, Satan leads them astray. The absence or tardiness of a Muslim would create barriers that would hinder peace, and why would any Muslim want to miss life at its fullest?

Allah sent the "Taurat" Torah to (Musa) Moses. The children of Israel received "Zabur" from David (Daud).The book of Psalms. A message from (Isa Ibn Maryam) Jesus to the children of Israel in the Book of "Ingel". The Bible. The Muslims received the "Quran" through the Prophet Muhammad.

In the Quran, Allah mentions the children of Israel frequently and the favors he has given to them. Whether Allah favors a nation or an individual depends on their negligence and disobedience. It was because of disobedience that Jews experienced exile twice. Jews in Israel who were once favored by Allah were exiled for disobedience, highlighting human arrogance. Allah's anger and wrath resulted in the relinquishing of favoritism.

Quran: Surah Baqarah 2:47.O children of Israel! Remember My Favor, which I gave to you, and that I preferred you over all the nations.

Revelations of the Quran to the Bedouin people of the Desert of Saudi Arabia through Prophet Muhammad. The Quran is the only book to reach the Saudi Hot Desert from the Arabian Peninsula. The children of Israel received other books from Allah. Allah revealed the revelations of Islam to humanity as the last testament.

Islam has five pillars.

The first belief is Shahada's belief in One Allah and Prophet Muhammad, his servant, and his messenger. It is the testimony of a Muslim. Performing the Second Salat mandatory ritual prayers with body and mind five times a day is mandatory for Muslims. There are no exceptions or excuses.

Third: Zakat almsgiving. This pillar of Islam is compulsory for the gainful, who can afford to contribute 2.5% of their earnings. If you cannot give, you are eligible to receive. Helping humanity is at the heart of these funds. Fourth Sawm fasting Muslims observe the fast in Ramadan from sunup to sun down.

Allah mandated fasting for this month, although restrictions for ill health apply to sick, pregnant, menstruating women, and breastfeeding women. The fast is for Allah and the complete and total observance of self-jihad self-correction and spirituality.

Allah says Ramadan is for him. Fasting is a relationship between a person and Allah. The benefits of spirituality and worship of Allah outweigh hunger. The generosity of giving and sharing during this blessed month outweighs the poverty of materials and the poverty of the heart. After the completion of the fast of thirty days,

Muslims celebrate (EID Ul-Fitr). Offering Eid prayer with other Muslims. (EID returns each year) Muslims distribute Fitra money grains given before the EID prayer, distributed to the needy in the community. Giving is an integral part of Islam. This is not a gesture or a handout but an opportunity to share. Sharing is a privilege for a believer, not a burden. Learning culture and faith are all wrapped up in one for Muslims.

Fifth Hajj Pilgrimage to Mecca (Dhu Al Hijjah), the last month of the Islamic calendar. Muslims perform (tawaf), the ritual of circumambulating the Kaaba house of Allah Abraham built with his son Ismael. There is no implication Muslims are venerating the building, but the ritual of circumambulating in a circle implies the circle has no end. Only Allah is worthy of any worship.

The dream of Abraham conveyed that he was sacrificing his son. He was the most obedient servant of Allah. He informed his son without hesitation. He replied, "Father, do as the Lord tells you." As he prepared to sacrifice his son for his Lord, he blindfolded himself and his son. Allah presented a lamb instead of a human sacrifice, as Allah had mercy on him and us. Allah is merciful, but he is not shy about testing his beloved servants.

Allah continuously tested Abraham. He earned the legitimacy of the title through the trials Allah gave him. Islam clarifies Allah has tested Abraham, referred to as (Khareen), as the closest of Prophets. Best friend by Allah. Muslims journey to the Kaaba and purify themselves in the house of Allah. An unending circle implies unity and oneness because its central point has no end. To acknowledge Allah's omnipresence, they circle it.

The Kaaba is the center of the world. The world map may show Kaaba as a central point in the world. This map is accessible to both Muslims and non-Muslims. In the end, humanity will explore the truth, investigate Islam, and experience seamless unity. They will prevail in all societies except those with disbelievers.

In this society, they deemed human research more significant than Allah's message. Because of his observations and research, Armstrong concluded the Kaaba was at the center of the universe. The gate above it is a gate to heaven, he declared. Muslims do not need a human to justify the central point of the world. In worship, the Creator has gathered in unity to purify the soul.

As Muslims devote their worship to Allah alone for the purification of souls, it is untrue that they worship Kaaba. Upon the completion of the Kaaba with his son, Abraham placed all the stones with the help of his son. A stone was missing, which he intended to be a beginning or an end. His father asked him to bring a different colored stone. Instead, Allah sent the white stone known as Hajar Al Aswad.

It is the culmination of the Kaaba and the starting point for pilgrims. Neither of them regards the stone as sacred. It was a gift from Allah, but it was not to be worshiped. Black became the stone's color, as Muslims touched and kissed the stone (Hajr e Aswad) only because Prophet Muhammad kissed it as a gift from Allah. The stone was milk white when it arrived from heaven, but the sins of humans and their touch have made it black. The heart of humanity requires spiritual cleansing through Allah's worship and prescribed prayers.

A pilgrimage to Kaaba is a visit to the house of Allah built by Abraham, and his son Ismael, the father of the Abrahamic faith, is Abraham. It is a place of meeting for Muslims from every land on earth, with peace and Muslims seeking the same countenance of Allah. Neither includes the worship of stones nor square buildings in Muslim worship. Everything in Islam has its rhyme and reason. As a focal point for Muslims, it focuses on the world of Muslims. Islam defines the Kaaba as the Qibla (direction).

Allah has limited worship and entrance to the Kaaba to Muslims only. This angered many non-Muslims, and blamed Saudi Arabia for not allowing non-Muslims to enter the holy site of Muslims. The Quran is clear that the Kaaba was accessible to every faith and later was a place of worship for Muslims No non-Muslims may enter the Kaaba. The holy site of Mecca is only accessible to Muslims.

Humans cannot enter government buildings and restricted areas without permission and access granted by humans. Humanity accepts human laws but frowns on Allah's laws. There are no questions for a Muslim, as the answers are self-explanatory.

Quran: Surah Tauba. 9; 28 O you who have believed the polytheists are unclean, so let them not approach Al-Masjid al-Haram after this, their [final] year. And if you fear privation, Allah will enrich you with His bounty if He wills. Indeed, Allah is Knowing and Wise.

The soul is clean when it is pure. It can only enter this sacred union of visiting the most sacred site for Muslims through complete commitment and submission to Allah. Passports are required to enter different countries around the world. A passport is also required to enter Allah's center of worship.

We can describe its delicacies with simple metaphors. To enter Haram Kaaba, Muslims must stamp the passport of Allah, not literally, but this is a requirement for entry. As a Muslim, it is necessary to renounce all self-will and submit fully to Allah's power and will, with no partners or deities.

To enter Haram (Kaaba). Allah is not shy about imposing his laws on humanity. Though it may sound restrictive and narrow-minded to some, human laws do not allow all humans entry to restricted areas. Kaaba was open to anyone in medieval times. Many believed this place was a sanctuary and a place of worship. Disbelievers worshiped pagan statues. The practice ceased embargo after the emergence of Islam.

Through Allah's permission, Abraham and Ismail built the first building together, marking the beginning of an era in the role of father and son. Islam has mercy but strict laws, no additions or subtractions to the laws of Allah, and no partners.

Kaaba was the first building in the world built by a prophet. Abraham is a complete monotheist who invites believers to gain solace through worship. Non-Muslims have rubber-stamped many myths, but the Quran commands only Muslims to enter the Kaaba for worship and cleansing. The acceptance of Islam is an entry point into Kaaba.

There is only one faith in the world that prevents non-Muslims from entering this place of worship on the Arabian Peninsula. The restrictions imposed by Allah are a full clearance and understanding of this faith, Islam. It requires complete submission and fulfillment of understanding and acknowledgment of the delivery of each Abrahamic prophet sent by Allah. And fully submitting to the will of Allah.The strict entrance policy to Kabba for Muslims only is a divine decree from Allah, emphasizing the purity of worship to Allah and prophet Muhammad as the last messenger.

Quran: Surah Imran.3;85. And whoever seeks a religion other than Islam, we will never accept it of him,"

By defining monotheism clearly, this verse clarifies its meaning. The worship of Allah is acceptable as long as it is based on a belief in only one God, Allah. And acceptance of the Prophet Muhammad as the last and final messenger of Allah. With these belief systems, one is classified as a Muslim.

It is not monotheistic to worship deities or idols alongside God. Allah hears all humans' desires, but it is Allah who fulfills their desires, not the deities. Humans will have full fulfillment only in the next life. Accountability for who he used to worship after the truth became apparent. All humanity is aware that there are no more excuses to be made.

Non-Muslims can enter and view other mosques. They can attend Salat with the cleanliness of body and mind, except for one place in Kaaba. This place **Kaaba** is only for Muslims. The act of worshiping Allah makes a Muslim understand the privilege of attending. Men and women wear the same uniform: white Ihram for men and mostly black for women, both modestly covered. To visit the holy site in Mecca.

Women are to be escorted by a mahram, a family member, or someone with clean relations, such as a father, brother, uncle, son, or husband. It is for protecting women to travel with a mahram. Allah knows his rules and regulations. A Muslim does not fight Allah's laws because humans impose their laws, which are fully regulated or have consequences.

In the year 1154, Muslims first drew a map with the Kaaba at its center. During his time with Roger, he worked as a geographer. His name was Muhammad al-Idrisi, and he was a Muslim Arab. The South is in the upper section. The North is in the lower section. As the chapters progressed, the theme of the world map shifted from its initial findings and placement.

During the Medieval Islamic era, this was the most detailed map available. His intellect was sublime, and he was a scholar. He also traveled extensively. There is no better teacher than to travel.

Muslims used their time wisely. They shared knowledge and improved the well-being of others. Islam taught the graciousness of belief and excelled in all avenues of life. (Qadar) belief in predestination is a belief in Islam. Muslims believe they know the decree as predestination. The resolution of the issue will take place as predestined by Allah, every Muslim believes in (Qadar) predestination.

Islam is fair if you analyze the five pillars. The first two have no exceptions. The other three have benefits and restrictions. If the qualifications converge and no limitations prevent the individual from proceeding, the last three pillars will become mandated.

For visitation to Hajj, every Muslim is mandated. But the fulfillment of obligations is necessary. Muslims are advised to pay their debtors as soon as possible. When the debts are less, the mind is free. If there are elderly or caregivers at home, some travel arrangements need to be made before traveling. Islam survives in reality, not in an illusion.

It is Allah's design that this system brings happiness to its users by following the straight path, not the constricting and narrow path that most humans take. (Qadar) belief is not a choice. Destiny is part of the divine and Islamic mandate, not a choice a believer believes in (Qadar) destiny. The concept of modesty for Muslim women is called (Haya). Every faith has a core. The core of Islam is modesty. This is not restricted to women, only the same rules apply to men. The curious eye can fall prey to (Zina) evil of the eyes when there are fewer clothes on.

This leads to unforbidden sinister acts, just like when Satan lets the first creation see their private parts for the first time. It is the plot of Satan to take away a person or a country's shame through penalization. It is much worse than the battles fought to destroy countries on the ground. There has been a decline in respectability dating back to the era when humans wore less clothing and worshiped pagan deities. Those days are returning, and most nations are contributing, except for Muslim countries.

Reforms and regulations of pleasing that precede outdated cultures, wrapped in the deceit of modernity especially the newer dynamic evil spreading from newer forces of less moral reforms from newly formed countries. It serves best to understand how the evil was employed as its origin can serve as an epidemic and influence Muslims and Muslim countries as well. No need to mention names as servitude of actions suffices.

A culture easily manipulated will consider believers out of date. The risk of disobedience to Allah is transgression when Muslims indulge in practices not sanctioned by Allah. It's to please humanity or to be accepted by societies that disregard Islamic law. This could be a special reminder for Muslims, especially for Muslim youth.

They will give the liars credibility, while the truth-tellers will be cross-examined and called outdated and non-credible. When the truth is revealed to disbelievers and tainted hearts, the believers will be accused of being jealous of their estranged ways.

The instincts at bay allow disbelievers and complicit believers to believe and swap lust for pleasure and passion. The eye that lurks looking for ills and being assured that what they are doing is right. Curbing certain impulses can help restore clarity for the most effective performance of a person who follows Allah's commands. It is this clarity that allows the believer to rise above their instincts and focus on the pleasures of the hereafter.

Decisions and acts that bring believers closer to Allah's pleasure. It is the only way to attain spiritual bliss far greater than worldly pleasure. Satan visits those who disturb others' lives, especially those who pray his envy is malicious. Satan is weak, so his deceit stands in the silent shadow. He wastes time for others by straying from the straight, wide path to a narrow path of suffocation.

The believer eventually sees Satan's attacks and continues on the righteous path. The truth is slow in receiving credence. Most Abrahamic scriptures warn of such harsh times. Those who put the evil ways of humans above the will of Allah will eventually face dire consequences.

Quran: Surah Rum: 30;26. All those in the heavens and the earth belong to Him (and serve Him); all are obedient to Him.

Both women and men value modesty and dress codes in Islam. Islam does not downplay any of Allah's laws. Following or not is up to the individual, but no longer is it contested, as the rules are not about to change to please any society. Allah brought reforms for a reason.

Through reforms, truth and falsehood will emerge for believers to see. Disbelievers will walk blindly because their eyes cannot see. With its dress reforms, Islam gave humanity rights in a feathered society. The elites later wore more clothing, and donning more clothing was a sign of wealth and dignity. For Muslims, it was a law of Allah to cover up.

Among the many factors contributing to the spread of this evil harming home privacy is social media. Rather than seeing their homes as a sanctuary, they turn to the house of devils, as these acts are accessible. Allah knows their hearts and the chaos this epidemic can cause.

Several obvious reasons have been categorized, along with the weaknesses and destruction caused by the epidemic. As a result, decay and decline are inevitable. Organizations have proven successful in expanding revenue because of nudity acceptance.

At the risk of sacrificing the dignity of women, which is acceptable at all levels for most in these cultures. Men also contribute to this society and take part in illicit doings and nudity as they are the contributors to too many magazines' strip clubs and their performances. Not forgoing social media, which is free.

Social media is not only used to break down barriers but also to invite others into sin. Technology can serve both benevolently and evilly. Muslims need to integrate the use of the system and share knowledge. Muslims, since ancient times, have been renowned for their commitment to disseminating knowledge and actively participating in endeavors that benefit humanity.

The best way for oneself and the Muslim race to invite humanity towards good is to strive to share the best during difficult times. Bringing revolutions from darkness to light is the Muslim motto, not following the darkness.

Money is the driving force behind many ill-doings in these cultures, and nudity drives the decline of society. Many civilizations, including Muslim countries, are following suit, as this epidemic is worse than wars. This is not a match with the theology of Islam. Modesty's adequacy is questionable in diverse societies, not aligning with Islamic modesty.

Quran: Surah Nur 24:31.O Prophet! Tell the believing men to lower their gaze and guard their chastity. That is pure for them. Allah is aware of what they do.

The Bedouins converted to Islam during that time. Those who undermined their belief were excluded. They never returned to familiar surroundings or people. Believers constantly improve survival skills and attitudes. They understood the principles of Islam. The changes in dress, discipline, and faith were significant. Paganism was prevalent while adapting to Islam was strange. It imposed conservative dress code rules for worshipers. Allah was the exclusive fashion designer.

Prophet Muhammad informed the Muslims that Islam came as something strange, and it would return as something strange. With blessing tidings to the strangers who follow Islam. Prophet Muhammad is the last prophet of Islam. The closing statement of the books that preceded the Quran is the last revelation sent by Allah.

Quran: Surah Taha 20:16 Therefore, do not be the one who disbelieves. Follow his lusts, but keep away from them lest you perish.

Angels are part of Islamic belief and angels are described as having no free will. Humans and jinns have free will. On the day of the resurrection, man will answer for the deeds he performed in this world. Angel Gabriel is the Archangel who acts as an intermediary between Allah and humans. He is the bearer of revelations to the Prophets. He delivered the Quran to the Prophet Muhammad. Moses was the only one to whom Allah spoke directly.

For centuries, hadiths have been circulating. Bukhari, Tirmidhi, and Muslim are some of the most well-known hadiths. The Islamic way of life, designed by Allah without human imagination or blueprints, needed a true general, a commander-in-chief. The delivery of a direct message leads a man in the right direction.

Through the angel Gabriel, Muhammad peace be upon him received the word of Allah, free from the corrupting influence of any society. Muhammad's heart was the only one capable of enduring this Quran if any other or even a mountain had received it. This task is beyond the capability of any other. Eventually, it would diminish to ashes. Prophet Muhammad could only handle this Quran without affecting and altering the words Allah conveyed through the angel (Jibril). Gabriel. The Angel

Jinns also have free will, but humans are more powerful than Jinns, although they have powers humans cannot imagine. Any species with free will, such as Jinns, and humans will face the consequences of their deeds.

The story of the wise decision in a noble family some decades ago:

The noble aristocrat was humble, always seeking Allah's help. He owned a palace in Mukalla, the southern part of Saudi Arabia, on the shores of the Arabian Sea. This imposing irresistible beauty stood by Yemen's seaport. He learned seventeen languages. He read the Quran daily. Knowing the human was stronger than the Jinn, he held the command of one Jinn who was at his service.

He dreamt of his imminent death. He asked humans for forgiveness if he had displeased them as a king. His sad informative dream saddened relatives, staff, and friends, leaving uncertainty. He didn't know the date but knew the time had come. Tearfully, he returned the grandson to his parents, leaving behind his mansion.

The grandson had to go back to his family. Initially unfamiliar with his siblings, he grew closer to them. Eventually, he felt at home after understanding his grandfather had passed away. His grandfather took him to the palace to ensure his mild health conditions were taken care of. The grandfather promised to take care of him. He loved his maternal grandfather. The mother and father agreed, prioritizing her son's welfare. Destiny reunites one with their family.

The Jinn offered to stay after his passing. He said I would serve your family as I served you. He released Jinn and set him free. He said if I did not release you, the family might not treat you with fairness, kindness, and respect. The Jinn loved him so much it disheartened him to leave him. He knew he was a beautiful human being. He was a humble and a believing king. The family would have fought for the Jinn if he had stayed, driven by their greed and the desire to control him, unable to maintain the peace he had with the king.

Their competitiveness would stem from greed. He liberated him. The king died shortly. Jinn can form emotional bonds with humans. He saw his relatives at the king's funeral, though they couldn't see him. With tears, he observed the family's lack of royal qualities. Jinn understood why the king had released him. He experienced immense pain at the funeral and observed the king's compassionate nature.

He observed in the king the qualities of belief, integrity, kindness, and intelligence that were lacking in his family. The king emphasized character and truthfulness in helping his family. The Jinn may have helped this family in times of distress with Allah's permission, but it remains unknown.

The family neglected to claim the king's riches or remember his habits. He understood why the king set him free. He had a luxurious library and enjoyed learning. The Palace in Yemen was taken away by unrelated sources as his family had already relocated and did not pursue ownership of his belongings. Allah may have intended it. He spoke seventeen languages, but his family lacked mastery in one language, which undermined the king's credibility. Memories turned to faded pictures. There are stories worth mentioning.

Quran: Surah Araf: 7; 179. Certainly, we have created Hell for many of the Jin and humanity by creating hearts that cannot understand. The eyes that can't see, ears that can't hear. They are like cattle—indeed, even more astray. Such are utterly heedless.

Quran: Surah Fatir: 35;39. He made you vicegerents on earth who made you. So whoever disbelieves will bear the burden of his unbelief. The unbelievers' unbelief adds Nothing to Allah's wrath against them. The unbelievers' unbelief adds nothing but to their loss.

Quran: Surah Maidah 5:68. The Prophet by your Lord is bound to make many of them more stubborn in their arrogance and denial of the truth. Do not worry about the unbelievers.

Quran: Surah Hijar, 1.2. Alif Lam Ra. It is the verses of the book and a clear Quran that make things clear. Those who disbelieve often wish they were Muslims.

It's difficult to understand the attitudes and similarities of low thinking, ingratitude, doubt, arrogance, and recklessness. Kindness and humanity make being human beautiful, and faith and trust enhance this beauty. Allah doesn't pair non-believers with believers. Cursed are the fallible with congested hearts. They are mentioned in the Quran. Disbelievers often express a lack of interest in hearing the truth repeatedly. Allah reveals the truth. Satan and his supporters prefer lies over constant truth.

The Quran is repetitive. Their reading is shaped by what they hear. A disbelieving reader's disbelief and blackened heart hinder their understanding of deception and fraud. Believers sense evil harshness and the disbeliever's pungent odor. Therefore, believers distance themselves from such individuals.

Allah has repeated the word Quran sixty-eight times in the Quran. In the Quran, Allah promises to protect the last revelation sent to humanity as a mercy. No book in the world takes such an oath directly from the Lord of the worlds. Allah.

Quran: Surah Hijar 15:9 Indeed, it is we who sent down the Quran. And indeed, we will be its guardians.

No alterations or falsifications are allowed for the preserved words in the original text. Quran revelations lasted 23 years. The initial revelation occurred at forty. His lifetime marked the completion of a significant chapter for Muslims and humanity. Prophet Muhammad consulted the Quran for decisions and rulings.

(Tawakkul) is a definition of faith. It is a trait of Muslims. The Quran is Allah's last revelation. Success is the only outcome for nations following the Quran's laws. Chaos continues in the world. The Quran is a source of solace for those searching for peace.

He delivers when he knows the human is ready. In Mecca and Medina, Allah revealed the Quran in stages. Allah completed the Quran before the demise of Prophet Muhammad. The revelations arrived in stages until it delivered the final closing statement. Depicting the past, present, and future to ponder.

Prophet Muhammad declared in his last sermon that he fulfilled his mission with Allah as his witness. He clearly explained to the crowd, pleading for Allah's help in their understanding. A Muslim's understanding of the Quran is as clear as if he were present at the Prophet's last sermon. Peace is found within a clear heart.

Quran: Surah ISRA 17:78. Observe prayer from the setting of the sun until the darkness of the night.

During the early hours of the morning, angels witness and record prayer and the reading of the Quran. Allah witnesses the reading of the Quran at dawn by a believer. Humanity has no reason to doubt Allah. One who seeks the Quran will ponder this book individually or collectively. Muslims read this book over and over.

The peace from this book is bewildering. The reader seeks solace in the Quran's proximity. Prophet Muhammad emphasized learning and teaching the Quran. Dhikr dialogue of Allah is the practice of following Prophet Muhammad's (Sunnah) his ways and practices.

When humans' emotions and spiritual needs falter, we learn not to agonize over those who fall short of faith. Allah drives this world and keeps believers in check, so man has no failures. In today's world, an illiterate man may have stronger faith than a literate one. The arrogant may view academic learning as a sign of power and arrogance, causing them to lose faith in Allah and credit themselves for their achievements.

Prioritizing society's influence and affirming one's own merits over Allah. Without trying, nothing can be achieved. Success eludes some individuals throughout their entire lives. Allah provided all from His Treasury. Humans can be ignorant of Allah's obvious gifts. Some easily forget the source of their intellectual capacity. Allah is the source of all gifts.

Intellect is for those who endure it with gratitude. Allah and for those who lead them on the right path. Shallow humans have no gratitude, only self-aggrandizement. Man-made books and history contribute to better salaries in today's world, but the Quran is wealth for a believer. Some people push the Quran to the back burner.

This book has more knowledge and prestige than any classroom-taught book or degree. One verse of the Quran suffices for a believer's mastery. Life's forces live in the Quran. In the realm of peace, a believer's wealth is their peace.

Material wealth and travel facilitate the attainment of peace, but we can only find true inner peace through spirituality. What does the Quran mean? "The recitation." The Quran was sent by Allah for recitation, not for storage. It is meant to be learned through communication, verbal reading, listening, and sharing Dhirk dialogue with believers.

Allah clearly states that a believer's conversation is incomplete without Allah's remembrance. Humanity can't learn from ignorant people. Information is readily available to them from knowledgeable people who can provide it for them. Allah would not give away his divinity to someone or something. Allah does not change his divinity, but humanity can worship who they will.

Quran: Surah Baqarah verse 256. Let there be no compulsion in religion; for the truth stands out clearly from falsehood. So, whoever renounces false Gods and believes in Allah has certainly grasped the firmest, unfailing handhold. And Allah is all-knowing.

Islam is the only faith that declares no force in faith. Finally, it ensures it will pay the consequences after it clarifies that the truth is available but denied. No other can take or share in Allah's divinity. Nor does he get tired. Allah hears all humans. Knows hearts that do not speak and eyes that don't see. Human writing has a price tag, and this is a compelling truth. And delivery. Time is a source of revenue, and human knowledge comes with a price tag. It takes time to commit hours to write, in particular.

The Quran was sent by Allah to promote peace and balance among humanity. Does a Muslim not value truth? Allah's books were free, and information given to Prophets had no revenue attached, except for soul purification. Seeing these values with truth and honesty, it is clear that they are priceless.

CHAPTER 2

VALUES AND CONDUCT INFLUENCE FAITH AND BEHAVIOR.

Islam's commands serve the interests of humans, not Allah. It teaches adherents to live harmoniously, be honest, and assist those in need. Its teachings emphasize mercy, compassion, and justice. Islam encourages followers to be ethical and moral. It values individualism and rejects individual or collective evil deeds. Core virtues and deeds determine how individuals are judged.

A balanced and excellence-driven company always succeeds. Muslims must unite and collaborate for societal improvement. Emphasizing the collective creates a stronger sense of community and support. Individuals are accountable for themselves. Not obligated to conform to group structure or peer-imposed beliefs. Islam values independent thinking and action.

Individuality embodies conduct, morality, discipline, and reliance on core values. Prioritize self-care before helping others. Each person has a moral compass for decision-making. Those decisions are up to them alone. Inevitably, there will be differences among individuals. It fosters acceptance and understanding. One's demeanor in loneliness and attentiveness to their creator defines them. In loneliness, some turn to evil, deceived by Satan, while others submit to their creator. A person's aptitude depends on their desire for self-improvement.

Conduct and values define a Muslim believer, but individuality describes the person. Their conduct can be influenced by others or their improvisation and shadows, which can hold positive or negative images. Your spirit can deceive you. It depends on a Muslim's perception of their duties to Allah.

Every day is a new beginning in this temporary world. Enhancing conduct and clarity of mind. A different attitude can improve life more than daily efforts. Inner conduct determines everything. Muhammad's trustworthiness was evident before prophethood.

Souls that jump into the river, ocean, or sea can be dirty or cleansed. Personal behavior creates barriers in these waters. Even after washing, some are still dirty. Industrial pollutants, sewage, and agricultural runoff cause pollution. The presence of a filthy soul repulses water. Conduct can alter truth-based environments. Contaminated water is unsuitable for humans and animals. Pollution negatively impacts habitats and ecosystems.

People's expanding desires and ecosystem damage make these circumstances unavoidable. Impurity comes from the soul, while purity comes from within. The soul greatly affects conduct. Both believers and disbelievers use this behavior to emphasize their differences. Shady individuals exploit Islam for their benefit. Crush evil where it belongs.

A striving soul seeks truth.Believers seek dialogue, good relationships, and righteousness. Allah is the ultimate master of all deliveries, even when he provides delivery through human contact. Maintaining "dhikr" and conversation to nourish the brain and heart is ultimate bliss. Water causes trees to be green. Eco-consciousness and accountability. Believers need Islam for inner growth.

Islam advocates for environmental stewardship. Islam emphasizes abstaining from disrespecting trees, including hunting for leisure. People are taught to avoid polluting the environment and care for nature. Environmental respect is essential in Islam. The soul is the gateway and compass of preservation. By being aware of our thoughts and actions, we can pursue a virtuous and purified life.

Quran: Surah Rahman: 55;19. He released the two seas, meeting [side by side];

Quran: Surah Rahman: 55:20.Between them is a barrier [so] neither of them transgresses.

Quran: Surah Rahman: 55:21.So which of the favors of your Lord would you deny?

Examples in the Quran are only for those who seek truth. Those who choose the compensation of finality to fulfill their inner surge of balance can benefit from stories or examples.

The story of a man and his wishes.

Once, there lived a Muslim man. He was committed to his faith. He saw the poor behavior of many people and wished he were an animal. He envisioned what it's like to be a dog. According to him, being a dog is a simple task for humans, as they don't have to face others' conduct. The human's desire for what they lack stems from not knowing the animal's experiences.

Being human is more prestigious than being a dog. He longed to be an animal to avoid human problems. He expressed his preference not to depend on humans for food and care. Unfortunately, he would rely on humans for his needs. They would silence him to prioritize their desires over his. It would be impossible for him to express his needs or make choices. Lastly, he would have no autonomy and rely on humans entirely. So he passed on this wish.

He wished to be a road for people to use. A road might serve many people they could walk along, he wished he was the road people appreciated. A clean road would be beautiful and useful for too many people. To gain respect, he knew the road needed to be wide and have reliable conductors.

The hope was for people to appreciate and respectfully use this road. Traveling on the road would be a joyful experience. He expressed his desire to assist those with better conduct. With hope, he advocated for treating the road with respect and joy. Hoping for universal adherence to a common code of conduct.

He desired equal enjoyment of this road for everyone. With sadness, he accepted everyone is different and has their journey. Accepting truth is refreshing and being a role model of respect and joy on the road. Despite the guidance, humans choose the wrong path. Regrettably, he abandoned the idea of his imagination to being a road.

Suddenly, he longed to be like the sea. His imagination took him to lengths of colorful images he could offer them serenity in his ocean. The tranquility and the ocean's colors would surround them once they came in. Sun, sand, and waves would provide them enjoyment.

The sound of waves and the calm sea would soothe them. Regardless of the sea's actions, dirty and clean souls would walk into it, he said. Consequently, he claimed that those with less integrity would be drawn into my paradise. The possibility of being surrounded by people who didn't meet his criteria was dismaying as he tried to handle everything.

Supporting people from all walks of life was too much for him. His eyes filled with tears, haunted by the idea of being the ocean. Sea creatures will be present. The sea creatures looked up to him for help, but he could not provide it and felt overwhelmed. Powerlessness and defeat consumed him. There was no other option but to depart from his thoughts. Although he wasn't afraid of the animals, he had a fear of humans, envisioning himself as the ocean. There was no choice left except to pass on this wish.

His busy mind was filled with wishes and ideas, imagining himself as a tree, providing shade and fruit to others. Trees represented life and growth, which he wanted to provide for people. The greenery and gardens bring joy and shade to the world. He envisioned a tree becoming shade for many. The idea that he could provide nourishment and enjoyment for everyone is captivating.

He aspired to be strong and optimistic, imagining growth and becoming a haven for wildlife. The image of someone leaning on him, with adults and children under the enormous tree's shade. The tree represented the blissful respite sought by humans in the warm hours.

He could imagine the adults talking and the children playing games. The vision of children laughing, and adults sharing stories. The desire to actualize this dream gave him a smile on his face. The realization hit him he would rely on humans for water, and they would dispose of the tree. Sadly, he abandoned his dream of becoming a tree. This wish too, like his other ideas, faded away as a passing phase.

He strived to escape mediocrity in every aspect. The problems made him appreciate being human and gave him a unique perspective on life. Understanding Allah's mercy, he displayed the best of character as a human. People are free to conduct themselves as they choose and express gratitude to Allah for their prayers and behavior. He surrounded himself with those who believed. We can make wise decisions with Allah's witness to our conduct.

He finally found an answer he understood and shared with the world. Allah knows my purpose as a human. "How would I know what to be?" Being human is the greatest blessing, and he thanked Allah for it. Misusing and demeaning oneself is not understanding the gifts of being human. Stories like these inspire Muslims to follow the (Sunnah) practices of Prophet Muhammad. People in this society lack individuality and follow a unified belief system of deceit from Satan. Those who know the truth will always find their way back to happiness and peace.

Peer pressure arises from the clash between pre-dated cultures and Islamic beliefs. Weak individuals will seek others to engage in improper behavior. The strong survive alone, not as followers. They are aware of Prophet Muhammad's legacy in his struggles, truth, and efforts to guide Muslims. Those who seek the truth with the authentic Quran will find it.

Guidance from observations and authentic hadiths to follow the prophet is left behind. Rules dictate a person's conduct. No negotiations are allowed for a Muslim in a closed channel. Islam is finalized by Allah, and the book is closed. Creator's rules are prioritized over humanity for Muslims. Survival requires law-abiding behavior. Most Muslims acknowledge the truth, but a few devalue themselves by not adhering to it. Return is anticipated from a believer without a doubt.

One day all Muslims will face the prophet as his "ummah" people, and the world will face Allah in the finality of reckoning. Allah sent the prophet Muhammad as our last and final messenger. Followers of Islam are Muslims. Few may base the conception of their tradition. Islam is not to be mixed with culture. The (Deen) is a way of life. Prophet Muhammad was an illustration of empathy, communication, honesty, and trust among the Muslim (Ummah) his people and extended toward all humanity.

As the old saying goes, "Charity begins at home." One who is kind to his Muslim (Ummah) people will be kind to others. Islam banished insecurities by adhering to sounds and cues and then practicing sustained self-discipline. Along with the company of a believer or believers to complement the efforts of transformation. Ability to appreciate and recognize another's efforts, not see them as motives or agendas. Or the untrusting world views, as they cannot deem themselves trustable.

Aesthetic and sentimental senses can be lost by some individuals. Because of compromised beliefs. Muslims advocate for youth studying Islam. Faith enables humanity to benefit now and in the next world. Islam and academia can guide the world to righteousness.

If Allah had not considered youth an influential stage of life, he would not have used them as an example in Surah Kahf. Muslims are told to read this surah every Friday (Jumuah) is the Friday prayers attended by Muslims in a (Jamaat) congregation.

Quran: Surah Jumuah 62;9. Believers, when they call for prayer on Friday. Give up all trading and remember Allah. ... That would be better for you if you only knew.

Muslims shut down offices and take leave, but they make their way to the Mosque on "Jummah" Friday prayers. Allah prescribes congregational prayer in the Quran. Most men attend this prayer, while women pray at home. This attendance of men in the congregation is mandatory.

Allah knows about the responsibilities women have with family and sometimes transportation and has not mandated nor exempted women from attending prayer at home or a mosque. It is compulsory and mandatory on all Muslims regardless of gender.

Women are welcome to attend the mosque, but they are not required to do so. Men and women perform the same acts. "Salat" ritual prayer is mandatory except for mentally ill individuals. The benefits of attendees attending the Mosque on Friday are tremendous. Benefits far outweigh the loss of the material world or academia for a brief period.

One must attend alone if congregational attendance is impossible, but there are no excuses for a Muslim not to attend alone or by himself. In the Quran, Allah mentions (Salat) as a mandatory act for a Muslim, but Allah gave Friday (Jummah) special significance. Do some Muslims' actions conflict with Islam?

The practice is defamatory against oneself and the Muslim community if it makes Muslims aware of disobeying Allah in public. It is also defamatory if it gives non-Muslims a chance to point fingers. This practice can lead to a negative image of the Muslim community, as well as a false perception of Islam.

In such cases, Muslims should avoid public displays of disobedience with the tap of fingers in the aggressive climate through social media. Instead, focus on repenting and reforming their behavior. Muslims can embody the best of Islam and lead an exemplary life. Striving to be the best version of themselves and to be role models in their communities.

It's the ultimate way to maintain the honor of Islam and the Muslim community. Behaving against Islam's teachings, particularly in public, undermines the reputation of a Muslim. For Muslims, repentance is an effective way to fix their woes and discontentment. This task poses a challenge for some. Dedication, humility, and Islamic understanding are required. This effort is the correct way for Muslims to honor Islam.

Most Muslims will return to the path if Allah commands. Peer pressures cater to corrupt societies' desires and cultures. Are Muslims unaware of Prophet Muhammad's struggle for Islam? How would Prophet Muhammad would view his followers?

Understanding the history of Islam is crucial for Muslims. Adapting to progressive and conservative ways, avoiding pagan practices. Unsettling period. Some societies or countries couldn't escape this demon contract in the name of modernization.

Life is full of intricate mysteries. Our conduct in this life reflects our conduct in the afterlife. The heart communicates, not the mouth. Their struggle was significant.

If someone wasted their life distracting others and jeopardizing themselves, it would be sad for them to confront Prophet Muhammad. The (Ummah) his people , which comprises his followers. Muslims make mistakes in a society that demands no restrictions, as Islam aligns with its moral compass. Some Muslims rebel against and follow corrupt, outdated cultures because of their belief that they can't follow the rules. Humans sometimes follow false rules disguised as independence.

They belong to a morally corrupt society compared to Islam. Allah holds our hope for a swift return to the righteous path. Islam conflicts with paganistic morals. Weak-minded individuals can only hope to escape from a corrupt organization if they don't value faith. Islam believes in the potential for change with Allah's will.

People born into this faith, including new converts, pay attention to the sound of kindness that drips like water from the sea over picturesque rocks. They see the marks of the constant downpours. A Muslim's kindness cannot change based on the attitudes of another.

A man's faith and strength change from time to time. Those in need benefit from his kind attitude and faith. Allah has told us to be kind to his people. The victorious are those who are kind to humanity and pray to their creator. Some view material wealth as success far beyond that of a believer, claiming world travel and academia can surpass the success of a Muslim without attending to Allah. There is no such succession for believers who are not in touch with the master of the world, Allah.

Quran: Surah Ghafir 40:51. Indeed, we shall make victorious our messengers and the believers in the world. And on the day witnesses will stand.

The realization of negative thoughts impedes moral decisions, prevents advancement, and ultimately promotes stagnation. This allows one to remain disdainful of a stagnant society where there is no advancement. Islam encourages a positive attitude, as Muslims have no room for negativity, as Allah is in charge of what's right or incorrect. According to Islam, the Muslim honors this responsibility by continuing to strive for righteousness and never doubting the path of goodness.

Asking and begging Allah for ease in the trials of life. Ask Allah in (Dua) prayer for anything and everything. He is a creator, Lord of the worlds, who cannot wait to hear from his servants. Muslims refer to him as the Lord of the Worlds. He is the owner of both the seen and the unseen worlds. (Rabul Alameen) Praise be to the Lord of the Universe.

Muslims seek help from Allah in times of difficulty or decision-making through a prayer called (Istikhara). One prays to Allah, asking Him to show direction through a dream. Most Muslims who perform this prayer see something positive or negative in their dreams. When Muslims see this in a dream, they fully rely on Allah. We must encourage them to seek the help of Allah. There are many ways to get closer to your creator before you make any big decisions. Those who seek will find answers.

The benefits of reliance on Allah are abundant. If one has seen positive results in a dream and does not receive immediate results, it's not the time of delivery. The answer is from Allah. Any obstruction or delay is no reason for panic. The one who holds one's life is the one who answers. Having faith in Allah is beneficial. Seeing positive results in a dream and not receiving immediate results does not imply delivery time.

Answers come from Allah. Before making any big decisions, Prophet Muhammad advised Muslims to read "Salat" (Istikhara). Doubts and negativity are only from the accursed Satan. The Muslim (Ummah) people have always been a threat to disbelievers because of a lack of understanding, which has caused many to revolt against it. In Islam, the justice system is just, and if someone disturbs one's peace of worship or property. You have the option to either defend yourself or take retaliatory action in the pursuit of justice.

Fairness is the hallmark of the Islamic justice system. Some laws and principles can withstand any decade. Through the diplomacy of entering for aid, taking what does not belong, and walking away with self-interest, the hypocritical world has not thrived but created more imbalances. The attitudes contradict Jesus' instructions to turn the other cheek. There's no place at the entrance, only blockages.

Bible: Mathew: 58:38;40. If anyone slaps you on the right cheek, turn to the other cheek. And if anyone wants to sue you and take your shirt, hand over your coat as well.

Refusing to seek justice does not justify doing the opposite of this verse. It is illogical to blame and embrace evil, just as it is illogical for someone to bear their own sins. Islam is a faith that resonates with the average person because it makes sense.

Therefore, following it can be quite challenging if it doesn't align with one's understanding. As a result, the script has undergone modifications and adaptations throughout its rich history, incorporating its own regulations and changes to the Biblical text. In contrast, the Quran remains unchanged and unaltered.

If Abraham prayed to Jesus, Muslims would also pray to him.Abraham prayed to Allah one God.

It wouldn't be fair if one stood by and did nothing. During the time of the Prophet Muhammad, faith flourished. Islam emphasizes the importance of (self-Jihad) the spiritual struggle within oneself. The word (Jihad) has two meanings: one is a spiritual struggle within oneself, and the other is a struggle to fight against the enemies of Islam.

They commonly use this word on social media that control masses in certain societies to depict anger or rage, but none of those are correct.The corruption is not from civilians its filtered through social media from higher ups corrupting the masses and making them believe they are giving them independence. While they get rich the poor keep getting poorer.

Through the name (Jihad), they breed Muslim terrorists or extremists showcasing them on social media. Islam is a faith of honor. They match anyone falling short of this demeanor and conduct by naming them followers of Islam. This name is incompatible with corroded behaviors. Islam means submission to Allah, not violence. Therefore, the names are incompatible. A political move, and the justice system and behaviors associated with it, do not coincide with Islam.

Both stand in contrast to the dignity, serenity, and justice of Islam. Taking advantage of others is incompatible with the character of Islam. The Quran, the legacy the Prophet Muhammad left behind, is an example.

Quran: Surah Baqarah 2:126. We have enjoined fighting upon you while it is hateful to you. But perhaps you hate a thing, and it is good for you. And perhaps you love a thing, and it is bad for you. And Allah knows while you know not.

The company places a strong emphasis on Islam at any age. If used incorrectly damages credibility. Or sustains credible behavior through inner strengths and the company one holds. It's said you're judged by the company one keeps, and small-minded gossipers are the most damaging. Focus on inner worth and self-worth.

The pursuit of spiritual development and worldly affairs composes the life of this world. A single believer is better than a thousand disbelievers misdirecting one's affairs. Islamic hangouts must be of the highest quality to bring out one's finest qualities. Islam encourages one to ignore the naysayers.

To entertain the good with understanding, one may ask, how does one get rid of negativity? Knowing that the blackened heart of a negligent person will never shine, he knows that the heart of a negligent person will continue to wander in doubt.

The only true heart-turner is Allah. Nothing is impossible. Even the most inhuman of humans or a non-believer can become exceptional. Nothing can change if one doesn't do something. Some use the phrase "you cannot change the individual," which contradicts Islam.

If Allah sees a sincere heart, he can transform anyone. Allah knows the innate nature of man. He can fool himself or others, but Allah holds the reins to the seen and the unseen, allowing the dark soul to wander into darkness.

Quran: Surah Araf Verse 185 *Have they ever reflected on the wonders of the heavens and the earth, and everything Allah has created? Their end is near? So what message after this Quran would they believe in?*

Quran: Surah Araf Verse 186. *If Allah allows someone to stray, no one can guide them. Leaving, they wander blindly in defiance.*

Quran: Surah Baqarah: 2;221.*And a believing slave is better than a polytheist, even though he might please you. Those invite [you] to the Fire, but Allah invites you to Paradise.*

The same concept applies to Muslim women and Muslim men who sanction their beliefs for altering Islam and pleasing disbelievers. They also engage in immoral activities that are not compatible with Islam. Eventually, they see themselves committing self-inflicted destruction and walking out of Islam and still say, "I am a Muslim," but don't follow all the laws of Islam.

Islam did not authorize Muslims or non-Muslims to rearrange law and order. As if to say they are not pleased with Allah's order but follow people's court system. Hypocrites have no place in Islam. Mistakes and repentance are expected. Allah loves to forgive.

Nevertheless, hypocrisy has its demon; even Satan is bored with the followers he has. He seeks new victims. Ill conduct and unjust are unacceptable to Islam. There is a crossroads where mishaps are bound to occur, but change is always possible with a change of heart and company.

Restoring conduct and morality is an open field, just as destruction has many options to choose from. Destiny leads humans. Muslim communities have faced a challenging time living in unproductive liberal ideologies compatible with pagan worlds.

Some seek alternative lifestyles and false modernization. Some get even closer to studying their faith by watching the conduct of many and seeing the disturbed souls. In Islam, the source of conduct is continuous foreplay. Those who please Allah never fail. Those who please Satan never succeed. The facade was short-lived. Expression of different facades and facets to indulge the mind and tame the fleeting impulses of continual habits and indulge in the change to understand. Why is so much said if every different example examines the mind and heart if it's heading towards one goal, belief in Allah,

Clarity with examples to see the truth of Islam. If one cannot grasp the concept, it is not for you, as Islam is not for everyone. Neither is its delivery or my expression.

In believing homes, disobeying Allah is unconstructive when a Muslim mother imposes barricades of correction. When Allah holds the heart, obedience shines brightly both internally and externally. The destination of a person who defies Allah is like that of a dark well. Disobedience to Allah is strong; what does it matter to a human? This can also happen to women and men living in corroded societies or any part of the world. Disobedience has no destination. It's prevalent worldwide. The only difference is access is easy in some countries.

In an age when disrespect and disobedience to Allah come first, it is fully expected for a mother or a believing Muslim to correct the moral code of ethics concerning Islam. A backward society is familiar with hurling words and disrespect when it comes to the concept of saying harsh words.

Especially in morally bankrupt hemispheres, reaching the worldly public minds of corruption is a dilemma of the pleasing nature of those who adapt to the currents of the weak society. This lures weak minds who don't oppose the concept of moral bankruptcy. People who instilled Allah's laws and orders become a burden. Defiance, however, leads to walking in depression's shadow.

Keeping psychiatrist offices paid well for the disobedient Satan and his company. The only time a Muslim holds and walks out is if he is stopped by a disbelieving family, spouse, or surroundings from practicing Islam. Then migrating is better than stagnation.

The families are so conjugated that no one is worried if one disrespects Allah, but certain Muslims are worried if they disrespect them. Accordingly, those who accept advice from disbelievers who never participated in growth are first to give advice such that the criminals of Satan have no interest in Allah's laws, self-worth, or the dimmed society. By obeying Allah, we maintain a heart and treat others with respect.

The story of Ghauz E Azam (Abdul Qadar Jelani) his lineage is about Prophet Muhammad.

The intricacy of respect for his mother: along with the laws of Allah, brought him ultimate success. The mother of Ghauz E Azam raised the young boy alone. He was sensitive to their surroundings and understood she had many responsibilities. He made sure he was of help to her.

She experienced severe sickness one day. He lived with her alone after his father's passing. She asked him for water. As a young lad, he approached her with water. He observed her sleeping. Recognizing her need for water and sickness. The young man stayed by her side all night in case she got thirsty. He knew his mother was important and rarely fell ill.

When she woke up for dawn prayers, she saw her son beside her with a jug of water. Her heart softened, and she spoke with a trembling voice. Were you standing with water for me throughout the night?". He said he didn't want her to wake up thirsty and sick and find him asleep.

The mother's heart was fulfilled by prayer. He became a saint and traveled extensively. Muslims are familiar with his name. Despite her attachment to him, she would be alone after he left. She urged him to leave home and explore travel and learning. She encouraged him to pursue education by attending school. Following her advice, he succeeded in his studies. He became a respected scholar and influential community leader. His legacy teaches that a mother's prayer can move mountains and succeed.

Disobeying a righteous mother can move mountains. The current epidemic is teaching parents important lessons. Allah's name isn't mentioned in the place of darkness, where the sun never rises in the hearts.

Harsh climates without sunlight weaken the immune system and lead to depression, the primary cause of death. Humans rely on the light of Allah for survival. The effects are known only to those within that body. When happiness is proclaimed but actions don't match, it is an inner loss from not knowing the creator. Bright light always welcomes return, but hope is mercy from Allah.

His mother exemplified adherence to Allah's laws and taught her son the values of learning, travel, dress, and moral compass in life. He was a highly intelligent young man. His ancestry goes back to the Prophet Muhammad. His mother sent him to a madrasa school at a young age. He pursued higher education and aimed to travel to Baghdad for spiritual and academic enrichment. His mother had grown older and was now alone. She acknowledged his capabilities and didn't interfere. She inspired him to travel and learn. He remained loyal to Allah.

He left for educational travel at a young age, bidding his mother farewell with her blessings. Allah was with him. Mothers can influence their children's success or lack thereof. Holds truth for all caregivers. But destiny will take its course, and its plans. The consolation was his moral compass. She sewed 40 dinars under his coat. She offered prayers and advice to him. Stay truthful and committed to your creator, regardless of the circumstances. He took leave of his mother.

Traveling alone, he was left alone by a gang of thieves who looted people because of his young age. He informed the thieves of their failure to take anything from him. The thieves were surprised. Why did you inform us? He responded. My mother warned me against lying. Allah is with me, even though she is not. I can't go against her. Before I left her, she advised me. She told me to know Allah is always with me, and her dua prayers stick with me. The thieves embraced the Muslim faith. The beauty of this advice she gave her son was even though she is not with him, Allah is.

The story reflects how she shaped her son's character. She didn't block his path to excellence. She knew the importance of self-education. Both learning and self-improvement necessitate persistence and life experiences. Learning does not involve immorality and mishaps. The defiance of Allah contributes to the discourse dilemma.

He was handsome and well-dressed underneath his outer garment. He always enjoyed a stylish ensemble. His clothing did not contribute to his concreteness. Stability, morality, learning, and a yearning for wisdom through serving his creator - that was his motto.

His mother raised him and filled in all the gaps he needed. He personified gratitude to Allah and his mother's time. Despite not being a prophet, he had the power to perform miracles with the permission of Allah. Not a prophet, but a saint. Many lessons can be learned from the name he carries.

His father passed away when he was young. Allah helps single mothers in their trials. Hannah's husband passed away before Mary was born. Women of faith and parentless children have proven their resilience under Allah's guidance. Prophet Muhammad is a perfect example. He lost his father before his birth and lost his mother very young. Excuses are futile if Allah has a plan. He possessed generosity, truthfulness, and bravery. Fearlessly, he exposed the truth on the pulpit about a cruel man named Qazi. Oppressors in Islam must be confronted or removed. He was known as a saint with education and travel experiences who was able to spread and share his knowledge.

Strong mothers and fathers mold strengths in their children. His stories depict him being raised by his mother and losing his grandfather and father at a very young age. These stories are examples of Allah's laws that strengthen families. Muslims and saints left stories to inspire truth, morality, and belief in Allah.

In Islam, mothers' prayers lead to success, along with early independence. Strengthening the rooting system strengthens roots. Without Allah, the roots lack strength. Declaring independence with defiance corrupts the world and breeds chaotic civilizations. Satan preys on the weak. The steadfast remain with Allah. The human body contains a mechanism intricately created by Allah.

Despite man's complexity, Allah empowers medical professionals to heal injuries and defects. Success is granted by Allah to the worthy. Allah's design ensures humans are created with intricacy. Allah stated that humanity is designed better than angels. Unlike angels, humans and jinns can choose their behavior. Humanity is the peak of creation. Allah created man perfectly. Humans acknowledge their distinct qualities. No human artist could make this complex work. Knowing your Creator is a heart's blessing from Allah. Only a believer can lead him to his creator, becoming his friend.

Can disbelievers succeed in worldly pursuits? Allah can grant success to anyone. Only Allah knows how the story of (Firon),Pharaoh, a disbeliever, ended. The tension is felt by those without faith, even if the world is oblivious. The end marks the start of the next journey, known only to Allah for the disbeliever. Muslims do not claim someone is in heaven; we can only hope they rest in peace. Defying Allah and being kind to humans won't lead them to heaven in Islam.

The next step is to increase goodness, not decrease. (Fitra) is the innate yearning within all humans to pray to the Creator installed by Allah. All children are born with a knowledge of their Creator. His advocacy aligns with his parents' and family's scriptures and interests.

A Muslim returning to their original state after being lost is a blessing from Allah. This process is Allah's gift to his servants, explained simply. Allah invites those he wishes to his faith. A heart distant from Allah is astray. Bowing to his creator is a blessed gift. Humanity receives a promotion from humans. He starts work hours early, he hopes to excel even further in worldly affairs.

Allah's surveillance surpasses human capabilities. He cannot recognize that the petition comes from the most powerful creator because he refuses to acknowledge him. Devotion to Allah erases differences and reveals the soul of the believer. If this component is missing, he avoids ever experiencing this delight.Spirituality's death is worse than surgery. It's true for many ailments of life, cure can become too late. The Creator's kindness provides abundant opportunities for seekers. Ailments plague life. The address lives in the heart. The Quran emphasizes the importance of the heart. Allah welcomes a pure heart.

Quran: Suran Ashura 26:89. But only one who comes to Allah with a sound heart.

Assumptions are made about Muslims battling illness before their death. Islamic principles bind Muslims. Allah will determine the outcome when he returns to a similar catastrophe, provided he cleanses himself or subtracts sins in this life. The torture in the next life is severe for the defiant without repentance it's better to pay your dues in this world.

Islamic belief records good and evil by angels. Healing is seen as Allah's method for restoring Muslims to their core. A person who turns to Allah in all circumstances is a devotee. The soul and character's ill health is the lowest disorder. The heart craves Satan's company because it lacks familiarity with productivity, positivity, and resistance to evil. Humans can suffer a catastrophic defeat.

Doctors prescribe medication and band-aids to prevent issues. Seeking penance can provide reliable spiritual solutions. A surgery survivor appreciates the rebirth, soul, and healing process. Without change, spiritual surgery is needed. The association of honest believers is crucial. Human sentiments and metaphysical needs should align. Islam encourages permissible heterosexual marriages. Inner discontent can result in forbidden relationships caused by negativity.

Spirit and character are foundational to the human spirit. Allah emphasizes the root's solvency. The heart is a central organ in human anatomy. Nutrition and liberty are luxuries for the wealthy. It is the responsibility of those who are fortunate and capable to support Muslims and others in need. Allah gives according to a person's capacity. Nothing surpasses the value of health.

'Health before illness' quoted prophet Muhammad. Islam highly values health and prioritizes physical and mental well-being. True devotion to Islam requires organization and restraint within boundaries. People are depicted as the engine of blunders from disregarding laws. Those who trust Allah always find the right path. Faith is vital. In Islam, astronomy, astrology, and embryology are subjects governed by scientific laws but the Quran exposes them first which affects relationships with all genders and age groups.

The Quran is a comprehensive book of laws that covers finance, wealth distribution, and the laws of the state. Mannerism, discipline, justice system. Allah's laws cannot be changed. The uninformed cultures of the world have an expression that says I don't care. It's not the care, it's the result of finality one will face that is eminent for preparation.

Muslims consider the Quran as a guidebook for life. Life prescription: flawless and beneficial. Allah revealed a book beyond human sight. Even the smallest things are emphasized in Islamic teachings.

Muslims are required to respond to greetings with better ones. In Islam, the greeting is significant as Allah greets Muslims daily during prayer and prostration, upon believers showing devotion to their creator. Islam's doctrine is explicit. Muslim values are a paradox of inner wealth. Created with rules and regulations for Islam's followers. A man's psychological profile must match someone with similar interests. Shared beliefs trump his relationships. Medication dosage is remembered spiritual health is neglected for some.

The Quran endures tests and trials of each decade, like a placed episode. Allah dared humanity to surpass the Quran with just one verse. The literate Arabs didn't meet the criteria. Talent = skill. Allah is the cause. They couldn't match the Quran's rhythm and delivery.

Quran: Surah ISRA 17:88. Say: Surely, if humanity and the Jinn were to get together to produce the like of this Qur'an, they could never produce the like. However, they might help one another.

Musicians and pop stars connect with youth and the confused. Contributed to corrupting the masses. Politics greatly influences lifestyles and mindsets. Allah sees the heart without a lens. Photography changes your perception of modern society by capturing expressions through retakes.

These visual images depict the subconscious mind, showing emotions and life's journey's. Emotions and thoughts are visible through a lens. Identity is the foundation. Modern technology showcases human expressions through appearance. A believer's spirituality is evident without pictures. Calm expressions are seen in believers. Models take multiple pictures for the desired look.

Allah does not require pictures. He can see through his lenses clearly. Happiness from Allah doesn't demand flawlessness. Islam discourages images. Photography exploits images and influences minds in various aspects of life, not limited to capturing happy memories. Islam discourages mixed gender relations, or provocative pictures to invite people to sin but in this society, any gender can have flings and develop interest in friendships. Therefore, believers must be cautious in this climate. Particularly in Western countries, where morality is seen as a political intrusion on domestic lifestyles.

These regulations are seen as outdated by some societies. Muslims should exercise caution regarding climate and societal restrictions in their actions. Grasping these ideologies can restrict the mind, making acceptance of good seem burdensome. Satan is causing fear and wasting time on fruitless tasks. Islam's methodology enhances permissible relationships without burdening them.

Khadija, wife of Prophet Muhammad, proposed to him, seeking an honest and credible man. He worked for her as her employee, strengthening their bondage through marriage. Western societies are experiencing upheaval and spiritual emptiness. Those who fear commitments are bound by fear but following the laws of defiance not Allah's laws. Throughout their proposal and acceptance of marriage, Khadija and Muhammad demonstrate many lessons to humanity. The right cannot meet the wrong in life, and the wrong cannot meet the right. Destiny is determined by Allah

Islam is unwavering in its rules and regulations, not swayed by corrupt societies. Conforming laws rejuvenated humanity with its moral application in daily life. The rules will remain unchanged when humanity reverts to ancient times. The rules are exceptional. Some see Islamic laws as outdated. Implementing pagan laws that permit unrestricted behavior doesn't make up for progress. It's the same road to calamity that has destroyed many countries despite warnings from the Prophets.

Continual hangouts with your former husband also have regulations. Islam has clear rulings. Reunite if mutually desired. Mishandling an individual's character can be complex and damaging. Allah's prescription is timeless. He undoubtedly acknowledges the humanity he created. Neither the Muslims nor the companions of Prophet Muhammad restored their compromised friendships. They formed stronger unions and improved their company.

In some cases, they left their families after embracing their new faith because other religions refused to accept their new faith. A believer would detach from such an environment if it was negative and unaccepted. Islam does not stop new Muslims from committing obligations to their family.

If they need help with the payments of life and obligations in this world taking care of them is acceptable. Survival in the same surroundings is impossible. They did not return to the same reminders, which were a reminder of disobedience to Allah once the truth had become obvious. In Islam, human beings advance, not regress.

Allah appreciates the patience displayed by humanity. Human beings are weak and impatient. Life is half won when one masters the skill of patience. God heard and understood the subconscious and conscious pleas of humanity. When spirituality and duality do not merge, they can create an untrue belief, resulting in disbelief. The rich seek spirituality. The same is true for the poor. In seeking inner peace, we all desire closeness to Allah.

From the Quran, Hadiths, and true narratives, we learn how these phenomena and examples can encourage us to contemplate life's cycle. Certain stories and reminders rearrange or arrange certain seekers' interests. Stories envelop understanding in various ways.

Story of a king and a pious man:

Once, a king visited a poor, pious man. The pious man caught the king's attention with his stories about Allah and his unwavering belief in God. He kept his longing for close friendship and connection with a believer to himself. His stern demeanor did not allow him to share his desires for belief. He longed for belief and friendship with someone who told him about Allah. Allah understood his heart. He satisfies the heart's longings. Unexpectedly, he encountered the pious man.

He invited the devout man to live in his palace. He lived in a small shack he called home. The pious man agreed after the king's persuasion. He asked for a room as compensation. The request was so small; he didn't want anyone in his living quarters. He wanted a simple room without furniture or frills. Despite receiving a palace title, he didn't want to forget his origins. He cleaned it himself, rejecting any help. No furniture or decorations. The King accepted the simple request.

The king made him the palace minister. His company and stories brought him joy. Jealousy arose among the palace residents because of this relationship. The new minister's stories were the most interesting. The friendship deepened. It was highly spiritual.

The spiritual stories made the king forget his kingship and he was in awe of the power of God. His power as a king seemed insignificant compared to the power of God. He aimed to be a fair and compassionate king. The king's knowledge expanded while he waited to hear more about God. It improved his kingship, but people disliked the new king due to their dislike of the new minister.

Problems arose from Satan's envy. He wanted the king to prioritize material wealth and people. He disliked the reformed king. The king received everything from Allah. The well and the believers are Satan's only concern. To destroy out of envy. No need for him to visit the underworlds, as he already has them.

The servants warned the king about the man. Why did he refuse entry to his room? The king dismissed the accusations against the pious man. Satan takes various forms and sends followers to sow doubt. The pious man asked for leave and the king granted it.

He can take time off. I'll spend a few days visiting my family. The staff suggested investigating his reasons for not allowing anyone in the room. What made him so secretive? The king agreed with the staff and they entered his room. Some of his old clothes and books were found. The man observed signs of unauthorized entry upon arrival. He asked the king. He answered. I permitted my staff to enter your room.

The pious man said I wore my old clothes and read my book, so I didn't forget who I was. I can no longer live here. You broke my trust and the agreement we agreed upon. If your spirituality reaches mine, you are welcome to knock on my door. I will now leave. The pious man returned to his tent. The grieving king lost a beloved friend who attended to his spirituality and shared his interests. As time passed the king felt lonely.

He longed for him but pushed away memories of their good times. On a certain day, he couldn't restrain himself. He knocked on the tent door of the pious man and invited him to return to the palace.

"Your spirituality has reached mine," the pious man replied.

He acknowledged the king's message. The return is something I've eagerly anticipated. This story emphasizes that spirituality is synonymous with unity. There is nothing that can sever that friendship. For a believer, spirituality is crucial in fostering friendship. Those who lead us to Allah are sought after by believers. Our loyal companions, handpicked by Allah, share our same interests.

Shared spirituality and a dual devotion to Allah form the foundation of genuine friendship. The person who reminds you of Allah is a friend. (Khareen)

Allah chose prophet Muhammad to be the last prophet and guide believers through his example. Practices and customs derived from the Sunnah. The concept of Prophet Muhammad without a security guard may seem theoretical. This prophet could walk without security due to Allah's protection. He welcomed everyone, gaining the leadership of Muslims and non-Muslims. Some people cannot grasp the Prophet of Islam's unique qualities and lifestyle. Humanity can display the prophet's practices by mirroring his customs. Every test strengthened Prophet Muhammad. Despite the challenges, he showed kindness and patience. He was equipped for the journey. His influence left a mark on the Muslim world. Many stories highlight the kindness, tenacity, and humor of this prophet.

Prophet's acquaintance with elderly women:

His reaction to the elderly woman shows the prophet's patience and endurance. An older, feeble woman's action of throwing rubble at Prophet Muhammad set a pattern for her. After a few days, he observed as he passed. She neglected to get rid of her rubbish for a few days. Upon inquiry, he learned she was old and sick. He knocked on the door, looking to lend a hand. His kindness and generosity moved her. Later on, she accepted Islam. Unkindness towards the teacher of this faith is not tolerated.

He taught with a caring approach to humanity. He cleaned her home until she regained strength. Her inner condition was repaired through spirituality. The maker revived her soul. Being patient and faithful during life's struggles is complex. Positive reactions can convert disbelievers into followers. Islam abolished pagan rituals. Allah alone deserves devotion. Prophet Muhammad is his helper and prophet. Besides unanimity, he showed no signs of careless behavior and left a living tradition and trademark traits to follow.

Quran: Surah Ahzab 33:40. Muhammad is not the father of [any] one of your men, [he is] the messenger of Allah and the last of the Prophets. And ever is Allah, of all things.

The body, mind, and soul are crucial to Islam. Man can call his creator anytime. Islam sets guidelines on ritual prayers and cleanliness. It describes the state of purity as water is crucial for cleanliness in Islam. Muslims must cleanse themselves with water standing before Allah. Clean people hesitate to be with unclean individuals.

The subject is discussed in the Quran. Man's questioning continues. Allah did not send a human to wander. He wants to expand our learning through researching the answers he has given. Those unaware of Allah are spiritually asleep. Humans cannot be satisfied by a synthetic world. Life without Allah is meaningless. Allah values truth, not material possessions. Islam followers achieve balance through repetition.

Islamic way of life has distinct stages of survival. Death is the transcendent stage according to the Quran, with life after death determined by Allah's ruling and questioning. Muslims envision the end of an earth chapter. The key to stability and balance lies in cherishing this life and preparing for the next.

The Quran portrays Prophets as role models. They endured numerous trials in their lives. They left behind communication and examples.

Prophet Muhammad came from a lineage of Quraish and the clan of Banu Hashim. His lineage branched from the prestigious and influential Quraysh tribe. Rather than a lineage that has left a mark in this world, it was Allah's chosen prophet for Muslims, and humanity was the delivery of Islam. Without social media, he endured his trials and walked away with the titles of (Al-Amin) trustworthy and (As-Sadiq) truthful.

His achievements are unmatched by any writer today. It cannot justify my writing or anyone else's writing based on his accomplishments. His followers adored him and considered him a legendary, highly successful prophet. Muslims react emotionally when they encounter disrespect for the prophet because of their love for him. They have no tolerance for disrespect towards Islam's prophet or the Quran, which has become an issue in certain cultures and through instigation.

It is incomprehensible that social or political motives cause these dilemmas. The amount of information I share is slender. Learning his faith from a non-Muslim is the most destructive thing a Muslim can do.

How can a non-Muslim teach the faith of a Muslim or advise a Muslim on his faith? Encrypted society's social media are full of interpretations of Islam. It is a poisonous source for the ignorant. Man cannot alter the Quran. Allah's last revelation, untouched by man, is the only book surviving. He will preserve the book he revealed. In Islam, obedience and faith are the basis of spirituality. In a nutshell, to be attentive to you, he must be attentive to his creator. Therefore, virtue and evil are not equal.

Quran: Surah Fussilat 41:34. O Prophet, Good and evil are not equal. Repel (evil) with that which is good, and you witness that he between whom and you there was enmity shall become as if he were a bosom friend of yours

People who are averse to Islam provide continuous criticism regarding Islam and Muslims. Is it possible for a Muslim to respond in words to evil acts? Imposition is not worth the efforts in retaliation unless necessary. The appraisal of this faith requires the understanding that there is no price except for time. Time is valued more than any currency, along with our health.

Quran: Surah Imran 3:159. So, by mercy from Allah Muhammad, you were lenient with them. And if you had been rude [in speech] and harsh in heart, they would have disbanded from you. So, pardon them and ask forgiveness for them.

Islam is the pure monotheistic faith of worship of one Allah alone. The colored world is fully aware that Muslims do not allow statues or pictures of the Prophet Muhammad as a sign of respect. Soon, they were delighted in inciting Muslims by showing disrespect to Prophet Muhammad, some of whom were prone to anger and retaliation.

Charlie Hebdo, a French magazine publisher, republished a cartoon defaming the Prophet Muhammad in the wake of a deadly attack in 2015. Immediately, more cartoons depicting disrespect appeared, causing political havoc and anger among Muslims, antagonizing repeated broadcasts by the Western media.

Charlie Hebdo satirical magazine incited many Muslims by showing controversial pictures depicting Prophet Muhammad. As a result, Islamist gunmen with a no-tolerance policy for disrespecting the Prophet launched attacks. He persevered and republished his article, letting anger get the better of him. In these incidents, the alleged accomplices of those who lost their lives faced trials.

BBC: Sep 1, 2020 — French satirical magazine **Charlie Hebdo** has republished cartoons of the **Prophet Mohammed** that made them the target of a deadly terror **attack**

Many Muslims have expressed anger in this way. Muslims often overlook the fact that they cannot control the feelings they feel. Because pulsating the Muslims by disrespecting the Prophet by direct instigation and provocation has consequences. Some people may challenge the instigator and end up in a brutal fight. This is not a representation of Islam but merely a play of emotions between the two parties. They can prevent such purposeful crimes. Charlie Hebdo was already aware of this act of instigation and provocation.

This resulted in retaliation and anger from the Muslim Islamists. This act of anger reflects the emotion and has no bearing on Islam. Muslims respect all faiths and do not intend to disrespect them by making negative remarks or drawing cartoons of their Gods or idols. This act created an outrage in the Muslim world, seeing disrespect for Prophet Muhammad. A massacre and attack took place at the offices of Charlie Hebdo.

BBC: Dec 16, 2020 — **Charlie Hebdo attack**: Three days of terror · Seven people detained over Paris knife **attack** · Fourteen on trial over **Charlie Hebdo** massacre.

This still did not stop the cartoonist from producing more disrespectful cartoons of the Prophet and the innocent suffering. All Muslims in the Western world were under attack after the incident. France banned the niqab face covering worn by some Muslim women. It became law, and they imposed a fine for violating the law.

Wikipedia: Act prohibiting concealment of the face in public space") is an act of parliament passed by the Senate of France on 14 September 2010, resulting in the ban on the wearing of face-covering

Face covering later became an essential element in the world because of COVID-19. The mercy of Allah has many patterns. This mercy of the Creator led to the world standing in a (niqab) face covering after COVID-19. Allah knows best. Throughout every decade, Allah will subject Muslims to all kinds of tests and trials. Although the restrictions on wearing a face covering (Niqab) have been relaxed, there are still those who wear this preventive mask and a new uniform of defense. Diseases come and go in news alerts. But Islam remains the same.

Quran: Surah Ra'd 13:11. For there are successive angels before and behind him, who protect him by the decree of Allah. Indeed, Allah will not change the condition of a people until they change what is in themselves.

And when Allah intends a nation to suffer, there is no repelling it. No patron besides Allah. Unreasonable hostility towards Muslims has also spread to the East. The most passive group, known as Buddhists, has conflicts with the Rohingya Muslims, who have perpetrated gang rapes and other forms of sexual violence and killing. According to Wikipedia, Buddhists have killed at least 24,000 victims. The numbers continue to add up.

For many Muslims, a harsh climate and unfavorable conditions have made them targets. The persecution of Muslims in Myanmar is a continuing disaster for Muslims. Rohingya Muslims face hardships. No concern for humanity is an ongoing effort in some places. Myanmar is a predominantly Buddhist country. The Mandalay riots of 1997 were a trying time. Tensions continued between Muslims and Buddhists regarding the statue of Buddha.

Wikipedia:1997 Mandalay riots: Tension grew between Buddhists and Muslims during the renovation of a Buddha statue. The bronze Buddha statue in the Maha Muni pagoda, originally from the Arakan, brought to Mandalay by King Bodawpaya in 1784 was renovated by the authorities.

BBC: Jul 3, 2014 — Myanmar's second city, Mandalay, is put under curfew after ... Vehicles, shops and mosques have been attacked during the unrest in Mandalay.

Buddhist monks destroyed Islamic books and mosques. Women and children were being violated by them. They were looting vehicles. Muslims and Buddhists were at odds with the statue of Buddha. Buddhist monks raped women, attacked mosques, and burned Islamic religious books. Buddha would not be pleased with these actions. They refer to themselves as Buddhists. We recount China's persecution of Muslims, putting them in concentration camps, and repression of Uighurs.

BBC: May 24, 2022 — China has been accused by the US of genocide and crimes against humanity against the Muslim minority group.

Many incidents of unrest, violence, and deadly attacks. This list could go on and on. The Palestine War began in 1947. Israel annexed the land of Palestinians. This war has been costly, with millions displaced from their homes by violent attacks.

History Central: 1947 Civil War in Palestine.

The support of certain regions led to the loss of many lives and the disruption of medical and clean water supplies to families suffering at the hands of distress. Losses in economic warfare and lives are costly. The conflict between Israel and Palestine is ongoing.

The world has seen harsh health conditions this land has faced for centuries: The mental and physical health of children and the elderly is at stake, not to mention the habitation of all kinds, including animals and plants. Ironically, they face a tyranny of ambushes imposed by greedy sources and vandalism toward the innocent. Allah examines Muslims, and they will continue to be tested in the future. The most difficult situation for believers is when disbelievers have the upper hand. Most believers pray our weaknesses don't shame us and strengthen our beliefs to face our enemies and finish stronger.

Islam encourages the dead to be buried as soon as possible, as the dead no longer have a place on earth after the soul departs. But the souls living in unrest appear to face death before it visits them. The dead and the oppressed only find peace when they are alone and away from humanity. The world becomes burdensome for the deceased after it departs the same for the oppressed. Continued efforts to shed light on Islam and incidents that impact this society, along with stories that have a deep impact on faith.

Nevertheless, the support of humanity or friendships regardless of political changes and arenas changes the counterfoil implications and thoughts towards humans, and friendships are not based on political agendas in any circumstance in the world. This does not affect humans, but teaching culture regimes greed is based on the separation of humanity but keeps kindness intact for those who know each other. Education, in the literal sense, is brought to life when one understands the academic framework of a classroom is structured and formatted in literature.

The delivery is a heartfelt and open form that appeals to those who think and understand with an open mind directly from a Muslim. Conduct is a solid character trait. It is not extinct for anyone of faith but for those who choose to live by morals and ethics; it forms the strength.

CHAPTER 3

ISLAM FOR HEALTH, WEALTH, AND ACHIEVEMENTS.

Islam's wealth is a valuable advantage for promoting good health. Is health primarily influenced by the physical or the spiritual? Lack of moral integrity is not exclusive to physically fit individuals. Balance is necessary for both spiritual and physical needs. The shades of Muslims vary depending on the shadower. Despite challenges, believers find solace in the presence of Allah.

The hold of Allah is the most powerful. Islam plays a crucial role in advancing human progress. Islam emphasizes personal growth through stability, consistency, and endurance, diligently neglecting oneself for others is a valid concern. Does Islam consider believers' avoidance of challenges and pursuit of different paths contradictory? Islam provides hope for individuals who repent instead of writing them off.

The belief in Allah's mercy, and forgiveness, and the importance of Islam drive believers to aid others. It encompasses the irreligious as well. Time does not affect faith. The poorest hearts can become the wealthiest through time, as in Islam. Hope endures, but the dead cannot be brought back. Hope in human deeds concludes when the soul departs.

Believers view distress as an opportunity for growth and closeness to Allah. How do believers respond to the unexpected arrival of hurricanes and tornadoes? Hope connects to every path for betterment.

True believers prioritize learning consistency and keeping approved believers in life. The human race is not neglected, despite its differences. Each person has their beauty that is appreciated by others. Humanity is designed to be cordial, helpful, and learn from one another. Walking away is a wise choice in the face of chaos.

Every living being has a duty towards Allah. Humans share the strongest connection with a creator. Believer maximizes his or her performance for Allah, the employer. Understanding validity and time constraints is necessary for this job. Humanity's duration is unknown, but daily performance remains consistent and evaluated. The office everyone wants to work at, where self-expectation drives performance. Employment lasts until one's demise.

Life's progressions necessitate a duty to health. Allah grants humans the ability to differentiate between right and wrong without supervision. He has both a job and control over his spirit, mind, and body. Each human has their deeds recorded by angels. Writings are determined by actions. Allah's accounting is speedy.

Better than any human accountant who erases errors and displeasing actions. Powerful companies and governments demand high performance from employees. Would the employer terminate the employee for underperforming? Most likely, yes.

The expectations for academic and sports performance are equal. Exceeding the bounds of human laws. Expulsion is typically the consequence of poor performance. Allah grants abundant opportunities until death. Humans frequently acknowledge their role as their responsibility and the significance of self-worth. Despite differing opinions, both Commander Allah and human enhancements are the main authorities challenging societal norms and harmful self-deprecation. The challenge for every individual is clear: prioritize personal growth and self-awareness above everything else. While followers and leaders are present, self-leadership is essential for personal success.

Understanding is crucial for health, as seen through numerous examples. When you see yourself as your thoughts' employee. Visualize the best version of life to achieve success. Deception through assumptions or impersonation of evil is not tolerated in any society. The major drawback of self-inflicted thoughts is deception. Constructive thinking is required for productivity. Progress is not inspired by negative sources.

Surround yourself with positive individuals and avoid negative influences. Inertia is the biggest influence on oneself, inspiring ideas. Muslims prioritized progress over negativity in the Golden Age. They filled the table with an abundance of food, positivity, and knowledge. This is the mindset of aspiring individuals. Allah observes the truth within the heart and allows life to unfold. Understanding the revisions makes the reading worthwhile for those compatible with Islam. And for those interested in understanding Islam and tallying the differences.

The best employer prioritizes time over currency. Making the most revenue in the least amount of time is success. Same strategy is applicable to those who don't value time.Make the most of life in the least amount of time. Time gets subtracted daily from life. Health is influenced by company and thoughts. Inner health manifests through behavior, not appearance. Thoughts and molecules nourish unseen tissues. Outer health is a mirage of societal expectations. This reminder for Muslims helps brush up on Islamic beliefs.

Employers who prioritize mental and physical health. Witness the success. One fosters the application of this concept within oneself as the employer of all thoughts. To foster a positive work environment and increase productivity, start with healthy minds and bodies. The best place to start is by being your most effective employer. Behaviors are self-imposed. Taking advice from poorly-behaved individuals hinders positive attitudes and decisions. Seeking guidance from Allah is the most appropriate behavior. Positive community involvement is crucial.

It's paramount to acknowledge the contributions of others, alongside Allah, in any successful endeavor. In today's world, people forget Muslims' history and repeat ingratitude. After handling their worldly affairs, they attempt to change the teacher's course. Weakness shifts the curve, strength remains deep. Constructive conversations and meaningful relationships foster holistic growth.

Our companions influence our character. The decision on which company to choose is up to you. The demands of life influence whether individuals keep or reject their family members. Disregarding laws of enforcement highlights the significance of family and expressing gratitude for maintaining familial bonds. How did Allah transform this into a positive experience for the family?

He is aware of the poor nature of the humans he created and knows their mentality; they lead themselves to forbidden paths. Kindness in Islam starts at home. The force of Islam's communities strengthens when family holds together, but weakens when separated. The imitators of Satan disrupt positive actions. Islam prioritizes strength and stability, not weakness and family division. Islam places a high value on family relationships. Secrets, attitudes, envy, competition, greed, deceit, hypocrisy, and restrictions are causing division among people.

Despite family discord, Muslims must uphold their values. The best course of action is separation. If they won't accept Islam, then try again. Over time, some people learn to embrace truth instead of resistance. Prioritizing and not neglecting building relationships is crucial. Relationships can develop either early in life or later through various events.

Chaos arises when a convert or Muslim strengthens their faith and stays in a disapproving family. Tension and misunderstanding can arise from the unfamiliarity of the new faith and its fusion. Faith is challenging to uphold in certain environments, so support and acceptance are crucial. In Islam, your companions in this life are your partners in the afterlife.

People are defined by the company they keep. The people we associate with can profoundly impact our lives. Right choices bring substantial rewards in this life and beyond. Our goal is to find people who bring out our best and facilitate our development. Nothing stays the same as seasons change. Seasons move in cycles. Life includes focusing on the timeline. Unexpected challenges strengthen those who wish to progress. Strengthening one's core involves unexpected challenges.

For some, it points to stagnation and a return to the same dust, never leaving the familiar core. Company is always the essence of Islam's climb or downfall, staying on the same surface and never experiencing the climb. Saturation and stagnation are not Islam's protocol.

Prophet Muhammad's (Sunnah) ways and practices are parameters of survival and depth of understanding the world as a human. It leaves the remnants of the positive cycle with no pedal corrosion and rust. Ray of hope is the climb's persistence. Islamic concepts cannot be neglected or discouraged, as academic wealth is the brutal source of independence. Along with travel, a strong sense of self-help and provisions for assisting others.

The spiritual enactment offers boundless riches and freedom. True freedom lies within on a journey of self-discovery. The result is purpose and fulfillment. The simple joys of life often go unnoticed. Continuous learning is familiar to Muslims. You cannot fix the perfection of something made by Allah. What is below is above, and what is outside is within. Believers who assist other believers are abundantly blessed. By Allah's mercy, it is unexpectedly transported and implemented as a surprise.

Promoting health involves prioritizing exercise in healthy environments. The individuals maintain a healthy diet and can relate to people with similar interests. Those who engage in similar habits can give advice, support, and understanding. It solidifies their bond and establishes a lasting relationship. Similar birds flock together. An old saying is correct. Believers remind each other of their shared bonds.

Befriending someone with opposing habits is impossible. It's hard to relate to someone with different health habits. Thus, forming a meaningful connection with them is difficult. This also applies to spiritual realms. Unhealthy individuals cannot be competent advisors. It is crucial to find the right mentor for accurate advice. The forthcoming advice applies to any lifestyle and the company relates to any field of life.

Humans seek companies that match their souls. Finding a company or your inner self that values your skills and appreciates your unique talents is crucial. Building relationships with people with similar interests can open up new opportunities and create a strong network of support. Having a positive working environment is key to success. These principles hold to Islam.

Envy is a treacherous accusation from the envier who has less experience of life. Still seeks the vantage and time of life he missed. Beauty is in the eye of the beholder. The soul of the confused carries him to meaningless conversations and unimportant places. Finding plastic blitz and defiance to Allah as success is not the life of a Muslim.

The chronological age of a man has no limits on health conditions. Islam has given utmost priority to health, placing it second next to faith. Showing disrespect to health is showing disrespect to Allah and his (Deen) way of life.

The Mediterranean diet will keep humanity healthy. Righteous and healthy women and men were raising happy families. The inherent culture of food, diet, and discipline in the Islamic world also prohibits overeating. Most doctors suggest a Mediterranean diet for a healthy lifestyle. Accepting obesity and feeling comfortable in your skin is a hallmark of the defiant. Overeating is taboo in Islam, which limits the use and consumption of food. Allah has given many health benefits through the food he has provided.

The Quran refers to various fruits, vegetables, and grains like olives, bananas, figs, grapes, pomegranates, onions, garlic, cucumbers, watermelon, and lentils. We use herbs mentioned in the Quran for both consumption and medicine.

Lentils provide ample folate, iron, and vitamin B1, supporting heart health as well. Consuming lentils may lower the risk of heart disease by reducing bad cholesterol and blood pressure. In a study, lentils were more effective than chickpeas, peas, or beans in lowering blood pressure. The Quran reveals what humans should prioritize in their pursuit of knowledge.

Quran: Surah Baqarah 2:173. He has only forbidden to you dead animals, blood, the flesh of swine, and that which has been dedicated to others other than Allah.

Quran: Surah Insan 76:17. We shall serve them a cup flavored with ginger.

The seeker's quest unlocks the answers within the Quran. The search has arrived. Ginger is mentioned in the Quran. Ginger offers numerous advantages. Ginger-based drinks are commonly served by Arab people. In Islam, individuals with certain underlying health conditions cannot use purposeful actions or neglecting health as excuses. Decadence is not a part of human evolution, rather it is characterized by progress in mentality and learning. A person's health is determined by their behavior and habits. Nevertheless, Muslims have to care for the principles of life.

Health is a gift from Allah to humanity and a loan is a payment of self-care from humanity to Allah. The body, mind, and spirit rely on regular attendance for optimal health. Obesity, depression, and ill health are consequences of excessive eating.

Certain regions experience weight gain due to excessive food and alcohol intake, and obesity can be considered an illness unless internal health factors are involved. Overeating goes against Islamic practices. Prophet Muhammad emphasized etiquette and food consumption.

He advised Muslims to eat in unity, not isolation. Eating meals together is linked to blessings. Be generous and share your food with others. Chew your food slowly to maintain self-control and avoid exceeding your limits. Avoid reclining while eating. The (Sunnah), left by Prophet Muhammad, guides Muslims. He showcased the eating habits that adhere to Muslim etiquette. Humans are at their lowest point when they overeat. Ensure one-third of the stomach remains empty.

Divide it into one-third for food and one-third for liquids. This dieting practice was left behind by Prophet Muhammad. Society has come to accept the consumption of hookah, shisha, chewing tobacco, and cigarettes over many years. Life's highs always bring lows, especially for those addicted to the burdens of unattractive attachments.

People who are addicted to this recurring pattern of extreme emotions develop a dependence on the rush it brings. The attempt to find meaning or fill a void only amplifies the sense of emptiness. Prophet Muhammad's (Sunnah) customs and practices do not mention any deficiencies of this nature. The praying mind and heart don't need to attend to unhealthy habits.

People continue to jeopardize their health over extended periods, unaware of the risks involved. Sometimes fully aware but apathetic towards personal well-being. Both tobacco and shisha smoke carry dangers from carbon monoxide and toxicity. The list comprises cancers, heart attacks, lung diseases, and nicotine dependence. The potential harms for users are a list of tragedies. Nicotine has a tremendous effect on the human body. Secondhand smoke is also highly destructive.

Monitoring the updates of this silent killer is highly addictive and can lead to throat cancers, emphysema, lung disease, or heart attacks. This spreads to every organ of the body, allowing the user to believe he is coping with anxiety, but continued usage can damage more than he bargained for.

Blockage of arteries by plaques can lead to heart disease, stroke, and other bodily issues. Familial disorders often result in elevated cholesterol levels that are challenging to regulate. Since smokers face higher risks in managing underlying health conditions. Exercise and healthy eating are encouraged in Islam.

Those who maintain a healthy lifestyle typically abstain from harming their bodies, recognizing that the body exemplifies optimal health for those who value their physical well-being. Spiritual health becomes important alongside physical health due to the damaging effects of poor health on peace. Spiritual and physical respect become habitual, transforming daily life and fostering personal growth. Through our actions and words, we invite others to grow and showcase an admiration for life.

Ignoring the guidelines of the Quran can lead to serious health implications. Nicotine and cigarettes are not mentioned in the Quran, but they emphasize health as a primary obligation. Going against the tide guarantees failure in any aspect of life. The Creator personally created the laws. Medicinal purposes and mind-altering experiences have been derived from plants.

Despite each substance not being mentioned in the Quran, these woes of destruction are (makrooh) detestable. For a believer, health is wealth, and every person who faces ill health understands it cannot compare the value to material possessions.

Drinking alcohol is prohibited in Islam. The Quranic verses refer to it. Prophet Muhammad's (Sunnah) customs and practices delineate any mind-altering intoxicant. There are no excuses for claiming that a few drinks do not alter the mind; it is prohibited and does not change the amount consumed. Islam has vetoed such acts and performances.

Qatar, a Muslim country, banned stadium beer sales after sponsoring the most recent episode in 2022.

BBC. Nov 18th, 2022. Alcohol sales banned at World Cup stadiums in Qatar.

Budweiser has been a sponsor of World Cup tournaments since 1986. To abide by Islamic principles and avoid contradicting the laws of Allah and the Quran. The significance of the huge gathering of public outrage was negligible. Muslims opted out of serving alcoholic beverages at the stadium during the show. Intoxication and drinks are often seen as a luxury.

Muslims consider alcohol consumption and serving to be contradictory to their religious law which prohibits it. It's impossible to stop someone from drinking, but it's recommended for Muslims to refrain from serving or consuming alcohol. There is a common link between foreign countries and the pleasure of drinking alcohol. The need for a superficial high is highlighted to appreciate life's intricacies, and simple enjoyment is connected to some sort of high. A content Muslim can fully enjoy life when all the human vibes and currents are in place.

Despite Western conflicts and resentments, many people find empowerment by respecting their values. Muslims consistently during this event prioritized Allah's rules and Islam above all else. The alcohol ban at Qatar Stadium during the 2022 World Cup left many spectators disappointed, especially those excited to see their team play, enjoying the personal high and addictions to superficial enjoyment. Allah's orders took priority over human needs. They soon found out dependence on highs is not necessary. Life can be enjoyed in its true self.

BBC. Nov 18th, 2022. Wales fans have voiced anger and disappointment at the last-minute ban on alcohol in Qatar World Cup stadiums.

Some may appreciate the strict moral laws imposed by Islam. However, humans can find pleasure in life with no intoxication. The Muslim world proved that it is possible. Allah allows humans to continue unless the harm exceeds the benefit. Alcohol use, especially over time, can cause damage. A portion of the brain damage is permanent. Impaired coordination leads to slurred speech and memory problems. Intoxicants cause gradual harm to the nervous system, with the negative effects surpassing any pleasure.

Through the examples in the Quran, one can find healing internally and outwardly. In the Quran, honey is mentioned by Allah as a healing source. Honey has anti-inflammatory properties and contains antioxidants. Honey can function as an antidepressant, relieve anxiety, and improve sleep. Aids in burn healing and memory disorder prevention. The skin benefits from it and it is advantageous for the cosmetic industry.

Muslims find justification for their actions in the Quran when Allah mentions something. In Islam, irrational behavior is not considered an experiment, multiple choice, or an act of defiance. Muslims were driven by a thirst for knowledge and a passion for Islam to embrace the teachings of the Prophet Muhammad. They wasted no time in sharing after finding out. Prophet Muhammad instructed us to learn and teach the Quran. The key to a thriving business today is to learn and exchange benefits. Benefit-sharing is a characteristic of successful companies.

Neglecting self-respect can lead to severe and damaging outcomes. When humans stop caring, they can become a burden on themselves and others. Islam places a strong emphasis on self-care and health.

Quran: Surah Nahl: 16;69.and feed from the flower of` any fruit you please and follow the ways your Lord has made easy for you." From their bellies comes forth liquid of varying colors, in which there is healing for people.

The Bible contains a more elaborate and vivid depiction of obesity for the believers of this religion. Despite its widespread prevalence, obesity remains the primary cause of heart attacks. Type 2 diabetes and cancer are among the various mental and physical ailments.

Bible: Deuteronomy 21:20. In the Bible, gluttony is closely linked with the sins of drunkenness, idolatry, lavishness, rebellion, disobedience, laziness, and wastefulness.

Islam takes health as part of respect for the gift from Allah. Every book Allah has sent has consistency, so if it falls out of consistency, questions arise since Allah is consistent. Life has played a role in keeping balance for most Muslims through Islam. After accepting Islam, Muslims did not dwell on the evil and destruction of body and mind. Successful Muslims have left behind a legacy of light and history. For decades, Muslims have respected all the forces of life granted to humanity and excelled in every avenue.

Playing an important role in changing the course of history and sharing knowledge for the betterment of the world. The Quran and the (Sunnah) customs and practices during the Prophet Muhammad's time governed reforms and legislation. During the Islamic golden age, the success of Muslims was a triumph. Following the waiting period, the Ottoman Empire filled in the gaps. A province of the Ottoman Empire. The Golden Age of Islam of this era gave Muslims the heights of literacy. The Ottoman Empire conquered the Byzantine Empire during its expansion into South Eastern Europe and beyond.

Britannica: Jul 3, 2023 — Ottoman Empire, empire created by Turkish tribes that grew to be one of the most powerful states in the world in the 15th and 16th centuries …

Wikipedia: The Ottoman Empire, historically and colloquially known as the Turkish Empire, was an empire that controlled much of <u>Southeast Europe</u>, Western Asia, and Northern Africa, between the 14th and early 20th centuries.

The Ottoman Empire flourished under Muslim leadership, experiencing prosperity in the economy, mental health, material security, and religious legislation. Regardless of their faith, Islam safeguards the rights of all individuals. Foreign forces caused evil to unfold and brought destruction that Muslims were unprepared for. Unexpected events occur as enemies envy successful believing Muslims. Malevolence encompasses more than just greed.

For a believer, failures are not a concern; they serve to strengthen and showcase the power of belief over the enemy's vengeance. Muslims possess the power to conquer evil and spread unity to the world, just as the Ottoman Empire did by sharing its success. The success achieved by deceitful foreign lands only brings harm to others, which is not true success but merely a temporary solution for their downfall. The world will witness Muslims leading with kindness, cooperation, and respect for all faiths, displaying the true essence of Islam.

The constant interference and enforcement of laws is exhausting for those who are aware of the truth and stay informed, and it hinders Muslims in societies that portray Islam negatively, leaving the world in a state of confusion while benefiting the higher-ups who exploit resources and destroy their own and other countries. When a community defies laws placed by Allah, it appoints a tyrant ruler who brings destruction to the country and its people. Better people, respecting Allah's laws and land, will be sent to help those oppressed by human command and follow Allah's commands.

In modern-day Turkey, it is still on the rise as it develops. The collapse of one empire is only the beginning of the next for Muslims. The Turkish people of descent are rulers at heart and givers who stand for justice and do not move away from the path of faith. They may not all practice Islam, but a Muslim's heart will practice it upon the summons of Allah. The heart yearns for those who believe and Allah answers those who call.

The architecture and legacy of Islamic culture still stand as a powerful reminder of the medieval Renaissance. Muslims had a powerful influence in these countries. During almost 800 years or more of Islamic rule, the peninsula of Europe flourished. Europeans and the world learned from the Islamic Golden Age. In the decade of Muslims, art, cuisine, education, and etiquette were all preserved.

It spread to Andalus, Sicily, Spain, and Portugal. Many streets still have Muslim names today, and the culture still shines in the countries they ruled and left behind in the past. It is not a pile of destruction and chaos caused by unexpected entrances. In addition, other Muslim countries should hinder from following the decadence of such minds.

The Muslim empire was at its highest peak before the British occupation and invasion. Nothing stayed the same after the meddling of the British. They copied most ideas of literacy from the Muslim world. As a result, they preyed upon this newly discovered renaissance, slowly but surely leading man into wars of greed. Faith must be the balance between this pendulum and hope in Allah.

The Muslim lands held the sunshine of success and the growth of an inherent culture that would leave a lasting effect on the world. During this time, the Muslim world faced compromising situations because of foreign interference. The entry of some uninvited guests into the Middle East destroyed plants, animals, and women. Many lost their health and lives as a result.

In Islam, wars are fought with fairness and without injustice it's a failed affair for a Muslim. Islam prohibits fighting for greed; fairness is emphasized. Out of greed, they have been waging wars in the Muslim world for decades. The climate and oppression in this world mirror the situation in Palestine. Unity is crucial for Muslim countries to fight for justice instead of greed.

Quran: Surah Baqarah 2:212. Beautified for those who disbelieve in the life of this world, and they ridicule those who believe. But those who fear Allah are above them on the day of the resurrection. And Allah gives provision to whom He wills without account.

Prophet Muhammad predicted the Muslims would conquer Constantinople, making it a victorious Muslim nation. If this prophecy did not happen as expected, Allah postponed it for 600 years. Islam's credibility would be questionable. If Prophet Muhammad's prophecies didn't materialize.

Those who oppose Islam would question its integrity. Without a doubt, it happened. Allah's oath reflects the truth. The Quran refers to the Romans' defeat. Allah's time is not the same as human time. The conquest of Constantinople was a game-changing event for Muslims, allowing them to take over the Byzantine Empire and establish the Ottoman Empire, which excelled in all aspects.

Quran: Surah Rum 1-6. *Alif, Lam, Meem, and The Romans were defeated. In the nearest lowest land. But they, after their defeat, will overcome within three to nine years. To Allah belongs the command before and after. And on that day, the believers will rejoice in the victory of Allah. He gives victory to whom He wills. And He is the Exalted in Might, the Merciful. [It is] the promise of Allah. It is Allah's promise that never fails, but most are unaware of this.*

It was a good time for the Muslims. If this had not happened, Islam would have been at a crossroads. Constantinople became a Muslim country under Ottoman rule. Today's social media often fails to deliver precise information about Muslims or the conquest and flourishing times of the Muslim era and those who continue still flourish, keeping victories within reach. The Muslim world is at the forefront of teaching and learning. It's not money, it's teachings that bring the blitz along with worldly gratification, which is the Muslim appraisal of life per Islamic doctrine.

Muslims who focus on learning and teaching succeed, but outside interference can cause division and deceit. Satan's dwelling is a source of disturbance for successful believers who prosper and instruct. Muslims have a motto of never stagnating, and believers follow suit. This was one of the most significant events in the history of the Islamic era.

After Prophet Muhammad's passing, the chapter reached its conclusion. The Prophet's predictions of Muslims taking over Constantinople came to pass. This event solidified Islam's integrity, but Muslims do not let their beliefs be altered by others. Prophet Muhammad didn't shy away from the truth. He was shielded from lies, not truth. The truth will never be feared by a Muslim who is a believer. The Ottoman Empire was a healthy time. Muslims had conquered most of the land and flourished in all aspects of life.

Islam and Muslims brought a new renaissance to this world. There was a light in this empire that shone brighter than any light bulb available in today's markets. The Ottoman Empire holds history tall as the biggest expansion in history, one of the largest empires known after they conquered Constantinople. Muslims were at their peak. Sultan Mehmet conquered Constantinople from the Byzantine Empire. Many feared the Muslim world was taking control, and jealousy continued to rise. Fear and conflict were the leading factors.

The world has always wanted the literacy of Muslims. Their achievements were a benchmark in society. Christians and Muslims continued the crusades and wars to gain control. With the Muslim conquest of lands, they flourished, but greed unleashed a massacre of morality for those who sought to destroy Muslims' ventures and accomplishments. Teachers are Muslims, not followers. We rule by truth, not with arrogance. The invasions and interference of outside sources led to an all-encompassing decline in spirituality, trade, economics, and degrading dress codes.

Free trade in sex and acceptance has led to many misguided actions by humanity, as was not the case with the Muslim world. Jews confined themselves, as they, too, were victims of tragedies. They worked quietly to gain control and had plans of their own. Muslims extended a helping hand to Jews during difficult times, considering them as friends and relatives. Islam assists everyone, regardless of their color, creed, or religion.

Their exile from the land of Israel from Allah resulted from disobedience to Allah's command and manifesting their laws. The Western world maintained a pattern of consistent behavior, making plans to destroy and dismantle the accomplishments of the Muslim world. Although they copied and enjoyed the culture of most of Europe, Spain, and Italy still hold the architecture of the Muslim world.

They composed the empire of many lands: Bulgaria, Egypt, Greece, Hungary, Jordan, Lebanon, Israel, Palestine, Macedonia, Romania, Spain, Eastern Europe, and parts of Syria, Arabia, also the north coast of Africa. These territories were under the control of the Muslim empire. The common language spoken was Arabic.

During the Golden Age of Islam, which spanned from the 8th to the 14th century, Muslims made significant advancements in various fields. In the realm of cultural and intellectual pursuits, Islamic scholars translated and preserved ancient Greek and Roman texts, ensuring their survival and eventual dissemination to Europe. This period witnessed the establishment of renowned centers of learning, such as the House of Wisdom in Baghdad, where scholars from diverse backgrounds gathered to exchange knowledge. Islamic scholars made groundbreaking contributions to mathematics, introducing concepts like algebra and the decimal system, which revolutionized the field.

They also made significant advancements in astronomy, developing precise astronomical instruments and accurately calculating celestial movements. In the field of medicine, Muslim physicians compiled and expanded upon the knowledge of ancient Greek, Indian, and Persian scholars, developing sophisticated medical techniques and creating influential medical encyclopedias.

These achievements not only shaped the Islamic world but also influenced European intellectual development during the Middle Ages. Therefore, it is crucial to include the Golden Age of Islam in school and university curriculum to highlight the contributions made by Muslims and promote a more comprehensive understanding of world history.

In the expression of delivery, if only the Golden Age of Islam and the Ottoman Empire were truly understood and appreciated, it would provide a comprehensive understanding of the remarkable achievements and contributions of the Muslim world. This period, known as the Golden Age of Islam,

witnessed extraordinary advancements in various fields such as science, mathematics, medicine, philosophy, and architecture. Scholars like Al-Khwarizmi, Ibn Sina, and Ibn Rushd made groundbreaking discoveries and laid the foundation for modern knowledge. Additionally, the Ottoman Empire, established in the 13th century, expanded to become a powerful and influential state that encompassed diverse cultures, religions, and territories.

Its success was attributed to its efficient administration, military prowess, and cultural tolerance. Understanding the profound impact of these periods in history is crucial for a comprehensive understanding of the Muslim world and its rich heritage. Therefore, it is imperative to educate people who lack knowledge about these achievements in Muslim history, as it would undoubtedly shake their perception and deepen their appreciation for this exotic era of knowledge and success.

Muslim empowerment and success in the past decade brought contentment, learning, and extravagance to the world. Muslims experienced a decade of success, leaving behind numerous examples of awakening. Muslims' enthusiasm for exploring the wonders of architecture, science, math, cuisine, and the military, while celebrating the joys of life. The world has been positively impacted by these accomplishments.

Modern-day Turkey results from Muslims gaining control of lands in the basin of Mediterranean Constantinople. It spread literacy and conscious learning in the Muslim world. They shared it with the rest of the world. The empire maintained strength in the economy, a driving force, and a powerful military. The world would never be the same, and Muslims earned a prominent place in history.

Love of learning and intelligence was given to them by none other than Allah. The shift in the new Renaissance Muslim world succession was brought to the world. Muslims do not seek praise; instead, they seek excellence and share knowledge. Success belonged to the Muslims during this era, and they shared it with the world. The European rivals and Russians plotted and planned to crush the Muslim empire. All colors are teachers in history, including success, greed, jealousy, and downfall. But Muslims are the best teachers.

Those who share the beauty with others. Nothing is kept out of selfishness but shared with open hearts are the hearts of giving and believing Muslims who give more than knowledge. They bleed the hearts to truth, which is the motto and the expression of Islam through the truth. The Golden Age of Islam and every era is golden for a Muslim who knows giving and receiving.

By adapting to Western ways of life, Ataturk, a native of Turkey. He led comprehensive reforms and modernization of Ottoman society after suffering losses. Ataturk, the leader of the New Modern Turkey, soon joined hands with the West and slowly adapted to the ways of Western society. He was not following Islam.

He was an atheist who did not believe in Islam. It is impossible to rule any country effectively if one does not pay heed to Allah. That certainly was a drowning downfall of the Muslim world, inviting the Western world to guide the Muslim world, alas!

Satan was at work. The accursed Satan is jealous of good. Man can return to a more meaningful meaning of life by resisting and pursuing a straight path. Life can be cynical and full of trials. Those from the West, who have never experienced Middle-Eastern culture only through books or social media, struggle with understanding reality.

They waged wars to get the lands and knowledge the Muslims brought to the table of learning. They did this in an endless series of campaigns against Muslims. Despite this inherent culture of destruction and values in Islam, they continue to exploit Muslim countries today. Islam will continue to spread regardless of attempts to corrupt the Muslim world. When Muslims conquered lands, they improved the lands and protected the people of the land. Jews suffered the most during these wars.

Everyone has indeed had their turn in losses, Muslims have suffered their share, and continue to suffer. Muslims are not hypocrites; they seek the creator, not the human who has no power over another except for their deceit.

Muslims protected the Jews even during the reign of Omar E Farooq, the man who conquered many lands and spread Islam, as his destiny called. The world has focused its attention on the evil spread of religious differences among Abrahamic faiths, but Islam has always been at the forefront of helping others during turbulent times. Any human can practice Islam in any country because Allah is the owner of both this world and the next.

Muslims ruled India in the 13th and 14th centuries. The dominance of Muslims pushed back the Hindu kingdoms against the heavy tides of the Muslim era. Also known as the Mughal Empire. The laws of the Hindus and their resistance led many Muslim empires to lose control of India. Muslim rule continued from the 12 century.

Wikipedia: The Muslim period in the Indian subcontinent is conventionally said to have started in 712, after the conquest of Sindh and Multan by the Umayyad caliphate.

This conquest continued in Northern India. People knew Islam. These regions still have friendships and bonds. The empire dominated the subcontinent of India, including the Delhi Sultanate and the thriving Mughal Empire. They expanded to South Asia from the mid-14th to the 18th centuries. The lands included Bahmani, Bengal, Gujarat, Malwa, Mysore, Carnatic, and Deccan Sultanates.

India (Andhra Pradesh) Hyderabad had a major influence from Muslims, and they ruled passionately. This was before the European empire conquered India and made colonies, and then later, India gained independence.

Unfamiliar laws and regulations were at a crossroads as the country shifted in a new direction. India still possesses stunning mosque architecture constructed by Muslims. One of the seven wonders of the world is the Taj Mahal, constructed by Shah Jehan, the Mughal Emperor. India is home to more than ten historic mosques. Jama Masjid is located in Delhi, Mecca Masjid is in Hyderabad, and Nagina

Masjid is in Agra. There's no way to mention each one in a short amount of time. There are countless Muslim victories yet to be recorded in the world. There's more to come that the world will witness in the future.

There are mosques all over India. Muslims and Hindus have a long history and fought against the Europeans during colonization to gain independence from the Europeans in 1947.

Greed separated the two nations, resulting in the separation between India and Pakistan. The dominance of Muslims was strong, especially in certain parts of India. Mediterranean cuisines are an integral part of Indian history, and everyone continues to enjoy eating them. It continued for many years, and they enjoyed the cultural differences. The Muslim empire gradually withdrew with changing laws and regulations and time.

The "Nawabs" controlled certain regions of India, administering and following the Mogul emperors, who were part of their legacy. "Paigahs" was the independent state of India. Part of the Deccan areas. They had their army and printed their own money.

Their architecture was explicit. These Muslims were noble aristocrats and ruled many provinces. The police action of 1947 derailed the (Nawabs), the (Jagirdars) land owners autocrats, and the (Paigahs) noble aristocrats in India.

The new control did not reflect the lucid and caring ways of the Muslim dynasty. It turned several palaces and lands under the amended law into academic and government buildings. They lost homes and moved out to accommodate the snatching of residences that took place during the regime change.

The turmoil was a masterful change. Almost no compensation could resolve this dilemma. Many Muslims migrated to foreign lands, not wanting to be under the rule of the newly formed government. Compensation for unfair acts was scant or non-existent.

The servants were distraught to see their masters move. Many migrated to the Western lands, and the generations to come adapted to the Western ways. Many of these people were more obedient to Islam because of this change as Muslims on new turf.

Some aristocrats adapted to the changes and survived the new era. Academic education consistently helped the new way of rationalization despite its difficulty. The next generations did not know of this thriving legacy and history their parents and ancestors held and left behind.

The legacy of the dynasty forced a grueling change in lifestyles and a new adaptation to life with migrations, still succeeding but in a brand-new setting. In those days of ruling countries, history was a history that generations would read and look back on with elegance and contentment.

Muslims strive to be notable in any land, especially the one to which they migrate, and show their gratitude in every situation. Except for a belief or longing to better understand the faith of Allah, it is challenging to explain what they did not witness.

Some individuals adapt to harsh times and get closer to Allah. They have a seamless belief system. In every country, not everyone leaves; because of new reforms or when the rulers change the regime. Some adjust to the changes and remain in the same country. Allah also destined migration. But Islam has not migrated; it remains strong in any country.

In addition, we continue to call for a focus on our youth, considering we have seen how corruption destroys many societies. The issue is not material wealth but spiritual bankruptcy. The Muslim's destiny is to achieve inner wealth, and Allah writes for him the (Rizq) maintenance.

Islam has left a legacy and architecture in every country it has ruled, which has been the price of the country's legacy. These wealthy nobles married from the same families or someone of equal status and kept their wealth and Islam intact. Though social media continues to report constant Hindu and Muslim fights, they continue to show hospitality and follow many Muslim customs. Fights do happen there is no doubt but evil is not continual neither is happiness it's the turning of time that shifts the epitomes of life.

Many people value unity and friendships. Troubles persist due to human greed, with social media manipulating events to suit their narrative. The negativity of news about Islam and Muslims varies based on the country presenting it.

All countries, excluding those that are predominantly Muslim. Allah is the source of all that is good. The flaw is in humanity. Muslims can flourish in any land they reside in. It is Allah who will grant benefits to a Muslim and his land. In reverence to Allah, he bows his head to the ground, forehead touching. Humility is like a constant rainstorm of movements and phrases.

Quran: Surah Nisa 4:79 What comes to you of good is from Allah. What comes to you of evil [of man] is from yourself. And we have sent Muhammad to the people as a messenger.

The paradox of learning and gaining ideas from the Muslim world was copied by the world. Coffee, a simple discovery of the Muslim world, has now been globally appreciated since the 15th century. After consuming coffee beans, Khalid, an Arab man, observed that his goats became more lively. Turkish coffee holds the title of the oldest brewing system. Drinking coffee at night was a common practice among most Muslims in the previous era to engage in dedicated prayers to Allah.

Muslims have influenced and shared their rich culture to promote unity. Jealousy and greed have harmed the Muslim world in certain societies. The lack of support among Muslim countries has negative consequences for society and culture. Non-Muslims become closer, while Muslims often feel like outsiders in daily life. We need to continue progressing and achieving greater things. The world is entrusted with the sharing of cultural differences within Allah's given time.

The cultural, culinary, and religious differences have blended in Western societies for Muslims in interfaith marriages. And traveled to distant lands. They are referred to as converts who marry Muslim women. People in the book were marrying Muslim men. The change came from the clash of cultures, not the religious structure. Islam advocates for strict adherence to laws with no compromises.

Islamic law served as a unifying force, fostering a shared identity among diverse cultures in the Islamic world. This led to the emergence of a unique Islamic civilization that was tolerant and distinctive. It was a culture conducive to progress and enlightenment.

Regulations aimed at benefiting society. The ongoing changes occurred because of migrations from faraway places. Flourishing in the realm of marriage is imperative for Muslims when presented with such opportunities by Allah.

The unity of diverse people fostered harmony and acceptance of differences, cultivating a diverse environment. A strong foundation was established for a society built on mutual understanding and cooperation. The checklist always included Islam because of these interactions. Specifically, raising children in the Islamic faith.

This created a strong bond between generations, enabling Islamic values to be passed down from one generation to the next. This ensured that these values and beliefs were maintained in society, allowing a culture of unity and respect to persist. Beneficiaries are likely to benefit more than they expected by following Allah's laws, not decadence.

Humanity's continued efforts are seen in all aspects of life that want to extend their ways. This creates a virtuous cycle of positive benefits, resulting in a more harmonious society. As a result, Islamic values are respected and upheld, leading to a more peaceful and prosperous world.

Islamic culture contributes to peace by spreading a continuous barrage of positive messages. The USA switched from tea to coffee after the Boston Tea Party in 1773. Islam and Muslims have been a driving force of learning in the world. They derived our rich cultures from Islam. Belief in Allah is, for Muslims, a pivotal and final achievement in success. Satan strives to disrupt good.

While development looks close. It's a handshake with turmoil, It is closing in faster than one can imagine. Without Allah, progress is in a slow and steady decline. While Satan's continued efforts are treacherous, their roots remain invisible.

Turkish society was transforming the Ottoman Empire's succession, mirroring Muslim achievements after years of waiting. Mustafa Kemal Ataturk, an atheist, persuaded the Turks to adopt Western culture and influence to boost the declining Ottoman economy. Precious metals experienced a surge. Trade between the East and the West was unbalanced.

Globally, the world improved as the Muslim world implemented its ideas and thoughts. The Turkish people welcomed the change and hoped that embracing Western culture would benefit the economy.

However, spirituality was taking a back seat to capitalism. His most recent declaration was Modern-Day Turkey. In promoting the backward cultures of Western civilization, he took the country backward. They viewed him as a leader and father of the nation. The deceiving ideas of Satan are glamorous and successful for a short period when times are dense.

As a result, the downfall is more significant than the success. Turkey was undergoing a major transformation. In the world's history, the Ottoman Empire was one of the strongest and mightiest dynasties. The Ottoman era saw Turks speaking Arabic, along with Farsi, and following Islam. Even though the language took a shift, the spoken language was not Arabic by the majority.

Regrettably, the rise of Constantinople brought wealth later the downfall of Western glamor and a resurgence of Islamic solidarity. It takes decades for cultures impacted by Western civilization to return to Islamic wealth.

Corruption primarily targets the youth. In addition to the dress codes and dances of the West, he incorporated various other elements of Western culture. The glamorization of chaos resulted in defiance of Islam. The finality didn't lead to any success. Ataturk filmed Turkey, a newly formed republic, with a glamorous leader. What is the price of obtaining something? Defying Allah will never lead to long-term success.

A Muslim country cannot be uplifted by an atheist statue. No statues are permitted in Islam. Muslims adopt the Sunnah practices and ways of the last Prophet of Islam. Ataturk became the man who reformed Turkey, and they erected a statue in his honor as if he was the embodiment of spreading and shifting ideas from the Western world. He showed indifference towards the clash of beliefs. Faith was non-existent to him. He is both a witness and a statue in Turkey, accused of corrupting the Muslims.

Rather than Muslim habits and adherence to Islamic principles conflicting with Western civilization, their beliefs, and ideas collide when portraying statues that embrace ideas and methods of idle worship from other civilizations.

These actions do not align with Islam's fundamental principles. For decades statues served as a form of pagan worship making it inappropriate for Islamic countries or Muslims to mimic these practices. It may be years before his statue is removed from Turkey but it will be (Insha Allah) God willing.

The hope is that Turkey will return to its vantage point of growth and Islam at the forefront, not a memory of an atheist who shifted and created imbalance corrupting Muslim youth for generations. Amid all the good and bad things, they are still balancing faith. The adjustment process takes time. Even if disturbances occur, Islam will always win. We need to fix the woes, set better examples, and share the inner wealth that makes us Muslims.

The country, which is newer than three hundred years, corrupts the old along with their defused concepts and ideas copied from the old paganistic world. Others who undermine Islam target our youth. Sometimes they rebel against their own families and call them backward. Has Satan not created chaos for the weak-minded for decades? He is weak and his temporal wins are losses.

The war is the epidemic of infrastructure and families. Nudity beats war followed by illicit relationships and acts. In Islam, they placed youth at the forefront of interest in teaching. If the elders die, they will rule. Their lies contradict the belief of Muslims that they are entering a modern age. Indeed, they are entering the phase of Satan. Islam is recent and contemporary, yet its existence is from the first man Adam, and Eve.

It tricked them by exploiting pre-existing pagan cultures. Like a farmer who hides his seeds, Satan deceives without knowing the outcome. Young adults, weak Muslims, and new converts who lack knowledge of progressive Islam or strong convictions serve as examples for us to guide and support in their journey to Islam. In this chaotic era, we must keep them closely connected to Islam. Allah's planned destiny. Muslims must recognize and express gratitude to Allah for providing the lands and air that they rely on.

Quran: Surah Waqiah: 63:73 Have you considered what they sow? Is it you who caused it to grow, or is it we who do so? If we willed, we would simply reduce this harvest to husks, leaving one to lament. They have truly suffered a loss.

Islam is the pinnacle of knowledge. Muslims, by teaching the world what it didn't know, are immune to corruption by the turn of the century. The country's economic progress will be hindered if Islam is neglected. Satan will never achieve success. Atheist leaders, aiming to improve the economy, deceived Turkey's youth with false modernization. The allure of evil, which had new elements, fascinated him as an atheist.

Kemal Ataturk undeniably enhanced the aftermath of the downfall and his image captivated with false allure and new attributes. The majority of his ideas did not conform to Islam. Glamor may have enhanced, but Islamic doctrine took a halt for the youth in this era.

Muslims who understand the beauty of Islam won't be deceived by false allurements of disbelievers. Educating the youth about Islam and the Quran is crucial. Specifically targeted towards Muslim youth from childhood. Copying Western ways didn't bring lasting success to Muslims. Muslims were the teachers of Islam's golden age. Satan uses regression as a manipulative tactic. Islam possesses greater strength than them. For Muslims, temporary deviation results in a stronger return.

Despite Ataturk's adaptation of opposition to Islamic ways, foreign capital was a major improvement for the economy, but anything gained by compromising Islam was disastrous. Turkey still undergoes the repercussions of the past. When a man listens to Ataturk's whispers of the accursed, it's never a win.

The (Muezzin) the man who calls Muslims to prayer recites (Adhan) the Muslim call to prayer five times a day. Even though Ataturk was bringing further downfall to modern-day Turkey, appearing glamorous, and defying Allah was a short success it ended in turmoil. The Islamic call to prayer continued in all mosques throughout Istanbul and all regions of Turkey. The downfall was an imminent imitation of Western society that backfired.

Turkey is the hub and heart of many Muslims. Although it has been through many changes, it will continue to flourish. No earthquake can take away Muslims' faith. Allah tests everyone, but Muslims who believe have a seat in bliss. Originally, Hagia Sophia was a church of the Byzantine Empire. They later converted the building into a museum. Today, it is a mosque where heads endow in humility. Allah's plans are unknown to man. A man in haste is off track because Allah has the best plan for him.

Quran: Surah Anfal 30. And remember. O Prophet, when the disbelievers conspired to capture and kill, exile you. They planned, but Allah also planned. And Allah is the best of planners.

Allah's plan for Muslims encompasses a grander purpose that extends beyond our limited perception. It is evident that Western influence often clashes with the values and principles of the Muslim world, creating a clash of cultures. However, regardless of the era we find ourselves in, Islam continues to prevail and withstand the test of time.

Islam stands firm, upholding its values without the need for justification or excuses. As Muslims, it is essential for us to demonstrate kindness not only towards fellow Muslims but also towards individuals of different faiths and backgrounds. By doing so, we foster solidarity within the Muslim community and reach out to people from diverse religious beliefs and professions. This inclusive approach allows us to build bridges of understanding and cooperation, promoting harmony and unity among all individuals, regardless of their faith or trade.

Muhammad ibn Musa Al-Khwarizmi, born in the 9th century, was a prominent scholar and mathematician from the Islamic Golden Age. He made significant contributions to the field of mathematics, particularly in the areas of algebra and algorithms. Al-Khwarizmi's work, particularly his book "Kitab al-Jabr wa al-Muqabala" (The Compendious Book on Calculation by Completion and Balancing), laid the foundation for modern algebra and introduced systematic methods for solving equations. This book introduced the concept of algorithms, which are step-by-step procedures or instructions for solving mathematical problems.

These algorithms revolutionized mathematics and had a profound impact on various fields, including technology and computer science. Baghdad recognized Al-Khwarizmi's expertise and appointed him as the head of the House of Wisdom (Darul Hikma), a renowned center for learning and translation of scientific works. Al-Khwarizmi's contributions to mathematics and his development of algorithms have had a lasting influence on the modern world, shaping the way we approach problem-solving and computation. Al-Khwarizmi's work was his dedication to knowledge and intellectual pursuits, which was highly valued in the Islamic civilization during that time. Muslims are not stingy, they share true knowledge, not corruption history can speak for itself.

Following the conquest of Persia, Baghdad became the epicenter of scientific studies and trade. Many merchants and scientists traveled to this part of the Muslim world to gain and share knowledge.During this time, the Islamic world saw a flourishing of intellectual pursuits and advancements. Islamic scholars developed a sophisticated system of accounting known as the double-entry bookkeeping, which revolutionized the field of commerce. This system ensured accurate recording of financial transactions and allowed for a better understanding of profit and loss.

The importance of accounting in Islam can be traced back to the concept of accountability and the belief that individuals will be held responsible for their actions in the afterlife. Thus, keeping meticulous records of one's deeds, including financial transactions, became an integral part of Islamic practice.

The city of Baghdad, with its vibrant intellectual and commercial atmosphere, became a hub for scholars and traders from various parts of the Muslim world. These individuals brought with them their knowledge and expertise, contributing to the growth of scientific studies and trade in the region. The exchange of ideas and knowledge in Baghdad played a crucial role in the development and dissemination of various fields, including mathematics, astronomy, medicine, and commerce.

Muhammad ibn Musa Al Khwarizmi, an Orthodox Muslim, made significant contributions to the world of Real Estate trigonometry. He not only used cosmic tables to accurately measure the longitudes and latitudes of cities and localities, but he also wrote about calendar works, Astrolabe, and Sundial.

These works provided invaluable tools for accurately determining property boundaries and surveying land. Additionally, Al Khwarizmi's advancements in calendar works helped establish a standardized system for tracking time, which was crucial for real estate transactions and property management. His contributions have had a lasting impact on the field of real estate and have helped shape the accuracy and precision of property measurements and calculations.

The Quran, the holy book of Islam, contains numerous verses that align with scientific discoveries made centuries later. For example, the Quran mentions the stages of embryonic development, the water cycle, and the expansion of the universe, all of which were confirmed by modern science. This connection between religion and science is highly valued by Muslims, as it reinforces their belief in the divine nature of the Quran. Additionally, Islam promotes intellectual freedom and encourages Muslims to seek knowledge and understanding of the world around them.

This pursuit of knowledge led Muslim scholars to make significant contributions to various fields, including mathematics, astronomy, medicine, and philosophy. These advancements greatly influenced the development of clocks and timekeeping, as Muslims recognized the importance of accurate time measurement for prayer. Through their fascination with clocks and their commitment to intellectual growth, Muslims played a crucial role in the advancement of timekeeping technology, benefiting not only their own religious practices but also the wider world.

Quran: Surah Yasin 36; 38. Sun runs on its fixed course for a term.

Quran: Surah Zumar 39:5.He created the heavens and earth. He wraps the night over the day and wraps the day over the night and has subjected the sun and the moon. Each runs its course for a specified term. Unquestionably, He is the Exalted in Might, the Perpetual Forgiver.

Quran: Surah Ra'd 13:2.It is Allah who erected the heavens without pillars. He established Himself above the Throne, and the sun and the moon, each running its course for a specified term, fixed each matter; details the signs the meeting with your Lord is certain.

Quran: Surah Anbiya 21:33. And he is who has created the night and the day and the sun and the moon each in orbit.

Ongoing research by scientists is focused on subjects that have not been made known to humanity. The Quran serves as a valuable resource for our learning. The level of understanding regarding everything is not complete. Certain aspects have been concealed by Allah from humanity, while granting humans the capability to research and uncover a portion of the knowledge He has revealed. Only Allah possesses complete knowledge of everything that exists.

Quran: Surah Luqman 31:29. Allah merges the night into the day and joins the day into the night, and has subjected the sun and the moon each, running its course for a term appointed; and Allah is aware of what you do.

Quran: Surah Yasin 36:38. Sun runs on its fixed course for a term.

Allah told us about science. Science found this first in the Quran. Allah explained the recurrence of the sunlight and the moon.

Quran: Surah Anbiya 21:33 "And he is who has created the night and the day and the sun and the moon each in orbit running."

Quran: Surah Luqman 31:29 Allah merges the night into the day and joins the day into the night, and has subjected the sun and the moon each, running its course for a term appointed; and that Allah is aware of what you do.

As humanity continues to explore this universe, Allah has described points in the Quran as undisputable. Look for answers in-depth. The Quran may take a lifetime for people who understand and recite it. Humans need to be reminded of the guidelines of Islam. There is a legacy of intelligent exploration in the Muslim world.

Learning about Baghdad, Persia, should be a prevalent topic taught in schools today. These regions continued to extend the influence of Muslims on history, algebra, mathematics, and geography. The scholars traveled from different parts of the world. Besides sharing their interests in learning, they spent hours exploring experiments and ideas from the Muslim world.

The process of learning provided both deep meaning and a significant challenge for the mind. In Islam, the wind is regarded as a magnificent blessing bestowed upon humanity. It is important to note that windmills are still present and functional in the present time. The current global movement is focused on harnessing the power of windmills to generate electricity, as it offers a sustainable and pollution-free source of energy.

The expense of generating electricity through the use of windmills is significant. In addition to their other contributions, the Muslims also introduced windmills, which have since become widely used across the globe. In the Quran, Allah specifically references the wind a total of 29 times.

Quran: Surah Araf 7:57. And it is he who sends the winds as good tidings before his mercy, until, when they have carried heavy rain clouds. We drive them to a dead land, and we send down rain and bring forth some fruits. Thus will we bring forth the dead: perhaps to remind you.

Throughout history, humanity has always had a desire to catch a glimpse of itself through the reflection of mirrors. In order to view shadows of themselves, they utilized the combination of water and metal. It is a common human behavior to take pleasure in looking at their own reflection in mirrors. When light reflects, the direction of the image is reversed. For decades, mirrors have played a significant role in the lives of humans.

Each and every day, the world is presented with the reflection of its own image. Mirrors play a significant role in enhancing the decor of the room. You will notice that the focal point of the room is the area where you can see your own reflections. When a human looks at themselves using a mirror, they are able to see their own reflection. The inner image of a person can only be seen by Allah. A person's image can be reflected through their expression.

The reflections of people can either be positive or negative, serving as a mirror of the world. Humanity views itself as a mirror, mirroring its values through the way it acts and behaves. The Muslims made a significant contribution to the world by introducing the mirror. Hasan Ibn Haytham's innovative mind led him to invent not only the camera but also make significant contributions to the field of optics.

His understanding was that when light passes through the pinhole, the image becomes reversed. The camera plays such a vital role in our modern world that without it, our society would struggle to function. Time management is highly valued in the Muslim community, and they prioritize productivity over wasting time. Through their consistent efforts, they made significant contributions towards the advancement of society. Ibn al Haytham, also known as Alhazen, was born in Basra, Iraq, which was a part of the Buyld emirate, to a prominent Arab family. 965. During the Golden Age of Islam, he made significant contributions to the fields of mathematics, astronomy, and light physics.

Prophet Muhammad holds the distinction of being the pioneer in using a toothbrush. To clean his teeth, he utilized a twig known as a miswak. Muslims followed his Sunnah, customs, and practices, and it is interesting to note that the first toothbrush was invented during this time. In today's modern society, advancements have led to the creation of a toothbrush that incorporates bristles. The balance between the health of the mouth and the health of the heart is interconnected.

The condition of your mouth is closely linked to the condition of your heart, so an unhealthy heart often means an unhealthy mouth. The cardiovascular system can be adversely affected by poor oral hygiene habits. Prior to the arrival of the angel of death, Prophet Muhammad would clean his teeth using a twig. In a state of complete cleanliness, both physically and spiritually, he was preparing himself to meet his creator.

Islam places great importance on cleanliness and personal hygiene as an integral part of its worship practices. The value of the Quran and the hadiths of Prophet Muhammad is emphasized in various ways. It was the Muslims who first introduced the concept of soap-making to the world. In order to achieve their desired outcome, they utilized a combination of both oils and glycerine.

A Muslim scientist by the name of Mohammed Ibn Zakariya Al Razi is credited with the initial discovery of the recipe for hard toilet soap with a pleasant fragrance. Muslims in Egypt were ahead of their time, using soap in the bathroom even before it was known to the rest of the world. Hygiene is given significant importance in the teachings of Islam. When a Muslim is in a state of impurity, he is unable to engage in his prayer directly before his Lord.

The relevance and understanding of the knowledge gained by the Western world from Muslims is crucial for both present and future generations. Muslims, as part of their faith, have diligently adhered to rules and regulations for centuries. These ideas, which were originally conceived by the Muslims, were eventually embraced and improved upon, leading to notable advancements in personal hygiene and extensive welfare enhancements.

The progress made in technology now allows airplanes to successfully make international flights, moving from one country to another. Allah has bestowed upon humans the imaginative mind, which enables us to explore and venture into new territories. A Muslim man was the innovator who successfully designed and built the world's first flying machine.

Abbas Ibn Firnas is the name by which he was known. Many significant achievements have been contributed to the world by the Muslim community. In order to succeed and flourish in this world, it is crucial to have a deep understanding of the culture and richness of Islam. The pen that was created first is a creation of Allah. With his commanding presence, he ordered the pen to write. The method of teaching employed by Allah involved the use of a pen. In the beginning, he gave the command for the pen to start writing. Allah, the divine entity, was the sender of the revelations, while it was the responsibility of human beings to meticulously transcribe and document them. The Quran was meticulously transmitted, as the Prophet Muhammad was purified for the task, enabling him to remember the words precisely, which were then recorded by scribes under his careful supervision.

Quran: Surah Alaq. 96:4. Allah taught by the pen.

It was Muslims who created the very first fountain pen. The act of dipping a pen in ink was performed by Muslims. The writing exhibited a high level of artistry and was carefully preserved. One of life's greatest joys is discovering and showcasing our unique talents and unwavering faith. Similar to how Muslims have done, the person in need will seek Allah's guidance in order to contribute towards the improvement of society and education. During the Dark Ages, Europe found itself under the dominance of a period characterized by various challenges and setbacks. While Muslims successfully illuminated the darkness, they failed to acknowledge the importance of history in serving as a reminder.

Attempts to darken the Muslim world are commonly observed in countries that find themselves in a state of darkness. It won't be long before they step in to help the world once more. Muslims should take this as a fair warning and consider changing their ways in order to come together and provide global assistance. In order to stay strong, it is crucial that you remain steadfast in your beliefs.

Those who sought knowledge in Islam and identified as Muslims were provided with assistance. Stained clothes were not to the liking of the Sultan of Egypt. The invention of the pen was immediately attributed to Muslims. Moved by the spectacle, and talent the Egyptian king took out a pen and started writing, inadvertently starting a trend that would become popular worldwide. When we delve into history, we discover the remarkable creations and contributions that Muslims have made to the world, often hidden from some but revealed to others.

This pen has failed to leave any stains on his clothes. The introduction of any reform or gift inevitably gives rise to a new need. The exploration of humans is only possible when there is a need. In the year 953, Al-Numan made a note of it. The advisor to the Sultan of Egypt, he was credited for the construction of the fountain pen. In various parts of the world, people use a pen as a tool for writing. The practice of using ink-dipped pens for writing was common among people from different regions. Muslims generously showcased their talents while extending an invitation to the global community to partake in this journey of exploration.

The ballpoint pen, which replaced the fountain pen, was a significant breakthrough for humanity. The original pen was created by Allah and He gave it the command to write. Prior to their arrival on earth, Allah has already determined a will for every individual. Muslim countries have the potential to make significant contributions to the world through their unity, just as they have done in the past. In order to avoid appearing hypocritical and weak, Muslims should not hesitate to confront the enemy and take action rather than being passive. In the Islamic faith, it is important to stand firmly for truth and reject falsehoods.

The achievements that have been made over the span of this decade are lasting and cannot be forgotten. Across the globe, there is an overwhelming quest for peace as nations and individuals seek to establish harmony. A key requirement for attaining serenity and a good quality of life is to possess an open mind. The achievements that are accomplished on a daily basis have a lasting impact on both oneself and society. Learning and exploration are actively encouraged by Islam as important values. Allah, in his infinite wisdom, does not compel individuals to adopt his beliefs against their will. The beauty of Allah is astounding.

Islam seekers will find like-minded partners. Allah provides for sincere believers who seek Islam with purity and let go of past demons. Allah beautifies humanity as he sees fit. Many questions about the Quran and the Muslim world's history have affirmative answers.

The building that is most needed in every decade is undoubtedly the hospital. The most crucial structure in our society today is undoubtedly the hospital. The first documented hospital in history was established by the Muslim world. Harun al-Rashid, who belonged to the Muslim faith, constructed the inaugural hospital in Baghdad. The Muslim world experienced progress due to the presence of a mind that was both inquisitive and intelligent. Throughout history, individuals have embarked on journeys to distant lands with the aim of acquiring knowledge and making valuable contributions to the advancement of society.

In its early days, the Muslim community established a hospital that primarily functioned as a sanctuary for those suffering from leprosy. Muslim hospitals were a notable feature during the medieval period. The reason why Al-Andalus, located in Spain, was culturally rich was due to the significant influence of Muslims and the exceptional treatment they received. Muslims are taught by Islam to approach the world with curiosity and interest, allowing them to learn and explore. Using time wisely is a skill they acquire to actively contribute to societal norms.

One of the things they do is learn how to make the most of their time together, which leads to personal growth. Damascus, Syria, specifically during the time of Umayyad caliph Walid Ibn Abd Al-Malik, was where this occurred. The government, during his tenure, focused on both strengthening and preserving the Arabic language.

Expressing gratitude is something that Muslims are recognized for. Muslim Arabs in Baghdad constructed the first psychiatric hospital in 705, marking a significant milestone in the history of mental healthcare. The year 1270 witnessed a notable rise in the popularity of psychiatric hospitals that catered specifically to the Muslim community. Taking the initiative, they were the ones who first assigned hospital wards specifically for the mentally challenged. Patients with mental health concerns were acknowledged by Muslims as individuals with a health condition and received treatment.

With the growth of Islam, Muslims began actively searching for ways to find cures and treatments. Their belief and faith were centered around Allah. Through the combination of their mental prowess and strong belief in Allah, they were able to uncover treatments for ailments. Giving high importance to hygiene was a key focus.

The needles and syringes were subjected to boiling as a means of bacteria eradication. Generous salaries were given to the helpers as a form of recognition. In the Islamic faith, it is customary to extend hands of friendship and truce in order to resolve any lingering hard feelings. The concept of reciprocity is highly valued within the Muslim community. There are certain societies where the act of giving presents may be refused. According to Islamic teachings, it is deemed impolite to refuse a gift.Muslims strengthen bonds with gift giving and exchanges are part of Islamic culture.

According to Islamic teachings, it is deemed unethical for an individual to not express gratitude. The Quran provides extensive coverage and includes intricate details. In the course of our lives, there is nothing that goes unnoticed or unattended to. The presence of spoils and remnants from pagan days contributes to the decadence of this society, which in turn leads to its lack of culture.

In contemporary society, ideologies are frequently concealed through the use of lies and deceit. Even though there have been some advancements, Islam and its progressive lifestyle are still way ahead, leaving a significant gap to catch up. In Islam, it is believed that the person who initiates the gesture of extending their hand holds greater significance, as Muslims are encouraged to accept gifts even from those they may consider as enemies.

Kindness is seen as a fundamental aspect of Islam, and one way this is demonstrated is through the exchange of gifts with both Muslims and non-Muslims. Giving is something that Muslims take pleasure in, following the example set by Prophet Muhammad. Throughout history, Prophet Muhammad has left behind a remarkable legacy that encompasses his exceptional treatment of not only people but also animals and plants. This faith encompasses all aspects of life that pertain to humanity.

One can experience the mercy of Allah in their heart as a manifestation of His kindness towards humanity. Being a Muslim in Islam entails embracing the importance of continuous learning. The longevity of a building greatly depends on its maintenance and the quality of its construction; if both are properly taken care of, the building can last for many years. Without strong foundations, a building will not be able to stand. Such is the faith that resides within humanity. The strength of the foundation in all hearts is crucial for enduring turbulence.

Overcoming challenges is possible for believers when they receive support from the Creator and their fellow believers. An individual who disregards the guidelines set forth by the creator. The chances of him staying loyal to you are slim. Those who firmly believe in the supremacy of human laws often face a fear of openly expressing their authentic selves. When it comes to their personal beliefs, Muslims hold the view that Allah's laws hold more importance than human laws.

One has an obligation to abide by the laws of the land. Allah's laws come first. Human laws are designed to impose punishment on those who exercise jurisdiction, legislative features, or both. The Quran and Sunnah serve as sources that elucidate the ways and practices of Prophet Muhammad, shedding light on Allah's laws.

While it is academically and socially acceptable, it is important to note that Allah's law should not be overlooked or disobeyed, especially in cases of omission and defiance. Muslims who find themselves in such circumstances often face challenging times, with turbulent tides and a sense of uncertainty surrounding their faith. The presence of tides is not limited to rough waters, as even smooth bodies of water can be affected.

Plagues have been a familiar occurrence throughout history, and one way that Muslims protect themselves from sickness is through the practice of Wudu, which involves ritual washing before prayer five times a day. There is nothing purer in terms of cleanliness than water. The COVID-19 pandemic, which was a global health crisis, instilled fear in the hearts of countless individuals and tragically claimed numerous lives. This plague that has happened in recent years will receive a substantial amount of coverage in history. The spread of it was not limited to just one country; in fact, it was observed and noted worldwide.

The people, without any fear of defying Allah's laws, were soon scheduled to receive injections as a preventive measure against the sickness caused by this plague. Blaming other humans how the plague came about.Believers can perceive every plague as a mercy granted to them, along with a warning. The fear of death, rather than the defiance of Allah, is what scares a disbeliever. The concept of death, as understood by believers, is not the cessation of life but rather a transformative process that opens the door to the afterlife.

The occurrence of a plague should be viewed as a chance to enhance our faith and reliance on the promises of Allah. Believers don't fear but embrace Allah's divine mercy and guidance. Through divine mercy and guidance, we find strength and direction. The practice in medieval times was to quarantine Muslims for forty days, using this period to instruct them in mannerisms and etiquette. Muslim history goes back hundreds of years. Doctors and hospitals used face masks to keep patients safe.

There are individuals who have knowledge about the Muslim world dating back to prehistoric times. These customs and cultures have been established and practiced for a significant period of time. The practice of personal hygiene finds its roots in the teachings of Islam. Due to the widespread transmission of COVID-19, people all over the world were required to wear masks as a preventive measure. Muslims had taken precautions with face masks after the spread of the plague before they even realized it, during times older than today.

Islam, as a religion, is known for its progressive nature. The cultures that existed before Islam, with their pagan beliefs and practices, are not compatible with the teachings and principles of Islam. The emergence and spread of the COVID-19 virus is set to become a significant turning point in the annals of history. In order to protect against germs and viruses, the world takes precautions by masking itself. For centuries, Muslims have been engaging in this practice.

The Muslims were responsible for maintaining the health records of their patients. The expansion of these minds has brought great benefits to humanity. Throughout history, plagues have been a persistent presence for thousands of years, yet man often chooses to disregard their existence. Throughout history, humans have encountered and endured various plagues. The tasks at hand are not typically designated for men to perform. The works that they have created are believed to be the result of the divine power of the Almighty.

Plagues, earthquakes, floods, and diseases are examples of natural disasters. Muslims believe plagues have participated in a man's journey. The presence of plagues along belie's journey can sometimes be seen as a mercy. Prophet Muhammed taught that believers may perceive plagues as acts of mercy and opportunities for martyrdom. In case of plague outbreaks, he specifically advised to stay stationed and avoid entering any other land. There is no aspect or question that Islam has not addressed. The answers can be found in multiple sources, including the book of records, the Quran, and the Sunnah customs and practices. Syria was struck by the plague while Omar Bin Khattab was in power. He remained unfazed and unafraid in the face of the plague.

Despite the circumstances, Omar bin Khattab chose to remain in place and implemented precautionary measures for safety. He made the decision to not accompany anyone into Syria and instead chose to stop at different entry points. The city of Cairo experienced the devastating impact of the black death plague during both the 14th and 15th centuries. Due to the large number of deaths, they resorted to disposing of the bodies by dumping them into the river. The experience of attending funerals was overwhelming.

Muslims in ancient times were known to practice social distancing. In Islam, it is obligatory for followers to follow specific guidelines during times of epidemic. To seek the satisfaction of Allah, they carried out the ritual of sacrificing animals and subsequently divided the meat amongst each other. During times of plague and distress, they pleaded and begged fervently for forgiveness. Muslims fervently pleaded for forgiveness and a pardon from Allah. The appeal made was solely in silence, without any criticism or anguish expressed.

In times of difficulty, one can observe the absence of cruel or selfish acts. During times of hardship, it is important to refrain from criticizing the actions of others. They conducted themselves in a manner that was admirable and commendable. One of the core tenets of Islam is to aid and support humanity, without engaging in blame towards others. The reason Allah has made this drought visible is because the heart does not feel the need for forgiveness and mercy. A drought in one's heart could potentially occur. Whenever a plague strikes, it serves as a warning for those humans who have faith.

The sole means for a nonbeliever to find contentment is by adhering to the guidance of medical professionals, while lacking any faith. When surrounded by darkness, individuals yearn for survival, yet the most effective remedy lies in the combination of faith and medical treatment.

Quran: Surah Araf 7:133. So they may reflect on being mindful) we sent upon them floods and (plagues of locusts, vermin frogs, and water turning into blood: distinct signs one after another. Yet they remained arrogant, and they were criminals committed to accumulating sin.

Throughout history, Allah has consistently issued warnings to mankind about the occurrence of plagues. The fortunate believers are shown mercy, whereas the unfortunate disbelievers are consumed by doubt. If the hearts of disbelievers yearn for change, Allah may grant them the cure they seek. The effectiveness of the COVID-19 vaccine was measured at 90 percent. The development of this was done by a couple from Turkey who follow the Islamic faith.

The field of medicine regarded this as a significant breakthrough. In the early Islamic times, individuals would use a combination of herbs and honey as a means of healing those who were ill. In no time, they were able to develop advanced technologies and successfully perform surgeries with utmost cleanliness. According to the teachings of Islam, Muslims are obligated to perform ablution before each of the five daily prayers and engage in ritual washing prior to praying.

In response to the epidemic, humans implemented rules that included the use of sanitizers and mandated hand washing. Given the historical precedence, with Islam leading the way in emphasizing cleanliness for several decades. The Muslim community has been faithfully practicing Islamic law since the time of Prophet Muhammad. For those individuals who are in search of peace and clarity, the reality of Muslims will finally be attainable.

Ibn Hazm took it upon himself to adapt clothing and hygiene practices specifically for the benefit of doctors and patients. In a recent article, a jurist provides a detailed overview of the essential qualities that physicians must possess. The Muslim world is an integral part of life's minor details that cannot be overlooked. Palermo, a city located in Sicily, and Salerno, which is situated in Italy, serve as prime examples of European colleges. One of the ways that Islam has had an impact on European society is through its influence on education, as a result of the blending of different cultures.

Muslims conquered and advanced through Egypt, Spain, and Europe, including all the Persian empires. Old Rome was under Islamic rule for decades. Islam spread through North Africa and became a dominant faith. Following its customs and cultures for centuries. Muslims ruled the Iberian peninsula and Spain for over seven centuries. Muslims left behind marks of grandeur and learning, as well as their belief in monotheism, which left no destruction except grandeur.

Education and learning need to be revitalized this decade. Muslims left a legacy that is hard to replicate in today's society. Muslims come together as a unifying force to share and teach what the Quran teaches, as well as excel at imparting ideas. Andalusia was a destination for many travelers from Asia and Persia.

The translation of medical books into Arabic resulted in their wide availability in libraries across the Muslim world. The Andalusian living model, characterized by its architectural splendor, can be traced back to the Moors in Andalusia and the Middle East. Among the breathtaking architectural wonders mentioned are the Alhambra Palace in Granada, Spain, the Taj Mahal in Agra, India, and the Dome of the Rock in Jerusalem, Israel.

These magnificent structures serve as a testament to the grandeur of Islamic civilization and continue to astound with their exquisite display of Islamic art and architecture. The inclusion of art, arches, and Arabic writing in the design made it a perfect example for them to follow. The influence of this style extended to various regions of the Islamic world, including Persia, Turkey, and India.

Moreover, it played a crucial role in shaping European architecture, especially in Spain and Italy. Even in present times, the influence of the Islamic style can still be observed in numerous countries. The act of copying was done by them towards the Muslim world. Muslim architecture was characterized by its unique design, with the dome being a prominent element.

They were able to infuse their architecture with Muslim design elements, resulting in a one-of-a-kind hybrid style. Many churches and other buildings started incorporating the iconic shape of the dome, which became a symbol of copying Muslim architecture. The way this man gauges success could be through the accomplishments that are recognized and assessed by others. The greatness of belief is acknowledged by Allah.

Muslims are constantly striving to improve themselves in order to please Allah, and they also aim to utilize their unique talents to enhance and contribute to the world around them. The Middle East is known for its abundant cultural wealth and diversity. The presence of mosques and buildings stands as a testament to the integrity and dedication of the builders and architects involved.

They stood tall, appearing as if they had left a man behind to gaze at them. The dismantling of hospitals, schools, and buildings took place during the invasions in the Middle East, and this action, which was labeled as "help," has been criticized as hypocritical, causing others to become frenzied.

The entrance of superpowers into Muslim lands has not resulted in assistance but rather in their destruction. Muslims fought for noble causes, driven by their convictions rather than materialistic desires, resulting in devastated homes and families torn apart by the consequences of deceitful rhetoric. Despite this, the individuals in positions of power insist that their actions are motivated by a sense of noble duty, even as their own nations continue to suffer from poverty, overlooked in favor of personal gain.

Man destroyed monumental legacies created over decades by a pile of dust. Inquisitive individuals interested in the Middle East and beyond. Make preparations for journeys to distant lands. Travel to the shores to see these lands. The cognitive abilities of the Middle East prove a genuine success in hearts. Islam emphasizes sharing. This fosters a sense of community and mutual respect. The ignorant mentalities accuse the privileged. Insults fulfill the spiritually bankrupt.

Discontent breeds sarcastic jokes for the insecure. They accuse others of having issues they have. Although it may appear harmless, this behavior can be non conducive to others.

Time is valuable. Don't waste it on unproductive negativity. Confidence comes from Allah. Satan and his followers falsify the truth, leading to attacks. Muslims taught unknown skills to the world, but today some accuse them of jealousy. Insulting fellow Muslims is common among Muslims. Competing with meager means and unproductive conversations.

This global epidemic is straining spiritually undernourished families dabbling with faith and relatives in the Islamic community. Competing mentality instead of sharing beauty and skills. Starving societies with a lack of faith and false individuality promote selfishness in the underprivileged. Spiritual equipping fosters a positive mindset in those lacking depth. Beauty is subjective to those who pursue it. Inner beauty beautifies the human, while the outer being shines.

It is the connection to the universe that brings a feeling of belonging and understanding. Beauty is often found within one's soul, not just in its physical features. Beauty is everywhere. One finds what he seeks. What you're searching for seeks you.

This kind of mindset of accusation and envy has been passed down for centuries and needs to be eradicated. If we want a more cohesive and compassionate society, ignorance needs attendance. The employer, Satan, will create doubts and assumptions without consultation with the one he accuses through instigation. Which is the evil within. It is necessary to teach the younger generations the importance of collaboration rather than competition.

Islam promotes unity, not competition or soiled affairs. A believer's affair is powerful. He is content in any situation. Striving for mutual respect and understanding is possible through this. Understanding the desire for change requires removing the shackles. He will make it happen, no need for new sections. The fabricated name of Islam, Wahhabism, is not genuine.

Corruption has the ability to infiltrate and impact various sectors and sections. One of the central tenets of Islam is the belief in monotheism.

The employer, who is spreading lies, can be likened to Satan. There are those who assert that Wahhabism holds the position of being the prevailing belief system within the Islamic faith in Saudi

Arabia. Untrue. Islam is a unified and indivisible entity. Islam is widely perceived by the world as austere. The Quran is a source of balance rather than chaos. Evil individuals who thrive on creating divisions must be stopped, and this includes those within the Islamic faith.

There is absolutely no need or requirement to alter or modify the name of Islam, as it will continue to remain unchanged. There is no need for an examiner or council to be present. The Quran's way of life emphasizes that purity stems from one's belief. The emergence of the sects occurred after the passing of Prophet Muhammad. It is imperative for Muslims to put a stop to this kind of rhetoric.

The religion of Islam and its sacred text, the Quran, are a testament to the belief in pure monotheism and the finality of Prophet Muhammad's message. The divine revelations of Allah conclude with this profound statement. If they hadn't formed corrupt alliances, their actions might have involved copying the Muslim world in order to accommodate and please their own culture. Muslims have a long-standing history of excellence in the field of teaching, which spans centuries.

The practice of referring to Muslims as "Mohammedans," which was once common, is unacceptable. Mohammedan is not synonymous with Muslim. The followers of Islam, known as Muslims, willingly surrender and submit themselves to the divine will of Allah..Prophet Muhammad was Muslim. Muslims willingly surrender themselves to the will of Allah.

Those who follow the teachings of the Prophet willingly submit themselves to the will of Allah and strive to emulate his Sunnah. It is recommended to follow the Sunnah, which is the way of life and teachings of the Prophet Muhammad, but Muslims don't worship him. Understanding the potential dangers that come with the act of replacing Jesus as the Messiah and assuming the role of a Godhead.

In a hadith, Prophet Muhammed made a prediction about the future of Islam, stating that it would eventually be divided into seventy-three sects. The approach of Islam towards Muslims is consistent and does not change. (Adubhullah hi minash shaitan nir rajeem) I seek protection from Satan and his deceptive words, O Allah.

Abu Huraira narrated that the Prophet Muhammad, may peace and blessings be upon him, said the following. The Jews will be divided into a total of seventy-one sects by them. It is believed that in Christianity, there will be a total of seventy-two sects. The intention is to divide my nation into seventy-three sects, as they have stated.

Within the framework of Islam, numerous nations have come into existence. These nations are often associated with Islam, but they do not actually practice its teachings. Instead of dividing Muslims and focusing solely on financial gain, the true solution lies in embracing the teachings of the Quran. Muslims, as a collective, belong to a single nation under the guidance and sovereignty of Allah, rather than being divided by newly formed nations and brotherhoods.

Hadith: al-Tirmidhī 2640. Indeed, those who divide their religion and become sects,

Quran: Surah Anam Verse 159. The affair belongs to Allah. You must not associate with them, Prophet.

All past behavior will be revealed and brought to light through Allah. The Quran is a valuable resource for Muslims and followers of Islam, as it offers answers to numerous inquiries. For individuals who find self-battling challenging, it is recommended that they consider not attending this event as it may not be suitable for them. Those who are actively searching for specific answers can trust that Allah will definitely provide them with the information they seek.

The process of Muslims assimilating into new countries involves navigating a complex mix of cultures and beliefs as they hold on to their traditional practices and customs. It is important to note that this corrupt ideology does not align with the values and principles that are embraced by contemporary society.

The return of ignorant times and the deepest decadence that the world has ever known is a recurring theme in many biblical texts. The results of this study on decadence and society reveal that although many individuals have received academic education, their actual knowledge is quite limited.

Independent women on their travels. The pursuit of peace and betterment will carry on across vast territories. Today's society has witnessed the fulfillment of various predictions made by Islamic sources. The shifts that are easily noticeable can be observed by individuals who regularly consume water from the seven seas. While the traveler observes and explores, they gain a deeper understanding of the place.

The experience of traveling to Allah's lands offers a perspective that cannot be found anywhere else. People who observe Muslims and Islam have witnessed their presence on a global scale. They witnessed the way in which both groups worshiped and faced trials, finding similarities in their approaches. Muslims prioritize the significance of both learning and teaching. My determination to share persists, especially for those who are curious and dedicated to seeking the truth.

Immerse yourself in the fascinating concepts and remarkable achievements of the Muslim world as I share my thoughts and expressions. While the expense of traveling to this pass may be low, the knowledge and insights one can acquire about the Muslim world are absolutely priceless.

CHAPTER 4
CONTINUED EFFORTS TO ENSURE MUSLIMS' SUCCESS

Rewards are granted to all living beings, irrespective of their species, in recognition of their hard work. It is important to give your maximum effort, even in situations where the outcome appears to be impossible. Achievements are the result of overcoming the challenges and obstacles faced throughout a series of trials. Similar to the Prophet of Islam, Muslims had to endure a multitude of trials in the scorching desert of Saudi Arabia.

The Arab community was known for their expertise in language, as well as their profound affection for poetry and literature. The Quran's linguistic excellence is so remarkable that it goes far beyond what our minds can conceive. Through unconventional means, Faith was able to amass a dedicated following, completely bypassing the need for pamphlets or door-to-door outreach.

Despite not physically moving, social media creates the illusion of travel. What about the person who chooses to remain stagnant, constantly contemplating loneliness for years on end? The decision to embrace solitude was made based on the undeniable and eminent results that it brings, whether they are characterized by progress or stagnation. The evidence is easily noticeable when examining the results. What about the person who actively pursues every single idea that comes their way? Allah, in His infinite wisdom, always recognizes and acknowledges the success of humans, serving as a shining example by appreciating their tireless efforts.

The mind, with its incredible capacity, absorbs all information it encounters, effortlessly navigating through the vast realms of knowledge at the speed of light. The remarkable capacity of the human mind to absorb information exceeds that of any available technology. Allah rewards those who put in effort. The act of sharing knowledge is a powerful way to bring enlightenment, not just to oneself, but to others as well.

The main priority for Muslims is Salat, which brings great rewards.

Quran: Surah Hud: 11:114.And establish the Prayer at the two ends of the day and in the first hours of the night.[113] Indeed the good deeds drive away the evil deeds. This is a Reminder to those who are mindful of Allah.

The consistency of the Quran is so remarkable that it surpasses what our imaginations can comprehend. The key to avoiding failure in everyday events lies in the establishment of strong habits. Among the options presented, which one would be your preference: having someone who is partially deceased, having someone who coexists with the deceased, or having someone who faces ongoing temporal challenges? In the example, the metaphorical depiction of the deceased does not signify physical death, but rather a state of spiritual struggle.

Difficulties in time enhance a Muslim's dedication and resilience. The dedication and resilience of Muslims is widely known and acknowledged. Having balance in life brings durability to the challenges one faces, regardless of whether they have faith or not. Hope, on the other hand, serves as a commander of choice for everyone.

Allah, in His mercy, blesses us with precious hours to share joy, kindness, laughter, smiles, and happiness, as well as to fulfill our deepest desires. The quality of life is the foundation from which dignity arises. Characters understand the importance of holding onto their words and actively work to keep them, instead of allowing them to slip away. The expression of the light becomes evident as it illuminates its surroundings with its rays. It's impossible to miss because it's so bright.

Quran: Surah Hud; 11:111.Surely your Lord will recompense all to the full for their deeds. For indeed He is well aware of all that they do.

The efforts of a person who consistently puts in the work. The length of success in all his venues is contingent upon the duration of his behavior. Allah has a special love for those slaves who remain consistent in their worship. Achieving success becomes challenging when there is a lack of persistent and consistent effort. Inconsistency and neglect are the prevailing characteristics of the situation.

The neglect of Allah or the neglect of a believer is clearly apparent among those Muslims who fail to prioritize their faith. The results have turned out just as we had anticipated. However, for those individuals who put in maximum effort and strive relentlessly, success arrives more swiftly than one can pursue it. The strength of character lies in one's self-behavior and attitude, as confidence disregards other behaviors. This lack of validation comes from individuals who do not believe in Allah and refuse to acknowledge the existence of others.

Quran: Surah Hud: 11:113. And do not incline towards the wrong-doers lest the Fire might seize you and you will have none as your protector against Allah, and then you will not be helped from anywhere.

It is a soldier of Allah who knows the truth has no limits. How could a Muslim not spread the truth they encounter? Islamic concepts and doctrines have a major impact on believers' lives. Nothing falls until a human falls deeply. The land suffers, not the doings of the land, but the doings of humans who use space in neglect or appreciation.

Quran: Surah Hud: 11:1117. And your Lord is not such as would wrongfully destroy human habitations while their inhabitants are righteous.

Muslims are expected to share the knowledge they have with others so that Allah's truth can be spread to all. The truth should be shared without fear or hesitation, regardless of the consequences. This is a sign of faith and dedication to Allah. There is no doubt that those who fuse beliefs leave indelible traces on the lives of those who fuse them.

The bond between the two individuals is formed through the shared experiences and beliefs they have, even if their paths end up going in different directions. Ultimately, these connections transcend ordinary words and actions and have a lasting effect on all those who are part of them.

The application of sharing content and teachings of Allah goes beyond its initial purpose and serves to strengthen the bond between parents and children at its core, which is truly remarkable. Those individuals who enthusiastically engaged in events that were designed to educate and enlighten others about the righteous path and fundamental principles of Islamic concepts deserve acknowledgement.

The purpose of this is to emphasize that the impact of stories about Allah is far greater than any other story, and this is specifically for those who remember and reflect on them. The same applies to both relatives and strangers who actively engaged in learning and following Allah's teachings, and who were fortunate enough to have teachers who shared profound stories that deeply resonated with them. The divisions among people become insignificant as the shared truth of the divine resonates, primarily because of the distractions created by Satan and his people.

These teachings are ingrained in the core of the family and protect them from negative influences. This bond ensures that the family remains true to Allah's teachings and never strays from righteousness. The application of this is not limited to family but also to those who come to the path in search of Allah. He places conformity and durability in the lives of those who seek deeper threads.

This application is not just exclusive to families but also to those who participated in the spiritual caveat of life. This is to balance the world with an inner strength that material life cannot fulfill. This strength encourages staying on the right path and provides courage and confidence in times of difficulty. It allows faith in the divine plan and to accept Allah's will with patience.

These connections bring peace and contentment that is invaluable and irreplaceable. All connections gained by the premise of purity are guided to clarity and fulfillment of life.

On the righteous path, along with accommodations to achieve in this world provided by Allah. These words are for those who believe, and they are merely an attempt to explain to those who hold conditional faith or solidarity in faith.

Those who pursue hollow connections devoid of substance, ultimately leaving their souls unsatisfied, invariably find themselves in a similar situation. Unless there has been a reform in the foundation of life to accommodate spirituality and souls, it is difficult to envision any substantial development. The absence of a spiritual connection often leads to a state of misery for most individuals. While blitz may not equate to contentment, it is undeniable that material possessions often lead to independence.

Those who don't communicate can remain entrenched behind each defending their position but Islam has no defense except to maintain its course for those who wish to follow it. Faith's primal instincts and impulses are appreciated, but logic and reason are essential components of truth. True believers follow with fully addressing challenges, but the Quran insists upon understanding deliverance since Islam is the master of faultless delivery.

It is through soul clarity and connection with the divine that one gains peace, tranquility, and materiality. It becomes more useful for oneself and for others. When it is received with the prosperity of the inner soul and a sense of connection to the divine.

Those who suffer from depression are seeking contentment in things that leave them empty at all costs. Academic pursuits transform lives. Travels bring closure to the unknown by introducing and experiencing people from all walks of life. Those who go through the pendulum of metamorphosis change their minds in all experiences. Small connections with Allah are greater than evil milestones.

The power of belief is the most important element of faith, and it can lead to remarkable changes in a person's life. It gives a person the strength to face any trial and tribulation with patience and trust in Allah's will. With faith, a person can find solace and hope in any situation.

It can be anything for a believer who looks for the easy way out but discovers the path they took has a major impact on life. Leading to dissatisfaction for those who find belief obscure after finding it and letting it slip away. Are bound by contaminated surroundings.

Organized religion or way of life symbolizes the inner teacher. This inner teacher helps us to understand the deeper meanings behind religious rituals and practices. It is a guide to help us find our spiritual path and reach a higher level of awareness. It offers us a way to connect with something larger than ourselves. The triumph over superficial matters does not supersede the divine. As the events unfold, thoughts and attitudes are restored.

In conversations that are related to the creator, a sense of connection can be ingrained. In reality, communication cannot be seen as a backend but rather as a memory of pleasant encounters. This connection can be a source of strength and emotional support. It can also help to create a sense of belonging and shared values.

Ultimately, communication is essential for creating meaningful relationships. The most meaningful connection is from a believer to a believer. True communication bordered by spiritual connection creates a bond that is difficult to break and can be a source of strength and comfort in times of need.

When the heart leads, possibilities are abundant as Allah says to come to him with a sound heart. It's all possible when the heart leads toward truth, the creator. Thus, humans will seek traders who share their belief systems in a medley of commerce. This commerce of reliance on Allah is more lucrative than any revenue humanity can bank on.

Along with doing one's most effective performance and holding on to faith. Acting with decorum and tact is the world's way. Allah's pursuit requires purity of the heart and a desire to seek gratitude's heights. Ultimately leading to possibilities one never envisioned. The hybrid of all attempts to savor this world and the next is (dua) prayer. This is a symphony that is directed and heard daily by attendees as mercy dispatch continues for a believer. The semblance of tranquility is best chosen as dedication and creativity in alliance with Allah.

It is important to remember that Satan is committed to his job if the confused believer has doubts about the impending decision. Believers have a job of worshiping Allah. However, humans do not find this job attainable or meaningful for those swayed easily or living in conditions not conducive to Islam.

It is important to remember that one doesn't need to be in a certain environment to practice their faith. One can still practice his or her faith wherever they are, regardless of their situation. Faith is an integral part of life and must be practiced regularly to ensure spiritual well-being.

Spiritual journeys are individual and should not be hindered by external factors. Faith is a personal journey and must be respected as such. Although nonbelievers are given commodities, the peace they receive is short-lived. Even an animal chased by humans or threatened loses its peace. So does a human without the assistance of Allah.

As the demons chase him he permits the weakness of his soul to take over the primary time of his life on earth which decorates the colors of life in this world and prepares for the next underestimating the whispers of Satan rather dim but loud for those who attend to the worst evils within to confront the demons further not peace.

The demons of evil that reside within us can be shared with others through false notions of independence and happiness, or through the misuse of technology to perpetrate even greater acts of evil. Muslims who hold the belief that repentance is the solution to all their troubles have the option to either walk away feeling dissatisfied or take the opportunity to address their problems and come back even stronger.

Although there are numerous religions practiced worldwide, it is important to note that there is only one God. Muslim individuals are part of the population in every nation, but it is incorrect to assume that any nation is entirely Muslim. Despite the shared existence of humans within the realms of humanity, their presence does not influence the steadfast convictions of the faithful.

Misleading individuals who are easily influenced can be accomplished through the distribution of handouts or the intentional spread of misinformation. Those individuals who lack mental strength have the option to either be liberated or restrained without any requirement to go through a formal registration process.

Deception dilemmas are often accompanied by lies brought forth by individuals from various organizations, regardless of their faith or creed. The Quran, remaining unchanged, reflects Allah's conception of truth which does not need advertisement. The Muslims do not learn their way of life from a distant memory or bygone era; rather, they derive it from the Quran and Sunnah customs and practices.

Muslims regard the Quran, which has existed for a duration of 1400 years, as a source of eternal wisdom. Consequently, every page they learn and memorize is cherished, reminiscent of a rejuvenating breath of fresh air. The clarity of this statement is evident whenever it is read. The preservation of this text remains completely intact. This recitation is a continuous practice in the homes of Muslims. The Quran is recited by each and every Muslim during the practice of Salat.

Both Arabic and non-Arabic speakers, ranging from children to adults, continuously memorize the Quran, making it the only book in the world with such a distinction. A significant number of individuals who do not practice the Islamic faith or those who have uncertainties about it have raised inquiries regarding the ability of the Quran to exert influence over the thoughts and beliefs of Muslims.

Whether an individual has received academic education or not, the impact remains consistent for someone who believes. It is a fundamental belief in Islam that Allah has blessed us with the heart, mind, and all of our organs as sacred gifts. For every Muslim, the Quran serves as a powerful testimony of faith. The Book of Records stands alone as the ultimate testament to His creation, encapsulating the very essence of law and direction.

The delivery of the Quran encompasses a set of rules and principles that govern its existence. Unlike books written by humans, which may become tedious with repeated reading, the Quran is the divine word of Allah. This statement stands in stark contrast to the texts that were previously conveyed by the Abrahamic faith. The book Quran holds a special place of significance as it surpasses all other texts, serving as the final revelation from Allah for both Muslims and all of humanity.

Similar to the way human laws function, once a newly formed government is in place, it promptly introduces amended laws and implements reforms. Furthermore, not only are old laws rescinded, but also new and updated laws are adopted. Prophet Muhammad is recognized as the final Prophet of all Abrahamic faiths, and this significant declaration is made in the Quran, which is considered the ultimate testament of Allah.

Salat is a mandatory act for Muslims as it represents a sacred meeting between Allah and a devoted servant. If a human were to have a meeting with an individual of great importance, it is highly unlikely that they would willingly forgo such an opportunity; instead, they would eagerly anticipate the momentous occasion, constantly counting down the hours until they can finally meet this significant person. In the event that someone does not show up, the important person would not feel the absence of that individual. However, despite Allah being the owner of the world, there is a sense of longing for the presence of the human who used to regularly show up.

While salat is an important aspect of being a Muslim, it is crucial to understand that the deen way of life encompasses a holistic practice. The true value of a human being can be measured by how they treat themselves and others. Muslims and non-Muslims both acknowledge the significance of humanity in their lives, as Islam emphasizes the importance of respecting and caring for both the earth and fellow human beings, thereby promoting harmonious coexistence with Muslims.

For a Muslim, the act of Salat is not only a means of connecting with Allah, but it is also a powerful practice that has the ability to soften the heart, reminding individuals that mistreating the humanity Allah has created is not a privilege granted. The theological differences, which are always present, never intend to disrespect humanity in any way. It is crucial to exercise care and understanding when it comes to Islam, as it is a comprehensive faith and a holistic way of life.

When you seek repentance from Allah for any wrongdoing you have done to yourself, Allah will grant forgiveness. However, it is important to note that Allah will also instruct you to seek forgiveness from the person you have wronged. The teachings of Islam highlight the significance of seeking forgiveness from both humans and animals whom we may have mistreated, showcasing its commitment to justice. The importance of gift-giving in Islam stems from its ability to clarify the uncomplicated nature of the religion and its role in promoting reconciliation.

There is a distinction between engaging in private acts of sin and actively encouraging others to sin, as well as spreading gossip about the sins committed by oneself and others. In addition to seeking forgiveness from Allah, one can also engage in acts of "Sadaqah", voluntary giving, and fasting as means of repentance and seeking spiritual purification. The best approach is to ask the person you are gossiping about, as it is most suitable for preventing the repetition of mistakes. Islam encompasses more than just Salat; it is a complete way of life, a deen.

Muslims are encouraged to surround themselves with like-minded individuals who share our interests and engage in meaningful conversations about the way of life in this deen. The act of acquiring knowledge about the faith of Islam from disbelievers or non-Muslims can have negative consequences for a Muslim. The disobedience of humanity has led Allah to destroy countless cities. The passion of an individual who loves his faith is what drives them to seek romance within their faith. The importance of manners in Islam cannot be stressed enough, as they extend to everyone, encompassing all of humanity. It is crucial to treat others with care, using kind speech and reciprocating with a kind word or a smile. This exchange can be seen as a form of exchanging gifts, and all of these aspects are integral to being a practicing Muslim.

Salat serves as a spiritual practice for your soul, yet it is essential for Muslims to embody a demeanor of attending to all aspects of life in this world. To truly embody the faith of Islam, it is crucial to refrain from engaging in actions that would bring shame to the Muslim ummah. It is important to practice what you preach and ensure that your actions align with the principles of the faith you identify with. Muslims are strongly discouraged from making their private sins public or sharing them with others. Instead, they are advised to give voluntary charity (Sadaqah) and refrain from repeating actions that displease Allah. Muslims, like everyone else, are prone to making mistakes, but it is always preferable to be conscious and aware rather than negligent.

Believers can apply these same qualities to their everyday lives as well. While combative behavior may have the potential to intimidate certain individuals, it is essential for an individual to make sacrifices in order to achieve their objectives and take a stance of truth rather than remaining stagnant. It is crucial for us to work together to protect and preserve the world, rather than causing its destruction or being subjected to its destruction.

When an individual speaks with a strong sense of conviction, a calm and composed voice has the power to clarify and emphasize their message. At the appropriate moment, Allah assures that He will guide you along the path you are meant to take. Known for his unwavering trustworthiness, King Faisal of Saud stands out as one of the most respected kings. The person who shows reverence to Allah does not experience fear towards other individuals.

The New York Times: Nov 23rd, 1973: Saudi Arabia warns U.S. against Oil countermoves:

King Faisal, the leader of Saudi Arabia, issued a warning to the United States regarding the potential cut-off of oil supply. A man of great courage and conviction, he boldly advocated for fairness. The greed they were exhibiting did not instill fear in him. He had a deep fear and reverence for Allah. In the annals of history, he will forever be remembered as a Saudi king. In contrast to becoming a puppet of Western culture, he remained true to his Muslim identity. In response to the warning from the USA, King Faisal, who was known for his bravery, confidently stated that the Bedouin Arabs were accustomed to consuming dates and quenching their thirst with water.

Hunger did not instill fear in him. During a televised interview, he made it known to the entire world that he had no intention of lending his support to Zionism. He was aware that Israel did not adhere to the moral code that is expected within the Muslim world.

There is a possibility that his stance could have consequences for the relationship with the United States of America, but it did not pose any threat to him. Around the year 1973, the Arab nations made a collective choice to refuse selling crude oil and petroleum to the United States. The reason behind this embargo was the United States' decision to support Israel, which in turn caused a significant amount of distress and hardship for the people of Palestine.

While petroleum was being rationed in America, it was common to see long lines of cars waiting to be filled up. In the end, it was the Middle East that took control of the situation and negotiated the embargo, completely disregarding the wishes of the late King Faisal. The system made a mistake by not following the decisions recommended and supported by King Faisal. The negotiations that they engaged in unfortunately did not work in favor of the cause of Palestine, and as a result, they fell prey to them. If rightful decisions had been made decades ago, this could have all come to an end.

If crude oil had been traded in Dinar at a higher rate instead of U.S currency, Muslims would have shown support to other Muslim countries. Despite the devaluation of the currency, the Saudi currency would have been stronger, giving Muslims a greater advantage in commerce and benefiting the economies of all Muslim nations, ultimately leading to an increase in the value of Muslim lands' currencies. Muslims would be fair in trade with rules set as this is part of Islam Prophet Muhammad was a tradesman he traded goods and sold in Syria before he married Khadija his wife.. Saudi Arabia ranks among the top oil producers in the world. Is there anything that Allah has not given to the Muslim world? How are they leveraging their wealth?

Since the 1970s, Riyadh has chosen to sell and trade its crude in dollars, a decision that has played a significant role in upholding the global dominance of the greenback as the reserve currency. The

Muslim world has the potential to contribute to the global community and combat greed by implementing strategies such as raising the currency and engaging in trade at various rates.

The situation drastically changed following the passing of King Faisal. Muslims who faithfully follow Islamic law and have a deep understanding of Allah's blessings are able to effectively engage in trade and provide support to the world. The comprehension of the system is crucial for its improvement, however, those who hold altered doctrines may impose negative consequences on Muslims who fail to recognize it.

Muslims must step up and take control of the system to protect the world from the perils of greed, dishonest speeches, spreading gossip, and fraudulent victories. During the Dark Ages, it was the Muslims who took charge and led the way, and now it is crucial for all individuals to come together and lend their support to the Muslim community and extend a helping hand to Muslims across the globe.

The sole voice of reason for Muslims cannot be attributed to just one nation or two alone. Greed and the pursuit of stealing land, crude oil, and wealth have created a predicament that the majority of Muslims are currently facing. It is imperative that we strive to protect and uphold the principles of truth and justice.

Impoverished nations that are heavily indebted to others and possess non-believing mentalities cannot be relied upon as educators, and the world should not look to them for guidance. Muslims do not simply follow, but rather they take on the role of teachers, recognizing that remaining in darkness and going against Allah's commands is not the solution.

In order to combat the destructive consequences that arise from the exploitation of nudity and deception by technology, it is imperative that we prioritize the education of both our youth and Muslims. Access to alcohol, porn, and drugs has been denied in many Muslim nations, as part of efforts to educate and uplift society. Muslims have a crucial role to play in guiding the world out of its state of ignorance and darkness, and this can be achieved through unity and educational assistance. It is imperative for the Muslim community to lend their assistance during this critical period.

Regrettably, it can be concluded that the ongoing negotiations have not been successful. The Middle East has been blessed with wealth by Allah, but it is essential for Muslims to strive for unity. Make it your goal to avoid surpassing the choices made by the system and to prevent exploitation from causing changes to the existing regimes in their respective countries.

It is essential for Muslims to come together and foster a sense of unity. Countries are exploited by systems and regimes who engage in manipulation due to their insatiable greed. The matter remained unresolved as they did not come to a settlement. Allah had a divine purpose or destiny that he was meant to fulfill. Regrettably, King Faisal is no longer with us as he has passed away.

Their failure to implement the justice system of King Faisal is evident. The negotiations, which were conducted under the terms imposed by the U.S., did not meet the expectations of the late King Faisal. The country of Saud, which is the birthplace of the Prophet Muhammad, continues to function as a monarchy.

Unfortunately, in recent times, external influences have been allowed to interfere and manipulate the Muslim world, exploiting their vulnerabilities and pitting them against each other in acts of greed, tyranny, and injustice. In an attempt to combat the detrimental forces of greed and selfishness, forming an alliance with Muslims would prove to be a formidable and impactful approach. Kindness, awareness, and humanity are essential aspects demanded by Islam, especially considering the prevalent misunderstandings surrounding this faith in various areas.

Quran: Surah Baqarah 2:222, Allah says in the Qur'an: indeed Allah loves those who are constantly repentant and loves those who purify themselves.

Muslims need to educate themselves about their own enriching "deen" way of life. There is absolutely no intention or desire to engage in any form of sabotage. If we consistently demonstrate progress, the learning process in today's society would remain free from any sabotage. Rather than progressing, they are moving backwards and returning to the principles that Islam had once evolved from.

Progress cannot solely be measured by material achievements, but also by the well-roundedness of individuals and their concern for humanity. While individual comfort may be seen as progress, it is unfortunate that some countries prioritize greed over the welfare of their people, focusing only on the prosperity of a select few. The act of taking resources from impoverished individuals in order to provide for the wealthy is not in alignment with the principles of truth or justice.

The reason that these countries have tyrants ruling over them is due to the fact that the overall morality of the society displays a blatant disregard for the principles and rules that govern life, with the exception of a small minority of individuals who adhere to the integral rules set forth by Allah, which promote a society that prioritizes the well-being of others over self-centered behaviors.

The periods in which Muslims have governed, spanning every decade, have consistently demonstrated advancements. In this decade, if you visit Muslim households, you will witness the incredible hospitality that one showers upon another. It is not just a matter of faith, but a demonstration of humanity. Islam, by its very nature, attends to every aspect of life, not solely limited to Salat.

European countries, including Spain, have a vibrant and diverse Muslim culture that is deeply rooted in history. When it comes to Islam, people from different cultures and backgrounds all come together under one common color, which is humanity. Even though this spread has reached worldwide, the most effective way to advance is by promoting the learning of Islam. This is because Islam is specifically designed for human progress and improvement, rather than allowing stagnation.

During this decade, a pair of thieves found themselves running from the law. As hunger struck one of them, he made the decision to seek food at the nearest church, while the other thief opted to approach a Muslim home, confident that they would be welcomed with open arms and offered a meal. Both individuals took different paths, with one heading towards the church and the other towards a Muslim home. The man who went to the church discovered that there was nobody present, as the lunch hour had already concluded.

On the other hand, the man who visited the Muslim home expressed his satisfaction with a full stomach. He recounted how he had informed the lady of his hunger, and she kindly prepared a special plate for him. This incident exemplifies the incredible hospitality often found in Muslim households, where no one leaves unsatisfied. The absence of hunger was a notable aspect of life under Muslim rule, highlighting their commitment to ensuring that no one went hungry. In this decade, the need for Muslims to actively respond to the call and provide assistance to those in need is becoming increasingly urgent.

To attain their destiny, individuals must exclusively traverse the path. Despite taking a temporary detour, it is indeed possible to find one's way back to the path of Allah. The act of converting to Islam marks the start of a transformative journey. Those who are interested in uncovering the truth can find enlightenment by gaining insight into Islam.

Manners, such as politeness and respect for others, play a significant role in distinguishing us from one another. The unfolding of Islam brings with it a tremendous amount of unity. Regardless of whether time stretches or shrinks, we always remember the profound events that brought humanity closer to Allah and forever changed our lives.

The aspect of hospitality plays a crucial role in the achievements of the Muslim community. The establishment of hospitals to care for the sick was seen as a gesture of kindness and generosity from the Muslim world. Without any acts of kindness or faith in the Muslim religion, the essence of its teachings may be lost. When individuals lend a helping hand to others, their talent and credibility become apparent.

Throughout history, hospitals have played a crucial and influential role in transforming the healthcare landscape. In today's greed-driven climate, hospitals that were originally founded by Muslims have suffered destruction, leading to the unfortunate loss of lives among the patient population. The selfless actions of Muslims included saving lives and ensuring the well-being of the sick, in stark contrast to the destructive impact of this system on hospitals and lands.

Muslims were the ones who established the first hospitals, which had separate wards specifically for the sick. Muslims were making significant progress in various fields and sectors. In Islam, one of the teachings includes the act of giving gifts and expressing gratitude.

Just like in Islam, a man or a woman can consistently demonstrate integrity and politeness. The character of a person is best revealed through their actions rather than through their words, speaking volumes about who they truly are. In order to ensure quality healthcare, they made sure to provide doctors' helpers with extensive remuneration and generous salaries.

Giving is what drives the Islamic world to thrive. Despite the fact that Allah gives abundantly to whomever He chooses, it is perplexing to contemplate how a Muslim man or woman could exhibit the characteristics of stinginess.

When you give, you will receive ten times as much in return. Building upon the accomplishments of the Muslim world, we are continuing to make significant advancements. Muslims were the pioneers in developing the art of ophthalmology and cataract surgery. In Egypt, there was a Muslim Iraqi named Amar Ibn Ali Al Mawsili who conducted the earliest cataract extraction.

The way in which he skillfully approaches the most delicate part of the human eye is truly remarkable. It is within the power of humanity to decide whether to use these eyes for benevolent or malevolent purposes. This experience will teach them valuable skills in observing and admiring the beauty that the world has to offer.

Or participate in forbidden mischief displacing and disobedience to Allah's laws. When one consciously decides to continuously break or mend the laws of Allah, it is possible to rectify this behavior by engaging in clear thinking and seeking the company of good people. The act of repeating and continuously delivering the message plays a crucial role in helping individuals comprehend the importance of repentance.

The eyes, which are a beautiful part of the human body, possess a lens that allows us to see. Interestingly, it was the Muslims who pioneered the restoration of the lens through surgery, specifically in the removal of cataracts. His attention to detail and carefulness remained intact, even in the absence of modern equipment.

The medical professional opted for a hollow needle as the instrument to operate on the eye. He was the one who carried out the surgery. While the patient was seated in an upright position, they took the initiative to bandage him. In order to perform cataract surgery, the modern world heavily depends on advanced high-tech equipment.

Without the aid of modern technology, Muslims were pioneers in performing this intricate eye surgery. In the Quran, there are a total of 40 references made to the eyes. The creator, in his book, highlights the significance of having a vision in life. There are individuals who possess a susceptibility to external influence and struggle to discern between right and wrong, even when faced with actions that go against the teachings of Allah.

It is important to remember that every action, no matter how small, carries its own set of consequences. Individuals who once had impeccable eyesight often encounter challenges when they endeavor to enhance their vision through the utilization of spectacles, contact lenses, or surgical procedures.

Is the significance of vision on par with the significance of all the other bodily functions for survival on our planet? Allah holds each body part accountable for its actions. The effectiveness of repentance is maximized when it is practiced in the present moment, rather than postponing it until the time of judgment. By selecting to partake in actions that are morally superior, individuals increase their likelihood of achieving more desirable consequences.

With those eyes, certain Muslims read the Quran and the words of Allah, and they offer prayers, seeking the clarity of vision to perceive the words that profoundly resonate with their souls. Those who engage in reading the Quran are well aware of the worth it possesses. When individuals engage in reading the Quran, they find themselves shielded from the allure of forbidden things and discover a deep contentment that becomes an irreplaceable part of their lives.

The way in which a Muslim or believer employs their eyes to challenge Allah does not negate the fact that their sight serves as evidence for the things they have witnessed. Whether they share or view it in person or on social media, the significance remains constant. In the eyes of the believer, repentance is characterized by a conscious effort to refrain from making the same errors again. While forgiveness is not guaranteed, it is hope that ultimately prevails.

The fear of loss is prevalent among those who lack perception and sight, leading them to go to extraordinary measures in order to comprehend the tests bestowed upon them by Allah. The reason why some individuals misuse this vision remains known solely to him. Can the combination of righteous and evil branding lead to the revival of Islam's solv's solvency or dependence? The possibilities for the future are limitless, and the destitution of destiny serves as a clear indication for the need for peace and reconciliation.

One of the benefits that a follower recognizes is the advantages. Vision, similar to all the other parts of the human body, holds great importance and is crucial for our overall well-being. The person who has faith comprehends the significance of having a clear vision, and the individual's heart wholeheartedly embraces and adopts its unique perspective. The person who is reciting the Quran is able to avoid forbidden things, unlike the person who does not have Allah's guidance and cannot differentiate between choosing evil and engaging in negative forms of entertainment. Once the heart forms a connection with its vision, the believer starts to feel fear when confronted with evil. This person can be described as a devout believer.

The absence of faith in one's actions can ultimately bring about misery, regret, and anguish. Thus, it is of paramount importance to stay committed to the right path and steer clear of any temptations that could veer you off course. The eyes and speech of an individual can be considered as the pulsating beats of their heart. Those who understand the rulings of Islam will find that the heart carries a heavy burden when one observes the forbidden with their eyes.

If a person who believes in Islam were to lose his eyes, he would be unable to read the Quran. It is disheartening to observe that a considerable number of people continue to allocate their time and energy towards activities that do not contribute to a reformed and clearer way of living. The proximity of evil is just a hand span away, whereas the pursuit of a positive life requires traversing miles of distance. Trust is attainable for individuals who possess the eyes, heart, and mouth necessary to remain steadfast in their vision.

Make a conscious effort to utilize your eyes, heart, and mouth solely for engaging in activities that promote peace and invite the blessings of Allah. The allure of worldly temptations can lead to a decreased desire for goodness, highlighting the importance of focusing on the abilities to seek Allah's pleasure.

Allah, who is known for His infinite mercy, bestows upon us rewards for our righteous deeds. When an individual acknowledges their blindness, their subconscious mind relinquishes its endeavor to perceive the genuine essence of spirituality. Until the blinders are taken off, individuals who are unable to see the truth are cursed as a consequence of their disobedience to Allah. When evil is present, Satan has the ability to gain control over the weak. Continuous cleansing efforts are the only means by which it can be removed. Pure beings are not exempt from encountering Satan, as he does make his presence known to them. In a regretful manner, he walks away from the believers who have witnessed his malicious tactics. Filth is the environment in which he chooses to live. Personal hygiene is given great importance in the religion of Islam which includes the eyes.

The eyes that look upon the forbidden images of humanity and other things are in need of cleanliness in order to maintain their hygiene, while those who lack vision face struggles in their ability to see. Those who use their vision to defy Allah require correction, with the intention of not expressing turmoil, but rather fostering hope for restoration and a renewed appreciation for the gift of eyes. In their supplications, Muslims beseech Allah to grant them the gift of perceptive vision, capable of recognizing and comprehending the absolute truth. It is important to have eyes that possess the ability to see clearly and distinguish between negative and harmful influences.

Quran: Surah Imran 3:13 Already there have been signs in the two armies that came together - one fighting in the cause of Allah, and another of unbelievers. Whose eyesight caused them to appear twice as many. With Allah's victory, he supports whomever he will. Indeed, that is a lesson for those with vision.

The truth lies within the depths of the soul, and the lights that enlightened the streets were all created by Muslims; as they illuminated the souls, they also illuminated the streets. Knowledge of Islam prevents one from joining darkness. Those who have experienced light do not prefer darkness.

In the beautiful city of Cordoba, situated in Andalucia, Spain, Islam and its followers found a thriving environment. The lights that illuminate the city at night, which are a legacy of Muslims, create a captivating atmosphere that people in this region and around the world truly enjoy.

Recognized as a prominent figure of the Islamic golden age, Abu Al-Qasim Al-Zahrawi excelled in the fields of surgery and medicine. Alongside his given name, he was also recognized as the Albucasis. That name was given to him by the Western world. The surgical procedure involved operating on the patient's eyes, ears, and throat, and he executed it flawlessly. His literary contributions include medical textbooks as well as the famous Kitab Al Tafsir. When he departed, he left a remarkable legacy behind. Intelligence and talents are bestowed upon individuals by Allah according to His will.

AL-Zahrawi, a Muslim innovator, made significant contributions to the world by pioneering the use of internal stitches, which are also commonly referred to as catgut. In today's society, his surgical instruments continue to be employed in surgeries that are performed. Muslims have made significant contributions to society and have brought a plethora of valuable assets to the table. The positive reputation of Islamic culture is widely recognized and cherished in today's society, primarily due to its abundant and inherent characteristics.

Muslim individuals must be educated in order to gain a comprehensive understanding of the background of the disciplined society and rich culture that characterized their faith during historic times. The understanding and appreciation of the truth and love of learning and sharing will spread throughout the world. It becomes challenging to ignore the truth for a significant amount of time once it has been presented.

The consciousness that most humans possess is similar to this. The European world in the Dark Ages was enlightened by the teachings of Muslims. Muslims have had a significant impact on Europe, particularly in the fields of medicine and architecture. The primary area of their work revolved around addressing and enhancing human mental health.

The religion of Islam places a strong emphasis on the mental health and general well-being of humanity, recognizing its utmost value. If a disease of mental illness is present, it must be acknowledged and addressed. However, it is important to differentiate between self-induced drug use and illicit acts that result in depression and the actual disease of mental health. The focus of the Muslim community's address was on a specific disease, rather than a series of unfortunate events leading to self-inflicted depression. The latter situation requires repentance and a change of course for a Muslim. Or any human willing to change course.

Islam not only encourages visiting the sick but also emphasizes the importance of sending gifts as a way of showing care and compassion. Whenever there was a need for medicine, they were always the first ones to take the initiative and explore potential solutions. Muslims were responsible for opening the very first mental hospital in the world.

One of the key teachings in Islam is the encouragement to seek medical treatment while also placing trust and reliance on Allah for the remainder. Instead of abandoning those who are weak and incapable, Islam teaches that they should receive assistance. An essential aspect of Islam is the provision of care for the sick and weak, showcasing the religion's commitment to humanitarian values. Care was given to both those who were less fortunate and those who were fortunate. Within the teachings of Islam, discrimination is not tolerated or encouraged. This faith places a strong emphasis on the importance of kindness as a necessary virtue.

By establishing pharmacies and hospitals in countries that have ample material opportunities, they positioned themselves as the preferred option for stock investments. Although medical care can often be exceptional, it is important to note that hospitals primarily thrive by billing insurance in certain situations. The health and accessibility of hospitals are greatly valued by humanity, regardless of the associated costs.

Some individuals are deprived of complete care due to the absence of proper insurance. The interests of individuals play a crucial role in determining the success of any given system. Conversely, the complete aid granted to the land that holds deep meaning for all Abrahamic faiths has only led to turmoil in the Palestinian territories.

The act of inhumanity that has occurred is deemed completely unacceptable by both Orthodoxies and individuals who deeply value the principles of humanity. Rather than impeding progress, allocating funds to the underprivileged within their nation could potentially serve as a positive means of advancement for many who are facing challenges. Poverty is an undeniable reality, however, it often remains unnoticed and unacknowledged by the major players in the world, especially for those who are grappling with financial difficulties or barely making ends meet.

In today's societies, there are medical professionals who are well-equipped to handle various situations, but unfortunately, corruption within the world's systems has also had an impact on this particular society. The act of destroying the core values that define humanity. The assistance provided for the sick and underprivileged individuals may experience an impact. The outcome of the situation may vary depending on the income bracket of the individuals involved. In societies where medicine is rapidly advancing and daily survival depends on it, having health insurance is absolutely necessary.

As depression and health issues are not far from their entrenched lives, medicine is consumed daily in these societies. Serving the destitute of doings with man-made infusions of pills found on shelves and cupboards costs a precise price.

After seeing that medicine is taken daily more than adherence to food, some regain their faith. Some continue to visit doctors and add more medicine to the shelves thinking the last days of lingering youth or old age are numbered, or those who dare to admit the course has been so evil that nothing can stop it except a longer life, to destroy themselves and others.

There are individuals who express their dissatisfaction with the trajectory of their lives and actively strive for improvement. Muslims, as well as all individuals who understand the value of time, recognize that once time passes, it cannot be retrieved. It is therefore wiser to focus on doing our best rather than acting on the whims of others.

It is always preferable for a Muslim to do what is morally right, rather than following the path of those who exhibit doubt and lack the qualities of practicing Islam, despite being labeled as Muslims. Opting to provide ongoing assistance to Muslims who have gone astray is a more favorable choice, as Allah does not disregard any individual and there is perpetual opportunity for progress.

Commitment is not hindered by any barriers, rather it is determined by what an individual considers important. The focus should not be on those who are naturally given material and academic advantages from birth. The individualized nature of home births and ways of life is a result of Allah's careful tailoring. Academic or familial privileges granted to those in affluent or successful families cause those less fortunate to feel resentful and often victimized. Others give up easily and dwell on sarcasm, misery, or hatred. Faced with trials, Islam is firm. Each human faces the path he or she will take, but Islam teaches that trying is a must.

In addition, injustice can never last until the end of time, and goodness is also a thriving factor for believers. The Muslim world has left footprints as a man walks on the sand. These footprints are reminders.

However, they can research the technology of today from the right sources. Since many are unaware of Muslims' history, sharing the successes of the Muslim (Ummah) his people with humanity is a primal task. History will remind the world of their accomplishments.

The intimidated society's repeated attempts to alienate the Muslim world's progress only contribute more challenge and endurance to succeed in the personal growth of Muslims. Haters keep you on your toes to ensure you are on the right track. If no one bothers with someone, then growth must be stagnant. Islam has been a threat to many due to their consistent beliefs, persistent challenges, and strong faith and progress.

When Muslim people are averse to learning accuracy, it leads to their downfall and ignorance. An adulterated version of the newer society does not teach progression. They have altered the Bible to suit their needs. What are the reasons a society dimmed by deceit would present Islam or its history as a counterbalance?

It's impossible to learn from non-Muslims about Muslims' history, Islam, or the Quran. Muslims have participated in the most intricate ways of human health and gift-giving through the sharing of knowledge. For generations to come, all the values of shared knowledge are gifts. The world can continue expanding the search for improving the types of equipment to perform surgeries.

It was the Muslims who played a crucial role in providing the core balance and learning for these ventures. Abu Al Qasim Zahrawi, who is historically recognized, holds the distinction of being the first Muslim to successfully identify cases of hemophilia occurring in both abdominal and ectopic pregnancies. This particular kind of pregnancy has the potential to go unnoticed. If this condition is not treated, it has the potential to result in serious health complications or even mortality.

In order to aid with cesarean deliveries where the fetus was in a breech position, he developed surgical instruments. The occurrence of pregnancy complications during that specific period ultimately resulted in fatal consequences. In predated times, Muslims would offer care and support in the event of any complications that may arise during this delicate period.

Cesarean sections have become a standard procedure in today's modern era. The influence of the Muslim century cannot be easily dismissed, as history itself testifies to its significance. The continuity of this beauty was not limited to its initial scope, as it continued to extend its reach to Andalusia and further expanded due to the profound impact of Muslims on the development of our world.

Andalusia, which happens to be the most populous city of Cordoba, was a city that flourished in various aspects. It was not only an international hub for art and science but also a center of culture and economic growth. During that time, the Muslim world was experiencing a period of great prosperity and growth. The continent of Europe faced numerous challenges and struggles during the Dark Ages. The Islamic golden age, which was a significant period in history, had a profound impact on the world by establishing benchmarks for progress and contributing to Europe's emergence from the dark ages.

After achieving a sense of equilibrium, they proceeded to betray their lands, after receiving assistance and learning from the Muslims. The city of Cordoba, which was located in a different region, was actually larger in size compared to the combined cities of London and Paris. The visual splendor of the Muslim world was a spectacle that delighted and captivated those who had the privilege of witnessing it. In order to enhance its beauty and charm, the citizens of the city decided to line its streets with citrus trees, so that even during the dark ages in Europe, people could still revel in the magnificence and embellishment of the city.

The Muslims were the first to install streetlights. The man had not known about street lights until the Muslim world first lit up Andalucia's city of Cordoba. The entrances of the houses were lit with lights that welcomed guests and occupants. European streets and homes remained in darkness as the lights lit up. Cordoba. They soon copied the Muslim world. Western world lighting, such as street lights and recessed lighting, is used to draw attention to a home to sell Real Estate. Muslim and Islamic traditions dictate that the front of the home should be lit.

The Quran has always shed light on knowledge and eradicated darkness. Muslims understand these concepts are new to others, but to Muslims, light is of significance. So is knowledge. During the Golden Age of Islam, Muslims illuminated countries and cities, leaving history to record our achievements.

Quran: Surah Baqarah 2:257 He brings them out of darkness into light.

As for the disbelievers, the route is darkness. No street lights can lighten such darkness.

Quran: Surah Baqarah 2;257 Allah drives them out of light into darkness. They shall be the inmates of the fire, and they shall remain in it forever.

Knowledge is powerful and cannot be unless Allah wills it. Muslims have received and shared it with the world. Muslims have never been stingy about sharing knowledge and improving society. It's part and parcel of Islam.

Quran: Surah Qasas 29:77. He said he had given them all the knowledge that was given to him.

Quran: Surah Muhammad 47:11. That is because Allah is the supporter of those who believe. Disbelievers have no supporters.

In the same way that the Western world emerged from the dark ages, continuing to be at odds with the Islamic world. All Muslim countries joining could complement the world, not destroy it, as history shows. Taking what benefits them and revolting against teachers are historic traits. History repeating is consistent. Western society still has them. Obviously, in every society, there are a few who remain integral, but the majority has repeatedly shown in the history of Western ideologies to remain consistent.

In the country of Saudi Arabia, the punishment for theft is the amputation of the thief's hands. Some individuals may view this punishment as being harsh. In the religion of Islam, individuals who engage in theft or cause destruction are subjected to a certain punishment. The question arises as to who possesses the ability to sever the hands of individuals who engage in the act of waging wars driven by greed, disseminating falsehoods and deceit, while those very hands should be devoted to cultivating virtues, self-education, and benevolently assisting others.

The young Muslims must be educated about the variations in critical thinking in order to be capable of assisting the world and assuming responsibility for ensuring validity and safety on this planet, as

Allah has entrusted humanity with the responsibility of preserving, rather than destroying, the earth. The completion of the faith of Islam lies in its role as the ultimate safeguard for the world, with the responsibility of protecting humanity resting solely in the hands of Muslims.

They will inevitably face scrutiny and questioning, as it is only through their proactive efforts that the oppressors can be prevented from prevailing. By assuming a prominent position on the global stage, Muslim nations can actively contribute towards positive change and alter the current trajectory. Through my writing, I aim to alter the trajectory and expand the horizons of Muslims and non-Muslims alike, guiding them towards a deeper understanding of the truth. The court system, which is responsible for determining justice laws and rules, is not typically disapproved of by humans. The act of bargaining with the laws of Allah is both paradoxical and serves as a clear indication of disbelief for those who are corrupted disbelievers.

The truth does not hinder friendships. However, theology is known for its inherent ability to mirror truth. Knowledge is a means of expressing gratitude to Allah. One of the teachings of the Qur'an is the guidance it provides on how to progress in life and avoid being consumed by greed and unproductive desires.

Education is of utmost importance in the Muslim world and plays a crucial role in shaping its future. The possession of this strength has proven to be advantageous in various aspects such as facilitating learning engagements, attracting scholars for recruitment, and extending invitations to share knowledge. Islam encourages individuals to pursue knowledge as a way to achieve personal success and to positively impact others through the sharing of knowledge. Humanity thrives when knowledge is shared among individuals. Throughout history, the motto of Islam and Muslims has remained unchanged.

The first university was established by a Muslim woman named Fatima Fihri, which is quite an impressive accomplishment. Following the passing of her father, both she and her sister became the recipients of his wealth. Not long after that, her husband passed away. She dedicated all her efforts to making progress in various aspects of her life and striving to achieve a state of positive equilibrium.

Instead of squandering it, she made a deliberate effort to use the money effectively. Both she and her sister, Maryam, had received their education in Islam and the teachings of the Quran. She did not receive a formal education, as she was the pioneering individual in her family to establish a university, prioritizing the comprehension of the Quran as their primary form of education.

Islam granted her the capacity to comprehend the importance of education and extend invitations to others. Additionally, as a Muslim woman, Islam motivated her to strive for progress and bestowed upon her various rights. She diligently utilized every right to further her own advancement, just like her sister Maryam.

In order to fulfill my role as a Muslim woman, I actively exercise my rights to spread the knowledge I have gained, with the aim of sharing it with the world as a preliminary introduction to my faith in Islam. It is noteworthy that I am pioneering in this endeavor, being the Muslim woman to do so. Fatima Fihri shared her vast knowledge with others. By opening the doors, she extended a warm welcome to all those seeking literacy. While in Fez, Morocco, she decided to name her university Al-Qairwan.

The Al-Andalus mosque in Fez was inaugurated by Maryam's sister. Without wasting any time, Fatima took immediate action and made a strategic investment in real estate by acquiring the adjacent properties. The expansion project was undertaken, even though there was no prior experience in the industry. Despite her inexperience, she successfully managed and supervised the project she had started.

Her leadership was granted by Allah as a result of her devoted prayers and unwavering faith in Him. Fasting as a devotion to Allah, she found solace in prayer which became her constant companion.

In an act of pure joy, she graciously shared her happiness, shared her thoughts, and placed her unwavering faith in Allah, all with the ultimate goal of finding success for her project. Despite dedicating numerous hours to work and prayer, she acknowledges that her achievements would not have been possible without the assistance of Allah. There is nothing that can exceed the support and guidance offered by the creator in one's life. The distinctive architecture and luxurious design of the mosque set it apart from others. A time period of eighteen years was needed to bring the project to its completion. It has been documented by historians that she would fast and pray to Allah until the task was accomplished.

Muslims believe that Allah is the answer to every task they face. Happiness, sadness, and hope all originate from Allah, the ultimate source. Such are the circumstances that a person of faith encounters. The University of Al-Qarawiyyin in Fes Morocco, which was established in 859 CE, has been recognized by the United Nations as the oldest operating university in the world.

The distinction of being the first University to grant degrees to its students belongs to this institution. Fatima Fihri took the necessary steps and successfully became a student at her school. This experience not only nurtured her spiritual growth but also contributed significantly to her intellectual development.

The school had a reputation for attracting the most brilliant, highly intelligent, and inquisitive individuals. Alongside its mosque, the school provided classes in music, logic, astronomy, mathematics, chemistry, medicine, and various other disciplines.

The Islamic world, as it ascended, experienced remarkable progress and achievements in areas such as science, medicine, and beyond. The writings extensively discuss the developments in the Muslim world, and it is worth noting that there is still ample documented evidence available. When we make choices, we need to remember that they have repercussions for both ourselves and the people around us. It is worth noting that Muslims achieved remarkable progress during that specific period.

Despite the groundbreaking achievement of a Muslim woman founding the First World University, Muslim women are still subject to negative stereotypes and considered backward in Western society. A lack of understanding about the empowering nature of the Islamic faith is the source of this misconception. It is not only a duty but also a responsibility for both Muslim women and men to actively engage in the pursuit of truth and to actively share knowledge with others, as well as with oneself.

Unlike the Bible or Torah, which tend to treat women as property, the Quran acknowledges and upholds women's rights. The rights that Muslim women possess are inherent to their religion, rather than being a result of societal progress. Muslim women can break free from imposed backwardness by prioritizing education, as it plays a crucial role in their empowerment.

It is abundantly clear that there are only two options in this situation: either they renounce the Bible and abide by their laws or they cannot continue preaching the Bible and assert a desire for governance.

Bible: ESV: 1 Timothy. 2:11-12. "Let a woman learn in silence with full submission. I permit no woman to teach or to have authority over a man; she is to keep silent"

Bible: Matthew: 5:31:32. "It has been said, 'Anyone who divorces his wife must give her a certificate of divorce.' But I tell you that anyone who divorces his wife, except for sexual immorality, makes her the victim of adultery, and anyone who marries a divorced woman commits adultery.

As per the scriptures of the Bible, if one were to marry a woman with such attributes, it would be regarded as an act of adultery, consequently making her unappealing. Women are esteemed and given recognition for their value in the Islamic faith. Muslim women have been granted their rights.

The theological disparity is quite extensive, rather than limited. Despite the close proximity of human beings, theological disparities continue to exist, even though the unchanging and non-negotiable role of women in the Bible is overlooked. While biblical books do not grant them rights, it is only the Quran that provides them with such entitlements.

In this society, the laws derived from the Bible strictly forbid women from ruling, making decisions, or initiating divorce. In the context of the Bible, divorce is permissible when one fails to uphold the vows of marriage.

According to some, gender equality and success can only be attained by following the teachings of Islam. In the context of Islam, it is acknowledged that women have been granted their inherent rights, while men are tasked with certain responsibilities. While adhering to the Quran, women in Islam have the ability to assert their status.

The assertion that women are striving for higher positions while simultaneously being prohibited from doing so by the Bible is hypocritical. Will they confront both the system and the Bible, or will they promote religious harmony or defy the teachings of the Bible?

Within the Islamic faith, women are regarded with prestige rather than engaging in a battle against a regressive societal structure. Islam encompasses more than just a faith; it serves as a comprehensive system of law and governance for its adherents. Culture is something that can be found in most societies.

Throughout history, educated women who follow the Muslim faith have made significant contributions to society. This is something that should be celebrated and recognized, rather than being ignored. In today's modern society, lies have become pervasive due to the influence of pagan and pseudo cultural influence. This trap is not limited to any particular group; it can ensnare both Muslims and non-Muslims alike. Certain faiths are dominated by pagan rituals, which are familiar to those who have an understanding of the delicate balance between monotheism and polytheism. The existence of this imbalance is closely connected to the allure and sparkle of glamor.

With their commitment to education and spreading knowledge, Muslim women demonstrate their unwavering faith in Allah. The struggle for independence is an ongoing battle that Western women are actively involved in.

Despite the struggles faced by Western women in their fight for rights, Muslim women managed to achieve significant levels of power. The act of having their voices heard had a powerful impact on future generations, empowering them.

Western women continue to strive for complete equality and liberation, making it an ongoing goal. Despite the existence of truth in society, the media continues to utilize the framework as a means to spread falsehoods and deception.

This information is specifically intended for individuals who may not be aware of the significant changes that occurred in literacy during the emergence and growth of Islam. The way in which they rely on modernity as a means to demonstrate their independence ultimately leads to a backward movement.

The relevance of these comments lies in their direct connection to a particular group of people, and it is important to acknowledge that misconceptions play a vital role in shaping the utilization of information. This statement does not imply that all humans are being categorized together. Despite the Muslim world's strong belief in independence, the current situation appears to be quite bleak.

The reaction towards immodest clothing in the Muslim world does not solely represent independence. As a result, this conspiracy is seen as wicked and is believed to have originated in a bygone age, leaving a lasting impact on society even now. The origin of this collection of rituals and beliefs can be traced back to a prehistoric era, and interestingly, it has managed to survive and remain prominent in the Western world throughout history.

This statement is especially applicable to individuals who dismiss rules as outdated or irrelevant. In today's modern world, the fashion in Islam is centered around the principle of modesty. Islam firmly upholds its values and does not compromise its integrity or the modesty of both men and women. The attire worn by Muslims reflects their appearance and adherence to these principles in the modern times.

Their unfortunate dilemma lies in their deep attachment to backward regimes. The world is currently being plagued by an evil force, which has significantly increased the level of difficulty in living within this society compared to previous times.

The advancements in technology that have taken place over the course of this decade have been substantial, resulting in the ability to easily access a vast array of accomplishments, advertisements, and any other imaginable content right at your fingertips. The purification of one's soul is contingent upon the wise and thoughtful utilization of one's faculties.

Once they have obtained their rights from Islam, Muslim women and men focus on prioritizing learning, teaching, and sharing, rather than cultural practices. The Middle East was the destination chosen for young Westerners and the elderly to pursue their studies. Through their enrollment in Muslim schools and colleges in the Middle East, they fully immersed themselves in the rich culture and vast knowledge of Islam. The university where they studied and graduated from was Fatima Al Fihri University.

With their mixed ideas colliding together, their ultimate goal was to corrupt the Muslims, a community that once held the prestigious title of being the world's educators during those dark and grim days. This state of affairs is seen as a source of sadness for some individuals who follow the Islamic faith. The presence of peer pressure within academic circles, combined with the lack of clear rules and regulations in society, gives rise to a collective illusion of diverse ideas.

Lack of education about the history of Muslims and Islam among some Muslims can lead to ignorance, often motivated by the pursuit of financial gain. False amusement has a strong hold on Western culture and easily ensnares it. Allah, in his infinite wisdom, bestowed independence upon Muslim women, thus highlighting their immense value and magnificence.

Within the framework of Islam, women hold certain rights that are recognized and respected. Both dreams and hope play a crucial role in maintaining a sense of balance. When inspiration serves as a guiding force, it allows the mind to break free from limitations and venture into boundless possibilities.

The justice system was deeply ingrained within us as Muslims, ensuring that we had a strong foundation in it. One of the key aspects of Islam is its emphasis on upholding values such as integrity and balance. When it comes to education, especially for women, it takes on a leading role and plays a crucial part.

When faced with challenges, they will not succumb to reliance on others, ensuring they do not grant someone else a position of power. Besides being a matter of faith, Islam is a reality that exists in our world. Our intention is to benefit both ourselves and others by making use of all available resources and not wasting time on insignificant issues.

The ability to obtain higher education is significantly influenced by the burden of student debt. The expense of education acts as a deterrent for certain students who wish to pursue higher education. Their monopolization of education out of greed has caused significant trouble for students. What are the possible outcomes for students who are unable to finish their studies due to factors beyond their control or financial limitations? Until the debt is paid off, it will remain outstanding.

Similar to actions performed in this world, they persist until they are resolved. Repentance, unlike the financial transactions of life that involve human payments and debts, plays a unique role in cleansing evil deeds. Washing away this owed sum requires finding a solution that does not involve dropping out. There are certain students who perceive college life as a theatrical performance and actively participate in order to completely immerse themselves in the overall experience. Throughout history, education has consistently demanded a significant amount of effort, as individuals have gone to extraordinary measures to acquire knowledge. The education of the Quran holds equal importance for Muslims, and there is a significant gain associated with leading a virtuous life.

The difference in mindset towards education is what sets apart the newer countries and their development from foreigners, as well as individuals of lower economic standing or the wealthy. The act of empowering themselves through education allows these individuals to open numerous doors for those who are in search of knowledge.

It is a rarity for a person to receive praise for engaging in behaviors that violate ethical standards. In the realm of education, we often encounter a multitude of individuals who, albeit reluctantly, eventually learn their lessons; regrettably, however, there exists another group of individuals who, tragically, never learn at all.

The persistent rise in college debt is causing students to be more exposed to the possibility of not finding employment. Muslims have always played a significant role in history by consistently making the pursuit of knowledge more accessible. This is evident through their active sharing of knowledge and their emphasis on the importance of learning. Additionally, the Quran itself highlights the crucial role that learning and understanding play, further emphasizing their significance.

A society that is corrupt lacks the ability to fulfill the role of a teacher, and it is even more incapable of assuming the role of a student. Allah's teachings remind us to actively pursue knowledge, engage in entrepreneurship, and prioritize our family life, all while embracing the unpredictable nature of life.

The phenomenon of light attracting light and darkness attracting darkness is widely observed and studied. In Islam, believers are characterized by their focus on spirituality and their desire to cultivate partnerships across various domains of life.

The guidance of destiny will continue to direct and lead every individual along their unique journey. As time continues to move forward, so too will the passing years of our lives. The passing of time has been so swift that it feels as if decades and ages have slipped away in the blink of an eye. When stuck in a life that lacks growth or change, the passage of time can either drive you forward or impede your journey towards your ultimate goal.

When discussing things that hold true value, nothing can match the importance of both time and health.

The elephant clock, created by Al Jazari, is widely regarded as his greatest masterpiece. Shouldn't we address the elephant in the room at this point in time? Muslims have a strong passion and interest in clocks, as evidenced by their historical fascination with intricate timepieces. The sophisticated devices that were developed during this time period defied the limitations of the Middle Ages. Muslim civilization made remarkable progress in the field of timekeeping, with clocks being one of their most noteworthy achievements.

Muslims can seize the opportunity to highlight the multitude of achievements by Muslims throughout history, alongside their continuous endeavors. The act of teaching and sharing enhances the approach, complexity, and balance of Islam, thereby contributing to its enrichment. This document includes the all-encompassing rules and regulations that govern the practice of Islam. Muslims have made noteworthy contributions across diverse fields, with Islam playing a central role in these achievements.

The act of getting out of a difficult situation has the potential to empower a Muslim and enable them to return even stronger. In order to effectively share the significance of time and a clock with the world, it is necessary to possess the appropriate tools and mindset, especially for a Muslim individual who comprehends the value of shared beliefs and time. Allah plays the part of a guide in this relationship, with time serving as the motivating factor. Within the Quran, there are references made to Allah's concept of time. If "Surah Al-Asr" were the sole "Surah" in the Quran, its inclusion alone would be enough to effectively communicate the importance of time.

Quran: Surah Hajj 22:47. And they urge you to hasten the punishment. But Allah will never fail in his promise. And indeed, a day with your Lord is like a thousand years of those that you count.

How is it that man fails to recognize the importance of nurturing time and spirituality? Cultivating a deep and meaningful connection with the one who created you. In what way could a meeting between a Muslim man and a woman be perceived as a mere coincidence? It is possible for this event to happen specifically between two Muslims who share the same gender. When family members become lost, it is heartwarming to witness their journey towards rediscovering their faith and reconnecting with their loved ones. When there are two believers, it is like receiving a wonderful gift.

Negligence of spirituality and disobedience to the Creator, as well as associating with evil company, can sometimes lead to self-induced pain. The question may arise as to whether individuals who do not have faith in Allah can still achieve success in different aspects of life. The truth is, success goes beyond material possessions. Even those who don't believe in it can achieve academic and travel success if it's solely based on material gains.

The concept of success in the spiritual realm is a paradoxical one, one that can only be comprehended and found solace in by those who hold faith. The option is available to either complete both tasks simultaneously or to tackle one task individually. Ultimately, it is Allah's prerogative to bestow his favors upon whomever he pleases. There is no experience that can match the profound bliss of prostrating to Him.

Intelligence, material wealth, academics, and families are just a few examples among many others. Therefore, it is possible that certain individuals may question the rationale behind having faith in an unseen entity such as Allah. Individuals who hold no belief system are unable to fully understand the concept of a higher power, as it is often obscured by the limitations and vulnerabilities inherent in human nature. Its defining characteristic is weakness. In the next phase of life, humanity will confront the entity that brought it into existence and come face to face with the consequences of its actions. The outcome of any test is expected when preparation doesn't matter.

The surface world is not the final destination, there are endless possibilities beyond it. Achieving this goal is impossible if we associate ourselves with evil company or if we have disbelief. Simultaneously justifying both good and evil company and belief is a possible task. Similar to how converting to Islam marks the beginning rather than the end for someone, the same can be said for a believer who has strayed and has now returned.

People who don't believe ask when trials become more difficult: why me? Through their devotion, the believer is able to establish a stronger connection with Allah. Engaging in testing can serve as a catalyst for significant shifts in one's beliefs, ultimately leading the believer to develop a deeper bond with Allah. The process of conducting comprehensive tests can result in profound and essential modifications. Islam discourages the act of playing the blame game. Even in the face of unexpected setbacks, it is only through persistence and hope that one can stay on track.

The success of destruction depends on the assistance of rebellious humans, and those who count on them are disappointed. By the grace of Allah, even a slight modification has the potential to create a massive impact, like moving mountains. With time, people will gradually realize the hopeful viewpoint of believers and free themselves from the sole preoccupation with empty possessions. Disbelievers are now free from the constraints imposed by the thoughts and values of believers. Until Allah rectifies the inherent trials, is it possible for one to lose hope? In any given situation, a believer never loses hope, as they believe there is always a triumph to be found.

It is believed that every individual on this planet has a specific purpose for their existence. Destiny has the ability to locate you in any place, and every aspect of life is consistently recorded. The decree of Allah has been permanently recorded in ink. Trusting Allah, who is renowned for being the best listener, is a better alternative to confiding in humans. It is recommended that, in today's world, individuals refrain from confiding in either believers or disbelievers when discussing their own lives.

The ideal approach is to place your trust solely in Allah and not in any of his creatures when sharing confidential matters. The primary goal of Islam is to provide assistance and support to every individual, regardless of their background or circumstances. The aim of Muslims is to provide assistance to all human beings and guide those who have deviated towards approved values established by the creator. Faith, regardless of colors or beliefs, has the power to bring balance through dialogue. Kindness is the cornerstone upon which the foundation of faith is built. Islam is known for its kindness, and it is believed that Allah, the Supreme Nur light, is both fair and merciful.

CHAPTER 5

THE QURAN LEAVES NOTHING BEHIND.

Humans are paradoxically united despite their differences, and life remains vibrant. Our dissimilarity doesn't hinder the bond created by our shared experiences. Our diversity allows us to learn and appreciate each other's differences's differences.

Life is like a kaleidoscope, full of colors and opportunities for growth and adventure. We're all on this amazing journey together, and it's our responsibility to maintain its diversity and enrichment. Recognize our commonalities as we embrace our differences. The power of this action can shape a world that is more vibrant and cohesive.

Unity is our goal, despite our differences. The foundation of a unified world lies in finding beauty and richness in diversity. We are all connected as a greater whole, despite our differences.

The ability to innovate lies within every individual, and it flourishes when we join forces to create on a larger scale. The paradox of unification necessitates accepting our differences and embracing diversity

Quran: Surah Hujurat: 49:13.O humanity! Indeed, We created you from a male and a female and made you into peoples and tribes so that you may get to know one another.

Understanding the cultures and ways of other humans and countries summarizes the beauty of diversity. Staying faithful builds strength, not weakness. Strength is valued by most humans, not weakness. Altered attitudes of defiance are displayed by those influenced by their own beliefs. Those who respect their core beliefs and values are respected by others. Their fear is for Allah, not for humans.

Safety lies in fearing Allah. Following His guidance leads to success. Honor awaits those who walk the path of righteousness. Neglecting oneself while caring for others makes it impossible to balance life's demands. Understanding the value of self-care makes it a top priority for maintaining physical and mental well-being. Attending to oneself is a vital aspect of life, and then extending that assistance to others.

Spiritual life, like physical life, also requires balance. Proper fluid and food intake in balanced proportions are necessary for the human body and animals. All things, including plants, the earth, mountains, and more, require nourishment. It's crucial to filter and nurture the beauty and correctness in life for the body and spirituality. Self-care includes taking time to rest, reflect, and connect with one's inner self.

A healthy, balanced life can be achieved with this key. The man is being interrogated for his actions. If a person's actions contradict their beliefs, they cannot respect the rights of others. Surrendering rights to others infringes upon one's rights. The person consumes their food and doesn't request someone else to do it. Sacrificing one's rights is not done to benefit someone else. This act of selflessness, while not mandatory, is against one's ethical code, and serves as a demonstration of compassion and empathy but it's damaging. The first responsibility is to oneself, then others. If you can't nourish your spirituality and physique, you can't nourish others.

The belief takes precedence over the individual. When internal beliefs lack precedence, false human dignity becomes the priority, making it easier to prioritize humans over faith. Sometimes, the person who makes such a choice can become the strongest believer, as only Allah knows how to bring humans to Him. Islam remains hopeful and faultless until the revenue allotted as time collapses, but some individuals require jolts to strengthen their faith.

Conversely, those lacking empathy, respect, or confidence are unable to help others. Finding balance while maintaining an ethical code of life is a delicate task. The beginning lies in the development of a resilient character. Inner life starts, and help is offered to others. The inner aura does not hoard its light. The light should be spread. People who prioritize pleasing others tend to lack initiative. Their success as followers is short-lived. Those who emulate strength, become strong themselves.

Those who followed the Prophet Muhammad became examples of life for others to learn from. It is the strength of the strong that matters. Positive thinking is always based on the law of attraction.

Positivity attracts positivity, and negativity attracts negativity according to the law of attraction. The unknown positives can lead to a negative environment out of fear. Using the positives is crucial for achieving balance and peace. The teachings of Islam aid in finding balance and fostering harmony. Prioritizing the inner journey of a soul over others is essential. Prioritizing one's personal needs is vital. Self-assured and confident individuals tend to be more giving and empathetic towards others. There are those who claim my time is limited. Ultimately, one should prioritize self and the principles of life and faith, rather than others. This balance enables one to assist others.

Helping and unifying with others is a beauty within, but not at the cost of neglec's own needs. Serving oneself and others is possible when core needs are met and balance is found. Engaging in self-nurturing can empower individuals to face the world's challenges. Taking care of oneself is essential for mental and physical well-being.Islam views the body, mind, and heart as a loan to humanity, entrusted by Allah with great responsibility.

The full repayment of this loan is achieved by repaying oneself in the best possible manner. Assimilating gratitude in mandated prayers is done for the benefit of humanity, not just Allah. How we feed and nourish a hungry soul can make an impact. Within the Muslim faith, there is a focus on caring for the body, mind, and soul. The five daily prayers maintain discipline and foster cleanliness of body and mind.

Regular self-care routines are essential for maintaining physical and mental health. Allah mandated Muslims to pray five times a day for balance in their lives. The integrity of a person is improved by limiting food intake and following the associated morals. Islam asserts that Allah knows creation and its benefits. He is characterized by giving, not taking. Modesty is a cornerstone of Islam, protecting its followers. Modesty is essential for preserving the souls of both genders. Satan lures the vices that support promiscuity and annoying public eye displays.

Social media promotes an unhealthy lifestyle in regions with anti-Islamophobic sentiments. A person's dignity can be destroyed due to this, leading to a lack of awareness. Preserving one's soul requires the practice of modesty and self-respect. Satan's narrow ways can expand into a wide range of deceit for those who fall into his trap. When one engages in sin and encourages others to do the same, through deceptive actions or inappropriate content, along with immoral behavior that is accepted by deception but rejected by Islam, it amplifies the sins.

The perspective of another person can serve an observer of the wicked actions or truthful delivery of others. Through social media, individuals disclose the harm they cause to others. To protect our eyes and preserve self worth, it's wise to avoid negative influences like gossip, social media, and participating in immoral activities. Deception is a correction, not an act of continuous evil.

The best course of action is to repent, give voluntary giving (Sadaqa), and avoid dealing with evil. It is important for Muslims to use social media as a platform to educate people about the Quran, the only remaining truth in this world. It is the duty of Muslims to educate people in every possible manner, while the decision to listen or not lies with individuals. However, genuine clarity reaches those who seek answers amidst the noise and disruptions of everyday life.

The allure of corrupting new-age technologies can captivate those who crave chaos, but those who strive for success and have faith in progress do not seek evil. The retrospective view of new-age technology is undeniably beneficial, and only its misuse is discouraged. However, the pursuit of progress and global outreach through technology is encouraged, as it can transmit positive signals to the world.

Regions that promote independence but suffocate the soul with deception, while presenting lies as truth, must be corrected by Muslims who have taught the world enlightenment. The discontentment array resides in those who neglect the spiritual sense while pursuing independence. While coercing the truth may be easy, adapting to lies in theology and daily life becomes troublesome in a colorful and diverse environment where expressing contrasts is crucial. Staying away from immoral activities is crucial for maintaining mental and physical health. Refrain from being carried away and endangering their values and reputation.

Harness technology for positive purposes to mitigate distress. It is essential for Muslims to play an active role in driving progress and impart the wisdom they previously shared to aid Europe's recovery from the dark ages. In this era of technological manipulation, deceitful rulers exploit less educated people by leveraging islamophobia and greed, using their lands and loyalty to them. To help the world, Muslims must actively participate and unite, relying on Allah for the rest. Watching the downfall is not in the nature of a Muslim believer. By prioritizing self-welfare, offering truthful education, and aiding oppressors through actions and words, a Muslim remains steadfast. The oppression of Muslim lands extends beyond certain regions; it is fueled by the evil spreading from Islamophobic areas, deceiving people with false truths.

Quran: Surah Zumar: 39;27.THUS, INDEED, have We propounded unto men all kinds of parables in this Qur'an, so that they might bethink themselves; [and We have revealed it].

Hadith: Muslim."They will fornicate like donkeys" means that men will have intercourse with women in the presence of other people, as donkeys do.

Islamophobic regions exploit human nature through technology, promoting illicit activities and pornography on social media. The entry of acts demeaned by Islam, labeled as independence and exploiting social media, into Muslim countries must be stopped to prevent the progress of ills. The high achievers abstain from corruption and understand how these regions manipulate their people with outdated eras and theology, spreading harmful beliefs to the world under the guise of independence. Similar to the past, when Moses was receiving the ten commandments from Allah, the same nature of defiance persists.

In Moses' absence, the deceivers reverted to paganism and immoral practices, unable to contain their wickedness. The contrast cannot be ignored - it involves the same conjecture and upheaval of societal trends through the exploitation of technology, manipulation of sex, false leadership, and greed-driven lies, all while fueling Islamophobia and spreading fear.

Hasn't the time of prophecy arrived for the world mentioned in the Quran and all Abrahamic scriptures, with the understanding that Muslims can only refer to what is unaltered truth? This society is promoting pornography and obscenity, which tempts morality and ethics, exploits individuals, and encourages same-gender relationships and illicit acts that lead to immoral behavior and the spread of evil.

Those who lack restraint cause mayhem by promoting porn and nudity, encouraging others to engage in sinful behavior. Both young and elderly individuals engage in hidden evil on social media, but Allah knows all and rewards accordingly. It is important for Muslims to have awareness and respond to the truth, utilizing their voices and social media platforms to consistently express the truth and prevent society from being influenced by darkness, as was the case in the dark ages.

Those who constantly break laws and stage falsehoods use the daunting light as a cover. Muslims have the ability to recognize and acknowledge the truth. Our youth must engage in efforts to combat Islamophobia and defend oppressed lands. We must protect the world from those who manipulate scriptures and spread deceit. It is crucial to put an end to this common sense violation. This is not about labeling any faith as right or wrong, but rather preserving the history of Abrahamic faiths.

Today's staged event on social media, targeting Muslims in Islamophobic regions, is spreading false narratives about Muslims and Islam, distorting the truth. Certain Muslim nations experience oppression, while others thrive economically. The oppressed and wealthy alike hear the Azan, as it is the duty of accomplished Muslims to assist the world and their fellow Muslims. Ultimately, Islam will prevail as the sole religion, governing regions with pure monotheism, before humanity faces Allah's final judgment.

A Muslim has to help the oppressed. Giving back brings more blessings than it takes away. The effects of oppression can take many forms. The oppression of knowledge is a drawback also for those Muslims who are drowning without knowledge of Islam and those who waste time. Isn't the Muslim world the wealthiest, with unaltered knowledge of the truth? Why is there a lack of support for other Muslim countries? Allah provided wealth to share through voluntary (Zakat) and non-voluntary (Sadaqa). This is the moment to rotate our time, wealth, knowledge, and delivery.

Why does a Muslim not understand the need to help oppressed people and not join forces to show the world that Muslims are humane? Is there greed when times are tough? For a believer, this is impossible. Justice can be achieved by refusing to submit to unjust proposals. Although wars will endure until the end of time, every Muslim must remain true to his or her beliefs. Muslim countries can be a force for positive change in the world if they are united. It is necessary to recall the beginning of Islam if we are to achieve a better ending.

In Islam, learning from disbelievers is not a goal. Muslims prioritize truth over the fear of many people, as their motto is centered around seeking truth and knowledge. Repentance has the power to quiet our sins. When a Muslim is tempted to sin, it only makes the wrong deeds more severe but exchange of reversal is better than continuation of evil.

Rather than pursuing evil, an organization should strive to encourage righteousness for believers who may be struggling. Seeking forgiveness and making amends is what one must do after realizing that Allah sent a fellow believer to help correct their understanding in the first place. This realization shapes their beliefs and values.

Muslims need education rather than ignorance. Many self-proclaimed believers surprise both disbelievers and true believers. Therefore, it is important for those who believe to behave by their faith and set an example of righteousness. Our objective is to inspire and educate young people, guiding them away from evil temptations. Stay vigilant, guarding against Satan's schemes. Depend on self-love to fill the emptiness. Unification of the inner self brings contentment.

Taking care of your inner self is crucial. To achieve this, it's important to submit to Allah, practice self-care, and engage in internal dialogue. By doing so, you can find a balance that aligns with your desires. Remember to prioritize your own well-being before helping others. Just like it's difficult to dress someone else if you're not dressed in your style, it's challenging to assist others if you haven't taken care of yourself first.

Prophet Muhammad made it his top priority to serve Allah and attend to his duties. He constantly monitored himself, forsaking his ways and practices to improve his spirituality. As a result, Islam's numbers continue to grow with new converts joining the faith. Prophet Muhammad is a well-known figure to both Muslims and non-Muslims alike, and he left behind a legacy of life, endurance, and spirituality.

The belief system does not allow for compromise of Islamic faith and guidelines. The highest priority is given to Allah, then humanity. Prioritizing spirituality over exploring sexuality is not suggestive. Sexuality is not negated in Islam, as Allah has made it permissible only in halal relationships between a man and a woman. However, he didn't suggest to fall prey to prioritizing sexuality above spirituality or break laws by attributing it to human physical needs. A complete human is spiritually and physically aligned, taking care of the body and nurturing the soul.

Some people, at their worst, attempt to change the thoughts of the believers but fail to achieve their objective and end up dissatisfied. In the search for spirituality, believers prioritize Allah over mankind. Integrity is the combination of leadership and individuality, which benefits not only oneself but humanity as a whole. Fitrah, on the other hand, refers to the inherent presence of purity, innocence, and light in every human being at birth.

Humanity's limited time on earth is both a blessing and an acceptance of our mortality. Positive energy paves the way for positive outcomes. While the world is increasingly embracing pluralism, it still falls short in embodying individualistic values. Society has undergone numerous changes that have led to the acceptance of previously forbidden and frowned upon behaviors. It seems that evil is more prevalent in the world today. However, by respecting people's morality and acting with conviction, society can uphold its pluralistic beliefs without being close-minded or biased.

Pluralism promotes individualism, but sometimes it can lead to a society where people think alike as if they were brainwashed by a cult. The formative sentences seem to have originated from the same institution, and this can promote illiteracy instead of literacy.

Pluralism has historically been used to deceive society, particularly in Islamophobic societies, also known as democracies. This democracy lacks full democratic principles and staged pluralism at individualism. Islamic democracy fosters pluralism and trust in individuals, highlighting the value of individualism before a unified system.

This explanation does not represent humanity as a whole but is aimed at Islamophobes who seek to spread their false independence and decadence to the world. Islamophobia has been a persistent fear in history, with different approaches over the decades.

Knowledge of changed scriptures and realizing one's own deceit is an arduous task. Focusing specifically on the Abrahamic faith. Humans can only freely worship if society corrects, not accepts, the misleading approach of fear and Islamophobia. Many view ignoring the truth for our desired beliefs as a sign of independence. In spite of this, we should stay vigilant and pursue the truth, viewing the conflicts created by foreign interference to stage lies with our beliefs as falsifiers.

In a world where conflicting beliefs and ideologies often clash, individuals are left to battle with their conscience to determine right from wrong. However, the principles of democracy can be challenged in such a state of affairs. Islam, on the other hand, provides a clear and unwavering framework for democratic governance. While the tenets of Islam are non-negotiable and everyone will be held accountable for their actions, it is important to note that Allah did not create everyone equal.

Each person possesses their unique individuality, so we cannot force ourselves to conform to a society that seeks to homogenize everyone. Islam provides laws and regulations for Muslims, but they are not imposed - judgment and consequences are assured, as this life serves as a trial for the next.

It is crucial for affluent individuals to redistribute their wealth and for knowledgeable individuals to share their knowledge. By studying the Quran and spreading the teachings of Prophet Muhammad, we can understand the significance of knowledge sharing.

Without disseminating his knowledge, Prophet Muhammad would not have gained followers of Islam. It is important to note that the projected number of Muslims in 2050 is estimated to be 2.9 billion, and this number is expected to continue increasing.

Like any jurisdiction, core values involve understanding Islam's faith and adhering to statutory laws. Allah's laws surpass human laws by far. Gain knowledge of the Quran and Islam to spread their teachings. Despite their struggle for independence, individuals in this society are being governed by the majority in most actions, leading to a loss of individuality. The constant efforts of Satanic forces aim to normalize and justify evil in society.

Consequently, society will grow more accepting of encrypted beliefs, opinions, and evil. Satan's strategy is to make evil seem more acceptable than virtue. Who has the authority to define what is disorienting or cryptic in a world without boundaries? It's challenging to code the masses with a moral code and justice system unless they are willing. The soul's desires and the people we surround ourselves with matter.

When living in a non-Muslim society, a Muslim can either uphold their values or modify them to fit in with others. Morality is seen as an obstacle in today's society, conflicting with the notion of freedom. Independence was disguised in a web of deception.The Islamic faith promotes human growth, not decadence. For decades, primitive paganism ideologies have resurfaced under the guise of fake modernization. Instead, it offers a false sense of independence to those who are deprived and Muslims seek inner wealth while enjoying the benefits of this life and preparing for the next.

It is crucial to stay away from this evil under any circumstances. Muslims can demonstrate light by adhering to Islam's prescribed rules and guiding others accordingly.Life is devoid of luck and chance. People prefer peace over misery, and adhering to moral principles can greatly enhance the lives of many. Pseudo-cultures and so-called progressive societies have led to deceptive behavior and impure lifestyles becoming widespread.

By infiltrating their lives, this demon has spread its infection to humans. Evidence of tolerance within Islam's history supports pluralism in its belief system. In the pursuit of modernization, certain influential Islamophobic societies lack individuality and corrupt the masses.

Contagious events are happening at business parties and higher education. Regardless, some manage to escape this scenario and perceive immoral conduct as taboo. Some people become dissatisfied when they alter their morals to please others. Alcohol consumption is a common practice in these societies to make up for the absence of inner joy during celebrations. You must either accept the illusion of deception or risk losing the company unless it happens regularly in business environments. There are instances where attending is unavoidable.

The incompatibilities that make relationships impossible to withstand are present at the onset of marriages or joyous celebrations. Islamic beliefs prohibit drinking alcohol during joyous events. Especially when it's served by Muslims. Calling oneself Muslim while displaying hypocrisy and disrespect is contradictory.

This is intended to please insignificant individuals in the grand scheme. It would be regrettable for a Muslim to adopt such a malevolent situation. Regrettably, this situation is cursed and compromised. It can be a challenge to organize a celebration that caters to everyone's preferences and beliefs, especially when considering Islamic concepts disseminated by peer pressure. Those who conform to societal norms are preferred over those who remain steadfast in the beliefs of Islamophobes.

People of faith expect others to adhere to their own faith, but pseudo society and Islamophobes depict all evil as good, particularly influencing Muslims who succumb to peer pressure and perceive serving alcohol at events as a source of happiness for misguided individuals driven by selfish desires. A society without individualism, promoting the ills of society while wrongly associating them with Islam, is not cohesive. Advocating for Islamic rights means expressing ourselves to remind Muslims, especially our youth, who shape the future of the Islamic world. This scenario is similar to Muslims abstaining from pork but cooking it for those who eat it. Similar to alcohol or mind-altering substances, it's not permitted.

Attendees who see Islam as a barrier between good and evil may find the inclusion of forbidden items in an Islamic celebration unsuitable. The pressured subconscious mind by peer pressure of this society captures those who go against Allah in order to satisfy the demands of the staged world. The majority of humanity values those who advocate for their rights. If a Muslim falls short of his rights he needs to exercise he needs reminders of Islamic values and support not exclusion. Helping Muslims who are struggling is a duty, not a difficult task.

There are consequences for defying Allah. Respecting one's own beliefs earns respect from others. One who compromises for appeasement is like many others who compromise their core. Satan uncovers weaknesses that unsettle his evil followers. Practicing Muslims find joy in philosophical spirituality, free from contaminants. In Islam, alcohol or wine consumption is not allowed. Some people refuse to drink if they encounter a Muslim or someone who expresses their beliefs. It's unpleasant to watch their vulnerability after a few drinks.

Instead of relying on the abundant security Allah provides, believers may indulge in evil due to inadequate insecurity. Peer pressure can divert a believer's attention in specific circumstances. Healthy survival necessitates good company. When one slips into making an error, one can continue with the process of rectification, repentance, and a forward stance. Unfortunately, certain behaviors of Muslims show Islam in a different light. Islam is not through people. But Islam is from Allah. Muslims cannot justify their faith. They can only try to follow as prescribed.

It is acceptable for some to remain in this setting because their souls are still bound to the material world. Humans who are successful walk away from evil and invest their time in bettering themselves, rather than clinging to the deception of modernization of Islamophobic regions, which harkens back to prehistoric times. Every Prophet faced the trials of life and endured without a dispute. They showed leadership, gratitude, and charisma.

It's the parents that direct them to Allah or different deities; few revert and never return to anything but the monotheistic faith and the company of believers. Many live in doubt since light isn't pure, and belief is shady. Transformation occurs gradually or not at all. Success comes to those who keep a stern eye on the objectives of triumph, unity, and solace. One who seeks it from Allah will find it. Allah has shown humanity miracles through the Prophets; miracles were for the people of those times.

Erasers cannot be used to erase the writings of destiny and the untold history of Muslims around the world. Every decade and every time has seen man's quest for inner peace paradoxically reflected. Allah attended to curious minds in the way a man would understand. Miracles exist, but only a few can see the special grants from Allah. There is no expiration date for a Quran written in Arabic; it is a book of peace, tales of history, battles, laws, contracts, a book of friendship, study, discipline, and consequences.

Justice contracts relationships that are halal, not haram, and promote learning. It's also pertinent to note that the sound it's recited in has a melody in the Quran that can transport someone who doesn't understand the language to a different dimension. Any man would understand the sweetness of this language. Allah has made the Quran accessible to anyone who cares to indulge in learning.

Quran: Surah Qamar 54;17. And we have certainly made the Quran easy to remember. Is there anyone who will be mindful?

Only Allah knows the hidden secrets, drawbacks, and endeavors of humanity. It is Allah who gives him time to endure this life and prepare for the next. The known miracle of Prophet Muhammad was that he split the moon in half with the permission of Allah. These divine interventions were miracles for the people of those times. The Quran is timeless. Each miracle performed by the Prophets by permission of Allah was according to the mindset of people during those times. Throughout history, the Quran has stood the test of time. The miracle of the Quran is that it stands for all centuries and will continue.

Surah Al Qamar [Quran 54:1] The hour has come closer, and the moon has split.

[Quran 54:2] Then they saw a miracle, but they turned away and said, "Old magic."

[Quran 54:3] They disbelieved, followed their opinions, and adhered to their old traditions.

Quran Surah Qamar 54, memorized by most Muslims, was revealed after the splitting of the moon.

Muslims don't live by miracles. Of the splitting of the moon. Every decade has questioned the existence of the creator despite every visible sign within, and every living thing outwardly conforming to Allah as the creator of all. Every person endures tests and trials in their lives, but looking back on history, Allah has always put humanity to the test. **Every Prophet in history was sent miracles by Allah to address the people of their time. However, it is impossible to prove the validity of these miracles beyond the stories that have been passed down through generations. Despite evidence presented on the lands where the miracles began and where they will end, there are still many people today who doubt the authenticity of these miracles and events.**

Prophets have performed countless miracles that cannot be listed. According to Islamic belief, the Quran is the last and eternal miracle of Allah that cannot be altered unless He wills it. Muslims believe in the Quran without any time restrictions, and it remains a timeless miracle for them.The ability to see the beauty that surrounds us is solely dependent on Allah's grace, which grants us a clear perspective. The miraculous events bestowed upon the Prophets by Allah are recorded in history, but they are not just a memory. The Quran, on the other hand, is a current memory, not just a written record of the past. As per news reports, a man landed on the moon in 1969. The New York Times reported that they attributed the cracks on the moon's surface to Earth.

New York Times: Sep 21, 2015 — The moon is shrinking, and Earth is to blame for how the moon's crust has cracked.

All the emphasis for Muslims is on the Quran, not the physical miracles performed by Prophet Muhammad. The stories can be narrated and depicted but not observed, hence the miracles are recorded. The Quran remains an unaltered, living miracle that guides intelligent and seeking minds. Muslims consider the Quran as the ultimate unchallengeable truth. Prophet Muhammad is regarded as a role model by Muslims, and they hold the Quran in high regard.Muslims believe that devout believers enhance human understanding. Descendants who follow Islam and acquire knowledge play a vital role.Truth takes precedence over greed in the foundations of Islam. It is crucial for the youth and the young upcoming Muslims to follow their beliefs and contribute to Islam, academics, and worldly affairs in order to determine their relationship with Allah.

The concept of death is significant, especially when considering spiritual death, which is more severe than physical death. This is particularly true for Muslims who are astray and fail to comprehend the sudden arrival of death, leaving them no opportunity to repent, resulting in unexpected sorrow.

Sometimes sickness provides warnings, while other times death comes without warning. Doctors and transportation are blamed for not getting patients to the hospital fast enough, but regardless of belief, time is fixed for leaving this world. The angel of death has no control over when he takes a soul; Allah determines the timing. Martyrdom is exclusively meant for believers of Islam who believe in the one God Allah. Killing a nonbeliever does not mean becoming a martyr. It's the conclusion of a life devoid of faith. In Islam, saving one life is equivalent to saving all of humanity, as Allah's judgment surpasses human understanding.

The Angel of Death, Izrail, begged Allah not to assign him the task of taking human souls, fearing their hatred towards him. He did not defy Allah, but rather begged for mercy, as he is an angel and did not wish to be detested by anyone. It was over fifty thousand years before Allah sent humans to earth. The existence of Allah was revealed to souls.

Before arriving on this earth, every soul affirmed that Allah was their sole belief. Deceit ensued, causing souls to be swayed in ways that undermine the affirmation of truth. When truth conflicts with lies, disbelievers or the doubtful often forget their promises to Allah or to a believer, and feel inner anxiety as their subconscious mind acknowledges the inconsistency. All goodness originates from Allah. Satan is responsible for negative distractions, doubts, suspicions, and delays. Without Allah's permission, he, like everyone else, is powerless.

But Allah examines each person through trials. Satan's true identity is not hidden; He comes through friends and family, creating havoc. Envious disbelievers mock the contentment of two believers. Satan the Jinn can perceive and hear humans, but they cannot perceive him, even in the presence of wind. He studies the behaviors of humans. He is made of a substance that is fire without smoke, and he desires to bring humans who obey him to fire.

Those closest to someone can be tricked into doing his and his practitioners bidding. There is no mercy for those who disobey him, he leads them with no mercy knowing they are bound for hell. A believer's friends or family can turn into enemies if they deceive and destroy their own souls temporarily. Those who have faith will discover their path to paradise and experience everlasting bliss. Eternal torture awaits disbelievers.

Quran; Surah Fatir: 36;6.Surely Satan is an enemy to you, so take him as an enemy. He only invites his followers to become inmates of the Blaze.

The only genuine friend in Islam is the one who leads you towards Allah. Genuine friendships guide towards the path of Allah, while Satan encourages division among believers or between a believer and their faith. Misunderstanding and lack of understanding often lead to believers separating. Two believers sharing unpleasant stories face Satan's attempts to silence Allah's word in their hearts. Allah has the power to bring believers together and separate disbelievers. Satan takes advantage of the weak through his ploys. Through Allah's grace, believers can stay strong in their faith and conquer any challenges.

The Muslim who seeks guidance from disbelievers lacks self-awareness. Studying your soul and core is the deepest form of self-awareness. Your inner being will speak to you as you discover yourself. During this journey of self-discovery, the true purpose of life and a sense of direction will be found. Consequently, individuals will make improved choices and experience a more satisfying existence.

Muslims find joy in this life and prepare for the next. Humans seek compensation after years of work, just like stock dividends seek retirement funds. The same applies to deeds done in this world that yield rewards in the next. Humans struggle to understand this world due to the changing seasons, not because permanence is untrustworthy. Death is inevitable. It's more beneficial to correct the (akhira) at the end rather than avoiding it.

Quran: Surah Anbiya: 21:35. Every soul will taste death. We will test you with good and evil, and then return you to us.

When souls existed without bodies, all humans acknowledged Allah as the ultimate authority. There are those who state they feel acquainted with you. There's a possibility that souls were once gathered together. They grasp and acknowledge souls, but are uncertain about past meetings.A few individuals emit negative auras, while others emit positive ones. The righteous and the wicked cannot coexist. It is not compatible or congruent. Virtue and evil cannot coexist; one will either retreat from the other or the other will resurface.

Humanity does not have power over life or death bestowed by Allah. He holds a position in the decision-making hierarchy, but his powers are not limited. Praying for the deceased is a practice in the Muslim faith. The judgment of those who die believing in one God rests with Allah. Humans will experience death just as they experience life in this world. Only Allah knows the inner struggles of a disbeliever or a believer. The attendee will answer the questionnaire about their life, and the answers lie in the grave.

Dust to dust, they bury Muslim corpses. Islam prohibits cremation. The departed can be disposed of in the water, ocean, or sea. (Janazah) is a funeral prayer performed for the deceased. A departed Muslim's soul prepares for his final meeting with his creator. Upon learning of the deceased's passing, Muslims pray for the deceased. No comments can be made upon the death of a disbeliever who did not believe in Allah from a Muslim except Allah's judgment.

As an example, he passed away both as a nonbeliever or a philanthropist. In Islam, belief in one God is essential; any other form of worship is not acceptable, but Allah is the ultimate judge. Laws in Islam are the basis for establishing rules. Humans cannot be punished until the doctrine is evident. It's time to take responsibility, no more excuses. If a person can find filth, they can surely find Allah if they choose.

This happens despite irrelevant comments that describe themselves as a nice guy and a kind woman who prioritized human courtship over Allah.It is possible that individuals who entertain, give gifts, and engage with humanity while disregarding Allah and finding fulfillment and kindness within themselves are an example of deficient comprehension for not recognizing Allah. However, it is important to remember that it is Allah who has control over life and death, and that even such individuals are ultimately controlled by Allah. They can also serve as reminders for believers that even those who have no control over their lives are not in control of the system and are also ultimately controlled by Allah.

Allah has the ultimate say in decision-making. Using a disbeliever to aid believers would not contradict a believer's devotion to their creator. Rest in peace " is the most appropriate comment a Muslim can make to a nonbeliever. Muslim society denies the idea of resting in heaven without belief in the creator. According to Islam, one's entry into heaven or hell is not contingent upon their belief in or knowledge of Allah. It's better to refrain from speculating on whether the deceased is in heaven or hell. Allah is the final arbiter of defiance.

After death, the battle between good and evil ends, and all tests and trials are suspended until the day of reckoning, except for those related to the grave. For those who have witnessed the death of others, it is important to remember that life takes things without warning. Warnings are rare, and most of the time, life leaves one by surprise. This equality is a reminder or awakening for most people, and Allah has made us aware of his blessings ever since mankind and jinns were created.

Some individuals have encountered near-death situations but survived, leading to transformative changes caused by diseases, surgeries, accidents, or comas, where their silent minds undergo diverse and unfamiliar experiences. Without warning, they came across this aspect of life. Such people either transform their lives positively or fail to appreciate their existence.

Closure's uncertainty and impermanence diminish the significance of frivolous enjoyment. Despite facing death multiple times, some individuals prioritize defiance over fearlessness. They fail to grasp life's unpredictability and the potential for sudden change. Nevertheless, certain individuals transform their lives and recognize the uncertainty of time. The most fulfilling way to conclude our lives is by appreciating the time we have. The ultimate goal of a true believer is to understand ourselves and our creator with not only the outbreak of materialistic desires.

Quran: Surah Baqarah verse 156. Dua (prayer) *Inna lillahi wa ina ilayhi raji'oon* **Surely to Allah, we belong, and to Him, we shall return.**

Quran: Surah Nisa 4:78. Wherever you may be, death will overtake you, even if you should be within towers of lofty construction.

Quran: Surah Anfal:8:50 (And if you could see when the angels take the souls of those who disbelieved.

In Muslim tradition, the deceased are given a final bath to prepare them for their journey to meet their creator. The success of their meeting with Allah depends on how they lived their lives. After death, the soul of a Muslim looks for its resting place, which is no longer in this world but in the earth, so it is important to bury the body as soon as possible according to Islamic law. It is important to note that Allah does not ask for the money one has earned in their lifetime. Instead, a person's meeting with Allah is based on their good deeds in this world.

The Quran explains life and death. A disbeliever is commanded by an angel of death to extract his own soul from his body. Angels are repelled by a pungent, smelly odor. The angel of death finally extracts the soul from the body after inflicting torment. Despite knowing it's impossible, the disbeliever in his final moments cries out in pain as they forcefully remove his soul. Disbelievers experience torment in this world before their souls depart.

Before he leaves, he is haunted by the sounds of his own screams, the noises, the whips, the awful smell, and the terrifying faces. This self-inflicted pain is only witnessed by those who disobey Allah. There are some nearby, while others are oblivious, but the journey is individual. The soul of a believer departs as if they are ready to meet their maker. The angels are happy to escort those who prayed to Allah for their return. Allah created us as human beings to confront our actions in this life and ready ourselves for the next.

It is crucial to believe in life after death because everyone will inevitably face this reality. In Islam, it is highly encouraged to remember death regularly as it serves as a reminder to lead a righteous life that pleases Allah, regardless of one's faith. Death is often a difficult topic to discuss, but it is an inevitable truth that we must all face. Our time on earth is limited, and therefore, we must use the time we have wisely. It is essential to focus on our journey and make the most of it by doing good deeds that will help us in this world and the hereafter.

The ticket will be checked before the train stops. This is because a person who fears death will not disrespect time or disobey Allah. Life can be compared to a train journey that often ends abruptly, just like death. Although death does not have a specific timetable, sickness can give indications. Nevertheless, time is the most valuable commodity that many people fail to appreciate.

Islamic survival and self-discipline rely on rational, diplomatic, and reconciliatory behavior within oneself. Occasionally, humans might express boredom and the desire to pass the time. However, it's important to avoid spending time with people who exude a negative and evil energy. Such individuals emit an unpleasant aura that can be sensed by believers, who should then distance themselves from such people.

Especially, individuals who embrace Islam or are practicing Muslims but choose to ignore truth and reality in favor of finding comfort in wrongdoing will experience significant repercussions for a period of time. Procrastination undermines progress. Sacrificing one's ideology for evil only leads to loss for the believer.

In a diverse society, a religious person can influence people through their actions, while a non-believer may simply conform to society's ideologies. However, if a person who follows Islam accepts evil while being aware of their beliefs and circumstances, they risk losing their credibility. Those who believe in one God will eventually enter heaven, but they will still be judged for their good or bad deeds.

Quran: Surah Anfal 8:50. "And if you could see when the angels take away the souls of those who disbelieve (at death), they smite their faces and their backs (saying): "Taste the punishment of the blazing fire.

Quran: Surah Ra'd 13:23. Gardens of perpetual residence. They will enter them with whoever was righteous among their fathers, their spouses, and their descendants. Angels will enter upon them from every gate, saying.

Quran: Surah Ra'd 13:24. The peace of God is upon you for what you have endured with patience. Excellent is the last home.

The idea that Jesus died to redeem human sins. Islam rejects this belief and emphasizes individual responsibility, stating that no one can bear the sins of another. Consequently, every person will be accountable for their righteous or evil actions. Islam is the logical choice for someone seeking truth. Believing someone would bear another's sins is a difficult struggle.

It is believed that Allah created the world fairly and he treats everyone with fairness as his rules are clear. Faith is a matter of personal choice but it has consequences that need to be considered in the present as well as in the future. Every action is recorded by the angels who document the day, and each action has a consequence. After death, one waits for the day of judgment in the purgatory of Barzaq, until the day of judgment arrives.

Muslims believe that their faith in Allah is the most important aspect of their lives. They prioritize their religion above everything else, and anything that obstructs them from practicing their faith must be removed. They need to stay true to their beliefs and not compromise, even if it means leaving a situation that hinders their practice. Muslims understand that their faith will be tested, whether it is by their family, friends, or society. However, they believe Islam is here to stay and will remain a constant in their lives.

People unintentionally accept others' opinions as absolute truths, hindering personal development and trust. The trials of faith are deeply connected to the lives of believers. The same principle holds for those who embrace Islam later in life. Even among Muslim groups, there may be resistance to this application due to its unfamiliarity. Muslims have a responsibility to defend their beliefs. Chaos arises from the disbelievers' impact on the weak-minded, caused by their indiscipline and disobedience to Allah.

The only solution is to escape a hostile environment. Serving and being grateful to Allah are the primary obligations of a human being. Allah is the one who grants life and death. The illusion of life is real. It's not the end of the journey, but the start of the next adventure. Allah holds the ultimate judgment. Muslims in this world experience both freedoms and restrictions. (shirking). Associating partners with Allah is the one sin that cannot be forgiven in Islam.

Quran: Surah Nisa: 4:48. Surely Allah does not forgive that a partner be ascribed to Him, although He forgives any other sins for whomever He wills. He who associates anyone with Allah in His divinity has indeed forged a mighty lie and committed a huge sin.

Quran: Surah Taha 20:15.Indeed, the Hour is coming - I almost conceal it1 - so that every soul receives according to that for which it strives.

Allah's punishments may seem harsh to some, but it is important to remember that He is the creator and has sent laws for humanity to follow. It is up to us to adhere to these laws. However, Allah cannot be replaced by any human, deity, animal, or jinn, and He will never surrender His supreme position.

For believers, Allah is the only God, unseen until the day of judgment.The Islamic faith has a limited lifespan. Eventually, the Quran will no longer be available to read, and only those who have memorized it will have it in their hearts. The day of judgment is drawing near, and according to biblical texts, there will be destruction before the end of time.

Signs of the hour are many as they keep coming closer to humans who are knowledgeable enough to see the destruction close at hand. The believer sinks into sadness as he notices the signs of the hour are clear.

And sometimes content as he has prepared for the hour. This period had plenty of preparation time. Allah gave some more time to prepare for meeting him than any human school. He gave humanity years to prepare for meeting their creator.The length of life could even reach twenty years or sixty, sometimes more, sometimes less, once puberty is over. In Allah's court, Allah judges a person as an adult. Allah's testing timeline is plenty for those who enjoy this world and prepare for the next.

If a human fails the preparation to meet his creator, the results are exactly how the preparation was. In this life, preparation is required for the confrontation with Allah. This is because, for Muslims, answers rest on your deeds. Education will be higher academically, but knowledge will decline. Per the Islamic concept. If immorality prevails, the person attempting to correct it will appear ineffectual and backward.

As ignorance spreads in the name of modernization, morality will disappear from most homes, including Muslim families that do not practice Salat or recite the Quran. These homes will adhere to a backward society with a lack of morality.The morally bankrupt will view people who refuse to partake in such evils as backward. They will also resist any advice to improve their morals. Peer pressure from the opposition will lead the jaded to surrender to evil, regardless of whether they are Muslims or non-Muslims.

Alcohol and wine will become part of social gatherings and give credence and adaptation to behavior. Islam forbids Muslims from participating in such societies. One who sets the bar for truth and belief controls the masses. Evil and Satan are weak. The apparent downfall is near. Music will be the most significant aspect of survival. This evokes unforeseen performances and gatherings among humans. Music and concert bars destroy and degrade humanity, targeting youth and confused adults. Along with mind-altering drugs. These affairs can lead to violence and sexual debauchery.

It can drain young and restless minds. Idle minds are the devil's workshops. The messages and discolored language send shock waves even to those who enjoy the music beats.

They can also lead to a distorted view of reality, where individuals are more likely to engage in reckless and irresponsible behavior. This ultimately creates a society of damaged individuals.

Mind-altering drugs are a grenade of evil for those who find superficial, temporary excitement more plausible. By inviting the forbidden into others' lives, the inner sadness increases. Selling and purchasing such chemicals called drugs destroys the minds of many upcoming generations and older generations.

In today's societies, evil is always compensated for. These drugs often lead to various health problems, such as addiction, physical and mental health issues, and even death. Mind-altering drugs have severe consequences and can impact individuals, families, and communities. Evil can multiply so can virtue. It is imperative to know the risks and prevent drug abuse. Islam promotes a healthy lifestyle, leaving all the ills behind.

Islamic teachings provide clear guidance on any form of substance abuse that alters the mind unless it is for medicinal purposes. Emphasize the importance of moderation and self-restraint. Muslims are encouraged to stay away from all intoxicants and seek a healthy and balanced lifestyle for their body, mind, and soul. It is especially problematic when the engagement is from a believer who purposefully engages in acts not permissible in Islam. By employing others to harm oneself and others, not unintentionally or intentionally.

This knowledge will provide them with the strength to resist Satan's temptations and remain firm in their faith. Ultimately, remembrance will bring peace and guidance to those who seek it. Destruction of others. Propagating sin is the most evil thing you can do. Photography and technology have improved and taken a toll on society, by taking pictures of humans and displaying acts inappropriate for those who seek chaos.

This has led to a decrease in values and morals and an increase in violence in certain communities. It has also led to a culture of desensitization and normalization of certain behaviors that would have been considered unacceptable in the past. Islam knew life's plasma as it unfolded. **The rise of pornography leads to a closer encounter with evil. By exploiting the minds of the weak through images that do not accord with any faith, the idea of pictures is limited in the long run. Memories are attached to images. Discretion is imperative in this society.**

Hadith: Bukhari:3226: "The angels do not enter a house in which there is an image."

Pay attention to the signs. Tall buildings will take center stage. Gog and Magog appear. (Yajuj and Majuj) There will be three sliding areas. One is from the East, one from the West, and a third is from the Arabian Peninsula. Temperature changes will reveal earthquakes, landslides, and floods. Fires will become frequent. There will be no discrimination against illicit sexual conduct or nudity. Time flies by quickly. There will be an overflow of money in society.

The number of murders will increase. Women will travel solo. Loss of shame among both genders will become prevalent. Evildoers will inevitably associate themselves with evil. Limited availability and high prices of rations in the markets will make it challenging for people to purchase, especially for those with limited funds. A correction results in resentment. Muslims can be Muslim in the morning and (Kafir) disbelievers in the evening. Faith can be called backward a Muslim can deny it. Besides the fire in the heart, actual fires will become part of life. Those who commit murder will not know the reason. The biggest fire will come from Yemen.

Soft winds will take believers' souls before the trumpet blows. A person outside the grave will wish he was in the place of the deceased, and honesty and oaths will have no meaning. In this chapter, Euphrates uncovers his gold treasure. It will be a fight between people for this treasure. Regardless of the current pluralistic society wrapped in deceit, a major war will break out between Muslims, Jews, and Christians. Muslims who know their faith know all these signs, which are apparent in Quranic texts and hadiths. The basis I have touched guides my curiosity and interests.

It's occurring in this society because of disorientation. The precursor to culture mixing with faith provides the encrypted beliefs. Islam categorically rejects any union not aligned with Islamic principles. Engaging in such evil undermines Muslim families' morale and undermines Islamic law. All Quran rules are not interchangeable laws in Islam.

Imams and top clerics have no right to accept or change anything in the Quran. Sometimes Imams are also uneducated about Islam. They are handpicked to collude with lies and misinformation to youth at the risk of not knowing themselves.

Or those seeking advice are turned away with answers not satisfactory to believers. This leads to erroneous faith interpretations and falsehood propagation. Imams must be knowledgeable about Islamic teachings and well-versed in the interpretation of the Quran and the Hadith. This is the only way to ensure Islam's true message is shared.

The process of adapting to an atheist environment requires the removal of Islamic concepts to replace the divine with human desires. The failure of such unions to keep up with modernization or please disbelievers is also a sign of the last days. Common sense and Islamic beliefs are compatible. One creator is the only source of submission and proof in creation. Islam believes that if a Muslim collaborates with paganism and their ideologies.

And await Allah's wrath. Rational explanations might help us comprehend the dogma, but the dilemma it created for monotheists is unsuitable. Allah designed humanity in such a way that the only way to see Allah is in the next phase of existence.

Non-believers' acceptance and social pressure have no bearing on Muslims. They proposed to Prophet Muhammad a repeal to share faiths: they would believe in their Gods half the time and Islam half the time. As a compromise, Muslims were asked to do the same, which Islam rejected. Pagan believers made this plea to Prophet Muhammad, and Allah revealed a surah showing no compromise between the Quran and Islam. Islam is infallible, but the followers of Islam aren't.

They continue to employ the same tactics, attempting to exploit unaware Muslims and undermine the significance of Islamic ways. Exercising the Islamic belief involves strict adherence to the Quran, Sunnah, and the ways of Prophet Muhammad, without adjusting to pagan history or societal dogmas. By not conforming to their tactics, he set an example for Muslims. Muslims in today's society must adhere to the understanding that the approach may vary, but deceit remains constant.

The last testament of Islam is incomparable and prohibits human alteration or intervention. Allah sent the "surah kafirun" in response to their request for clarification. Muslims cannot and will not compromise their faith to appease persistent requesters. Even those who deceive themselves, Allah knows their hearts. The Quran unequivocally states that they won't be satisfied until you adopt their ways.

Quran; Surah Kafirun: Say: O disbelievers, I do not worship what you worship.Nor are you worshippers of what I worship. I will not worship what you worship. Nor will you be worshippers of what I worship. You have your religion, and I have mine.

The conflict between Islam and a paganistic society is novel. Instead, it has been an ongoing battle since the Prophet Muhammad introduced Islam in the Quran's closing statement. When Allah's laws become less relevant in society, families and societies become closer to Allah's doom surrounding their environment. By agreeing to the ills prohibited by Islam, you cannot gain momentum to resolve hardship. Compensation can only last for so long. This is another example of the last days.

There are many examples of resentment and stubbornness in today's society that lead to evil endings. This society will become accustomed to disrespecting Muslim parents who condone Islamic concepts and ideologies and undermining and overriding their advice. There are many families that this epidemic has affected. Words that are twisted and unfounded allegations mark the end times.

Responsibility and scrutiny come hand in hand with honor. Neglecting to teach Allah's word makes the first teacher, the mother, a failure, regardless of grade. If some family members stray after being taught, it is not the responsibility of the mother.

This is because Allah's word echoes in every Muslim's home. Helping the lost find their way is the ultimate goal of our actions. As Muslim mothers, it is their responsibility to guide their children in Allah's ways, while also working on themselves to set the right example. What one instructs must be implemented personally. Furthermore, households that do not pray cannot force children to pray; it is a joint effort.

Children have the right to be taught at a young age in Islam. Those who are not good examples as mothers, fathers, or caregivers, cannot be teachers. Respect is an essential element in Islam, and Allah evaluates behavior while parents instill discipline. If your parents direct you towards paganism or non-acceptance of Islam after your belief, Islam says not to listen to them. Such premises require a graceful exit. The key to success in life is to do what you see and not what you're told. In the majority of life facades. Seeing is believing. A household that prays to Allah is not destined for destruction.

Quran: Surah Isra 17:23.And your Lord has decreed that you do not worship except Him, and to parents, good treatment. Whether one or both of them reach old age.

Advertisement dominates business, followed by social media ads, and repetition is a significant factor. It works on the human mind.The nurturing father and mother who pray will influence the family and lead them to submit to Allah for those who practice Islam. The seeds that are planted by the young and old reap the benefits sooner than later. A Muslim family faces doom if a woman or man does not attend the Salat and read the Quran.

The ripple effects become obvious as life proceeds. The Quran provides guidance and wisdom for a successful life. Salat along with the complete discipline of life helps to restore the inner peace and mental strength of an individual. Thus, fulfilling the spiritual and religious obligations of an individual can be rewarding in the long run. Additionally, these points signify a society where money, academics, and social status are more important than Salat for women and men. There is a significant problem with certain parents' low literacy rates. The absence of fruitful behavior is consistent with the literate epidemic and dominance.

Economic setbacks and disinterest in non-education have mostly been responsible. Education is a major part of Islam's upbringing process for both sexes. It is a major priority for women, as they will need it when they least expect it. Mainly economics prevents the parents from being able to attend to the children.

Despite cultivating driven children, these families become their drivers of good and mishaps. As a result of their offspring dominating academia over the experience of their parents. In an insecure society, individuals sometimes dictate and disrespect words that are not pleasing to the eyes or ears.Muslim families have less prevalence in this matter, as the rules of the household are dictated by Islam. Learning the Quran is considered a disciplined practice from an early age.

People who assisted their rise are mistreated in Islamophobic regions, which goes against Islamic doctrine. Muslims have a strong passion for gratitude. The Islamic perspective emphasizes the importance of education for both the less fortunate and the fortunate.

It's the force that motivates life and learning. Education, whether formal or through self-learning, is essential for survival. It is crucial to educate young Muslims, despite opposition seeking to sway them. Thriving Muslims should support one another and avoid pride and grudges, preventing them from falling deeper into the ditch. It is essential to come together to ensure that such episodes do not happen in our society.

Those who believe are constantly targeted by Satan and his followers. Satan invites them to his fire, while Allah fills hell with the deceitful; yet Allah shows mercy, understanding the benefits of Muslims helping one another. Understanding morality is a gift for Muslims and those seeking knowledge of Islam's fundamental beliefs. The act of praying Salat indicates helpfulness, not deceitfulness. Deceit and Salat are incompatible.

There is dignity in education in every aspect, as well as consistency in learning. Survivors and teachers are those who learn. Islam-based education cannot be traded. Those who succeed are dedicated and have the mind Allah has given them. Education is the only way to progress in life. It is a noble trait to ensure knowledge and understanding of the world. It is the foundation for success and a better future. This will ensure that they do not struggle to reach the heights of this spectrum.

Common sense and belief can be lacking in highly educated individuals at times. Parental rights in Islamic cultures allow Muslim parents to correct their offspring, regardless of their higher education or academic jobs. In certain families and societies, the bonds of an Islamic family remain strong as they age. Islamophobic societies impose ideas on the weak-minded, luring them into an incompatible society with progressive Islamic laws. Obeying God's commands brings a feeling of peace and satisfaction. To achieve inner and worldly success, it is crucial to prioritize faith over worldly achievements. Spiritual values are key to achieving true and lasting success. Those who abandon Islam to be controlled by worldly desires will suffer a grim fate, remaining ignorant and blind. Muslims achieve success by promoting global prosperity and embracing the joy of Islam.

Quran: Surah Ghafir: 40:58.Those blind ˹to the truth˺ and those who can see are not equal, nor are those who believe and do good ˹equal˺ to those who do evil. Yet you are hardly mindful.

Truth-tellers will be silenced while lies gain acceptance, and defiance and arrogance become inseparable. Those in the correctional belief system will be deemed outcasts due to their intolerant views on societal issues. When the truth is denied, fear and distrust can arise

Acceptance of lies without question increases and those who challenge them are viewed as a threat to the status quo. Smoke will appear on earth as a sign of the Dajjal antichrist's arrival. The Dajjal the antichrist will bear a mark on his forehead and will have an army of jinns and men. According to Islamic concepts, he will be described as having one eye that is blind, thick-skinned, and protruding. He will possess a ruddy complexion and curly hair.

He will be the symbol of evil and bring chaos and destruction to the world. People must remain vigilant and prepare for his arrival. Dajal appears to have been fishing for decades. Satan's job is taken very seriously, as is Dajjal's arrival, which wires those who fall for evil's ploys. The people of Lot will be indulgent and more in numbers.

He will usher in a new era of hope, only to deceive his people with false promises. He will present a fresh approach to life and a more promising future. In his presence, they will experience joy and realize they are not alone. True believers can always distinguish between truth and falsehood. Dajjal's total stay is 40 days. He will bear the mark of the beast, a one-eyed monster with one eye protruding. Prior to Jesus' arrival, the false Messiah known as Dajjal will have been identified.

Hadith: Tirmidhi 2245; Many Hadith describe the attributes of Dajjal. He will be a young man with a ruddy complexion, with thick curly hair, blind or defective in the right eye, his left eye will be covered with a thick piece of flesh growing at the edge of his eye. Separate Arabic letters "Kaf, Fa, Ra " ('Kafir' when letters are joined) will be written between his eyes and every believer will be able to read it.

Hadith: Sahih Muslim: 2944.Dajjal will emerge from the East, from Khurasan and he will be followed by 70,000 Jews of Isfahan, wearing Persian shawls.

Hadith: Sahih Muslim: 2942.After his emergence, he will travel all over the world and will never leave a city without entering it, except Makkah and Medina.

Hadith:Tirmidhi: 2244, Sahih Muslim: 2420(a) During Dajjal's stay on earth, all people, other than his followers, will be in extreme trouble. Then Allah will send the Son of Maryam, Isa (A.S.), who will chase Dajjal. Isa (A.S.) will catch up with him at the gate of Ludd (Lod), a place in Palestine near Bayt al-Maqdis where He (A.S.) will kill Dajjal.

He will be sterile and have no children. To most people, it will seem like 1 year, 1 month, and 1 weak day. Many of Allah's creations have yet to surpass this world, with more miracles and destructions to come before the end of time. Some doubt, but those who know have seen consistent signs of the hour. His stay will seem longer despite being short. His mission is to deceive and mislead people on a large scale, turning them away from faith and righteousness. Dajjal and his followers will be defeated and brought to justice.Non-believers may view faith outcomes as unrealistic stories.

Those who observe the results of faith contribute to societies striving for material and academic achievement. Faith seeks everything and beyond from Allah. Muslims are advised by Islam to read the Quran and ten verses of Surah Kahf on Friday for protection from Dajjal. Islam covers everything, even exposing false Messiahs in countries with limited theological knowledge. The search for truth and knowledge about Islam is crucial for those interested in learning and overcoming illiteracy. Islam possesses truth, devoid of hidden motives or adapted rhetoric to fit the times; the times will ultimately have to accommodate Islam. Those seeking to understand Islam should be educated by Muslims.

Dajjal's army is of evil Jinns and people already visible. Each gesture emits fumes that reach humanity individually. Knowing and watching evil plots is better than walking like the blind when Allah has given vision. Success cannot be attained through evil means like arguments, attachments, mishaps, or destructive conversations. Believers are advised to avoid and not enter such a setting. It cautions against deceit. Satan's tricks are deceptive and unpredictable. A fume destroys comfort from within. Believers are closer to the truth's validity. Maintaining distance from harmful individuals.

Islamic theology has defined stages. Mehdi the Imam will precede the appearance of the Dajjal. Mehdi's appearance establishes him as a descendant of Muhammad, the last Prophet. Black banners will be worn by the supporters. The Mehdi will bring prosperity and prayer, but will not defeat the Dajjal, the anti-Christ. He will bring justice, and peace, and lead people on the right path.

Hadith: TIRMIDHI 2269:Black standards will come from Khorasan, nothing shall turn them back until they are planted in Jerusalem.

Hadith: Ibn Majah: 4082. The people of my Household will face calamity, expulsion and exile after I am gone, until some people will come from the east carrying black banners. They will ask for something good but will not be given it. Then they will fight and will be victorious, then they will be given what they wanted, but they will not accept it and will give leadership to a man from my family.

Hadith: Ibn Majah. 4084. When you see them, then pledge your allegiance to them even if you have to crawl over the snow, for that is the caliph of Allah, Al-Mahdi.

The hadiths align with the beliefs and actions of those who manipulate truth and lies, exploiting the vulnerable and oppressed. Young Muslims are being manipulated and led astray towards evil by promises of fame and progress in a staged world. Believers receive what's theirs without resorting to manipulation or compromising Islamic values, only by educating against Islamophobia. The wait for Jerusalem to be under Muslim rule, like in the time of Omar bin Khattab, will appear long, but Muslims should continue helping the oppressed and showing humanity to all. Assume the responsibility of being ambassadors for Islam, rather than becoming detractors or blind adherents to evil. As the war erupts, men are expected to join and demonstrate their unwavering faith in Islam.

The prophecy of Prophet Muhammad was fulfilled when the Byzantines were succeeded by the Muslim Ottomans after six hundred years. The final war is where the winners are determined, not through losses in other wars. Islam holds the ultimate truth and will triumph in the final war. Regardless of the land taken from Muslims, it ultimately belongs to Allah. Muslims fight for truth, not for land. The truth of Islam, the monotheistic faith, stands alone and stands tall, leaving everything else behind.

Mehdi will establish a new government and ensure justice. Restored Islam will spread globally. Only Allah, the belief in one God, will be worshiped, not triune Gods or others. Jesus will come next. The coming of Jesus. Two angels will accompany him on each side when he descends from Syria.

His mission starts after praying behind Mehdi. He will offer Fajr prayer and request Jesus to lead. He declines and prays behind the Mahdi.The Islamic principle of prayer requires a leader to lead the prayer.His faith in one God will be the same as that of the other Prophets. It is Jesus who is the brethren of all the Prophets of Allah. The glimpse of the Quranic stories can be seen as of interest to those who believe. A believer prepares for the hour for those who are not ignorant of their faith need reminders not exclusion.

In the eyes of those who are not aware, daily life without preparation results from disobedience to Allah. Islam has moved on and cannot regress backward. Conservatism is revolutionary. It cannot return to ancient times. Adapting to the changing times is key to progress while upholding our values.Being flexible and open to new ideas, while still staying true to our core beliefs. We must find a balance between progress and tradition.

Western and Islamophobic societies mimic prehistoric habits and culture. Learning to embrace change and adapt to the times while preserving our cultural values and faith is critical. Balance is crucial for our survival and success. It enables growth and evolution while maintaining roots.Modified clothing and buildings from earlier, amoral eras do not console the believer of modernity. Most of society is governed by their false temptations. However, been tempted by glitz and glamor? Misinformation and prejudice have widened the divide between Islamic and non-Islamic societies. Islamophobia is a significant issue that requires attention. In the end, it's not the glitz that's to blame, but knowing Islam. The rest depends on the core of the soul and belief system.

Education is one of the most effective tools for bridging this gap, as it can reduce misinformation and prejudice. Additionally, tolerance and mutual understanding are essential for fostering positive relationships between Islamic and non-Islamic societies.

Finally, governments and other institutions' participation can be a proactive approach to tackling Islamophobia and fostering a more inclusive society. Around the world, schools teach Islam. The question is whether Islam is being taught in its true form, as it stands at the forefront of the curious.

People tend not to negate the differences between culture and Islam in many Muslim countries as well. The difference between culture and faith is similar in some venues but not the same, as culture does not dictate faith, but perhaps cuisine does. Islamic theories altered to suit the times of today have no validity in learning. The studies are sometimes subjected to conformity for some to alter the venues or leave the faith. Some question the teachings of Islam and have taken extensive studies of studying abroad and learned the core of Islam.

Questions teach through answers. Answers make the mind learn. If the answer is unsatisfactory, the questionnaire may continue searching until finding a suitable option. Islam's truth is not discourteous. It is based on a Muslim understanding of faith, making the differences and contrasts easy to show. Easily influenced Muslims in newer Western countries struggle for individuality. Conforming to peer pressure leads to loss of individuality. Those who cling to their beliefs no matter what.

The restrictions of Islam are not a way to suffocate a person's soul, but a path to a better life monitored by self-control. Ignoring the rules and customs of society, whose decisions are based on desires, causes more harm and distress later.

Muslim populations are increasing in new Western countries. It is crucial to explain the differences between the Abrahamic faiths. Despite many adhering to the faith, many have compromised the revenue of faith for the world. Islam lacks remorse for these Muslims. Apart from punishment. Comparative theology and Islam's belief in one God are infinite. Islamic rules are non-negotiable. Mistakes happen, but repentance is always available.

When contract and theology are assimilated, the friendships associated with multiple faiths are not overlooked. However, deception cannot be used as a cover for friendship. References and understanding of Abrahamic faiths and theology can be enhanced through understanding and correlation of differences.

Islam prioritizes faith over symbols. A cross symbolizes hope and Jesus's suffering, death, and resurrection. The Jewish community named the star after David, of ancient Israel. It dates back to the Middle Ages as a symbol. Islam doesn't endorse the crescent and star symbols. The new moon phase signifies progress. The star represents light and knowledge. This can be patented as a monogram, not a religious symbol, unrelated to Islam.

Islam denies the resurrection of Jesus. In Islamic teachings, he did not die on the cross. Searching for theology is crucial for developing personal beliefs. Muslims accept Jesus as the Messiah, but most Jews deny him. Islamic practices promote harmony, not friction.

Islam will not be afraid of the truth. Blood symbolizes faith for Christians. Monotheism prohibits blood sacrifices. Islam has no attachment to mortals and believes in Allah as the only God. The substitution of deeds to Jesus as a blood sacrifice opposes Islamic beliefs. Jesus is a symbol of truth for the faithful, but hypocrites distort his message.

Clarity is found in obvious points when discussing tranquility in theology and comparisons. Islam's gradual dominance of conversion is increasing in Western society doesn't pose a problem for mixed cultures, but interfaith mixing can have unfamiliar effects on families and homes.

Jesus will bring peace to the world by clarifying for those who hear him.

While no one knows when the last day will come, man can learn all signs as he researches the truth daily. There are various differences in faith, and even Jews anticipate the arrival of another Prophet. Muslims and Christians share a belief in the return of Jesus, but their perceptions of him are vastly different. Jesus' arrival is expected in both Muslim and Christian faiths, but Jews do not believe he will return as the Messiah. Instead, they interpret a different belief and await another Prophet from David's lineage.

Time will tell who will witness if they are alive, and it will be Jesus.

The reason these faiths are called Abrahamic faiths is that Abraham was a monotheist. Jesus was a monotheist, and attaching him to Allah is polytheistic and outside the fold of monotheism. The comparative study of these faiths is Christianity, Judaism, and Islam. All came with the same concept of one God to worship Allah.

From the perspective of most Christians, Jesus is commonly referred to as God or the Son of God. This concept has no roots in the Abrahamic faiths, which have been followed since the beginning of time, beginning with Adam and Eve and culminating in Abraham the monotheist. By exploring the minor differences in theology, it is possible to gain a clearer understanding of the distinctions that exist and to satisfy the curiosity of inquisitive minds.

There is a thin line between monotheism and polytheism when it comes to beliefs. In the USA, the widely celebrated holiday of Christmas was banned until 1836 due to the Puritanical beliefs of the earliest American settlers. The holiday was considered to be a pagan festival by the Americans at that time.

Time Magazine: The holiday was prohibited.The Surprising First Fighters in the War on Christmas.Dec 25, 2014 — Dec. 25, 1659: Puritan settlers eschew Christmas celebrations, which are illegal in the colonies from 1659 to 1681.

In other areas of New England throughout the 17th century. It wasn't until the 19th century that Christmas was widely celebrated in the US. This ban was enforced by the Puritans in the 17th century. The first Christmas celebration in Boston was held in 1856. Although initially banned in some countries due to its non-religious origins, Christmas is now celebrated across many nations. This holiday has a long history that dates back to pagan times.

Many people formally requested to keep the statues as a reminder of their ancestors, which later turned into reminders of their pagan roots. In Islam, the worship of Allah, one God, and no paganistic ritual is solace. Unlike human courts, deception does not exist in Allah's court, and his laws are not shaped to please humans but Islam is to conform to divine will.

Courts have been known to bend the rules in favor of human happiness, but such actions are rarely justified by the jury. It is important to note that the tribute paid has no connection with Jesus, the son of Mary. The similarity between the two is that their origins both stem from Mitra, the God of the same birthday who orchestrated the birth of Jesus.

It is a known fact that Jesus did not celebrate Christmas, nor did he mention his birthday. In addition, his birthday was not on December 25th. The Bible prohibits the lighting and decoration of Christmas trees. The practice of decorating fir trees and homes with lights originated with the Pagans during the Roman and Egyptian eras, who did so to celebrate Saturnalia.

Bible: Jeremiah 10-3-4. For the customs of the people are vain: for one cutteth a tree out of the forest, the work of the hands of the workman, with the ax.

The first Nativity festival spread throughout Egypt in 432, and Christendom subsequently adopted many pagan practices, including the worship of Jesus as a deity during later years. Man-made holidays exist because they were adopted as celebrations.The essence of truth and reality cannot be suppressed. It takes courage to reveal the truth in any situation. Islam does not force anyone to believe, but a religion that emphasizes purity and authenticity requires us to reject falsehoods and fake beliefs.

Muslims need to understand that, despite historical intrusions caused by humans, Allah remains consistent and never changes his pattern, in contrast to humans who often seek excitement. Governing impulses and passions with ingenuity requires courage to control human desires, taming fierce lions through the strength of truth. Jesus did not instruct people to worship him.

After the ascension of Jesus, significant changes occurred in the beliefs and practices of his followers. Prophet Muhammad, in his teachings to the ummah, emphasized that his people should not worship him like the followers of Jesus did, because he was only a servant of Allah. It is not possible to convert monotheistic beliefs into pagan ones, and any form of worship directed towards a mortal being is considered a pagan practice.

Although the beliefs of paganism are similar, certain stories have been removed from specific texts. This history is accessible to anyone willing to research and explore it. In contrast to monotheism, these ideologies have unfamiliar bounds. However, the diversity of human thoughts, experiences, and religious histories and principles presents an infinite number of learning opportunities.True wealth originates from knowledge, education, and a contented soul. Islam does not make exceptions to please any particular society. Faith cannot compromise to please humanity. Humans will have to change for Islam, as it will not change for them. The Abrahamic faith has answers to certain questions that some may seek.

Both Judaism and Islam are monotheistic religions that believe in one God. However, there are significant differences and divergences in their doctrines compared to Islamic beliefs. Islam has a strong stance against any attempts by humans to disobey or modify Allah's will. The Quran repeatedly assures the protection of Allah's last testament, previous Abrahamic scripts were compromised due to human disobedience and the alteration.

Quran: Surah 24:50 Do their hearts suffer from the disease of hypocrisy? Or have they fallen prey to doubts? Are they afraid Allah and His Messenger will wrong them?

It is said that at some point in their lives, every person will encounter someone who will share the truth about Allah with them. It is important to respect their beliefs and opinions, even if they differ from one's own.

Islam does not condone attacking or belittling the beliefs of others. However, it is important to explain the differences in beliefs respectfully and peacefully, without trying to force one's own beliefs onto others. Ultimately, it is up to each individual to choose their path, and Allah grants them the freedom to do so. However, Allah also guarantees that there will be consequences for one's actions and choices.

It is crucial to keep in mind that even if someone is dishonest, the truth will eventually come out. It's always better to be truthful and have strong moral principles. Life poses many challenges, and according to the Islamic faith, Allah is the giver of life and death. At times, humans wish they could be given another chance to do things differently.

After seeing the truth, humans will plead with Allah for another chance on earth. However, Allah exposes people's true nature by stating that if given another chance on earth, they would repeat the same mistakes. Humans have a single opportunity to learn, educate themselves, and enjoy or suffer the consequences of their choices. Choice of faith is not imposed either after knowing the truth; it's up to the human.

Quran: Surah Imran 3:185. Every soul will taste death. Allah will repay it only on the day of judgment.

Mercy from the fire and admission to paradise will indeed triumph, while this world is only a fantasy of pleasure. The last exit from this world is death. As Prophet Muhammad stood up, the corpse of a Jewish man passed by. The (Sahabah) companions of Prophet Muhammad asked him why he had stood up. Should I not respect the dead? As part of following up with condolences after losing loved ones, food gatherings, and attending to the needs of the bereaved families.

There are no eulogies in Islam; there are only prayers for the deceased and help for families who have lost a family member. As the deceased has faced a transition that the living has not, Islam forbids slandering or mentioning anything negative about him. His own trials await him. Words can accompany positivity, not negativity or sarcasm. An angry Muslim doesn't need our attention. He needs our prayers.

Quran: Surah Hajj 22:46. Have they not journeyed into the land that their hearts might understand and their ears might listen? Indeed, it is not the eyes that are blind. It is the hearts of the breasts that are blind.

"What is the Islamic perspective on martyrs?"

Quran: Surah Hajj Verse 154. And say not of those who are dead in God's cause, dead? Nay, they are alive. But you perceive it not.

Allah asserts that humans may consider those who died in martyrdom to be deceased. The truth of humanity's existence remains unknown.

Quran: Surah Baqarah 170. Exulting in that (martyrdom) which Allah gave them out of his bounty.

The ones who have departed face their course. Their loved ones left behind need not grieve for too long; they too will join soon. Trials and tribulations can lead to happiness. Death is inevitable, so humans should not fear it. For a believer, losing faith is a greater fear than death. Letting go of positive values and people can reveal the negative ones.

Grave-related inquiries are part of Islam. When waking the dead, three questions will be asked. The mouth echoes the heart's past life. Who is the Lord of the world? It's Allah, my Lord. What do you believe in? Islam's submission to life's way. Who is your final Prophet? Peace be upon him, Muhammad. Angels question humans in the grave. The duo Munkar and Nakir. The journey starts alone as the family leaves the burial site. Believers find contentment in each other's company. Without belief, earthly choices are meaningless. Defying Allah carries a heavy price for Muslims.

People worldwide celebrate birthdays with gifts and parties. Virtuous deeds were the genuine gifts for a Muslim, not superficial ones. The creator succumbed to the invest's investments. Abiding by the highest standards. Allah, the Lord of all existence. Interest in global actions is reciprocated. Time is valuable to believers and achievers with or without faith.

Quran: Surah Kahf 18;26. Say: "Allah knows best how long they remained in it. Only he knows what lies in the heavens and the earth. How sharply he sees; how well he hears! The creatures have no other guardian than him; he allows none to share his authority.

Islam teaches man's existence. From conception to birth, the Quran explains embryology. After living in the body of a mother for forty days, the sperm of the man mixed with the sperm of the mother becomes a clot of thick blood in her womb. Allah sends an angel to write four things for the child in the mother's womb. He writes of his deeds, livelihood, blessed or wretched, and the time of his death. The angel then breathes a soul into the fetus.

How does a human become so proud when he comes from utter fluid? The womb of a mother nurtures him or her. The Quran is the only book that talks about death, human conception, and the formation of the fetus. Using a microscope, humans discovered the information later. Allah has revealed this in the Quran. Islam has fully described this process. Another significant part of Islam is (Qadar) destiny. "Qadar" Belief in Allah's predestination. The Quran clarifies that Allah has preserved the record in the (Lauh Al-Mahfouz), known as the preserved tablet.

Allah's knowledge has no boundaries. The written record documents its destiny.

Allah knew the path humanity would choose. His knowledge empowered the world he created. Pens no longer write, the ink is dry.

The provision of (Rizq) is sustenance before a human is born. He will travel to the farthest lands to attain what already belongs to him. No one can take what belongs to a human given by Allah before birth.The environment one travels in is fertile soil for future success and fulfillment. Nothing is unattainable. Allah can fulfill all worthwhile desires in life.Perseverance, strength, and optimism endure turbulent trials as a believer clings to belief and spirituality. When Allah wrote something for one, he ensured that what he wrote reached one. No one can take it. Allah scribed one's name on it. Islam clarifies this mark of life.

Quran: Surah Qaf 50:16. Indeed, ˹it is˺it is We who created humankind and fully know what their souls whisper to them, and we are closer to them than ˹their˺ jugular vein.

Humans may become anchored to the trials and tribulations of unexpected timing.

If time were just, humans would know how to react to time and work on assignments given by Allah. A man works in haste. One must learn to adjust to the unexpected blows of life without knowing the synchronicity of trials. An individual seeks appeal and acceptance from sources who agree with him. The most valuable agreement a man can have is when he agrees with the laws of Allah.

According to Allah, the most appropriate place to share stories is closest to the jugular veins. It's best to turn to Allah for problem-solving instead of creating more problems. With his light, he illuminates the hearts of genuine believers. Allah always has the well-being and interests of his servants in mind when they worship and praise him. To endure the challenges of life and grow spiritually, humanity can choose to exhibit enthusiasm and tenacity without giving up.

Developing healthy eating habits and practicing internal cleansing can help nourish the body, while prayer and attending religious gatherings can help nurture the soul. It's important to focus on the positive aspects of life instead of dwelling on negativity. Sometimes, what people are searching for is not far away but may be closer than they think. The mystery of life can be a journey to find the gold we desire.

One can see the gold of life presented to one by Allah. The gold that a human seeks is not material. Someone who believes in the same path Allah prescribed. Peace within is better than any precious metal sold in the marketplace or panned from the ocean.

Humanity or any living creature can find Allah. He is near. There is no unattentive boss in his office. When the caller calls, he answers. Any caller is welcome.

A person's love for Allah is the clearest evidence of their actions: a union of believers is sacred, irreplaceable, and priceless. The lasting love of believers who remind one of Allah. In Islam, tenderness, compassion, and generosity characterize such relationships.

A healthy relationship starts with a belief in Allah and worshiping one God together. Life is ironic. It signifies purity and hope for believers. Islam warns to control anger. Prophet Muhammad advises Muslims to calm their anger by sitting down and drinking water.

Forgiveness in Islam occurs after three days. Anger and misunderstanding are not long, no hateful periods. Speech can be kind or cruel and must be renegotiated within.

Quran: Surah Nahl 16:127. And be patient, O Muhammad and your patience is through Allah. And do not grieve and do not be in distress over what they conspired.

Quran: Surah Muhammad 47:26 That is because they said to those who disliked what Allah sent down, "We will obey you in part of the matter." Allah knows what they conceal.

Satan's influence can separate humanity from the truth. Resolute behavior can strengthen faith in the face of hardships. Islam brought clarity to spiritual seekers' minds. Allah operates on His own clock, not the seeker's. The Almighty is near to us. Allah is all-seeing and all-hearing. Allah knows the secrets hidden in man's heart. Confessing heart. The concealed heart.

Those who are close to their Lord experience contentment and can endure life's challenges. They consistently obey their Lord and relish the adventures that life brings. The differences that exist among Abrahamic faiths don't affect how humanity gets along, regardless of their faith. Islam doesn't force non-believers to accept the faith, as it is restricted to believers only. Belief and faith cannot be forced upon anyone. Allah invites whomever he wills to His faith. The constant life changes lead to new horizons and opportunities.

Living in an endless dream and belief system is true enlightenment, which can wash away all fears and doubts. Allah guides us in all aspects of life and puts us on the path to success. However, success requires effort and hard work.

Recognizing the stakes and taking the necessary steps are important in achieving success. Changing the environment is the first step towards success, and it is important to take enlightened actions to fuel inner illumination. The contagious bliss of that light reveals the divine forces at work and leads us to success.

CHAPTER 6

GRATITUDE TO ATTITUDE, COVERS ISLAM.

Uncovering gratitude is an endeavor to enchant the truth, for those who perceive it as more than mere words. This results in a life that is more meaningful and fulfilling, leading to increased happiness and contentment. Practicing gratitude is essential for unlocking Allah's blessings. The significance of expressing gratitude in daily life is based on a spiritual bond. Individuals who possess gratitude exhibit a distinct mindset. This will aid in establishing a sense of peace and contentment with life. It will assist in cultivating self-awareness and comprehending one's position in the world. Engaging in this will help individuals to truly appreciate Allah's blessings and find greater fulfillment in life.

Muslims, as evidenced by records and examples, would pick up garbage while traveling to maintain clean streets. If people observe garbage on the road, it is believed that a Muslim has not passed by because the garbage remains. The Muslim traveler ensured the roads stayed clean for others. They thanked Allah for giving them a path to travel. Finding these Muslims is rare, as they avoid cleansing the inner garbage in their souls, making it difficult to clean the path for others.

Muslims set examples and clean paths and hearts to allow for picking up existing garbage in sharing knowledge and stories, uniting humanity with truth and leading with gratitude. Those who neglect Islam and time, and fail to improve roads and paths, cannot purify their hearts, let alone the roads. Those who neglect Islam and time, and fail to improve roads and paths, cannot purify their hearts, let alone the roads. within yourself by purifying your heart. They used this help as an advantage to clear the way for others in gratitude to Allah. Muslims who have passed away ensured the road stayed clean, demonstrating strength, compassion, and gratitude. Finding these qualities is rare in a world filled with uncertainty and unawareness of the end.

Society's influence diminishes the gratitude expected from Muslims, forgetting the fortitude that once brought balance. Unexpected imbalances arise from a lack of gratitude. People who offered water or shared knowledge of Allah always remembered them. The gratitude and attitude of most people are changing as society advances. Graciousness persists in business, academic, sports, and travel settings.

This impact can decrease domestically as society trends shift in Muslim families and beyond. Certain Muslim families tolerate the disregard for Allah's laws, as long as it's not directed at them. The significance of obeying Allah's laws and regulations outweighs human grandeur. All that matters in the end are the deeds we leave behind. Prioritizing true mannerism and gratitude is more important than anything else. Gratitude to Allah and humans should be sincere, not just empty words, regardless of faith.

This lack of gratitude has spread to all aspects of life. People no longer value the efforts of others and are less likely to show appreciation for the help they receive. Boredom often takes over illicit activities that are not conducive to the soul's health in social media users. Social media and its extended reach could be beneficial to learning and betterment, but many people use it for activities and viewing conversations that do not benefit the integrity of their inner being.

Those who use social media and their minds for the betterment of themselves and others can become powerful tools. The gift of Allah can produce a thread that human technology cannot reach.

120

What Muslims are doing with this thread is a question for their souls, not for others. The same social media can become a means of an invitation to seekers of truth through reminders for those who understand. It is in the making of gratitude that provisions are made and tailored to each individual.

Illicit actions cause pain to those who disobey Allah. The false air of happiness is a cover-up for the discourse one endures from disobeying Allah. As a result, relationships suffer, and people become more isolated. There is a lack of respect and imbalance in gratitude in certain settings, and their complexes are imposed on others.

For those who lead the way of righteousness but fail to follow through, it is not a matter of vilification, but a battle within for those easily swayed and in poor company. A believer is someone who knows how to correct the wrongs. The instruction was given for all believers and Muslims to pray to Allah, however, pagan worshippers chose to adhere to their ancestral traditions. Despite the truth being evident, they resisted change. Many people are willing to ignore the truth and continue making careless mistakes in life. To remind another Muslim, one must have both kindness and gratitude for being chosen as the reminder.

Quran; Surah Luqman: 31:21:-27 When Allah says, "Follow what Allah has revealed," they reply, "No! We only follow what our forefathers practiced.

Those who show gratitude to Allah experience happiness. He keeps showering them with more when they continue to be grateful in any situation. A believer's affair is always pleasant in every circumstance. The happiest person is the one who derives the greatest joy from their proximity to Allah. Doubts and disturbances from external sources undermine the belief system, causing it to lose momentum. Consequently, even the most sincere believers are influenced by these scenes and bad companies. The path for believers is to clear the restrictions that influence evil and continue with gratitude, without blaming anyone.

Negative setbacks and impositions are usually the traits within themselves imposed on those who live and exist in a different world and lifestyle. When adversity strikes, a search for better avenues is a better solution than confidants or disbelievers who are unable to solve the dilemmas. Making things worse for the individual after the intrusion, which ends in chaos. Doubts and deceit quickly creep into the minds of believers and non-believers if one's faith foundation is shaky.

People who practice gratitude leave the situations of life behind and look for gratitude in other areas of their lives. In the pursuit of monopolizing the best of themselves and trusting in Allah at the highest level. Those familiar with the dark side gravitate towards it. Those familiar with light see trials as temporary realms and tests of faith and endurance. Exposure to light in the past keeps the believer seeking truth in all aspects of life. Some believers stay true no matter what. They reap all the benefits granted to them.

Humanity understands that thank you is not a slogan, but an appreciation for actions that represent symbolism. A daily exchange of gratitude between the creator and the human. All living things give thanks to Allah, except certain humans who compromise their humility. Human arrogance is the only thing that depletes gratitude to Allah. Such a creature can't be grateful to others. Repentance is the only remedy for loss of self-realization. Knowing why gratitude is a part of our existence is imperative. One who is grateful to Allah is grateful to humans. Including animals who show kindness and care to humans.

The plants that provide fruit and shelter on hot days, the mountains that allow a human to climb, or the oceans and seas that allow human entry into their privacy are all sources of gratitude Allah has given those who grasp this exchange. The home that gave shelter and transportation that provided means and a body that one pushed to limits. A mind that gives comprehension and a heart that brings solace. The human who showed you the rope to Allah is the one whom you are most grateful for. Until life ends, focusing on gratitude is enough to balance the list.

One can hide or bolster the character flaw of forgetting what Allah has done for such creatures. Therefore, it is difficult for such evil transformers to thank a human who reminds them of Allah. Not everyone, from small means or large, expresses gratitude. Allah does not distinguish between people's means. It is he who grants the soul peace and human shows gratefulness.

The gratitude of (Firon) Pharaoh's wife, Asiya Bint Muzahim, was such that she asked Allah to take away everything from her and give her a house in Jannah. Riches alone didn't buy peace, except faith in one God. Allah grants this wisdom to whom he wills. Human houses do not matter; it is the heart that seeks escape from evil, not the house. Similarly, a heart that yearns for peace in its home through faith in Allah rather than material or worldly desires. A person's soul yearns for peace within as the world creates challenges. As humans were created as subservient beings, faith completes the person.

Unseen consequences result from being ungrateful or lashing out at Allah or a believer who assists one on one's journey. Evil has a plan, just as goodness and the rewards are the same for both acts. Each act pays its debt in full. When believers overcome challenges and achieve their goals, their dreams become triumphant victories. In contrast, the justice system represents purity and messages from the creator himself. Sleep is the grandeur of bliss.

A believer will see the truth in his dreams. The Prophet Muhammad said the dream of a believer is truth. While one cannot lie while he sleeps.

Gratitude for beautiful subliminal messages is to a believer from his creator. Each day is the beginning of thankfulness, and each night is the end.

A believer even expresses thanks while sleeping. Even during sleep, the mind is still working, albeit in a restful mode. There are many people throughout the world who cannot sleep peacefully at night. Muslims who are far from Allah also face this dilemma.

The realization of a Muslim's never-ending potential will turn his dreams into reality. In the dream of a Muslim, anything and everything is possible. Humans must strive, but Allah has the last word on everything that exists. Muslims live with gratitude, forgetting the episodes of life that could have fallen apart, for Allah saved every episode of this facade of life. Each human and living thing experiences trials unique to themselves, but gratitude to Allah has no limitations.

The wanderer wanders the hallways at night, drinking water, eating unnecessary food, or watching television, computers, and phones. Some are privileged to have the technology to rest their tired minds. Some wander the streets or in darkness, unsure of where to find such peace. It is Allah's allowance for the believer's heart that brings peace to their hearts. This is not satisfactory either, as the night passes for such people, and the next morning begins with the same journey. They travel to distant lands in their minds, places that are repetitive and mostly living through the life of others or promoting rhetoric.

This is to keep the wandering soul occupied with fruitless situations. A believer knows his path. It may seem repetitive to disbelievers, but those believers who understand its value will find contentment in praying, reading the Quran, and attending Salat.

When a soul believes, it receives peace within itself, which lightens the mind and heart. In disobedience to Allah, some indulge in lawless lewd nights. Muslims know that sleep is for resting preparation for a better day ahead, so they enjoy their nights. The most comfortable beds, mattresses, and pillows are sold for the best sleep. The believers slept on cots and mats on the floor. Less sleep and more prayers were their aspirations as sleep is not foreign to the dead, it's a long rest before the awakening of judgment so keep sleep minimal and prayers in odd hours and prescribed hours are the desires of a believer.

Mischief can be found at any hour and any place but darkness has its flare for good and evil. Even though most people find mischief in the late hours through technology and secrecy, they live multiple lives. Allah knows the heart's truth. Though they can fool people they cannot fool Allah, whether it is daylight or dark. It has been said many times that you can fool some of the people some of the time. However, you can't fool all the people all of the time. This saying is a meaningful slogan of understanding who pulls the rug over the dust. However, upon lifting the rug the dust is still under the rug and even worse.

To clean the dust filth needs to be swept away as evil deeds need to exit to become the individual Allah deems. Laws are clear. Islam does not have bendable laws. Similarly to how a Muslim's back bends in worship every day, so does his or her life in a variety of ways. Islam writes that no one is excluded until the last day. The chance to return to Allah is available to everyone until the day he departs from this world.

Faith and gratitude solidly support desires that do not conflict with temptations and exhilaration. It's Allah's solidarity for those who believe, The worship of Allah and its connection to worldly achievements allows Muslims to share both this world and the next. Some Muslims sleep less to stand in the worship of Allah and have more energy than most.

Quran: Surah Hashr: 59:19. And be not like those who forgot Allah, so He made them forget themselves. Those are disobedient.

Quran: Surah Ibrahim 14;7 .*If you* express *gratitude*, I *shall* certainly *give you more*, and *if you are ungrateful, then your punishment is severe.*

In the Qur'an, Allah says to be grateful, and I will give you more. Those who pilot this (Deen) way of life and some who do not respect such guidance are irrational and show spiritual and intellectual malaise. A believer receives what he asks for and expects from Allah. Believers are not controlled by evil. There are only disbelievers or conditional believers on shaky ground. Grateful believers will recognize the mistake, correct it, and be grateful for the correct directions sent by Allah.

Quran: Surah Hijr: 15;42.*Indeed as for My servants, you do not have any authority over them, except the perverse who follow you*.

Disbelievers, however, neither bargain nor expect from Allah. Even though they receive, they give the contentment to themselves. The belief is that what they have is all due to them. It is the believer who believes in Allah and strives to achieve, not sitting back and waiting but trying hard to achieve. As a result of reaching his goal, he thanks Allah and is satisfied with his resourceful mind and efforts.

Disbelievers try too but upon accomplishing their goals they become engulfed with pride as they believe they did it. The success of worldly affairs is a grant to those selected by Allah, but the success of a peaceful heart is only for believers.

Islam's pillars are the dress code for Muslims

Human laws require a dress code in business and society. These are the factors that make a person significant. A person's dress speaks volumes about his or her identity. An address can be a home, a chapel, a mosque, or a street, but where humanity sleeps in peace is Allah's shaded address. Addresses can stipulate status, but it's the depth of the heart that reveals a person's true personality through his face and demeanor. These are the factors that make a person valuable, and the dress speaks loudly about what identity the person carries.

Every society has a dress code. Temperature affects a person's need to keep warm or cool. This source of information allows one to see how a human communicates through his or her dress. Some people do not have the financial means to purchase an outfit, while others can. In extreme climate conditions, clothing becomes a luxury item.

Regarding the matter of dress and address, some believe it matters, and some don't, but for some, it is an accurate measure of identity. It changes the attitude of the person who carries the persona. Fashion and appearance can change your demeanor; living in an immense mansion or a sizable one. Home in the most desirable area is a privilege in today's society.

But being at peace is the greatest reward; one's home is the wall of one's heart. An attitude of self-possession and a house filled with prayers to Allah are blissful.

It's not the size of this address that counts, but how it speaks to the soul, showing where the proper residence of a human is his heart. In Islam, Muslims live with disbelievers only if they have common ground for survival. Sometimes, this is because of necessity. As the heart beats in obedience to Allah, the Muslim lives by obeying him.

When a Muslim is born into a Muslim family, or either converts to Islam. Especially in societies where relaxation and entertainment involve illicit activities. It's not the living a Muslim seeks as such hangouts can become consistent. Sometimes peer pressure can swoop you in and it is best to exit as daily mixing can only be with people of the same interests. Can infiltrating loneliness through social media effectively help the lonely with low self-esteem or exploit weaknesses? Prophet Muhammad wouldn't have spoken about Islam in public if Islam advised isolation. The (dhikr) conversation of Allah is the perfect ending to every conversation for a Muslim.

People who are conscious about their health often choose to visit the gym or set certain parameters to maintain their body weight rather than focusing on obesity. Those who prioritize healthy eating habits and encourage it, tend to overlook those who overeat or never exercise. Their hangouts are persistent with people who have similarities. Instead of progress, conflict only leads to stagnation. Likewise, someone who regularly engages in Salat (Islamic prayer) may struggle to fit in with a crowd that holds contradictory beliefs and values, due to differing lifestyles and mindsets.

It's challenging to constantly interact with opposing beliefs, but it's not about not getting along with humanity. Humans can explore these waters through faith, trust, money, travel, and cohabitation. In the darkness, believers find their way, while non-believers reveal their true colors. Whomever Allah desires, he has the power to command. Even skeptics can offer support to believers. Expressing gratitude to Allah for sending assistance is essential.

When a person regards human laws as superior to Allah's laws, they are erroneously trading with Allah. Steadfastness is clear in all aspects of Islam. Coincidences are not acknowledged; there is a documented and written plan in place. If Allah does not allow it, it cannot enter a human's life. Opening the mind to accept life's utilities brings liberation. It's too restrictive for those who don't understand.

Surah Qalam 17:23.The Lord has decreed that you worship only Him and do well to your parents. Don't say anything to them that shows anger or contempt if one or both of them reach old age. Do not scold them, and address them respectfully.

The only difference is that modern technology has been added. There was more respect for humanity and families even in the pre-dated days. There is a theme here regarding humans' desire to bow before something that Allah created for us to be subordinate to. Humans were created subservient; they will bow to something.

Even before Allah sent books humans bowed to something. According to the knowledge reciprocated, there have been approximately 125,000 Prophets sent, but the Quran only mentions 25. Especially the Quran, which has fewer pages with deeper substance to consider and laws that outshine any document produced,

For some Muslims, following one Quran has become an impossible task. Leave alone the research, which leaves one with a lack of awareness of what is in front of them. Those who believed in higher forces taught their families about those forces in the past. How can a Muslim not teach the Quran?

Today's society is so arrogant that it exasperates all sources of defiance in order to break the rituals of religious sects and cultures. And perceive their outdated preconceived ideas to express and declare independence at a price that is ultimately costly. Life's dilemmas and losing control in disparity do not lead to prosperity, nor did they help in the past or will help in the future. Here is the answer: Quran. Following Islam is a choice, but Allah knows who will and who won't. The destiny of every human is predetermined.

For his defiance, the ruling king of Egypt, Allah, finally drowned Pharaoh (Firon).

To progress in a better direction, one needs to entrust oneself to better conditioning of the soul. In any decade, the soul seeks peace. To achieve this, one must have an open heart and a willingness to learn and grow from the experience.

With a pure heart, one can navigate life, even in the most difficult situations. Remaining steadfast and never giving up is the key to success. In contrast to the lifestyles of the past, today's lifestyles touch the majority of homes.The generic platform of the plastic lifestyle wrapped as fake independence today does not align with the moral code and also does not correspond with previous lifestyles

or the present for most believers. An alternative is for a rebel to convert to Islam.

Silent prayers can be more powerful than loud ones in reaching Allah's throne. When one's hope reaches its highest point, and faith becomes the answer for a believer, those who disrespect Allah and His laws are left in a state of dismay. In addition to not sitting back and waiting, Islam's motto encourages believers to keep trying, do their part, and await answers.

They plead with Allah to have mercy on the concerns of believers. Despite the world's changing course, believers are only strengthening their endurance and hope in Allah. Break a mosque or temple, but don't break the heart of someone who helps as the cries of those who leave silent complaints or give loud complaints reach Allah.

Checkpoints help monitor and correct any ill behavior and reward positive behavior. It helps to create a culture of accountability and encourages individuals to act responsibly. As a result, trust between people is also built. The result is a culture of collaboration and mutual respect, which can lead to stronger relationships and better teamwork.

Rewards systems can motivate and incentivize employees who adhere to a moral code and discipline of work. Those who adhere to a moral code of life are employees of faith, not just human concepts. Not just Islamic concepts are displayed in this application, but the world as a whole. This doctrine can be accepted by people of any religion. Or people of no faith. Kindness and morality are instilled in most humans, religious and non-religious.

It's a test for those who fix themselves not to fall further into the ditch that makes them change their venue and trust due to harsh experiences of life. As a result, some impose their complexes upon others as if they were not content within themselves. Seeking accusations rather than facts expressed by the other.

Chaos is intentionally created to create negative experiences. It is apparent that this is satisfactory to a negative person. Parity of morals is distinguished by how a person conducts himself through religious principles.

All humans are implanted with the core value of helping one another. The sadness and the happiness we feel for each other. Common respect and gratitude for those who contribute to the survival of others on earth. In contrast, religion shapes the human core, not just the superficial balance of the world, as it brings a code different from regulations humanity imposes.

The core within, however, seeks solace to feed the soul, and kindness and capabilities shine even brighter. Bringing the light that cannot be missed. An emblem of pleasantries that doesn't go unnoticed. As with deliberate instigation and provocation, it can have different consequences and reactions. Islam does not condone inciting others, reacting, and blaming them. To determine how an individual reacts, Certain forces use minuscule acts of evil to harm relationships. In Islam, it is void.

Islam's morality emphasizes kindness, fairness, and justice for Muslims and non-Muslims alike. Despite social conditions, and contrast to cultures Islam remains committed to its principles. Separating Islam from other cultures requires not bartering with it in opposition to its beliefs and principles, especially in non-Islamic dimensions. A Muslim can live anywhere as long as he or she holds truth within Islam's belief system.

To challenge someone's claim, one might use certain words casually. However, for Muslims, these words hold a much deeper significance than mere superficiality. The only way to convey the intensity of meaning is through language. A believer's words can manifest in the way they are spoken, and many angels can say "Ameen" in unison.

As per the teachings of Islam, believers are instructed to hold onto words that resonate with the holy book Quran and keep them close to their hearts. The words we speak hold immense power and should be used in a positive sense, even during times of hardship. For believers, choosing the best words and manifesting them into actions is crucial. It is the beat of a true believer.

When words accurately convey their meaning, their consideration is valid. Self-defeating words and promises can be challenging to accept. In Islam, a person's inner characteristics are revealed through their words.

Quran: Surah Isra: 17;34.Allah says in the Quran: "And be true to every promise, for verily you will be called to account for every promise which you have made."

The Islamic faith places great emphasis on the importance of keeping one's word. According to this faith, if one doesn't mean what they say, they should not say it at all. This is because, in the absence of meaning, words have no value. Therefore, followers of Islam are willing to do anything to keep their word. In the Muslim world, integrity is highly valued, and it is seen as an essential trait, rather than just a document. While documents can bind words, it is the understanding of the terrain and processes of the Muslim world that truly matters.Today, symbolic values of integrity are being reexamined and held to a higher standard than ever before to ensure their survival. Building boundaries within relationships begins with self-awareness and self-correction, which are essential traits for maintaining integrity.

We need to bring up concerns for young individuals leaving home for education or economic improvement. At times, they return and adopt a quasi-atheist position, deviating from the principles of Islam. Some grasp ideas that do not align with Islamic beliefs. Modifying rules to give priority to self-wants. It is important to address the young as they are the future of Islam and hold its teachings for the next generations. Protecting them is our responsibility and not an infringement. This application of information about Islam is intended for all Muslims, including those born into the faith, those who have converted to Islam, and those who have strayed away from it. It is also a reminder for all Muslims to uphold our fundamental beliefs, as it is our duty to do so.

Islam does not permit modifications or adjustments to conform to human desires. The rules and laws prescribed in the holy book are not based on human inclinations, but rather on divine guidance. The purpose of these laws is to benefit humanity and not to cause any harm. Some people may convert to Islam without fully understanding its teachings, while others may follow it as a fad. There are converts in Muslim households who are more devoted than those who were born into the faith. Similarly, some people born and raised as Muslims may lose their way and follow societal trends instead of the true teachings of Islam.

Throughout their lives, humans can change their path and make different choices. Age does not necessarily determine whether someone is honest or deceitful. It may surprise some to know that a person's character can be as malleable as a rubber band, but ultimately their actions and words reflect their true nature. Allah understands the challenges that humans face in navigating the unknown and has written the story of each individual's life. However, the presence of deception in various environments can make it easier for individuals to act dishonestly.

The story of the noble aristocrat a Muslim cannot be amiss:

Migration has always been a part of life for Muslims and all humans. This event took place in times when the nobles ruled India. The rich and the nobles, although they knew alcohol was not permissible in Islam took to drinking habits and some kept it secretive while some indulged openly. Although Islam did not permit it, people accepted it as this is between Allah and the Muslims.

Dreams are a calling for many and a premonition for others. The nobleman had a dream and a voice called him to Mecca. The noble woke up crying and he said my call has come and I must answer. In his palace, he disposed of all alcohol. Soon he asked everyone to forgive him as he knew he would not return. The family was saddened by his words when they packed to sail the ship to Mecca.

As he said goodbye to his grounds of bliss and his palace he knew the upcoming land would not be like this. His young children, his wife, and servants sailed across the waters, eager to see Mecca. Soon the family and the servants fell ill upon reaching. Nurses and Doctors were called to cure the illness. He was told they had influenza. As a result, he urged the Doctors to give them medicine first, then come to him last.

Allah had a plan when it came to the nobleman's turn there was not enough medicine for him. After that, the doctors rushed to get more. He said don't worry I don't have much time. After he paid homage to Allah in Mecca. His time had come and his dream was true. Allah called him to his place to finish his last moments. He died in Mecca. He was buried by Prophet Muhammad's family.

The story is true. And many such stories live in families where dreams become the destiny of those who receive truth from Allah. It has become a part of families to deliver unforeseen results in the future. Only those whom Allah sees fit to see the dreams as truth he shows them. What most can't fathom this could happen to a common man. It's not what the deeds or the person did, it is the heart of the human Allah knows and he calls his humans to the path they seek. Had he not paid attention to his dreams, he would have missed the opportunity. Those who are aware of gratitude never miss the target, because Allah knows they know what's coming.

Story of a mother who made Salat a gift of Allah for her young son with sugar he loved:

Baba Fariduddin was a young boy whose mother wanted him to pray Salat. She placed sugar underneath his prayer rug every day, and he believed that Allah had given him the sugar. The mother's devotion to Allah and her son's education led her to use sugar to engage him in learning about Islam when he was a young boy.

With great enthusiasm, he performed Salat five times daily, in search of the hidden sugar beneath his prayer rug. His love for sugar drove him to become a devoted attendee of Salat at a young age; he desired Salat as much as he desired sugar. Although the mother's commitment never wavered, she forgot to place the sugar under the rug one day, and she was afraid that her son wouldn't find it after praying Salat. To her surprise and joy, she saw him eating the sugar in front of her.

She asked him if the sugar was under his rug. He replied affirmatively, stating that it was there every day. Allah kept her face in front of the little boy, and she expressed her gratitude to Him. All she wanted from him was to pray, and she no longer put sugar. Nevertheless, Allah rewarded her intention. He placed the sugar for the young boy.

Despite her unintentional forgetfulness, Allah never forgot her intention. Consequently, the story of Baba Sheikh Farid Shakar Gung spread widely, earning him the name of Saint Baba Sheikh Farid Shakar Gung. He was given the name "Saint Baba Sheikh Farid Shakar Gung," which means he received sugar. He not only received sugar, but also Allah's mercy and fulfilled his mother's wish to learn recitation and love Salat. He became renowned as a saint. Some mothers who are unfamiliar with Salat still pray to Allah and teach their children. Hope and desire are embodied in stories. Certain individuals, regardless of age, find no significance in Salat. It is of immeasurable value to numerous Muslims.

Islam's five pillars are non-negotiable. Muslims believe in monotheism and accept Muhammad as the last prophet. Salat is also mandatory.

Giving (Zakat) alms is not mandatory if the giver is incapable. Islam is a logical and fact-based religion. Women who are pregnant, nursing, or menstruating are exempt from fasting for some time. Common sense is the foundation of faith, with legal laws and regulations that cannot be altered by humans. Hajj is a pilgrimage that is meant only for those who are capable of affording it and making necessary arrangements. In Islam, a modest dress code applies to all venues. Ramadan is a holy month for Muslims and is mandatory for those who are able to fast. Following the rules prescribed by doctors is not a burden, but rather Allah's laws become a burden for those who fail to understand their benefits. Ramadan is a time of gratitude for Muslims. What does Ramadan mean for Muslims?

During Ramadan, Muslims fast from dawn until sunset for 30 days. Suhoor, which is the pre-dawn meal, is the time Muslims wake up to eat. During the fast, one refrains from eating, drinking, and having sexual relations with their spouse during fast. However, daily activities such as work continue as usual. Muslims break their fast (iftar) after sunset with food preparation and aroma. Heartfelt invitations are sent to bring together non-Muslims and Muslims alike.

Ramadan is a time of festivities and worship for Muslims. It is a time of joy, abundance, and extended prayers (Taraweeh) at the mosque or at home. Throughout the month, the Quran is read from cover to cover, and women showcase their culinary skills. Guests who visit during Ramadan are aware of the significance of this month, which is all about worship and giving.

The month of Ramadan, the focus for Muslims is not on bling and gift-giving. Instead, they seek forgiveness and practice forgiving others for any wrongs committed. Muslims spend time asking for repentance and hoping for blessings during this blessed month. Despite facing hunger, those who fast remain steadfast in their devotion, with every part of their body and mind participating in the fast.

Fasting is not just about keeping yourself hungry, it is a spiritual act of devotion that brings us closer to our belief in Allah. It is believed that one cannot endure fasting unless it is for Allah alone. While some may argue that Allah doesn't want us to go hungry, the truth is that fasting is about spirituality and control of the soul (nafs). Fasting dates back to the Prophets, and Allah has prescribed it as a way to cleanse our souls and draw closer to Him.

During Ramadan, Muslims observe fasting as a way to gain a closer relationship with Allah and seek solace. It is an act of mercy to believers and an opportunity to spend time with oneself and keep company with other believers who are also seeking spiritual growth. Therefore, fasting should not be seen as a mere act of hunger, but rather a means to purify the mind, body, and soul.

Ramadan is more than just abstaining from food and water. It is a spiritual dependence on the Creator that involves the whole being, not just the body. For Muslims, it is a blessing that is given without any expectations of who is fasting. Believers eagerly wait for this month each year, knowing the blissfulness of it, something that non-fasting individuals cannot understand. During Ramadan, Muslims exchange food and gifts to rebuild friendships and relationships. Fasting Muslims have a different attitude than non-fasting Muslims during Ramadan.

People have different ways of spending their time - some work long hours, some pursue academic interests, sports, or travel. For some, the month of Ramadan is a time to test their faith and prioritize their spiritual pursuits by refraining from eating. Ramadan has a special atmosphere that is both inviting and spiritual. During Ramadan, Muslims fast and correct their flaws, which helps them filter out behaviors that are not acceptable to Allah. Despite the physical hunger, a Muslim's heart remains free of hatred or malice and instead is filled with a spirit of sharing and worship. This month creates time for reflection, devotion, and understanding.

Allah has granted a Muslim the chance to invoke the supreme ruler, the possessor of the world. Muslims consider this month sacred, so how can they disregard it? The beauty of this month often moves Muslims to tears as they beseech Allah for forgiveness. The world brims with happiness. The prayer is a way for humans to connect with Allah. Fasting is common in all Abrahamic faiths, but Islam dedicated an entire month, Ramadan, as a mercy to humanity for purifying the body, mind, and devotion to Allah. Muslims invite neighbors to share by sending food trays during Ramadan. Each year of Ramadan is highly anticipated by sharers and Muslims. During the blessed month of Ramadan, angels visit Muslim homes as Satan remains bound. After hearing the Quran, a few Jinns embraced Islam. Evil is not inherent in all jinns. Just Satan and his followers.

Quran: Surah Ahqaf: 46:29. Mention O Muhammad when WE directed to you a few of the jinn listening to the Quran. They attended it and said 'Listen quietly" When it was concluded, they went back to their people as warners.

During Ramadan, Satan is chained for one month while leaving his army behind. His legacy of evil lives on through his people. Jinns belong to Satan's family. Similar to humans, Jinns can be either good or bad. Similarly, they can choose to embrace or reject the faith of Allah. The day of judgment will also examine their actions.

Ramadan is a time of spiritual reflection and giving for believers. Although it is dedicated to Allah, everything we do during this time benefits us as humans. Believers' worship of Allah does not increase his divinity nor bring any benefit to Allah, but it is only beneficial for the soul. During Ramadan, Muslims focus on self-correction, spirituality, and self-worth. The act of worship itself is a gift and not all humans are blessed with it. Ultimately, Allah is the only one worthy of worship.

Starving the soul while feeding the mouth is worse than starving the soul while feeding the mouth. Starving the mouth but feeding the soul is the best strategy. It is only a believer who can understand this statement. Disbelievers may view the concept as heedless. However, a believer knows that spiritual nourishment is more important than physical nourishment. Nevertheless, maintaining a healthy physical and spiritual balance is essential.Worldly gains are temporary and fleeting, and should not be pursued at the cost of one's spiritual well-being. Feeding your soul and resisting temptation can lead to a life free of guilt and regret. Accumulating possessions that do not please Allah have no true value or benefit, and often come at a high price or are short-lived.

When the soul is neglected, the body cannot be nourished. Ramadan provides Muslims with an opportunity to reflect on their blessings and express gratitude for them through fasting, prayer, and spiritual contemplation. Ultimately, the purpose of Ramadan is to draw closer to God by purifying the soul. Understanding the value of this juncture can help a person structure their desires, wants, and discipline in life. For Muslims, the significance of this short month of worship can sometimes feel underestimated. It requires many hours of repeating prayers and listening to and reading the Quran.

Only Allah and a believer can truly understand a believer's affairs. There's so much happiness in the world and the sky appears beautiful, providing shelter without any pillars. Even when rain showers come, they bring pleasantries. The earth welcomes believers and the relationship between a servant and their creator is a grand affair. During this time, Muslims put aside their prejudices or disagreements and share kind words and gifts to please Allah.The soul's core is found within the heart. The heart's stance is evident in its actions.

The actions of Muslims in this month reveal their innermost desires. Blaming Satan is not an option. He left his people to endorse the acts that Allah detests. If Allah wishes, he can bring about change. He will populate hell with humans and jinns. Jinns are Satan's family. He's not a fallen angel or a dark angel. Those who search for truth will discover that Allah resolves all doubts in Islam and the Quran. Repentance is an option, but consistent defiance after being warned has consequences. Why do people follow human laws instead of Allah's? Both the defiant and the obedient can discover the answer.

Quran: Surah Araf: 172 We have destined for hell multitudes of jinn and humans.

They have hearts with which they do not understand; eyes with which they do not see, and ears with which they do not hear. These are like cattle. They are further astray. These are heedless.

Sick people are exempt from fasting for Ramadan. But encouraged to feed at least one person per day. Muslims see this month as a privilege to share (iftar) break of fast customs with both Muslims and non-Muslims. The reformation of a Muslim during Ramadan is like a renaissance of behavior. It is a time of spiritual awakening that makes the soul aware of its true nature as the world becomes more alive.

As a part of the spiritual cleansing process, every part of the body fasts and refrains from prohibited acts. The departure of Ramadan is mourned by Muslims as if a close friend has left. Although Islam requires five daily prayers, the depth of spirituality experienced during Ramadan cannot be explained. This is a journey that only a Muslim can truly understand. For non-Muslims, merging with Muslims and fasting can be a challenge. This sparkle marks the start of their journey as Allah wills. The day of celebration is when EID returns every year. Once the 30-day fast is over. This day is celebrated by all Muslims. The starting point is the mosque. Morning prayer. Celebrating Eid al fitr.

Quran: Surah Baqarah 2:183. Allah guides whom he wills O, believers! We prescribe fasting for you—as it was for those before you—so perhaps you will become mindful.

Gratefulness for Ramadan, and allowance to worship Allah, a Muslim, is happiness.

Quran: Surah Hud 120: Everything we narrate to you of the history of the messengers is to strengthen your heart therewith. The truth has come to you in this, and a lesson reminder for believers.

Sustenance, known as "Rizq" to Muslims, is a crucial part of their faith. According to Islamic belief, Allah has already determined the extent of everything in this world, including sustenance. Both believers and non-believers receive sustenance from Allah, but it is the believers who understand its true value. Allah provides for the needs of a believer, from a companion to a believing home, a faithful spouse, and offspring, to money, health, and spirituality, all covered under a maintenance allowance. However, it's worth noting that not everyone receives the same allowances from Allah.

While Allah provides sustenance to both believers and non-believers, it's the believers who derive more pleasure from it. They recognize and appreciate Allah's blessings, and their hearts are filled with gratitude and abundance. It is a blessing from Allah that one can achieve success in both materialism and spirituality. Wealth originates from within and reflects the genuine virtues of kindness, hope, and patience, honoring Allah's grace and kindness towards them.

Quran: Surah Hadid 57: On the day you shall see the believing men and the believing women, their light running forward before them and by their right hands. Glad tidings for you today! Gardens under which rivers flow (Paradise) to dwell forever! This is a great success!

Quran: Surah Rahman 55:38. Gratitude remains the key ingredient of this faith in Islam. So which of the favors of your Lord would you deny?

Islamic stories serve as a way for Muslims to align their moral compass and be guided towards goodness. When one's heart is pure and desires kindness without seeking validation from others, Allah rewards them with His kindness and mercy. Throughout many stories of gratitude and kindness, Allah has blessed those who have shown compassion and generosity with tenfold rewards. Giving is a privilege that should be embraced. In Islam, it is believed that jinns and animals share a similar sense of courtesy towards each other and their own kind. Giving solely to show off is not considered true giving, but rather a self-serving display of ego. Allah, the Almighty, knows the intentions and motivations behind every act of giving.

On a scorching hot day in Arabia, a woman stumbled upon a stray dog panting with its mouth wide open, clearly in need of water. Without hesitation, the woman took off her shoe and poured water into it. Despite the pain from walking barefoot on the hot ground, she didn't think twice about quenching the dog's thirst. This selfless act of kindness was witnessed by Allah, who recognized it as a pure and genuine form of giving. Allah sees the deeds of His slaves and rewards good intentions. The kindness of Allah towards His slaves has no bounds, regardless of doubts, grandeur, or self-attributed accomplishments. Whenever a Muslim refrains from doing something impermissible for the sake of Allah, an angel records it as a good deed..

Allah's mercy brings a tenfold compensation. Retribution is not the purpose of the delay. Obeying Allah leads to victory. The strength given by Allah is not weakness. It's possible to go against a person's expectations. Allah's power becomes evident when humans abstain from their desires and are fearful of disobeying Allah. Allah allows for fluctuations in faith, but the path to redemption always involves returning to worship and repentance. In Islam, kindness cannot be selective.

The religion promotes unity and equality among all people and expects its followers to exhibit kindness and compassion towards everyone. By embracing the simplicity of this faith, individuals can find peace and blessings from Allah. It is important to note that Allah understands that humans are inherently flawed and unjust. However, choosing Islam as one's religion means striving towards justice and righteousness.

Having a lack of understanding of the Islamic faith can lead a person to behave negligently. This can result in a person disregarding manners and becoming arrogant, which is a behavior that is not acceptable in Islam. The act of pride is reserved only for Allah. As a Muslim, the ultimate goal is to achieve the best version of Islam and succeed in this world. It is important to hold on to this world while keeping Islam in our hearts. Muslims should aim to thrive in this life by doing good deeds that will benefit them in the afterlife as well. In Islam, family involvement is not a factor in determining pride in one's achievements. Pride belongs solely to Allah.

Quran: Surah Ibrahim 14:34 Who gave you all that you asked Him for? Were you to count the favors of Allah? You shall never be able to encompass them. Verily, man is highly unjust and exceedingly ungrateful.

Doom is heavier than bliss in the hearts of the proud. The story of the man Allah gave two gardens is an example of pride (Kibr). He said that his garden would never perish. He gave no thanks to Allah. The darkness within him overtook his pride.

Quran: Surah Kahf 18:32:44.And present to them an example of two men: We granted one of them two gardens of grapevines. We bordered them with palm trees and placed them between them [fields of] crops.

The story in Surah Kahf displays the wealth of a man including picturesque gardens, silver, and gold, as well as flowing clear water with rivers. Having virtuous, wealthy, and spiritual children is Allah's gift to parents. Such a family is the envy of many and a blessing from Allah. A good mind, heart, and body are part of their possessions. Those who are always subservient and grateful receive more. The greater their gratitude, the more blessings they receive. Lack of gratitude leads to perpetual dissatisfaction. The blessings go beyond material wealth and encompass spiritual and intellectual riches as well. It's crucial to appreciate the gifts we have been given.

Gratitude is the key to unlocking even more blessings. The predominant infection in stories of bliss versus contempt for family or gatherings is a loss of spirituality that leads to malice. Each individual's external beauty is subjective. Discontent believers accuse others of jealousy when it comes to an individual's exterior appearance.

Sometimes even the happy disposition of others comes at the cost of sarcasm and insults. The power of gratitude is low as those who believe know their looks are granted to them by Allah. Certain premature believers find external appearances appealing added spirituality makes a human beautiful. The hope to see within oneself is the best of prayers for a destitute of solace within. Success in worldly pursuits and self-solace are prime indicators of wealth in this society. Prophets have been granted riches, so minting money is not evil. Its effectiveness depends on how it is used. To apply this methodology, it is crucial to understand how it was accomplished. Every avenue plays a role in life.

Having been granted (Rizq) sustenance in every season, there is no need to fight for riches. Trying is a daily factor, not knowing the unknown is a preliminary worry, but ultimately, what is yours will reach you. When spirituality is present, the inner beauty makes the outer even more attractive for those seeking serenity. Those with spirituality often view someone without spirituality as incomplete. They strive to nurture and develop their spirituality, creating a more fulfilling life.

Neither academic skills nor understanding could be achieved without a mind from Allah. Any resource, for that matter, unless it is allotted to each individual temporarily or permanently cannot reach until Allah gives it. Without compassion, a human wouldn't see the beauty of stories that could change human attitudes. The overconfident man in Surah Kahf attributed all his gifts and accomplishments to himself. He idolized his actions and showed no gratitude to Allah.

Quran: Surah Kahf 18:32.And his fruits were ruined, so he began to turn his hands about [in dismay] over what he had spent on it. While it had collapsed upon its trellises, and said, "Oh, I wish I had not associated with my Lord anyone."

In the end, the downfall outweighed the gains. He cried out to Allah in dismay. There is nothing owned by a human. A human is a taker of the gifts Allah gives. As his pride overpowers his gratitude, Allah gradually takes it away from him. This discourse affects humans in some fashion. Some may never see an individual's downfall. Sometimes it is apparent, and sometimes only he sees it. Stories in the Quran emphasize the importance of gratitude over pride. It also ensures the protection of all humanity, not just Muslims. Both men and women can benefit from this.

The Quranic stories can be paraphrased, but when one understands Arabic, the beauty in words becomes more profound. It is said that the Quranic words have a power that can move a human heart. It is an extraordinary and beautiful experience to understand the words in Arabic, the original language of the Quran.

Evil plays a role in corrupting the hearts of those who answer his calls, as his pride got him out of heaven. Pride is a disease without gratitude in Islam, just as the ego endures harsh life experiences. One's ego sometimes gets in the way, and he refuses to accept good so he can prove he is right.

Humans can't compete with Allah's rules, as they are unalterable. The structure of Islam has left nothing for man to wonder about. Allah covers every intricate detail of this plateau of life. Allah has also shown Muslims how to worship him at specified times. A human can pray countless times and have intimate talks with his creator, but mandatory Salat ritual prayers are not to be negated. Tahajud is the voluntary prayer that Muslims aspire to attend in the early hours after sleep.

Each fiber of our being is attentive to Allah during Salat's ritual prayers. The body bends in humility, and the heart fills with worship of God. All parts of a human in submission to Allah attest that the mouth, tongue, heart, brain, and body work together in worship. No segregation in prayer. All Muslims must perform Salat ritual prayers in Arabic. Muslims were required to pray the five daily ritual prayers. The choice to follow the rules is the responsibility of every Muslim, but Allah did not command forces.

It linked the consequence of disobedience to the dissatisfaction of the soul.

Having a responsibility requires a parent to explain Islam's faith to their children. They are to be taught, not given choices. Should they learn about Allah or not?

Islam holds parents responsible for their offspring.

Allah will question parents why they did not teach their children Islam and the Quran if they were born to Muslim parents.Islam is not a force, but an aid to understanding the beliefs and practices of the faith. This is a method of learning where parents only supervise. It is possible that the stories on certain social media platforms are not accurate. They could confuse the reader when they read the text of the Quran and the hadiths.

(Salat) ritual prayer is also available on social media, but parents should monitor it for children and first-time converts or beginners learning Islam. A human being is the most influential player in his own life. His attendees serve as watchers, whereas he plays an active role as he progresses or regresses in the time allotted to him by Allah. There are serious implications to following or not following the justice system of Allah, which will have the final say.

They have accused Muslims of being too religious if their attendance to daily ritualistic prayers is consistent. It's called being a Muslim. People who pray most humbly are incapable of not showing gratitude and kindness. True worshipers have their own space and place.

The ground is fertile, and gratitude comes when Allah deems one fit to pray to him.

Allah granted believers allowances and mercy through prayer. If the soul shifts to arrogantly disobeying Allah, he finds himself in turmoil or in nonexistence. Such souls are heavy. Some born into this faith or converts to Islam may pacify others by saying all faiths are the same.

Although all faiths in Islam acknowledge the existence of each individual following their creed, they are not equal. Just as a polytheist is not the same as a monotheist. Keeping society in mind while coming to terms with Islam. Showing cordial behavior towards others, but compromising Islam at the expense of deviant behavior, is not Islamic.

As an Abrahamic faith Christianity. In gratitude they thank Jesus as a holy central figure, seen as someone to be worshiped. The worship of these sects is the same. Jesus is the figure attached to God. Muslims have no God but Allah. Islam sees mortal worship as paganism. Facts can be crucial to understanding the differences.

Across all professional, academic, and social settings, people get along. A dilemma arises when these humans intrude their belief systems on the lives of Muslim families.

In unions where Muslims are weak, pagan rituals can infiltrate at the risk of adapting peer pressure. Muslims cannot survive in such circumstances, since Islam is a monotheistic religion. Losing faith to impress a human is a poison that feeds death.

As a society, we get along with each other and accept others regardless of their faith or lack thereof. Despite being a Muslim, you cannot follow Islam when you combine it with paganism. Genuine Muslims will never compromise their faith for the benefit of others' beliefs. Muslims will stand firm in their faith no matter what. It is Islam that comes first, then a human being for a practicing Muslim. Since human beings can change. Actions that have consequences are more important than forceful acts. To please a human, we cannot deceive the highest.

Some Muslims are also seeking and embracing change and integration with current environments, or are bewildered by laws and regulations that don't match current society and are therefore rebelling against them to demonstrate that they are modern. Regardless of the outcome, Islam won't appease humans. Human courts have laws. The laws of Allah will not change to appease human desires. Islam is a closing statement.

Revisions have removed certain texts and added others in other biblical texts.

Allah sets rules, and Jesus is his servant and Messiah. All other Prophets hold the same as bringers of good news and consistently worship one God (Allah), not a human. In terms of belief systems, these faiths do not mix, but there are many friendships between them and Muslims. The friendship between Muslims and Christians dates back to the time of the Prophet Muhammad. The king of Abyssinia was a Christian. While Muslims were being persecuted by the clan of opposition, the Quraish, he gave them asylum. King Negus of Abyssinia. Known as present-day Ethiopia. Later converted to Islam and became a follower of the Prophet Muhammad's teachings.

It is only when lifestyles are at a crossroads with Islamic beliefs becoming a paradox of opposition that the environment becomes incompatible. This can even happen within Muslim families. It occurs when conflicts arise among those who follow the faith to see the members of the family affected by the motion of disobedience to Islam. In any land, anyone can survive as long as the foundation of their core is strong and rooted in their place.

As long as the foundation helps others gain balance along the way, a believer cannot oscillate on the whims of disbelievers. The affliction affects families that break ties of faith, usually resulting from pseudo-cultures or women and men not following the values and scripts of their respective faiths. This can destroy Muslim families and cause resentment. As for Muslims, they put Allah first, not humans. Despite their differences, these faiths remained friendly. The only time this cannot work is with morally corrupt individuals.

Exposure to such an environment may have intensified the beliefs of Muslims. Those invited by Allah receive a balanced gift that leads them to faith. Humans naturally tend to be drawn to others who share their beliefs and habits. "I can tell who you are by looking at your friends," says Prophet Muhammad. The customs and practices of the Prophet Muhammad are followed by Muslims.

He preferred the company of men over women as friends. Women sought his guidance for faith and family matters, not for friendships or socializing. He preferred spending time with the women in his own family rather than befriending women from other men's families. He kept friendships with men and respectfully addressed concerns from both men and women.

This dilemma is sometimes exaggerated. Nevertheless, every scenario and necessity varies. Help is different from socialization when it comes to unauthorized relationships. Within specific acceptable contexts. It becomes a habit for a woman to spend time with a forbidden man. Islam discourages such acts because they have caused many broken relationships. In the realm of deceptive connections, desire, and fake bonds. Islam alluded to this before it gained mainstream recognition. Marriage is the ideal setting for attraction, not fornication.

However, interference and neglect pose problems for Muslims when they affect their faith and relationships with Muslim life partners. Dilution of morals may occur, but change is always necessary. In these societies, it is common for people to hold delusional views or for Muslims raised in misguided environments to adopt different cultures. Muslim youth and mature Muslims have a keen interest in sports and business, process ideologies, theology, and career paths. Some Muslim youth and mature Muslims are not affected by false teachings or cultural influences.

Plant a fruit-bearing tree, not a thorny one. When a man rubs against it, it leaves thorns. Such is the example of disbelievers to believers. It does not impose gratitude on the smallest things and gifts. It's not forced, it's willful.Life is a continuous process of sharing and caring in private, in person, and in others' company. These traits are not exclusive to certain individuals. Islam is not guided by human might. It's destined. Those born into Muslim families or who convert to Islam remain grateful to Allah.

Quran: Surah An'am 6:116. O Prophet!` If you obeyed most of those on earth, they would lead you away from Allah's Way. They follow assumptions and lie.

Quran: Surah Talaq 65 (Whoever fears Allah keeps his duty to him, he will make a way for him to get out from every difficulty provisions from sources he never could imagine.

And whosoever puts his trust in Allah, then he will suffice him. Verily, Allah will accomplish his purpose. Indeed, Allah has set a measure for all things.

Quran: Surah Imran.3:31–32. Tell people: 'If you indeed love Allah, follow me, and Allah will love you and will forgive you your sins. Allah is All-Forgiving and all-compassionate.

Confidence is a priceless quality that is unparalleled by individuals. The fear of Allah eradicates human fear. Surrendering to Allah dispels all uncertainties and instills optimism and aspiration into the magnificence of life. Virtue lies in excellence. A believer's actions are guided by Allah. Allah has charted all paths and directions. The disbelievers' actions are a reflection of his use of the accursed Satan.

Excellence and virtue come from a continuous process of learning and sharing. The defining characteristic of discipline is consistency. Having the courage to defend one's beliefs is a testament to inner strength and self-confidence.Those who believe find Allah. Perseverance belongs to the believers. The pursuit of belief is not limited to believers, it can also be embraced by disbelievers.

CHAPTER 7

ISLAM REACHED ITS ZENITH WITH THE PROPHET MUHAMMAD.

Believers' convictions possess the power to move mountains, shift water in the meadows, change inertia, and more. The power of belief knows no limits. Fear is the priority for a hypocrite, not belief.The presence of belief can be observed amidst apparent chaos when a strong bond weaves with passion. Those who understand the power and beauty of faith can achieve the impossible. The quantum belief rule must be understood to have knowledge of this system. Faith in Allah can work miracles for a devoted believer, even without logic. If the truth exists, why can't logic reconcile with the belief? Islam isn't opposed to logic, but it rejects fiction and offers truth to seekers.

Blaming is a distraction from learning to change the subject or grasp negativity's undertones. This results in dissatisfaction. Muslims possess an unshakable belief due to the logic and facts of Islam. It's not compelled, it's about choosing and comprehending the methodology. Thriving in a society that falsely labels Islam as terror is not scary for those who are aware of the truth. Islam will persevere, unfazed by the unjust claims as the true winner is fearless against manufactured threats. The truth is obscured by lies in the literal evidence.

Times Magazine: Jan 21, 2021 — It said that more than 60,000 books were written against Islam, in 150 years. ...

Npr: Muslims are erased and stereotyped in TV series, a study.

Islami City: Mar 14, 2006 — Islam has had many enemies over the centuries and still has. One of the most persistent lies repeated by its detractors is that Muslims spread ...

Cnn: Sep 11, 2022 — Despite making up one-quarter of the world's population, Muslims are severely underrepresented on television – and when they are represented ...

To counter Islam in a threatened society, the best approach is to exploit Muslims to create division and disrupt families. If there was no fear of Islam distorting the truth and gaining followers through deception, there would be no negative attention or mention of a growing faith. Understanding the core beliefs of a personal shift in faith is crucial, but social media platforms spreading Islamophobia cannot serve as credible teachers of Islam.

However, they can contribute to the propagation of evil. Many comedians use this drama to gain an audience by showing the address or regress used in comedy, which has become comical. The humor is for those who can tolerate the rationale. Comedians have the power to distort truth or speak truth through jokes, sometimes targeting Islam or supporting it, but Muslims remain unaffected as life goes on. When lies encounter truth, it becomes easier for humans to believe it's natural. Mixing previous scriptures with truth makes it easier to believe, but lies are easily distinguishable, so the tactic of evil is to mix with truth.

Islamophobic politicians exploit Islam for their own gain by capitalizing on the fears and prejudices of the population. They often make grand promises of fighting Islamophobia and ensuring national safety, but in reality, they only perpetuate lies and deceit to maintain their power. This exploitation not only harms the Muslim community but also undermines the principles of democracy and equality.

In order to break free from this cycle of deceit and manipulation, it becomes a duty for young Muslims born in these regions to educate themselves and challenge the dogma of deceit. By promoting a more inclusive and tolerant understanding of Islam, they can help their fellow citizens overcome their prejudices and foster a society that values diversity and mutual respect.

It is important to note that the effects of this exploitation are felt most strongly by those who struggle to make ends meet or belong to the shrinking middle class. The wealthy, often shielded from the consequences of Islamophobia, may even exploit their own people for personal gains.

However, at its core, this issue is not solely about faith or belief; it is about recognizing the humanity and dignity of all individuals, regardless of their religious background. While many benefit from challenging Islamophobia, it is the Muslims who thrive in this climate that become shining examples of how their faith can inspire them to help all of humanity, transcending religious boundaries.

Society is lacking in knowledge and awareness. Picturesque scenes are utilized to spread fabricated lies as news. Islam is devoid of fear. Those who twist and fabricate the truth are threatened by fear of Islam. Fabricating falsehoods and orchestrating attacks on Islam and Muslims wouldn't be a realistic course of action.

Instead of acquiring knowledge about these catalysts for regime change, persist in spreading deceitful negative rhetoric. The dilemma lies in referring to the wrong sources, despite the availability of free classes and donations for knowledge. Muslims need to combat evil with the truth. They can use their creativity to excel.

In order to combat the lack of knowledge and awareness in society, it is important for Muslims to actively engage in spreading the truth and dispelling falsehoods. This can be done through various means, such as utilizing their creativity and imagination to create satire news channels that highlight ignorance and misconceptions about Islam. Muslims can also play a crucial role as teachers, guiding those who struggle to educate themselves and providing accurate information about their faith

. However, it is essential to be cautious of those who manipulate thawed-out regimes and conceal the truth with deceit. Muslims must question oppositions and be aware of Islamophobia, who resort to falsehoods, deception, scheming, and shifting blame in order to gain power and target Islam. It is disheartening to see shows that perpetuate ignorance about Muslims and portray them as backward, when in reality, Muslims have helped to bring light and knowledge to the world during the dark ages of Europe and continue to excel.

Muslims will not stoop to the level of making fun of their opposition or resorting to demeaning tactics. Instead, they focus on excelling in various fields such as social media, theater, politics, law, medicine, real estate, mortgage, psychiatry, contrasting theology, teachers, chefs, pilots, politicians, and any other field that benefits humanity.

By actively contributing to these areas, Muslims can help the world progress and move away from the dark ages, rather than joining the repressed darkness. It is the duty of every Muslim to excel and teach the world in order to uplift humanity and promote self-worth. They should stand firm on their progress and not compromise their faith to gain popularity or spread lies. Muslims have a responsibility to represent Islam in a positive light and contribute positively to society, bringing about positive change and dispelling misconceptions.

Establishing a front line of faith, truth stands strong against the world's lies. For those who do not identify as Muslims, Islam's concerns are not the most common. They do not echo through news headlines or political debates. However, Islam does not blame anyone and does not need to blame anyone. Muslims will have to endure many trials to stand for the truth at the end of time. Many misunderstand Islam and become servants to its facade. Regardless of one's beliefs or disagreements, Islam has never disrespected any faith. Its theology is based on truth, not lies. You can either accept it or reject it. There is no fear in truth, but there is fear in lies.

Muslims must support Muslim countries under oppression and distress until the world appendix changes. Deception cannot be used to barricade oneself from acceptance by society. This is causing harm and setting up stages to control the minions who believe and fall for the rhetoric. The light of reason cannot value darkness under the false guise of assistance. When truth becomes visible, lies can be confronted. If one knows the stager, how can one fall for the stage where the curtain closes before drawing? Evidence will prove itself.

Muslim countries must support weaker Muslim countries. The issue is not about prejudice; it is about strength to strengthen the world. Muslims have brought strength, learning, and teaching to the world. They will continue to do so if they stand together and include all humanity in our endeavors. Many youths have contemplated whether they should refer to themselves as Muslims after watching these evil performances, printed rhetoric shows, and false portrayals of Islam and Muslims. Having a firm understanding of academic and social life within this society will enable one to mix with other cultures.

It is expected to excuse intentional acts that become fake apologies for human shortcomings. Islam represents itself. When something is fair and sure of its actions, no apology is required. Mistakes require apologies, but fair contracts and deliveries do not require them. A faith uncorroded and unapologetic, Islam will finally be the only one standing before the world winds down. Why is the Muslim so sure? Didn't worship originate from the first creation of one god? The one God worshiped is Allah, whatever you want to call him.

Islam is not based on shaky grounds appealing to the common mind if the basis of understanding is clear. Know Islam in its entirety, not through followers who also make mistakes. Allah gave intelligence to a human, who cannot expect to believe without logic and sense.

In the absence of knowledge, this rhetoric can lead to regime changes among Muslims. Social peer pressure compels newly converted converts, ignorant individuals, and Muslims who are impersonated by society to demonstrate modernity and follow trends. Faded and corroded backward ways are for the uninformed. They isolate and learn from social media, or negative sources, which portray Islam as violent and ignorant without a basic understanding of Islam.

It's a dangerous game, but Islamophobia needs to be addressed by educated Muslims and monitored. Islam's fear is so high that they spend all their time staging Muslims. Most humans challenge lies, as loss is inevitable. Hiding in hypocrisy is another source that becomes visible as evil reveals itself, as the source is weak. The Prophet of Islam did not have to lie and exploit others to triumph. Truth is the only way to win, not staged lies.

Media portrayals of illiterate and young people who spread lies and make fun of themselves have to be stopped in an era of multiculturalism. Muslims are not using Biblical books to mock them. It is rhetorical that the world documents their changes, but Islam does not thrive on downing other cultures, or religious beliefs it thrives on its foundation. Theological contrast is about learning beliefs, not exploiting others, but expressing truth in Abrahamic faith and differences. Truth-seeking humanity doesn't get offended because insults hold no power.

They blame most wars on Muslims. The rhetoric thrives on blame. The more Muslims are blamed, the less likely to weaken sources but strengthen humanity. Instigation and battle are different strategies. If one has fewer means, don't overpower the other. Islam is fair in all aspects of life. Islam teaches such simple lessons as morals, ethics, science logic, and empowering knowledge, but dumbing down Muslims by showcasing ignorance in this society is not Islam. Muslims are teachers and will be for years to come.

The Quran introduced numerous subjects that were unfamiliar to humans until they started exploring. Some topics to discuss are: science, astronomy, embryology, laws and contracts, big bang theory, and expansion of the universe.

Islam is both logical and factual, therefore no fallacy exists within it. Cross-referencing the Quran is advantageous for truth seekers. The Quran brings provision, peace, and answers to questions, transforming strangers into confidants on the path to Islam. Knowledge leads to bliss, while ignorance leads to tragedy. Curious minds and critics prefer exploration-based choices, while truth-seekers have a unique style. Some individuals have faith without question, while others insist on receiving answers. The most effective way to converse and seek answers is by reading the Quran and learning daily with a practicing Muslim.

Water is essential for all living organisms, and the ocean acts as a major source of freshwater through the global water cycle. The process begins with the ocean's vast surface area, which allows for evaporation to occur. As the sun's heat causes water to evaporate from the ocean's surface, it forms clouds in the atmosphere.

These clouds eventually release the condensed water as precipitation, which falls onto the land and replenishes rivers, lakes, and groundwater sources. In this way, the ocean plays a crucial role in maintaining the earth's water supply and sustaining life on land. Additionally, the ocean's diverse ecosystems support a wide range of species that contribute to the overall health of the planet.

From phytoplankton that produce oxygen through photosynthesis to large marine mammals that help regulate populations of other marine organisms, the ocean's biodiversity is vital for maintaining a balanced and thriving ecosystem. Furthermore, the ocean's vast expanse offers an exciting opportunity for exploration and discovery.

Scientists have only explored a small fraction of the ocean's depths, leaving much of its mysteries yet to be uncovered. From uncovering ancient shipwrecks to discovering new species, the ocean continues to captivate and inspire researchers and explorers. In summary, the ocean is not only vital for regulating the climate and providing sustenance but also offers a world of untapped potential and endless possibilities for humanity.

Islam, as a religion, encompasses a vast array of teachings and principles that cover every aspect of life. It acknowledges the importance of the natural world and the wonders it holds, including the vastness of the ocean and the intricacies of the Earth. In the Quran, there are references to scientific concepts, such as the Big Bang theory, which have been seen by many as an affirmation of the compatibility between Islam and science. One intriguing example is the mention of the separation between two seas, one bitter and one sweet. This phenomenon, known as a halocline, occurs when two bodies of water with different salinity levels meet but do not mix. The Quran provides this information as a means to inspire contemplation and awe in the believers, as it highlights the intricate design and balance in the natural world.

Quran: Surah Furqan:25:53.And He it is Who has joined the two seas: one sweet and palatable and the other saltish and bitter; and He has set a barrier and an insurmountable obstruction between the two that keeps them apart.

When someone seeks Islam as their faith and embraces its teachings, they often experience a deep longing to know more about the truth and explore the depths of their newfound faith. This journey of seeking knowledge and understanding is encouraged in Islam, as it fosters a stronger connection with Allah and deepens one's faith.

The Quran encourages Muslims to question, reflect, and seek answers, as long as it is done with sincerity and the intention to seek truth. Once a person discovers the truth within Islam, it is rare for them to leave, as they have found a sense of purpose, guidance, and fulfillment. However, it is important to note that some individuals may still struggle with doubts or misinformation that may cause them to question their faith. Islam encourages believers to seek knowledge, to critically analyze information, and to discern between truth and falsehood.

Explaining the truth of Islam to others is considered a great benefit and Allah acknowledges the one who tries. Muslims are encouraged to share their knowledge and understanding of Islam with others, as long as it is done with respect, compassion, and a genuine desire to guide others towards the truth. It is through education, dialogue, and open-mindedness that misconceptions can be dispelled, and a greater understanding of Islam can be fostered. Ultimately, the goal is to invite others to embrace the truth and beauty of Islam, while leaving the decision of accepting or rejecting it to the individual.

Quran: Surah Anbiya: 21;20.Do the disbelievers not realize that the heavens and earth were once one mass then We split them apart? And We created from water every living thing. Will they not then believe?

Quran: Surah Al Muminun:23:18.And We have sent down rain from the sky in a measured amount and settled it in the earth. And indeed, We can take it away.

Quran: Surah Anbiya: 21:30:41. Life, therefore, depends entirely on the strange properties of water. Protoplasm is the basis of all living matter and the vital power of protoplasm.

Water is essential for the survival and functioning of every cell, tissue, and organ in the human body. It plays a crucial role in numerous bodily functions, such as regulating body temperature, transporting nutrients and oxygen, lubricating joints, and aiding in digestion. Without water, our bodies would not be able to carry out these vital processes. Additionally, water is vital for maintaining overall health and well-being. It helps to flush out toxins, supports healthy skin and hair, and promotes proper organ function. The importance of water is not only recognized by science and medicine but also emphasized in religious texts, including the Quran.

The Quran acknowledges the significance of water and its role in sustaining life on Earth, highlighting it as one of the blessings bestowed upon humanity. In the Quran, lush gardens with flowing rivers are described as a symbol of water and a promise of paradise. The beauty of greenery and flowers is enhanced by water.

However, those who deny will still be held accountable. Those who fail to understand the subtleties of truth can't understand the gravity of this punishment, yet they embrace defiance. Water replenishes the body and quenches thirst. Isn't it natural for a Muslim to have a strong desire for Islam? Wouldn't a Muslim naturally desire Islam considering water's importance to life? The body is mainly made of water and craves it, just as the soul longs for worshiping Allah for those who comprehend His essence.

Quran: Surah Muminon: 23:18.We send down rain from the sky in perfect measure, causing it to soak into the earth. And We are surely able to take it away.

Has the Quran addressed all possible subjects? Those in search of answers turn to the Quran as their only source. Those who have doubts never find what they're looking for. Doubters are not suited for Islam.

It's designed for those who believe and want clarity through knowledge, not blind faith. Questions meant for pondering have answers, rather than unanswered questions leading to answers. Islam is here to answer questions and verify the Quran''s truth.

Integrating the Quran into daily life is crucial for a Muslim's complete learning. Confusion arises when one fails to follow the virtues and discipline of Islam, leading to reliance on unreliable sources for answers.

A company that embodies virtues and beliefs enlivens believers.The deceiver uses negative connotations from deception to lull the believer into ignorance by envying those who adhere to truth. Sometimes Muslims show envy towards Muslims.

Deception leads to turmoil and pain, while genuine faith promotes peace and success. A person's actions are not isolated from society's deeds or drama. For some, the journey involves experiencing glitter, blitz, and pain in the temporal world. A human body's limbs and every aspect of creation that breathes have a purpose. Nothing he makes is without purpose. All parts of human anatomy will bear witness against you or for you on the day of judgment.

Islam's Prophet will witness how his (ummah) people followed or defied or followed his ways. Has the Quran made a difference? How one acts in solitude is his true self to analyze the person within.

The seasons of life can hold glimpses of light and shades of different colors. For some, all events and experiences of life can trigger a storm of delight or constructive thinking of avenues that bring the human to not replicating life as time passes.

Nothing remains the same except the deeds that accumulate like revenue that one cannot see. In Islam, angels are considered to be accounting agents for writing deeds as time progresses.

The beauty of these angels is that if one was planning an evil deed and refrained from it before committing the act displeasing to Allah, stopping and thinking and refraining from committing the impermissible act is written as an honorable deed. The good deeds can scratch out the bad deeds.

There is no accounting system or judgment in human transactions more fair than Allah's. Most believers think about not displeasing a human, but displeasing Allah is so simple. He is not visible, but he is nearer to us than anything visible.

In his weakened state, man is unable to perceive Allah in this life. Anyone who says they've seen God is making false statements. The key to facing Allah in the next life is preparation, as he is currently veiled.Muslims who adapted to Islam during Muhammad's time used rational beliefs and logic.

Because modern society's demand for self-desire and passion for lust, money, and greed are driving forces. Islam does not deem these qualities as serenity. Prophet Muhammad's triumph of Prophethood was a victory in both the secular and religious spheres.

Prophet Muhammad implemented the rules of both religious and secular combat jurisdictions. He partook in jihad struggles, efforts and combat with the people. He was not only a commander he was also a soldier with his people he did not waver to what he said, he did more than he told. By following his path and journey, he introduced a cleaner alternative to a cleaner path and tolerance in society.

Expressing the potential to grow mentally, physically, economically spiritually, balancing all fronts of human self-improvement. Islam benefits humans, not Allah. Muslims follow Islam's direction, rules, and regulations. People who live by their own rules emphasize their own rules and delegate right and wrong according to what suits them. In their corrections, the voices are harsh. In explaining rights and wrongs, Islam uses kindness.

Allah's voice is not harsh, but compassionate. Have humans truly heard the enigmatic voice of Allah? Humans use his voice metaphorically, not as a literal sound, but as mercy and kindness rest in his voice with justice. Those who believe and feel compassion give it back to the world instead of harshness. Through practicing believers and Allah's will.

Forgiveness and understanding lead those seeking kindness down the path of truth. Whomever he chooses, he guides his path. Islam does not provide people with any self-inflicted nuance, as no individual knows what offers the greatest benefit to themselves. Misbehavior that preserves one's values might contradict Islam's values but remains acceptable to the pseudo-society.

Integrating the Quran into daily life is crucial for a Muslim's complete learning. Confusion arises when one fails to follow the virtues and discipline of Islam, leading to reliance on unreliable sources for answers.

A company that embodies virtues and beliefs enlivens believers. It is best for believers to avoid evildoers who shamelessly propagate immorality and the acceptance of all evils in society. Society's standards may not align with Islam's beliefs. There are varying beliefs. In this world, there are both good and bad people, so choosing the right company is crucial.

Believers are not affected by inept societies and tough times, however, accepting all societal ills and social media can trigger unbridled human desires. For the weak and restless. Throughout history, all Prophets and the faithful to Allah have demonstrated the positive impacts of believers on society, as opposed to detracting from it.

Who says in a society where anything goes who becomes the voice of the correction especially when Divine laws are concerned? It's impossible to break human laws, but breaking Allah's laws or labeling them outdated is the cover-up of the deceitful.

Following the Quran for a Muslim is a must, a doctrine of beliefs spelled out. Allah's deliverance gave the Prophet of Islam a serious task for the people. Bowing to Allah is mercy allotted to humanity.

Allah does not need the prayers of his creation. Prophet Muhammed had all the endurance and tenacity to succumb to the upheavals, challenges, and turmoil phases of humanity. Humans respond to familiar or unfamiliar evil when truth delivery turns into anger and resentment from the opposition. This can apply to Muslims or non-Muslims.

Yet, hope outweighs the challenges of deceit that typically accompany a Muslim's defiance of Allah. A believer who follows the wrong path in temperance. Return to the path of truth stronger. In terms of the success of Islam and humanity as a whole, Prophet Muhammad was the most successful Prophet. In a matter of decades, he revolutionized the world, and his teachings continue to guide millions of people today. He taught the world how-to live-in harmony and peace with one another. He exemplified compassion and mercy. Millions of people around the world continue to be inspired by his example of a good life. Throughout his life, he taught and left behind the importance of kindness, justice, and equality. He left a lasting legacy that continues to shape the world today. People of all faiths, cultures, and backgrounds have embraced his teachings.

Generations to come will be influenced by his legacy. When stillness is present, doubts may seem promising, but isolation can sometimes end negativity and lead to positive certainty. Negative can be fleeting when we disconnect, but positive brings ultimate assurance to a seeking mind. Balance must be maintained between stillness and engagement. Even in the quiet times of solitude, Doubts can disturb the premise of those attempting to reason within and for betterment.

Focusing on corrections and solitude will help believers get closer to Allah. The most propitious period in human life is personal growth. The demons and predators are always seeking to destroy something perfectly spiritual, but coming to evil would be no cause, as it already belongs to them. Therefore, they invade believers' privacy. Disarray and nuisance are notable, and a change, of course, and believers return to Allah stronger. The essence of recognition lies in time. It is the strongest currency a human can hold for a short period of time.

To motivate and encourage someone to keep pushing forward, acknowledging their efforts or success is important. A lack of appreciation can, on the other hand, be detrimental to relationships and trust. Showing appreciation requires acknowledging people quickly and sincerely. An individual who comes to Allah in dependence and hope is appreciated by Allah. It goes far beyond a human who is a believer and does not show appreciation. These are not the traits of a believer. Those who are arrogant and look to feed enemies' spoils.

Even those who do not hold any religious belief sometimes hold their morals and integrity as a form of integrated internal mechanism a human has. However, a believer's rules are in communication with Allah. Some might comment that those who have no mind believe in books from the past. It outperforms any decade, as the Quran is not a product of the past, but of the present. Due to the challenge of bringing one verse, the most competent could not compete. The rules are set in stone by the creator, and the only hope for a believer is forgiveness.

The believer seeks solace in appreciation and gratitude to Allah through self-reform. Appreciation for those who assist in bringing a believer back to ground zero with reminders of truth when they slip or slide from faith. Believers who appreciate each other are those who are grateful for each other.For a believer, he sees evil ploys and walks away. He leans back to Allah, asking for His abundant mercy. Allah lavishes with an open fist without expectations. This mirage describes Allah's giving. A believer gives without expecting. Allah gives to whomever he wills without an account.

Surah: Nur: 24:21. O you who have believed, do not follow the footsteps of Satan. And whoever follows the footsteps of Satan - indeed, he enjoins immorality and wrongdoing. And if not for the favor of Allāh upon you and His mercy, not one of you would have been pure, ever, but Allāh purifies whom He wills, and Allāh is Hearing and Knowing.

The framework of a believer is humility to Allah and preservation of faith by avoiding alliances and counsels of disbelievers intended to misdirect believers. Prophet Muhammad mingled with everyone but kept believers company. Humans may have detours but reach the finality of success uprooted just for those who face trials and still maintain their positive behavior. They may also concentrate on correctional life. Presented and wrapped in a bow for those who believe and face the truth is Islam.

Believers have no doubts about Allah, both in trials and in good times. There are no failures for those who believe. Allah changed the Muslim world through the Prophet Muhammad. In renunciation of paganism, he created a fully monotheistic world unbeknown to the Bedouins' worship of one God, Allah.

Throughout every successful relationship, Prophet Muhammad held on to God's strength. He offered his prayers to Allah with sincerity and wept for mercy for long hours. Arabs were camel herders and traders who adapted to legal and political frameworks.

As well as writing poetry and competing. Although the new concepts and delivery were new, literacy didn't falter. But when they reformed their ways, they did not turn back. By adapting to the new methods of learning, they became more proficient in literacy over time. It shows the resilience of the human spirit and the willingness to embrace change in order to progress. In scorching days in Saudi Arabia, many Bedouins lacked shoes on their feet, and it was a privilege to own them.

Rather than wearing shoes, they were kept in the house as status symbols. Coins, beads, and sequins decorated these fabric shoes. Consequently, they became valuable and were often given as wedding gifts or other special occasions.

These shoes were designed with bright colors and intricate patterns inspired by the culture and environment of the Bedouins. The tradition of crafting and giving fabric shoes is still alive today, with Bedouins still making them and giving them as gifts. It is Allah who can change a person's fate. The world is envious of those with petrol, gold, and gas pipelines, and zam zam water. The riches are endless for those who can see Allah gives to whom he wishes. With gratitude, you spread the wealth and use it in a non-selfish way for progress and the opportunity to give back.

Islam was drafted and implemented into the structure of the Saud, and many converted to Islam and never reverted to pagan practices. Soon spread throughout the world. As a result, they gained prestige they could never have imagined. However, the conversion rate is pretty high in Islam. And the numbers have been growing. Acceptance of the Shahada testimony of faith between Allah and acceptance that Prophet Muhammad as the last Prophet is the beginning of this testimony.

Many converts who are coming to Islam are diligent in learning and exploring their faith. They make progress in making families with Muslims practice (Dhikr) dialogue of Allah, pray to Allah, conform to the discipline of Islam, and much more. They rarely return to the same quarters and are most grateful for the changes they see in their own lives. Many Muslims and converts do not educate themselves about their faith from the right sources. Few live the same lives, which are not compatible with Islam.

The adjustment to a new faith, or strayed Muslims on the other hand, can be more challenging. As a result, they may repeatedly backslide as they struggle to reconcile their beliefs with Islam's teachings. By ricocheting beliefs between themselves and their evil companions, distrust walls bounce back and forth. A better reason to prove oneself is that if Islam was an invitation from Allah, then every fight is worth it to reach the goal. Life events shake a Muslim's belief, but returning to Islam is the key to victory.

Even Muslims born and raised in Islam can experience this. The return solidifies the belief that the creator is merciful and forgiving. Belief is restored to a Muslim and a believer through hope and trust. Prophet Muhammad told Muslims to keep striving for knowledge and faith. Nothing stays the same but change is an evolution within the human mind some for betterment some for worse. The Almighty may send believers to guide the swayed, for sometimes those who hit rock bottom seek to rise again.

A practicing Muslim who leaves the path of righteousness to act contrary to it and treat others in a demeaning manner still has hope. In comparison to today's society, the stories of the early Muslims are unmatched. Islam acceptance by converted or strayed Muslims does not require applause. It's to their benefit. Islam benefits not from their acceptance. Over time and as changes come, conduct will tell the tale. Employees who disrespect their employers are usually terminated. Although Islam never fails to dismiss or terminate the forgiveness of the creator, there is no termination for an employee of Islam, only repentance and return.

Those who repent and return can be rehired. Neither a human company nor a stock gives better dividends than Allah in Islam. There is no successful human company that gives humans continuous chances to progress in this wealth. Continuous examples become a spotlight for those who understand.

The examples or messages that bring light are for those who seek solace and understanding. Words impact society. They can be used to encourage, motivate, and inspire. They can also be used to create awareness and spark conversations about social issues.

Words have the power to bring people together, create understanding, and foster peace. Prophet Muhammad's words resonate. He taught us that words can build bridges instead of walls. To create a peaceful world, we must use our words to spread positivity. When certain Muslims do not understand the simple concepts of Islam, they look for human resources to learn when Islam is the platform of knowledge of morals and conversation.

People who lack conversations with mindful and literate people always turn to sources that are not productive. In the Arab world, learning was a constant endeavor. Islam traces its roots back to the Arabian peninsula, but its birth is from the birth of a man who worships Allah. It was only presented as a reform in the last destitute Quran. Prophet Muhammad's revelations came to an end. For those who see the Quran as leading mankind through all centuries of life without expiration or alterations, the delivery was front and center.

The beauty of Islam is that it is accessible to anyone from any country or region. Essentially, respect for the moral code of modesty and justice as well as upholding laws of character. Integrity and mandated prayers are bundled into a simple package for believers' benefit. Islam encourages learning knowledge and development of human physical and spiritual development as a constant learning factor. A person can gain prestige by their moral character, not by their wealth.

Moral character is the basis of the Islamic concept. The world might consider the materialistically well-off prestigious. Without character, wealth leads to poverty. If Allah wills, it is not difficult to have both. The other loses appetite for an individual who loses morals and expresses demeaning character because they do not know that a person can stoop to such levels. In this society, the least expected from the most unexpected is possible. Especially looting this demeanor in public to show self-characteristics through social media of the Islamophobes.

Flaunting sins is never progressive in a Muslim society. A believer must uphold moral character. For those who receive Allah's gifts, money and glitz are the means of spending and circulating.Saudi Arabia in the past did not possess the prestige of today, when Saudi money, petrol, and glitz are seen as a luxury almost unimaginable to the average person. High-rise buildings and lush gardens in Saudi Arabia are signs of the hour predicted by the Prophet Muhammad.

Islam has elevated the status of those who were overlooked in this world. Despite all its calamities, Islam has become the epitome of admiration.Islamic Prophet attained Islam and status. Before becoming a Prophet, he obtained the position of being the most truthful and honest person in the world. Islam gave him a grandeur that nothing could rival. Allah can allow any unrecognized person to gain status. Allah can grant status to those he chooses. Saud gained status after Islam. Muslims may fail to recognize what Islam has done for Muslims is more than anyone can do for another.

Allah says that every beginning has a finality. The finality of those who believe in Allah is not feared but awaited as they plan just as a human would plan a retirement fund. A believer also plans to justify the perpetuated plan given by Allah without being forced to do so. Employing humans requires adherence to the law. No laws are imposed by Islam, by force, but the consequences can be awaited when justification is begun.

Quran: Surah A'shura 26:47. They said, "We believe in the Lord of the worlds.

The Bedouins reformed during the time of the Prophet Muhammad, but many fought and negotiated to preserve their pagan beliefs. Islam was the faith of the vast majority of Saudis. This Muslim country holds Kabba within its grasp, and worship gets intense during Ramadan.

Saud has given many jobs to expats, and visitors are welcome, except at the Kabba. Only Muslims have access to entry. Some receive housing, transportation, and education packages, which can be appealing to foreign expats and students.

In healthy learning and relationships, disagreements and misunderstandings are the result of animosity. As evil animosity antagonizes those who listen to calls of dilemma and separation from believers.A company or act that captured the understanding and outlook once familiar can become a memory for those who stepped away from the right path. Others do return as time passes.

There are no sects in Islam, according to Allah, but Muslims keep dividing as it gives the other groups ammunition to separate and build up the stigma that they don't like one another. Who today claims that Islam sects did not emerge soon after the Prophet Muhammad's death? Is it possible for humans to alter Quranic texts? What makes you think they wouldn't? Humanity can do good and bad things.

Allah's last scripture will remain intact no matter how many sects form. Allah knew the outcome of the previous scriptures. He did not give Muslims the responsibility to protect the Quran. Humans are flawed; Allah will protect his last revelation, not Muslims. Islam is one, and the Quran remains the same. Those who differ and do not follow the ways and practices of Muhammad are answerable to Allah alone.

Muslims are the only ones who acknowledge all the Prophets of Allah. Jews don't accept Jesus as the Messiah. Christians don't recognize Muhammad as Allah's last Prophet. Islam is the only religion sent by Allah, honoring every Prophet in the Quran as truth deliverers. Not deciding who to accept or not is contrary to Muslim protocol. Islam is the faith organized by Allah, not rearranged by humans.

Individuals who did not exist during the Prophet Muhammad's lifetime have created divisions. Muslims, however, recite the same Quran. As opposed to any other sect of Islam, Sunnis follow the sunnah customs and practices of Prophet Muhammad. Dubai is the hub of global transformation and wealth accumulation for many carriers. Diverse backgrounds make up the community.

Muslim countries have welcomed many Westerners, Asians, Jews, and people from all over the world. Migration has been a way of life for decades for both humans and animals, including birds. Many Muslims have migrated to Western and Asian countries and prospered. Humans have accepted diversity and travel for centuries, as well as cultural mixing and blending. There is only one place where there can be no compromise, and that is Islam cannot mix with culture - it stands on its own for a Muslim.

Islam opposes man-made laws, in theology which are prone to corruption unless they are the law of the land. By eradicating companies that are incompatible with Islamic principles, one can eventually return. Despite understanding Islam, they still test the waters, but deep down, they know they are Muslims and are remorseful. Muslim roots uphold Muslims together, and it would be a shame if they lost sight of them. The ways of a colluding world cannot be adapted to a tree without a strong root system. Allah has brought the Bedouins who could not afford shoes to riches. This empire could dominate the world if the Muslim world enjoined together and did not follow the whims and distractions of Western influences.

But collisions with wrong have been the way of the world. Explaining the issues to others and helping them reform is the plea of a believer to believers, the barricaded Muslims who believe this plague is modernization. The goal is to appease the unreformed with outdated paganistic rituals and morals in the name of modernization, which affects the entire world.

There are people with more knowledge than others, and some speak as if they are comfortable with the opinions of the majority. Meanwhile, there are Muslims who believe that their views are different from those of the majority. Not agreeing with the majority is not a failure, but delivering without hesitation is like the lion who is the king of the jungle.

If Prophet Muhammad worried about what the majority was saying, he would stand still. Those were the days when paganism was at the forefront, and veneration was prevalent. Islam stood alone and was not concerned about majority regulations. As a believer who believes in delivery, to disbelievers, it finds itself alone today.It is not the followers of the masses who make a dent in society; it is the leaders who hold the stage without compromising their beliefs. Leaders leading societies cater to the masses' needs. Every chapter of life is won by leaders who stand alone on stage. Truth is shed by some, and deceit is shed by others. The true believer knows the difference.

As a single-handed reformer of the Muslim world, Prophet Muhammad's teachings resonate worldwide with Muslims and non-Muslims alike who seek the truth. The corrupters are in order to seize power for themselves and to make empty promises that have no foundation in reality.

Understanding and knowing the faith are more critical than following the crowd. The Quran guides one's convictions without arguments. It's not the observer who holds the reins, it's the rider. If one's belief is strong, stay with the strong, not with the majority.

Following others to appease the majority leads to losing oneself if one follows the norms of a corrupted society. A believer exits the company of disbelievers to adapt to the recent changes. Islam makes no adjustments. Whispers of Satan from a stalemate company were never a benefit, only destruction. Not understanding the duality of faith requires a separation from the past to the present.

Afraid to leave the familiar compound, sometimes neglecting the path or person Allah chooses where introduction can come from, the purity of paths is only determined by the will of Allah. Ensuring the fulfillment of the (deen) way of life requires undivided attention, leaving the constraints that paralyze the growth of man towards a breath of fresh air achieved by no other than Allah.

The propensity to approach truth and let go of social norms that tie one to a negative lifestyle or people, who makes justice within adapting to the new life offered by no other than Allah." He" sent the Prophet Muhammad to humanity as a beautiful breeze man enjoys on a warm summer day or a cold winter when the sun shines brightly. The man feels that subtle warmth, the one who follows this Prophet. Those who extend their hands in prayer to Allah win all. Not the doubter. Allah says he is to the believer what the believer believes he is. No faith, no kindness, no belief, no victory.

Quran: Surah Muhammad 47:2. And those who believe and do righteous deeds, and believe in what I have sent down upon Muhammad - and it is the truth from their Lord - he will remove from them their misdeeds and amend their condition.

Prophet Muhammad endured patience despite the harsh challenges, along with the turbulent times he faced. The strenuous job and position were more important than any other executive position in society. He delivered the Quran's last testament.It gave the importance of this delivery from Allah to the best of his servants. The most truthful, the most honest. (As-Sadiq. Al-Ameen) His courage was of the bravest, and his compassion was of the sweetest. The excellence of his character has left no doubt in the minds of humanity. Will Muslims follow the practices he left behind and the Quran?

Quran: Surah Qalam:4. Inshallah (if Allah wills) ask Allah for forgiveness "and verily. For you (Muhammad (s)) are of an exalted (standard of) character."

As a servant of Allah, Prophet Muhammad is not to be worshiped, as he was on earth to lead humanity for a short while. It was Allah who sent the Quran and the Prophets. Muhammad's character and mannerisms, as a symbol of good for the entire world. Rather than just sending him to Muslims, he sent him to the entire world.

Quran: Surah Anbiya verse 107. We have only sent you as a mercy to the world.

Quran: Surah Qasas verse 56 "Indeed, (o Muhammad) you do not guide whom you like, but Allah guides whom he wills.

Having a long-term relationship with someone committed to just causes is a sign that Allah chose him for humanity's advancement. Allah has tested the faith of Muslims time and time again. Our failures don't account for our beliefs. Disbelievers can question our faith, but we don't question their disbelief. According to several media outlets, Islam in Western countries is backward, not leaving the imperialistic society that cannot stay away from the Middle East, returning in remorse and depression. Social media anchors don't understand Islam or some have never been to Middle Eastern countries, contributing to the turbulent effects on those who believe social media is gospel truth.

While some Muslims take social media at face value, Muslim youth, and converts are increasing in number despite the negative connotations portrayed by many. Muslims held office recently, on foreign lands where the faith brandished itself only because they were Muslim.

They described their identity as Muslims without proclaiming their ability to hold office. Muslim women who have had civil union marriages to advance their careers are not representing the Islamic faith, particularly in the Western Hemisphere.There are not only women who identify as Muslims; many men follow their own rules, which is why the Western media embraces them to portray Islam. This is a false representation of a Muslim who does not follow Islam and cannot serve as a model to portray Muslim women or Muslim men or Islam.

Islam has rules, and regulations, as the government of any country does. Laws govern Islam. Allah did not send Islam without laws, just as no government can function without laws. Islam is a sensible faith devoid of fantasy. At every step, it makes sense, unaffected by the influence of this society and its alterations.When one steps outside the boundaries of Islam to join any society not in compliance with Islam and then makes excuses, they are already outside Islam. Identifying persons of either gender as Muslims in politics or the movie industry who rebel against Islam is not an example of Muslims.

Cultures that intermix with interfaith marriages or individuals from the Islamic faith who do not follow Islam's structure are examples of Islam's defiance. Unions will fade, but Islam is here to stay. Political or movie industries or colluding Muslims in this world understand Islamic laws, but filter truth and add their twists.This faith will not tolerate alterations. There is plenty of mercy in Islam. As the Lord is merciful, but he has rules. Compromised Muslims are not clerics of Islam. This faith of Allah does not live through them. Neither celebrity nor office can hold Islam up; Islam stands alone.

Social pressures are surmounting in certain lives, with more people joining the adherent society of privileges wrapped in the guise of modern living. Muslim flaws don't change Islam but affect Muslims. Maintaining a separate private life, we continue to serve the world in all positions held by Muslims. Our last attempt is to find solace in Allah.

Islam says you should take your share of both this world and the next. Being your top self on all counts is what one should strive for. Despite Islamophobia, with our cultural and religious differences, most countries are diverse in religions and cultures. Some States are epics of a cultured society.

In the same society, few don't know Islam or have never heard of it. In addition, others have converted to Islam, and a few succumb to peer pressure. When one leaves a fertile environment and continues in the same infertile soil, growth ceases, just as in Islam. Social media sites or television become the primary teachers for many, damaging the mind more than teaching.

Travel is the most effective teacher if one can afford the trip. A lack of knowledge from a lack of learning makes an ignorant human. Believers strive to learn from believers. Education in Islam can shape a person's life. Prophet Muhammad had no degree, but he left his mark and living legacy throughout the world.Society compels human beings to improve their lives by educating themselves. Humanity can be self-taught and needs the intelligence to seek the right sources. A Muslim must have the companionship of a believer. In most cases, you are the religion of your friend.

To educate the young and curious through example and debauchery with some truths and some falsified rhetoric, they set examples. New Western settings or colleges teach Islam's theology differently than sources who practice and read the Quran.

"Access Islam" is an indoctrination program implemented in public schools. In this country and around the world, inaccurate information and videos are used to portray Islam as a threat. Thousands of dollars are spent spreading lies and falsified information to deceive those who seek to understand Islam.

Politifact:"The United States Department of Education has introduced an Islamic indoctrination program for the public schools, called 'Access Islam.' "

Despite attempts to spread lies, more people are joining Islam. However, finding the true version of Islam and educating the young and old is the struggle within. Allah knows best. It appears the program would educate people about Muslim prayer and belief. A faith that is widely spread and unknown to most people.

Despite this, the spread was not intended to educate the masses, but to allow minds to collide with truth. Theology has been corrupted to corrupt masses, but truth always sets the world free. In all spheres of life. Allah says don't learn Islam from unbelievers. We can't change this faith or deliver it differently. Human history has seen upheavals, challenges, and periods of turmoil.

Quran stands as a victory they cannot change, unlike other scripts. It is based on monotheism, humility, kindness to all humanity, not excluding oneself, and the opportunity to grow despite all odds. The ability to grow is the ultimate success. Because all life requires application and persistence.To see what the ancestors went through, Allah says to explore his land. It encourages people to travel per Islam. A believer may not take a vacation and destroy the land. Not participating in illegal acts, drinking, or using mind-altering substances is not part of the protocol.

Travelers journey to distant lands for culture, food, and religion. Many people travel to explore and participate in sports and academia. Some travel to pollute the land, contributing to drinking alcohol and drugs. Acts of an illicit nature. Not condoned by Islam or religious sects. They drift from their lands to corrupt others. Bad conduct in new lands will be the story of their travels. The conduct of such affairs would not be acceptable to a believer. Muslim travelers have left their mark on the lands they have visited. Land migration is a means of bettering ourselves, not destroying it. Traveling through learning and enjoying it is a privilege. Travel applied correctly is a brilliant teacher.

Quran: Surah Qasas 28:77 But seek through that which Allah has given you the home of the, and [yet] do not forget your share of the world. Allah has done well for you, so do good. And desire, not corruption, in the land. Indeed, Allah does not like corrupters.

The traveler exudes an unfamiliar warmth. While a traveler can tell a tale of what he has seen, an observer of television or social media cannot. An observer of social media continues to tell tales as if he had visited the land personally.

Also, he spreads fake news and falsified rhetoric around the world without understanding the news broadcast or the Islam it depicts. Especially those who don't leave the land and believe that what they hear is gospel truth. Unlike a traveler who saw the shore, felt the breeze, and traveled through the land, he did not rely on someone he heard or saw on social media. Allah gives the traveler permission to explore his land. Travel is permission from Allah that cannot be reversed, and the one who never leaves the shores cannot teach.

152

The most valuable teacher in life is traveling. Islam encourages travel and migration because they lead to personal improvement. Traveling to destroy a land does not promote solidarity within the individual. The vacationers of this society travel to disobey Allah. Muslims traveled to better societies to spread goodness, not evil. Certain allegations against Muslims today are unwarranted, as their history shows contentment and teaching for the world. Rather than a loss of morals brought about by technology. Muslims did not lose their morals in gaining knowledge.

However, it was the moral standing of Islamic laws that enabled them to advance their endeavor to share learning with the world. As the upcoming decade approached, certain Muslims saw the Western World as a source of progress. However, they forgot that Muslim morals are, for many, the most meaningful thing in life. Few returned stronger and even became teachers after experiencing both sides of the spectrum.

Quran: Surah Ankabut 20. Say ˹o Prophet ˺ "travel throughout the land and see how he originated the creation".."

Quran: Surah Hajj 22:46 So have they not traveled through the earth, and have hearts by which to reason, and ears by which to hear? Indeed, it is not the eyes that are blinded, but the hearts within the breasts.

Have you noticed the madness and upset from watching social media? Ignorant people who have never left their country will say, "Get back to your country.". All countries belong to Allah. Human beings will ultimately travel to their provisions and death. Thomas Jefferson loved Islam and had a pluralistic vision. He kept the Quran in the White House. Many people think he was a secret Muslim. They drafted the first amendment to the Constitution in 1777. It became law in 1786 in the USA.

They accused Obama of being Muslim after 200 years, but he didn't proclaim he was Muslim. Despite faithfully describing Islam in a positive light, he never admitted to being a Muslim. Though he carried a Muslim name, the accusations were not valid. In Islam, we honor integrity, one voice. He is not a Muslim. We have to go by his word. Unless they were misconstruing to protect, their lives could be permissible, but the actions did not add up.

Despite disorderly morality in the sphere, the fear of Islamic law and order has been present, calling it dated. The majority of people who tell stories about Islam enjoy stepping into the Muslim world as much as they can. Islam or true believers never fear anyone. Islam stands alone with no pillars and remains uncorrected.

Quran: Surah Imran 3:190 Verily! In creating the heavens and the earth, and in the alternation of night and day, there are indeed signs for men of understanding.

Has a human noticed? that the sky stands without pillars? Can a man design a house without pillars? It's impossible.

Quran: Surah Luqman 31:10 He created the heavens without pillars and has cast into the earth, firmly set mountains, lest it should shift with you, dispersed, from every creature. And we sent down rain from the sky and made to grow [plants] of every noble kind.

The noticed prejudice cannot go unnoticed and continues as a daily life projected on social media and certain settings. During a certain regime executive order banning immigration from seven Muslim countries created chaos and curiosity for many to look into Islam. A suggestive blanket Muslim ban and wearing badges carrying identification badges on the news media, which many feared is part of history.

During World War 11, they forcibly sent 120, 000 people who held Japanese ancestry back, leaving their homes and locked up in camps. The Muslims had trials of their own. Most Muslims did not fear the government shake-ups. Destiny documented the trials of life predestined; such is the faith of a believer.Youth and business continued to operate as usual, and humorous people jokes, and some of us laughed together. Are you still here? The concept of life mortality, regime changes, and doctrines that are incompatible with the concept of belief, friendship, and treatment of human beings mostly keep a cordial relationship.

It remains important to keep the focus on the betterment of society, even if some have felt the effects and aftereffects. As Muslims contribute to the progress of the world, it would be a shame not to participate in this progress and educate the world about Islam.Rather than regress, Muslims have brought the world to contentment and blitz in Muslim countries by teaching melodies and beating the myths of chaos as Saud where Islam started is not the only factor of life, but belief in Allah is unanimous for Muslims.

Regime changes don't affect morality, false advertising, or fallible concepts. Muslims endow their heads in prayer in the humblest of positions. While engaging both their bodies and minds in prayer. The gesture of wearing a badge was not offensive or upsetting. This is because Muslims already wear the mark of faith. It should hardly offend any Muslim, to be asked to wear a badge of faith. The only thing that could frighten a Muslim is that he may not represent Islam to the best.

Quran: Surah Hud 11:56. I put my trust in Allah, my Lord, and your Lord! There is not a moving living creature, but he has a grasp of its forelock. Verily, my Lord is on the straight path of the truth.

Higher-ranking individuals who have visited the Saudi world have received extravagant gifts and bowed to humans in gratitude, but bowing to Allah is a chore for certain Muslims, in some cases. Similarly, hypocrisy is to receive from humans or Allah and not shift the pendulum. Allah has provided even to those who are not thankful. In contrast, it is hypocritical to use those benefits without gratitude. Repentance cures all heart evils.

As a sign of respect. After Islam solidified its rules, Muslims could not bow to others except to Allah. The overwhelming hospitality throughout the world shows the culture of the Muslim world. Muslims thrive on hospitality and gifts. They shower with gifts. The attitude of Muslims does not change depending on the attitude of others. Muslims are consistent in showing gratitude for guests.

Given the source, it shouldn't be surprising to see leaders endowed, in humble bows, to the Muslim world in Saudi Arabia, in a display of hypocrisy. These are the same hypocrites who spread lies about Islam, but eventually, the pendulum for all evil is always exposed sooner rather than later. Muslims testify to the authenticity of the Quran when Allah promises the preservation of this book,not the human,

Quran: Surah Nisa: 4;145.The hypocrites will be committed to the lowest pit of Hell, and you will find no one to help them.

Quran: Surah Munafiqoon: 63;4.When you see them, their appearance impresses you. And when they speak, you listen to their ˈimpressiveˈ speech. But they are just like ˈworthlessˈ planks of wood leaned against a wallˈ. They think every cry is against them.

They are the enemy, so beware of them. May Allah condemn them! How can they delude from the truth

Guests, whether they come from faraway lands or nearby, are held in high regard in Islamic culture. Every guest holds a special place. Welcoming a guest involves preparing, providing, and cleaning to ensure their comfort and satisfaction.The host's gesture of welcoming the guest at the door is a distinctive characteristic of this society and faith. Waiting until the guests had completely departed on their transportation before waving goodbye, a bittersweet smile on their faces has been the memorandum of exchanges for decades with humanity.

Exchanges filled with laughter and tearful goodbyes of the joy of spending time together forge cherished memories in the minds of all involved. Islam stresses humanity's needs daily.

The story of a man who expected from his guests:

In the olden days, when times were hard, a man spent hours preparing a festival for his guests. He was pleasantly surprised by what he had accomplished on his own. As the guests arrived, he expected them to tell him how well he did. Not receiving the recognition he expected, he complained to Allah.

Waiting for his reply, he realized he did not appreciate everything he had been given. He changed his attitude immensely his heart was pure, the realization and thought became clear he could never repay what he was given. It serves Muslims to see that they have been given an unchanged Quran, Salat as a gift and if a believer can participate in shared beliefs then all other trials will be trivial.

Being able to share food with guests is a blessing. When people break bread together, they form relationships that remind them of the guests who came miles to see one another. An individual who makes time to see another in a world where he rarely has time for himself or herself cannot dismiss such memories. These are gestures Islam takes as gifts of Allah.

Respect embodies love. Without respect, there is no love. Humans who respect their faith can respect others' faith. The obvious differences in theology don't disrespect others' faith, only clarify them, especially in Abrahamic faiths. Despite some worshiping a hundred Gods, Muslims believe in one God but do not differentiate between them when it comes to helping people. That judgment awaits from Allah,to humans.When individuals emigrate, they are visitors until they complete the required documents to gain citizenship of the land. The country's law determines their legitimate home.

Humanity cannot leave the land unless Allah provides food at the destination. Allah provides for survival and travels for humanity. Some never leave their birthplace. It is common for some to travel only short distances, and some to travel through many lands. For some who die in foreign lands, death is like an invitation to the land.

Some travel to distant lands. Muslims flourish in migratory nations and benefit the region they inhabit. Patronage is required in Islam. In a culture of communal instruments and antagonism, most Muslim youths are educated and begin trade and professional careers in Western regions and all parts of the world. Any part of the world where destiny companions those who expand their horizons in life. Performing outstanding ventures. Salat, submission to the creator, softens a Muslim's face.

Quran: Surah Rahman 55:41 The Mujrimun (polytheists, criminals, sinners, etc.), you will know them by their marks (black faces) and their forelocks, and their feet will seize them.

It is the face that tells the tale of a smooth life or a raspy one. It's all in the face of a human. It's not amiss that a believer's face is soft. The harshness of the face is also not amiss in life. One can change its ways, but sometimes the scars of the past take time to soften. Only through faith can life change. It's the belief of a believer. Most individuals never left the country, so there is no factual truth to what their brains absorbed. Without social media, one man, Prophet Muhammad, conquered pagan minds with Allah's permission.

This also applies to Muslims who change their Islam ideology and say they are Muslims, but they do not follow. Checkpoints are very helpful for inept friends or self-inflicted individuals who want to fit in with their social group.There is no greater faith than worshiping Allah. Call him whatever you want, but he is the ruler of the universe. Comments or words can spark some people's psyches. Man will find only one God. This concept of belief that rules and regulations apply to both men and women.

It can become a terrain of disobedience to Allah should Muslims break away from binding laws. Any country's laws and human courts have these regulations as well, so one cannot negotiate them. Because of Allah's laws, Islam is a state within itself that cannot change or compromise the rules.

But the world knows Islam has no force. Islam does not force Muslim men or women to convert. Conservative Jews refuse interfaith marriages. The modern equality they created for themselves does not allow Christians to marry from other religious sects.

Bible: 1 Corinthians 6;14:15. Do not be yoked with unbelievers. For what do righteousness and wickedness have in common? Or what fellowship can light have with darkness? What harmony is there between Christ and Belial?

Breaking religious rules and regulations costs defiance. Disobeying religious rules and regulations can lead to guilt and shame. The result can also be alienation from the community or even expulsion. Whether it is family issues or personal issues, they are not conducive. When the faiths of two divisions do not align, chaos results.

Muslim men could marry chaste and believing women of the book. Such women are scarce in modern times. Western societies, in particular. Most Muslims will not agree with Jesus' baptism. Unabated concept: Muslim women can only marry a Muslim man born and raised in Islam or a Muslim convert. Therefore, it is difficult to agree between the two religions. A couple with two different faiths faces a challenge.

There is no point in selling Islam for self-inflicted desires without faith-based decisions. However, pseudo-cultures are governed by atheist rules. Only believers are subject to these rules. True Muslims firmly establish their faith before marriage or any faith-related relationship.The Christian faith dominates Western cultures, although not widely practiced, and the differences are vast to adjust to as a marital union. In most cases, however, friendships are acceptable and lasting. Despite its constant adjustments to satisfy self-desires, its stories and mythology starkly contrast with Hinduism.

Christianity has been used to justify wars, the oppression of minorities, and other atrocities. Its emphasis on individualism and materialism has led to a culture of consumerism and selfishness that has negatively impacted the environment and society at large. Cultures and faiths are particularly prone to some alterations especially in newly formed regions exploiting the old. They need constant adjustments to survive. Islam's rules remain the same, so follow them or ignore them. They are harsh trials for humankind that confuse; most humans are wonderful.

There are some who are misdirected, and most are searching for peace. Humans exchange kindness constantly, even without faith. Humanity getting along does not mean faith is the same or can live on the same threshold. Allah has rules on when and how this is permissible and when it is not.

Muslims cannot change Islam's doctrine. The differences are significant unless they meet Islamic guidelines. Muslims either disobey laws or follow laws. Islam has laws, not force, but promises consequences. These subjects have become increasingly relevant as the world develops. Infiltrating Muslim households and many others, the demon of defiance brings its own rules.

In many countries, especially in the Middle East, watching people pass by and observing their actions is one of the greatest pleasures of life. It did not say Muhammad should be worshiped based on his legacy. The consistent message never deviated from Islam. Worship is only for Allah. Because of its deemed value and prestige, they regarded the Middle East as an icon gateway to greed and destruction from Western countries.Soldiers return from the Middle East. With post-traumatic stress disorder. Veterans of these regimes have a higher suicide rate and depression than civilians. Sometimes they accept Islam and return as Muslim converts.

Some have faced heavy trauma. Irreversible damage is irreparable. They continue to live in a post-depression world. Every unfair trait in humanity has a cost. Allah does not miss minuscule details, never amiss. The conversion rate to Islam has surpassed many and continues to grow. The Islamic military commander-in-chief during the wars was Muhammad.

Converts to Islam are attracted to this faith for its democratic values that grant rights to all people, regardless of color or creed. Converting to Islam increases a person's status; it doesn't decrease it.

The democracy of Islam, being the first in the world, offers countless examples to write about, leaving no one unfamiliar with it. It has remained unchanged, never shifting. Would you like to see democracy in action at the mosque or embark on a journey to Mecca for Hajj? Anyone can attend Salat, but Mecca is exclusively for Muslims. This highlights that democracy is for Muslims, while humanity encompasses all humans who comprehend this faith. For the lost, this faith is a valuable treasure.

Prophet Muhammad was a leader, a commander, and a Prophet. Islam stipulates that when the enemy attacks, the opposition is prepared for war. Hypocrisy is so rampant that they are told to "turn the other cheek while Christian countries fight most wars."

In Islam's history, Prophet Muhammad led three wars that were pivotal. As a new religion, Islam faced many wars against its adversaries. It is important to note the significance of the three wars. The number of Muslims was smaller compared to the opposition, who had more than a military.

But Muslims had the commander-in-chief, the Prophet. He presented multiple instances of genuine life and Islam free from illusion or hypocrisy. Having him as the commander who ensured all his people left the battlefield after the finality of any war is a great honor for Muslims. In Islam, there are no illusions except reality. A hypocritical society's commanders are good at talking the game which is mostly lies and shielded with hypocrisy which is not clear to Muslims and foreign to those whose nature is concealed.

In certain countries, Muslims are being mercilessly attacked while they try to gain more power. Palestine serves as a vivid illustration of oppression. The change in the stretch occurred when Muslims gained power and began treating all of humanity with respect, allowing religious freedom. Wars driven by greed demolish lands, homes, trees, animals, and civilians. Islam promotes self-defense and retaliation without aggression or anger, but rather in the context of a just war with equal means and protection for all.

Countries seeking salvation in Jesus provide support. Israel has significant power, yet Allah's power exceeds that of man. Losing the soul before death is a fate worse than death, which humans have experienced for decades.

Having properties and wealth is meaningless if one's heart is filled with deceit and lacks true belief in Allah's laws. The world's creator controls life and death, testing humanity's attachment to the temporary land. The soul departs from the earth, defying Allah. Remember the worth of avoiding spiritual death and imitating evil. Muslims fought for truth throughout history.

Muslims must resist the persuasive evil rhetoric to gain acceptance from wrongdoers due to social pressure. The richest nations on earth are Muslim countries if they unite under Islam. In so-called modern and powerful lands, peace and safety are non-existent, as they are still present in Muslim countries.

The superpower of evil stems from the exhibition of lies painted as truth, not a write-off when deceit is a continual habit. Muslim countries are falsely portrayed as unsafe when in reality the only unsafe place to walk alone is their own territory. Foreigners often find success in foreign lands.

While they face poverty of the heart and sometimes material while pursuing their greed for more. When hearts are unaware of the truth, ethics can be deciphered through kind expressions. The visible signs are clear, but no statement can include everyone in this dilemma, only the majority speaks. However, the minority can hold the truth if it is only held by one Muslim.

Muslims fought crucial wars based on their religion. The Battle of Badr was an attack by the Quraish, and over a thousand people participated in this war. They came in herds and prepared for war. Muslims had three hundred and thirteen combatants ready for combat. Muslims were outnumbered by a thousand fighters.

Although few in numbers compared to the opposition, who came fully prepared. Muslims won the battle of Badr. This victory spread throughout the Arabian peninsula. Allah grants victory to whom he wills. Muslims fought for rights, not greed. If battle rules are based on greed and killings, humans representing such episodes cannot be happy. Muslims who fought with Prophet Muhammad never suffered trauma.

It was all in the cause of justice for Islam's faith and protection. They could not stop Muslims from worshiping Allah. Prophet Muhammad was the last to leave the battleground, ensuring all his people were safe; such was his leadership. Neither he nor the youths were hypocrites.

Greed is unIslamic. He distributed the war booty to the needy but kept nothing. No women, children, or trees were part of the war. The Muslims' army was small. Allah sent three thousand angels to help the Muslims. Muslims' victory shocked many, but it was not a match. And neither were the equipment and animals involved in this war.

Quran: Surah 3:123 Allah sent 3000 angels in the battle of Badr in weak times, so be thankful to Allah

Muslims were few but the enemy outnumbered them. Muslims won the Battle of Badr. Six years later, the Jews surrendered to the Muslims. Prophet Muhammad gained the reputation of being a powerful leader who did not fear a large headcount from the opposition in the battle of Badr. The

Muslim community and Islam were protected by Allah, and he prayed for their protection. Allah helps without full stops or commas.

During the battle of Uhud, Abu Sufyan led three thousand camels, infantry horses, and trained soldiers outside Madina. Muslims had very few resources and no preparation. They injured those who participated in this battle. Along with the Prophet Muhammad, they were left brutally wounded on the battlefield. They lost in this battle. Allah granted the first win, whereas the second was a loss.

The people of Quraish killed and injured Muslims in their attempt to eliminate Islam and kill the Prophet Muhammad. The Battle of the Trench, known as "Khandaq," was another war led by Quraish Jews against Muslims.

They estimated that at least ten thousand people rode camels and used archery. In those days, there were only three thousand Muslims, fewer animals, and less archery. Despite the well-prepared people who came to fight, Muslims won this war. They finally gave up and accepted Islam as a dominant force.

Only got stronger. Muslims ruled the surrounding areas and conquered many. There was nothing they left behind that the Muslim world hadn't already educated the rest of the world about. Islam's youth, the Quran, and Prophet Muhammad's Sunnah were all included in this study. Due to Allah's mercy, Islam remained, although some faced setbacks along the way. It was the Prophet Muhammad who held the commander-in-chief position. He moved the earth himself along with others by digging the trench, known as the Battle of the Trench. In the trenches, people hid as they arrived by the dozens. In the trenches, his army hid from the enemy.

Muslims introduced the concept of digging trenches in combat, which the rest of the world copied. Keeping the enemy at bay. Islam has even educated the world in wars. They sent no missiles to destroy the universe. The commander was on the front lines with his people. Prophet Muhammad. That cannot be dismissed; he was successful in every field.

Quran: Surah Imran: 31;40. If a wound has befallen you a similar wound has already befallen the people who are opposed to you. We make such movements to men in turn so that Allah might mark out those who are the true men of faith and select from among you those who do really bear witness (to the Truth): for Allah does not love the wrong-doers, 100.

The elephant year of this century was a war, Abraha, viceroy of Saba, attacked Kabba. Ethiopian Christian emperors employed him. Men riding white elephants launched the battle. They did not prepare Muslims for what was about to happen. There were tremendous trials. Every trial strengthens faith.

Quran: Surah Al Fil: 105:1-5.*Have you not considered, O Muhammad], how your Lord dealt with the companions of the elephant? Did He not make their plan into misguidance? And He sent against them birds in flocks. Striking them with stones of hard clay. And He made them like eaten straw.*

Allah sent flocks of birds with pebbles in their beaks. They destroyed elephants and men riding them. The year in Surah Fil was the year of elephants. The elephant year was the birth of Prophet Muhammad. Muslims celebrate not the year or the elephant but the word of a Muslim with integrity and character.

In retrospect, when a Muslim honors a Muslim's word, authenticity and integrity are balanced. Skeptics can create doubt among faithful believers when disbelievers are included in groups that collude and sway believers. Since Islam stands alone, it needs its own appraisal. Islam has no flaws. Islam's hallmark is infallibility.

Quran: Surah Luqman 31:2. Each verse in the book is full of wisdom. They found every teaching on wisdom.

Quran: Surah Imran 3:106. On the day, some faces will turn white, and some faces will turn black. As for those whose faces become black, to them, it will be said "Did you disbelieve after your belief? Then taste the punishment for what you used to reject?"

The Quran mentions the destruction of an army by small birds carrying pebbles, resulting in the army's demise and Abraha's death. The incident in Surah Fil is depicted clearly in the Quran. Omar introduced the Islamic calendar with the intention of augmenting the magnificence of Islam, not replacing any aspect of it.

Omar ruled as the second Rashidun Caliph from 634 to 644. Omar's caliphate achieved remarkable conquests, expanding its territory to include present-day Iraq, Iran, Azerbaijan, Armenia, Georgia, Syria, Jordan, Palestine, Lebanon, Egypt, and parts of Afghanistan, Turkmenistan, and southwestern Pakistan. While Omar reigned in Persia, the Byzantines saw a loss of over 75% of their territory.

If the ancient chiefs were present today, Muslims wouldn't be passive - with the charisma and strength of Prophet Muhammad, and the knowledge of Omar as his successor, second in position after Abu Bark but conquered many lands. Islam and Muslim territories would have flourished.

His dedication to Islam was evident in his following of the Prophet and his ongoing pursuit of knowledge in the Quran. The Quran is not a fictional book; it reflects the reality of life as decreed by Allah. The laws of Islam are practical and fighting for the true cause is an internal struggle. The hypocrites are too preoccupied with their own battles to save themselves, let alone others. Learning about the strengths of men and women in Islam can inspire someone to study the Quran with practicing Muslims.

Tremendous responsibility delegated with extreme kindness and not forced to accept this way of life. Islam restored peace to greedy, wicked people's hearts by abolishing pagan worship and embracing monotheism. One Allah, one God. In humanity's soul, everyone craves solace from one creator.

And no human does not yearn for peace. Muslims believe in destiny. Some might blame destiny for everything they do. Some might say that if destiny is written, I have to do nothing. No one knows destiny except Allah. As a result, the human will continue his life mission, and destiny will guide him to the right path. Sitting and hoping is not the answer; trying and seeing where destiny takes one is the outcome of destiny.

As the robber told Omar E. Farroq, why are you punishing me? It was my destiny to steal. Omar replied that it was my destiny to punish you. Life's examples show that although destiny is set, one must find the path and follow it. Life's path involves everyone. No one misses out.

Quran: Surah ISRA 17:13. We have bound everyone's destiny to their necks. And on the day of judgment, we will bring forth to each person a record which they will find laid open.

Quran: Surah ISRA 17:14. And we will say, "Read your record." You alone are sufficient for this day to consider yourself.

The accountant and record keeper is Allah. Allah sent the Prophet Muhammad as the seal of the Prophets. Allah owns everything that lives. Angel Jibril brought good news to Prophet Muhammad and all Prophets except (Musa) Moses. Allah directly spoke to him. Islam would reform the arrogant and ignorant. Arabian Peninsula in a society, when little or no change was expected in warm deserts.

Islam spreads worldwide. The world will know Islam's beauty, but Islam is not for everyone. Some will find reasons to excuse themselves, while others will ignore them completely. Allah will give every human an opportunity. Never use substantial force. Islam is a voluntary religion. Those who choose Islam as their religion are Muslims by choice. Rather than ordaining Allah's paths for all of creation, he guides those who seek him.

Surah Baqarah 2:256. We shall not compel religion. It distinguishes between the right and wrong course of action. Accordingly, those who disbelieve in taghut refer to a focus other than Allah, whereas those who believe in Allah are holding on to the most reliable handhold that cannot be shaken. And Allah hears you.

By his delivery style and credibility, Muhammad gained fame as a member of the community known as (Al-Amin) the most honest. Allah gave him the self-confidence to tell the truth to arrogant and ignorant people. Islam reforms society. The upheavals of society are particularly conducive to the emergence of heightened opportunities and a belief in one Creator, Allah. He transformed the Arabian Peninsula and Islam spread throughout the world.

It is not the spread of Islam or the number of Muslims that matters; it is the faith that guides a Muslim's convictions that matters most. Although many see Muslims as representatives of Islam, Islam has no flaws. Some see Islam as a cultural experience, not feeling the depth of the shores, not feeling the beauty beneath the depths of the sea that only a diver can discover.

Islam's essence lies deeper than any surface. Its purity is as clear as water, something one cannot discern from the surface. The only way to understand contrasts and examples is by diving deep. Unless one knows Islam's faith and follows the laws and regulations, it's difficult to be a role model for Islam.

Laws mixed with Islamic laws cannot intertwine. It is impossible to coexist based on other faiths' laws. As the tree cannot carry different branches, friendships, and associates survive, but faith is only understood through laws that survive within the same branches. All branches on the tree are rooted in the same tree, just as faith survives with the same roots and branches.

Some people ask how you know faith is truth. It is obvious from creation's beginnings that humanity prayed to Allah, not to man. It sought truth, not man-made rhetoric, which eventually failed. Islam needs no stabilization. Allah before humans, and they will continue to worship Allah until the last human is on earth.

Allah is the only God with no partners in Islam. Therefore, Muslims cannot adhere to the regulations of other religions. Islam will remain unchanged. It's in the forefront, advancing, and refusing to back down. Islam's growth includes a strong emphasis on learning and teaching. Once the truth is revealed, performance, not neglect, determines productivity and potential. If you're a Muslim, you'll know the importance of Islam. If you're not, learn about Islam and Muslims.

Excuses won't help those who want to learn; they need to find a way. This is the motto of successful individuals in all endeavors. Muslims and seekers alike will find what they seek, and it will find them too.

CHAPTER 8

IGNORANCE IN THE FAITH OF ISLAM IS DANGEROUS.

Life is a journey that includes elements such as progress, success, ambition, determination, willpower, control, self-discipline, focus, and continuous learning. Instead of remaining stagnant and ignorant. With determination and drive, one can be motivated to complete everything within their capabilities. In its entirety, the concept of existence encompasses an array of infinite forms, spanning across all things.

Muslims achieved success in all of their endeavors. Dealing with irregularities or irrelevant subjects should be neglected despite the challenges. It's an accurate observation of growth, not a lack of awareness.

Mistakes become sources of improvement for achievers and mistakes slow down those in compromised surroundings. It's a way to stagnate. Faith is guided by principles and practices that impact daily life. In Islam, Allah's teachings are essential for self-improvement. Rules are designed to free, not constrain, humans. Ignorance is dangerous, so seek knowledge and strive for self-improvement.

An individual would not intentionally descend from a road of success, knowing exactly where it leads. Everyone prioritizes their own self-preservation. It's natural to avoid actions that could potentially harm oneself.

On the other hand, some find joy in climbing and feel the adrenaline rush with each step. The climb becomes worthwhile upon reaching the destination. Only the climber is aware of the route they took, and no one can dispute it. The real dilemma isn't losing the path, it's not finding the path. This might stem from a lack of understanding, negative influences, or personal insecurities.

Those who have not experienced the journey themselves may try to discourage others, strategy is not let their doubts affect our determination. This is especially true in Islam, where the reward for our efforts is so great that no believer would willingly give up their place on the path to ultimate success.

Success is the result of unwavering determination and an unyielding desire to keep going, while others grow weary from not achieving instant results. Believers are unstoppable, as their vision goes beyond any obstacle.

Perseverance and consistency have made winners, not stagnation what Salat means to a Muslim. One who prays Salat cannot lose if they are consistent in their perseverance and visitation to Allah.

If someone's actions are derogatory despite claiming to attend Salat, where is their attendance? Is it possible for perseverance to be sublime without yielding results? A believer's dedication is evident through their actions. The participant in (Salat) displays various strands. Hope persists for non-attendees. Consistent attendance in any aspect of life leads to success.

It is the finality of the world's journey as one closes their eyes and prepares for the next sunrise. There is no scuffling on this journey. It is equally critical to prepare for the enjoyment of this world as well as to make conscious preparations by following Allah's laws.

Emblazoning the spiritual influence that enlightened the forces within is a structure that keeps the feet on the earth grounded. Despite entrapping oneself into different dimensions.

The heart stays focused on the serenity Allah once infused into the heart that asked for peace. Reminded of the truth and mesmerized by sounds that bring one closer to the creator, the passion that makes the believer return stronger.

Despite winding turns and detours, the believer seeks the sounds and the passions of the same time when bliss was at the forefront, not confusion. The soul needs to revert to the place where Allah once provided it with a place of peace and a canopy that shaded its route. Confidently a believer will succeed.

Each individual's journey through life is prepared by the creator. Enacting the heart and simplicity that make life beautiful for those who shed light on themselves and others.Such souls thrive on light and receive attention from most people. They are energetic and happy, but some see this light and express dark remarks with sarcasm.

Ignorant outbursts come from not satisfying the creator's rules. Discontents attack believers who display happiness and contentment in every aspect of their lives.This behavior reflects their inner turmoil and dissatisfaction.

Ultimately, it generates a hostile, poisonous, and negative atmosphere. Ignorance and lack of understanding of human qualities lead to malicious language. In the same way, failing to study something to improve our worldly conditions is equally ignorant. Using similar examples, we can contrast ignorance in daily life and non-adherence to Islam, despite claiming to be Muslim.

For a Muslim, reciprocating with the Quran brings individual and collective well-being, serenity, and self-realization. There are hard and soft aspects of humanity, and knowing the truth can be difficult for some, and for others, a quick breeze can stabilize the balance, and for the arrogant ignorance remains unabated.

The rekindling of the Quran and Sunnah is a practice most Muslims continue, even if the distance was unintentional. The destiny was written as Allah saw and knew where the human heart would lead him. Allah knows both the unseen and the seen, so the actions are predetermined.

A Muslim who is ignorant of his faith is considered the worst kind of Muslim. In the modern era, there are no valid reasons or justifications for neglecting the need to find a harmonious balance between personal growth in this world and spiritual preparation for the next.

Muslims strive to find a balance in life by seeking knowledge from the world around them and taking pleasure in their rightful portion, but those who are committed to learning understand that ignorance has no place in their lives. The only way to unravel the mysteries of the universe is through the acquisition of knowledge.

Reading the Quran over and over again reveals the truth as fresh information to a seeking mind. Never content with the status quo. But the curious are always striving to learn daily. Neither ungrateful nor unappreciative but seeking knowledge daily as food for the soul. Appreciation is for those who are aware of receiving.

One of the greatest journeys one can embark on is the pursuit of knowledge. For those seeking a balance between their daily worldly affairs and their spiritual journey. A believer who learns daily has no revenue from ignorance. The Islamic belief system includes learning as part of its platform.

Every aspect of the faith is programmed to benefit humans, not Allah. The worship of a human does not increase or decrease his divinity. A human's heart is soothed by worshiping Allah.

A Muslim's ability to perform in this world will be determined by the rules and regulations of Islam he follows. To prepare for the next examination. Education in the right format of Islam's theology puts the ignorant to rest so that they can live to the fullest.

People who comprehend the caveats of rules made to benefit human indoctrination can reap the benefits of bliss. The rules are not oppressive, but liberating, allowing you to live a peaceful and content existence. Through the divine beauty of Islam's teachings, joy and spiritual growth can be found. As with every subject, the quest for knowledge gives rise to succession, and the same is true for the Islamic faith. Having the right understanding and knowledge is equally important.

After years of formal education or employment, one is expected to reap the benefits. Depending on the performance and reliability of the actions, time is not wasted. The same applies to learning and living according to the rulings of Islam for a Muslim or any faith, for that matter. Following one's belief, the due is compensated by their actions. The ignorant cannot live in arrogance. Learning and performance hold the venue for progression in any field.

To explore this intricate process, self-investment is necessary. Besides academic gatherings and travel. It would be a treacherous waste of time to spend time with disbelievers or anyone who doesn't contribute to soul and mind improvement.

But focusing on the inner soul, which brings tranquility into life, heralds prosperity on all avenues. The lack of knowledge has been a painful experience for Muslims and a waste of time. Years passed without knowledge and obedience to Allah are a curse on a Muslim who knows Allah. It is a painful event for those Muslims who watch the downfall of once-believers.

The religion of Islam is specifically designed to address human problems and bring harmony to individuals' personalities in order to achieve success, especially in a world that is striving for peace. It is fascinating to note that the human mind is capable of engaging in thought processes and transmitting vibrations to other minds. The power of vibrations and thought messages is incredibly strong. The universe is filled with vibrations of both negative and positive energy, and it is these vibrations that contribute to certain individuals being more appealing than others.

It's the way they express themselves. All energy comes from the vibrations they send to each other. In some instances, one can feel this vibration through a crowd, a distant person, or an entertainer who holds the crowd. Depicts enthusiasm and desire to connect with one person. Sometimes the same vibrations attend to the crowd.

The positive energy and vibes emitted by a single individual have the power to spread happiness and joy throughout a multitude of people. There are certain individuals who have the ability to create such negative vibrations that they can effectively silence the entire room. The connections mentioned earlier become more evident when observing the behavior and attitude of the individual as they display both their sense of security and their vulnerabilities.

A person who exudes positive energy has the ability to captivate a crowd, whereas someone else may have the opposite effect and make people feel bored.

The pureness of thoughts is most apparent when their manifestation leads to the desired results. The solar plexus is the focal point and core of self-understanding for a human being. Without the will of Allah, nothing can occur, however, the combination of goodwill and the purity of thoughts contribute significantly to the achievement of an individual.

The presence of negative and impure thoughts has a dampening effect on the environment. The same application can also be applied to the faith of Islam. It is crucial for a Muslim to avoid investing in the fundamentals without having a clear understanding of their faith, as this can result in disaster.

When it comes to wealth, Islam is considered to be the most affluent faith. Wealth cannot be obtained in exchange for poverty, as the two are not interchangeable. Islam holds immense value and cannot be equated with impoverished ideas when it comes to monotheism.

It is a profound truth that provides clarity to an inquisitive mind, rejecting the notion of allowing poverty to interfere with the richness bestowed upon Islam by Allah. Islam stands independently prosperous, untouched by human interference. Ignorance is detrimental to one's own well-being. The reason why exploration is a public venue that is open to everyone is because it allows individuals to seek inner wealth.

The act of compromising in order to entertain evil is often a consequence of ignorance within the Islamic faith, or among those who choose to compromise or disbelieve in the fluctuating nature of faith that impacts all religions. The act of giving priority to one's own desires can ultimately lead to the emergence of a new faith that is marked by deceitfulness and arrogance.

This ignorance has been formative for decades and continues in different shades. The text emphasizes the importance of addressing character flaws, spiritual clarity, and promptly implementing updates. It can be challenging for the conscious mind to fail to recognize individual changes within and for others to notice.

The negative person tends to close in on themselves as a result of their insecurities. What one thinks and reflects upon is commonly projected onto others. They find themselves questioning their choices as a consequence of the internal frustration, the challenges they confronted, and the attitudes they encountered.

Satan specifically targets individuals who are weak and causes disturbance among those who devoutly pray to Allah. The aura provides an opportunity for re-invitation, offering another chance to rectify the issues faced by those who don't believe in unity under Allah's laws.

Believers are invited by Allah to embrace Him in their lives, whereas disbelievers' laws are influenced by Satan. It might be argued that having a temporary loss of faith in Allah is a better outcome than losing it entirely.

Those who maintain a belief in their ability to bounce back stronger from challenges often exhibit a strong sense of camaraderie and support for their fellow believers. By taking the initial step, individuals have the opportunity to immerse themselves in a multi-dimensional living experience, which ultimately serves as a valuable educational journey. In Islam, the concept of duty is highly valued and not taken lightly, with a particular emphasis on the role of the mother as the primary educator.

Among its followers, the Islamic faith places significant emphasis on the nurturing of the womb, highlighting its importance. The act of nurturing, which encompasses feeding, bathing, and tending to all the infant's needs, is how the significance and safeguarding of the mother's offspring are expressed. This guidance remains with them until they embark on their journey into the world, emerging from the very depths of the mother's being. Due to Allah's divine nature, he does not have the capability to be nurtured or guided in the same way as humans.

Additionally, he does not possess human qualities that would enable him to send a human to be born and later evolve into a God through the process of being carried by a human. There is no doubt that the birth of Jesus, which occurred within the Abrahamic faith, a monotheistic religion that takes its name from Abraham, is not only supported by common sense but also by all logical explanations. Mary, just like any devoted mother, dedicatedly nurtured her womb and lovingly took care of her offspring.

Humans are not required to nurture Allah, nor do they need to provide nourishment for him. The idea that evolution and the retrospective view can coexist is implausible, as the notion of transitioning from a human to a God is entirely invalidated and considered unachievable.

The justification for this lies in the fact that the qualities associated with a divine entity are inherently distinct from those of an ordinary person, thereby presenting a formidable challenge to the preconceived notions of individuals who possess misconceptions about the Abrahamic faith. In addition, the act of comparing Gods and mythological deities contradicts the fundamental beliefs of monotheistic faith.

A human born in a mother's womb may be considered weak, while God cannot be carried within a woman's womb. It is impossible to imagine that Allah, the creator of humanity, could be carried and nurtured in a womb. Only when a human is willing to abandon all common sense would they believe that Allah would send a son to be carried by a human, as it would diminish the exalted nature of Allah, who is the highest being.

Hence, according to the theological beliefs of Islam, Jesus cannot be considered as half god and half divine, the son of God, or God himself. This notion is refuted and denied based on logical reasoning. However, it is acknowledged in Islamic theology that Jesus is the Messiah, sent as a miraculous creation for a virgin to bear him. Allah, who is never shy of performing miracles, can accomplish anything effortlessly. His highness is characterized by being all-knowing and all-seeing, and his divine nature cannot be achieved through any form of birth, or conception.

As an alternative viewpoint, one might contemplate the existence of a birth that contradicts the customary concept of conception, involving the fusion of male and female sperm. Islam provides a comprehensive framework that delves into the intricate details of Allah's immense power, extending far beyond the boundaries of the visible world experienced by humans. By mimicking the historical epoch that existed prior to the present time, the paganistic ideologies of previous cultures are adapted going back to Hinduism, where human deities are called Gods and Greeks and the Romans implored humans as Gods.

In light of Jesus' lineage within the Abrahamic faiths, Islam refutes this claim and emphasizes the importance of providing concise and coherent explanations, given that Jesus shares the same message as a representative of monotheism. It is evident that open minds have a clear advantage over closed minds in terms of superiority. By merging the fields of theology and contrast, individuals have found new avenues to expand their perspectives and knowledge.The introduction of contrasting ideologies can serve as a catalyst for opening minds, although those who are closed-minded may be unable to grasp the concept.

There have been significant downfalls and pitfalls. More organized groups with revised versions of indoctrinated beliefs have been established through human influence, leading to misinformation. As human beings strive to submit to something intrinsic to their nature, evil is a continuous process. Islamic laws, contracts, and worshiping only Allah are priorities for Muslims. Behaviors must align with the Quran's commands and laws, benefiting humans. Allah knows what's most beneficial. There have been many defiant humans, but many fortunate people have realized the beauty of worshiping Allah, the one GOD.

Ignorance can lead to damaging upheavals. Evil uses ignorance to distract the weak and the strong. Satan promises to distract his humans, and Allah forgives those who repent and change their evil ways. But continued defiance is not unintentional; it becomes a poisonous state of mind that blocks all good. Many schisms have been diverting weak minds.

Based on his desires, a Muslim can be unaware, arrogant, or submissive to humanity. Failing on various fronts is a potential outcome. Continuous success is attainable as well. Opening doors to prosperity allows truth and mindfulness to thrive. A Muslim's motto is to hold the world in their hands, but Allah in their heart.

Having an unbalanced life in this temporal world to avoid the climate of truth. Having eternal life is more likely to be a longer existence than simply existing in this temporal one. The world is a test, it teaches daily how it works by striving for success while also being mindful of our actions. The positive impact of our good deeds can last for years, with revenue. If one rejects Allah's will, one may be lost and struggling. As Muslims, it's imperative to adapt knowledge about Islam from trustworthy sources. It becomes public either through the lips of sinners or Satanic whispers.

Alternatively, he sends hypocrites to spread the word. Gossip and unreliable advice instead of repentance characterize sinful telling without being asked instead of repentance. Evil's deception is obvious.

Confidential statements are typically from believers or former believers to disbelievers who believe in fowl. One who is not friends with Allah cannot be friends with humans. Humans can change, but the company has to change to adapt to the cocoon metamorphosis.

Quran: Surah Nisa: 4:148.Allah does not like speaking evil publicly unless one has been wronged. Allah is All-Hearing, All-Knowing.

Paganism and Satanism have a significant influence. This application is not suitable for everyone, but it is widely used. The Satan church in the USA was founded by Anton Szandor Lavey. The region saw the merging of false independence and the cult of evil, leading to moral concerns. Certain individuals can become victims of these modernization acceptance ideologies. The world is being affected by a contagious event that's spreading.

The quantum regime is independent in most academic settings on certain lands, despite lacking truth. Young minds are burdened with absorbing unnecessary rhetoric, hindering academic progress and invading personal and family lives. Part of the mission of Satanic temples is to advocate for false empathy, freedom, resistance to tyranny, and protests against injustice. Those easily deceived are manipulated by evil disguised as a satanic cult.

Deceit manifests in different forms, often with lies at the forefront. Ideologies are followed by people without them consciously incorporating them into their minds, not knowing the consequences of returns are paybacks from evil. If the cult makes the rules, they bow to someone.

When a victim follows the satanic cult, his or her self-inflicted woes are returned with a great deal of independence and disregard for Allah's laws in return. In some cases, cults serve this system openly, whereas others practice unhealthy acts due to distrust of the truth. The lie appeals to them more than the truth. In these cults that do not believe in an unseen God, he is associated with something human and divine. But a monotheist does not worship mortals or pagan Gods. Anything falling into paganistic rituals is out of monotheism.

Or cults deceive their followers by proclaiming themselves to be Gods. They do not see divine rules that pertain to their desires. A similar cult system. During the Roman Empire, erecting statues of humans and referring to them as Greek Gods was a pedagogy of falsehood wrapped in deceit that exposed nudity through statues and architecture.

On most buildings with a combination of domes copied from Muslim architecture, it serves as an emblem of belief and a reminder bringing nudists. The presence of human remains is observed in ancient churches and roads. In addition to the reminders of worship and colorful rituals showcased through cultic practices. These days are characterized by ignorance. Islamic doctrine includes rules and strict laws that reject all these principles without any changes in their implementation. People are safeguarded from cult deception and lies by these laws.

As a result, society becomes more just and honest. Islam reveals nothing unless it benefits humans and their souls and the environment and their survival in this temperate world. Islam stands against such rhetoric and questions parents' validity. Since Allah created humans to be subservient, it is impossible to be content in the long run with idol or material worship. Islam considers ignorance detrimental, and progress is meant to benefit the human soul, not Allah. He is Allah. With or without human worship.

Humans benefit from worshiping Allah. Islam says ignorant Muslims are dangerous to themselves and others. Because they can be influenced by self-interest at the expense of losing faith. This is a cunning way academic leadership in Islamophobic regions undermines belief systems. Decoding lies continue to display the barrel of independence.

Nevertheless, the consequence is typically surrendering to Satan and his deceptive tactics, resulting in the loss of freedom. Why would a Muslim choose to remain ignorant about their faith? Jahiliyah is the term used to describe ignorance and opposition to Islam. Arabs in the pre-Islamic era followed their own ways and called it Jahilliyyah.

Even in this modern era, if a Muslim recalls committing actions displeasing to Allah, they may refer to it as their past ignorance (Jahiliyah), repent, and strive to forget, as no one wishes to be reminded or remember their sins. It is best to move forward, repent, and trust that Allah will be the ultimate judge. Moving forward with learning requires a reasonable, diplomatic, and reconciliatory approach to eliminate ignorance. Seekers find faith, peace, and contentment through Allah.

Islam's dominance led to the spelling out of their ways in laws and rules. All opposing ideologies of old and new civilizations incompatible with Islamic beliefs are condemned. The convenience of the modern era is beneficial for those living in the pre-modern era, which closely resembles the pre-dated era. Islam brings new reforms instead of following old ways, making it a modern and progressive religion.

This doctrine of independence, from Isamophobes catering to the majority, will prevail and bring about the downfall of the deceitful. Many individuals in this cultic practice have depression and have high suicide rates. Islam prohibits engaging in fornication and adultery. Alcohol consumption is prohibited. Avoid engaging in gambling, polytheistic rituals, and idol worship. Islamic concepts bring order to life, despite apparent dissimilarities or exposure to incompatible ideologies.

A lack of humility towards Allah is evident when an educated Muslim or an uneducated Muslim presents themselves with arrogance. Their behavior is shaped by the culture around them, not by Islam. The culture is defined by rules that prioritize character and a lack of discipline, resulting in collisions for the conscientious and those who witness the downfall of loved ones. Correcting arrogant or ego-centric Muslims is a duty for a Muslim.

Fear is absent in those who have hope, and lies and deceit are like a bothersome thorn in the mind of those with a pure heart. Despite this, the wise or swayed can deviate. When arrogance mixes with Islamic concepts, there is no harmony, just as Satan's arrogance serves as an example for all of humanity. Self-inflicted suffering leads to feelings that are overwhelming and all-encompassing, erasing rationality and causing baffling actions.

Normalities and contrasts of the believer's endurance of rooting dispel the transgression. This becomes increasingly compelling as the heart is in a state of euphoria, of cleansing as a believer. As a result, your perception of any stimulus or emotion will be amplified. Islam has distinctive characteristics. There are no weak, tainted, or aggressive elements to it. To destitute and discipline their character, those who recognize and understand the faith often look for reconciliation with the faith that documents and withdraws evil. By changing course, you can leave the weaker surroundings behind and discover a primal company that complements your beliefs and unlocks treasures.

What is worse, ignorance or arrogance? Ignorance can be fixed, but arrogance is Satan's characteristic. On many fronts under Satan's influence. Such evils can persist for decades and years until ignorance leaves and clarity sinks in. If a Muslim defies Allah's laws to gain human acceptance, an episode of happiness is not contentment. After being exposed to Islam's truth. When defiance of Allah becomes a habit to please others, malice within will cause damage in the future. Sometimes the payback comes sooner rather than later.

Hadith: Muslim Tirmidhi: The Prophet Muhammad said: "One will not enter paradise if one has an atom's weight of arrogance in his/her heart."

To whom does arrogance belong? Those individuals who choose to oppose Allah, even when the truth is clearly apparent. Especially individuals who have had previous exposure to Islam. The Muslims who do not possess a deep understanding of their faith often find themselves in a state of confusion. Intentionally neglecting to learn is something that cannot be overlooked or forgiven.

The council of disbelievers, with their misguided beliefs, can be compared to lost sheep who have strayed from the right path. Instead of remaining vigilant against ignorance of Islam, believers who are not studying to expand their knowledge risk being visited by Satan.

In 610 CE, the Arabian Peninsula witnessed Islam, which marked the end of the pre-Islamic era of ignorance. Certain individuals possess the ability to vividly depict this significant period in history.

170

Individuals who possess faith frequently strive to adhere to regulations that are in accordance with the laws of Allah and are widely acknowledged, as they perceive them to hold greater significance and appeal. Only believers have the privilege of understanding Allah's timing, and this understanding can bring about a distinct feeling of sweetness or negativity.

How a person uses their time will have a significant impact on the outcome of various situations. The wretched past of humanity might surprisingly give birth to the most promising future. There is no price that can be placed on the experience of spending time with someone who has a greater love for Allah than for you.

More people are gravitating towards evil due to its spreading. Why do men seek relationships with other men and women with other women? Did Allah create man to satisfy another man? No, he did not, so why is it frowned upon to express this truth that goes against Allah's creation?

Were Adam and Eve created as a male and female couple? It is fine to go against Allah's commands. The status quo can be disregarded when confronting the defiant in this world. The arrogant and ignorant can be deceived by evil, but those who understand prioritize the laws of Allah.

In what way does human disobedience contribute to the spread of diseases? Wasn't COVID-19, the recent pandemic, sufficient to make those with underlying health conditions more vulnerable? Didn't evil return after they were given a chance to survive? Humanity was not created by Allah to survive to do evil.

Additional diseases and warnings are coming for those who defy Allah and harm society. The righteous will die, but Allah has prepared a place for them to return. The disturbed perspectives never shift. If this is an alarm to read to change your ways then the read was worth it.

Can defiances be countered as ignorance, or is it futile in a world with easy access to social media? Those who perceive reminders as invitations to improve have gained from individuals who remind others of Allah and his laws.

Abraham's faith in Allah earned him the title of the father of all Prophets; divisions and lack of faith are the root causes of the world's suffering.The mosque doors close after hours, while Satan's venues remain open and inviting. Evil tendencies arise for some when mosques close and illicit activities are available.

The Kabba in Mecca is open for worship at all times, unlike mosques that have set hours. This is a global issue as some countries are afraid to keep mosques open. However, Mecca in Saudi Arabia remains accessible for worship at any hour. The Dajjal, the antichrist, will not be able to enter this sacred place. The Dajjal antiChrist will invade all lands except Mecca in Saudi Arabia. Prayer is never restricted in this beautiful city. The house of Allah is open for worshipers at any hour.

In order to gain a complete understanding of the new Islamophobic modernized independence, it becomes essential to delve into its origins and acquire a comprehensive comprehension of their significant influence on the global stage.

Since the emergence of Islam, all faiths have been deeply influenced, making it nearly impossible to find a religious community untouched as Islam and its impact throughout history. Islam's reform, characterized by the idea of regaining freedom through walls without barriers, has had a profound and far-reaching effect.

Regrettably, the implementation of this reform has resulted in negative outcomes for the global community, including the emergence of fear, arrogance, and misrepresentation primarily driven by Islamophobia and widespread unrest.

Ignorance is often the result of a lack of understanding, whereas the presence of corruption creates an environment where true beliefs and laws are undermined, allowing evil to thrive and spread. To truly understand those who sow evil and their inability to sow good, one must delve into the study of history, examining the roots of those who invited and created the house of Satan as a place of worship.

Whether a believer disagrees with the disbeliever's belief system or not, grave loss caused by negligence cannot justify silence. This evil is especially dangerous if it strikes believers' homes.Not allowing ignorance to persist on the believer's journey is key.

Standing up for your beliefs despite opposition is the truth. The faith of a believer who knows Allah is on their side is unbreakable, unlike Satan and his followers. Correction is necessary to restore the lost minds, and Allah's mercy is greater than his anger toward the ignorant if a believer helps them. But those who receive help have to help themselves to gain knowledge.

Ill health of spirituality and deprivation of blessings from Allah can lead to a toxic environment or ignorance of faith. This is a corruption of the mind, and believers must avoid toxic individuals and surroundings that do not align with Islam's beliefs.

Throughout history, individuals have interacted with many people from diverse societies and formed mutually beneficial friendships. However, adapting to their social and moral principles can be difficult for Islam followers, as they may be incompatible with their beliefs.

Despite this, a believer can reside in any country and still follow his belief system. Allah determines their destiny, and their place of residence is also pre-determined. A believer needs to have their heart as close to their beliefs as possible and guard against allowing evil to enter.When ignorant individuals act recklessly, they can upset the human balance, which relies on inner peace.

This can lead to anxiety, depression, and other mental health disorders, especially for Muslims who intentionally disobey Allah. The problems of the heart can cause a once-devout follower to become corrupted by self-desire and failure to obey Allah's laws.This can lead to the development of ill habits that are detrimental to one's health and ultimately stem from ignorance, known as (jahiliyah). And self-imposed desires lead people to sacrifice their spiritual and physical health to conform to a corrupt society.

Hadith Tirmidhi:2414.Whoever seeks pleasure from Allah by displeasure from people. Allah suffices against the people. Whoever seeks the pleasure of people by displeasing Allah, Allah will leave him to the patronage of the people.

In the long term, going against the laws of Allah is harmful to both the physical and spiritual well-being of humans. The pleasure of Allah is more important than the misguided actions of humans. Disobeying the creator who made humanity is too risky. However, everyone must accept the consequences of their actions. Repeatedly disobeying Allah is not ignorance, but arrogance. Society cannot dismiss the laws of Allah. Unfortunately, many people, particularly Muslims, suffer unnoticed ills when they ignore Allah's laws.

Life's highs are fleeting, but the lows can seem endless. These lows help believers return to ground zero. Some people never overcome their challenges. However, those who are fortunate enough to see the dilemma and push through it become even stronger. The most valuable friend is the one who reminds us of Allah and helps us stay true to our beliefs. Other friends may listen to our problems or offer advice, but they cannot support our belief system like a friend who shares our faith.

Quran: Surah Imran: 3:28. The believers may not take unbelievers for their allies in preference to those who believe.

Quran: Surah Imran: 3:19. Indeed, the religion in the sight of Allah is Islam. And those who were given the Scripture did not differ except after knowledge had come to them – out of jealous animosity between themselves.

The Quran explicitly warns against forming alliances with disbelievers due to historical and current incidents of betrayal. In a world where believers can change their demeanor, it is difficult to trust disbelievers. Do not doubt the Quran; doubt is from Satan. A true believer will follow the advice of the Quran.

Common sense suggests that the creator is revealing humanity's potential to his followers. Shouldn't people listen to their creator? Anyone with logic will ensure that they understand the words and advice for their own protection.

The message being delivered does not contain any indication that forming friendships with non-Muslims should be avoided, even though it is acknowledged that certain non-Muslims may display better behavior than some Muslims. In this day and age, even those who previously had faith can easily shift their beliefs, which poses a challenge as the majority without faith can abandon the human and its words and arrangements.

However, it is still possible to rectify this situation. It is interesting to note that even those who do not believe in their creator can still surprise someone when they least expect it.

This can be seen through the knowledge of the history of solid friendships and destruction in Muslim lands. Simply observing the entry into these lands is enough to witness the continuous process of envy, from Islamophobes, which extends beyond daily life and it is mostly not prevalent among commoners.

Surprisingly, these small friendships with non-Muslims have remained strong for decades. It is important to mention that Allah does not explicitly forbid befriending humanity from other faiths nor does Islam suggest discrimination at any point. However, caution is advised when it comes to placing trust in others.

The climate can be harsh for both believers and disbelievers, but what sets certain individuals apart is their unwavering commitment to upholding a moral code, irrespective of their faith. Theological differences are not a barrier that separates humanity; instead, both Muslims and non-Muslims can count on each other and find common ground.

Why did the Quran suddenly assert that Islam is the preferred belief by Allah? The answer is straightforward: the initial creation's faith was Islam, and the father of all Prophets believed in one God. Muslims believe in one God and also believe in all Prophets.

Humans have no authority to choose or refuse Prophets if they are all sent from Allah. The belief in one God is central to Islam, which is why it is a rapidly growing faith. The Quran asserts that animosity developed after the truth was acknowledged and rejected, driven by their inherent envy-fueled defiance.

When all attempts, whether successful or unsuccessful, have been made to uncover the truth for those who are arrogant and confused. In order to comprehend the delivery and existence of truth, it is necessary to have an open mind.

The verdict, whether it is accepted or rejected, will ultimately be determined by Quranic judgment. In anticipation of the impending judgment, it is important to value and appreciate the clothes we have now, for the time will come when we will stand naked and full of hope, just as we entered this world.

Quran: Surah Fath 48:28. It is He who sent His Messenger with the True Guidance and the Religion of Truth that He may make it prevail over every religion. Sufficient is Allah as a witness to this.

Prophet Muhammad is the final messenger of Allah, sent to address alterations made to previous scriptures; whether one chooses to believe in him is a personal decision. Despite his character potentially being reexamined, it remains firm in every aspect desired by a human seeking fulfillment in every avenue. His departures symbolize the end of Islam's final chapter of revelations. Prophet Muhammad consistently showed compassion and fair judgment, despite facing presumptions and judgment. Whenever issues arose, he was always available to address them.

To live by Allah's wishes, believers must maintain their individuality and follow their path. Prophet Muhammad was greatly admired for his compassion and love for all. Upon hearing the camel's complaint about its hurting back from the heavy merchandise, he made a fair judgment and instructed the owner to alleviate the weight. He could communicate with animals, humans, and jinns; he was a Prophet. Prophet Muhammad's actions are an example of kindness. He exhibited composure, endurance, and sustainability, which were challenging traits for humanity to possess.

However, many were convinced of Islam's sweetness through his compassionate and firm message. Islam's teachings and message are precise and reliable, with a strong emphasis on Allah's mercy. Despite being a religion that dates back centuries, it attracts millions of followers in contemporary society.

It's not just individuals, but entire nations and even a whole church that are converting to Islam in today's day and age. Shahada is the starting point of your journey after conversion. The best person to share this with is someone who believes, not necessarily a Muslim by name, but someone who embraces Islam upon receiving a direct invitation from Allah. If Allah wills, even the strayed Muslims can return, for He knows the heart.

When Prophet Muhammad traveled to the small city of Taif in Arabia to teach about Islam, he faced a harsh climate of rudeness and disbelief from his opponents. Despite his strenuous journey, he received an unwelcoming reception.Islam requires guests to treat guests with respect and positivity.

When someone travels a distance to visit, it is especially fitting to honor them as a guest. Although some may find certain aspects of repetition in Islamic practices tedious, repetition actually helps build awareness in the subconscious mind and is therefore sustainable. Honoring guests is considered the most significant value in Islam. The Quran demands to honor a guest who travels to see you.

Quran: Surah Dhariyat 51:24:37 (O Prophet), did the story of Abraham's honored guests reach you?

Quran: Surah Hud 11:78 And his people came to him rushing. Before, they wanted to commit evil deeds. Lot said: 'My people! Here are my daughters; they are purer for you.

The inhabitants of Taif disrespected the Prophet Muhammad by treating him cruelly as a guest. He came with sincere intentions to teach Islam's goodness and faith, but instead, they sent children to pelt him with stones. Adults can determine their behavior, whether favorable or bad, and it is up to adults to guide the young.

The sight of his bloody shoes and clothes filled him with sorrow, and during moments of vulnerability, he cried out to his creator. Despite being a guest, he was met with a harsh and mocking welcome.

It's unfortunate how cruel humans can be when they don't believe in Allah and lack kindness towards each other. A person installed with Satan's whispers can easily engage in treasonous behavior. These exchanges have played a crucial role in the past and continue to do so today. Contrasts aid learning, and one can express manners and gratitude through actions and comments, as shown by Prophet Muhammad's experiences.

By leaving behind a legacy of welcome or evil, Allah establishes documentation of what has happened.He prayed to Allah that his enemies wouldn't have an advantage over him. Quraish's wealthy leaders owned a stunning garden. Atabah and Shaibah watched with sadness and regret as the Prophet was treated poorly. To make amends, they sent their servant Ada's grapes from the garden. The Prophet thanked Allah and ate the grapes.

Angel Gabriel visited Prophet Muhammad after the incident. Gabriel asked him which punishment he preferred for those responsible. He did not seek revenge despite his suffering. The angel asked if he wanted the city buried between two mountains.

His wish was for Taif's city and youth to embrace Islam. He wanted everyone to know and experience the beauty of this faith. Prophet Muhammad's prayers for Taif were for Islam's future spread. Taif's story highlights the value of honoring our character and not harboring anger or hate towards oppressors. Pride and ego lead to misunderstandings and a lack of kindness. He set a precedent for all by showing kindness and praying for Taif.

Taif, being a Muslim country, boasts beautiful water and scenery, and five daily prayers. Many devout Muslims bow to Allah, even those who previously did not. This is a testament to Allah's mercy and the Prophet Muhammad's teachings. Taif is a popular tourist destination and is blessed by Allah. The once detrimental and negative has transformed into a source of empowerment and optimism. There are countless examples for humanity to reflect on.

This city is filled with kindness, motivating people to create positive transformations within themselves. Taif's reputation lies in its hospitality and friendliness, offering humanity hope. The city that once caused mischief has transformed into a beautiful tourist town through prayer.

Lack of awareness can cause problems for Muslims if not addressed properly. The environment plays a crucial role in shaping self-esteem and conduct, as emphasized by Muslims. Following their conversion to Islam, the Bedouins of Arabia experienced a significant transformation during Prophet Muhammad's era. They refrained from reverting back to their old habits or social circles. The Quran showcases how Islam transformed human behavior and mindset. Prophet Abraham, born to an idolater named Azar, rejected his pagan roots and embraced monotheism.

Quran: Surah Fussilat 41:34(Good and evil cannot be equal. Respond 'to evil' with what is best, then the one you are in a feud with will be like a close friend).

Quran: Surah Ahzab 33:34 And remember what it recited in your houses of the verses of Allah and wisdom. Indeed, Allah is ever Subtle and acquainted with all things.

Faith is fostered and strengthened by being in the company of fellow Muslims. Muslims should use their influence to spread the truth, not falsehoods. Muslims globally desire the best for humanity and would not hide the truth if it were real. Allah's love is clear when certain individuals are universally loved.

Angel Gabriel along with other angels share crucial information to foster recognition and appreciation of the devotee of Allah. Individuals with strong faith in Allah are recognized for their positive influence, while those who are envious and unbelieving are excluded.

Those who are mindful of Allah are the ones that Allah favors, not those who choose to disobey him. The brightness of their smiles clearly indicates the level of their happiness. Even brief interactions with them have the power to touch hearts and leave a lasting impact.

The company we keep greatly influences our lives, as emphasized in Islam. Satan disrupts those who interact with negative individuals, causing doubt. A devout individual outshines a disbeliever. These disliked individuals are seen as negative symbols, even by Allah. Allah's kindness allows true believers to sense non-believers' ' presence. Certain individuals have lasting impacts, while others are fleeting. Allah distinguishes between wrong and good.

Finding guidance in the Quran and performing Salat can purify the heart. A true believer doesn't trust ignorant and uneducated individuals who serve as judges and jurors. Building character is akin to crafting a better life, with the best design and companionship, and embracing it completely.

Witness testimonies started in Saudi Arabia with Prophet Muhammad and are now universally accepted. Islam is recognized as a symbol of truth. Inaccurate sources of information are used by people globally, with inadequate knowledge. Their understanding of Islam and Muslim cultures is insufficient for discussion. Trustworthy sources are necessary for learning about these topics. The Creator's environment determines the ability to excel.

Bowing to Allah in prayer is not a burden, but a humble and gracious gift. To maintain sobriety, individuals struggling with alcohol addiction avoid their old drinking buddies. They avoid bars and other places that tempt them to drink. Likewise, faithful followers are cautious of their social circle and choose companions who share their values and beliefs.

"You are the company you keep," as stated by the Prophet Muhammad. Our actions and behavior are a reflection of our faith and self-image. Through closeness to Allah, believers seek to eliminate negative influences. The environment and social circle have a significant impact on personal growth and development. Islam regards the careful selection of company and surroundings as essential.

Quran: Surah ISRA 17:72. Whoever lived in this world as blind shall live as blind in the life to come; rather, he will be even farther astray than if he were just blind.

According to Hadith Bukhari, narrated by Uthman, Prophet Muhammad stated that the most excellent Muslims are those who learn the Qur'an and teach it.

It is common to feel uncertain in a dangerous environment. The Shahada is recited when someone converts to Islam to accept the faith. Nevertheless, this is merely the onset of a substantial expedition.

Islam does not impose its ways on people. Similar to the Bedouins during Prophet Muhammad's time, those who decided to follow anticipated significant transformations in their lives. Islam remains unchanged; it's not for people's convenience.

Names hold great significance in Islam. Many converts to Islam seek a new name to symbolize their spiritual transformation and enlightenment in Islam. This is a critical moment for individuals to contemplate their self-image, and there is no need to announce any change as it will be evident to others. Status in Islam is not determined by material revenue, color, or creed. The beauty of it lies in its simplicity.

Although the teachings of Islam may not always match one's lifestyle, true repentance requires stopping harmful actions. Ignorance often leads people to prioritize their desires over Allah's rules and regulatio's rules and regulations. Temporary ignorance or disobedience caused by self-desire can be corrected through repentance once knowledge is gained.

Allah's forgiveness is renowned, so it is wise to avoid repeating mistakes made by others or oneself, as Allah may have already pardoned them. Beauty is encompassed in every aspect of life in Islam. Believers should steer clear of gossip and sinful conversations to avoid Satan resurfacing forgiven sins by Allah. Evil promotes sin by enslaving believers to their past or present emotions. Poverty of the heart can result in destructive behavior, self-harm, and negative influences. Repairing oneself is crucial for a successful future, especially for Muslims. Reform and repentance are the starting point.

Quran: Surah Luqman:14:15. And We have commanded people to honor their parents. Their mothers bore them through hardship upon hardship, and their weaning takes two years)

Bible: Exodus 20:12:The fifth commandment says, "Honor your father and your mother, that your days may be long in the land that the Lord your God is giving you.

Disrespect is frequently encountered by individuals who strive for independence in a society that is fixated on age, particularly those who find themselves in antiquated environments during this modern era. The proper upbringing of parents or caregivers in Muslim communities is of utmost importance as it plays a vital role in ensuring the future success and well-being of the younger generation.

Mothers who play an active role in molding their children's knowledge and awareness of Allah bear the burden of accountability. The mother's role holds great significance in Islam as it has a profound impact on molding the faith of her children. If she has granted the rights for teaching a child to learn and understand Allah and Islam, she will be questioned, as it is the rightful entitlement of a child born into the Islamic faith. Developing the character of children who disregard obedience to Allah requires the early implementation of discipline. The absence of faith often leads individuals to lean on their own doomed ideologies, much like the ruler of Egypt who famously placed his trust in the mystical realm of magic.

Ideologies are inherent to every person, yet it is an undeniable truth that certain ideologies are destined to meet failure in due course. Within the teachings of Islam, there are various aspects that are covered including material laws, contracts, discipline, and manners. Despite having knowledge of the truth, there are individuals who opt to disregard it and face the resulting repercussions, especially those who endure a slow demise.

Alqamah's story is an example of contemplation:

Muslims prioritize obeying a believing mother as they align her with Allah''s interests. Islamic laws take precedence over a mother's request if they contradict. The purpose of this respect is not to give mothers the right to meddle in their offspring's life at any age; however, teaching them the foundations of Islam was their duty when they were young. However, her advice remains valid regardless of age.

The reason they will come back is that walking on solid ground is a more common experience compared to having no ground at all. Envision a world where the extraordinary ability to walk on air is within your grasp. In the context of Islam, it is recommended to prioritize the respectful treatment of mothers rather than resorting to negative reactions.

In addition, mothers will also be asked about their treatment of their child and specifically, Muslim mothers will be questioned about how they instilled teachings of their faith in their children. While the mother's authority does not replace that of God, it is important to acknowledge and respect the role she plays in our lives, leaving the ultimate decision-making to Allah.

The plot of making the mother co-equal to her children by Islamophobic societies is the same as those who plant deceit.Equating Jesus to Allah and a mother to her children is easy for deceitful individuals in this society.

The story of Alqamah serves as a cautionary tale, highlighting the consequences of both time wasted and arrogance:

.Alqama's story holds truth as he was a believer he did everything right in obedience to Allah he chose to speak negatively and harshly towards his mother who taught him about Allah how could he forget Allah also said to have respect for his believing mother who attended to the most important part of life taught him about Allah. It was not intentional but he chose his self desires instead of talking nice he made her upset some mothers forgive some don't she did not forgive him for his rudeness. The issue at hand was connected to a specific woman in his life, however, the words that were exchanged indicated a lack of respect for her legitimate concerns.

As the moment of his demise drew near, he faced immense difficulty in uttering the shahada, the sacred testimony of his faith. Prophet Muhammad was aware of his arduous struggle towards the end, with each breath becoming a challenge. It seemed as if life itself was anticipating the conclusion, with an unknown element that perplexed him. Despite being a wonderful man, he possessed a demeanor of arrogance that should have been set aside, especially when it concerned his own mother.

The better option was to walk away from him rather than boasting about his arrogant nature and the way he treated her in the past. Despite her anger towards him, she was unwilling to forgive him and instead held onto it. He didn't come around to apologize, but rather chose to spend his time in worship, following her teachings and practicing everything she had taught him. He prayed salat, gave tidings, and adhered to all the Islamic concepts she had imparted to him.

Islam is a comprehensive religion that not only discourages rudeness towards one's mother, but also rejects any harsh words that contradict its principles. It is expected that once anger subsides, one must apologize; otherwise, conflicts can persist for years, which is not in accordance with Islamic teachings, but unfortunately, such conflicts have occurred within the Muslim community. This particular occurrence serves as a flawless illustration, even taking place during the time of Prophet Muhammad.

Prophet Muhammad asked about his mother's health, she was well, but she hesitated to forgive him despite his dedication to Allah. He assigned Bilal the task of collecting wood for burning him. It was worth a try to have his mother forgive him, despite the event not taking place. He made it clear that he wouldn't read his shahada testimony until he was forgiven by the mother, leading to his suffering.

In response, the mother expressed her refusal to forgive him, stating that he had never visited her. He then proposed that the only remaining option was his suffering. This caused her heart to tremble as she revealed that she had been waiting eagerly for him to come see her, which was the reason behind her anger.

The situation was emotional for her, as she had deep affection for Alqama. Unfortunately, he had already made the wrong choice and by the time he realized it, it was too late to change it. Having received forgiveness from his mother, he peacefully passed away, forever cherishing the knowledge of being a respected member of the Islamic community.

Regrettably, within the context of this narrative, precious time was wasted, leading to missed chances to share moments with his mother. Despite her longing for him, he remained patient and hopeful for her to eventually have a change of heart, but that never came to fruition. The mother's inability to forgive was primarily due to the hurtful display of arrogance exhibited by him, but it was also exacerbated by the prolonged wait to see her son. The mother, in her teachings, imparted knowledge about Allah to him. The source of her upsetness did not stem from his choices, but rather from his failure to come home and see her, which caused her anger.

Although he may have misunderstood, the son who knows his mother well comprehends her simple desire to spend time with him. The arrival of their son or daughter is considered a blessing, and there isn't a single mother who doesn't eagerly anticipate their children's return. The climate can be harsh for those who fail to comprehend that it is not the choices that hinder the bond between a mother and child, but rather the mere sound of the child, regardless of their age.

The arrival of a child is sufficient to establish and solidify this relationship, even if it is only for a limited duration. Alaqama, being a devout follower of Allah, sadly missed the opportunity to spend time with his mother. His arrogance caused her to wait for him, resulting in wasted time.

It turns out she was not wrong; he never returned home. The mother does not seek apologies, but rather finds enlightenment in the presence of her child. This is the belief that defines a mother, and this tenderness is a common trait among most mothers. Alqama died with the misunderstanding that she resented his choices and was angry at him for not coming to see her.

After the Janazah, the final prayers for the deceased Prophet Muhammad delivered a khutbah emphasizing the importance of mothers and their close bond with their children compared to fathers. While nations may have suffered defeat, it is never right to speak harshly to a mother or anyone else. Believers have wins ahead, so there's no need to self-defeat.

A Muslim has the freedom to do as they please, but it's wise to hear their mother's advice and follow the path Allah has set. All mothers have a common desire, which is to ensure the best for their children. Nevertheless, it is essential to remember that while individuals have the ultimate authority over their decisions, sharing opinions should not lead to the deterioration of relationships.

Humanity benefits from discoveries. Comparisons are only informative for those seeking, but the truth is what humans seek, and for those searching, they can find it. Listening to Allah's laws is a battle for some although disobedience has its own price tag. It is usually those who are not familiar with Islam who give advice.

A chameleon's attitude is dangerous-not knowing the do's but convincing the don'ts leads to arrogance mixed with ignorance.Muslims prioritize Islam over everything else. Disobeying its teachings can lead to lack of understanding and faith. Allah meticulously records every action taken by humans, leaving nothing undocumented or void. One of the reasons why forgiveness holds a high value in Islam is because time, once wasted, can never be regained.

This thorough record-keeping reminds believers to stay on the right path. Islam notates doubts in disbelievers' minds and hopes in believers. Each human is assigned two angels to record their daily events, as well as a good and an evil Jinn since birth. The impact of these forces on an individual's daily life depends on which one carries more weight. In Islam, not all sins are equal as each sin has its measure.

This is because Islam is a factual faith and just like human faults are not treated equally in court, Allah punishes sin differently. When someone unexpectedly indulges in negative actions, it can reduce others' respect for them until they reform. If Muslims believed that Prophet Muhammad would take their sins by dying for them, they would likely be inclined to do as they please. The love for this Prophet is so strong that it can surpass all boundaries when it comes to following the laws of life in this world.

If Allah could make a human sacrifice take his dignity to appease other humans, then what is stopping another human from committing acts of deceit when they know that someone else has taken the brunt of the blame for their misdeeds?

In a society that believes in Jesus dying for their sins, blaming others for their own mistakes is common. Those who hold this concept have deeply embedded the blame game in their minds. In Islam, associating partners with Allah is unforgivable. Unlike Christianity, which believes in the forgiveness of all sins through salvation and acceptance of Jesus as a Savior, this belief sets itself apart. Islam considers adding partners to be polytheism due to its adherence to monotheism.

Muslims worship Allah, who created heaven for believers and Hell for those who do not believe or rebel against him. Islam's justice system emphasizes fairness, and individuals are responsible for their actions and deeds. Allah did not create hell for luxury; it has a destination for every type of evil. Palliating lies is not an invitation to Islam. It's straight and simple. I like it, dislike it, or leave it. But those who leave always return tenfold. Apostasy can cause greater distress than disobedience. Some people live in more turmoil than they bargained for.

Bible: ESV Mathew 5:21: You shall not murder, and anyone who murders will be subject to judgment.

According to the verse provided, murder is explicitly prohibited. Christians believe that Jesus was hanged and killed, which raises the question of how such a heinous act can be revered and celebrated as dying for the sins of others. Additionally, the symbol of the cross serves as a constant reminder of the tragic events and inhumane treatment that Jesus endured, without anyone stepping forward to help him.

The idea that onlookers would just passively observe and then later decide that it was in their best interest to take on the responsibility for the wrongdoings of others seems to defy common sense. The story presented seems to be not only unfair but also goes against biblical principles, as it portrays a betrayal towards an individual who was left in a state of hopelessness and helplessness.

Furthermore, the concept of Allah sacrificing his son for them appears to lack logical reasoning and does not align with common sense. However, the theatrical experience of evil can be witnessed in our daily lives, as Islamophobes target nations that lack the means to defend themselves against their own forces. This same scenario can be seen in the portrayal of an individual bearing the burden of human suffering solely for the sins of deceitful individuals whom he had no knowledge of.

Although the biblical text clearly states the commandment "You shall not commit murder," the interpretation within different belief systems has elevated the killing of this Prophet to a sacred act. The concept in question has been understood by humans throughout history, and the theology associated with it sheds light on this development. Understanding coherently is of utmost importance due to the unbreakable nature of Allah's word.

In contrast, Islam takes a different theological position on this concept, as it does not accept the notion of Jesus's death but instead advocates for the succession of another individual in his place. This is not a minor difference in belief, as the entire faith is centered around death and his role in salvation.

The allegations made against Jesus are insufficient because, like all Prophets, he referred to himself as a servant of Allah. Additionally, there is no record of him ever proclaiming himself as the king of the Jews, even from the moment of his birth. Another blasphemous lie against him is the reason he will return as the Messiah and the one who will rectify the allegations placed against him.

In Pilate's court, Jesus was brought before the Jewish elders who urged Pontius Pilate to pass judgment and condemn him. However, instead of receiving a fair trial, Jesus was subjected to even harsher punishment, thereby bringing together both Romans and Jews in this episode. The truth, which Muslims firmly believe in, will become evident as time goes by. It is believed that a significant figure Jesus will return and proclaim this truth. Furthermore, he is alive, unlike other humans who only experience death once.

Hence, when this individual Prophet and the Messiah returns to the world, he will only die once. It is important to note that he will not be coming to countries that harbor Islamophobia, but rather from a Muslim country, Syria. Since the theology discussed in each chapter resonates with Islamic concepts and beliefs, it is evident that Muslims hold the truth. Therefore, there is no valid reason to deny this truth. Additionally, differences in theology should not be viewed as a source of conflict or debate, as belief is ultimately a personal choice and should not be forced upon anyone.

Quran: Surah Nisa: 4:157 And for their, saying, "Indeed, we have killed the Messiah, Jesus the son of Mary, the messenger of Allāh." And they did not kill him, nor did they crucify him, but another was made to resemble him to them. And indeed, those who differ over it are in doubt about it. They have no knowledge of it except the following assumption. And they did not kill him, for certain.

Quran: Surah Nisa: 4:171.O People of the Scripture, do not commit excess in your religion1 or say about Allāh except the truth. The Messiah, Jesus, the son of Mary, was but a messenger of Allāh. His word, which He directed to Mary and a soul created at a command from Him.

So believe in Allāh and His messengers. And do not say, "Three"; desist - it is better for you. Indeed, Allāh is but one God. Exalted is He above having a son. To Him belongs whatever is in the heavens and whatever is on the earth. And sufficient is Allāh as Disposer of affairs.

Quran: Surah Nisa: 4;159.Every one of the People of the Book will definitely believe in him before his death. And on the Day of Judgment, Jesus will be a witness against them.

The disparity in beliefs between these two religions is significant, with stark differences even in their stories. It is a crucial factor that distinguishes them. Muslims must confront these stories and facts rather than remain ignorant. While friendships may be strong, it is not worth compromising religious beliefs. Compromising one's beliefs to maintain a relationship is not worth it.

Learning to progress in life is paramount. It is valuable to understand and appreciate the faith diversity in our world. Learning about theology is a fundamental aspect of personal growth. Rejecting or altering religious beliefs is incompatible with monotheistic principles. As monotheistic faiths, the Abrahamic religions believed in one God. However, Christianity differs from Islam in accepting the sacrifice of a man, a Messiah the Prophet Jesus, who is not considered divine in Islam.

This deviates from the belief in one God without additions, is pragmatic and focused on monotheism which was upheld by Abraham, the father of all Orthodox faiths. The Quran, which is unchanging, is central to the Muslim belief system, and remaining ignorant of its teachings is not an option. Allah, the God the owner of the two worlds, and owner of all creation is not a human being. The idea of him being co-equal with anyone or anything is beyond rational comprehension. Unlike Christianity, Islam does not depend on a human messenger sent by Allah to wash away the sins of humans. Jesus, who submitted to Allah's will, was a Muslim, not a Christian. He worshiped Allah, the one God, and not himself. While some may find these differences appealing, others may resent them.

The belief system of Islam has a long history and is not something that has been recently established. The absence of comprehension regarding Islam's teachings can result in doubts and misconceptions arising. Islam, a religion that is free from fear, can be easily understood by individuals who possess an open mind. Due to the concept of submission in Islam, all Prophets, including Jesus, are considered Muslims as they submitted to Allah. Allah chose the name Islam for the faith of Adam and Eve when humanity was deemed ready, but Islamic concepts uphold that its essence has remained constant.

In a particular instance, a child directed his question towards his mother, inquiring about the presence of God in the room while pointing to the statue of Jesus. The mother was taken aback by the child's question, her surprise evident, and she wondered aloud why he was contemplating the concept of God at such a young age. The child then went on to express his belief that God had passed away and raised the question of whether it made sense to pray to a deceased entity.

The mother responded by saying that she would provide a more detailed explanation of the concept when the child reached a more mature age.The understanding of God or religious texts should not be limited by the age of children. The truth cannot be considered when it comes to concepts that are difficult to comprehend. Throughout history, Allah has always been portrayed as a singular entity, which makes it possible for people of any age to comprehend the teachings of Islam.

The questioning of concepts, especially within the Abrahamic faiths, can arise from the fact that Abraham was a monotheist. However, it is worth noting that the concept of Allah in Islam deviates from this. Allah, who is an unseen God that no human has ever laid eyes on, is described as a light. Despite being concealed from our sight, he is actually in closer proximity than those who are visible to us. In Islam, there is a belief that Jesus did not die, rather Allah chose to take him to Himself and appointed another individual to take on his role.

As Allah has demonstrated through numerous miracles, He is capable of accomplishing such a remarkable feat. It is a widely held belief among Muslims that questioning Allah's divinity is not something that is done. One common misconception that many people have is that Jews were responsible for the death of Jesus.

Despite this, there is a significant number of individuals who argue that this belief lacks any solid foundation. It is worth noting that Islam also holds the same perspective. One important point to consider is that the Bible was actually written approximately 40 years following Jesus' ascension, while the First Testament was written around 300 years after his lifetime.

The timelines for these projects might differ based on the research being conducted. In addition to that, it is important to note that the Bible was written in a time when Jesus was not physically present, which raises the question of who actually authored it. The Ingel Bible was revealed to Jesus rather than being revealed to those who came before him. Conversely, it is important to note that the Quran was not only revealed to Prophet Muhammad but also written and finalized prior to the passing of Muhammad the Prophet of Islam and humanity.

The Quran explicitly cautions against any attempts to modify sacred scriptures, as it is Allah who ensures the preservation of the final testament, not human beings. Muslims, especially those who are new converts or have limited knowledge, can greatly benefit from gaining a deeper understanding of this history. Although true friendships have the ability to endure for a lifetime, a genuine friend consistently prioritizes honesty when interacting with their friend.

Despite this, it is ultimately the individual's responsibility to accept and adhere to the truth. According to Islam, ignorance is characterized by the failure to acknowledge and embrace the truth, even when it is presented in a clear and evident manner. Although it is unfortunate that stupidity cannot be cured, ignorance can be effectively addressed and remedied through education and continuous learning.

In numerous societies, a pseudo-culture is prevalent and spreads rapidly, with the exception of Muslim countries and among individuals who are true believers. One of the obligations of a Muslim is to guide those who may be misinformed about Islam, particularly those who have strayed from the right path. Self-imposed failures manifest in continuous resentment, a lack of understanding of social pressures, personal desires, negative influences, and a corrupted heart that is unable to see the good. While it is true that challenging experiences can sometimes foster faith, it is important to remember that with Allah's will, nothing is unachievable. Faith is the key that unlocks all possibilities, and it is Allah who serves as the source of these endless opportunities. The essence of conviction is encapsulated in this statement. Assisting fellow believers is not perceived as a burden by Muslims; rather, it is regarded as both a duty and an honor.

Quran: Surah Sajdah: 2. The revelation of this Book is—beyond doubt—from the Lord of all worlds.

Those who seek serenity and truth, and obey Allah's laws instead of defying them, will thrive in Islam's bliss. Success comes from sharing rather than selfishness, arrogance, or ignorance. When Islam is practiced at its finest, it illuminates homes with its beauty, making it impossible not to embrace it. Sharing Islam benefits both the giver and the receiver, and differences in beliefs should not be used to deny humanity among people with or without faith.

Caring for each other's needs is a fundamental courtesy established by the creator to foster human connections. It is often misunderstandings that lead to destruction, but if the believer's heart is clear in its delivery, keeping Allah close all the time, then the rest is always up to Allah, not alienation, or reevaluation of humanity, or people who refuse to obey Allah's orders.

The core values of the heart are at the center of peace, and friendships that come from faith have a deeper understanding of these values. Through courtesy and care, humanity thrives in all humans. The core of inner peace and friendship is rooted in faith, leading to a profound comprehension of these values. By showing kindness and concern, humanity flourishes within us all.

The semblance of tranquility is not its own lucid illusion. Instead, persistence in governing the soul's emotions and intuitions with Allah's help is the key to success. Islam's ideologies have always been based on logical belief shaped and understood by a believer as the Quran has dispelled no doubts except for clarity. What human does not seek clarity of life and soul? Everyone! In the depths of the shores, where one seeks light even in the darkest hours, one will find it

CHAPTER 9

GROWTH, NOT DECADENCE, IN ISLAM

Throughout the ages, Islam has groomed humanity. It emphasizes respect and dignity in all aspects of life. Islam is a symbolic concept that emphasizes the importance of performing actions repeatedly, which are preferred by Allah. Despite being bothersome to humans, Allah finds it pleasing. The importance of consistency in expanding humanity's horizons cannot be overstated. Despite the monotony of the routine, this draw results in success, not failure.

Consistency is the key to success in business and everyday life. The risk of falling out of this facade is inconsistent behavior. Muslim discipline is programmed as a pathway to success. The key is Salat which is the game changer for a Muslim.

The diversity and mobility of friendships only make it easier for others to understand their actions. Islamic beliefs are rooted in the etiquette of the Islamic faith and the teachings of Muhammad. They are designed for practicing Muslims or even for those who have strayed but returned due to incompatible values.

In the Islamic faith, one of the key teachings is to refrain from comparing sins and instead, entrust the outcome to Allah. Strive for a sense of balance and harmony within your own being, and make a conscious effort to associate with individuals who share your beliefs in order to foster a positive and uplifting atmosphere. In order to counteract negativity, it is important to shift our focus towards attaining success and embracing a positive mindset.

Additionally, when a believer becomes distant from their prayer (Salat), it can be seen as a sign that enemies are deliberately trying to create a divide and keep them away from the path of success that they are familiar with. If humanity was to call another human five times every day, he would quickly become exhausted and find the frequent calls bothersome.

The act of paying homage to Allah, which involves praying five times a day and even more, is not only heard but also greatly appreciated by Allah. When Allah receives the call he promptly answers it when the caller calls.

Islam is thought to encourage personal growth and balance through five daily prayers to Allah. Many successful people follow similar habits. Humans are naturally inclined to seek guidance. While we must submit to society's rules, we are not weak. Submitting to Allah can lead to a greater sense of fulfillment. Allah's teachings take precedence over society's rules. Islam trains its followers to excel in any task, without it being excessive. Adhering to Allah's laws can feel excessively restrictive. Only those who do not grasp Allah's laws have the potential to help humanity.

Those individuals who faithfully adhere to these laws are blessed with an extended duration of connection to Allah, whereas those who disregard His commandments will have their time shortened. Among all the faiths, Islam stands out as the only one that proclaims that Allah has perfected the religion in the present time. It is possible that certain individuals may have doubts as to why Allah did not create it flawlessly from the very beginning.

The teacher has the ability to determine when the student is ready, and that is the answer. In His creation, time, and teachings, Allah is the ultimate and supreme teacher. Is it possible for any individual, no matter their stature or intellect, to challenge and engage in a discourse with the Creator of everything, even including humanity?

The episode's true power resides in the act of understanding, a gift bestowed upon us by the Creator. Regrettably, there are individuals who are unable to comprehend written, visual, or auditory information due to mental barriers that impose restrictions. Muslims hold a deep appreciation for all aspects of life, viewing each moment as a valuable opportunity for learning and never taking anything for granted. When a believer possesses a humble heart and lives their life according to Allah's guidance, their facial expressions reveal the softening of their heart.

Quran: Surah Maidah: 5:3. Do not fear them: fear Me. Today I have perfected your religion for you, completed My blessings upon you, and chosen Islam.

Although the recovery time may vary from person to person, those who have undergone this experience understand that their return to the same demanding and draining routine is uncertain.

However, it would be advisable to explore alternative methods and redirect your efforts towards finding more effective means. In light of the addiction to social media, it is evident to those who are influenced that news does not always maintain a state of impartiality.

Humans have a tendency to present episodes of their lives to one another. Rather than leading their own lives, they prefer to experience life through the experiences of others. There are certain individuals who, when they adapt to someone else's way of life, discover it to be far more fascinating than their own, leading to a monotonous existence and a toxic atmosphere.

Life that remains static and stagnant lacks the ability to grow, and negativity is unable to infiltrate it. Muhammad the Prophet displayed his versatility by walking, swimming, and riding horses, and even if you can't do all of that, you can still find balance by incorporating some of those activities into your routine. If a human calls out to Allah, they can expect to receive an answer from Him.

Given that a Muslim is aware of the proximity of being questioned, it seems inconceivable for them not to be attentive. When mistakes are acknowledged, they have the potential to transform into acts of repentance, and when there is distance between individuals or groups, it can evolve into a powerful alliance.

The absence of sound slowly evolves into a delicate symphony of language and intricate links. The individual who comprehends their difficulties and takes steps to rectify them is someone who practices the Muslim faith. In his prayers to Allah, he fervently asks for the gifts bestowed upon him to function as a means of equilibrium, rather than becoming a hindrance that distorts the line between truth and deceit.

Quran: Surah Kahf: 16:26: And We have already created man and know what his soul whispers to him, and We are closer to him than his jugular vein.

The faith of Islam thrives and expands when provided with nourishment. As it continues to develop, it becomes essential for it to have a supportive habitat where belief and regular discussions about Allah, known as "dhikr," take place with a like-minded believer. An environment that lacks movement or change does not support progress or growth. Islam made significant advancements that brought an end to the era of decadence for both women and men.

Muslims frequently excel in academic, physical, and travel accomplishments, often achieving the highest levels of success. They spend hours praying to Allah, hoping to experience all the thrills and frills that life has to offer. Only Allah has knowledge of the outcome. His actions are predetermined and can be found in what is written in His destiny. There are instances when humans tend to overlook the opportunities and pathways that life offers.

The ruins are contaminated by evil when a spoiled fish is present. The genuine believer, with unwavering faith, always remembers and acknowledges the divine power that made this climb possible. Thus, it is impossible for the mind, body, and soul to resist the captivating allure of these gifts that greatly enhance overall performance. The practice of expressing gratitude can significantly contribute to the success of Muslims in various aspects of their lives. Similar to how ideas evolve, the implications of global changes also undergo a transformative process.

Islam will remain firm and unwavering, bolstered by both substantial evidence and an unyielding resilience to withstand any attempt at change, as Allah bestowed his divine book upon each successive generation. The crucial role that women play in the attainment of independence worldwide cannot be understated, and the challenges they face are more pertinent than ever. Even though the world is rife with deceit, the traditions of paganism manage to endure. In a world characterized by excess and decline, women had to confront marginalization. Throughout history, the remarkable achievements of Muslim women have left an indelible mark.

It is a common occurrence for humans to frequently overlook the needs of others and occasionally experience remorse for not prioritizing their visits. The most high, Allah, eagerly awaits the prayers of his servant who dutifully engages in the practice of performing five daily prayers. The lord of the entire universe feels the absence of his servant deeply whenever the servant neglects to perform Salat, and this is truly remarkable. While it is natural for humans to miss one another, it is important to remember that Allah, the creator, is constantly aware of and attentive to every individual he has created, and he is the ultimate owner of the entire world. If a Muslim were to read a sincere appeal or receive a reminder from someone, it would be quite challenging for them to not attend (Salat).

The purpose of performing (Salat) is not solely to satisfy Allah, but it also serves other important functions. Those who have faith receive it as a source of mercy and blessing. The act of refusing a gift is commonly interpreted as a display of incompetence, illiteracy, and ungratefulness. Muslims are bestowed with (Salat) as a divine gift from Allah. The second pillar of Islam is the act of praying, also referred to as Salat, which is mandatory for Muslims. The attendees of (Salat) make it a priority to arrive on time so that they can better understand and internalize the belief.

Muslims have a designated time for each prayer and they make sure to pray during that time. The loss that a Muslim experiences when they miss Salat cannot be understated; it is indeed grave. Many individuals hold the belief that the world is governed by people, however, this perception is nothing more than a delusion. Despite mankind's ignorance, Allah, the Most Merciful and Forgiving, bestows his mercy and forgiveness upon us.

It is impossible for any other rules to take precedence over those established by Allah. From the very beginning, both humans and Jinns were created with the sole purpose of submitting to Allah. While it may be challenging to escape evil, one must remember that discord ultimately results in emptiness. The only source of happiness lies in abiding by Allah's rules. The Creator, who is responsible for the creation of humanity, possesses knowledge about the benefits that a soul can derive.

In the Muslim community, it emphasizes the importance of well-being, serenity, and self-realization for each individual and for us as a whole. By addressing life's obstacles and implementing laws that enhance the quality of life, we can navigate through trials and make positive changes. A Muslim who follows Allah's laws experiences a unique union that brings immense bliss, a bliss unknown to those who have never married, just as the growth of a Muslim without offspring differs, as this responsibility teaches and shatters barriers that believers, believers may not have been aware of

Laws vary from laws that are concrete and unadjustable, but mistakes turn to repentance and fixing is the beauty of Islam for Muslims. When a society is marked by love without laws, it is imperative to seek differences, especially from settings that prescribe different ethical standards.

Those who do not abide by the laws of the Islamic scriptures do not take into account the violation of moral laws. As an illustration, let's consider the case of someone who shows negligence towards Islam or is not a Muslim. This individual may find themselves involved in a romantic relationship that occurs outside of the institution of marriage, ultimately resulting in the conception of a child born out of wedlock.

The intended users of this application are exclusively those who adhere to the prescribed laws of Islam. Individuals who fail to comply with these laws demonstrate a lack of comprehension regarding the consequences on both aspects. It is of utmost importance to comprehend that those who do not abide by Allah's laws are incapable of exerting any influence over them.

The actions of someone who does not believe in Allah do not affect the laws set by Allah. Whether individuals choose to violate laws on a daily basis or abide by human-made laws instead of those prescribed by Allah, the outcome of their ultimate destiny being either heaven or hell remains unaffected.

Questioning the final destination of any individual, regardless of their belief or lack thereof, is rendered meaningless since Allah extends the chance for anyone to transform their lives and embrace His faith, provided their heart remains pure.This matter carries significant weight and requires serious consideration. As an adherent of the Islamic faith, one recognizes the deep significance of its fundamental doctrines. The intention behind this is not to cater to the desires of humanity or to conform to the shifting society. On the contrary, its objective is not to manipulate society by enforcing laws that are in servitude to a world shaped by Allah.

Many people engage in conversations about the possibility of a one-world order. In accordance with Islamic beliefs, it is believed that this order is the sole faith accepted by Allah before the finality approaching the doomsday. The reason behind this is that Allah, being the creator of the world, was worshiped and invoked by all Prophets who conveyed a unified message.

As a society, who are we to even contemplate altering the laws that have been set by a divine entity? Chaos is permitted by Allah, temporarily but there is a designated time for everything to come to an end. Countries, much like life itself, have the potential to be submerged in dust and water, ultimately leading to their burial. Islam, being an eternal religion, holds the belief that Jesus will clarify to those who considered him as God that he is not acquainted with them, since he too worshiped Allah.

Whether individuals are believers or non-believers, it is important to refrain from questioning their fate as it serves no purpose. Allah, in His infinite wisdom, has granted every individual the ability to transform themselves whenever they desire, as long as their hearts remain pure. Allah bestows the opportunity for individuals to embrace the world of faith at any given time. The doctrine of beliefs followed by Muslims is characterized by serenity, as it is not intended to cater to societal expectations, but rather to provide guidance to humanity through laws that are derived from Allah, rather than from human creation.

In the realm of Abrahamic faiths, it is widely believed that none of these faiths have managed to survive solely through human intervention, but rather through a combination of human effort and divine guidance. Islam is regarded as a comprehensive belief system that is inherently resistant to change. While Muslims do not oppose trials, they firmly believe in conquering them by engaging in repentance, humbling themselves before Allah, and fervently seeking His assistance to transform their sorrows into moments of joy.

Humans have the ability to design and produce robots, toys, and other mechanical gadgets, and these inventions are typically packaged with a manual for guidance on how to use them correctly. Nevertheless, once Allah dispatched humans to Earth, He made sure to provide them with a comprehensive guide in the form of Islam as a final chapter and a closing statement is the Quran. This comprehensive guide encompasses all aspects and serves as a definitive statement for the entirety of humanity.

When Muslims invoke Allah, they do so with humility and a commitment to abide by His guidance in their day-to-day existence. Muslim women have made remarkable strides in society, effectively dismantling barriers and defying stereotypes. The contentment of a Muslim can be compared to a serene sea that is softly ruffled by a gentle breeze, which is the result of adhering to Allah's guidance and fulfilling one's responsibilities.

The act of referring to the women of Islam as backward has sparked a significant uproar. Throughout history, it is possible for us to compare the achievements of Muslim women. The advancement of Islam took place by granting rights to Muslim women instead of engaging in a struggle for rights. In this society of Islamophobic regions that is constantly evolving, women who do not meet the established criteria and expectations are derogatorily referred to as female canine dogs.

Many women use the term "female dogs" to describe themselves. In societies different from ours, words that are considered acceptable in this climate can be seen as demeaning. The use of derogatory terms not only undermines and degrades women, but it also serves as a clear example of the prevailing sexism that still exists in society today. It is not permissible to use language of that nature. While the idea is often brushed off as mundane, it is not acknowledged in different environments.

The act of observing this facade of independence with open eyes reveals its tainted nature. In this society that has grown dim, the freedom of speech is subject to certain restrictions. The concept of free speech does not encompass the act of insulting or disturbing the peace of others. Mannerisms are often used to characterize Islamic culture. Despite the fact that individuals in this society hold diverse opinions and beliefs, they are frequently subjected to generalizations that assume uniformity in their perspectives.

The act of wearing a man's suit for work or choosing to dress in revealing clothing is frequently interpreted as a representation of personal independence. Nevertheless, there is a counterargument that can be made against the idea of incorporating ancient cultures as a means of advancement in developing societies.

A more preferable approach would be for individuals to focus on cultivating their own individuality instead of trying to copy others. The manner in which we dress has a substantial impact on our freedom in today's society, particularly in the realms of education and travel. The comprehension of this concept can provide women with the tools to steer clear of participating in regressive societal practices.

Islam is a religion that encourages forward-thinking and advancement rather than embracing regressive ideologies. The various aspects of our lives, such as our fashion choices, academic pursuits, travel experiences, family values, and religious beliefs, greatly shape who we are as individuals, and as Muslims, we hold them in high regard and cherish them. Our commitment to maintaining our dignity is paramount, and we strive to do so while also practicing modesty.

Attaining achievements is within reach and having a mindset that everything is possible is crucial. Before the introduction of the concept and religions, certain cultures had already been in existence for centuries. While there are both similarities and differences, the fundamental connection that unites us is our shared belief in one God. It is unfair to associate Islam with the confusion and chaos that characterizes modern society. The emphasis on modesty, morals, and ethics, which is prescribed by Allah, is one of its most notable features.

The prevailing belief suggests that Islam's purpose was to bring about a transformation in the ignorant practices of the people. The path it is currently on is progressive, indicating that it will not return to its previous state. Throughout the world, various countries have embraced and upheld cultural traditions that have endured for decades. However, it is important to note that Islam should not be regarded as simply a culture. Any modifications or subtle changes to this message from Allah are absolutely unacceptable. Islam is committed to never returning to the ignorant times of the past.

The principles and standards of this cannot be interchanged with any other. A society that boasts progress and advancement, yet fails to uphold moral values, cannot truly be considered advanced, except in domains like medicine, technology, and transportation. The behavior of certain individuals who identify as Muslims and act in contradiction to their religious beliefs, while being portrayed in a negative light by the media, does not accurately reflect the core principles and values of Islam.

Within the Islamic faith, women are held in high esteem, with their independence and ability to pursue their goals and desires being acknowledged and supported. It is unfortunate that the remarkable achievements of women in the Muslim world have frequently gone unnoticed or unacknowledged. In contrast to archaic societies that disregard women's entitlements, women in Islam are granted equal rights.

Even though the Muslim world has encountered various types of sexism, from false sources it has wholeheartedly embraced the idea of including women in the workforce, proving that this is not a novel concept for Muslims. In the future, when history reflects on the achievements of Muslim women, it will also acknowledge that the Western world only granted women access to the workforce out of necessity for revenue generation, particularly during times of war.

Women face a constant struggle in their ongoing fight for rights, as they are frequently exploited for financial gain in establishments such as nightclubs, strip clubs, conjugated political arena of mishaps and the porn industry, often being degraded by men. This exploitation has unfortunately become a means for many women in the Western world to support their daily lives. In contrast, women in Islamic societies do not have to endure such exploitation in order to earn money.

Another avenue for selling beauty is through modeling, where attractiveness and high pay are often intertwined with manipulation within Western society. Women have been sacrificing their well-being in pursuit of attractiveness and glamor, which has now become the epitome of revenue generation. In addition to that, the women of Islam have not only imparted crucial lessons to the world but have also been a constant source of inspiration for women in the Western world.

These women in the West are still tirelessly fighting for equal rights and equal pay. Khadija, the renowned wife of the Prophet Muhammad, managed to establish herself as a prosperous businesswoman. His employment of Prophet Muhammad under her is a testament to the fact that in Islam, women were not restrained but rather treated with dignity and respect. Muslim women have made significant progress rather than remaining stagnant, thanks to the rights granted to them by Islam, which were not available in other human societies. The Islamic culture ensures that women are granted their rights under Islam, eliminating the necessity for protests or demonstrations. It is imperative that the justice system not only recognizes but also acknowledges these fundamental rights.

Throughout history, the presence of both genders in educational settings has consistently posed challenges when it comes to fostering and preserving respect between them. Furthermore, the promotion of activities that are not in line with Islamic beliefs not only undermines the dignity of women but also contradicts our core values.

The exploitation of women is widespread and can be found in numerous domains, such as pornography sites, where people of all genders, including those of the same gender, participate in illicit activities in order to make money or provide entertainment. If this society, despite all the progress in technology, is not progressing, in moral code of ethics.

The utilization of new technology in this context of Islamophobic regions is reminiscent of the behavior in comparison to the ancient Stone Age, catering to individuals who don't possess the discernment to perceive the variances. When it comes to tackling the problem of hypocrisy, nations have a range of strategies at their disposal. Gender rivalry is prevalent in these nations, leading to intense competition.

In advanced societies, both men and women tend to exploit the concept of retribution. Although it has been kept under wraps, this epidemic has been rapidly spreading across the globe. As a result, individuals take measures to safeguard their belongings, ensuring that their valuable possessions remain under their ownership in the event that their union comes to an end. To embark on a journey of self-reform, one must maintain vigilance and constantly remember Allah.

By cultivating self-contentment and continuously working on improving their character, individuals can achieve inner peace. The true wealth of a Muslim lies in their faith and beliefs, as everything else is determined by the handiwork of Allah and human destiny. The call of destiny beckons us and it is through human effort that we find our way to our destined path.

The significance of effort cannot be understated, as it is the driving force behind achieving anything and shaping our lives. Women in Islam are granted dignity by Allah. For many years in Saudi Arabia, there was a cultural outrage surrounding women's inability to drive, but now they have been granted the freedom to do so. The Western world has been fascinated by tabloids for decades.

The society in question persisted in exploiting Muslim women on Western social media, highlighting a clear distinction between the Islamic faith and the perception of women as being antiquated in comparison to Western society. Despite not monitoring themselves, they continue to imitate a culture rooted in ancient paganism and the customs of previous generations. Their ability to drive a car, in Saudi Arabia which was a cultural rather than Islamic practice. They completely disregarded the fact that women in the western world are still struggling for their rights and facing daily exploitation.

However, the portrayal of these individuals as individuals who require assistance is not being depicted by Middle Eastern media. Interfering in the affairs of Muslims, specifically in matters of regime changes and destructive actions, is a consistent and unwarranted endeavor on their part. Furthermore, they have a tendency to portray Muslim women as backward, conveniently ignoring the fact that if it weren't for the first Muslim women who discovered the first university in the world, they wouldn't have knowledge about degrees and classes.

The Muslim women who, with Islam as their driving force, played a significant role in advancing education and shaping history, cannot be overlooked. However, it is unfortunate that many Muslims themselves are unaware of their own history. Therefore, it is essential to repeatedly explain and highlight these historical accomplishments, even if it means repeating the announcements.

This is crucial in countering the repeated lies staged by Islamophobes, as Muslims have the power to repeatedly present the truth. It is intriguing to observe how an activity as commonplace as driving, which countless individuals engage in on a daily basis or opt for public transportation, has become the primary subject of discussion regarding the complexities of operating a vehicle. While Muslim women in Saudi Arabia may have independence from Allah, their independence from Saudi men is not relevant. Despite the presence of cultural differences across nations, Islam remains a universal faith that embraces all Muslims and welcomes those who wish to join.

Nevertheless, the ability to observe positive changes in a culture becomes challenging when one refuses to open their eyes to them. The progress that Saudi Arabia has made towards women's rights holds great cultural significance not Islamic. It is alarming to witness the negative impact of social media and gossip, as they often result in verbal attacks and ignorant behavior in public.

The countries that are interrogating or interrogating Muslims. The dress code culture and lives contrary to Islam are not subjects of debate in other Muslim countries, as Muslims do not question them. Despite this, they still feel compelled to insert themselves into situations that have no relevance to them.

Treating it as a duty, there are those who believe in the necessity of bringing about regime changes. In order to maintain privacy and avoid unnecessary interference, it is advisable not to disclose personal matters, particularly to individuals who display a keen interest in the lives of Muslims. It is truly disheartening to witness the way in which certain individuals regard news as an absolute truth and exploit rumors as a means to propagate malevolence, ultimately resulting in utter turmoil.

In the religion of Islam, the concept of privacy is deeply rooted and regarded as a core belief, as it serves to prevent the spread of sin and evil (known as fitna). Private repentance holds great significance when it comes to acknowledging and seeking forgiveness for both intentional and unintentional wrongdoings.

Throughout history, societies have never regarded engaging in illicit relationships with either men or women as a form of flattery. Personal relationships are subject to privacy law acts in these societies, however, they often end up interfering in the larger scope of the world. The harm caused to humanity can also be a result of self-inflicted problems, such as gossip or harmful words being posted on social media.

Unlike the public billboards that defame women, Allah sees them as both strong and fragile. To prevent any form of defamation, numerous Islamic men and women opt to maintain their personal lives in privacy. Regrettably, there are still certain societies that have not acquired the understanding of respecting personal privacy. Witnessing the global dissemination of this culture is a distressing experience, as it is utterly futile to subject oneself to the noxious repercussions of such behaviors.

A helpful resource for educating colleges and schools about Islamic etiquette would be a book that offers in-depth information about Islam. On the other hand, it is of utmost importance to utilize sources that can be trusted and are reliable when seeking information about Islam, avoiding any distortion or misinterpretation that may arise from personal biases. The suggestion is to prioritize seeking forgiveness from Allah (Astaghfar) instead of engaging in discussions about sins and weaknesses, as this approach brings preventive and curative measures closer together.

One of the core values in Islam is the high regard for both men and women. Women in countries that assert their independence and strive for equality have a strong desire to occupy prominent political positions and actively work towards leading their nations; however, in Western arena especially promoting Islamophobia is constantly demoting them they frequently encounter a lack of respect and are compelled to go to extreme measures in pursuit of power and material advancement. The issue at hand has been effectively addressed within Islam, as women are granted a high moral status and are encouraged to pursue education from a young age.

Muslim women, even before they began ruling countries, had already made remarkable contributions by occupying prestigious positions. If you have a keen interest in discovering the remarkable female leaders who shaped the Islamic world in the 7th century, this is an opportunity you won't want to miss. Fatimah, daughter of Prophet Muhammad, and Aisha, daughter of Abu Bakr and wife of Prophet Muhammad. Zaynab, daughter of Ali, and Hafsa, daughter of Omar, and wife of Prophet Muhammad along with Umm Darda as Sughra, Umm Hakim, Al-Shifa, daughter of Abdullah, and Hafsa, daughter of Sirin, are all over achievers and left their mark behind. Did not fight for rights as women Islam gave them rights.

Even though these nations claim to be modern and influential, do they still struggle with the challenge of electing women into positions of power? The only strategy some individuals employ to make progress is by spreading negative rhetoric about Muslim countries and promoting Islamophobia. However, this approach does not contribute to the advancement of their own credentials. Instead, they exploit the progressive societies and cultures that have historically fostered education and knowledge, ultimately perpetuating Islamophobic sentiments. It is essential that we take a stand for truth, ensuring that the younger generations, equipped with fresh ideas and education, prioritize the pursuit of truth over the influences of an unfiltered society.

Even though they are staging Muslims to claim that they will protect them from Islamophobia, the unfortunate reality is that social media exploitation is being used to deceive the general public. Instead, social media should be utilized for educating and uniting people, promoting truth and transparency, and working towards a better world. Muslims, like many others, have always strived for progress rather than regression. Muslims have a responsibility to contribute to the betterment of the world by offering assistance and promoting understanding, rather than focusing on hostility and theological disparities that hinder the pursuit of truth.

Muslim women have successfully defied false notions and shattered stereotypes by assuming prominent roles and positions of power within ruling nations, thus serving as a prime example of the progressive essence of Islam. The men and women of Islam have contributed to the world with their educated creative ideas and inventions. Now is the time to step up and assist the world instead of remaining passive.

Let's shed light on the corrupt individuals who are hiding the truth in order to benefit a select few. They are enduring internal struggles that are not visible to the naked eye. The reflection of truth is essential for unity, as Muslims have historically played a significant role in fostering unity. By embracing truth and working towards progress, they have the power to strengthen unity in the present, which will be visible to the entire world.

They assume all women are the same, falsely believing they know Muslim women. Muslim women demonstrate strength, resilience, and confidence, never compromising their dignity as they lead nations. These examples are Benazir Bhutto, the Prime Minister of Pakistan. Khaleda Zia Prime Minister of Bangladesh, Tansu Ciller Prime Minister of Turkey, Sheikh Hasina Prime Minister of Bangladesh, Mame Madior Boye Prime Minister of Senegal, Halima Yaqub President of Singapore.I've identified some Muslim women who are powerful leaders.

The nations have been ruled by 16 or more individuals. Muslim women don't rely on others promising to live long enough to witness a woman in office. Female rulers have held power in Islam for centuries. Muslim women find confidence in Islam as it allows them to pursue their goals without hindrance. The strength of a household lies in the strong Muslim woman. Khadija exemplifies the ideal wife of the Prophet Muhammad.

Muslim women have historically held high offices and made educational contributions worldwide. Countries that perceive Islam and women in Islam as backward have not had a female ruler yet. The struggle for women to achieve higher positions is still ongoing in many societies. In these newer countries, where women have been fighting for rights for centuries, the desire for power has become an epidemic, as centuries of oppression have left them hungry for recognition and respect in societies they call modern. Unfortunately, some women may use degrading actions to advance, which are exposed on social media.

While there are always exceptions, most icons and political figures in these societies are characterized by sexist competition. Both men and women may take advantage of others to advance themselves, leaving their peers behind.The current state of politics in this society is concerning and disappointing. It is disheartening to see that within the Christian religion, there are teachings that prohibit women from holding positions of power. Ironically, many individuals in this society look to the Middle East for examples of oppressive regimes when similar or worse issues exist within their community.

These attitudes hinder progress and do not contribute to a healthy society. On the other hand, in Islam, women are granted certain rights despite some cultures limiting them. Both men and women must learn about these rights granted by Allah. Muslim men have a cultural and religious obligation to support women while refraining from derogatory language.

Resolving disputes without academic training is possible, but learning is crucial for progress. Formal education and experiences gained from learned teachers can be powerful tools for personal growth. They should be embraced and used to enhance the quality of our lives, rather than being used to demean the system of living or limit humanity's potential.

In Islam, our dignity is of utmost importance, and a recognized marriage contract known as a Nikah is required not wedlock. Allah prohibits wasteful acts such as rejection and living in wedlock for years, as they do not lead to a happy marriage. In some cases, individuals may choose to live together outside of marriage for an extended period, ranging from seven to twenty years or more. These relationships are commonly called common-law marriages but may not be legally recognized in some states if certain criteria are not met. According to Islamic beliefs, such relationships are considered cursed by Allah.

Although disobedience to Allah may be viewed as acceptable in certain societies, it contradicts the Islamic belief in the possibility of change and repentance. Both believers and non-believers are capable of experiencing changes of heart, but ultimately, Allah's will supersedes human will. For believers, especially new converts or Muslims struggling to hold onto their faith, being in such a situation can be challenging, and seeking forgiveness through (Astaghfar) becomes necessary. Allah protects us from such situations. Despite the laws imposed by various governments, Islamic laws remain unaltered.

Islamic laws remain constant despite changes in government. It is important to maintain alignment between the body, mind, and spirit for overall well-being. However, this may be difficult for some to fully comprehend. Muslim women have entered the workforce and education system without compromising their dignity, and families have been successfully raised with their contributions. Furthermore, Muslim women are not dependent on marriage to support their families or to access education. In Western societies, cultural differences do not grant Muslim women immunity from emotions or temptations as per Islamic teachings.

Muslims can be tempted by certain cultures and societies, but their values and clothing may not always align with Islamic morality. However, Muslims always repent and return to their faith. Deliberate disobedience as a cause of sin is quite uncommon. Sometimes, unintentionally. Muslims who aim to please Allah refrain from spending time with those who persistently disobey His laws. Muslims in Western society may make mistakes, but they can strengthen themselves by repenting and gaining a deeper understanding of Islamic concepts and laws.

The role of gender is not significant when it comes to dealing with challenges and conquering obstacles. Prior to the advent of Islam, women did not receive the respect they deserved; however, with the arrival of Islam, their rights were recognized and they were elevated to a position of high status. Muslim women have the ability to uphold their rights, maintain their dignity, and preserve their honor.

The niqab that they wear not only serves as a shield but also as a cover, reflecting their modesty. A Muslim woman can preserve her dignity and dedication to progress by choosing to be independent. The feminist movements that emerged in the wake of the riots in the USA during the 1960s were often marked by the symbolic acts of burning bras and embracing nudity; however, it is important to note that such actions are not condoned within the context of Islam.

Jul 19, 2023 — On July 19, 1848, the Seneca Falls Convention convened. Heralded as the first American women's rights convention the two-day event was held.

Sep 5, 2008 — A New York Post story on the protest included a reference to bra burning as a way to link the movement to war protesters burning draft cards.

These countries, which faltered under false modernization, sought independence in the following manner. The introduction of birth control not only provided a means for contraception but also gave rise to the prevalence of free-living abortions and illicit sexual activities.

Islam is a religion that has its own distinct set of rules and regulations, which are generally compatible with humanity, unless they infringe upon the rights of Allah. It is mandatory for Muslims to follow the laws of Islam, and one of the obligatory requirements for couples who give their consent is to activate the Nikah contract and proceed with the marriage. The marriage ceremony in Islam involves the signing of a written contract by two parties, which is then witnessed by two Muslims, as part of the Islamic tradition of documenting important agreements as contracts.

In the context of a marriage conducted through (Nikah), it is important to note that the concept of Dower for the wife is directly linked to the Islamic laws, whereas her maintenance from her husband is a significant aspect. The concept of Maher, which is a bridal gift, signifies a financial obligation that the husband owes to his wife, and she has the authority to either enforce it or forgive it.

Muslim women enjoy protection of their rights through both Quranic laws and their birthright. Consequently, there is no justification for engaging in protests, whether they occur prior to marriage, subsequent to marriage, or in the event of choosing not to marry. During the time of Prophet Muhammad, as well as in the present day, Maher known as dover bridal gift from the husband can be given as payment in various forms such as dates, grains, lands, or even through the teaching of the Quran, as long as both parties mutually agree.

Quran: Surah Nisa: 4:4.Give women ʿyou wedʾ their due dowries graciously. But if they waive some of it willingly, then you may enjoy it freely with a clear conscience.

In a halal relationship, if all parties involved come to an agreement, it is possible to negotiate the Maher, and the inability to afford a significant Maher should not serve as an obstacle to getting married. The institution of marriage plays a crucial role in establishing a permissible and morally upright relationship, and its regulations are divinely ordained by Allah.

The terms of the marriage are determined by the agreement reached between both parties involved. Islam is a faith that places great importance on contracts, emphasizing the significance of fulfilling obligations and holding individuals responsible for their commitments. The principle behind this is to ensure that the rights and laws of all living beings on this earth, such as jinn, plants, and animals, are respected. The husband traditionally presents his wife with the Maher during the Nikah ceremony. Payments can be made either upfront or throughout the duration of the marriage. The husband is responsible for taking care of his wife and children.

Despite any financial ability or level of education, women are not limited from offering assistance to their families and husbands. Khadija, who was the wife of Prophet Muhammad, not only played a crucial role in managing finances but also provided assistance to those in need, showcasing her skills as a businesswoman.

It is not within a husband's rights to compel his wife to seek employment outside the home in order to contribute financially and simultaneously manage the household. In the event that the wife is capable, her contributions can prove to be a valuable asset to her husband. In Islam, there is encouragement for women to attain financial independence and education, while also having the right to be protected by their husbands. The completion of a woman's (deen) way of life occurs after she gets married. While Islam does not require women to be the primary earners, there have been numerous cases where women have taken on the role of household leaders.

Due to various circumstances in life, many households in today's world find it necessary to have two sources of income in order to sustain themselves. However, it is possible for married couples to sustain their lifestyle without the requirement of supplementary earnings. In the event that they desire expansion, both parties will need to contribute financially, except if one of them is already financially stable. Within Islam, material possessions are considered of little importance when it comes to a marriage. On the contrary, it is the spiritual and religious beliefs that contribute to bringing a sense of inner peace to one's home.

Former husbands are obligated to provide maintenance to divorced women and their children until the women can become self-sufficient. The father assumes responsibility for the rights of children's provision if he is alive and capable. There is no negotiation with Islam. This duty is obligatory for the father. The Western system acknowledges it, but Islam requires it. Muslim countries, like Western societies, also have laws.

In Western countries, many men in this divided society resent their former responsibilities after the marriage ends. Leaving the women with the sole responsibility of raising the family. Debts accumulate over time and eventually need to be paid, just like deeds that accumulate and must be paid. However, some women thrive on their own, especially Muslim women who consider it their duty and responsibility. Family support is crucial, but many women rely on their strong belief in Allah rather than humans. In Islam, a marriage where the wife helps or gives is considered to enhance her beauty.Understanding the laws of Islam is a mind-boggling experience, revealing its comprehensive guidance for human survival in this world.

Understanding can excel from both knowledge and ignorance, but it ultimately depends on the individual's ability to comprehend. While a child may grasp the concept of Islam as a fact, they may struggle with understanding the idea of three in one or one in three. The message is hard to absorb. Islam does not recognize a marriage without the (Nikah) in the civil court system ruled by Western pseudo society laws as legitimate. Why would a Muslim disregard Islamic laws and adopt the laws of a system that opposes Islamic beliefs and spreads Islamophobia? Prophet Muhammad conducted the (Nikah), a contractual affair in Islam that involves an exchange of Meher, a bridal gift. However, disbelievers do not perform this contract for Muslims.

The presence of evil encourages Muslims to go against their own faith by conforming to a system that permits marriage without Islamic doctrine. Marriage in Islam is deemed sacred and fully acceptable in a Muslim court in a Muslim country. Corruption of young adults is becoming prevalent due to the persistence in undermining religious laws in this system. Islam stresses the importance of youth and young adults as supporters of the faith. This system challenges religious laws and embraces alternative lifestyles. Muslims who fall into this trap require enlightenment to recognize its purpose of eradicating all religious sects.

Islam gave no rights to Muslims or non-Muslims to alter Islam's laws. It's a straight path, not narrow or constricted. Alteration of laws violates contracts. We can fix faith matters by adjusting our path and repenting to Allah. Considering the plethora of rules, one must adhere to these rules while remaining aware of Allah's rules. It is detrimental for a Muslim not to be loyal to his own faith. Especially if the adjustments to Allah's laws are for disbelievers. It's a curse, not a blessing.

In Islam, actions are addressed after puberty, not at 18 or 21. If a teenager can do things that Allah forbids, this faith also holds you accountable for your actions as an adult. There are no excuses for not comprehending Islamic contracts, as young adults can learn their faith's laws. At the age of 9, Edward VI ascended the throne. Able to speak and write fluently in Latin and Greek. At the age of 3, King Oyo of Uganda began his rule. Alexander the Great became ruler at 20, following his father's reign. At only 13 years old, Akbar became the ruler of the Mughal Empire. He inherited the throne from his father, Humayun. The list is endless.

During the 1960s, women devoured the feminist movement in the USA and entered the workforce. World War 11 was the turning point for these women who were deprived of independence to showcase their abilities. They took charge and helped men and raised families as their men rushed into the army fighting wars. Women in these countries were empowered to show that they were capable during this economic time of scarcity.

Women did not attempt political independence in Islam. This independence was given by the creator through Islam. Right to choose a profession, right to ownership, ability to seek knowledge, entitlement to divorce. A right to propose, a right to participate in politics. Women have extensive rights in Islam. A bland life would result from a lack of culture, followed by Islam, which is a tasty combination. Women may own property in the USA. Freedom autonomy did not become effective until the 20th century.Only in the mid-1970s could women in the USA access a line of credit without a man, independently, and without a male co-signer. Muslim women had the right to own property without a fight in the times of Muhammed. Islam was progressive then, and it is progressive now. This faith has no expiration date.

Despite the Western world's struggles for decades, it is a shame that the Muslim world cannot see how deep Islam's threads have gone. Islam has pierced the deepest waters of humanity's awareness with only a glimpse of my words. The misconceptions and misunderstandings of the Muslim world need clarity and education on this inherent force that gushes. Stronger than any ocean tide. Allah has raised women's status in Islam. He named Surah Nisa after them. We must preserve dignity at all costs.

Quran: Surah Baqarah 2:221. Do not marry polytheistic women until they believe; for a believing slave-woman is better than a free polytheist, too, even though she may look pleasant to you. And do not marry your women to polytheistic men until they believe, for a believing slave-man is better than a free polytheist, even though he may look pleasant to you. They invite you to the fire, while Allah invites you to Paradise and forgiveness by his grace. He makes his revelations clear to the people so that perhaps they will be mindful.

Language plays a role in Islam. Imprecation is not expressive. Obscene words are (makrooh) distasteful. Prophet Muhammed quotes, "A believer does not use curse words to express" Obscenity and vulgarity are both not compatible with Islam. Laughter and cry are both from Allah. The one with harsh speech makes one upset, or the one with kindness leaves you with sweet memories. Islam prohibits loud, continuous laughter, especially among women, as it weakens the heart. Allah blesses those who cry in front of their Creator. Because tears soften the heart. A human exposing his tears in front of another is the strongest form of nudity, as emotions, laughter, and sadness are from Allah.

The act of expressing this genuine emotion in the company of non-believers may provide them with ammunition to use against a believer. It is important to keep our emotions solely for Allah. Relationships between individuals who are not mahram (non-mahram) and forbidden by Allah are not permissible, as they can result in both physical and emotional vulnerability, leaving lasting marks of danger due to disobedience to Allah. Hypocrisy is the term used in Islam to describe the act of betraying secrets.

The power of speech lies in the ability to influence and control one's emotions and desires. Satan, the accursed one, tempts individuals through the comprehensive ear that embraces and spreads gossip. Downtrodden anger is a manifestation of harsh language. A person's language is often a reflection of their emotional state, and when they are happy, their language becomes happy as well.The existence of language acts as a barrier that separates and hinders communication between individuals.

The essence of Islam lies within the profound words of understanding. The beauty of acts of kindness is that they require no words to be understood. The comprehension of this language is within the grasp of every human. For a man who fails to recognize the divine blessings bestowed upon him by Allah, the emphasis on life's hardships can lead to feelings of despair.

Frivolous, shallow, and superficial topics have always been incomprehensible to achievers. Besides the talk of witty speeches or people, there is also gossip being shared. Throughout various instances, Allah consistently emphasizes the significance of time. Have you ever considered acquiring the finesse necessary to captivate and hold the attention of a crowd with your words? The weakened state of the environment forces him to endure an environment that is not suitable for human existence.

Islam does not waste any time whatsoever. With all the demands and responsibilities we face, it is important to set aside any bruised or hurtful ego as there is no time for it. In the Islamic faith, it is emphasized that humanity should not have any ego. It is the divine command of Allah for us to humbly walk upon the earth. The feeling of pride should only be directed towards Allah. The angels diligently keep track of each and every word uttered by humans. It is important to exercise caution when dealing with the recordings. There is no eraser available that can effectively erase the recorded markup. The fact is recorded in the clear book of records from Allah.

Quran: Surah Qaf 50:18 'Not a word does he (or she) utter, but there is a watcher by him ready.

Quran: Al Imran: 3:122.Let the believers put their trust in Allah.

Quran: Talaq: 65;3. Allah is enough for those who put their trust in him.

The Quran has a profound meaning behind every word, every sound, and every syllable. Each syllable is repeated several times throughout the Quran. Rhythmic sounds cannot be compared to poetry or to any book in any era. Allah's writing is a melody. Allah's word is unambiguous and clear. Some people may not understand the exact meaning of what they are saying, despite using many words. When Allah speaks, everything he says has profound clarity for a believer. The hearts that yearn for the same solace find it together when a believer speaks to a believer.

CHAPTER 10

BOOK OF LIFE GUIDES HUMANITY QURAN

Even though Allah mandated Salat for Muslims, is it permissible for Muslims to claim fatigue as a reason for not waking up early to pray?Wouldn't it be expected that individuals would rise before sunrise in order to attend to their personal needs and fulfill their obligations? Given that Allah is the provider of sustenance (Rizq), it is perplexing why a Muslim would deliberately choose to disobey Him. Who is the source of his granted health and in what way does he derive pleasure from the act of sleeping, defying the statistical probability of another day?

In all forms of adversity, whether physical or emotional, there are remarkable comebacks that demonstrate both strength and purity, serving as powerful reminders to reassess and improve our lives. The consistent reminders that we receive are truly a blessing. In the absence of reminders and persistent defiance, even evil becomes tired of such individuals, leading Satan to find excitement in those who maintain a strong prayer practice. The army that he commands is weak because it is made up of individuals who do not pray.

Daily devotion to Allah brings about a sense of happiness in one's life. Truth, although highly valuable, is often perceived as impolite in a society that is obsessed with following trends. The act of instructing and expecting individuals to respond in a uniform, monotonous manner is being carried out. Are trends sometimes a guise for the corruption of evils and the acceptance of actions that oppose the divine? It is hard to imagine anyone who is not aware of such tactics. By praying to Allah, we are granted with knowledge and bestowed with the capability to provide assistance to those who require it.

Take heed and give careful consideration to the rhythmic patterns that govern divine laws. Conveying a facade of contentment by defiantly issuing calls that do not reflect true emotions. How can an individual find peace within themselves despite going against the will of Allah? Was he forced to find satisfaction in disobedience?Choosing to ignore the laws of Allah ultimately results in a sense of emptiness rather than true contentment.

If an individual chooses to share their joy in rebelling against the creator with a believer, they should be aware that the consequences they face will be far from rewarding. In Islam, Muslims are both rewarded with special gifts and faced with severe trials, however, it is important to note that repentance is accessible to all individuals.

The ultimate source of contentment for the soul lies in worshiping Allah, and not in worshiping any human being. How can the person making the call not be able to identify the highest ranking individual? Society has a tendency to either adore or abandon individuals who express themselves with a different tune.

In a society that is corrupted and lacks the ability to restrain its desires or uphold honesty, what activities or pursuits are truly worth dedicating our time and energy to? Does the purpose of this society revolve around diverting the attention of the person responsible for error correction by constantly reminding them of their mistakes?

The truth is not confined by any boundaries. Those who seek Allah's help at all times, even if they make mistakes, are granted mercy as long as they refrain from repeating their wrongdoings and strive to learn from them. Diverting Muslims can prove difficult as they express themselves sincerely.

Daily bowing to the highest eliminates fear in the lowest humans on earth. Allah created humanity in a weak state. The absence of fear for Allah leads to fear of others. Humans are not feared by those who fear Allah. Admitting weakness to Allah is the best antidote that doesn't compromise the truth.

He already knows.Believers' support empowers fellow believers in times of challenges. It is incumbent upon believers to ask Allah for help. Ignoring the creator's finest gifts is a futile search for something better. Allah's mercy includes distinguishing between virtues and evil.

Believers gain strength by supporting each other rather than staying silent or feeling alienated during challenges. Weaknesses should be elevated rather than isolated. Believers need unification and bury each other's sins instead of allowing evil influences to divide them. Seeking guidance from Allah is an act of mercy while rejecting His gifts and seeking better opportunities is a tragedy. Acknowledging Allah's blessings is a blessing for a believer.

Those lacking confidence often feel compelled to explain themselves, unlike confident individuals. Prophet Muhammad's legacy continues to serve as a source of reminders, admired by Muslims and non-Muslims alike.

A book on life would elicit comments and advocacy for its successes and failures from many people. A book of life and a precise manual has been given to Muslims by Allah. Its name is the Quran. To stay on the right path, emulate the ways and practices of Prophet Muhammad. (Sunni) is the term used to describe people who follow the path of Muhammad.

In addition to identifying and sidelining one's desires, putting them at rest and eliminating one's woes is beneficial to the soul. Everything permissible is beautified by Allah. What drives the desire to find evil? Can it lessen the difficult times we try to avoid? Islam's laws prioritize integrity. Muslims living in vulnerable societies need to be assertive, especially those who are easily influenced.

Once new converts have acquired knowledge and strength, which can happen either through marriage or by associating with fellow believers, they have the potential to become teachers.

The best teacher that leads someone to understand the change in Islam is the change of demeanor. Passing trends have no power to define Islam. It is crucial to always bear in mind that the choice to adopt or abandon Islam is an intensely personal decision that cannot be delegated to anyone else. The connection that exists between us is not something that we intentionally started, but rather it is a connection that Allah Himself initiated.

The ability of Muslims to convert others is contingent upon Allah's permission, as destiny and faith are believed to be predetermined. The final decision, despite human efforts to resist their predetermined fate, ultimately lies with the creator. The act of addressing oneself in chaos is not the preferred course of action when compared to the goal of pleasing Allah.

The results that have been obtained with chaos and bad company are not satisfactory because they fail to align with the principles of Islam. One way to make individuals more acquainted with the moral rights mentioned in the Quran is by providing them with a thorough understanding of these principles. Regardless of the direct or indirect influence, Muslims tend to defy and interact with disbelievers. Blame, in the context of Islam, is not utilized as a means to attain salvation or atonement.

The clash that arises between entitlements, specifically neglecting Allah's laws and rights, and the desires, wants, and liberties of humans, taking precedence leads to speculation of doubts being invoked and consequently encroaching on personal territory.

This is particularly true for those who defy the affluent belief that Allah's laws are progressive and view mistakes as opportunities for repentance. In a society that is consumed by self-desires and aggression, it is important to remember that the laws of Allah remain unchangeable.

Although Muslim mistakes are penalized, society tends to glorify those who do not believe. Breaking laws has become a regular aspect of our daily lives. People who hold strong beliefs have the understanding to acknowledge their own flaws and actively work towards resolving them. According to the teachings of the Quran, there is a wholesome belief that mistakes can be corrected, but there are consequences for persistent inappropriate or irrational behavior.

Most jobs require training before joining any firm. Islam is the strongest firm at accepting a human at the face value of his (Shahada) and the creed of Islam. It's the heart Allah purifies when a human accepts Islam. He does not need training, but a pure heart. His sins become obsolete, making fresh waves to better his life. Most come to Islam as converts or returning Muslims in the best of hearts.

The highest firm has the least rules to join. How then does a Muslim deceive himself after joining the best firm of Allah? Mistakes don't take a human out of this association. The only chance to fix one's demeanor is present. Is there a firm faith company that allows human rights like Islam? One who does not see is off-course, but the hope of being rooted in is radiance for a believer.

Righteous company is necessary for souls who entrust their lives to Allah. Keeping a Muslim's faith and proclamation in mixed societies is not a trial, but a triumph of his faith. Humans tend to watch unsavory lives.

But making your own life palatable and watching your show of reality is much more rewarding. Islam does not transfer sin. And no one will proffer another's life for another's sin. These unpalatable venues contradict Islam. But Islam has explained it's erroneously deceptive. Your deeds are yours. Work on your life series, and this story, too, shall end with a beginning one day. Humans will live in a world where death and life are nonexistent, just life and deeds.

Fostering a stable temperament is the king of all avenues. While pleasing others and ignoring your dimensions leads to failure. When you believe in Islam and stay on the path, you're guaranteed a win. The only one who holds the laws of the book of the Quran ventures to true success.

Individually or in tandem with reciprocity and sincerity to Allah has taken the strongest hold.In the Quran, the last testament of Allah, rules, regulations, justice, contracts, morals, dress codes, and worship are all explained. For those who seek solace and answers, there is no guesswork. Keep the world at a distance, claiming your share while keeping Allah, Islam, and the Quran at heart. Preparation for the next world, as this one is temporary.

When believers speak to each other, some people understand the deep words spoken. However, others dismiss them as if society has conditioned them to take things lightly when it comes to depth. Those who study the Quran understand the syntax of each sentence and word. They know believers' words are precious and hold great weight. Truth should not be discarded, as it holds value. Those who speak from the heart carry lightness, while those who hold back carry heavy burdens. The grudgeful suffer, while the forgiving lead to mercy distributed by Allah.

Those who are frequent travelers are easily identifiable by their noticeable bags or suitcases. As inhabitants of this world, humans embark on a journey, carrying suitcases filled with their actions and deeds. Once the call for departure is announced, the human journey will officially commence. In an incredibly short amount of time, the soul will quickly expose the complex intricacies of a person's life, granting the opportunity to witness the multitude of actions and events that have shaped the world they are preparing to leave behind.

It is of utmost importance to take note that the station of life, regardless of whether it is referred to as an airport, train station, or road, can only be accessed once, thereby eliminating any possibility of a return. The significance of submitting oneself to Allah and dedicating time to Him should never be underestimated. Certain individuals opt to associate themselves with those who have influenced them towards wickedness, which ultimately leads them to share the same fate as their companions. Friends who remind us of Allah are the ones we can consider loyal.

Each and every individual will be tested by Allah, as Islam places the responsibility for one's actions on every person. In the context of Islam, it is emphasized that each person is solely responsible for their own actions and not those of others. The justice and fairness system in Islam is truly remarkable. Many alterations have occurred to the other biblical books that Allah gave to the children of Israel. Although they may be older in terms of chronological years, it is important to note that Prophet Muhammad holds a significant position as the final Prophet and serves as a conclusive figure for Islam and all Abrahamic faiths.

The Quran, which was sent to the Arabian peninsula, has proven its longevity over the years. As the last testament revealed by Allah, it will remain uncorrected. Although dreams and intuitions were once relied upon by humans for answers, the cessation of revelations occurred after the Quran was revealed. Allah possesses the power and determination necessary to ensure the protection of His final book. In order for a Muslim to accept prior scriptures that involve human participation, it is necessary for these stories to be correlated with the Quran.

This can be attributed to the fact that the narratives found in the Bible are not solely divine in nature, but also incorporate valuable human perspectives and experiences. The completion of the Quran took place prior to the departure of the Prophet Muhammad, and it was diligently protected by Allah. The ability to adjust or decrypt the divine revelations of the final testament of the Quran is beyond the capability of human hands.

The Prophet Muhammad carefully examined each parchment and provided guidance to Muslims for the Jewish community, encouraging them to seek the counsel of their book Torah; later they distorted all previous scriptures regarding their laws and also advised Muslims on matters pertaining to the Quran. Over the course of time, as it steadily progressed, it also accommodated the shifting desires and alterations of mankind. The books underwent significant alterations, resulting in drastic changes within the prior scriptures. Despite Jesus observing and abiding by the same laws, the followers of Christendom still worshiped him as the Lord himself.

Quran: Surah Nisa: 4:159. There are none among the People of the Book but will believe in him before his death, and he will be a witness against them on the Day of Resurrection.

Quran: Surah Maidah:5:73 They have certainly disbelieved who say, "Allah is the third of three." And there is no God except one God. And if they do not desist from what they are saying, there will surely afflict the disbelievers among them a painful punishment.

Although the Bible doesn't mention the word Trinity, the idea of God's triune nature is suggested in numerous verses. The doctrine of the Trinity took shape over centuries and amidst numerous controversies. The Bible does not explicitly state the Trinity, but it does reveal God as the Father, the Son, and the Holy Spirit.

The concept is strongly challenged as humans can only become Gods through close association with Hinduism in reincarnation. Abraham is the central figure in Abrahamic faiths, not any other human involved in these concepts. Abraham worshiped Allah alone before any books were available.

Once the Quran came with unaltered laws, it became challenging to follow any altered laws from other jurisdictions. Islam promotes acceptance of all faiths and freedom of worship, whereas contrasting theology highlights distinctions between Christianity and Islam. Jesus worshiped Allah, not himself - that's an undeniable fact.

It's sacrilegious to combine lies and truth, demonstrating disrespect and distorting the truth alongside blasphemy. Understanding the Quran completely reveals no unfamiliar concepts, but Bible concepts create resistance in accepting its truth. In the real world, there are consequences in human courts for falsification of truth but this dogma continues to celebrate historical falsified roots as gospel truth.

It centers on a human's death and their role as the son of God. Signifies the entirety of the Christian faith. The concept remains the same, regardless of the Christian sect you belong to. He is either the son of God or God himself, and he sacrificed himself for the sins of humanity. Jesus only prayed to Allah, which is the foundation of Abrahamic faiths.

Explaining the dogma's significance to Islam and Christianity, given our shared prophet, is crucial. Islam denies the divinity of Jesus, recognizing only Allah. Following an explanation of trinitarianism and its historical roots, many adherents of this faith refuse to accept this form of worship and instead profess belief in a single God..They credit their connection with God, whom they also identify as Jesus, and reject the Bible, disregarding stories that don't align with their beliefs. Muslims are required to complete the Quran at a young age.

The content of the Bible is not thoroughly explored by children at a young age; they pick and choose what they can transform into a play to make it appealing.

Muslims and Christians have contrasting views on the concept of Jesus in theology, despite both being aware of his second coming. There is no similarity between the concepts. Judaism's rejection of Jesus paved the way for Muhammad's arrival in the Arabian Peninsula, where he established Islam.

The central theme mandates Muslims to accept the Quran as a consistent law from Allah and to integrate Salat and the Quran into their learning and way of life. The last revelation cannot be altered by humans like other scriptures.

The fact that Christianity thrived despite Jesus not identifying as a Christian can be perplexing. Jesus received the book Ingeel, also referred to as the Gospel. On the other hand, it was modified. He was rejected by the Jews as the Messiah, but accepted by Christians as God's son, born of a

virgin. While some struggle to accept it, many people recognize this truth. The Quran explicitly mentions that he is the Messiah, the son of Mary. Neither the son of God nor God incarnate.

Over time, the book has undergone changes and reforms, including some for political reasons. The book retains some truth, but certain stories have been diluted. These stories were inconsistent with the concepts of the Quran.

Although some question Jesus' status, it is clear that he is the Messiah and a Prophet born of the Virgin Mary. It cannot be overstated that all Prophets, including Jesus, were Muslims. All the Prophets submitted to Allah's will.

Islam is a monotheistic faith. Although it received its name as a closing statement. Islam remains the faith of all Prophets with the missions and miracles they performed for the people of those times. However, the Quran is a living miracle unchanged and unaltered. This religion centers on submitting to one God, Allah, and seeking truth through clarity.

Consistency is a strong trait found in human character. Helping new converts and supporting believers is drafted into Islam's protocol. Muslims must address the questions and assist at all levels. Answers regarding Jesus' mission and identity will come directly from him. In the Christian faith, prayers are fulfilled by asking Jesus.

He is sometimes thanked by lighting candles, singing songs, and giving thanks to Jesus for his blessings and fulfillment of prayers. However, some may question whether Jesus is God. Those who pray receive answers only Allah answers all prayers of everyone regardless of who a human prays to as this world carries abundant religions and faiths. Ultimately, only time will tell who answered their prayers, and Allah is fair.

Quran: An'am: 6:108. Do not revile those whom they invoke other than Allah, because they will revile Allah in ignorance out of spite. For WE have indeed made the deeds of every person seem fair to them. Then, their return is to their Lord and He will inform them of what they have done.

Although the substitution of god for a deity is a common belief in many faiths, it becomes necessary to highlight this contrast only within the Abrahamic faith. A Prophet Jesus who is revered by two faiths. Christians reject Muhammad while Muslims accept Jesus, making them similar in anticipating his return, but their beliefs differ.

Everyone will eventually learn about Islam, but not everyone will follow it. Helping one another is a characteristic of humans, and showing gratitude to Allah for guidance is necessary. Misguided advice can create tension between Muslims and others. Instead of getting alarmed, it's better to continue doing the right thing and stay away from the wrong.

In Islam, Jesus is recognized as the Messiah, but it is considered blasphemous to associate Allah with spiritual attributes such as being the son of God. Allah is not a human, but the illuminating light of the world. His physical characteristics are difficult to explain since no human has seen him.

Jesus cannot be seen as a God if humans see him, as Allah cannot be visible and possess human qualities. While these clarifications may offend some, it's important to comprehend Islam and its beliefs. It is a misconception that Islam lacks color and variety; in reality, it is a vibrant and diverse religion. The Quran is the only holy book that remains unaltered by human hands, and it will remain unchanged forever.

Only those who study and recite the Quran truly grasp the foundations of this faith. Our role as fair and helpful assistants is to assist those who are converting to Islam or returning to the faith. We must go deeper and support those who require help, regardless of their attitudes or beliefs.

Quran: Surah Nisa: 4:157.and for boasting, "We killed the Messiah, Jesus, son of Mary, the messenger of Allah." But they neither killed nor crucified him—it was only made to appear so. Even those who argue for this ˹crucifixion˺ are in doubt. They do not know whatsoever—only making assumptions. They certainly did not kill him.

Therefore, the concept of death and killing is so far not derived from Islam. That is when these concepts enter Muslim families. They either strengthen the person of another faith or take the weak Muslim out of his faith. Because their laws differ a great deal from Islam. Throughout the years, these distinctions have been clarified many times. Two faiths have different conceptions. Friendships have continued, and many positive changes occurred.

As the environment is also a great teacher, travel is the most effective teacher. The common mind rejected the concept that many priests quit Christianity and joined Islam. There are more conversions from Christianity than from any other religion.

Despite the need for a tally, the numbers show 77% and rising. However, do they understand Islam? It is important to teach them with kindness. However, those unfortunate Muslims who compromise their faith, are only in a state of deception and ignorance. Any human can change an untrue statement. Islam gives hope. Not negativity backed by illusions.

The old saying you cannot teach an old dog any tricks is not Islam. Change can make the most unfit human the most efficient in belief and worldly life. Muslims also have divisions. The Quran will not be altered despite Muslim divisions. Muslims read the same Quran without any alterations.

Allah has guaranteed the protection of the Quran, his final testament and last revelation from him. As the updated testament of the Bible had 30,000 changes, it was revised many times and is still being revised.

Bible: Matthew 5;17-19. "Do not think that I have come to abolish the law or the Prophets; I have not come to abolish them but to fulfill them.

The verse clearly states that he came not to abolish the law, but to fulfill it. Therefore, there is no discrepancy in Islamic belief, as all Prophets prayed to Allah. No human can call himself the owner of the business he worked for when he was only an employee. Concepts and examples are plentiful for truth-seekers. This negates all contradictions and fully clarifies per Islamic conception that Allah is one and all Prophets brought the same message to worship Allah alone. Judgments among Muslims were based on the ideology of the Quran.

Muslims believe in Prophets who transmitted their scriptures from Allah, but a script is true if it complies with the Quran. Other biblical books do not align those stories with the Prophets' interpretations of Islam. As an example, Islam sees Jesus as pure, and Satan tempted Jesus of Christianity for forty days.

This is preposterous and blasphemous to Jesus. The Messiah Jesus was deceived by Satan, according to the Bible and Christian beliefs. Is it not possible for God to be deceived by the Satan he created, and do the followers of Jesus worship a God who followed and was tempted by Satan?

It's out of the question. How can God combat Satan if he is depicted as God's son or even as God himself? Who is the creator of whom? Didn't Allah bring Satan into existence? How does he manipulate his son into believing falsehoods? Why didn't Allah intervene to stop him? He hindered Satan from approaching believers. The idea of a believer witnessing Satan's tactics and Jesus following him goes against Islamic concepts and beliefs.

In the Quran, it is said that Satan does not have control over those who believe and pray to God. He authorized Satan to lead Jesus into diverse dimensions of deception. Despite his triumph, he persisted in following evil. The Jesus of Islam is highly revered, being born sinless and pure. Satan cannot harm him as he was born without sin following Satan would be sinful.

The contrasts between these two concepts cannot be dismissed or weakened. The fact is that Allah created Satan and Jesus in the womb of a virgin Mary. He is a human and a mortal, which leaves no doubt in the intelligent mind. For those who believe, truth has no fear. These answers may clarify the Islamic concepts for many and upset others, but for those who believe, truth has no fear.

The Bible presents Jesus as both vulnerable and tempted, personifying God. Preposterous statements are not welcome in a truth-seeking intelligent mind. Satan led him astray for a total of forty days. According to Islamic concepts, God cannot follow Satan, nor can a Prophet. Islamic doctrine contradicts these allegations.

If certain concepts can deceive God, then humans must also be vulnerable. While Jesus, who is considered divine, wandered for 40 days, a believer promptly acknowledges their wrongdoing. Ultimately, he emerged triumphant, but 40 days of his life were consumed by temptation. Jesus, son of Mary, is considered pure since birth in Islam and will return to clarify that he only prayed to Allah. He's not a god, he's the Messiah.

One God turned into three and accompanied Satan to the wild animals and wilderness, where angels protected him. This is a human-only occurrence, not something a god can go through. The focus here is on mythological concepts, not Abrahamic concepts. Angels observe without influencing human behavior they record deeds not influence actions. Islamic beliefs consider Jesus of Islam, son of Mary, to be pure in all aspects. Jesus of Islam is inherently pure and free from the sins of following evil; both he and his mother were purified by Allah. The theological disparity between the Bible and Islam cannot be simplified; it necessitates careful consideration to grasp the conflicting concepts.

The Prophet Muhammad was purified and made virtuous. Two Jinns exist to accompany every individual, one good and one bad, with one exerting a greater impact. If Jesus was human and divine in Christendom and then transformed into one, it would be difficult to worship a God in all senses who could be tempted by Satan when God himself created Satan. This theology is composed of ideologies that disagree with the human mind. This mesmerizes some to leave faith and some to put all religions in one basket.

Finally, some give up organized religions due to this discord of confusion and not agreeing with common sense. They call themselves spiritual and make up their own laws. Some believe this concept without questioning it. However, Islam says to question, read, understand then accept it. How can one believe when comprehension is scarce? A human who seeks truth wants answers, not illusions. Islam makes sense on every road for those who pray to smooth out rough edges. Their goal is to find like-minded people and believers.

Bible: Matthew. 4:1-11 *Satan* Tempts *Jesus* - Then *Jesus* was led up by the Spirit into the wilderness to be *tempted* by the *devil*. And when He had fasted *forty days* and forty.

Bible: Matthew 4:8, KJV: *Again, the devil takes him up into an exceeding high mountain, and show him all the kingdoms of the world, and the glory of them;*

Bible:MATT. 24:27 "For just as the lightning comes from the east and flashes even to the west, so will the coming of the Son of Man be.

Christians refer to the Lord or Son of God, Jesus, who was tempted not twice but three times by Satan. In the above verse he is referred to as the son of man.The irrational dogmas of Christianity and Bible stories make it difficult for Muslim minds to comprehend. The disrespectful portrayal of Prophets, including Jesus, whom they worship, adds to the challenge. Many Prophets in the Bible, including others, are mocked and defamed. The Quran is distinct, and most narratives offer a different outlook. The Quran corrects stories and reveals the truth, not taken from other scriptures.

Bible: Deuteronomy 6:13 When Satan tempted Jesus a third time, he took him to the highest point of the temple in Jerusalem and dared him to throw himself down.

Bible: Mathew: 4:11:1. Now when the tempter came to Him, he said, "If You are the Son of God, command that these stones become bread." But He answered and said, "It is written, 'Man shall not live by bread alone, but by every word that proceeds from the mouth of God.' " Then the devil took Him up into the holy city, set Him on the pinnacle of the temple, and said to Him, "If You are the Son of God, throw Yourself down. For it is written:'He shall give His angels charge over you.

Jesus acknowledged his identity as the son of Mary, affirming her motherly dignity from birth. He is the Prophet mentioned in the Quran who spoke at the time of his birth. In the Bible, Satan refers to him as the son of God, even though Satan has lived in heaven and knows that Allah is not human and Jesus is not the son of God, but rather the son of Mary who carried him just like any other mother. No woman can carry God in her uterus.

The Bible mentions Satan leading him towards suicide, contradicting Abrahamic faiths. In Islamic doctrine, it is believed that Jesus did not experience these encounters, suggesting that the idea of Jesus, who is considered divine, being tempted by Satan is misleading.

In the end, they made Jesus responsible for bearing the burden of sins, even though he was tempted to sin. Muslims believe in the concept of Jesus having no sin, but how can he resist the dajjal's corruption? According to the Bible, he may be seen as frail, but he defeated Satan and even an ordinary believer can do the same. The Bible portrays him as an adversary lured by the enemy. Only a weak individual will follow Satan, not the Prophet of Allah in Islam.

Jesus will come and announce his Muslim faith to the world, embodying the ultimate truth. Learning with an open mind is crucial to comprehend theology and contrast, especially when exploring the differences in concepts between the Bible and the Quran, both of which share the Prophet Jesus.

Viewing a man as superior through prayer implies that calling a man God diminishes women and places them inferior based on biblical ideas. In Islam, Allah is described as an luminous light, not human, and without a gender hierarchy. In Hinduism, the most important Gods that are men are Brahma, Shiva, Vishnu, Rama and many others. There are profound similarities between them

Bible: NIV: In John 14:3, Jesus said: "I will come back and take you to be with me that you also may be where I am"

This verse contrasts the belief that Jesus will return to gather those who believe in him as God or a Triune God. The Quran states he will come to reveal his identity, confront the dajjal antichrist, and address the accusations against him. He will establish peace and affirm his devotion to Allah, just like the other Prophets. These theological differences highlight the importance of knowledge over ignorance.

Bible: Mathew: 4:1:11. Jesus said to him, 'It is written again, 'You shall not [a]tempt the Lord your God.' " Again, the devil took Him up on an exceedingly high mountain, and showed Him all the kingdoms of the world and their glory. And he said to Him, "All these things I will give You if You will fall down and worship me." Then Jesus said to him, [b]"Away with you, Satan! For it is written, 'You shall worship the Lord your God, and Him only you shall serve.' " Then the devil left Him, and behold, angels came and ministered to Him.

The book is filled with confusion and contradiction that the average person cannot comprehend. The Quran contains strong declarations. The comprehension is beyond examination in the above verse from the bible that Satan offers Jesus the world when Allah is the creator of the world. How can he offer the world he didn't create? If Jesus is the embodiment of God and knows that Satan's request for respite was granted, why would he instruct him to pray? How could he fall for Satan's deceptive lies? Quranic concepts deem it impossible.

Omar, a Muslim convert and true believer, instilled fear in Satan and he walked on the other side on encountering Omar the "The Prince of believers" However, according to biblical doctrine, Jesus' faith appears unpredictable. In Islam, he is cleansed and never approached by Satan. Allah granted him purity from birth. Examining the conflicting beliefs in theology regarding the non compatibility of the Bible and Quran. In Islam, it is the responsibility of a Muslim to show humanity and kindness to all faiths. Valid differences contribute to the contrasting theology and experience.

The Quran offers numerous examples of Prophets to guide us away from blasphemous behavior. Neither the toy nor the robot can fight the toy maker. A human can't battle Allah. Therefore, precise observation concludes Jesus is not God and did not exist in the form of God. God would never subject himself to walking as a human. Allah is the creator of humans, including their inherent weakness, and He is all-powerful.

Comparing Allah to a human is a deceitful lie. Jesus, being Muslim, submitted to Allah's will instead of his own. The fact that he came to the Jews may raise questions about his Muslim identity. All Prophets of Abrahamic faiths are Muslims, as Islam is the submission to Allah's will.

The name "Islam" brings closure to all Abrahamic faiths. Being a mortal, he exemplified the clarity of Islam. Human hands later invented and added lies to the previous scriptures, conflicting with the truth. It caused a division in the Abrahamic faith and led to the differences in theology of Islam, leaving behind only scripture Quran that reveals the deceitful actions of humans.

Why do Muslims have to explain the traction and credibility of Jesus? Why does it matter? Anyone is liable for following their own beliefs. Why has explaining his identity been of significance to a Muslim? The answer is simple: he is part of the Abrahamic faith and also the Messiah, who will return as the closing statement to the finality of this earth.

Since he is part of the Abrahamic belief, allegations against him cannot be demobilized. Islam brings clearance to the table, as per Quranic doctrine, unchanged. After knowing both sides of the spectrum, how a human addresses his or her belief is up to the individual. A Muslim must express the truth.

Many people come to Islam, but they do not understand. Islam is characterized by clarity and does not hold back anything. Truth is not to be feared, but lies should not recommence. Clarity characterizes Islam along with modesty. There is no doubt that this has been exposed many times over, and many Muslims know the truth.

Several people have left their faith and Christianity, while others have joined pre-dated modernization. Fully knowing that it may not deliver what it seems to promise. Suppose Muslims join the collision of mishaps and an altered belief system. This is treason in itself.

The drunken Noah is another example in the Bible of disrespect, not respect. How would anyone want to listen to the prophecies of a drunk Prophet who exposes himself, let alone a drunk man? It's not even plausible in today's society that such characters would not get suitable employment, let alone be Prophets of God, to build arks.

Bible: Genesis 9:21. Noah got drunk on the wine from his new vineyard. In his *drunkenness*, he lay naked in his tent. *Noah's* son Ham walked in and saw him naked.

The book Bible contains many erotic stories. The Quran is read to a child and memorized by a child or an adult starting at four years. It is not surprising that those who do not study the Quran place all faiths under the same emblem. The differences are not minute; they are significant.

Bible ESV. Psalm 84 song of Soloman.

Few came here to resolve their depression, while others learned something and left. Those who stay and never leave are more faithful than Muslims born into this faith. The born Muslims who spend their whole lives calling on their creator find solace in Islam and Allah. There are so many things we can learn from Allah in so little time.

There are no different versions of the Quran. Muslims perform the Salat in Arabic throughout the world. They read the Quran in Arabic. The Quran is translated into many languages, but the true pleasure of reading lies in Arabic. Even non-Arabic-speaking Muslims memorize the Quran and pray Salat in Arabic. This ease of learning is from Allah.

Quran: Surah Qamar 54;17.Indeed, We made this Quran easy to understand w. Who,, then, is willing to take it to heart · The Clear Quran.

There is no adequate translation of the Quran that does justice to its words. Allah commands us to learn Arabic. His language.

Quran: Surah Nisa: 4:135.O you who have believed, be persistently standing firm in justice, witnesses for Allāh, even if it be against yourselves or parents and relatives.

Some struggle with Muslim families when Islam stands in the way of their own whims. Sometimes, converts struggle after accepting their faith and the approval of their families and peers. Islam is first, and truth cannot refrain from Allah's word. One who fears Allah is not afraid of human acceptance. Putting humans first would not be justice for a follower of Islam. Mistakes are many, but justice is at the forefront. Allah's mercy is plenty. But the rules, methodology, and design are impeccable and cannot be negated by any Muslim who practices Islam. These differences between Christendom and Islam are so wide it's impossible to comprehend how a human holding human qualities as Jesus is made to pose as God.

Allah says to be just and stand for justice, even if it is against you. The differences and clarifications are simplified as truth has no barriers to Islam's faith. As a result, they struggled to fathom how Jesus could have been born of a virgin birth, so they blasphemed and titled him the son of God. Islam views this as a major sin. This is the only sin Allah will not forgive, as his divinity possesses no flaws.

Bible: King James Version: John 1:14 And the Word was made flesh and dwelt among us, (and we beheld his glory, the glory as of the only begotten of the Father,) full of grace and truth.

Imagination cannot control the mind to say who Allah is until the next life when a face-to-face meeting occurs. He is not a human and cannot have a son. The explicit statement is from the Quran and not from a Muslim. Although vast differences can be bridged. By friendship and business, inviting this rhetoric into Muslim homes is a recipe for failure. Unless any seeker is willing to learn. Which only Allah can permit according to the disposition of the heart.

Witnessing Jesus transform into God and walk among humans would be seen as blasphemous because people would have seen Allah. He cannot enter a human body or be seen by anyone, although he knows his creatures and he is near to those who believe. Moses requested to witness God's presence and lost consciousness upon seeing a fraction of His radiance.

The human's weakness is evident from the moment of creation, and the blending of humans with mythological concepts, along with Jesus following Satan, adds to the complexity. This concept is rendered invalid by the Islamic understanding of Abrahamic faiths and monotheism.

If a person is weak in faith, this results in invitations to paganism. Yet there are blessings in store for those who are averse to learning Islam on their own. The term pseudo-culture and tolerant society refers more to friendship than to courtships involving Islam. Totalitarianism appears to lead many concepts of individual life through coercion and repression.

It does not permit individual freedom. Although the Western world is coerced to believe they are independent thinkers. However, the masses lead the minds and use repressive methods of expression. This is quite predictable in any society that suffers from spiritual literacy in the right order.

The only way Allah allowed Muslim men to marry people in the book is because Jesus is the Messiah and a Prophet sent by Allah. Only the women who believe in the book. Not the rebels who break Allah's rules. In the absence of repentance, they continue to follow their own rules, and they cannot bridge relationships.

Muslims are protected by Islam, not restricted by it. The layout of the differences is for the viewer to see. They include faith, friendship, and compatibility. Keep your faith close as a Muslim, and you will help others to see direction and balance without fear. Allah guides the believers. A curious mind and heart will find these differences pleasant, not upsetting or derogatory. Without questions, one cannot believe it.

Islam encourages one to think, reflect, and then believe. It endowed humans with an inquisitive mind that Allah created. Some drift through life in their comfort zone, never exploring their minds, souls, faith, and contentment of the heart. For those who stagnate, those are the wasted years of life. All of humanity, the jinns, and every living creature have access to time, and time is the ultimate wealth. The time's price beats all other materials. Except for the mentally challenged. Allah took the oath over time, demonstrating its importance.

The small surah of the Quran is al-Asr, which means Allah takes an oath over time in this surah. Pseudo-society members believe they are spiritual, but not religious. In metaphysics, the spiritual self distinguishes itself as a human governed by the spirit. However, it does not follow the rules and regulations of the guiding principles of biblical texts.

Advertently a borderline atheist who submits to his free will, even though he acknowledges that there is a higher power, understands the hierarchy of the universe. Expressions of gratitude and sorrow within the pseudo-culture do not express faith in God. Gratitude, as to the universe or the spirit, is worded, thankfully. It is painful for another Muslim to witness the dilemma of disobedience to Allah when a Muslim is involved.

Humanity's rules empower spirituality and acceptance of hierarchy as the supreme authority of the universe. For a society adhering to pseudo-cultures and laws, revelations of the divine and scripts are out of date and relegated to the background. These cultures measure success by travel, academia and material wealth, but submission to the will of Allah is a compromised issue for the troublesome.

Satan's calls aren't brand new. Humans have repeated them for centuries, only that the formats change, but the content does not. Later, changes occurred. All these scripts changed to match the times except the Quran. The Quran corresponds to the times, but this book will not conform to human desires. The Quran will stand the test of time regardless of comparisons.

A Muslim's dream cannot be told to a non-Muslim. Those who have malice or do not wish the best for the person may say something negative. It may be difficult for some to believe, but that is also true for weak believers. The interpretation of dreams is a gift from Allah given to Prophet Yusuf. Islam is true for a believer and a question mark for a disbeliever or a doubter.

Some might say I don't let a book written 1400 years ago dictate my life choices. The same individuals must realize they are completely under Allah's control. Especially confused Muslims and Muslim youth. When the most intelligent being cannot control death, the most significant part of life, then his understanding is lacking. Death controls life already.

Quran: Surah Ankaboot: 29:57. Every soul shall taste death, and to "US," you shall be returned.

Quran: Surah Imran: 3:185.Everyone is bound to taste death, and you shall receive your full reward on the Day of Resurrection.

When an individual gets sick despite exercising, eating right, and doing everything in their power, there is already no control. Faith, soul, body, and time are borrowed, and humanity can take control of their lives as long as they remember this. Life has its own clock, and it can stop at any time. It is understood by those who value this episode of time that Allah's worship is also timed.

A believer is driven to attend meetings (Salat) and discussions of Allah (dhikr) dialogue that benefit his soul and worldly affairs. Time passes at a continual range for those who believe and quickly for those who are skeptical. Access to time can sometimes lead to enhanced success. Some seek the world, others Allah, and some acquire both. The loan does not accrue interest, but deeds add up, whether positive or negative. As a Muslim, the believer accepts the faith of Islam as a gift from Allah.

Some life and health failures make some bitter, while others seek betterment and see this as a turning point in life. Others never change. Some are born wealthy with Islam and material wealth, and these are successful who never forget Allah. The wealthiest are those who have Allah close to their hearts and have complete faith in him. Some faiths might count the success of materials as a blessing, while others might say money is greed or beauty is conceited.

Quran: Surah Tin: 95:4."We have indeed created humankind in the best of molds."

Muslims believe everything that exists that all gifts are from Allah, and that they are not the result of human design. Those who alter their appearance and appear less attractive than when they started. A human's appearance will be altered by Satan's unrest in their hearts. Tattoos are improvised on bodies to make statements that it is forbidden by Islam to pierce a human body.

Quran: Surah Nisa: 4;119.I will order them, and they will change the creation of Allah." Whoever takes Satan as a guardian besides Allah, certainly has suffered a clear suffering.

Muslims are told that to succeed in this life, they must educate themselves, travel, spend, and give to others, all within the means of one. Islam encourages travel and learning. Faith in this world entertains the innermost thoughts of a believer. Although Allah created the world as a platform for humans, he did not prohibit humanity from enjoying nature, trees, water, animals, humanity, food, shelter, and family.

Allah orchestrated a temporary universe for humanity to enjoy worldly pleasures. Nature captivates humanity, and there's a specific form for entering heaven. There are instances where two individuals have different perspectives on the road they journey. Certain individuals witness identical things along the identical path simultaneously. However, their perspectives on life differ.

The entrance to destiny is foretold and fated. Many individuals, creatures, or spirits persist in this world for extended periods as old age gradually affects various aspects of life. Some credit their healthy lifestyle and good eating habits for their overall well-being. Some individuals with underlying health conditions may develop stress and eating disorders. Health is a fundamental component of Islam's pillars.

The duration of life is predetermined. Long life serves as a gift of realization and self-correction, setting an example for everyone. Some depart suddenly and without warning, but Allah knew their time on Earth had ended. The ability to survive, self-correct, be responsible, and be influenced by Islam is present in humans growing up in a practicing Muslim family. Seeking progress and aiming to assist others in finding the right path to Allah.

Humans can sometimes serve as shining examples of what not to do in life. They also give examples of how they excel and impact others' lives. When a person is coherent and alert to the evil they are pursuing, they are no longer living. A Muslim's house without Salat and Quran is like a graveyard.

Prophet Muhammad cautioned Muslims against turning their homes into graveyards. Every inhalation a person takes in good health is a blessing. Some people cannot breathe and others require medication daily, yet they do not practice Islam. There are no excuses for Muslims.

It's unfortunate when someone who converted to Islam and sought righteousness goes back to a darker path. Sometimes neglect is experienced by a born Muslim. Familiarity with laws and rules. The jurisdiction of justice rests with Allah. Even after receiving it as a solemn truth from Allah. Without the will of Allah, humans cannot accomplish anything. Without permission, one cannot attend to their faith or prostrate to Allah. Humility holds the utmost significance in Salat for Muslims.

Overachievers value the pursuit of knowledge and growth over staying stagnant and believe in the power of positive thinking. It's more important to keep one quality person who can lead you to Allah than to keep many people. Many people can ruin a dish, but one person can fix it. Muslims cannot have haters of Islam or resentful people as companions. They cannot be part of a network that goes against the rules of Islam.

Muslims also face exposure to a pseudo-cultural society. The fully devoted to their faith may stray, but Allah blesses those he selects with spiritual wealth. Predefined measures in place make the return more solidifying than the departure.

Quran: Surah Furqan. 25:29. *He led me astray from the admonition that had come to me. Satan proved to be a vengeful betrayer of man."*

Quran: Surah Al Fath 48:29 (Muhammad is the messenger of Allah. And those with him are severe against disbelievers and merciful among themselves. You see them bowing and falling prostrate (in prayer), seeking bounty from Allah and (his) good pleasure.

The mark of them (i.e., of their faith) is on their faces (foreheads) from the traces of prostration "during prayers."

Quran: Surah An'am 38. And no creature on or within the earth or bird flies with its wings, except that they are communities like you. We have not neglected a thing in the register. Then unto their Lord, they will gather.

Surrendering to Allah means letting go of bitterness in speech. To punish the tyrant, we can appeal to truth rather than obscenity. The launch focuses on factors that impact us in modern life. Addressing oppression. A genuine source is necessary for all humans. The advancement of material is a blessing. The highest form of ecstasy and contentment is found in spiritual gifts.

When views change, it's important not to ignore spiritual growth. Islam remains constant, but humans can adapt. Muslim endeavors to enrich themselves have adorned both Muslims and non-Muslims for decades. Constantly blaming Muslims and internalizing concepts has been an ongoing effort.

Ways to cope with life's unchanging episodes. The best way to help the world is by knowing the truth and expressing it. Discovering one's talents is important, but standing for truth is the ultimate gift of Islam. The jolts do not affect on the contrary; they amplify strength. Allah steers those whom he selects. It has been the daily broadcast of the Westward expansion that has perpetrated incidents and blamed Muslims.

Disguising the truth relishes unknown events with evidence, but fails to capture the truth of the perpetrators. Spirituality is no match for physicality. Any successful relationship requires them to work concurrently.

The unfortunate 911 incident in the US affected many and had a positive impact on seekers of Islam. Seeking Islam became important as Muslims were collectively blamed for the incident without full proof of who was responsible. The higher-ranking individuals were not present at the scene. The air was filled with sadness, leaving an array of heartache. Death is a visitor in every home. It manifests itself in strange and unexpected ways. The political agenda behind gaining access to Iraq led to retaliation.

A lot of resentment and unfulfilled promises resulted in loss due to their long-term friendship. They finally succeeded in setting the enemy for non-compliance with regime change after numerous allegations and court trials. Despite Iraq's lack of involvement, the opposition wasted no time in initiating their pursuit of entry by announcing intentions to demobilize.

The regime undoubtedly endorsed totalitarianism, which aimed to control every individual and guarantee protection through coercion and repression of non-participants. Even though 911 had no relevance to him, they proceeded with the plan to infiltrate Iraq. The absence of high-ranking officials during 9/11 has raised questions about whether it was coincidental or planned. Muslims collectively shouldered the blame.

Throughout history, corrupt puppeteers have plagued the Muslim world, while Europe and the world thrived under Muslim regimes. Becoming skilled at managing these situations. Educating and teaching the truth to the masses is crucial.

The invasion of Iraq legitimized evil and falsely portrayed Iraqis as evil. Throughout history, numerous Muslims have been subjected to the death penalty. There was also no real proof in their staging. Societies have developed animosity to maintain evil and foster opposition. Disbelievers' promises are unreliable and can be expensive.

Quran: Surah Nisa.4:144.O believers! Do not take disbelievers as allies instead of believers. Would you like to give Allah solid proof against yourselves?

This is the evil axis of civilizations. One can see this turmoil in daily life. These are eye-openers for Muslims. Some friendships understand the truth and continue, while the ones without basis fall apart as time is the friend of those who understand its value. There are many documented friendships, but the one that takes you to Allah is the one that counts.

Allah protects his believers. He will keep sending the highest quality of people and eradicate the negative from life. In this society of deceit, a handshake or written document does not suffice. There is always a positive in every society as we learn who not to trust and who to trust. In the replay of 9/11, the administration shifted its attention to Iraq, saying it was part of an "axis of evil" that pursued anti-American policies.

The New York Times Magazine the day I realized I would never find weapons of mass destruction in Iraq. ABC News reported.

Iraq has been forever changed by the aftermath of its turmoil and uninvited entry. They committed various crimes, including child murder, rape, tree burning, environmental contamination, and retaliation against a country they dubbed the evil axis. The wrongdoers will be repaid and compensated by Allah for their deeds. Occasionally delayed in receiving. Every human will be justified..

The fighters returned with posttraumatic stress disorder, confronting sorrows, and retired with battles of liability within. Many had stories to tell, and some surrendered to the truth, causing them to withdraw from further interactions and soul searching.

Nations, individuals, and families are still investigating answers. They produced many films during this period. It bears no presented concrete testimony. The people who blame a certain group without evidence are haters. The tragedy of September 9/11 2001 in the USA. Islam took a harsh pulsation in this society.

People who never travel and do not engage in certain channels of research are likely to receive undocumented lies and spread more evil without being aware of the truth. Humanity can keep exploring for truth until it finds what it's looking for or drowns in lies. The intelligence's unequivocal conclusion was not contradictory.

But the damage was massive and never paid back to the families. Mass destruction is not a response to accusations, but rather a pattern preferred by most con artists staging the Middle East to gain entry into the country. Former friends and promises have turned into the sword of victory for the opposition against Muslims on stage. Islam is clear: do not take unbelievers as allies.While the statement may not encompass every single person, it does encompass the majority not the minority, those of whom remain trustworthy.

Once the chaos and support for oppressive lands are witnessed, there is no denying the statement that every society, with experience, is considered good for humans. However, it is crucial to issue a warning when truth is explored, as truth cannot be merely brushed aside, but rather should be recorded in history.

The word "allies" can have two distinct meanings, which should not be confused with the concept of friendship. Allie is an individual who possesses the admirable quality of standing up for the truth, even if it means going against their own interests. In this world, there are still a few allies who have the courage to speak the truth, while others choose to remain silent and avoid expressing their opinions. However, it is the responsibility of a Muslim to act as an ally and support the truth, regardless of personal consequences. Strive to be your own best ally and advocate.

Quran: Surah Maidah: 5:51.Believers! Do not take the Jews and the Christians for your allies. They are the allies of each other. And among you, he who takes them for allies shall be regarded as one of them. Allah does not guide the wrong-doers.

The verse above can resonate with prejudice and point fingers at Islam. The fact remains, that they have altered their books to suit their edifice. As a result, changing testimony or shifting the truth to oppose Islam is happening in today's lifestyles. This rule does not apply to true believers. Instead, the majority of rules in this deceitful episode are a questionnaire answered simply for those who comprehend the delivery. Believers and disbelievers are not the same and can never stand on the same platform. If one can change Allah's books, going against a human is not a challenge for evil-doers. Clearly, this does not apply to believing souls.

Quran: Surah Maidah: 5;52. (Indeed, you see those afflicted with the disease of hypocrisy race towards them, saying:

'We fear lest some misfortune overtakes us.[84] And it may happen that Allah will either bring you a decisive victory or bring about something else from Himself? And then they will feel remorseful at the hypocrisy which they have kept concealed in their breasts.

The built-in hypocrisy of staging Muslims is continued efforts through social media and rhetoric created in the fascia they have portrayed. Islam says to stand against yourself for the truth.

Quran: Surah Nisa: 135. O believers! Stand firm for justice as witnesses for Allah, even if it is against yourselves, your parents, or close relatives. Be they rich or poor,

This led Americans to believe more lies as world affairs literacy is a conflict in the USA. Masses educated by social media. Especially the less empowered with a lack of education. As this country barely makes ends meet, although it often appears otherwise, it certainly does not apply to everyone. There is hardly any travel to Middle Eastern countries. Some don't even have a passport, let alone the ability to travel, and these masses can easily be corrupted.

The Western world remains unresolved and contradictory to many allegations against the Muslim world, saying Muslims did it. Many Muslims, regardless of what they said, helped in this unfortunate parley, as humanity was at stake, not to blame. The reports of this tragic episode are still a pursuit to point to the right origin. Leaving behind many to question Islam and many who rushed to bookstores to discover the truth about Islamic doctrines.

For many Muslims and non-Muslims, it was like the breeze that drove distantly through the gloom and prolonged vitality with fury. Fear subsequently outstripped and investigated Islam in pursuit of accuracy. The concern of Islam provided humanity with a glance at behavior considerably patiently.

Many established homes with Muslim women and households and pursued this adventure. As an inevitability, destiny has plans. The political theater of the iniquitous system or societies to enjoin evil or accusations has no foreplay in Islam. Allah's word resonates around the world. He is not shy of punishment, nor is he shy of giving in abundance, without an account, to whom he wills. He does what he wills and no one controls his giving.

Quran: Surah Imran 3:9 "Allah never breaks his promise."

Muslims continued life as usual in the US with diligence and perseverance, which offered help at every junction. As if all the Muslims handled another Muslim's action. Ludicrous in a society that alleges false allegations. All Muslims paid a price for the act, but it's obscure who did it. The Muslim community needs to help and respond to the angry society.

Abc news: 20 years after 9/11, Islamophobia continues to haunt Muslim.

Al Jazeera: Sep 11, 2022 — The September 11, 2001 attacks on the United States ushered in a new era of hate crimes and racism.

As matters calmed down, humor triumphed between the American acquaintances. Academic amenities, playgrounds, and marketplaces. Social gatherings for young or mature people had the same effect. Travel was affected when Muslim men had a beard or a Muslim woman wearing the (hijab) head cover set apart and checked rudely at airports as if they were criminals. Muslim youth shaved their beards before traveling. Some younger women did not wear the hijab during the serious walk through TSA, although some feared having a Muslim name.

Some said (bismillah) in the name of Allah and moved past the fear and prejudice after boarding the plane. Airports and the TSA made it difficult for Muslims to have a hard time traveling after these times. Muslims continued life to the best it had to give. Reaching Allah for forgiveness is what Muslims do in hard times. They brought many clerics into custody for questioning whether they were the target of suspicion, as mosques continued to be under surveillance. The Muslims gazed during seating or service on the airplane, depending on what flight they were boarding.

As if the Muslim boarding had not the slightest fear or anger, perhaps some concern. The Muslim pilots and crew on the airplanes continued to protect others. Prejudice remains a consistent battle for Muslims. Years don't alter an ignorant attitude.

Every news media illustrates Muslims collectively.

Fearing the tabloid aftereffects, Muslim children feared to admit they were from a Muslim household in academic facilities. Muslims working in professional fields carried out their duties with the utmost respect. As Muslims, we were fully aware this phase would pass. Allah tests faith either with curiosity, man's fear, hatred, or desire to learn about this religion not known to man.

Islam has been around for decades, perhaps not known to too many in the Western world, especially the USA, where the world got to know Islam. Perhaps the timing was harsh for Muslims and Islam, but Allah's timing has a clock of its own. Such are the tests of life for humanity. Islam tests our faith as Muslims.

We continue to have no animosity and only gratitude to Allah and the people of the USA. We continue to help each other. This attitude does not prevail in all humans. The court of law discharges the punishment against an offender not without collecting concrete evidence. However, tabloids and social media maneuvered against Muslims as collective punishment blamed by the US for these actions.

During the regime of the former higher-ups. This is a continuous effort from them toward Muslims using social media. To register them as a collective group. Despite ignorance, Muslims continue to strive to help this society in every way possible.

With the demeaning laws and rules they play to the youth, they are inducing the word modern. Their society dates back to pre-pagan times when they never took leave.

There is no assumption in Islam, only evidence and truth. This raises awareness of misunderstandings. Rather than hiding like hypocrites or claiming the victim. Evil can't succeed in a story. Greed is the dearest of too many. Later, exploring the ones serving them was a Muslim. It did not inform them of the faith they followed until later. To see the character was strength. Embarrassed, curiosity leads many to bookstores to purchase the Quran or question Muslims about Islam.

It is for this reason that Muslims need an education in Islam. If there is no explanation other than my parents being Muslims, one cannot explain why he follows Islam. The answer to that question is hardly satisfactory. A Muslim needs to consider why he follows the faith of Islam in his answer. Ignorance of a Muslim has no place in Islam.

Islam thrives on ethics, respect, and kindness. Ignorance or manipulative behavior can resort to evil. Allah keeps note of all humans and those who are disrupting the lifestyle of other humans, mentally or physically. All actions justified upon the approach of judgment day may be closer than man can fathom in this world. The Muslim world was unwanted in this society, although our children continued to thrive and do better than most. It was Allah's plan. It was time Islam was re-established with full strength, and curious minds were searching for the truth.

The tragic incident marks history in a sad train of thought for all humanity concerned during that time. Every decade. Islam has been at a crossroads. It has emerged as a conqueror in every decade and will continue until eternity. The angels questioned Allah about human existence since Jinns caused enough havoc before humans. The strongest form of creation is a human.

Understanding its capabilities is the battle within the self-awareness of those who conquer their strengths and weaknesses. Allah has hope in humans that even humans do not know their capabilities. It is with humility and gratitude to Allah that one leaves behind his deeds, examples, and accomplishments as a testament to his faith after coming out in a triumph of bliss.

The Muslim knows the value of himself and his faith. Humans can survive in ways that no machine can match. The mechanics of survival installed by Allah surpass any man-made robot or machine.

Quran: Surah Baqarah 2:30 Just think when your Lord said to the angels: "Lo! I am about to place a vicegerent on earth," they said: "Will You place on it one who will spread mischief and shed blood while we celebrate Your glory and extol Your holiness?" He said: "Surely I know what you do not know."

Quran: Surah Maidah 5:8 O you who have believed, be persistently standing firm for Allah, witnesses in justice, and do not let the hatred of a people prevent you from being just.

Allah protected his last document, the Quran and Islam. Every door, every home worldwide, knew about this faith. Tabloids and social media projected lies and altered truth. It was up to humanity to search for the truth. This led to the conversion of many to Islam. Islam may have a negative undertone for some through new Western communal instruments.

Allah permits humanity sufficient knowledge to delve into realism. Indeed, examining realism is a contribution of its own from Allah. Muslims receiving this assessment had questions. Muslims served the trials on offshore territory, for many of us and our offspring who relive these years perceive the fragility of this era. Deliberate annihilation destroyed humankind and substance, crushing spirits. Can the man in charge at the time provide answers? Collectively, the Muslim community took responsibility for the blame imposed on them. If Saudi Arabia held the blame, the US wouldn't be allies for someone who was harming their soil.

Accusing Muslims collectively of pointing fingers at Saudi and continuing to bow to Saud's autocrats. And showing they are in bed with the enemy devours no sense except hypocrisy. Humans do not bow to the opposition that destroys their lands and people, and shameful society has no remorse about enslaving and staging them and profiting from them.

People who take and talk badly about those they take from Islam have shown us immoral behavior. That's why learning about Islam is a must for both youth and new converts. Precisely, they would not invade Iraq to declare they encountered no weapons of mass destruction. People who come to Islam with a filtered heart never leave, because the passion is too strong to rebuke the faith.

There have been many decades of decadence for some who came to Islam with doubt.

Or a heart that is unclean and tainted. But Allah knows the hearts that seek him.

By living a pure life, the believer lives a full life. Many people became Muslims after traumatic heartbreak in the USA. Many found the contentment and answers they sought, while others remained empty and searching. The human will find what he seeks since it is the will of Allah.

Quran: Surah Nisa: 4:88. What has happened to you that you have two minds about the hypocrite even though Allah has reverted them, owing to the sins that they earned?

Do you want to lead those to the right way whom Allah let them go astray? And he whom Allah lets go astray, for him you can never find a way.

Quran: Surah Imran 3:134 Those who spend [charity] in prosperity and in adversity, who repress anger, and who forgive men; verily, God loves the good doers

Guardian: There were no weapons of mass destruction in Iraq.

NBC News: Apr 25, 2005 — In his final report, the CIA's top weapons inspector in Iraq said Monday that the hunt for weapons of mass destruction has gone "

But haters still blame Muslims without evidence in hand. But they do have evidence within the silent hate and prejudice they hold and accuse others. Islamophobia needs to be addressed, says the world, but Allah knows the truth. It will always come to terms sooner than later. They may remember the deaths, but they don't acknowledge the silent death within the soul they face. It is frightening

They clutched the Middle East as the grounding of game destruction and greed. This is not the first time. The number of bodies is unknown, but there has been much more injury in the Middle East and Baghdad, with allegations that have yet to be proven.

New York Times: Dec 14, 2008 — Prime Minister Nuri Kamal al-Maliki of Iraq tried to block a shoe that was thrown at President Bush at a news conference on Sunday in Baghdad.

The man is still looking for proof. Will this be hushed, or will Muslims have to shoulder the blame? A tennis shoe was pitched at him, the one visiting to console and make amends; the crowd was not so friendly. For most Muslims, honesty is of great value , and do not endorse hypocrisy. Speaking the truth is highly encouraged, and silence can be interpreted as hypocritical. The faith of Islam stresses the significance of taking action with integrity.

Muslims mostly admit mistakes and seek repentance instead of engaging in idle chatter. They are aware that the world can be misleading, and what is shown on social media may not always reflect the truth. To uncover the truth, it is important to travel and gain new experiences.

Muslims believe in the importance of sincerity and accountability, and they value justified actions. Allah commands Muslims to uphold justice both during war and negotiations. Hypocrisy is viewed as a sin and has consequences in both this world and the next.

It's crucial to recognize the realities of our society, where people often prioritize insignificant things and become consumed by social media instead of taking action to bring about change. Isolating oneself or refusing to engage with those who hold different beliefs does not promote progress; it leads to stagnation. Connecting with a fellow Muslim can bring immense value, especially if both individuals can positively impact each other's lives. While physical presence is important, prioritizing spiritual connection is crucial. When two Muslims connect on a spiritual level, the results can surpass any roundtable discussion. However, it is vital to prioritize Allah's laws in every interaction.

Quran: Surah Nisa: 4:145.Indeed, the hypocrites will be in the lowest depths of the Fire.

It's interesting to note that some countries that accuse others of wrongdoing are allies. It makes sense that if they truly had ill intentions towards your home or region, they wouldn't continue to interact with you in a kind and generous manner or accept gifts. Sadly, this type of deceit has led to jokes and comedic material, particularly about Muslims.

Nonetheless, Muslim individuals have been able to make a name for themselves in the entertainment industry and have made strides in countering the negative stereotypes that portray them as radical terrorists in the United States. The Muslim group has taken on a distinctive name that is recognized by almost everyone. Many found it amusing or a joke, but some were not pleased and became angered by the deception. Muslims are commonly associated by given names collectively with terms like terrorist or extremist.

Persecution of a certain religious group, such as Islam and Muslims, may seem unfair, but nothing is fair to a human who feels the strain of opposition. Islam spread like wildfire. Most Islam conversions came from the Big Apple, New York City. We cannot estimate Allah's power. Human allegations turned to the research of Islam.

Faithless and heedless, they acquiesced to Islam's principle after a continuous search for accuracy and exploring light from darkness. Justice in Islam is the cornerstone of this faith. Justice must prevail in all aspects of everyday life, and no human being can punish another. Islam does not recommend the spreading of lies and hypocrisy; instead, it promotes fair wars fought with integrity.

Quran: Surah Nisa: 04:135 - Stand out firmly for justice, as witnesses to Allah, even if it be against yourselves, or your parents and relatives.

There is no possibility that the enemy will interrupt what the future permits. That is Allah's grace. For a steadfast follower, the horizon is Allah. The truth uncovered is not a dilemma but lies kept under the rug eventually emerge; such is Islam's truth will rule. The dogma of ill literacy will present Islam as backward.

Despite this, even the most literate Arabs who practiced educational literacy and poetry could not compete with the phantom delivery of the Quran. There has never been a man on earth who can compete with the delivery of the smallest "surah" of the Quran. No challenge has been met and never will be met; it is the terrain of understanding the soul's grandeur that comprehends the truth.

As individuals, we have a finite amount of time to invest in ourselves. We hope that our exploration of worldly life and preparation for the next is successful for all who coexist. Islamic teachings provide significant benefits, and it's crucial to remember that fear is not the truth. Instead, we should fear Allah, not other humans. Those who revere Allah have no reason to fear other humans. Those who are afraid of humans are not entirely committed to following Allah, as they are always concerned about what others think of them. However, those who believe in Allah are content and find peace in their faith.

It's important to share the truth about Islam, but ultimately, each individual must decide if it's right for them. Regardless of one's beliefs, progress can be made by learning, listening, and reading.

CHAPTER 11

THE ACTIONS OF MUSLIMS DON'T MAGISTRATE ISLAM.

In today's world, do the actions of Muslim magistrates align with the principles and teachings of Islam? If the survival of Islam depended solely on the actions carried out by Muslims, it would have disappeared a long time ago.

The comprehensive and all-inclusive nature of Islam guarantees its resilience against the actions of individuals, as it shapes and influences the State and its legal system. In addition to influencing personal relationships, Islam also has an impact on mannerisms, justice, and discipline. Individuals who adhere to rules and regulations place a higher emphasis on the practical aspects of abiding by the law and preserving societal order.

Those who veer off course find their way back with Allah's guiding navigation for the pure-hearted. Who can get consumed by their responsibilities and miss out on exploring and experiencing spirituality?

Every person on earth can explore Allah's spiritual realm. Allah foresaw the journey of humankind and authored this path as a choice, not an obligation. A hidden power within destiny compels humans towards their destined path.

Many people have multifaceted personalities with hidden layers waiting to be discovered. Some individuals manipulate and blame others to avoid accountability for their actions. People with strong convictions take responsibility for their mistakes instead of blaming others.

A Muslim's words and actions should carry profound significance. While some prioritize actions over words, Muslims steadfastly uphold the belief that a Muslim's word is absolute. When someone breaks a promise, it reveals a deficit in their integrity.There is a palpable presence of honor and words that radiate from within. Character is the intangible force that adds weight to a Muslim's presence. The broken words resemble a fragmented puzzle, with their scattered and mismatched pieces making it impossible to grasp their truth. Solidarity is conveyed through words that reflect truth, not negligence or external influences.

Effective communication is vital for maintaining any relationship. While writing is a common way to connect, the sound of someone's voice adds depth and meaning to the conversation. A gentle conversation has the power to mend divides, fostering a sense of togetherness and restoring balance. Rather than being written down, prayer in Islam is spoken aloud as (dua) and directed towards Allah. While writing is widely used, there is something deeply personal about recalling the sounds and emotions that come with delivering a message.

In Islam, effective communication is highly valued, and Prophet Muhammad and other Prophets were diligent in delivering their messages. Their revelations were conveyed through spoken words, emphasizing the power of language and its undeniable impact.

In their daily lives, Muslims seamlessly blend the words of Allah and stories, even during business engagements or while on the move, to stay connected to their faith. Commonly used phrases in the Muslim world are "Insha Allah," which means "If God wills," and "God willing." It is crucial to seek out what nourishes the soul and fosters positive growth, instead of staying isolated and silent. To stay grounded in truth, Muslims should only share things that protect them from the dangers of deception and falsehood, regardless of who they come from.

Effective communication and open discussion about Allah are crucial aspects of Islam. Islamic laws strictly forbid immoral acts, considering them as regressions rather than advancements. Including references to Allah is an indispensable part of conversations among Muslims.

Solidarity is crucial for individuals of faith, achieved through patience and perseverance. It is not safe to assume that Islam is fully represented by Muslims, as many actions do not reflect Islam, even among those who practice or have converted to it. The essence of Islam lies in continuously returning, regardless of how many falls one takes, as repentance is the key to success.

Muslims who perceive Salat as burdensome may feel like they're wasting energy on a society that only offers minimal inner peace. Salat was created to benefit Muslims. Work hours in society are determined by the system.

Conversely, people willingly accept a job that devours their time but yields a source of income that adds value and advantages without any sense of burden. Excitement and planning surround retirement and finances, but health is unpredictable. It's a divine gift from Allah. Certainly, the work of this world is important, but not at the risk of compromising beliefs.

Some individuals and retirees who delay travel and fun for retirement may face health problems that prevent them from enjoying their plans. Allah determines all plans, but Muslims who don't realize the significance of (Salat) ritual prayer are bargaining for their time and growth in their personal life.

Spending time with a believer who reminds one of Allah, even if they have flaws, is like having a precious jewel who shares conversations, stories, and (dhikr) dialogue about Allah because time is not guaranteed.

It's not uncommon for some Muslims to stray from the guidelines of Islam, which can make it challenging to justify their faith. Nevertheless, the strength of Islam as a belief system endures regardless of the actions of its followers.

Even a single devout Muslim can uphold the values of the faith. To gain a comprehensive understanding and assessment of Islam, it's important to take into account both its positive and negative aspects of defiance or unexpected actions of those who know it was a mistake and rectify the demeanor.

However, ultimately it's Allah's assessment and the final Quranic revelations that hold the ultimate authority and cannot be surpassed by human evaluation. The change one makes in life augurs happiness. Or negativity, one welcomes.

Color shades are many, but inviting the right color into life is half the battle for success. Inviting evil or doubt into one's thoughts is negligence towards progress. Accepting Focus and morality: a sense of contentment based on faith and positive company.

The company of a believer is like a gleam of light that penetrates life with subtle rays benefitting our souls. The horizons display success for those who try. Never forget to reflect on the source of your efforts and believe in Allah.

Certain countries have developed academic education systems and social media to negatively portray Islam, which can have a detrimental effect on vulnerable individuals. Despite that, studying from the proper sources can be advantageous. Platforms that focus on showcasing negative depictions of Islam and Muslims are detrimental to those who only have access to distorted representations.

Those who convert to Islam and isolate themselves from fellow Muslims lead a solitary existence unless they participate in dialogues about Allah. Despite not being lonely, Islam educates about compassion, kindness, laws, contracts, forgiveness, and permissible relationships. Islam encompasses both the physical and mental aspects of humanity. Islam does not promote celibacy, but marriage completes the (deen) way of life, as humans are social animals and loneliness is a void of happiness for those who have never experienced Islam at its full command and demand.

Islamic clerics, whose credentials are sometimes dubious, are more concerned with pleasing the higher-ups and curtailing Islam's truth. Incompatibility and easy implementation of laws not enforced by Islam or misinterpreted for construal or softening. It is imperative to learn from practicing Muslims, however, because the Quran cannot be altered.

The rigid Islamic laws may be perceived as personal offenses by some, particularly those who have recently converted or are unfamiliar with Islamic ideologies. Those knowledgeable in Islamic laws can convey the truth without disrespecting their position.

It is possible to discuss the laws of Islam even if one makes mistakes since they are unchanging. This may offend non-Muslims or newcomers to Islam. Islam does not subscribe to the beliefs of other religions which emphasize love over laws. Respect comes before love for Muslims as laws take precedence over all love.

Certain sects' of Islamic creed not permissible by Islamic doctrine present temporal (Mutah) marrying for sexual needs for a few days or hours practice is considered barbaric by (Sunni) scholars due to the deception involved. It is considered impermissible in Islam to engage in sexual relations or enter into a financial or sexual barter transaction under the guise of (Mutah).

Denigrating women is not Islam as Islam gives rights to women in a society equipped and raised by finances is doing things any brothel would do only adding (Mutah) as content from Islam which is denied at all counts in an open society where some countries face hardships as they still use women and exploit Islam.

Temporary marriage for sexual needs is not in line known as (Nikah al Mutah). It is considered a deceptive means of satisfying desires not permissible in Islam. To comprehend the actions of those who become tabloid news of the enemy to stage Islam is a clear indication that they are not practicing the religion in its form. Many make mistakes, but entering into a union to deceive oneself is not Islam.

It's a juncture for confused Muslims to live in harmony to do less harm but harm societies at large with deception. Counting other Muslims' woes is also not Islam. For decades, women have been subjected to exploitation. The advent of Islam introduced a newfound respect for women. Economic conditions have delved into the heart of society's religious realms, bringing stillness. This exploitation is largely driven by revenue.

The story of two women in the old decade is a revival of truth and purity of heart:

224

Many years ago, two women occupied the same building, but their demeanors were contrasting. One of them was a prostitute, while the other was devoted to serving a God. The God-serving woman's gossip was intense as she recorded the visitors of the prostitute and praised her virtues.

As time elapsed, they both met their demise. Scholars were genuinely questioned in earlier times. Their opinion of this particular religious woman was not favorable. People were curious and asked about this surprising venue. It was said that the prostitute detested her job and turned to Allah in tears.

The exit was challenging for her in her unfavorable surroundings, but her heart pleaded for mercy for hours. The religious woman was preoccupied with speaking ill of the prostitute. Gossip is disliked by Allah. It goes against Islamic teachings and is considered a sin.

Like consuming the flesh of a deceased sibling. Repentance is always possible, no matter how late. Only Allah can understand the heart of a sinner. Engaging in gossip is detrimental to one's soul. The consequences could prevent one from entering heaven and facing unexpected consequences for unanticipated sins.

These stories remind Muslims that correction is preferable to ongoing deceit. Only Allah possesses knowledge of every individual's heart. In modern society, women willingly partake in acts that prostitutes once feared and wept over. The society that promotes prostitution exploits women and is not in line with Islamic teachings.

Islam recognizes marriage as the sole institution for fostering togetherness and sharing a home. What is the reason behind Allah's request for humanity, especially Muslims to sign contracts? Does the entire basis of faith in Islam revolve around a contract? Does belief in Allah and being a believer also involve a contract?

Islam encompasses laws, contracts, and beliefs that dictate jurisdiction. Failing to abide by the law fails in any society. Islam is also considered a doctrine. The laws of Allah are not meant to be enforced but prescribed. Penalties will be imposed for non-compliance, similar to any law. Believers find reminders valuable.

(Nikah) marriage ceremonies in the new trending society exposed to Western cultures are performed in certain settings with the agreement of Muslim parents on a trial basis when their young adult children begin dating in societies where this platform is acceptable. Continued dating with the new agreement of (Nikah) permits the actions of married couples which permits consummating a marriage.

The intention realm of entering a union is sacred and cannot be compromised by upcoming Muslims entering a society with challenges incompatible with Islam. Some clerics might agree to this arrangement, but (Nikah) is a sacred union in Islamic doctrine performed by Prophet Muhammad. It is not to be used as a tool to defy reciprocate in this world of compromises of moral compass. Marriage is the truth, not a made-up avenue. Once the (Nikah) takes place the couple can consummate the marriage.

But in this society, the consummation of marriage is not new and most people in these societies live in wedlock and trials before marriage. The Muslim families living in this society find no alternative and agree to (Nikah) but why can't they accept they are married? Allah's laws supersede all parents' and people's laws. Islam encourages real unions. It also permits divorce for couples not meeting marriage compliance or falling out of contract. It's encouraged to maintain harmony and guide the family to Allah and his laws. Despite the separation, the woman remains responsible for her family.

Assuming an executive role is not burdensome, but a responsibility endorsed by Allah. Every trial strengthens a Muslim, and every episode becomes a victory for believers. Necessity is the master of learning and teaching and exploration of traits one never knew one had. Since its creation, the Quran has been the final and complete source of guidance for Muslims. Following Muhammad's departure, Islamic dogma caused chaos for the liberals outside Islam and Muslims forming sects.

The use of hashish hookah is prevalent among some Muslims and has become a lucrative market for drug traffickers. Dubai, being the hub of entertainment for expats, accommodates ideas and activities that are not permissible by Islam. Although these activities are done in quiet settings and are fully quieted down during Ramadan. Muslims are blessed with great wealth that they can share with the world for its benefit. However, joining forces with evil is an act that condones today's society and pleases those who are against Islam, which is something Muslims can try to refrain from.

If Prophet Muhammad could witness the actions of Muslims today, how would he view them? It is important to stay disciplined and follow Islamic laws, which is appreciated by most people. Discipline is key to success, and communication is a result of Islam's teachings.If Muslims were to share their wealth and knowledge with the world, instead of conforming to a society driven by selfish desires and immoral behavior, it would benefit greatly. However, societies that fear commitment often limit commitment to truth, while immoral behavior is praised.

Muslims who commit to the five daily prayers (Salat) may stumble but always get back up and repent to Allah. Good deeds nullify bad deeds and trials become a source of contentment when a believer's prayers are answered. However, the imposition of equality and the spread of falsehoods have shattered the collective mindset of the people. Puppeteers use and manipulate youth, young adults, and strayed Muslims leading to corruption.

Modern democracies have roots in wars that can be repeated because of the aggression society is facing. In some Muslim countries, ancestral misconceptions lead to inaccurate understandings of Islam's truth. Education and socio-economic circumstances also contribute to these misunderstandings.

Correct education and understanding of Islam can benefit both poor and rich Muslims. Muslim countries base their laws on justice and morality, with no separation between state and religion. Christian architecture worldwide serves as evidence of their legacy, with modern democracies accepting state and church separation as a fundamental principle. While the goal is to separate religion and state, complete separation may not always be possible. Certain political regimes manipulate religious doctrines for reforms, leading to societal conflicts. It is essential to recognize one's woes and avoid relying on false assistance from deceitful individuals or countries.

In a secular belief system, the peaceful coexistence of different religious beliefs promotes a moral compass. Overall, it is critical to understand Islam's correct sources to avoid false fronts. Young countries may struggle with this concept, but it is necessary for peaceful coexistence. Christianity's architecture showcases an array of styles, both secular and religious, from past to present. These styles can be seen in various locations, including Rome, Spain, and much of Europe.

In contrast, Muslim art features domes and tombs, while pagan ideas are represented by statues of humans and nudity.

Understanding the beauty of ancient architecture can help foster inclusiveness and mutual respect, as it allows us to understand the shared history of different cultures. Islam emphasizes modesty and morality in educational settings.

However, some argue that teaching Islam alongside secular education can be harmful, as it may mix and corrupt the truth. Muslim exposure to other faiths or secularism isn't the issue, it's the imbalance within not the exposure. Additionally, some fear that Islamic teachings may be distorted to fit with Western societal norms, which are often at odds with conservative Islamic values. Western society is currently experiencing a shift in attitudes towards gender.

While laws relating to alcohol and tobacco are strictly enforced, individuals are free to choose their gender identity and express themselves accordingly. However, this can be a source of conflict for some Muslims, who believe that gender is divinely assigned and cannot be changed. It is important to remember that Muslims and non-Muslims can coexist peacefully and respectfully. By understanding and appreciating each other's beliefs and cultures, we can build a more inclusive and harmonious society. Following beliefs and morals becomes tandem not the exposure of criticism.

Quran: Surah Nisa: 4:119. *I will order them,* and they will change Allah's creation." Anyone who takes Satan as a guardian besides Allah has suffered clearly.

The Muslim countries have the Quran to follow the laws of Allah. It's not about equal opportunity, but society is trending towards challenging Biblical laws instead of human laws. Many of these laws originate from nations striving for independence through personal motivations and aspirations.

The Netherlands was the first country to expand marriage laws to include same-sex couples in 2001. Law has established same-sex marriage in 34 other countries, mostly in the Americas and Western Europe.

Muslims or believers of Abrahamic faiths living double lives will notice the shifts in defiance of Allah, which is not just a human criticism but also against the Quran and Biblical scripts. The world offers freedom to do as one pleases, with after-effects and inner peace is known only to oneself.

The human interior remains constant despite changes to the exterior. Same-sex marriage's impact on human morality is a trending topic in Western society. The US recognized same-gender marriages after a groundbreaking ruling in Massachusetts in 2004. The LGBT community's enthusiastic response prompted other states to follow suit.

The Supreme Court legalized same-sex marriage in all 50 states in 2015, transferring the responsibility of performing these marriages to the court system instead of religious institutions. Initially rejected by religious leaders, it was eventually accepted due to societal backlash.

New York Times: News about same-sex marriage, civil unions, and domestic partnerships …

In this society, the law takes priority even if some churches reject same-sex unions. The Islamic perspective on same-sex relationships is also highlighted in the text. The Quran forbids such unions, and they cannot compromise this position cannot be compromised to suit societal shifts. It's worth noting that other Abrahamic faiths hold the same perspective, as the Quran remains unchanged.

Changing rooms in school gyms and gender-neutral powder rooms are public spaces that can compromise privacy during changing. In Islam, men must cover their (aura) privates and avoid looking at other men as Prophet Lot's people did. The same laws apply to both genders, including women.

Only countries without moral objections have open attitudes toward change, although porn accessibility is a separate issue. Muslim countries prioritize privacy, with different areas for men and women to change privately. Islam values modesty and acknowledges the impact of viewing forbidden things.The eyes can be a source of temptation. Reflecting and seeking forgiveness is necessary for Muslims to correct mistakes, as the same eyes that read the Quran may make errors. A society that disregards morality may view this as outdated, but Islam shields humans from harm and eliminates confusion.

Bible: ESV:20:01. If a man lies with a male as with a woman, both of them have committed an abomination; they shall surely be put to death; their blood is upon them.

Quran: Surah Nisa: 4:16. If *two men among you are guilty of lewdness, punish them both*. If they repent and amend, leave them alone; for Allah is Oft-returning, Most Merciful.

Hadith Bukhari: 6474:Allah's Messenger (ﷺ) said, "Whoever can guarantee (the chastity of) what is between his two jaw-bones and what is between his two legs (i.e. his tongue and his private parts), I guarantee Paradise for him."

Allah's messenger recognized the fallibility of humans but stressed the value of self-restraint and avoiding actions that could harm relationships. Islam promotes finding solutions to challenges while upholding (halal), permissible acts rather than giving in to temptation.

Those who conquer self-control have a distinct position in this life and the hereafter. Trials don't mean giving up, only coming back stronger because Islam teaches hope and positivity, not negativity, and comebacks of mishaps are forgotten when better memories are made.

Individuals who partake in actions contrary to Islam can transform their behavior into permissible relationships, earning Allah's rewards. Islam consistently acknowledges positive deeds as Allah watches those who make an effort to abide by his laws. Societal approval does not change the fact that same-gender or bisexual relationships are not in line with Islam. Islam Quran and hadith provide us with countless stories that are a part of our daily lives as participants and teachers.

Do you happen to know the current location of Sodom and Gomorrah? Many believe that these cities were once located in the Ghor or Jordan Valley, which encompasses not only the valley itself but also the Dead Sea and the neighboring land in this hilly area.

In the cities of Sodom and Gomorrah, men engaged in sexual acts that resulted in death, including sodomy, which went against human nature and God's moral teachings. The land was punished when the Prophet Lot called out to Allah for mercy.

Both the Quran and biblical teachings denounce same-gender acts, but the Quran also offers forgiveness for those who change their ways in all aspects of life. Despite this, modern society often accepts and promotes pornography and illicit relationships, and those who oppose these behaviors are often labeled as rude or intolerant.

However, the laws of theology are clear in their rejection of these harmful patterns that are not approved by Allah. Even if society accepts and normalizes these actions, it does not change the theological perspective on the matter. This explanation is not intended to control anyone's behavior in a society that is often characterized by defiance and disregard for moral principles.

It is important to note that this piece is not intended to criticize or challenge modern society. Rather, it is a sincere expression of beliefs and truths from a divine source, rather than from human interpretation. Some economic systems promote harmful behaviors that may seem beneficial at first, but can ultimately lead to long-term health issues. It has been reported that individuals who identify as bisexual or part of the LGBT community have a higher rate of suicide. Higher depression.

Npr: May 5, 2022 — The survey found rising rates of suicidal thoughts, as well as significant disparities among trans youth and LGBTQ youth of color. Transgender.

Mental Health Foundation: half of LGBTIQ+ people had experienced depression, and three in five had experienced anxiety;

The rules are commanded by Allah. When human life is not in one hand, isn't it a sign of human weakness to question the creator who knows what benefits humanity and what doesn't? The scriptures of the Quran and previous texts are not determined by humans. Breaking laws has repercussions in all aspects of life.

Many individuals are curious about Allah's reasons for prohibiting certain actions and behaviors. They question His rationale for restricting humans despite desiring their free will. Nevertheless, humans frequently struggle to comprehend the wisdom within these laws. People frequently ignore the guidance in the Biblical scriptures and Quran, leading to self-inflicted harm.

Comprehending why Allah prohibits certain actions is crucial, as He knows the illnesses and negative impact on humans in the long run. Research has indicated that men who engage in sexual activity with other men, including those who identify as gay or bisexual, are at increased risk of contracting sexually transmitted infections such as chlamydia hepatitis, and gonorrhea. Moreover, HPV (Human papillomavirus) is a prevalent concern for this group.

Center for Disease Control and Prevention: Gay, bisexual, and other men who have sex with men often get other STDs, including chlamydia and gonorrhea infections. HPV (Human papillomavirus), syphilis, and genital warts.

In ancient Rome, men had the freedom to engage in sexual relations with other males without facing a perceived decline in their masculinity or social standing, as long as they assumed the dominant role. This role has remained constant in pagan cultures and also applied to the people of Lot. All Abrahamic faiths follow the same laws in this context.

Nonetheless, Islamic teachings disapprove of such practices and they are not widely accepted in Muslim countries. Despite being seen as outdated by some, Islamic law is not concerned with human approval. Our laws are subordinate to the laws of Allah.

The Quran's distinctions don't aim to please humans or highlight negativity. The truth remains independent, even when Allah's laws do not align with human values. Muslim individuals should not hesitate to express the truth because they are Allah's laws, not the laws of humans. Therefore, speaking truthfully is not seen as impolite or offensive. Nevertheless, humans have specific limitations assigned by the creator. Islam allows the wife to seek divorce if sodomy is practiced in a husband and wife relationship.

There will come a time when children born in wedlock will have a voice. The reason Islam has prescribed laws as every human has rights. Christians employ love to eliminate laws. Muslims prioritize laws and rules over love, and love can only flourish if these laws are followed consistently, otherwise, love will be discouraged; it's a delicate balance.

Quran: Suran An'am: 6:164.*And no soul earns (evil) but against itself, and no bearer of burden shall bear the burden of another...*1

Bible: Deuteronomy 23:2. A bastard shall not enter into the congregation of the Lord: even to his tenth generation shall he not enter into the congregation of the Lord.

There are no restrictions for a child born out of wedlock to take part in Salat or visit the mosque. The Bible prohibits him from attending church. Is he burdened with the sin of his parents? Islam states that sin cannot be passed on and only parents are responsible, not the child.

Bible: Hebrew: Niv: 12:8. If you are not disciplined—and everyone undergoes discipline —then you are not legitimate, not true sons and daughters at all.

The unveiling of laws during joyful occasions may result in resentment from those who prioritize human laws over Allah. Those who fear contracts also fear commitment, while those who disobey Allah's laws already obey Satan's laws. The rules that govern Contracts function as valid commitments. In Islam, the design of laws and contracts is governed by Allah's laws.

Bible Gateway: John 8:7.And while they continued asking him, he lifted himself up, and said unto them, Let him that is among you without sin, cast the first stone at her.

Bible followers frequently cite this verse, but the Bible is both divine and human. However, it doesn't affect laws. Committing sins is not justified by the fact that everyone else does. It appears to be a strategy to find another means of doing as one pleases, as quoted in this verse. In Islam, just because the whole world is doing wrong doesn't mean it's acceptable to follow suit; that's why knowing the laws is crucial.

Quran: Surah Nisa: 4;116. Surely Allah does not forgive associating 'others' with Him 'in worship' but forgives anything else of whoever He wills. Indeed, whoever associates others with Allah and his divinity has strayed far away.

Quran: Surah Isra: 17:32. Do not even approach fornication for it is an outrageous act and an evil way. And do not come near adultery. This commandment is meant for both individuals and society as a whole

While certain individuals use Bible verses to rationalize their sins and argue that all sins are equal because of original sin, the Quran presents a contrasting viewpoint. The Quran categorizes sins based on their severity in a comprehensive set of laws. Taking a loaf of bread is not on par with committing murder, for example. Forgiveness is possible for those who repent, except for associating partners with Allah. Although the punishment for murder, according to the law, is death. Every sin has a different price.

Religious affiliations are absent in secular court systems, making them accessible for all marriages. Opposite gender or same gender, it doesn't matter. The problem occurs when these systems don't acknowledge religious weddings. In Islam, marriage is the foundation of our faith, known as (Nikah) in the Quran and upheld as a tradition by the Prophet for heterosexual couples.

It is crucial to understand that Muslim marriages are exclusively conducted by Muslims and same-gender weddings are prohibited according to Islamic law. Islam has its own state with specific contractual obligations. If the ceremony is held in a Muslim country, the court may acknowledge it as per Islamic law. Following misconceptions would steer the Islamic faith toward a crossroads.

Certain people prioritize secularism and personal desires, even if they conflict with their faith. In modern society, numerous individuals identify as spiritualists who believe in a higher power governing the universe, even without following a particular religion.

The Quran suggests that Christians who grasp Islam can foster stronger relationships with Muslims and potentially convert after renouncing paganism. Muslims' peaceful and understanding message may be the reason for this, in contrast to Christendom's history. Islam's appeal lies in its ability to offer hope for a better future and motivate individuals to pursue higher goals. Christians who adopt Islam do it by their own free will, not because they are forced, and they renounce the worship of a deity.

Hadith: Tirmidhi: 74. The seeking of knowledge is obligatory for Muslims.

Those who reject the changed and re-written scriptures are called pre-dated. But they are still knocking on doors to give literature to invite to their faith. In the broad spectrum, they are unaware of the history. Unfortunately, academic settings are bombarded with misconceptions about Islamic beliefs.

However, Islam has a policy and effectiveness that increases society's durability. History has shown that Muslims' conquest was a complement to the world. The most desirable Muslim parents are those who have control and guidance over their offspring.

Single mothers or married couples can only succeed with endurance and perseverance. To raise their Muslim children in diverse societies or any part of the world, parents must be strong and disciplined, standing for the Quranic belief system, and not self-imposed ideas.

Youth and young adults are vulnerable to outside influences and social structures that can manipulate and corrupt them. Public school systems can be especially problematic as they often impose ideas that are not compatible with Islam, which remains unchanging even as times change.

Many Muslim youth and young people are breaking free from the influence of invasive ideas propagated by certain groups, but these ideas are not true reform and can lead to destruction. When observing global society, it is clear that the USA, among many other countries, uses the imperial measurement system instead of the metric system that Muslims have been using for decades.

The metric system, which is based on the decimal system, allows for basic arithmetic functions, as well as the extraction of square roots and cube roots, and Muslims have made many changes in this field through continuous learning. Islam is a religion of reform and progress that speaks to the modern world. If Muslims can teach Arithmetic to the world, shouldn't they also know the fundamental laws of Islam? Muslims possess knowledge of addition and subtraction that they have taught the world. What is the reason for not redefining the laws and contracts of Islam? Given that marriage holds great importance in Islam, is it necessary to clarify its components?

In a society full of technology, academia, travel, and human desires, Muslims coexist. What is the consequence of not following Islam? Desires of humans. Revisiting laws and providing reassurance is the key to uncovering the truth. In Islamic doctrine, marriage is restricted to opposite genders. Same-gender marriages are not allowed by contractual Islamic law. Will it be accepted by Islam? No? The answer is no, not yes. Conforming to humanity does not excuse changing Islamic laws.

Its laws are fixed and untouched, making sure the faith remains modern and applicable in both spiritual and temporal realms. Due to the impermanence of this world. In Muslim teachings, the emphasis is on learning and teaching from authentic sources, not mixing secular thoughts with Islam.

Muslim men were granted the privilege to marry chaste women from the people of the book, which was a benefit that other religions also enjoyed from this order. During that specific period, the number of people who belonged to the book was greater than the number of Muslim women. With the absence of an expiration date and governed by the new age law of Islam, these unions have the capacity to generate a positive impact on all individuals and facilitate the growth of Islam. In the event that these unions impede Islamic laws and infringe upon the laws and agreements of Islam, it is contrary to the principles of Islam.

Prophet Muhammad, in order to foster stronger relationships and promote unity among communities, entered into marriages with women who belonged to the people of the book. These women, in accordance with Islamic law, were entitled to a dower (Maher) or a payment that they were owed during the course of their marriage. This law is obligatory for all practicing Muslims and strict adherence is expected. His wives, in addition to being Muslim, also held the esteemed title of mothers of the believers.

Islam, unlike Judaism and Christianity, has specific regulations governing marriage, and interfaith unions are not generally permitted unless certain restrictions and laws are observed. In the Islamic faith, there is a strong belief that faith cannot be compromised by any individual, and therefore, interfaith marriages cannot impose conditions that would alter the fundamental principles of Islam. In addition, Christianity also prohibits interfaith marriages and places certain limitations on individuals who identify as Christians. The act of baptism serves as a symbolic gesture, representing the dedication of a couple to raise their children within the Christian faith.

Can righteousness and lawlessness possibly coexist? Throughout the centuries, the coexistence of light and darkness has been a recurring topic of inquiry and contemplation. The concept of faith is also associated with the contrasting forces of light and darkness. Those who remain steadfast in their faith experience the radiant glow of light piercing through the perpetual shadows of uncertainty, confusion, doubts, and anxiety.

Just like any other faith, Islam has its own specific limitations. While men have the freedom to marry individuals from the book, women face limitations and are only permitted to marry Muslim men or have the groom convert to Islam. Unlike other religions, Islam does not allow for any exceptions, making it crucial to comprehend that resistance and change are not tolerated.

Despite the hardships faced by the Prophet's daughters, it is important to note that divorce was permitted in Islam, and the Prophet's daughter exercised this right. Furthermore, they both daughters found happiness by marrying the best convert to Islam, who not only had the love and approval of their father but also embraced the faith wholeheartedly. It is important for Muslims to uphold the laws of Islam without compromise, as the truth knows no boundaries and falsehoods are likely to be confronted sooner or later.

Bible: Nkjv:6:14:15.(Do not be unequally yoked together with unbelievers.

One of the reasons why it is crucial to explain the potential complications of interfaith marriages is due to the tendency of non-Muslims to impose certain conditions. The presence of contaminants in various societies throughout history has resulted in a form of self-promotion and implications of self laws that can be seen as a declining market, and this practice predates the process of progression that exists in Islam.

Muslims who distort the teachings of Islam in order to appease non-believers demonstrate a lack of comprehension regarding Allah's divine laws and a limited understanding of historical context. In Islam, marriage holds great significance and is universally acknowledged.

It is a fundamental belief that both men and women require strong and lasting relationships that align with the ethical teachings and traditions set forth by Prophet Muhammad and the Quran of Allah's laws for a Muslim believer. Personal transformation must begin from within, and change is not to be questioned.

Muslim behavior cannot be used to gauge Islam. Listening to temptations or desires is a challenge for Muslims as they too face challenges and trials of human desires and temptations rectifying with plenty of (Astaghfar) repentance.Provocation or instigation can involve unalarmed behaviors not conducive to Islamic behavior. Attitudes or behaviors that change negatively contradict Islam.

Unified efforts to keep Muslim countries and Muslims connected would disable all events, and the ills and challenges Muslims face would dissipate. Nothing opposes fulfillment when enduring links and faith in Allah are present. Muslims should realize that most rhetoric and alienation created between Muslims originate from evil.

Similar to how humans deliberately incite and antagonize bulls through the cruel act of torturing them for the sake of entertainment and spectacle.The purpose of this is solely for the enjoyment of humans, with no consideration or empathy towards animals. In the Islamic faith, it is strictly forbidden to cause harm to animals. These bulls are intentionally made aggressive for the purpose of entertainment.

Demonstrating an elevated level of alertness, the Matador promptly reacts to the perilous circumstance, effectively triumphing over the bull through its demise. Once the bull is forcefully brought down, it is immediately slaughtered.

Their decision to transform him into a decorative ornament stems from their desire to entertain the audience. In the event that he is unable to perform, he will ultimately face his demise. The level of cruelty that humans display is truly astonishing and deeply unsettling. In the religion of Islam, there is absolutely no tolerance for any form of animal cruelty.

Newly formed regimes are implementing this logic by means of social media usage and by orchestrating the involvement of Muslims, all in an effort to entertain those individuals who are unacquainted with the Middle East.

In order to undo the gains that are shown on the graph, it is necessary for us to prevent the errors that facilitated their increase. It is important for Muslims to have access to education and to come together in unity. Differentiating the rhetoric that creates a divide between Muslim countries and individual Muslims. By Muslims actively engaging in efforts to improve society instead of indulging in decadence, you have the power to create a positive impact in the world.

Muslims joined together to help the masses. They left history to be read by many, not chaos. The youth must be educated and not fall prey to their devious plots. A mind that enjoys violence is offset by watching animals revolt and regress.

Muslim countries and regimes undergo frequent and unwelcome landings, which come at a high cost. The majority of them occur due to evil plots and greed.

An oncogenic scheme designed to provoke conflict between Islamic sects and countries to seize power and manipulate the formation of new regimes.

Their motto involves demolishing homes first and then using division as a conquering strategy. Societies have been deceived by this rhetoric for years. Instead of migrating and restoring peace, they choose to enter the ring of destruction. Driven by greed. History has only recently accepted the truth.

If they were to revert to their previous behavior after discovering the truth of Islam, it would be truly regrettable. The tabloid effect, similar to positivity, or negativity can spread and influence others, although it does not apply universally.

A person can become ill from having a negative attitude, despite the satisfaction it brings to malevolent minds. To be envious and desire the ruin of others. It is an evil trait but undeniable it exists.

The soul's intricacies involve choosing between positive and negative and navigating the barriers. A harsh soul is recognizable even to animals upon first encounter. Is the bull ignorant of its foe while understanding the malice in the minds of the humans who watch its performance?

A society that derives pleasure from exploiting animals for human entertainment cannot feel remorse towards humans who speak the truth, as their lies can easily overshadow it.

Islam emphasizes the importance of respecting all living things, particularly animals and plants that are unable to protect themselves. Islam teaches respect for animals, plants, and human rights.

Engaging in activities such as bullfighting, cockfighting, or shooting animals is not classified as entertainment. The disregard for Islamic concepts in provocation entitlement results in the mistreatment of animals and humans.

The animals are intensively trained to become aggressive, resulting in many bullfighters being fatally attacked by their own trained animals. Consequently, their lives are taken. The humane minds have led to the outlawing of such evil entertainment events in many countries. They derive pleasure from hurting animals for entertainment.

Quran: Surah An'am:6:38. And no animal walks upon the earth nor a bird that flies with its two wings but (they are) genera like yourselves; We have not neglected.

The 15th century marked the end of Muslim rule in Spain. Tournaments were the start of evil games that tortured or instigated animals to entertain autocrats.

Spain outlawed bullfighting. The newer countries engage in a common tactic of inciting issues and then observing the consequences of crimes committed. The historical pattern of cowardice behavior through instigation and blame persists in today's world.

Islam's value becomes clear, reminding us that divisions only worsen as countries suffer. Those who seek penance in greed and salvation from others fail to understand that it originates from within one's soul, not from others.

This also manifests itself in personal lives where education on Islamic values is scarce. Islam focuses on every episode and nature of human existence. As they are viceroys of all living things.

People who don't respect animals and find sadistic behavior a barrage of entertainment suffer from conscious behavior and selective empathy only if it belongs to them personally.

Animal shooting is prohibited in many countries and practiced as a sport or target practice by many people. Animals can only be killed if eaten. It is also inappropriate to use dogs as sled animals.

Animals like horses, donkeys, camels, and mules were transportation means for travel and war. They need rest and kindness, not instigation games for mortal sadistic minds. The enjoyment of such entertainment leads to sadism and animals attacking humans. They also find pleasure in attacking humans. This does not apply to Islam.

Many matadors fail to hit their target and instead puncture the bull's lungs and bronchial tubes, causing it to bleed from its mouth and nose. Islam strongly opposes such cruelty.

Severe consequences await those who commit such acts. These acts reveal their intent to target the helpless. Harsh chemicals and highly destructive materials are being sought after around the world. In Muslim territories, they seek to control and anticipate salvation.

Animals can be utilized for transportation and archery training in Islam. Because of the animal's limited capability. They need to be taken care of, rested, and fed properly. It's acceptable to engage in activities that do not cause harm to others or yourself. Your potential knows no bounds. Because of the foreign approach to power, in foreign lands habitats and families have seen the repercussions for generations and decades.

Alongside others who observe efforts to remove people from their homes where they have lived for decades. Funded and supported entirely by a deceitful society. Those who await Armageddon also await justification. Punishment is the only justification Islam has for cruelty.

Poverty slowly infiltrates this nation. The savior won't save them since hope stems from wicked actions. The bull's example is a perfect illustration. He is easily provoked and incapable of defending himself. Next, he confronts death and brutal injuries. When there is a lack of weapons on either side, they must be set aside, even in war. According to Islamic beliefs.

Despite the prevalence of injustice in this era, reading has the power to restore our sense of ethics. The bridge's false modernization is concealed through deception.

Youth and upcoming Muslim converts require education. They not only seek same-gender relationships, but their experimentation knows no bounds as they freely choose partners of any gender to fulfill their desires, which is traumatic for believers. However, believers are aware that those who are discontent will go to great lengths to defy Allah and ultimately find themselves in the same state of discontent. Muslim countries are often labeled as backward, but many converts and estranged Muslims rediscover Islam.

The majority of these remarks originate from nations that denigrate Muslim countries as regressive, harkening back to an era of punishment and divine retribution. Allah can replace disobedient humans with better ones who will worship him and abide by his laws.

Boredom and lack of interest drive them towards engaging in bestiality and forbidden sexual experiments. Nothing worthwhile can ever satisfy these souls, and nothing bad can bring them contentment. Without finding peace, death is imminent.

Quran: Surah Maidah: 5:54.O believers! Whoever among you abandons their faith, Allah will replace them with others who love Him and are loved by Him. They will be humble with the believers but firm towards the disbelievers, struggling in the Way of Allah; fearing no blame from anyone. This is the favor of Allah. He grants it to whoever He wills. And Allah is Ever-Bountiful, All-Knowing.

The disturbing consequences of characterless actions in new societies include false modernization that affects even the old and weary. Societal differences stem from a mismatch with Islam, not upheaval. When sexism, nudity, porn, and greed infiltrate a society, it forms an incompatible combination.

Society may break laws and create new ones, but the Quran remains a permanent law. Evil dominates this society, which is less than three hundred years old, and it's contagious nature. It is incorrectly perceived as a symbol of modernity as well.

Islam aims for the refined aspects of intimacy. Abstain from engaging in sexual activity with women during their menstrual cycle. Muslim women are prohibited from engaging in ritual prayers (Salat) and fasting during menstruation.

Prayer (Dua) is perpetually accessible without any exceptions. Engaging in sodomy can be considered a legitimate reason for divorce. In the context of Islam, this act is considered absolutely prohibited and entails a penalty. It disallows husbands and wives from engaging in sodomy, as well as two men from participating in such acts. Islam has had a profound impact on all facets of existence. Humanity was imparted by Allah with commands, not without them.

Mature individuals are utilizing social media without any limitations or restrictions. Both men and women are known to support and endorse indecent behavior. Not only do they demean themselves, but they also have the tendency to encourage others to reveal their true natures.Islam, which is a timeless faith bestowed upon humanity by Allah, imparts unwavering wisdom while harmoniously coexisting with humanity.

Books that specifically delve into the Hindu customs in Northern India shed light on the phenomenon of sexual arousal and its significance within intimate relationships. The Kamasutra, a book on ancient Indian sexual practices, has gained significant popularity and interest among individuals from Western cultures. The decision to incorporate Hindu ideologies into these settings was influenced by the similarities that exist between Christianity and this faith.

Despite its Abrahamic roots, there have been notable changes. In contrast with Hinduism. The Abrahamic faiths have a strict adherence to monotheism. Islam forbids discussing or sharing books, texts, or social media content about sexual intimacy between couples.

Faith signifies sexual excitement between spouses, not illicit relationships. Realizing that these actions are allowed and approved by the creator is the ultimate bliss of satisfaction. After marriage.

Angels, without needing any instructions, maintain their distance from intimate couples and shy away by sending blessings and delighting each other with Allah's permission.

Islam recognizes the importance of meeting others' needs and places a strong emphasis on marriage. Consequently, this sacred outset must begin in Allah's name and with the support of Muslim unions.

Not non-Muslims whose ideologies are far beyond Muslim theology or thinking. A (halal) permissible relationship between a couple is not cheap in Islam; rather, it is sacred and private.

Intimate moments are private. It is not a tabloid effect of immoral satisfaction through magazines, social media platforms, or filth. Islam gives chances to repair mistakes.

The Bible has explicit content that may not be suitable for children without guidance. These stories are often referred to as sexually stimulating novels. Islam encompasses all laws, without any restrictions on age. These theological comparisons and contrasts are truly eye-opening.

Islam's intricacies and laws also cover the etiquette of the entrance to a home. What has Islam left behind? Nothing a human needs to know to explore Islam. It is imperative to examine these differences to determine whether Islam is the starting point for freedom of life. Islam respects privacy. Do not enter homes from the back door.

Enter from the front and knock to let the occupants know you have arrived. Do not spy on each other or others in their absence. It is taboo to publish books about intimate acts or share them online.

Quran: Surah Nur: 24:27. O believers! *Do not enter any house other than your own until you ask for permission and greet its occupants*.

Quran: Surah Hujurat: 49:12. Some suspicion is sinful, so believers should avoid being overly suspicious. Do not spy on each other or backbite one another. Would you like to eat his dead brother's flesh? You would surely detest it.

The rules one develops determine effectiveness in life and gauge success in mind, body, and soul. Rest will follow. By fostering understanding in all avenues, those who question the truth are corrected.

Islam tells the story of animal kindness:

Prophet Muhammad traveled with many caravans accompanying him. He watched the bird flutter in his face as it flew by. Allah made him understand. She told him someone had stolen her eggs. The caravan came to a halt, and the Prophet Muhammad interrogated the individuals. He asked who had taken the bird's eggs. One individual affirmed his action of taking the birds' eggs.. The Prophet instructed him to give back the eggs to the bird in her nest. The bird expressed gratitude, returning to her eggs.

Respecting personal property and minimizing unnecessary distractions is of utmost importance in Islamic faith. Birds cannot be coerced into combat, and it is strictly forbidden to confine them. The Islamic faith profoundly permeates the core of every individual. Islam emphasizes the importance of personal accountability in dealing with animals. Additionally, it mandates that a Muslim treats all of humanity with justice, kindness, manners, and special regard for guests, irrespective of their faith or creed. In Islam, there are no distinctions of color or faith when it comes to humanity. Every living being is brought into existence by Allah and merits reverence and equitable treatment. In the pursuit of learning theology, it is required by Islam to treat every human with respect and fairness.

Exercise strengthens the human core. The core of a human is his heart, followed by his physical strength. Cores connect the upper and lower bodies. The spine, abdominal viscera, and hip all play a role in connective balance. Without one, the other isn't strong. Islam and the resulting balance cannot exist without a Muslim core. Which is Islam's faith for Muslims. Outside influences and interference taint the connection between the upper and lower bodies. Many episodes of life can serve as examples for those familiar with Muslims' facades.

Yet, actions adapted to satisfy doubters do not accurately portray Islam. Abu Hurairah stated that The Prophet Muhammad recounted the story of a righteous woman being sent to hell. She was in a state of agitation regarding her cat and proceeded to restrain her with a rope, neglecting to provide sustenance or hydration until her demise. Allah disapproves of both torture and animal abuse for entertainment purposes.

This is the nature of Islam. It is a well-documented tale that Prophet Muhammad observed a feline resting on his garment. He made a conscious effort not to disturb the cat. He carefully severed that portion of the garment so as not to interrupt her sleep.

Despite the existence of such stories, there are Muslims who do not display the same courtesy towards one another. However, it is important to note that repentance to Allah has the power to open all doors. Regardless of the possibility for individuals to change their viewpoints.

Allah grants forgiveness to Muslims in accordance with their transgressions. Sharing the sins of Muslims goes against the principles of Islam. Some individuals always derive joy from hearing about misfortunes, and frequently feel envious of self-control. Breaking such boundaries gives them contentment because they have broken the rules for decades. Islam says that if you sin at night, you should not share it in the light of day. Ask Allah for forgiveness, and do not share it with humans.

Some sins bring Muslims closer to Allah as he acknowledges evil and seeks forgiveness. Allah loves to forgive. Persistent evil is not an accident; it is a continuation of a lifestyle one chooses by choosing. Corrupt Islamophobic media will pick up on a Muslim who is not representative of Islam. They will portray this person as a Muslim. Humans do not need to be cited as Muslims or as a source of credit or discredit for their actions. Islam speaks for itself, not for individuals.

It is common for many people to judge Islam based on their shallow behaviors. Not privately, but publicly. All Muslims' actions don't represent Islam. The only clue that he or she is a Muslim is his or her Muslim name. You'll know if it's a Muslim by its attitude, gratitude, respect, discipline, modesty, and morality. When a mistake is made in private, it is between Allah and the believer, and unless it is made public, then it becomes a matter of gossip.

Quran: Surah Baqarah 2;120.*Never will the Jews be pleased with you*, (O Prophet), nor the Christians until you follow their way. Say: "Surely Allah's guidance is true guidance.

It is worth noting that Muslim needs and circumstances cannot be replaced by disobeying Islam's laws. Although the early Prophets were from Israel, they all shared a common belief in Allah. Islam's emergence from the Arabian Peninsula was remarkable and distinct. All Prophets including the Messiah Jesus son of Mary have conveyed the same message, which stems from the original belief in Allah that was instilled in Adam and Eve. It is interesting to note that Islam is a unique religion.Allah communicates his message to an Arab Prophet. Also, each Prophet has been designated Muslim, as Islam is the act of submitting to one.

Islam is the universal faith of all Prophets and people have been submitting to Allah since the dawn of existence. According to Christian doctrine, Jesus was conceived by a virgin and Allah is considered his father. While Muslims also believe in his miraculous birth from the virgin mother Mary, they do not attribute Allah as his father, as the Quran explicitly rejects such a blasphemous claim against Allah. Nevertheless, Allah brought forth Adam and Eve into existence without the need for parents, establishing Him as a creator not a progenitor, a maker of the initial creation through no conception and inception. It is crucial to acknowledge that Allah is not a mortal being, and Islam is unambiguous on this matter. It may not align with the beliefs or concepts of certain individuals, but truth remains unhidden.

The longstanding presence of Judaism and Christianity presents an intriguing opportunity to explore their disparities from Islam. The challenge of comprehension is not an understatement nor an indication of societal discord. The majority of individuals, regardless of their beliefs, possess empathy and social skills. Islam, however, presents itself as a ritualistic, disciplined, mandated, and consistent religion, in contrast to other Abrahamic faiths.

Quran: Surah Baqarah: 2:120. And the Jews will not be pleased with you, nor the Christians, until you follow their religion. Say: Surely Allah's guidance, that is the (true) guidance.

It's amazing how friendship can transcend religious differences and endure for years. Islam is not a competing religion, but rather emphasizes monotheism and promotes entitlements and reforms for humans with restrictive behavior. Throughout the course of history, Jews have faced expulsion on two occasions, once by divine decree and once by a totalitarian regime.

Both believers and non-believers exhibit benevolence and concern for humanity, yet this does not alter the essence of their devotion or convictions. Muslims require education in Islam, just as the world necessitates enlightenment in Islam as truth, not falsehoods, must be disseminated. A vast number of Arabs and Muslims played an active role in initiatives to assist in the preservation of Jewish citizens of Arab lands during the occupation by fascist regimes.

The Muslims clandestinely transported them through tunnels and concealed them within mosques, masquerading them as fellow Muslims. No other religious group offered assistance, except for the Muslims. During the Muslim rule of Jerusalem, they extended an invitation to Jews to coexist. History tells us that Muslims must reclaim authority rather than passively observe in order to contribute to the betterment of the world instead of its destruction. Muslims are the foremost to extend assistance, their origins are far removed from truth and reality. Muslims confront life with unwavering courage, as they are accountable to Allah. Numerous examples can prove significant in grasping the essence of Islam.

The Ottoman forces emerged victorious over the Mamluk armies and seized control of Bilad al-Sham, present day Syria encompassing Palestine. This marked the initiation of a period of nearly unbroken Ottoman control over Palestine for four centuries. Palestine is a predominantly Muslim nation, whereas Jerusalem is not recognized as a Jewish state according to Islamic laws.

Exile does not imply forced entry or violent conflicts, but rather emphasizes the protection of the vulnerable against Islamophobic agendas. The world experienced contentment during the golden age of Islam and the rise of the Ottoman Empire. It will only know true peace when Muslim rule prevails, preventing the threat of evil. As nations vie for power and greed, Muslims contribute sustenance to the table, not mere crumbs. It is not a formidable task to conquer this world; Allah will grant victory after enduring trials. It is the preparation for the next life that serves as the ultimate test.

The Quran does not allow for interchange between law and regulation, and Allah will not alter destiny. However, as followers of Islam, we have faced challenges while upholding our faith. If we were to compare the atoms of Islam to a living organism, they would have perished long ago. We are simply followers of the faith. Exigency refers to a critical time or state of affairs, but it specifically emphasizes the pressure of restrictions on humanity.

For Muslims, understanding Islam at its best is considered a compliment. In today's society, forced restrictions present a challenge that we must navigate through. It is neither wearisome nor difficult to join a community, but rather a dilemma that requires our attention. Islam's restrictions aim to protect the soul and mind of humanity. We are followers who seek forgiveness from Allah at every crossroad of life.

Quran: Surah Fussilat 41:34 O Prophet, goodness and evil are not equal. Repel (evil) with that which is right. And you will see that he, between whom and you there was enmity, shall become as if he were a close friend of yours.

Quran: Surah Imran: 3:28. The believers may not take the unbelievers for their allies in preference to those who believe.

The response of a disbeliever is often kind, but he is driven by his own agenda, fueled by doubt and disbelief, which is planted in the heart of a believer. Islam prohibits sharing intimate moments or dreams with unbelievers or believers not trustworthy.They often strike when least expected. The Quran, the Sunnah, and the Prophets exposed their hypocrisy. Society today lacks the trust needed to reveal the instincts or dreams granted by Allah.

Quran: Surah Ankaboot: 29:11. And Allah will surely make evident those who believe, and He will surely make evident the hypocrites.

Unless a Muslim embraces apostasy and departs from Islam. Perhaps he is a committed Muslim, but sometimes he feels disconnected from Islam.Venerating Designer Allah for a portion of this life is a delightful opportunity in later life. This life determines future millenniums. Islam highlights the connection between a believer and their beliefs.

A person who converts to Islam but stands up for disbelievers is a misguided soul longing for Allah's mercy. A person who is Muslim or has converted stands for believers not disbelievers. The magnificence of this faith is reserved for those who sow seeds in fertile ground, not for those who return to a tainted plot. The comparison between a toddler learning Islam and a convert has similarities.

The children of converts are observant and progressive in their understanding of Islam, recognizing the necessity of their parents' change to preserve their true faith. Unfortunate individuals oppose their parents' choice of Islam and seek alternative measures, turning to disbelievers who strip away the beauties that once adorned their homes. Slowly, darkness engulfs these households as the light of Islam fades away along with the familiarities it brought. Some return while others remain in darkness, distracted by superficial surroundings and forgetting the true light that once touched the hearts of Muslims.

Islam's adoption is evident in the roster of converts. The majority of new converts to Islam, or Muslims returning. Cognizance is free from apprehensions. It indicates a remarkable shift as he transitions from the known to the unknown, finding faith and gathering believers. Some people believed in the concept of Christendom and thought that humans are born with original sin. This concept is isolated in Islamic thought. According to Islam, everyone is born without sin.

Bible: Psalm *51:5* - Behold, I was brought forth in iniquity And sin, my mother conceived me.

(Fitra), the belief in goodness is present in every child from birth. He is untainted. Following his Christian conversion, they adopted the doctrine of original sin from St. Augustine. He was a theologian from North Africa. There was no allusion to Jesus or his teachings. Christianity's practicalities don't resonate with many young people and seekers.

Combining all faiths without guidance is detrimental to understanding Islam's essence. Distinctions persist, making it nearly impossible to overlook the stark contrasts between the beliefs and interpretations of biblical scripts in Islam and Christianity.

Despite identifying as Christians, Christian populations have been decreasing for decades. Without guidance, humans struggle to believe due to the mismatch between stories and their minds. Throughout history, politics has blended divine tales with human influence, resulting in a problematic fusion of theology in Christendom.

Annually, approximately 30,000 Americans convert to Islam according to studies. The numbers have quadrupled since 911. Before embracing it, Americans were interested in learning about the flaws of this faith. Islam is a truth that resonates with human cognition and personal responsibility.

CNN: "Islam has drawn converts from all walks of life, most notably African-Americans". Studies estimated about 30,000 people convert to Islam annually in the United States.

Assuming accountability for one's actions without placing blame on others. It lacks validity in human courts. Human laws do not approve of the preposterous behavior of someone else taking on others' actions.

It is something that Allah cannot approve of. Who embodies the most justice? His reasoning knows no bounds. Islam is logical throughout its entirety. Unlike Christians, Jews do not subscribe to the concept of original sin.

Sin is not transmitted like a disease in Islam, and humans cannot atone for sin. Muslims perceive the Divine Allah as destitute. You can't learn Islam through social media. It's only a temporary diversion. Dialog and interaction play a crucial role in the positive upbringing of Muslim children or adults.

Children often imitate adults. Prophet Muhammad's grandsons prayed alongside him and even climbed on him as he prayed to Allah. He adored his grandchildren. Their grandfather taught them about Allah. Faith is a common factor among humans. Some dive into this with unlimited strength. Some choose a longer timeframe to assess importance and reject diminishing positives. The company is always involved in every aspect of life. Delirium or confusion in understanding after embracing Islam is the chaos of inner health. The turbulent times allow no space for contemplation after belief.

In the era of Prophet Muhammad. The honor was held by the man. His words were truthful. The magnitude of their dependency cannot be adequately measured. Amidst numerous responsibilities,

Muslims should set aside time for self-reflection and evaluate their beliefs. Muslim duties involve introspection to meet spiritual needs and achieve ultimate bliss.

Quran: Surah Baqarah: 2:221.Do not marry polytheistic women until they believe; for a believing slave-woman is better than a free polytheist, even though she may look pleasant to you.

Islam's emphasis and beliefs prioritize Islam above any form of attraction. If faith is not surrendered and compromise is absent, the journey's commencement remains self-serving and materialistic. When plastic foundations in relationships melt, faith is uprooted even during their collapse. For Muslims who forget Allah, no faith can alleviate emptiness. In the disputed realm, people make uninformed claims about Islam's doctrine. It was the first and sole religion to grant women rights.

Islam is unique in that it does not compel individuals to worship. The laws are fully supported and accessible for learning without enforcement. Once the truth is revealed, there is no obligation to follow faith, but the consequences are guaranteed. Humans have the option to choose their own path. Allah already knows what will happen, but humans need to explore it for themselves.

Quran: Surah Baqarah :2:256.There is no compulsion in religion: true guidance has become distinct from error, so whoever rejects false Gods and believes in God has grasped the firmest hold.

Muslims have blended in different ways based on various factors, such as freedom, appeal, and cultural fit. In the USA, some people took Islam and made it a learning factor.

It is not necessary to give up Islamic values to survive in this society.

Youth is a captivating period filled with intimacy. Attendance includes both spiritual and worldly elements. The prime years of youth, as stated by Allah, will lead to questioning in the years to come. The time of judgment values youth as a gift, not to be underestimated, as these years bring strength and a mind open to absorbing anything. Allah has granted a short time known as youth, and how it is used is questioned. The success of the young is celebrated in history, making excuses based on youth is not valid.

Pseudo-culture for a Muslim does not have a monopoly on adaptability. Failed modernism conceals it, yet it bears the mark of a paganistic society. Islam successfully replaced it years ago with its monotheistic set of unchangeable rules for Muslims. To instill a sense of Muslim identity, it is important to teach Islam to the child. The rules were established by Islam, without any modifications. The subtlety of a Muslim woman and her desire to impart knowledge to her child is appreciated in Islam. Therefore, a Muslim woman cannot marry a non-Muslim man due to this reason. People of different religions will doubt these regulations and restrictions. Against the idea of letting their child decide their faith. Islam provides clear guidelines on the faith of Muslims.

Interchangeable laws cannot parallel the delivery of this message, and it cannot be replaced by appeasement. Being part of a diverse society, the expression holds truth with clarity. In regions where faith is not as common and pseudo-culture is accepted as modern. The laws of Islam cannot be determined by where a child is instructed to select their gender in these settings. Some may retaliate by citing their faith, asserting its lack of relevance.

Providing a safe home, food, and shelter, and teaching Islam are the rights of both children and parents according to contractual law. Father provides, mother nurtures and teaches Islam. In Islam, rights are present despite different circumstances. It is within Allah's ability to have made all nations

Muslim. However, he did not. He granted Islam to those with distinct laws that cannot be exchanged. Accept it or reject it. The script remains unchanged. In Islam and health, time is the most valued currency.

The earth speaks on your behalf or against you. How do your animals communicate about you? They will inform Allah about how you treat them at your home. Humans are entitled to rights. Ultimately, everything you utilize will either support or undermine you. Numerous examples demonstrate that Allah created everything with intention and purpose.

If you possess rights presently, they will possess rights in the future. Those who comprehend these rights acknowledge that time and health are fundamental, with health being a loan that cannot be overlooked. Attendance that fails to prioritize or fulfill obligations. Allah does not return to time. Conversely, it will oppose someone who values time. Learning is a way for believers to appreciate time, not hijack it. Disbelievers appreciate time but fail to acknowledge their creator. As he sees fit. It's all connected in this rotating, evolving world, where one person can bring benefits to another. Allah bestows upon those whom He chooses.

Quran: Surah Furqan 25:28 Oh, woe to me! I wish I had not taken that one as a friend.

Quran: Surah Isra 17:21 See, how We have exalted some above others in this world, and in the Life to Come, they will have higher ranks and greater degrees of excellence over others.

Islam is a groundbreaking movement, not a revival of an underdeveloped pagan era. The idea of (Halal) permissible relationships in society terrifies them. The (haram) impermissible relationship finds pleasure in what is forbidden. Allah, the architect, bestowed mercy upon humanity and all living beings, recognizing the legitimate rewards of a way of life. Repetition of truth is tiresome for few and a reminder for the grateful.

Countless stories can be inspired by belief and strength.

The narrative of Rabia Basri:

While in the palace, Rabia Basri faithfully prayed to Allah while attending to the king. She sobbed and begged for mercy in the depths of night. Being sold as a slave defined her childhood. While making rounds in his palace, the king was suddenly alerted by the sound of crying. He inched closer to the sound of Rabia Basri weeping for her Lord. Witnessing it left him feeling sad. It came as a complete surprise to him that he was oblivious to her unhappiness about something. At dawn, he started interrogating her.

She stated that she intended solely to demonstrate reverence to her Lord. Impressed by her commitment, he decided to propose. The woman replied that I requested my Lord's time, and he gave me a human. She refused. Crying to her Lord, she expressed, "I can only serve you after fulfilling my human responsibilities." The King granted her release from her palace duties in this tale. Belief transcends barriers, and formalities are irrelevant. She earned the title of a Saint and dedicated herself to a life of worship.

Belief is boundless for a man who believes:

A believer's heart desires a closeness to their Lord that goes beyond worldly attachments. In the era of Prophet Muhammad, a man embraced the Islamic faith.He had an affair with a pagan woman and enjoyed her company. But, after renewing his faith, he still hadn't seen her. Seeing him in the Kaaba, she witnessed him liberating the Muslims from the pagans.

She gave him an ultimatum: either return to her or face the consequences of being accused of supporting Muslim liberation. Upon returning to Prophet Muhammad, he suggested marrying her and supporting her. His nature seemed incapable of rejecting him. The Prophet possessed a kind heart. He had a comprehensive understanding.

He excelled in both secular and religious realms as a Prophet. Prophet Muhammad received a sudden revelation, instructing believers to marry fellow believers and non-believers to marry non-believers. His faith prepared him to receive divine revelation from Allah, enabling him to answer the new convert's questions directly. The hearts of Allah's faithful followers are observed by Him.

Quran: Surah Taubah 9:71.The believing men and believing women are allies of one another. They enjoin what is right and forbid what is wrong, establish prayer, give zakah, and obey Allah.

Quran: Surah Ahzab: 33:35.For men and women who are devoted to God- believing men and women, obedient men and women, truthful men and women, steadfast men and women, humble men and women.

She rejected the belief in Allah and was resistant to change. His methods, which were enlightened, would motivate her to make changes. However, she was not ready for it. With time, it can tarnish a calm heart that does not possess the ability to differentiate between right and wrong.

Muhammad, the Prophet, affirmed his faith. Instantly, he knew he was a believer. The affirmation of his faith brought him joy and satisfaction. Understanding that the prophet called him a believer was enough for him to set aside his desires. He prioritized his faith over the desires of a non-believer. With a smile on his face, he recalled how the Prophet Muhammad had labeled him a believer, and a revelation had been sent specifically for him. Rare to find believers like these and no more revelations to come. Listening to stories like this can inspire belief and seekers.

The Story of Noah:

The Quran presents a different depiction of Noah compared to other biblical narratives. He personified hope and belief for his future generations. In Noah's time, idol worship was widespread and his teachings were ignored. He had a divine calling to worship Allah, the sole God. His speaking skills were exceptional. Despite Noah's persistent pleas, they refused to abandon their paganism. He was a Prophet advocating for monotheism.

Their anger towards him intensified as they continued to defy him. Every Prophet, except Prophet Muhammad, cursed those who defied them despite their best efforts. Unlike the other Prophets, he never cursed or wished harm upon his people.

Quran: Surah Nur: 71:27 For if you leave them, they will lead your servants astray and spawn no other than those who deny the knowledge of the reality and who disobey the commands.

Quran: Surah Hud 11;44. And the command is given: 'Earth! Swallow up your water; , and: 'Heaven! Abate!' So the water subsided, the command was fulfilled, and the Ark settled.

Quran: Surah Ankabut:29:14. We certainly sent Noah to his people, and he remained among them a thousand years minus fifty years, and the flood seized.

Allah hears everything but accepts prayers based on His own will. Prophet Noah's prayers were answered by Allah, yielding fruitful results. The strength of faith eludes those who doubt, similar to building a ship on a hilltop far from the sea. Noah built this ark at Allah's command. The arc was a symbol of faith, trust, and strength. It was a testament to the power of Allah and a reminder of his divine capabilities. Noah was an example of the power of faith and the strength of perseverance.

The ark resting at Mount Judi can be found in present-day Turkey. Visitors can see the accessible history of these grounds. Exploring and traveling the world is an instruction from Allah to Muslims. Noah took pairs, and they came in twos. His wife and son were the only ones who didn't come to the arc. The disbelievers drowned as the water rushed. There is no mention of the raven sent to find dry land in the Quran. Allah stopped the rain when Noah prayed.

Bible: God promises in Genesis 9:11-14 that "neither shall all flesh be cut off anymore by the waters of a flood; neither shall there any more be a flood to destroy the earth"1 The world has flooded in many regions multiple times because of humanity's disbelief and disobedience. The Quran does not guarantee that Allah will not flood the world.

The flooding persists. The sins and floods show no sign of stopping. Noah begged Allah to spare his son. Allah replied, saying he is not one of you. A child in a family can possess different characteristics, as their destiny is determined by Allah.

Quran: Surah Hud: 11:45. And Nuh called upon his Lord, said he, 'O my Lord, my son too is of my family. Your promise is true, and you are the greatest of rulers.

Quran: Surah Hud: 11:46 He said, "O Noah, indeed he is not of your family; indeed, he is [one whose] work was other than righteous, so ask Me not for that about which you do not know.

The Prophet Noah of Islam was known for his eloquence and exceptional oratory skills. <u>His reputation was built upon his exceptional ability to communicate the message of God with eloquence, persuasiveness, and unwavering conviction.</u> Additionally, he exemplified qualities of compassion and humility as a leader.

Labeling someone as a fool is unkind. Various techniques for addressing a person. In the past, individuals who didn't understand the palace were called court fools. The definition of a fool is often someone who resists change, but this description can be patronizing. Teaching a prideful and arrogant egotistical person can be difficult, as evidenced by this. Help is ineffective for the foolish, but can benefit the ignorant. He clings to an unsuccessful endeavor, hesitant to begin again.

Embracing challenges and reforms, the Islamic world strives to learn and advance. Even if they offered him compensation to leave a dirty environment, he chose to stay. Would he be seen as a fool for staying? He haggled for the opportunity to uncover and pursue a better life, yet opposed the transformation. With Allah's will, even a fool can change. Help is only available from Allah. Prophets bring messages. The Prophets were fatigued by fools.

The story of Isa (Jesus) and the fool.

A man witnessed Jesus fleeing from someone. With Allah's permission, he was a Prophet who healed lepers and brought the dead back to life. He was fleeing from this individual. When asked, he claimed to have the ability to heal the sick, but not to assist a fool. This story teaches us that stupidity is incurable. The fool was beyond the Prophet's assistance, causing him to run away.

Allah can restore spirituality to anyone He chooses. He bestows intelligence on those he chooses. Intelligence alone is pointless without Allah's guidance. Many stories exist for those who believe in the power of a single word to change a believer's heart. A believer will always desire the companionship of another believer.

The focal point of life lies in correlating the events of its many dimensions, as long as there is balance and no stumbling or stalling. When nothing seems possible, the believer's affair becomes extinct. His faith lies in Allah.

CHAPTER 12

IMPORTANCE OF COMMUNICATION IN ISLAM

The communicative and unitarian belief of Islam affirms Allah's divinity and denies the worship of any man or entity. The five times a day Azan is a reminder for a Muslim to communicate with Allah.

Every Muslim country has heard this sound loud and deliberate as a communication tool for centuries.

The acoustic and melodic sounds bring Muslims to prayer, while non-Muslims perceive this loudness as a disruption to their vacation, in Muslim countries while others are mesmerized by it.

Throughout history, (Azan) has never been used as a call to action by any religion in the world. The Islamic call to prayer is broadcast around the clock in this world every single day. How can a Muslim wait to enter the bounty of Salat when Islam is being communicated to him at all times?

Technological progress enables phones to loudly announce the azan. With technology constantly reminding Muslims of the salat at specific times, there are no valid excuses for missing it. Who is blocking the path? Can the answer be found for intentional neglect or can the believer claim to answer every call-in attendance and solidarity with Allah and believers?

Those who do not understand Islam need a believer's attention. Surely this is a powerful reminder for humanity and all Muslims that communication is key to success. Muslims consider communication crucial. Body language, facial expressions, tone of voice, softness, direct words, kindness, and melody are universally understood. To a Muslim, kind words are never missed by angels; documented as good deeds.

A smile is a charitable act, and having intimacy with one's spouse is also charity. This statement might be deemed sexist in the current society. Why limit rewards? Every day, the gifts of communication keep adding up.

Through Salat, one can communicate with the creator. While communication is an important skill in all societies, Islam places particular importance on it and expects individuals to demonstrate responsible attitudes and behaviors. Actions speak louder than words; as a Muslim, be the most effective communicator by setting an example for young and new converts, and others will follow your lead.

Stronger trees also sway with harsh winds, but they stand up again after weathering the storm. People with deeper roots may also sway with harsh winds, but they stand up again after weathering the storm. Returning to where communication and strength were felt, those rooted in strong exchanges stay connected.

When combined with a positive attitude and an open-hearted recipient, open communication flourishes and the conversation can seamlessly continue. A captivating harmony draws one soul to another, concluding in a heartfelt conversation. Nothing can replace a divine connection except the waves of faith and belief that bring souls together.

Prophet Muhammad conveyed each revelation, resulting in the written Quran. Without his communication, Islam wouldn't exist. Islam is exemplified when a Muslim helps a lost Muslim. Allah will observe the hearts of those who assist lost Muslims who were once faithful but are influenced by a corrupt society. Help, not rejection, is what they need from a believer.

The act of prayer can soften a Muslim's heart and facilitate self-expression. Playing with fire without understanding its fumes can harm those nearby or leave clothes smelling of smoke.

Misunderstandings and miscommunication arise from a lack of communication. Interacting with negative people can lead to unproductive situations and hinder self-confidence. Engaging in actions that contradict Islam becomes a habit, not an error, and requires improved guidance and companionship.

Who doesn't know who Allah is? There's no better time than now to gain knowledge. Every one of his 99 names holds both mercy and importance. Allah, also known as Al Ghaffar, is ever forgiving and is also called Al Malik Al Quddus. The Pure, The Prefect, flawless and faultless.

One of Allah's names is (Al Muizz), the bestower of honor. Those honored with sharing their words become gifts of grandeur, conveying Allah's message to the world, especially to struggling Muslims or new converts.

While one can acquire wealth in this world, health is an invaluable gift that can be taken away. Prayer is the dialogue between Allah and his followers. By listening to the soul's messages, he finds contentment in the answers received.

Islam's gift cannot be kept to oneself by a Muslim. The laws of Islam the Quran and Sunnah have a universal impact on humanity, beyond just Muslims. The laws of Islam bring advantages to individuals in all aspects of life and serve as the ultimate means of communication between humans and the creator.

One believer helps another fill the questionable empty holes. Sometimes the search is a solitary journey until answers bring clarity.

Prophet Muhammad did not communicate his character traits; people did. The one who defines his character in opposition to the one he displays is a deceitful mirage for a Muslim.

Individuals who perform (Salat) ritual prayer and have faith in Islam embody the teachings of Allah. If an individual commits an error, the masses patiently anticipate the opportunity to assign blame, as this affords them a position of superiority.

Prophets faced their trials. Despite Jonah's failure to meet the challenges he was put through, the people didn't put him down but changed their ways because they missed his words. Allah is (Al-Fattah) The Opener of hearts.

The character of a Muslim is the word of communication without which getting a testimony of disbelievers to define nature is not conducive when a believer sees the distance of communication broken leading to venues one reaches out of loneliness. The communication of a believer is a platform for victory, not stagnation.

Some express hardness underlying difficulty in communicating the true kindness and restraint in proclaiming true truth or the emotional expressive side marked significantly by fusion of belief that lacks communication cannot flourish and negativity and intolerant behavior of enjoyment one shows while withdrawal is noncommunication.

(Salat) involves communicating with Allah, whereas those who don't attend don't experience that peace. Growth in Islam is determined by communication.

Those who don't attend to (Dhikr) dialogue of Allah can sway easily, while those who communicate with Allah discover flaws in themselves that need to be corrected, knowing Allah is merciful, and staying in communication with believers since one believer is better than a thousand disbelievers.

Ṣaḥīḥ al-Bukhārī 5534, Ṣaḥīḥ Muslim 2628. Abu Musa reported: The Prophet, peace and blessings be upon him, said, "Verily, the parable of good and bad company is that of a seller of musk and a blacksmith. The seller of musk will give you perfume, you will buy some, or you will notice a pleasant smell. As for the blacksmith, he will burn your clothes, or you will notice a bad smell."

Human communication of believers is conducted through words that bring the Quran and all biblical texts to humans. As words are sound bites that remain within the human mind, choosing the most appropriate words is beneficial. Don't misuse words. As a Muslim, it is a privilege to deliver the highest quality, says Islam.

Communication is at the forefront of success. Developing excellent communication skills is essential to any work. It allows for the efficient delivery of tasks and ideas, as well as the ability to effectively collaborate with others. It is also critical for resolving conflicts and creating healthy working and personal relationships. Although Allah understands the heart of human communication.

Muslims communicate using Salat, which is a mandated practice of every practicing Muslim. Some people scroll through life without direction, while others have a plan. A traveler is a person who travels through life. Some gain momentum, and some keep searching until time communicates life through higher sources unknown to man.

It remains to be seen whether or not time adjusts for those who leave communication with Allah at the expense of gains or losses. Life will speak for itself. The best investments are found by analyzing currency market data and trends carefully. Looking for currencies that are expected to appreciate shortly and have a positive outlook.

Diversifying your portfolio minimizes risk and maximizes returns. Stay on top of changes in the market by regularly monitoring it. There is no risk to morality and communication in such a market.

A diversified market can promote revenue as long as it does not risk mortality. Communication with markets outside of one's comfort zone is progress. There is no worse market than stagnation.

Investing in oneself is more prudent than gambling in a market that goes against one's morals. Muslims follow the guidelines of Islam and ensure that the outdoor intercom works. Assisting with communication and company selection is vital.

These laws were established by Islam to uphold Allah's order and safeguard integrity. The pursuit of pleasing others will result in chaos and division. Balancing one's equilibrium is crucial for believers, as honesty and helping others are top priorities. Striving for excellence means not compromising our highest values for temporary pleasures.

Staying focused on goals and prioritizing one's own needs. Remember that Allah's laws are supreme and a believer must adhere to them. Islam provides a firm foundation for those who seek it. A divine source that guides each step. Gaining Islam is a victory, but the competitors and enemies are many to sway the believer. Overthinking and being trapped in negative thoughts cripples victory-seekers.

The believers in Allah are full of confidence. Worldly measures could be seen by Satan and his prowlers. Jealousy has the power to sway believers if they allow disbelievers to scheme. Successful people share, not brag about, their accomplishments. Can light be measured? Islam emerged as the guiding light for humans tired of darkness. Balance and moderation define Islam as a religion. It promotes introspection and contemplation among its followers. Additionally, it encourages peaceful coexistence with other faiths and cultures.

In Islam, the connection between the velocity of light and the automatic transmission serves as a metaphorical comparison to highlight the significance of communication between Allah and humanity. The velocity of light, which is considered the fastest known speed, represents the swiftness and immediacy with which Allah's message can reach humankind. On the other hand, the automatic transmission symbolizes the smooth and effortless transmission of knowledge and guidance through the Quran.

It emphasizes the importance of voice or imprinted delivery in conveying Allah's teachings to believers. The Quran is regarded as the direct communication from Allah, and without it, humanity would be left adrift without clear answers to their questions. The Quran's role in providing guidance and addressing the needs of humanity is crucial in ensuring spiritual fulfillment and avoiding confusion or misinterpretation. Therefore, the Quran's delivery is seen as a high awareness requirement in Islam, as it bridges the gap between Allah and humankind, providing essential answers and guidance for a righteous and purposeful life.

Allah reveals that light moves at a rapid pace. The Quran is the only book that discusses the speed of light. According to the Quran, light travels at an absolute velocity. When a human corresponds with Allah. Praying and relying on Allah is faster than any speed of light. Overall. He is the master of all affairs. Humanity would be in a state of loss if Allah didn't communicate with his creation.

Islam has strongly stressed the importance of communication. A Muslim is instructed to establish communication with Allah through five daily prayers. This is not a viable choice for Muslims in a multiple-choice format. Allah is imparting the lesson that life holds no worth without communication. Muslims have long recognized the significance of this domain. Some argue that I do not require five daily prayers. My beliefs and practices align with spirituality. Rules, regulations, laws, and communication are encompassed in a comprehensive volume. Therefore, as Muslims, we have no doubts that an individual who lacks belief and associates with neglectful individuals is neglectful of their responsibilities.

Islam upholds the principle of effective communication. The ultimate manifestation of belief in Allah and his final messenger, Muhammad, was their unwavering communication. The Prophet of all of humanity, jinns, and all that is in existence. A human who adheres to the Islamic faith engages in communication with Allah five times daily. It's a requirement set by Allah. The barrier of communication between believers serves to thwart the entry of evil, as disbelievers seek to disrupt this connection.

There is (dhirk) conversation about Allah in the presence of two believers conversing.

Allah guides whom he wills. Islam has been clear in the voice of communication.

Defiance of Allah is not a spiritual act, but pure neglect and defiance for a Muslim is dangerous. Allah also communicates with those who ignore him. We can construe their material or academic gains as success. Allah provides sustenance with ease. He feeds the birds who go out hungry and ensures they return home full. The only success life can offer is peace within communication with Allah. When troubles escalate, people might raise their hands in fear of losing material or academic achievements.

The main motivation for life is health. Nothing can aid a human without good health. The unintended wealth distribution goes to hospitals or caregivers. Communication depends on the passage of time. There is no turnaround time for every minute. Ignorance and pride hinder communication. The communication registry with Allah commences with Salat. In his most humble position, with gentleness. The attendee has Allah's full attention.

It's common for people to experience being ignored or receiving no response when talking to someone. Even a slave standing before Allah receives his full attention. The person performing the Salat may lack attentiveness, but the one you're standing in front of is attentive to every individual's needs. What is rightfully yours has already been granted by him. If you raise your hands for it, Allah will grant it or you will stop asking for it. There's something better waiting for you if you didn't receive it.

Allah holds dominion over all planetary events. Allah is described as the light of heaven and earth in the Quran. The transparent glass allows the light to shine like a star, illuminating a blessed olive tree. In the past, earth and heaven were a single entity. Your life will be presented by Allah according to his judgment.

Quran: Surah Anbiya: 21:30.Have the unbelievers not ever considered that the heavens and the earth were one piece and that We tore them apart from one another.

If he can separate the universe, he can separate each phase of a human's life. Allah created the world in six days. According to Islam, the world exploded after the big bang. In the world of today, Allah has granted man the benefits of both worlds. There is a reference to Islam for the Big Bang when the world exploded.

He sent humans down for testing. They will run this course efficiently. This is the test of life. Allah offers man both worlds in the world of today. The junction to prepare and live in this world while preparing for the next is the key to progress.

Any life test, including a job, family, relationships, academia, sports, or travel, requires preparation. How can a human deny that life doesn't require preparation for the next? Except for those who believe there is no life after this, all bets are off. Do as you will, but judgment awaits everyone.

After humans exit this life, it will leave them with perpetuity and no shares of the earth. The only thing one will take with them is the weight of righteous and evil deeds on the scale of justice. In addition, a book is handed to the individual. Accounting is swift from Allah, but humans today can't add without a calculator and Muslims branched into Mathematics and shared achievements with the world. We share our knowledge, not hold back, and sharing abounds in bounties.

The Quran distinctly states that the human soul and every part is a reward from Allah. All recipients must regard Allah's loan with respect and sincerity. Without the harmony of the alternative, this life cannot be complete. Recognition of Allah is the key to establishing a belief in Him... Human minds can open up a world of possibilities.

Embracing Allah's abilities enables humans to realize their inherent capacities. If he is earnest in his exploration, a human can entertain the accuracy entirely if Allah chooses. The mind and spirit coexist if the stability is annexed. Spirit, mind, and frame.

Humankind lives in tranquility and alignment. Someone often misconstrues the concept of communication in life. If a human is not communicating with himself, communication with others is a minuscule effort.

Whenever you neglect your physical and spiritual needs, you cannot help others and rush to find a lesser being to make up for your inabilities. When social media works in a country that dumbs down minds by using a system for stagnant, uninformed, and untraveled citizens, it perpetuates the information of those who willingly spread rhetoric as if the information were real.

In certain settings, social media can generate hostility towards Islam and regimes. They use this as a threat to manipulate the uninformed, and untravelled by spreading rhetoric under the illiteracy of the subject. They present this information as gospel truth to the swayed, uneducated, untraveled, and uninformed. In these settings, gossip is abundant, and true information about the Muslim world is scarce.

Without publicity and communication, businesses can fail and relationships can fade. The loss of communication leads to losing touch with Allah. In Islam, communication takes the form of Salat five times with Allah, not multiple options. Communication is essential for believers. Satan's domain includes silence. He works his tricks and plants doubts by whispering in their ears, confusing their minds.

It encompasses individuals who disconnect from Allah and those who guide them towards Him. The doubtful mind contains numerous compartments filled with doubts, fictional scenarios, and baseless accusations against others.

A mind filled with doubt that always repeats "if I was this or that". The believer substitutes "If I was" with "Alhamdulillah" by the grace of Allah. This is a noteworthy milestone for those who appreciate the worth of Islam. Gold is the solitary commodity bought and sold in a flourishing market, where degraded metals have no value.

The strength of one's belief in Allah outweighs any amount of wealth or treasure. Faith is the key to conquering all challenges. Neglecting to appreciate the significance of solidarity results in missed chances. Negative experiences regain prominence as mindsets evolve under positive influences. Devoted to those who have faith, not those who deceive

A believer yearns to converse with a fellow believer about their successful communication with Allah. A subject without Allah's approval is a lost subject. Allah, the giver of peace and communication to believers, deems those subjects with pleasantries. Those who don't lead a Muslim on the path of Allah are not true companions. The system of survival can become weak when physical and spiritual health are disrespected. Those aiming for success rely on the support of their supporters.

Winners cannot be made by failing companies. Some high achievers see the world as a barren desert and are willing to work tirelessly for worldly success. Together with survival and surrender to Allah. Success is a gleam of light.

Balancing accomplishments in this realm, readying for the next. As hours elapse, eyes seek repose. Dream big, and you may achieve the impossible. When Allah and the right company of oneself in solitaire or with righteousness with a believer come together, there are no limits to what can be achieved. A company that changes one's Muslim beliefs is not helpful, but evil.

The addition of working out and having a chiseled physique for men and women is a physical fulfillment. It is Prophet Muhammad's advice that Islam does not neglect the physical body and encourages exercise, especially swimming.

Humans balance all three aspects of their being: if one or the other is disproportionate, the polarity of this disparity causes imbalance. The grappling confusion resting within is the soul or the mind? The soul clings to the matters of the heart. If the heart is sound, it adapts to goodness.

The world is currently focused on traveling to explore the beauty that Allah has created. Money and fame are a tantalizing combination. Power dynamics in academia. Human beauty and physique are attributes people desire and adorn. Allah has instructed Muslims to educate both genders, with a special emphasis on women. Exercise and proper eating habits lead to good health.

It enhances the beauty of both (Mahram) permissible men and women, and nurturing their attraction is crucial for spiritual life. Despite using all means and being given in all aspects, they still doubt whether they should worship Allah. All forms of ignorance can be corrected, but lack of comprehension defies explanation.

The same realm of bliss is reached when the heart and faith are in sync. Those seeking insight within are guided by Allah's light, while a purified heart seeks truth over superficial happiness.In societies with work expectations, women generally dress up for work and alter their appearance for relaxation, while their husbands typically desire attractive partners.

Similarly, men dress nicely for others but look unkempt at home, which is not universally attractive. In the Islamic faith, the importance of mutual attraction is emphasized in permissible relationships. Embracing pagan beliefs or imitating them goes against the teachings of Islam.Alterations occur continuously and change gradually. Islam remains unchanged and does not adapt to the times, so the times would need to change for Islam. When analyzing societal changes, it is important to examine end-of-life adjustments as well.

Bible; Leviticus *20:14* indirectly mentions cremation, since it involves capital punishment that requires the offender to be "burned with fire."

Leaving this world holds the same importance as entering it. Christians opt for cremation, contradicting Christian beliefs. What is the process for changing laws to support the revised system? Is the implication of this verse that they are being punished for the original sin?

Surprisingly, this falls under the category of Abrahamic faith. The rituals would be considered paganistic, as they do not align with the Abrahamic faith. As an exit, the Hindu faith opts for cremation. Hindus believe in God, which they consider as a primal source of belief called (Bhagavan).

Cremation is their chosen method of body disposal once the soul has departed. According to Hindu doctrine, reincarnation happens when the soul is released from the body through cremation. What was the reason behind Christendom's choice of this process? Cremation is not accepted by any Abrahamic faiths. Muslims are buried or disposed of in the sea as every part testifies to the deeds, even if it disintegrates. Allah's laws and orders are not altered by Muslims.

The unity of Islam is rooted in unification and discipline, surpassing any other faith. All Muslims recite the Salat in Arabic. The language of the Quran flows, even for non-Arabic speakers. Also, the call to prayer rotates five times a day throughout the globe. According to Islamic doctrine, laws and regulations exist to improve the long-term well-being of Muslims, not to limit them. Without understanding the core of the Islamic belief system, the literal sense is to liberate a human. Entrepreneurship, sports, faith marriages, or any successful endeavor cannot begin until one understands its value.

Understanding the value of success is the key to achieving it. Islam's impact on one's life is apparent solely to believers. Believing in this implies faith in wisdom, knowledge, understanding, and not mindlessly following Islamic dogma. A Muslim who comprehends its significance would not perceive Salat as a burden since this commitment is with Allah, not a person, and would never skip it. It's exclusive to those who appreciate provision and communication with those who guide towards Allah. Those who succeed should cling to Allah's word and collaborate with the world, rather than working for it.

Breaking laws is common in these societies. Looking into their history reveals that it is the result of defiance, which the world sees as false independence. While humans are drawn to temporary entertainment, they often turn to strength after experiencing both sides.Exploring the historical changes and societal contrasts can be challenging for those who struggle with adapting to a misleading culture. In times like these, sharing homes can help reduce living expenses as society trends towards recessions. A sign of the hour is the increasing cost of ration.

Etymology Online traces the origin of the term "boyfriend" back to 1909 when it meant a woman's paramour. Still, the term had a previous platonic connotation. Later, the system changed, allowing men and women to engage in guilt-free sexual intimacy. Collaboration between women and men highlighted the feminist movement in this case. Satan introduced a moral dilemma as he descended into destruction. They deceived the world by pretending to be progressive and desiring freedom while communicating evil.

Countries that implement self-imposed regulations use the term "boyfriend and girlfriend" instead of marriage, as marriage is defined by Allah as a union exclusively between a man and a woman. Relationships that are disapproved by laws in biblical texts, whether altered or intact, pose a risk to their core identity in society. Islam scrutinizes them through evaluations. Muslims are being educated on discerning disparities. Some perceived these blemished beliefs as emancipating. A minority vacillated but ultimately returned to the conviction that the erroneous would conquer the accurate. Covert romantic relationships have had detrimental effects on the psychological well-being of countless individuals and influenced the country's economic stability.

Additionally, there are other countries with comparable traits. Wrongs don't make them right. The signs lead to many women remaining single. Researchers anticipate a projected increase to 45% in the proportion of unmarried women in a decade. Islam promotes the institution of marriage. Society grew weary of commitments and contracts amidst a rise in illicit acts. This has caused economic distress as both women and men are refraining from growing their families. Married individuals of opposite genders contribute to the economic and moral compass, which is gradually declining. Same-sex unions are increasing and families are not increasing. The focus transitions from emerging nations to the global stage. Muslim countries tend to exhibit lower rates of observation, potentially leading to a slower spread.

Research indicates that 50% of individuals in upcoming modernized countries are unmarried, with increasing rates of divorce. Islam prioritizes matrimony over premarital relationships or trials. The legalization of same-sex marriage also impacted the economy and morality, as well as reshaped the balance of faiths.Ultimately, the laws originate from Western civilization and countries that have been dominating the world for less than three hundred years, deceiving the world of progress. Slow poisoning is more harmful than the fumes one inhales after smoking.

Influences play a role in shaping the new wave of thinking. Reformist Muslim countries and Muslims will resist defying Allah's commands. In a corrupt society, communication is a bargain for most. When unions are formed, sacrificing religious content or moral codes is always on the agenda. With opposing religious convictions. Likewise, communication is vital in both the business world and personal interactions. Allah's command in the Quran is to come with a sound heart.

The soul is important for foreplay to interact with the mind with a complete balance, with attendance to the body and staying healthy. The restless soul is missing the serenity of the worship of one Lord Allah.Some minds show less maturity or development of comprehension, or a way behind schedule. As life conjectures, constricted pathways occlude upheavals or missing links to survive in this arena of life.

 Some preliminary uses of substances may alter the brain, or some may have used opportunities for growth with the aid of superficial entertainment of this world. Foreign harmful substances do not enhance the mind or body; they only cause damage and rebellion against oneself. It is important to acknowledge that humans are created weak, considering the substance Allah used to create the first two humans.

The material used to create the first humans has been clearly described by Allah. Allah has the power to change the color. A man is bestowed with his color and distinct characteristics. He constructs each individual with purposeful ways of looking at the world. The soul can only be seen by Allah. Coincidences do not exist in Islam. Luck is nonexistent. The Book of Records contained everything he recorded before humans arrived on Earth. Islam teaches that there are no coincidences in life.

To create a sustainable future, not duplicating the same mistakes, moving forward. Positivity. Working on the alignment of soul, mind, and body is the focus of realization. Attainment within gives solace to even better sleep and dreams.

Following up with the company of believers, or a believer, will be the ticket to freedom.

Economic freedom will contain the human, but having it all is the key to success.

(Rizq) sustenance is already yours, written just for you. No one can snatch your treasures. Allah will direct you to them. Focus on inner consciousness, not on the fruitless advice of disbelievers.

Quran: Surah Anbiya 21:30 Have those who disbelieved. The heavens and the earth were a joined entity, and we separated them and made from water every living thing.Then will they not believe?

Allah leaves no gaps. The transmission of his messages to humanity, the Prophets he assigned, the books he sent, and the Qur'an he sent as a statement of a gift, is phenomenal. The strongest of conversations with believers, without which the human feels loss regardless of worldly contentment or travel.

The Quran has constantly communicated with humans as we explore from conception to death. At the time of judgment, the Quran will plead for a Muslim. For those who read daily.

Alternatively, you will have proof that you were vigilant in learning and seeking to understand the content and transmission of Allah. Or it will rank against affirming you were not attentive and never served the connection. Allah invested with his creatures through the Prophets of date.

The Quran is the last testimonial of truth for Muslims. It may unsettle many to question how a text can communicate. How can part of a human skeleton speak to the operations of life? Allah will give each part of your body to speak. It will speak for you or against you.

Quran: Surah Fussilat 17:14. Then his mouth will be sealed, and his limbs and organs will be asked to tell about his deeds. Every organ would speak up and give true evidence.

It's incomprehensible to an individual of the shady belief that a Muslim is mindful of the delicacies cited from Allah. If he can develop a human, form an egg from the drip of fluid. And lodge it in the mother's entrail and make up the original mortals Adam and Eve out of the mud. There is no uncertainty. He is Allah, and there is everything he can answer.

Quran: Surah Hijr 15:26 Surely we brought man into being out of dry clay, which was wrought from black mud.

Water and sand play a role in man's creation of Adam and Eve. A developing child rests in the mother's womb. Quran clarifies that a man's sperm nucleus, known as (nutfa), mixes with the egg of the woman. The mother carries many eggs, of which it fertilizes one egg and produces an embryo. The expectant mother delivers her baby in nine months or fewer.

Quran: Surah Muminoon 23:12 And certainly did we create man from an extract of clay.

Quran: Surah Muminoon 23:13 Then we placed him as a sperm-drop in a firm lodging.

Quran: Surah Muminoon 23:14. Then we made the sperm-drop into a clinging clot, and we made the clot into a lump of flesh, and we made the lump, bones, and we covered the bones with flesh, then we developed him into another creation. So blessed is Allah, the best of creators.

Many have explored human embryology. The latest is from Keith Moore, the scientist who found answers in the Quran. Man has always been inquisitive. Man has sought to investigate, through civilization's idols, manuscripts, prophecies, and saints, tapping into the universe for answers unknown to humanity. Before humanity examined the benefits of comprehensive exploration to discover the development of a fetus, it was the Quran that provided answers to Muslims.

Allah dispensed answers humanity cannot dismiss or weigh. It wasn't modern. The skilled analyst, or the new sophisticated techniques, who invented answers to embryology. Humans probed to explore the Quran, seeking answers under a microscopic lens. Allah presented the answers in the Quran.

And a direct declaration from Allah. Man cannot rebuff or be introspective. The authority leaves no corrections and simply answers what humanity seeks. Prophet Muhammad had no formal education; he was unlettered. There was no doubt he would not know of conception morphology, the various phases of intrauterine life inside. Scientists did not know of this until some decades later.

(Surahs) in the Quran depict various stages of human development. The Quran is not organized into chapters. The Quran mentions both Mecca and Medina as sources of revelations to Prophet

Muhammad. There were 91 surahs in Mecca and 23 surahs in Medina. There are one hundred and fourteen surahs in the Quran. The Quran has no versions other than translations.

Muslims believe that the heart is not just a physical organ but also the center of one's spiritual and emotional being. It is believed that the heart is where the connection with Allah is established and where true faith resides. The Quran emphasizes the importance of having a pure heart, free from negative qualities such as arrogance, envy, and hatred. Muslims are encouraged to purify their hearts through acts of worship, repentance, and seeking forgiveness.

By cultivating a pure heart, Muslims believe that they can attain closeness to Allah and receive His blessings and guidance. It is believed that a pure heart enables one to have a deeper understanding of the Quran, enhances spiritual growth, and allows for a stronger bond with the Creator. Therefore, while modern technology may allow us to witness the development of the fetal heart, Muslims understand the heart's significance beyond its physical function and strive to nurture and purify it in accordance with Allah's commands.

Quran Surah A'raf 7:179 "Having hearts wherewith they understand not and having eyes wherewith they see not." The Quran is clear on the formation and conception. "We " formed a heart within five to six weeks. After the formation of the heart, "we" form the skeleton in the seventh week. Muscles form in the eighth week.

Quran: Surah Muminoon 23:14. Then we made the sperm-drop into a clinging clot, and we made the clot into a lump [of flesh] we made [from] the lump bones. And we covered the bones with flesh; then we developed him into another creation. So blessed is Allah the best of the creator.

No book has undertaken the task of elucidating embryology, save for the Quran, thus how can a Muslim disregard Allah's decrees? Delving into the profound teachings of the Quran is an imperative for Muslims, and educators ought to disseminate knowledge while the curious should ardently pursue it. Muslims require education that prioritizes adherence to Quranic laws and the pursuit of knowledge. Familiarity with the Quran serves as a powerful motivator for individuals, irrespective of their faith, to actively seek intellectual growth instead of remaining uninformed.

Measuring 2mm, the embryo burrows into the uterine wall. It resides in the amniotic sac's fluid, also referred to as water. The fetus, floating in the water inside the womb, soon starts to move, sometimes becoming stuck in a breech position before being born. By getting closer and using advanced technology like an ultrasound, you can see the fetus's organs functioning properly.

During pregnancy, the fetus goes through continuous development, and in some cases, it may die naturally if unhealthy. Occasionally terminated voluntarily. By the end of the tenth week of pregnancy, the embryo develops into a fetus. The Quran's description of embryology provides a profound understanding of the intricate process of human development, inspiring Muslims to appreciate the beauty and complexity of life.

Islam's standpoint on abortion. Out of concern for financial insufficiency, the humans opted to terminate the fetus to guarantee provisions for the newborn. Allah gave assurance of sustenance for his designated representative. Refrain from ending the life of the fetus due to worries about provisions. Islam stands as the solitary progressive religion capable of enduring any era. Islam is a pragmatic belief system.

The recognition of the predicaments humans encounter in life is intricate and subdued, yet potent in its reactions and repercussions. In situations where the mother's well-being is compromised, specific fetal abnormalities may result in intrauterine mortality or graver outcomes. The exclusive choice is to abort the pregnancy. Abortion is not intended for the termination of pregnancies resulting from extramarital affairs. In their collective decision-making, neither of them has any interest in keeping the fetus. Relationships such as these are deemed taboo and strongly discouraged within the context of Islam. In a multitude of countries, self-induced abortions are a relic of the past.

Despite claiming to be free from religious influence, the regions in question are forcing Christianity on non-believers. And those who are believers but don't adhere to their modified regimes and faith. Which is mandated by the laws of the land. Abortion decisions should not be in the hands of this altered society.

The presented ethical code focuses on terminating a fetus, even if it hasn't fully developed. The society's acceptance of illicit relationships raises questions about the prevalence of abortions.

Not being able to feed one's child is not the reason here. Will they put in place measures to stop such acts and conduct surveillance on the country? There is no justification for their intervention. Many infants and fetuses have died because of the hypocrisy and changing regimes vandalizing and destroying hospitals in the Middle East.

In spite of its claim of secularism, the country is enforcing Christianity upon non-believers of this faith. And those who are believers resist their modified systems and beliefs. Which is mandated by the laws of the jurisdiction. Those who assert their authority to determine abortion policies reside in hypocrisy and endorse same-sex relationships, premarital sex, and meddle in personal choices.

These regions, who proclaim to harbor Islamophobia, exert control over their territories akin to a cult, dictating the personal conduct of their citizens. In due course, they may even dictate whom one can date, as they already impose their selective laws and rules, such as abortion, while disregarding the rights of other faiths within reasonable limits. This displays blatant hypocrisy.

However, these individuals with hypocritical and Islamophobic beliefs terminate the fetus, yet show no regret in annihilating the fetuses of others by destroying countries without engaging in war. They extend assistance to oppressors amidst the demise of numerous fetuses.

It's unjustifiable, regardless of greed, but especially if it risks the mothers' health and causes perpetual unrest. A country heavily focused on ethics deliberately invading other nations' infants. Abortion is considered ethically permissible in Islamic and Jewish doctrine when the mother's life is in danger.

Hypocrisy goes beyond this culture heavily influenced by altered regimes, but the subject remains sensitive. Out of greed, they have waged wars and caused the deaths of many innocent people, disregarding their families. Could illicit relationships be prohibited in a country with backward liberalism? What about the detrimental effects of porn on mental health and relationships?

This epidemic originated in countries to corrupt minds and promote nudity and pornography. It's even worse than war. Reflecting on thoughts that don't align with our beliefs can harm us and others in the silent war. They derive satisfaction from being belittled, as low self-esteem only mirrors negativity. It's not their sexual desires, but the illicit acts they derive pleasure from witnessing, in a world where Satan collaborates with evil in every possible manner. They promote ills to damage minds and corrupt the world Muslims need to step up to help the world.

Birth control is allowed in Islam. While it may not be harmful between spouses, it is not condoned in illicit relationships using it as an excuse to do as one pleases. Islam does not have a disparity when it comes to clarity. The faith that is universally understood is expounded upon in a suitable context. Their next move is to outlaw birth control, claiming it contradicts Christian religious doctrine. The criteria of selective rules in any faith cannot accommodate such alleged hypocrisy.

Some US states have prohibited abortion, causing outrage among Jewish Americans and leading them to seek justice and separation in the courts. In Jewish law, abortion is mandatory when needed. Muslims also face certain limitations, but the same principle applies.

New York Times: Tracking Abortion Bans Across the Country.

Abortion may also be necessary for the mother's health or the child's quality of life. Restrictions were enforced in some states to safeguard the fetus. Women who self-induce abortions after unplanned encounters face health risks due to certain state laws. Safety measures for the mother or unborn child are why we address health reasons. Mishaps occur because of disobedience towards the creator. The Quran encompasses all aspects of human existence in this world. It encompassed the remaining (Sunnah) practices of Prophet Muhammad.

The history of sexual activity in porn is not surprising, considering its origin and the country it came from.

Wikipedia: Reuben Sturman **(August 16, 1924–October 27, 1997), sometimes called the "Walt Disney of Porn", was an American pornographer and businessman from Ohio.**

The continuous indulgence in brainstorming corrupts minds and undermines moral codes, beginning a distortion that affects those who hear the evil from this land. The world has created illusions of ecstasy contrary to Islam, from men's and women's porn to illegal living to same-gender porn.

Taking cues from countries that developed under three hundred years ago. This is an inundation of closeness that is often linked to cults. It no longer hides behind lies, but instead speaks the truth to liberate Muslims and young individuals. Historical context can shed light on Muslims' behavior not aligning with the expectations of believers of prior days.

In Islam, the frontal cortex plays a significant role. The Quran (Surah Alaq), verse 16, refers to the frontal cortex located in the forehead. The forelock placed on the ground during Salat is for Muslims. Those who practice Salat to rid themselves of evil acts and promote peace are billed daily. The frontal area of the human brain governs truth and lies, as well as judgment and actions.

Watching pornography can be addictive and alter the prefrontal cortex. The negative effects of psychological aggression and commitment issues on the release of dopamine from porn can harm both the body and mind.

Newer countries offer global opportunities, but their societies are restricted and labor markets are competitive. Workers find a forty-hour workweek insufficient to meet their needs. The sudden pandemic emphasized the importance of system control and the advantages of working remotely and enjoying family time.

COVID-19 brought development for some, and decadence and isolation for others. Overachievers have been consistently achieving and climbing higher for decades, creating a pattern in the world. People are inclined towards darkness during distress and low self-esteem. Satan and his followers are wicked and can be influenced by the easily swayed. Praying Salat softens the heart, making it impossible to indulge in filth afterward.

The Quran is heavy on the Richter scale. The coherence and transparency in this book are the ultimate precision of Allah. Anyone can read the Quran. The believer understands each word, and we can leave an empty heart full of content. The body and heart would take a jolt, leaving it harsher than electric airways if the truth were told by hypocrites. Allah knew the servant he had picked for this strenuous job. Prophet Muhammad was not a scribe. He was the deliverer.

The Quran can bring tears and joy to the one who understands. How can anyone not want to know the direct word of Allah? He who sent the Quran has promised his upkeep. Who else could be a better keeper? Some Muslims find it burdensome to keep up their ritual prayers (Salat) Allah asked every living thing to come to him willingly or unwillingly.

They transpired willingly, and trees, animals, plants, and everything prayed to Allah without being told. Except for the defiant human. But Allah knows what he created and why. Muslims who miss Salat and woefully negate the hour of prayer (Salat). Satan makes an appearance and leaves them. The absentee did not make the mark. The attendance of the one present has accumulated credits. Completing the Ritual Prayers (Salat)

There is a rapid passage of time. For a believer, the allowance of (Sujood) prostration is a grant. Some people regret missing the ritual prayers (Salat) because of life's idiosyncrasies. There are no excuses to miss Salat Muslims praying during combat. Such is the heart of the believer, whose heart comprehends the value of this meeting with their creator, Allah. Angels asked Allah, don't we sing your praises daily? They will create havoc and bloodshed in the world.

Allah replied, "You know not what I know about them." Allah, who created humanity, knows the beauty within for the ones who know him. Trees to humans are all mentioned in this text of the Quran.

Those who disregard the value of Olive trees, mentioned by Allah, will be held responsible for their actions.

There are numerous health benefits associated with olive oil. Olive oil is used in everything from salads to beauty secrets. It is commonly used for cooking by most Middle Easterners. Human actions that involve uprooting olive trees, burning them, and killing their roots to take over land for more buildings are morally wrong.

Utilizing knowledge of Allah's unknown powers to sterilize humans. Vocalization and articulation of speech are exclusive to humans. Allah will grant every living being the ability to speak on Judgment Day, where even the earth and water will bear witness to Allah for every disobedient part of the human body that defied the laws of the creator.

Even in opposition to oneself. Every part of the body communicates with Allah. The day when everyone will be held accountable has come. One's work cannot be altered or augmented by anyone. Repentance to Allah is the sole alternative to finding a cure. He possesses the utmost mercy. Preventing the recurrence of wicked actions.

Quran: Surah Muminun 23:20 and [We brought forth] a tree issuing from Mount Sinai, which produces oil and food for those who eat.

The house that worships Allah possesses a gentle soul. Allah requires us to pray morning, midday, and evening to honor him. Unexpected rewards await those who remain dedicated to their worship. The world brings joy to more than just humans. They are provided with sustenance by Allah. Fruits and vegetables testify to him, those that humans pick and consume. How does humanity exhibit doubt or ingratitude?

The Quran lists figs, olives, grapes, and pomegranates as heavenly fruits. Just as eating these fruits promotes good health, following Allah's rules brings inner peace. Progress is crucial in every aspect of life. The act of sharing food is symbolic, such as breaking bread or sharing fruit. To share Islam is to unveil the truth to the world.

Sharing faith is more symbolic than sharing a meal. The ultimate joy for a believer is the divine ecstasy of faith bestowed by Allah. Destiny has the ultimate say in everyone's fate. It can bring both doom and the fireworks of happiness, with endless contentment through shared faith. In Islam, fate or destiny is predestined.

A story about the Boy and the King, also known as the people of the Ditch:

Surah Al-Burooj of the Qur'an (paraphrased)

During a bygone era, a king beseeched the court to find a young boy of innocence for magical instruction. A young boy was called upon to gain magical wisdom. Each day, as he neared the palace court, he encountered a monk who practiced worshiping Allah. The monk's teachings about Allah had a profound impact on him, leading him to repeatedly pursue them. He felt a strong affinity for the monk.

There were times when he would arrive late for his magic lessons and spend time with a monk beforehand. The monk's dedication to Allah, rather than the magic, fascinated him. He desired to gain knowledge from the monk. They believed he was disrespectful towards the position and didn't show gratitude for the coveted palace role. He continued to acquire knowledge about Allah from the monk. In the presence of a large animal, he turned to prayer, seeking Allah's assistance, and Allah rescued him.

Quran: Surah Buruj 85:8 And they resented them not except because they believed in Allah, the Exalted in Might, the Praiseworthy,

The boy developed the power to cure blindness and assist the ill. Despite facing a colossal creature, he triumphed in victory. He informed the monk of his abilities. Upon hearing that, the boy reached his full potential in learning and received a dedication that most spend a lifetime to attain. With his belief, he gained knowledge from Allah. Upon hearing what the boy's capabilities were, the monk warned him not to reveal that he taught him about Allah.

Please don't reveal my secret. The monk made a plea to the boy. The boy promised the monk he wouldn't expose his presence to the king, aware that the king would execute him if he discovered.

The king was thrilled when the magicians informed him that the boy could perform magic. The boy had unwavering faith and couldn't tell a lie. He denied any involvement of magic and instead credited Allah for his abilities. The king and his courtiers were displeased by this. When asked about the person who taught him about Allah, the boy said it was the monk, but he couldn't recall his words to safeguard the monk. The king persisted in torturing the monk to make the boy renounce his faith. The boy persisted in his faith in Allah. Despite facing persecution, the boy remained steadfast in his faith.

The King commanded his subjects to bring him to the tallest mountain and renounce his God. In case of refusal, push him down the mountain. While the army descended the mountain, the boy made his way back to the palace. The king commanded the army to escort him to the ocean. While the army perished, the boy survived and made it back to the palace.

The king was at a loss on what to do with the boy. This boy's faith knew no bounds. If you desire to end my life, bind me to a tree and release an arrow towards me. But before you proceed, utter the name of Allah. You will kill me. Gather everyone to watch, and I will die. The king assembled everyone and announced, "In the name of Allah," I will execute this boy. The boy passed away. The king faced opposition from his subjects, while the majority held a strong belief in Allah. The little boy's belief created believers, despite knowing the king was evil.

A story makes complete sense when faith is strong. A believer's heart remains unchanged. A believer will stay connected to another believer. The believers are in harmony with their creator, and with Allah's permission, the little boy converted the city and palace to believers of faith in Allah. Nothing occurs unless Allah permits it. Full belief is necessary for believers to resonate with stories about Allah and His plans.

However, believers can be deeply impacted by them. These stories and values are meant for those with believing hearts. Paraphrasing is the only way to present Hadiths and Quranic stories.

This story is for the believers who can see that age doesn't limit belief. The boy endured many hardships from the king and his subjects. The restored faith in believers' hearts is untouchable when their faith is strong. Despite being martyred by the king, he left behind an example for those who believe that even a single word from another believer can change the heart to believe. A tainted heart cannot be convinced by the presence of mountains or seas. Every believer's heart will be touched by the story of this boy.

The farmer plants the seeds and patiently waits for the crop to sprout. He doesn't reveal the number of seeds he has planted to anyone. The outcome hinges on the crop he anticipates, and Allah determines if the seeds will grow or perish. Humans are kept in the dark about the secrets of the heart. Disbelievers advising believers is unwarranted. They will sow the seeds of mistrust among believers and wait for the harvest to wither.

With Allah's will, any heart's belief can bring forth the revival of any crop. Whom Allah wills, he guides. He understands the essence of every person. He may unexpectedly find peace, sometimes startled by happiness. Was this deserved by me? The treasures bestowed by Allah are everlasting. The beauty of sustenance given by Allah cannot be taken away. Humanity escapes the lures of Satan sooner than expected. False treasures don't endure.

Quran: Surah Nahl:16;11. He causes you to grow for you thereby olives, palm trees, grapevines, and all the fruits. Indeed, that is a sign for people who give thought.

A true believer understands the heart of another true believer. The fusion they share is their belief in Allah. Stories that touch the hearts of believers are about finding Allah. Some people never find the gem they seek in life. Faith guides believers on their life journey, offering solace beneath Allah's shelter. Numerous individuals in life aspire to work in big corporations or further their education. Some people establish large companies to gain recognition and education, travel to far-off places, and succeed in sports.

Some people engage in hobbies to achieve a work-life balance. They engage with nature, acquire new abilities, and express their creativity through art. People devote their lives to animals, specifically their pets. Animal loyalty and helplessness overwhelm them. Loyalty to Allah is first and foremost, however, they do admire the dog's loyalty. They appreciate Allah's creations but neglect the giver. They overlook the fact that Allah is the creator of everything, and all beings, including animals, are devoted to their creator.

The Story of the Dog Named Mayday:

The unwavering loyalty of this dog symbolizes the Salat. She consistently ensured the human was awakened and alerted for prayer. Observing Salat five times a day is a mandatory obligation for a Muslim. Mayday was familiar with the prayer times throughout the day. In the moments preceding the performance of Salat, the dog let the humans know it was time to pray. It can be observed that her purpose, as designated by Allah, is to fervently pray and serve as a source of encouragement for others to follow suit. At the appointed time for prayer, she vocalized and exhibited signs of restlessness.

Muslims would realize the significance of Salat if this story had an impact on them. She never missed the early morning prayers of Fajr. Her priority was serving Allah, not her family. Despite being old, she sticks to her routine without any alterations. She displays unwavering devotion and purity and humbly bows down during Salat.

Allah can bestow humility upon those who pray to Him as He desires. Mayday refrains from licking or giving doggie kisses. The story embodies a belief and holds truth. She emphasized the importance of Allah and the need for punctual prayer, ensuring her legacy lives on.

As a believer who reminds you of Him, she ensures you won't forget Allah. A believer believes that a person who reminds you of Allah will never be forgotten. Like Mayday, she too leaves a lasting impression as time passes, but her dedication to prayer endures.

Due to her age, she will eventually leave, but her commitment teaches us to prioritize praying to Allah. Another aspect to consider is the unwavering loyalty people have towards their pets.

She has taken a more significant role in attendance to prayer This dog displayed a strong connection with his owner, Allah. Some do not acknowledge Allah's role in their creation. And overlook the fact he is the master. Mayday's loyalty reflects Allah's love and mercy. This dog has chosen Allah as her master, not a human. Salat is a mandated gift from Allah, and even a dog like Mayday can teach humanity its importance. If this story has taught you the importance of Salat, your next Salat could mark the start of your devotion as a Muslim.

Expressing gratitude for the blessings bestowed by Allah and maintaining faith in His provision. Our objective is to exhibit loyalty and obedience to Him in all areas of our being. Those who have faith in these symbols appreciate the reminders.

Animals worship Allah, while humans remain rebellious. Allah's anger is tempered by his mercy, and he grants those who seek him a chance in return. The key to wealth, knowledge, and inner peace is seeking Allah's pleasure. Allah is the only source of true happiness and contentment. Holding on to the world and Allah in your heart is an accomplishment, and words matter only to believers.

Those who are willing to make the effort can find strength and satisfaction by having a keen eye for life's offerings and a desire to resolve differences within. Allah rewards those who try, regardless of the trials they face in this world and the next. What about those who attempt and don't succeed? There are no failures, only lessons to improve for those who try. Challenges can be transformed into triumphs through Allah's mercy. Ameen!

What causes a once green and vibrant garden to become brown and dry? The invitation of a believer who prays to Allah to another human creates a welcoming green garden for everyone. Muslims invite you to explore the garden of beliefs and understandings.

CHAPTER 13

ENTANGLEMENT WITH TRUTH VERSUS ILLUSION

Islam, as a whole, enhances the stature of its adherents and embraces a positive outlook in all spheres. It maintains an optimistic worldview as a comprehensive belief system.

The truth represents reality, whereas illusions can metamorphose into manifestations and perceptions that ultimately mold and define reality. It is possible for the power of positive thinking to bring about the manifestation and transformation of illusions into reality. Positive behavior is an essential requirement for attaining success.

The forces of energy can transform the serene process of self-discovery, whether undertaken individually or within a group, into an actuality. The forces of energy strive for equilibrium.

Followers of the faith firmly hold the belief that Islam extends its reach like a radiant sun, surpassing the darkness of an eclipsed sky. One cannot fail to notice the luminosity of Islam if one comprehends it. For those with an eye for beauty, its manifestation is evident and pronounced.

A relationship with truth brings bliss, whereas one with deceit leads to emptiness. It strengthened faith through companionship between Muslims seeking solidarity. Sincerity, responsibility, and characteristics deepen the exchange of trustworthiness.

This deeper understanding contributes to strong, long-lasting relationships. The relationships formed by superficiality differ from spirituality.

The false notion that Islam is strict is simply not true; it is a balance with life that complements life. A mind with blinders cannot comprehend and understand explanations if one does not understand them.

There is nothing more beautiful than human romance, which is created by devotion and belief. This type of exchange brings out humans' highest qualities. Allowing them to form strong relationships through mutual understanding and respect. It is an exclusive connection that transcends uniformity and seeks the same creator, Allah.

Allah has provided companions to those who share the same search. Prophets who held beliefs received the best. This holds true since many Prophets and caliphs of Muslim history married believing women and men.

These companions can help each other in matters of faith and spiritual growth. Companions can also help create a supportive atmosphere. Finally, unity embodies Allah's mercy and grace. Believers trust Allah. All good actions are blessings from Allah. The bad side of humans always flares up unexpectedly.

Allah drafted the destiny for every living thing. Because of his destiny, man will lead a life filled with predetermined actions. Eventually, Allah will lead him to his destination. In a world where Allah decides destiny, where is the free will? A human picked it; Allah wrote it ahead of time. Does the master not know the heart of the humans he created? Allah will override human will. If he sees fit.

Humanity pays attention to Allah's meticulous observation. Sending for accurate observation of a believer and forgoing Satan's unimportant matters. This allows one to stay away from evil sources and focus on things that benefit them.

Following these observations will lead to a more meaningful and satisfying life. It will also help bring peace and harmony to the world.Environments are unpredictable, but man must control his sails for success. Allah's referents will have a warm relationship with an adherent.

In this society, entanglements are real.These woven threads can be of values or deceit that violates conservative principles. They are exposed through academic interventions in universities, schools and social media and see Islam as the enemy. The same fear of Islam rages in anti-Islamic rhetoric.

Time Magazine: Jan 21, 2021 — 1979. It said that more than 60,000 books were written against Islam, in a span of 150 years.

Negative books about Prophet Muhammad, written by people who do not believe in him and possess no knowledge of Islam, have been circulating, aiming to spread falsehoods and provoke Muslims. Shaded words are unnecessary in truth, as truth holds strength. The fact that the Bible is globally recognized for its historical support of divine and human writings does not imply any form of indoctrination or rhetoric except truth known to the world.While engaging in theatrical performances about Islam, they also simultaneously modify the bible.

The translators have removed the word "begotten "and say "only" Son. Muslims can not interchange the Quran. Withered branches result from altering the root. Misleading people with fabricated words installed by humans, not God, is causing them to revolt.

To clarify, "begotten" is an adjective derived from the verb "beget," which means to father or produce offspring. It is important to note that Allah, not being human, cannot have a child. This understanding challenges the beliefs of many faith followers, who may be hesitant to delve into research and confront potential misrepresentations of Abrahamic scripts, but it may also lead to future changes.

The Quran remains unchanged, and the world knows that Allah sent scriptures when creation was ready. However, the creation had to change the previous scripts due to their misalignment with lifestyles and political shifts; it is an ongoing process. Muslims and the Quran are painted as the reason for spreading Islamophobia, suggesting all faiths are equal. The direct delivery of the Quran and Islam is unparalleled, and it cannot be reiterated enough. Muslims have good relationships with all religions, but we can't overlook theological disagreements.

Bible: ESV:1:23."Behold, the virgin shall be with child, and bear a Son, and they shall call His name Immanuel," which is translated, "God with us." Matthew 1:23

Bible: KJV: John 3:16.For God so loved the world, that he gave his only begotten Son, that whosoever believed in him should not perish, but have everlasting life. The new versions have removed the word begotten.

Quran: Surah Iklas: 112:3."He begets not. (No other form of existence has ever originated from Him, thus, there is no other.) Nor was He begotten."

Islam's fearlessness is seen as a waste of time by those who embark on staging lies against it. Its popularity did not come from changing venues.

The elephant in Islam poses a threat that exceeds their capabilities. There was no fear of any faith among Muslims. Despite self-identifying as Muslims, their understanding of Islamic values and knowledge is lacking. For those who don't find their faith of importance. Young people who are incoherent are easily influenced by scandalous appeals. The world is rapidly changing and dealing with societies without clear disciplines.

Morality is challenged by falsified presentations. The history of tampered scriptures before the Quran is crucial for Muslims and non-Muslims to learn from. In a corrupt society that tampered with earlier scriptures, it is unlikely to recognize its flaws, allowing for the promotion of an evil methodology under the guise of freedom.Both Muslims and non-Muslims should learn this history in order to make informed decisions; the fear of change is the dilemma for those who avoid facing the truth.

The values and beliefs of emerging Muslims may become disconnected due to this phenomenon. This colored society includes the values and beliefs held by their peers and pressures of life. The risk of forgetting traditional Islamic values is high, as they may be replaced by contemporary, secular lifestyles that oppose tranquility. Furthermore, it's important to mention that within the Islamic community, there is a group of Muslims who cannot express their views due to limited education and literacy levels of Islamic doctrine.

While facts may blur into fiction or reality, the distinctions in worship remain, yet the sublime contentment lies in knowing Allah as one.

Diwali is a highly celebrated holiday for Hindus. Diwali, the festival of lights, illuminates the world where Hindus live, symbolizing the triumph of light over darkness.Happy lit celebrations and food friendship has been shared by humanity for decades.

The contrast with theology remains unchanged by the theme of friendship and acceptance of each other's beliefs. Both declarations of truth must be accepted and decisions made based on knowledge and the heart's calling to live in worship of Allah or whoever one chooses to worship, proclaiming their own truth. The Quran contains unaltered words from Allah, not from a man.

Every era of mankind has worked to combat darkness. Hinduism, a diverse and wide-ranging system of thought, includes metaphysics and mythology. Its special days are marked by exotic celebrations and an array of vibrant colors, promoting prosperity and well-being. While God is the central focus in all faiths, this religion also involves worshiping humans as deities.

The mythology of this ancient faith is undeniable, as it continues to exist and friendships persist. Seeking serenity, as any faith does the previous faiths accept humans as Gods, allowing them to display their greatness. Islam differs from other religions by rejecting the idea of humans as Gods, while Christianity also incorporates colorful festivities inspired by ancient cultures.

Islam connected self-cleansing of inner spirituality and rejected the notion of humans as Gods or sacred beings except Allah. The power of humanity lies in acknowledging darkness to value lightness, while the pursuit of peace amidst suffering involves exploring various ideologies and making individual decisions to attain personal tranquility.

Millennials and Gen Z are knowledgeable about academia and love to travel.They are commonly referred to as the first fully "digitally natives" Islam should be introduced to their age group and Muslims. Depending on their environment and guidance, some were directed by parents, others were self-directed. They will have a greater advantage in living and experiencing life at its best than any previous generation. This generation will be the most educated in decades, particularly in countries that previously undervalued education.

Moving forward, investing in education replaces job abundance without a high school diploma. Society's moral compass is lost, particularly for those easily corrupted by peer pressures. Nevertheless, independence distinguishes itself through its emphasis on self-care and collectivism, while still valuing individuality to protect one's own interests.

From a materialistic standpoint, the commitment to Islamic values may not always align with a collective society, as some academically educated and well-traveled individuals from the next generation are interested in exploring their faith, while others are satisfied with their early teachings during formative years.

Time investment and consistency are crucial for optimal exploration in any endeavor. In collective thinking, no comment has significance as each person possesses an individual mind. People from all societies are intrigued by Islam and many adhere to its principles, while others who lack knowledge of its teachings opt for a different approach. Those who possess knowledge flourish on a wide path, continuously increasing their understanding.

These settings promote a feeling of patriotic loyalty and demonstrate a notable change in values and admiration. The diamond era shouldn't be seen as a negative phenomenon. Muslims are now in an era of revealing the truth of Islam, just like during Europe's dark ages when Islam had its golden age. This time, it will shine as the diamond age of Islam. The greater the backlash, the more people join the faith of Islam. Humanity's search for truth leads to Islam, the faith of Muslims - one submission, one God.

Possessing self-assurance serves as an indication of effective parenting. Individuals who receive attention during their delicate formative years exhibit resistance to the evil that society embodies. They transform into achievers, rather than failures.

Prophet Muhammad encountered various challenges from birth onwards, however, he was greatly nurtured even amidst frequent relocations during his youth due to circumstances.

Allah orchestrated many trials to test and enhance his inner strength, while also exposing him to the world. The path to victory is open to all, regardless of unconventional family backgrounds. Their origins lie in the act of seeing life through a specific viewpoint.

If Allah shows mercy, He gives faith with endurance, stability, and teachings of truth. Those who succeed without faith often turn to a higher power and seek redemption later on.

Expanding one's perspectives in this world can be effective, yet embarking on a narrow path without the presence of Allah can be a challenging journey for those who compromise tranquility for duplicity.

Is this the perfect time for Muslims to succeed in their roles? Did Muslims not play a significant role in Europe's emergence from the Dark Ages? During the dark ages, teaching a society without extravagance was suitable, and it remains suitable today by not imparting the unchangeable truth from the Quran and knowledgeable Muslims.

As we pursue excellence in worldly matters, let us not forget the importance of Islamic education and its numerous benefits for our society.

The voices of individuals who speak truth have a resounding impact. The Muslim community consists of educators who aim to promote truth through teaching.

Has the world not derived benefits from the accomplishments of the Muslim community and is the evidence of history not self-evident? What developments have taken place for Muslims? Our focus is on numerical growth rather than pursuing Islamic knowledge, but both are vital for human success.

To ensure stability, it is important to have a thorough knowledge of Islam from credible and knowledgeable sources. Being a Muslim in a private Catholic school abroad, learning about Christianity offers a unique perspective on the Abrahamic faiths, where the central belief in Allah as God remains consistent, without any human deities, emphasizing monotheism for a Muslim.

The only way to learn is by blending with the teachers and the environment. Growing up in a Muslim household and being educated by Muslim family and teachers, leads to a deep understanding and appreciation of Islam. Education primarily originates from a fascination with faith and a quest for knowledge from various sources. The Quran is the ultimate source of direction.

Some Muslim parents exhibit unwavering confidence in their faith by sending their children to Catholic schools, despite Islam's prohibition of human worship. It is preferable to introduce the youth to diverse faiths instead of isolating them.

The wealthy have always prioritized education due to the opportunities it provides. Education is invaluable and cannot be taken away. Knowledge is power and should be pursued to the fullest extent. Muslims consider education valuable, and the Quran is regarded as limitless knowledge. The Quran is not just read once for an examination, but it is a lifelong study until death. It is an education from Allah that holds immeasurable worth.

The optimal approach to comprehend Islam is via exposure and engagement with diverse religious beliefs. Venerating mortals differs from venerating a solitary God Allah. Does mortal worship encompass the adoration of a human or a God? Neither of them practices monotheism. Jesus never gave his disciples instructions to worship him. He adhered to the Abrahamic faith.

Islam is a guiding force for its followers. Nevertheless, without fear of expanding one's knowledge and journeying to different shores.In this society, the age of adulthood is established at eighteen, while senior citizen status is granted at sixty two. In countries with a history of less than three centuries, the legal drinking age for alcohol is twenty one. Age is frequently associated with the occurrence of mistakes.

In Islam, the burden of responsibility is placed upon individuals upon reaching puberty, while the onset of old age is marked by shifts in hair color, behavior, and self-discipline.

Holding those who have conducted themselves righteously accountable for their guidance. Irrespective of one's manner of living, the passage of time on this planet unveils the narrative through physicality, yet those who live virtuously are characterized by their comportment, not their chronological age.

Society's ambiguity in defining adulthood and seniority arises from a lack of comprehension of bodily indicators rather than dependence on chronological age. In Islam, individuals who exhibit signs of puberty and engage in adult behavior are regarded as adults. With the passage of time, the visible impact of aging becomes evident on human faces.

A person's lifestyle can unveil virtuous and wicked deeds, enabling believers to distinguish the pious from the wayward. Those who are misguided will always find faults, as the lack of accomplishments can be perceived as a form of self-oppression. The ultimate happiness in this world lies in obtaining both.

Noah, the esteemed Prophet, had a remarkably long lifespan of nine hundred and fifty years. Prophet Muhammad passed away at the age of sixty three after fulfilling his mission with the Quran. According to him, the lifespan of my people ranges from sixty to seventy years, anything exceeding that is classified as extended life. Muslims engage in prayer to Allah in order to avoid imposing burdens on others.

Muslims possess the capacity to excel in the realm of education, and now is their moment to radiate in this current era. They must exhibit unwavering dedication to spreading the benefits of understanding Islam. Truth surpasses humans in every facet, providing benefits to humanity.

Individuals who unjustly accuse Islam for misfortunes cannot serve as educators, whereas Muslims possess the ability to educate the worldwide populace. There is no more opportune moment than the present to exhibit a positive attitude towards Islamic beliefs and those who hold contrary viewpoints.

Embracing a pseudo-religion that advocates for slavery undermines both morality and balanced values. Does it not constitute slavery to manipulate minds into perceiving freedom while depriving them of their precious time in service to the system?

Modernity is frequently perceived as synonymous with autonomy, but this society is predominantly characterized by collective thought. A Muslim is inherently granted rights from birth, while the corrupt society disassembles the fundamental bonds of the uninformed. Failure is an inescapable consequence when success is attained through falsehood and deception.

This, too, will be unsuccessful. Egypt adopted Islam as the empire of the Pharaoh fell. Authorities have been abusing their power and exerting undue influence, resulting in a persistent problem. To tackle this problem, we require enhanced education and awareness regarding the truth and its importance. Islam strikes a delicate balance between individualism and collectivism, adhering to the boundaries set by Allah. It should provide individuals with the ability to confidently voice their truth without worrying about backlash. The propagation of Islam serves as evidence of its lack of apprehension towards the truth. They categorize Islam as a malignant disease. However, cancer is exceedingly widespread in this society. Although cancer claims lives, Islam perseveres.

Death or birth are not experienced by Allah. If he did, he would not be Allah. The truth is held by Islam, and nothing can alter that fact. Islam will remain alive despite any challenges it may face, as Allah is eternal. Muslims don't need to protect Islam.

It provides protection for Muslims. The situation is not reversed. Despite the presence of social media, political fear and chaos persist. Disciplinary actions are a recognized part of Islam's inherent success, according to Islam. This will be the last and only faith left in the world before the end of time. Discipline plays a crucial role in succession.

Salat five times a day is a God-instituted discipline. A successful life begins with preparation and ends with success. Attending once a week to a church, synagogue, or mosque is a wonderful gesture of continued effort. During prayer time, a Muslim child asked his mother why we can't be like other faiths. Mother replied, "Why don't you look like everyone else?".

Islam is not like other faiths; its face is dictated and choreographed for Muslims. The best performance in showdowns that hold the best awards. From the moment 'We' created Adam and Eve, this is the sublime truth. One worship one God, Allah. But by colluding with false impressions and secular mixing, they impose falsehoods.

While Islam can listen to the views of others when it comes to secular ideas, as long as they do not alter the stance Muslims have towards Islam, there is no restriction on hearing their opinions. During the Prophet's lifetime, the Prophet of Islam was able to build a very successful relationship with both believers and disbelievers as well as people from other faiths.

Living in a diverse society, one cannot avoid hearing the concerns of those living there. It is important to keep in mind that Islam is a state in itself, with its laws, but following the standard laws of the country is mandatory as well. Clearly, this statement states that any country's laws must be followed by its citizens. However, the question arises: how come Islamic laws do not need to be adhered to by Muslims? In the absence of understanding one's faith, one becomes incomplete. This is a disservice to the religion's true teachings and a violation of its values.

It is imperative to ensure that the original texts are respected and understood in their original context. Ultimately, this is how we can ensure Islam is not misrepresented by people of no knowledge and its true message is shared.

Islam is a unified religion, yet various sects are emerging and creating nations and brotherhoods within the Islamic community. With little understanding of Islam, they try to elevate themselves as Gods. The uprooted changes proposed in advent for a rising culture go against the threshold of Islam and are not acceptable.

One Quran that unites all Muslims. Non-Muslims can use this approach to identify specific behaviors or select individuals who closely align with their objections to beliefs.

The evil epidemic moves from the West to the East. Social media, for the uninformed, is seen as the gospel of truth, causing confusion and misunderstanding about religion, particularly Islam.

To prevent the truth from being lost, Muslims should stay committed to their faith and the teachings of the Quran. Educating Muslims in the right settings about the truth about their faith in order to ensure that the Quran's teachings are maintained and practiced.

To combat misinterpretation, it is essential to promote an understanding of the religion rooted in its core values. Rather than being shaped by extremist views. Throughout history, Western society has used various threads that don't show the same material.

Islam is not in combat with anyone. The opposition, however, controls fear's visual effects and nature. As numbers increase and more people join Islam, the updated numbers state that 77% of newly converted converts to Islam come from Christianity, and 19% are from non-religion.

It's crucial to keep in mind that everyone can choose and pursue their own path. Stay consistent in stating the truth. When choices fall outside Islam, rely on divine judgment. Being truthful could make you a potential witness. If Muslim children go off course, their mothers will always correct them. Her children remain hers regardless of their age.

In these societies, there is a common age bracket where children become equals, which sets boundaries for parents and disrespects them. Islam does not set an age limit for disrespecting parents. Disobedience restricts peace and enjoyment, making it harmful at the highest level.

If Allah created everyone as he did Adam and Eve, there would be no need for mothers. He assigned women to carry the child after fertilization with male sperm. Allah opted for mothers to bear children instead of creating humanity effortlessly, like Adam and Eve from mud. Allah intended for men and women to create families and establish permissible relationships.

The plan aims to improve the standard of living and promote family values. Mary alone bore Jesus, conceived by the angel's blowing a spirit into her garment by Allah's permission. Like any mother, she carried him and gave birth. Allah, the only God, does not beget or die.

Quran: Surah Hijr: 15:26. Surely We brought man into being out of dry ringing clay which was wrought from black mud.

Quran: Surah Sajdah: 32:7.Who perfected everything which He created and began the creation of man from clay.

Jesus, who was born of a virgin, did not regard Allah as his father. As a mortal, he possessed a mother, lest he remain an unseen deity for eternity, yet Jesus was tangible, engaged in conversation, walked, slept, ate, had human necessities, and was denied by Jews.

No mortal on this planet would dare challenge the divine presence of Allah and take his life. If Moses, a revered Prophet, was unable to tolerate his presence, it becomes evident that a clear distinction exists between a divine radiance and human rebellion. However, marriage can be fated for someone and they may not experience it in their lifetime, but illicit relationships are not considered permissible actions.

There are no limits to what Allah can do. Jesus demonstrated reverence towards his mother and resisted societal influences. There was an observation of Prophetic activity during that era. Those who exhibit defiance will be met with consequences. Jesus exhibited human traits upon his birth due to God's eternal nature, which encompasses neither birth nor death.

Quran: Surah Maryam: 19:30.The child cried out: "Verily I am Allah's servant. He has granted me the Book and has made me a Prophet.

Quran: Surah Maryam :19:32.and has made me dutiful to my mother.[20a] He has not made me oppressive, nor bereft of God's blessings.

Quran: Surah Maryam:19:33. Peace be upon me the day I was born, and the day I will die, and the day I will be raised up alive."

In a manner reminiscent of the tale of Jesus, Mary was entrusted with carrying a child by Allah and brought forth a Prophet. In his infancy, Allah granted him permission to speak and show his mother's integrity. Pointing at him was the extent of her actions. From the moment he was born, he displayed reverence for his mother and spoke eloquently from infancy.

Quran: Surah Maryam: 19;29.Thereupon Mary pointed to the child. They exclaimed: "How can we speak to one who is in the cradle, a mere child?"[20]

Quran: Surah Ibrahim: 14;22.When the Judgement has been passed, Satan will say to them, God made you a true promise; I too made you promises, but I failed you.

Quran: Surah Nisa: 4:76."Those who believe fight in the cause of Allah,.

Quran: Surah Taubah:9:74.If they repent, it will be best for them; but if they turn back (to their evil ways), Allah will punish them with a grievous penalty in this life and in the ...

Those who undergo transformation pursue the path illuminated by light and escape from the shadows post-transformation. Consequences are a result of the choices made. The decision to embrace Islam is a thrilling transformation, yet remaining oblivious to its teachings and associating with the same group is equally dreadful. The price of hypocrisy is steep in Islam.

Mingling with lies when the truth suddenly becomes avoidable, and choices to accept Islam become personal. Instead of imposing, they accepted free choice. Those who converted to Islam left hope for new converts and Muslims. Muslims consider Omar Bin Khattab as an example of strength as a convert. An over achiever who left his mark for converts to know what change means. Most dedicated and disciplined in their faith, Omar and his companions set an example of faithfulness and commitment to Islam. They encouraged the truth and their demeanor made others accept Islam and live in line with its teachings. Omar and his companions spread Islam's message. Satan feared him. He was walking on the opposite road when he encountered his path.

Anyone with this name has a heavy load to carry and lives to a fraction of his standards will succeed. This would be an example of a person of profound faith and dedication to his religion who can inspire other Muslims. By carrying his name, others can strive to live up to his example and remember the high standards he set for himself and others. Omar (RadiAllah hu Anhu) May Allah be pleased with him and is remembered as an outstanding leader and teacher. He is a symbol of religious devotion and a reminder to Muslims of the importance of pursuing a life of faith and service. His legacy is one of strength and courage in the face of adversity.

This world is currently encountering legacies of a remarkable individual who embodies bravery, tenacity, justice, and faith, all while remaining modest and humble in his self-expression. His dedication to being a leader was evident through his unwavering commitment to following the laws and rules of Allah, as well as the teachings of Prophet Muhammad. What Surah is obligatory for a Muslim to recite during their Salat? The recitation of (Surah Fatiha) in every Salat signifies the start of the Quran and is crucial for completing a Salat.

Whose name is mentioned in every Salat? Prophet Abraham and Prophet Muhammad are mentioned in the (Surahs) recited in every (Salat). Abraham is acknowledged as the father of all Prophets, with Prophet Muhammad serving as the final Prophet. Muslims mention these two names in every Salat, acknowledging the elevated status granted by Allah, incomparable to any worldly pursuit.

How is it possible for a Muslim to be unaware of these delicacies? In light of Omar"s education from the last of the Prophets, how can he neglect to prioritize the propagation of Islam in his very being? The strong man demonstrated profound humility in the presence of Allah. Those Muslims in their roles are advocates of Islam, transformed from opponents to exemplars, becoming the best for the world to learn from.

Omar Bin Khattab was not just an ordinary man, but a powerful advocate of the simplicity of Islam who fearlessly spoke the truth. Satan understood that the man who possessed the truth had the potential to inflict greater harm upon him than he could upon a believer. Subsequently, he assumed the role of the second Caliph of the Muslim world. This job held great significance to him as he spread Islam across multiple continents. He displayed unwavering honesty in his rulings.

His dedication can demonstrate his passion as Muslim convert. The upstanding attitudes and unwavering commitment to truth, coupled with the absence of fear towards humans except Allah, are indicative of Muslim identity. Mere self-identification as a Muslim does not adequately reflect the actions required to embody the teachings of Islam. Making mistakes does not equate to renouncing Islam, but rather serves to fortify a believer's conviction upon their return.

He is an inspiration to many, and his name carries values of courage, faith, and service. His legacy reminds us of the power of determination and the importance of being true to his beliefs. From Prophet Muhammad to all the Caliph's of those times, they were Islam's viceroys. And their stories and names can be told for generations to come. The hardships and trials all stood tall, battling to expose the truth Muslims supported the royals of faith, Islam's truth followers.

Islam proves its longevity, no matter the circumstances. Islam's adversaries have remained and will continue to persist, but fighting against a faith ordained by Allah is futile. It is the only belief system that will endure due to its unalterable nature and monotheistic principles.

Pew Research states that in 2075, Islam will be the largest religion in the world.

Mankind yearns for ultimate truth. It is crucial to receive education on the veracity of this faith. In non-religious environments or through manipulation by religious leaders, it becomes exceedingly difficult to resist the allure and intellectual depth of Islam. Those who seek the approval of disbelievers while compromising their own beliefs are easily influenced.

Numerous territories eagerly anticipate the pinnacle of cultivation, while countless individuals yearn to sow life's finest seeds in those territories. In a gradual manner on a global scale. Those who experience the pinnacle of joy will derive the greatest pleasure from the ascent. Those who haven't witnessed the aerial perspective have never truly tasted bliss. As Pharaoh ascended to great heights, arrogance struck with even greater force.

Identifying yourself as a Muslim requires education from the right sources, reading the Quran, and understanding it. One who is unaware of Allah's disobedience will always seek disbelievers' comfort. Their treachery and insidiousness, along with resentment. In spite of disbelief, humans have a passion for humanity and animals. Faith is embedded in human nature, just have to look for it.

Quran: Surah Baqarah: 2:9.They seek to deceive Allah and the believers, yet they only deceive themselves, but they fail to perceive it.

Believers instinctively know right and wrong. The aura he feels is both favorable and evil. Being deceived by disbelievers is not plausible, as the aura is negative and alarming. A believer will always be conscious of his actions even if he succumbs to world temptations. Eventually. Strive to do good and be a role model for others. Islam emphasizes that a company's mark is an individual's mark. In the school of indoctrination, Allah directs and educates believers.What better teacher could a man ask for? This regiment school is repetitive.

Muslims read the same book, the Quran, over and over, pray Salat (ritual prayer), and worship. Muslims commit to improving their minds, bodies, and souls. Gratitude for the abundant peace from Quran readings and Salat ritual prayers. Islam is a comprehensive way of life, offering solutions to life's problems and promoting self-balance.

The Arabic Quran possesses a divine melodic rhythm bestowed by Allah. The Quran does not possess the qualities of singing or a song. Given their lack of familiarity with Arabic and Quranic languages, they could confuse it with singing.

The act of listening to the Quran unveils it as an invitation from Allah, be it conveyed directly or through a believer.In order to reestablish comprehension and tranquility within oneself, one must consistently partake in active listening. Peace cannot be acquired solely through the act of reading another book.

No human can alter the Quran. The Quran has a precise and concise cadence at the end of each verse. Allah's precise transparency is showcased through modulation and syntax in each verse.It's impossible for a writer to imitate another writer, so how can anyone modify a biblical book and expect others to accept it as truth?

Believers and non-believers play different roles when it comes to the validation and dissemination of truth. Believers often hold steadfast to their beliefs, using them as a foundation for their understanding of the world. They may impart valuable lessons to others by sharing their experiences and insights. However, when lies are mixed with the truth, it casts doubt on the authenticity of the information being presented.

This can lead to confusion and skepticism among individuals who are seeking the truth. Non-believers, on the other hand, approach information with a healthy level of skepticism and critical thinking. They question the validity of claims, seeking evidence and logical reasoning to support or refute them. Their role is to challenge beliefs and ensure that the truth is not distorted or manipulated. By engaging in open dialogue and exchanging perspectives, both believers and non-believers contribute to the pursuit of knowledge and the discovery of truth.

Compassion, tenderness, responses, glances, and voice communication are all essential aspects of human traits. Helping a fallen child, or older adult, or listening to a sorrowful tale all fall into compassion's rites. Islam demonstrates compassion towards others. Islam exemplifies consistent traits as directions. The absence of kindness leads to the absence of faith. In taking this action, we progress further towards unraveling the authentic nature of humanity.

Muslim but prideful people sometimes don't care if his family does not call out to Allah, but paying attention to them and calling out to them becomes prevalent. They are Islam deviants. However, it is essential to remember that Islam teaches humility and compassion towards others, regardless of their faith or beliefs. Engaging in simple acts of kindness, such as smiling at a stranger, can have a profound impact on someone's day.

This small gesture of warmth and acceptance can break down barriers and foster a sense of unity and understanding among individuals. It aligns with the teachings of Islam, which emphasize the importance of treating others with kindness and respect. Therefore, it is crucial for Muslims to not only prioritize their own spiritual journey but also actively engage with and uplift those around them, spreading human care, kindness and positivity in the process.

Small acts of kindness can create a ripple effect that spreads far and wide. Or jolt negativity in the same manner, causing a ripple effect of destruction. These societies have been manipulating for decades and propagating fear of truth.

Such issues need to be addressed and tackled to ensure everyone's safety and well-being. These societies shut down the truth, but Islam is clear that complete faith dictates self-awareness and accountability to oneself. Isn't that the premise of the world?

In Islam, justification is not fighting the weak or harming civilians, children, animals, or trees. Current stakes the strong are attacking the weak and destroying nations out of greed and desire for land. Retaliation is inherent in human nature, but displacement of people and land has occurred even before the Jinns disrespected the lands and humans were created. Similar or worse circumstances are occurring, but Allah knew that those who pray to Allah would eventually assume the position. During Muslim rule, prosperous cities, including Jerusalem, flourished, suggesting the potential for a better world if Muslim countries unite.

Omar Bin Khattab received the keys to Jerusalem without any resistance due to the Muslims' reputation for fairness and commitment to justice. They embodied honor and character while accomplishing significant milestones. Can a flawed character effectively rule? It's a shame for Muslims to observe injustice without assisting the oppressed. The world can be explored through human migration, but safeguarding it is our duty.

Joining Muslim countries to help the weak and oppressed is the only alternative. Educated Muslims speak to justify truth, not lies. Orthodox Jews are advocating for justice to prevent the unlawful seizure of land and property. Oppression of the heart is not standing up for the weak; stand for truth as humans, not just as Muslims. Understanding the importance of reminders for Muslims has become necessary for the education of Muslims and humanity.

No one can learn from societies that interpret lies as truth. Islam cannot accept these scenarios. In order to portray Islam as backward, manipulative deceivers employ conventional lies.

The Prophet's prediction has come true, leading to divisions and sects within his people, including the (Sunni) and (Shia) split, causing a misalignment in the faith of Islam. Neglecting Islam gives advantage to prowlers, who use divisions among Muslims to weaken nations.

Non-landowners have been confiscating land for centuries, but Islam emphasizes fair fights and cannot be imposed on the weak. The Evangelicals, seeking salvation, confront hypocrisy while others displace the rightful in search of lands to call home. These events foreshadow the end times, where the fair and just will prevail.

Those who bow to Allah will rule, and justice will serve humanity. To know whom to join is crucial, as winners are those who embody character, truth, endurance, piety, and the demands of their creator. Muslims should not be fooled into joining forces and transforming it into a catastrophic error. The task of Muslims is to join forces with Muslim countries and help the world emerge from the dark ages.

Muslims, can use voice to spread justice and fight against oppression, rejecting evil and standing up for the oppressed, with the hope of a brighter future for humanity.

The voice of a fearless Muslim stands for truth when it is the only voice. Those who lack control over their own lives shouldn't have the power to take lives. The martyred Muslims are still alive, while the oppressors who disregard faith are spiritually dead.

Let not the voices of humans suppress the voice of truth, as Allah has granted us the ability to speak and write. When Allah mutes a voice, no other voice can be heard until He permits the voice of truth to resound, even if you must stand alone. Let the voice be heard. Muslims prioritize the truth and live by it, undeterred by those who sow division and support the oppression of the vulnerable.

Such lies of hypocrites and greed mongers malign Islam's justified and progressive teachings. The best policy is to expose the truth at all times. Strive to reject and refute lies and promote truth.

They represent backward eras in fake modernity. Genuine kindness heals and brings people together. Kindness is a sign of true faith and humanity.

Secular pseudo-lifestyles also offer kindness, since humanity is born with it. Kindness connects people. Respect does not require monetary compensation or faith, but only sincerity. Kindness shows that we are all connected and can thrive together.Globally, truth prevails over lies. They wouldn't try so hard to alter the truth if they didn't fear it. It is for this reason that they focus on false interpretations and make accessing the truth difficult.

Pseudo-society and the religious establishment want people to remain silent on questions. As Islam will not regress, both agendas are unsuited to the Islamic context. Regardless of the decade, it remains progressive and balanced.It is appropriate to question Islam. Allah advises us to read and ponder before accepting rather than blindly. Blind faith would never run to darkness after light if the truth was evident.

In order to spread Islam's true teachings,voice deceptions.A Muslim cannot forefront truth. Isn't it amazing how passionate and caring Allah is to send humans the Book of Life? It brings pleasure, peace, and education. What makes a Muslim not want to learn from a believer? It is clear in the Quran.

Disbelievers should not teach Allah's book to believers. Teaching others and showing their skills and sharing is a Muslim tradition. The teachings of Muslims have been supported by historical evidence, proving their impact on the world. Semitic languages, such as Hebrew and Arabic, sometimes share the same cuisine. While sharing and caring are common traits, they are far apart on many other fronts.

As Muslims, we are obligated to reciprocate Islam's truth. Individuals and the world around them, human actions can profoundly affect them. As an honorable character, man should act to meet his deepest needs.Islam demands respect for trees and nature. They also worship Allah. Ignorant people ignore life's intricate details. Intense lies often undermine human morale when a man focuses on financial security.

For decades, man has dominated this world with materialism and power. Because of their greed and treachery, they became accustomed to ill health within themselves. Could one survive with neither too much nor too little? Islam brings balance by ensuring that each person's destiny does not affect others. Humanity has a responsibility for all living creatures, as nature cannot speak for itself and humans have been given more by Allah. Water waste is prohibited in Islam, as well as the reverence for the earth. Islam prohibits waste.

Allah has a strong dislike for pride and arrogance. An attitude of pride and arrogance often leads to disrespect and ungratefulness. The earth humans walk on cannot be destroyed by them. The earth will soon assert its rights over humans.

The Quran: Surah Isra: 17:37. Do not walk arrogantly on the earth. You cannot crack the earth or reach the height of the mountains.

The conflict of man's hope should be addressed in human communication. Prophet Muhammad sought answers during a drought on the Arabian Peninsula. It was the rise of another empire, not the collapse, that brought about the harsh climate. The faith of Islam. Paganism needed to be halted. The belief in a natural, internal force that guides humanity towards a single God (Allah) is becoming increasingly popular. The Muslim population is on the rise, with an increasing number of people embracing Islam. It has a subscriber base of around 2 billion people. The numbers are continuously rising on a daily basis and might not be exact.

In its faith, Islam considers the entirety of the universe. Islam entrusts humans with the environment. Humans are forbidden from wasting or destroying anything and disrespecting the universe. This loan will be questioned by Allah if it causes harm to human health. It is also imperative to care for their material interests, in addition to their care of self.

Greed versus peace in this world has destroyed the climate with superficial interests seeking to harm health. Harming nature raises questions about humanity in Islam.Building high-rise buildings by cutting down trees is the world's approach. Even the trees will protest to Allah about humanity. To attend to everyone, Prophet Muhammad leaned on a tree. Once a pulpit was constructed, Prophet Muhammad stopped delivering sermons by the tree.

The tree wept in longing for him. He soothed it by gently rubbing his hand against it. Omar bin Khattab reported it. In the eyes of disbelievers, the idea of inanimate objects speaking may seem absurd or like Muslim fantasies. Allah's miracles are for the believers, not the truth deniers. By straying, they miss out on life-changing stories. The purpose of Prophet Muhammad's arrival on earth was significant.

Allah has a purpose for everything He sends. There are no accidents in Islam, as it believes in the absence of coincidences. It is fortunate that humans, animals, and jinns comprehend the significance of this Prophet and the sunnah - his ways and practices that he left behind. It is unfortunate for those who do not learn about Prophet Muhammad. Lengthy friendships without progress can be detrimental. New friendships can bring a breath of fresh air, improving and revitalizing stagnant areas of life. Allah has the authority to send individuals as He sees fit, according to His own timing.

Understanding the significance of gifts is a gift for a believer. While evil may take years to achieve its objectives, the damage it inflicts is beyond imagination. The process took years to complete and did not happen overnight. In their pursuit of fighting climate change, they created weapons out of greed and a sense of superiority, aiming to destroy the universe. In prehistoric times, men fought with bows and arrows or engaged in fair fights. They relied on elephants, horses, and camels for transportation. Islam does not allow fighting against the weak. If the opponent is unarmed, one must lay down their weapon. It is evil to be excessively proud and ruthless.

The progress of technology has brought about both positive and negative impacts on human life. With the advancement of gunpowder explosives, dangerous attacks began utilizing the power of the mind to destroy humanity and the universe. The presence of harmful sources is causing climate change and pollution, which are detrimental to human health. Cancer, lung diseases, heart conditions, depression, and various other illnesses. The universe is being affected at the same time. Some take pride in their military capabilities and cache of weapons of mass destruction.

Certain nations have higher rankings in terms of military and weapons. The greed of Western and Asian countries leads to competitive destruction and preparation. Allah's strike will overpower the evil and manipulative sources, showcasing chaos and destruction as his exquisite mastery. Humans have intentionally caused the destruction of both the universe and themselves.

Human evil and natural causes are also credited for the increase. There have also been civilians who have died and suffered, but ultimately Allah is the judge. As long as greed exists, it is impossible to separate humans from the environment. Globally, there is a scarcity of water and air pollution is a pressing issue. To combat drought and climate change, water conservation is crucial. Interestingly, country clubs possess vast expanses of land for recreational purposes, improved real estate, and a more pleasant environment.

These country clubs allocate water resources to maintain lush green grass for golfers, while residents are required to adhere to water restrictions. Unfortunately, water shortages are on the rise while golf courses consume significant amounts of water. Some affluent individuals utilize golf as a status symbol or for business transactions, while others view it as a sport. The concern lies not in the game itself, but in the lack of water recycling on every golf course. Allah has provided humanity with the benefits of the sea and oceans. He made it clear 1400 years ago that Islam does not tolerate waste, including water.

Not everyone has access to clean water. The world requires unity to conserve water, even for those who have none. Humans become dehydrated without water. 1400 years ago, Islam alerted us to this environmental issue. Islam places importance on the environment, self-discipline, and company. Living in better conditions is attainable for those who strive for it, without any conflict. Functionality can only be affected by wasting. Flooding is widespread, and the issue of water scarcity is worsening.

Farmers suffer from water scarcity caused by overpriced and corrupt resources, limited usage, and inadequate supply. Crops and cattle dying cause markets to become overpriced and survival more challenging. The act of Prophets growing crops and caring for livestock established the foundation for human's bond with nature. Destroying nature and wasting water comes with a cost. These warnings about the last days have been heard by humans many times, as Allah offers chances to change, but the outcome is already known to him.

Quran: Surah Nahl :16:14.And He it is Who has subjected the sea that you may eat fresh fish from it and bring forth ornaments from it that you can wear.

Quran:: Surah Anbiya: 21:30. Do the disbelievers not realize that the heavens and earth were ˹once˺ one mass, then We split them apart? 1 And We created from water every living thing.

Quran: Surah Rum: 30;12. On that Day when the Hour will come to pass,[14] the criminals shall be dumbfounded.

Quran: Surah Anam verse 2, it is he who created you from clay, then decided a term—a term determined by him. Yet you doubt.

Quran: Surah Nisa 4:27 And it is Allah's will to turn to you in grace, but those who follow their desires wish to see you deviate entirely. ˹From Allah's way.

The tangible components of a mind can be influenced by external forces or companies. The offsetting of spirituality fails to capture its duality. In today's society, seclusion is just a hand span away, whether through social media or mischief. The search of a human for anything he desires is an arm's length to satisfy or corrode the soul.

Trusting Allah surpasses relying on a multitude of disbelievers. The key to inner peace lies in eliminating negativity. Everyone, regardless of faith, faces obstacles in a world that encompasses both good and evil. Prophet Muhammad, the world leader, had adversaries.

How can a believer not consider Satan and his followers as the biggest enemies? Caution is required when dealing with (astaghfar) as the Quran presents numerous surahs daily. If a world without enemies existed, reflection on the surahs wouldn't be necessary. Logic is a fundamental aspect of Islam and other faiths, where good and evil coexist. Evil can be found in surprising proximity. Finding the truth is an internal search that leads to Allah's friendship.

Quran: Surah Furqan 25:28 Oh woe to me! I wish I had not taken that one as a friend.

Allah gave certain people a mystical power that is challenging to comprehend. The supplicant and claimant joined the petitioner in the search, all seeking the same outcome. It affects belief, respect, and obedience through a sincere appeal to Allah. The supplicant and claimant sought the intercession of the petitioner, hoping to gain favor from Allah. The petitioner had the power to intercede with Allah on behalf of those in need.

It was a divine gift given to a select few, and it was a sign of Allah's immense mercy. People who pray for others ask Allah on behalf of others such as parents praying for their children or the Prophet of Islam asking for mercy for his people.Spirituality and faith are the foundation of this appeal.

Allah can grant a friend (the Khareen) that fulfills his dualistic needs. The company controls the balance between deception and acceptance, good and evil. It can be used in different scenarios, including personal, religious, and family contexts. The religion of humanity lies in friendship and the environment we embrace.

Symbolic differences exist between light and darkness. The Quran asserts that the Earth is the central point around which the sun and moon revolve. Motion occurs at specific intervals. The Quran has taught science valuable lessons, despite not being a science book. It was the creator who made all of this accessible for exploration by man. What is the mechanism for the sun''s rotation?

The Quran clarifies. Humans discovered that the sun rotates on its axis. The Quran already conveyed this knowledge to Muslims. However, man discovered it at a later time. Through extensive research, they found that it completes one rotation on its axis every 27 days. It informs mankind about planetary movements. Celestial bodies in space, including Earth, rotate on their axis. Earth's rotation on its axis is also responsible for the changing seasons and the movement of the stars across the sky. Astronomers have studied the movement of the stars and planets for centuries, trying to understand how the universe works.

Quran: Surah Anbiya 21:33 And it is he who created the night and the day and the sun and the moon; all in an orbit are swimming.

Quran: Surah Yaseen 36:40 It is not allowable for the sun to reach the moon, nor does the night overtake the day, but each in an orbit is swimming.

Quran: Surah Yasin 36:38, and the sun runs its course for a term and place, appointed for it. That is the decree of the all-mighty, the all-knowing.

Quran: Surah Furqan verses 27-29

The Quranic texts mentioned Earth's spherical shape over 1400 years ago. Humanity is commanded by Allah to respect the Earth. Every living organism possesses inherent rights. In the depths of the earth, growth occurs, wells are dug, and the deceased find their final resting place. Aristotle, in BC, proposed that the Earth is a sphere and suggested that its shadow is circular based on his study of astronomy. Late observations by astronomers revealed it was not round. The Quran asserts that the Lord of worlds, who created this world, declared that the earth is not round, but spherical. The Earth and other planets are in a constant state of change. The universe is in a state of constant change and expansion.

Quran: Surah Dhariyat. 51:47 refers to the expansion of the universe, a phenomenon that has been made known to us.

The observation that the universe was expanding was made by the scientist Edwin Hubble in 1929. In place of solely relying on microscopic observation and technological tools. The message that was received directly from the Quran dates back around 1400 years ago. In order to gain a comprehensive understanding of the mechanics that underlie the Big Bang theory. Elucidating the mechanics that led to the explosive separation of celestial bodies, as commanded by Allah, is an intriguing aspect of the big bang theory. This theory provides valuable insight into the way the universe works and has been widely accepted amongst scientists. It also helps us to better understand the relationship between science and Islam.

Quran: Surah Ambiya: 21;30.Do the disbelievers not realize that the heavens and earth were ˹once˺ one mass, then We split them apart? And We created from water every living thing. Will they not then believe?

There was a colossal explosion, named the Big Bang. In a microscopic society.Allah mentions all the metrics in the Quran, which were later discovered by man. Humans have explored galaxies and nebulae with their naked eyes, but microscopic research hasn't quenched their curiosity. Allah has created a universe with unexplored galaxies and lands beyond human reach. Travelers understand that it's impossible to explore the entire world in one lifetime.

A colossal explosion took place in a microscopic society known as the Big Bang Theory. Belgian astronomer and cosmologist Georges Lemaître developed the modern big-bang theory. Humanity was informed by the Quran before exploration. The theory claims that the universe is expanding from a finite, high-density singularity. The scientific community widely accepts it and it revolutionizes our understanding of the universe.

 Muslims are motivated to pursue knowledge through consistent reading of the Quran. Understanding the Quran goes beyond those with formal education. The Book discusses diverse subjects, including knowledge, comprehension, self-control, ethics, modesty in fashion, and nurturing children.

The virtuous company is an integral part of Islam's ongoing endeavors. Men and women's rights. Inertia and self-control: a concept that captivates. Education rights and the pursuit of knowledge. An equitable global system for distributing government and political funds. The artist created this timeless masterpiece. The conclusion of this masterpiece is known only to Allah.

The emphasis is on how evil acts can steer individuals away from righteousness and the significance of avoiding such temptations. It examines cognitive enhancement with substances, exploring benefits and consequences. The concept of enhancing quality of life amidst societal turmoil, acknowledging challenges and proposing the occasional sense of impossibility.

The importance of learning from exceptional leaders is emphasized for positive change. Islam cautions against experimenting with low-quality components and stresses the importance of living a clean life. Additionally, it addresses the lasting impact of artificial highs on brain function and advises against their use. The text underscores the importance of faith in Islam by focusing on (Salat) ritual prayer and the need to present oneself to Allah with a pure body and soul. It emphasizes that a strong connection with Allah can bring peace and life.

Politically and socially aware individuals disguised themselves as "woke" based on colloquial understanding. Describes a person who is trendy and open-minded. These politically ignorant and misled individuals are nowhere near finding common ground.

Hypocrites are indecisive, playing both sides of the coin without knowing where they stand. Educating the masses with corrections is affordable. The existence of Islam depends on Muhammad's fearlessness in speaking the truth. In Islam, hypocrites who know the truth but mix it with lies are condemned to the lowest level of hell.

Quran: Surah Nisa: 4:145. The hypocrites will be sent to Hell's lowest pit, and no one will be able to help them.

The Story of the Frog and the Scorpion:

The lack of Islamic origin doesn't diminish the fascination of the frog and scorpion story. The scorpion asked the frog if it could give it a ride on its back across the river.

The frog expressed doubt, saying that you are not reliable. The scorpion rejected the idea and expressed its determination to prove itself. If I were to harm you we would both get hurt. He successfully convinced the frog. The frog finally instructed to hop on its back. The frog eventually agreed with the scorpion, despite initial hesitation and distrust. When they were halfway across, he stung the frog. What was the reason behind stinging me?"Deceit is my nature," replied the Scorpion when asked by the frog.

The story cautions us to avoid scorpions. Their closeness should not be underestimated. Did the scorpion cause you to veer off your chosen path? Proceed with caution. A stinging sensation lingers after he departs. The outcome is a feeling of numbness and wasted time. Opt for the legitimate company instead of the fraudsters. It's smarter to stay alert around scorpions instead of trusting them as friends.

The story of a man who killed 99 people:

A man's life-changing story fueled by hope and belief. This story is familiar to numerous hadiths.The individual who ended the lives of 99 individuals. There was someone who lived in the distant past. His behavior was appalling and horrific. He demonstrated a lack of approval for his actions, unable to grasp the reasons behind his atrocious behavior. He deprived others of life. What influenced him to involve himself in such behavior? Did he experience an ongoing state of unhappiness?

It didn't take him long to enumerate the 99 deaths he was responsible for. The heart developed empathy and acknowledged its own lack of mercy, striving for self-improvement. Can the act of repentance and the presence of hope facilitate his transformation? ...What is unattainable within the realm of Allah... There are no limits to the realm of possibilities. Allah observes the human heart, distinguishing between its purity and impurity. Is it possible for attempts to upset the creator to bring about transformative results? Is it possible to perceive the stillness within a heart that yearns? Can a person take advice from a believer and alter their actions? Achieving all things is possible through Allah's will.

He encountered a feeling of being unable to breathe. In terms of being cruel, he didn't live up to human expectations. He diligently sought out individuals whom he believed could provide solace or instill hope. Can repentance effectively resolve his internal conflicts? The absence of kindness and shelter in humans made him doubt the potential for hope through repentance. He questioned if he would end up in heaven or hell.

In response, he was told, "You'll go to hell" He expressed his anger and exhibited more aggressive behavior. Can hope be found in humans? There were only a select few who saw no hope in a person who killed others without cause and desired amnesty. Ultimately, he was advised to approach an aged individual who was devout in his prayers to Allah. Filled with hope, he eagerly approached him and asked the same question, confiding in the man about his inner struggles and seeking solace in the possibility of redemption. The man responded affirmatively, expressing unwavering faith in the mercy of Allah.

He hurriedly moved from place to place, soliciting the viewpoints of those who invoke Allah in prayer. Eventually, as he ran in every direction, he came across a man of unwavering faith and hope who advised him to disassociate himself from the group he was affiliated with. Bursting with happiness and confidence, the man raced. His sole possessions consisted of hope and repentance. He was deeply and genuinely sorrowful. He was utterly unaware of the source of his malevolence. While he passionately implored Allah. He showed deep regret as tears cascaded down his face while sprinting. He beseeched Allah to grant him forgiveness. It is with utmost remorse that he acknowledged his unjust treatment of Allah's creatures. He fervently implored Allah for forgiveness, incessantly repeating his words.

As he sprinted and struggled to catch his breath, he persisted in running to the opposite side. The mountain peaks towered, and the road was rugged. It held no significance. He had absolutely nothing, not even a single drop of water to quench his thirst. He persisted in running.The final destination is predetermined as death draws near. The angels informed Allah that the man responsible for the deaths of 99 people had passed away. To which destination would you like to dispatch him? Heaven or hell?

Allah commanded the angels to calculate the distance between the mountains. In the event that the man is situated on the opposite side of the mountain, direct him towards heaven. He displayed mercy towards the remorseful soul. Following the measurement, the angels responded that he was situated on the opposite side of the mountain.

Allah observes the innermost being of his servant. Allah is abundant with mercy towards those who sincerely seek repentance. Allah extended the distance as he granted forgiveness to the man while the angels quantified the distance. Despite the angels' joyful report of his presence on the opposite side of the mountain, Allah's mercy extended to stretch the mountain, preventing him from reaching the other side of evil as he ran tirelessly. However, the heart of a believer was forgiven, enabling them to reach the opposite side.

This man is an impeccable embodiment; he was sincere in his repentance. Allah's rage has the power to annihilate the world, yet his compassion can flourish within the heart of a faithful follower.

Being affiliated with an unfavorable organization sometimes necessitates adaptation, resulting in individuals undertaking unfamiliar responsibilities. The selection of undesirable companions is a manifestation of personal vulnerability, but self-improvement can lead to transformation.

Seeking forgiveness from Allah is an act of compassion for those who earnestly seek Him and commit to avoiding displeasing actions. How can one convey their intention to transform in the future, considering the uncertain inevitability of mortality? The potency of intention surpasses temporal boundaries, and divine justice is preserved by Allah.

Like the person who swiftly crossed to the other side, he boldly proclaimed his intent for transformation as he sprinted to achieve it, abandoning his familiar realm in pursuit of a new world and redemption through regret.

The new world became both his end and a manifestation of Allah's grace. This narrative imparts the importance of time, emphasizing the necessity for prompt action to facilitate positive transformation. Moreover, it emphasizes the importance of surrounding oneself with individuals who share similar beliefs, emphasizing the superiority of one believer over many non-believers.

Time offers no guarantee, as the man who sought forgiveness was indeed forgiven, yet did not witness his transformation before passing away. He departed as a believer, holding onto the ultimate hope shared by all believers. This man surpassed many in his quest for forgiveness, and Allah, seeing his intentions, granted him forgiveness. He died as a faithful believer.

Prophet Idris' story:

The story of Idris the Prophet serves as a powerful illustration that demonstrates how human beings do not possess complete control over everything. Allah does.The Prophet Idris, commonly referred to as Enoch, is a truly captivating figure. Following the era of Abraham, he emerged as the second Prophet. With his intelligence and soft-spoken nature, he introduced the important skills of reading and writing.

He was the inaugural Prophet to introduce the concept of literacy, involving reading and writing. His people fell prey to Satan's influence. Allah told him to wage (Jihad), a war against his people.They were followers of (Qabil) Cain. His army defeated the transgressors as Allah ordered. With his victory, Idris was content.He desired an extended lifespan in order to assist a greater number of individuals.

Allah pledged him rewards in return for the virtuous conduct of his people.He implored Allah for a chance to meet with the angel of death. Muslims hold the belief of the existence of seven heavens. He traversed through the fabric of time on angels' wings until he arrived at the realm of fourth heaven as they are built with layers. At that precise moment, he was overwhelmed with delight upon encountering Azrael; the angel being responsible for guiding souls to the afterlife.Azrael the angel of death was told by Allah to take his soul back when he reached the fourth heaven.

Nevertheless, the angel of death was completely unaware of the means by which he could transport his soul to the fourth heaven; he was uncertain of how he would reach his desired location. Allah possesses knowledge of the measures a human will undertake to attain the ultimate end of their life. Allah issued a command to Azrael to retrieve his soul upon reaching the fourth heaven. Captured his soul, which explained his presence.

Little did he know, he was ascending towards his inevitable end. Thus is the divine summons of Allah. Humans are limited to mere speculation and reside in a realm of delusions. Only Allah possesses knowledge of the outcome of each episode of life and everything in it. The angel of death claimed Prophet Idris's life here before he could plead for a postponement. The timing of Allah is incomprehensible to humans. Repentance is an integral part of a Muslim's daily life. Ultimately, Idris, the esteemed Prophet, arrived at the destination beckoning him towards demise.

Allah has control over the hearts and the affairs of the soul. Those who believe that they have achieved something without acknowledging Allah first are truly at a loss. For a believer, relying solely on oneself is nothing more than an illusion. Every encounter with a story holds a valuable lesson for us. Allah is the ultimate overseer of the matters in this world. Having pride in oneself can be harmful, as it implies arrogance, whereas putting Allah first frees the human from this dilemma and acknowledges that all control belongs to Him.

This remains true, even though humans have been granted free will. They should attribute the good to Allah and take responsibility for the bad. Pride is reserved for those who heed Satan's whispers. Those who fail to comprehend the significance of safety and doubt in the affairs of believers are troubled. Believers are blessed to be able to share their beliefs and stories with others. They often dissuade those who doubt or disbelieve. A believer finds solace in sharing with another believer.

Quran: Surah Maryam 19:56.And mentioned in the Book, Idrees. Indeed, he was a man of truth and a Prophet. ... And mentioned in the Book (the Quran) Idris (Enoch). Verily! He was a man of truth.

Quran: Surah Furqan 25:70. "Except those who repent have faith and do good deeds for such people, Allah will change their sins for good deeds. Certainly, Allah is most forgiving and merciful."

Quran: Surah Zumar 39:53 Say, "O my servants who have transgressed against themselves [by sinning] do not despair of the mercy of Allah SWTswt. Indeed, Allah forgives all sins. Indeed, it is he who forgives the merciful."

The challenges we face in the present can eventually turn into cherished memories. Who has the ability to shake the faith of a believer? Those who invoke Allah are aware that difficult times will be followed by moments of ease. Every person experiences their own trials, without exception. The way individuals handle life's challenges may vary, but no one is exempt. Each individual is conscious of the challenges they encounter, often unexpectedly and without warning.

Dealing with these challenges and the significance of one's beliefs during trials are of utmost importance. Did their beliefs waver or become stronger? They expressed gratitude to Allah, resembling the Prophets who endured trials and declared, "I have experienced more favorable days" with the faith that this too shall fade away. Let's take the example of the Prophet Jacob. By demonstrating patience and understanding, believers can help each other strengthen their faith. The Almighty always allows for repentance and shows mercy, providing guidance when it is most needed.

CHAPTER 14

ALLAH CREATED MAN AND JINNS TO WORSHIP HIM

To live life to the fullest, you need to be completely free from any hindrances that may hinder your progress. To feel complete contentment in the present moment and be able to experience the warmth of the breeze passing by, one must experience the effects of what has just taken place.

It is the one who doesn't see the moment that loses what time has to offer. Some moments in life cannot be relieved. There are, however, some who return even better than they were before. Positive thinking is the best motion in life.

A powerful wind can leave one breathless. You will notice that your aura will become lighter when the wind blows through your hair or clothes. Imagine the delicate touch of nature brushing against your spirit as it gently touches your soul. The ability of water to allow purified souls to experience purity is another effect that water has on its users.

Nature's ability to revive dry areas and shift winds reminds believers to adapt and transform. There is no doubt that the way a person speaks, smiles, behaves, or even just a simple meeting can have a profound impact on another individual.

There is no limit to what Allah can do if it is in His will. What is the reason behind the creator of the world, the owner, the master of this world and the next, requiring humans and jinns to worship Him? The owner of the world, possessing absolute power, does not rely on humans or Jin to recognize his greatness; he is self-sufficient.

Worship is intended to serve humanity's interests rather than being solely focused on benefiting Allah. Although the human possesses numerous strengths, when faced with their creator, they are rendered weak. By engaging in worship and showing reverence to the creator, humans can attain the peace they so strongly desire, thereby achieving peaceful survival.

The tablet of events, which has remained unchanged, consistently delivers the truth to conscious minds, guiding humanity towards the worship of one God and helping the soul rather than sabotaging our time in this world. While finding enjoyment in this world is important, prioritizing the progression of getting closer to Allah is the ultimate form of well-being for a human.

Quran: Surah Dhariyat: 51; 56. The Jinns and humans were not created for any other purpose than to worship Me.

Bible: ESV 14:7. Then Jesus said to him, "Be gone, Satan! For it is written, "'You shall worship the Lord your God and him only shall you serve.'"

In the passage of the Bible, there is a consistent message where Jesus instructs people to direct their prayers to God (Allah ha), not to himself. The act of maintaining consistency brings about numerous benefits for humanity, particularly through efficient delivery. The shift towards Jesus as the central figure of worship implies inconsistencies with previous Abrahamic scriptures.

Since the beginning of time, Allah has been the exclusive God for worship and the source of Abrahamic Prophets. This message is the only one since Adam and Eve were created. He is a worshiper of (Allah-ha) as the God of Jesus.

Do religious beliefs depend on the ability to confront opposing views in conflict? That is not the case. Ultimately, the worship and judgment of a human is left in Allah's hands. Throughout the Abrahamic faiths, Prophets brought the same message, without contradicting Allah or claiming to be a combination of God and humanity at the same time.

There has been a fascination with the shimmering shadows of the Jinns surrounding humanity for decades. As there has been no information regarding Jinns in society, humanity has sought to find out more about the darkness that is lurking within the shadows one contemplates or the noises one hears without notice of a being, as there has been no information about Jinns in society.

The waves of silent winds that pass through the unseen world without one being aware of their existence more than a passing phase is something that makes a human wonder about the unobserved. In light of the intricacy of humanity, Islam makes evident the fact that they perceive you on a level far beyond what you can comprehend due to the unseen world of Jinns.

There is no doubt that the Jinns and their people share some responsibility for the silent whispers of evil people and the division between believers, which causes a temporary nuisance for both groups. A strong believer will not be afraid of evil and will not be able to let their beliefs be hindered by obstacles.

It is impossible to leave out the world of Jinns who lived on earth before humans as Islam mentions their presence in the world and explains that though they are not visible to humans, they still live in the world with them. Islam is the only faith in the world that mentions the existence of these entities in detail and warns its followers to be aware of the good and evil around them.

Man would not be able to survive if he did not know his enemy. It would be difficult for humans to deny that Satan is the enemy of a believer if a believer believes he has no enemies that would insinuate Satan is not seen as evil.

His awareness and manipulations of his people need accounting. Jinns can take different forms and change their bodies to cause mischief, while humans cannot do the same. The presence of these creatures can sometimes be unanticipated by humans. Depending on how you perceive it, Satan is one of the families of the Jinns, as a reminder from Islam.

People have personified these shadows not knowing their identities, some jinns are harmful and others more sinister but harmless. These shadows, while not harmful to humans, can still frighten them as they occupy space. While some jinns have the ability to harm humans, nothing happens without Allah's knowledge. The blueprint in Islam holds all the answers, but their completeness awaits the day of judgment.

Jinns and humans share similarities. They possess both virtue and evil. Choices are available to them, and angels are made of light and completely obedient to Allah. Clarification is necessary to verify the differences. The Quran clarifies that Jinns possess the ability to see what humans cannot, emphasizing their presence when humanity lacks awareness. Verifying the differences requires crucial clarification. For humans and Jinns, worship is significant, (Al-Khaaliq) The one Allah who creates.

The Quran is undoubtedly clear wherever it is read. Determining Satan's identity is highly critical. He is a Jinn made from fire that doesn't produce smoke. A Quran provides an explanation of the substance of Jinns and how they were created. Before humans, Earth was inhabited by Jinns.

'Iblis' is the name given to Satan, a member of the Jinn family. In the darkness, Iblis went against Allah's command. Allah cursed him and banished him from His presence. He promised to guide humanity away from light in his commitment to lead them into darkness.

The fascination humans have for the unseen world leads them to stay up all night watching movies. Investigating darkness and capturing the unseen world are manifestations of human curiosity. Rather than investigating darkness, why not search for light, truth, and the company of a believer? Knowing the source and avoiding it is vital for a believer. Delving into the shadows to expose the identity of evil.

Prophet Muhammad's shadow was not visible. His aura didn't create a shadow. Imagine the incredible stature Allah bestowed upon him. Many have been frightened by the number of shadows. Allah administered a test of faith to both jinns and humans.

People question why Allah requires humans and jinns for recognition. He is the sole truth recognized. The fleeting existence of humanity and Jinn underscores their lack of permanence and vulnerability.

The source of contentment for all mankind is worshiping Allah. It's optional, but the outcomes are non-negotiable. Devotees count on Him for strength and power, and He bestows hope upon them. Muslims seek Allah's guidance and protection by worshiping. Acts of forceful worship and insulting non-Muslims go against Islamic teachings.

Additionally, he did not appoint Muslims as managers over disbelievers or non-Muslims. It is uncertain if those who deviated from the correct path will find their way back.

Quran: Surah Anam: 6:108. And do not insult those they invoke other than Allah, lest they insult Allah in enmity without knowledge.

The truth requires conscious effort, yet many are enticed by lies, allowing Satan to exploit their negligence. They persist in arguing with both believing Muslims and their own souls. Muslims deviate from Islam when they abandon truth and embrace lies. Mindful individuals strive for better companies to improve themselves.

Some individuals search for inferior companies to feel superior. Tempting the uncertain is Satan's job who comes from a jinn family. Manipulating confused minds is easy. Satan's strategy to retain control over his followers involves instilling feelings of inferiority in them. Additionally, he exploits the hostility of those who resist integration by encouraging antagonism towards those with a modest lifestyle.

By resorting to name-calling, individuals can express their opinions in a derogatory manner. His strategy involves dispatching his followers to restless places, where they sow chaos and disrupt the tranquility.

His constant vigilance for original and creative methods to attain power demonstrates his refusal to accept the status quo. His ability to create confusion is well-known, and Satan and his associates possess a clear understanding of the necessary time required for each task.

Individuals who are familiar with his tactic tend to be more inclined to avoid associating with individuals who engage in evil behavior. His perseverance is one thing that humans can truly learn from him.

It is worth mentioning that there are jinns who are also good. Their lives are filled with happiness and contentment. Furthermore, they have demonstrated their commitment to their faith by rejecting evil and dedicating themselves to the worship of Allah.

A group of Good Jinns, who heard Prophet Muhammad reciting the Quran, accepted Islam, and they read the Quran regularly. Consistent with the general perception of humans, it can be agreed upon. For a Muslim, there is no comparison between the protection of Allah and any bodyguard.

Prophet Muhammad, without claiming any divine status, served as a beacon of guidance and a symbol for his followers. His level of security was such that he didn't have to rely on bodyguards for protection. The protection of Allah was sufficient to safeguard him as well as any devout Muslim who follows their faith. By engaging in the act of worship, one can effectively maintain a sense of balance and harmony between two distinct realms.

Moreover, it serves as a powerful reminder, highlighting both its power and mercy. This process serves as a means to instill gratitude and humility in individuals. The guidance of Allah is available for both humans and jinn, and it is up to them to either accept or reject it. In the Quran, Islam is mentioned and referred to as a guiding direction. None of the Bibles contain any references to Christianity.

Based on the absence of evidence, it can be inferred that Jesus did not identify as a Christian. His religious affiliation was with Islam, and he strongly identified with its teachings and beliefs. All Prophets, without a doubt, humbly bowed to Allah and faithfully conveyed the messages entrusted to them

. Like his fellow Prophets, he held Allah in high regard and communicated the very same message. All Prophets follow Islam as it is a religion centered around the worship of one God, Allah.

The first man and woman, whom Allah created, practiced monotheism by worshiping Allah alone. The message of Allah is so powerful and profound that it cannot be emphasized or reiterated enough.

It wasn't until the conclusion of the Quran that the term Islam was introduced, however, the message remained unaltered. Without fail, the prevailing belief system revolved around the adoration of a solitary God. In terms of divinity, Allah holds exclusivity as the one and only God. Humanity cannot be convinced by any means, nor will anyone make an attempt to do so. The message has been delivered, and it is up to each individual to choose whom they worship.

Quran: Surah Anam; 6:125.(Whoever Allah guides, He opens their heart to Islam. If He wants to leave someone astray, He makes their chests tight and constricted as if they were climbing up a mountain. A disbeliever's fate is determined by Allah in this way.

Both humans and Jinns possess the capacity to exercise their free will. Humans and Jinns were both given the opportunity to choose between light and darkness. Satan, who was the first Jinn, made the choice to disobey Allah and asked for respite. His request was granted by Allah.

Given the momentary pause, Satan's ultimate aim is to wreak havoc on humanity and lead them astray from the path ordained by Allah. The eternal battle between good and evil had its origins when he, in his attempt to tempt humans, assembled his own army, which consisted of his family of jinns. Is it possible for jinns to take on the form of humans? It has been confirmed that the answer is affirmative.

By providing explanations of the unseen, the Quran serves to deepen the understanding of the spiritual world for believers. Is it within the realm of possibility for Jinn to possess and control human bodies? Without a doubt, the answer is a resounding yes.

These individuals not only possess powers, but they also display a fondness for filth and are specifically drawn to individuals who neglect personal hygiene and avoid using water for cleaning purposes.

And for those individuals who do not have the privilege of seeking solace through prayer. These individuals who are possessed have the ability to mimic various personalities, often requiring them to seek assistance from clerics who engage in prayer and combat against the inner demon.

At times, this manifestation can reveal numerous malevolent personalities coexisting within a single person. On occasion, the individuals may find themselves defeated by the one who battles the jinn residing within them. These individuals, devoid of pain due to the jinn's resistance to prayer, are typically those afflicted by an evil jinn.

Muslims are advised to stay clean and read surahs of protection in their daily lives, as the natures of these episodes exist. The Quran, through its teachings, has provided warnings to humanity about every possible challenge that may arise in this world. There are no valid excuses for not being aware of these teachings. By engaging in reading, one can ignite their curiosity and embark on a journey of continuous learning, even within a short span of time.

The virtuous Jinns not only engage in religious practices and prayers, but they also have families. As part of their preparation for Salat, Muslims were instructed to keep themselves clean through the use of water. In order to fulfill our duty to Allah, it is necessary to perform ablution as part of the ritual prayer, known as Salat.

Ablution, which is a ritual purification practice, includes the act of washing the face, hands, arms, and feet. By practicing humility, devotion, and obedience to Allah, individuals can experience the purification of both their body and soul.

It is not possible for humans to freely roam in darkness and establish their own set of rules during their brief stay in this world. Allah sent the Quran and Islam as an unchangeable book, which serves to establish a final decree of law. Personal desires and opinions do not have any influence on Islamic laws.

Satan, with the intention of misleading people, has numerous agendas in this world, one of which involves placing other gods above Allah. Among Satan's followers, there is a popular trend of observing and enjoying the performance of various sexual acts by others. The excessive obsession with technology can give off a negative vibe that is reminiscent of evil spirits.

There are individuals who find fascination in watching paranormal spirits and even extend an invitation for them to enter their homes. The next move he plants in their minds is eagerly anticipated by the young and hopeless, who are enticed by the distasteful lyrics.

These are the companies that should be avoided at all costs due to their association with evil. Falsehood, hypocrisy, lies, and loss of character are all attributes associated with satanic behavior.

Dogs, cats, and donkeys displaying a change in behavior suggests they possess a perceptiveness, animals, notice jinns and angels. Evil spirits are invited into dirty homes that are not suitable for Islam by none other than Satan and his family. If individuals turn to reading as a source of solace, it has the potential to aid them in rectifying their ways.

The agendas that have been formulated are in complete accordance with the teachings of the Quran. The simplicity of faith lies in its comprehensibility, as it is described for anyone who reads it to comprehend.

It is a faith that operates with laws, without which even a household cannot survive. It is essential to seek the laws that align with your personal journey, as nations will crumble without them. Despite facing confrontations with evildoers, Allah's laws remain strong and the faith of believers remains unwavering.

By studying and understanding Islam, we can prevent the infiltration of destructive ideologies. Seeking Allah's help is a necessary step towards achieving success and contentment of the soul. True friends are the ones who remind you of Allah.

In certain communities, individuals who do not follow any religious practices tend to have a preference for sleeping without clothes. According to the teachings of Islam, angels do not visit or come into contact with nakedness or impurity.

Satan's declaration of nakedness began with the first act of disobedience to Allah, resulting in the removal of their clothes and the exposure of their privacy. He is continually promoting nudity without any hesitation. According to research, using the same dirty sheets daily can have adverse health effects due to the accumulation of human dander.

Although individuals who sleep in clothing have the luxury of changing their attire on a daily basis, the majority of people do not have the same luxury when it comes to changing their bedding sheets daily, resulting in the potential spread of unhealthy dander. Dirty sheets can harbor bacteria and germs, which can be observed crawling on them. The impact on their health from allergens and other illnesses is felt on a daily basis.

Tik Tok: Sep 9, 2021 — A new video on TikTok has gone viral after a plastic surgeon shed light on the gross reason why you may not want to sleep naked.

Generally, human minds seek guidance from doctors or other humans rather than doing their best to learn the truth from Islam. There can be a challenge in understanding what is allowed and what is prohibited when we delve into the smallest elements. Regulations and laws serve a purpose, just as worshiping Allah serves a purpose as well. It is easy to overlook the worth of rain if you do not appreciate its beauty. Just as an animal herder guides his flock, humanity is not abandoned without direction from the creator. Mothers will not abandon their young without guidance. Not all mothers are directors, but they are all here to unload their offspring.

Among the creations that Allah has revealed to humanity, only a few have been made known, such as humans, Jinns, and animals. Many of Allah's hidden creations still remain undiscovered by man. By teaching what is unknown to mankind, the Quran uncovers the mysteries that lie beyond human perception and reveals only what an individual is able to handle. Allah's creations are vast and diverse, encompassing even extraterrestrial beings, and this fact cannot be denied. The more we progress as a species, the clearer it becomes that Allah is the ultimate force, and with this realization, we begin to comprehend that the possibilities that await us are infinite. Rather than worrying about what is not revealed, focus on protecting yourself from what is revealed.

The inclusion of specific details serves as the primary objective to ensure the safety and well-being of individuals who follow the faith or are interested in embarking on their own spiritual journey.Regardless of whether humans are present or not, Allah's divinity remains constant. The laws that govern human inner health are responsible for determining our overall well-being. Just like being completely exposed and without any sort of protection, lacking knowledge about Islam can make someone vulnerable, as they choose to ignore the understanding of their own faith.The laws that govern Islam are intricately crafted with great attention to detail. Similar to how an uninformed Muslim lacks the ability to protect themselves from the malicious actions of the Jinn Satan and the Jinn family.

Throughout history, Islam has unveiled and presented an extensive range of discoveries and knowledge to the entire human race. Despite the aforementioned point, it is crucial to recognize that the responsibility for his adherence and learning ultimately falls on him. In accordance with the principles of the Islamic faith, it is recommended to sleep on the right side. According to a study conducted in 2003, it was found that sleeping on the right side might have beneficial impacts on the heart. Engaging in regular exercise is an important factor in the maintenance of a healthy heart.

Over 1400 years ago, the Prophet Muhammad said this in his practices. While Islam may dictate or prescribe the placement of these small delicacies in accordance with the (sunnah), it is important to remember that all threads are sewn for the benefit of humans. Allah's mercy knows no bounds and is infinite. The true concepts and delivery of both can only be grasped by those who truly understand. They find it easy to distinguish between what is right and what is wrong.

Satan is envious of pure souls and regularly visits to tempt them. His boundless fascination with beauty is on par with his other passions. Certain Jinns possess exquisitely stunning entities. Muslims maintain self-cleanliness through the practice of Salat and following the teachings of the Quran.

While it is suggested to keep dogs outside as per Islamic teachings, there are owners who defy this practice and permit their dogs to sleep in their beds. Islam strictly prohibits the practice of this activity. Consistently defying Allah's commands can lead to the development of dog dander infections and allergies. It is absolutely essential that rules are followed and adhered to. Rules can be established and exceptions can be granted, especially in cases where weather conditions or limited space are factors to consider, as is the case with him being a dog rather than a human. Grant him the freedom to live according to rules and treat him with kindness.

Dogs, just like any other animals, will greatly benefit and appreciate the structure and guidance that discipline provides. Research is the only way to discover the truth. Allah will also question the dogs about how their owners treated them today, allowing them to bark and provide a report on the treatment they received. Being kind to animals is an integral part of Islam. Under the protection of a human, not only dogs but every animal will have the ability to speak for or against you. When it comes to showcasing discipline, Islam leaves absolutely nothing behind.

When Allah warns a human, it is because He has knowledge of His creation. Accepting it at face value is a must for Muslims, without any room for skepticism. Given this reasoning, it is prudent for individuals to adhere to the principles outlined in the Quran and engage in thoughtful contemplation before accepting any beliefs, as this approach is most beneficial for the entirety of humankind. To achieve a lifestyle that is healthy and safe, it is imperative to adhere to comparisons..

By examining different instances of human behavior, the significance of cleanliness in relation to personal health and hygiene is underscored. The presence of filth in the mind is unhygienic and requires the need for both physical and mental cleansing. While many people prioritize physical hygiene, the main focus in this context lies on spiritual hygiene and the importance of cleansing one's inner self.

In light of the rising frequency of diseases, Hindus consider the Ganges as a revered destination where they imbibe and cleanse themselves in the same water that millions partake in. Faith knows no limits; it is inherent in all human beings. The intention behind this example is not to expose unsanitary conditions, but rather to emphasize the inherent human yearning for spirituality.

A significant number of cholera intestinal infections are caused by ongoing diseases that are transmitted through water contamination. The significance of that may not be relevant to those who find solace in its ability to purify their souls.

Despite this, Hindus persist in holding the Ganges in high reverence as a sacred river. The act of bathing in the Ganges holds great significance in their belief system as it is believed to absolve sins. According to Hindu beliefs, the consumption of water from the Ganges is thought to be a path to achieving liberation or moksha. These examples of humans seeking penance are ongoing and continuous.

Regardless of the deity or entity they choose to worship, no individual's faith can be invalidated. In the Islamic faith, it is strictly prohibited to show disrespect towards the beliefs of others. However, it is important to note that theological differences are not considered disrespectful. Instead, these differences are viewed as an opportunity for individuals to exercise their freedom of choice, highlighting the clear contrast between disrespect and personal decision-making.

Under the ownership and rule of Muslims, specifically during Omar Bin Khattab's era, Jerusalem saw the flourishing of all faiths, with no instances of forced conversion, and the inhabitants were given the rights to practice their respective religions freely. Our intention is to raise awareness about Islam, while simultaneously upholding the principle of granting individuals the freedom to choose their own faith, as Islam inherently respects this autonomy until the conclusion of one's earthly journey. The strong hold that Eastern religions have on Western societies is highly alluring.

Despite their lack of understanding of the practices of religions such as Hinduism and Buddhism, they are drawn to the attractiveness of glamor and spirituality, as it resonates with the shared experience of human worship. Despite this, it is important to note that Buddha did not demand or expect his disciples to worship him. In recognition of his extraordinary achievements, they raised him to the level of a divine being. Similar to Eastern religions, Jesus did not ask to be referred to as a God.

Similar to Jesus, Krishna also possessed the remarkable ability to walk on water, emphasizing yet another point of contrast between the two. With the exception of Jesus speaking at birth and performing miracles, the Quran does not provide any mention of him having the ability to walk on water. Christianity is unique among the Abrahamic faiths because it recognizes a Prophet who conveyed Allah's unified message as both a deity and the son of God, and this distinction is influenced by various historical factors. One of the reasons for the explainable differences is that Jesus holds a significant position in Islam, where he is respected as a Prophet and awaited Messiah.

Was Hinduism mentioned in the Quran? No. Only the Prophets of the Abrahamic faith were. If one cannot follow the example of a few, the previous ones are not a context of worry as only monotheism is relegated as it was the only message from the beginning to the end. People pollute truth, not Allah.

He is truth and mercy, no doubt. (As-Salam) is one of Allah's names sources of peace and flawlessness. Humanity is flawed, but he is perfect.

In Islam, scientific affirmation also focuses on matters of human health and sanitation. The well of (Zam-Zam), located in Mecca, Saudi Arabia, is well known among Muslims for its purifying properties.

Muslims do not engage in bathing and consuming the same water. With the advancements in technology, it is now being filtered and adopted by a significant number of Muslims. Additionally, Muslims hold the belief in the efficacy of prayer and meditation as a means of purifying the soul. As so do other faiths.

They also focus on charity and philanthropy, believing it is a way to gain righteous deeds and blessings. Lastly, Muslims practice fasting during the holy month of Ramadan, which is seen as a way to increase spiritual growth and closeness to Allah.

But all of these actions benefit humans, not Allah. The sole purpose of internal and external hygiene imposed by Islam is to cleanse a Muslim's soul.

His superiority stems from the difference in their creation - humans from altered mud clay, and him from smokeless fire. The existence of Jinns before humans leads to his condemnation of humans.

The scriptures contain a similar analogy. However, his defiance resulted in his expulsion. Previous scriptures lack authenticity due to their dual nature and exploitation of the Bible as human and divine. The Quran remains the only scripture untouched. Evidence forms the foundation of truth.

Only at the discretion of the Jinn can a human observe him. He can be visible to whomever he wills. Allah has given him such authority. His credentials are revealed to humans, however.

They must be vigilant against evil and stay clean. The Muslim purification process includes the prayer of Salats and the Quran. The Jinn can be beneficial to humans, but also a source of harm.

It is important to be aware of their presence and to seek the protection of Allah against their evil. Muslims must also stay away from activities that may attract their attention, such as sorcery and black magic. Satan and his partners lurk to destroy what is positive. Whispers and loud gossip are heard.

The plot is obvious, Satan and his malevolent followers strive to entice those who succumb to deception and wickedness.To destroy humans, especially believers. Not merging private and confidential matters is ideal.

The plot of his evil nature is to create enemies and friends who look around for gossip and mishaps. This is to trick the believer into believing they are friends. Falsified masters and disciples of Satan cannot be believers' friends. They are envious of any success and seek to destroy it before attaining contentment. It is easy to win the battle against Satan and his weak army by dumping evil out of life and forming alliances with believers.

One believer can defeat a thousand disbelievers. Believers are stronger when they come together in unity. Faith and prayer are forces Satan, and his followers cannot contend with.

Therefore, believers can stand together and fight Satan's temptations to win the battle against evil. When a believer stands with disbelievers and protects them instead of a believer. The fact is, he joined Satan's team. Only Allah's strength and mercy can return the person to his belief. Allah dislikes disbelievers. Allah has answered humanity in the Quran.

The Jinns lived on earth and worshiped Allah throughout history. Bloodshed and havoc ravaged the people as time on earth progressed because of their disobedience. But Allah also sent messengers to humanity to remind them of His commands and to lead them back to the right path.

These messengers reminded humanity of Allah's kindness and mercy. Through their teachings, humanity could find hope and salvation. Muslims handle their own actions, and there is no savior to save them. As in the modifications to Christendom. As per Islam, Jesus is not the savior since he also needs a savior - Allah.

Unlike all humans, Allah purified him and did not have benevolent and unbeneficial jinns born with him. It matters who humans listen to the most. Cleanliness of the heart, soul, and body will allow humans to serve righteous or evil. Purified hearts seek Allah.

As Allah will not approve of human activity of deceit at any cost, (shirk) is a sin unforgivable in Islam. Added partners to Allah. Having a human placed by a Jinn to worship is the highest form of ecstasy for a Jinn. Instead of Allah.

When he himself knows who Allah is as he dwelled in heaven with the angels before being exiled to earth. As long as this earth is a test for humanity and jinns, it will be a test for humans. Humans feel liberated from Satan's intervention by placing human deities in churches and temples as Gods.

Within the framework of Christendom, Jesus plays a crucial and esteemed role, as he is considered either the embodiment of God or the son of God. By exerting its influence, Islam offers a comprehensive understanding of Jesus, presenting the truth and his genuine identity.

The act of Jesus being submissive to Allah served as a powerful testament to the universe, emphasizing the value of embracing diversity. Nevertheless, Satan has cunningly manipulated human thinking, promoting the dangerous belief that humans can replace God.

The level of deceit displayed by him was already astonishing, but he managed to surpass it by planting something even more deceptive. The ultimate decision of where a person is placed in their destiny lies with Allah, and it is determined by the sincerity and purity of their heart when it comes to seeking peace.

The enforcement of pagan beliefs, which are not in accordance with the teachings of Jesus in Islam, goes against our values. The majority of the stories do not align with the teachings and beliefs of Islam. Jesus, despite being the central figure of the gospel, came to symbolize an Abrahamic faith.

The clash of satanic uncertainties can also manifest in individuals from Muslim backgrounds. Significantly impacted by corrupt ideologies. The return symbolizes the purity of one's heart and

Allah's permission for those granted entry. He possesses knowledge of all hearts. Despite one's knowledge of humans, the heart within remains unseen. Solely Allah Knows.

Quran: Surah Mulk: 67:13. Whether you speak in secrecy or aloud, (it is all the same to Allah). He even knows the secrets that lie hidden in the breasts of people.

Quran: Surah Nisa:4;48.(Surely, Allah does not forgive that a partner is ascribed to Him. He forgives anything short of that for whomsoever He wills. Whoever ascribes a partner to Allah commits a terrible sin.

Those who renounce their pagan notions and acquire an understanding of the principles concerning the divine entity aim for purity. When the day of reckoning arrives, they will come to realize that it is Allah who responds to their pleas, not the deities.

The Godlike qualities of God would lose their validity if He were to be observed by humans. Even the Prophets have not seen God. In this phase of life, humans are created weak and are unable to endure the sight of his radiance.

The assertion that Jesus walked in God's image is false. The most significant deception of Satan is to establish himself or a deity as God, exploiting his knowledge of God's identity from his time in heaven, which humans lack.

If Satan does not hold the title for being the most deceitful and evil, then who does? How is it conceivable for a human being to be oblivious to the deployment they have initiated and the alteration of the preceding scriptures facilitated by human intervention?

Does he possess the necessary abilities to achieve this, considering that his only recourse is deceit during his intermittent breaks? Every time he gives something, he has certain expectations attached to it. The act of receiving reminders can foster a stronger connection between humans and the intricacies of their own functionality, ultimately bolstering their resistance against evil.

The conclusive manuscript of the Quran, which was intended to be conveyed, aimed to expose the ability of humans to manipulate divine scriptures that existed before it. It is important to note that Allah's pledge is focused on preserving the Quran, rather than just protecting mankind. The delivery of the laws of the manuscript in the Quran is a means of delivering a message to humanity, and it is up to each individual to choose whether to seek the truth or remain stagnant in their understanding.

Christianity is placed under the category of Abrahamic religions primarily because of its close ties to Abraham. If one were to accept a mortal as divine or as the descendant of divinity. Unlike paganism, the Abrahamic faiths strictly adhere to the belief in monotheism. The shift from monotheism to paganism indicates a separation.

The reason for classifying it as an Abrahamic faith is solely based on Jesus being categorized under Abrahamic faith, rather than the worship of Jesus, unless Christians choose to believe in the oneness of God and Jesus as the Messiah, which would align them more closely with the Muslim belief.

<u>To be recognized as a Muslim, one must acknowledge Allah as the exclusive Lord to be worshiped and Muhammad as the ultimate and last messenger.</u> The existence of evident belief variations eliminates any discrepancies in understanding.

The discipline of theology is an avenue for acquiring knowledge, enabling individuals to recognize that their beliefs may diverge from those of others, empowering them to elucidate their adherence to Islam.

This self-discovery journey is often long and difficult, but ultimately rewarding. It is only through this process of self-reflection that we can truly understand ourselves and our place in the universe. This is the essence of true spirituality.

The act of telling lies is widely accepted, whereas speaking the truth is often seen as impolite. The statement being made is not representative of the teachings and principles of Islam. They are fearless and have no qualms about acknowledging the truth. Islam is not concerned with being a people pleaser or adapting to the changing reforms of contemporary society.

In the world of deceit, Islam stands firm and does not recognize the pagan and illicit days that lead to a loss of morality. For decades, Satan has been the one to make humans the God from the roots, especially within the Abrahamic faith, and he continues to corrupt the world, targeting those who fall prey to his manipulative tactics.

Quran: Surah Anam:6:100.(Yet they associate the jinn with Allah ˹in worship˺, even though He created them. They falsely attribute to Him sons and daughters out of ignorance. Glorified and Exalted, is He above what they claim!

Quran: Surah Anam: 101.He is˹ the Originator of the heavens and earth. How could He have children when He has no mate? He created all things and has ˹perfect˺ knowledge of all things.

When an individual has the ability to recognize their own deception, it is seen as a divine blessing bestowed upon them by Allah. In pursuit of knowledge and adherence to the truth, believers strive to follow Allah's commands. One way to effectively handle commands is by applying your knowledge to recognize evil and reject them. Employ your understanding to discern and dismiss the deceptive lies propagated by Satan, while also aiding others in achieving the same.

Be cautious and do not let yourself be swayed or manipulated by deceitful tactics. The virtuous Jinns, just like everyone else, have made the decision to reject Satan and instead choose the path of positivity that aligns with their own clan. Given that he is not composed of the same substance as the initial human, one would wonder how a human could fail to perceive the distinction.

Individuals who are open to receiving truth will have the ability to comprehend and understand the concepts. The mixing of lies with sacred words is strictly prohibited. In Islam, there is a strong discouragement against attaching partners to Allah, therefore it is strongly advised to avoid doing so. Strengthening faith and piety can be achieved by being mindful of one's actions and thoughts.

Quran: Surah Hijr 15:27 And the Jinn We created before from scorching fire.

In terms of their fundamental nature, there is no discernible distinction between modern-day humans and their historical counterparts. After giving severe warnings, Allah sent angels to destroy them. Before humans came into existence, it was the Jinns who disrupted the world. There were numerous warnings that lacked the necessary oversight to be changed. In the end, Allah decided to send angels in order to put an end to this chaos and destruction. As a dedicated worshiper, Satan sought Allah.

He dedicated his life to serving Allah and was known for his unwavering obedience. The people faithfully worshiped and diligently obeyed Allah. In the battle, he emerged victorious, triumphing over angels and even fighting alongside them. Satan, accompanied by the angels, was responsible for killing the majority of jinns. After he had defeated his own, he humbly pleaded with Allah, asking to be granted the privilege of joining the angels in heaven. Out of all the Jinn, he was the singular individual who had the privilege of residing alongside angels in the realm of heaven.

He was a Jinn who displayed unwavering devotion in his worship. Satan, possessing free will like a jinn, utilized it to carry out his tasks. The expected change was known only by Allah. As a jinn, Satan exercised his free will and went against Allah's commands. To gain a deep understanding of angels, it is crucial to keep in mind that they lack the capacity for free will.

He found himself aligning with persistence due to the animosity he felt towards humans, and this alignment became evident when a worshiper became an enemy to Allah's worshipers.

While he coexisted with angels, his qualities and attributes differed from those of angels. As a consequence of his disobedience, he was banished from the heavens. In response to his request, Allah granted him respite, giving him additional time. Despite Satan becoming the leader of evil and the destroyer, there were some jinns who chose not to follow him. Within the realm of jinn, it is important to note that there exist both benevolent and malevolent entities. Until the Day of judgment arrives, he will persist in being a source of temptation and distraction.

Despite this fact, those individuals who underwent changes did not anticipate the profound revolution that humans currently experience, characterized by the existence of free will. Instead of placing blame on him, it is important to take personal responsibility and make the necessary corrections. His departure from Paradise was a result of his pride, arrogance, and enmity, which manifested as disobedience to Allah.

As he resided in the heavenly realm of Jannah, he had the privilege of beholding its magnificent beauty. Initially, he found joy in being the sole Jinn amidst angels; however, his contentment waned when humans entered the picture. As a result of this, he became excessively arrogant and developed a strong sense of envy towards humans. Due to his inability to see, he was unable to grasp the concept of Allah creating humans from modified mud and commanding angels to show them respect by bowing down.

Since he resided among the angels, he did not receive a direct summons but rather accompanied them whenever Allah called them. He had a sense of superiority. However, he came with the angels at Allah's command. He declined the offer. The command belongs to someone or something. Despite being asked, he refused to comply.

Quran: Surah Araf: 7:12. [Allah] said, "What prevented you from prostrating when I commanded you?" [Satan] said, "I am better than him.

Quran: Surah Araf 7:14. 'Give me respite till the Day they shall be raised.'

Quran: Surah Araf 7:15.) Allah said: 'You are granted respite.'

Quran: Surah Araf 7:16.Satan said: 'Since You have led me astray, I shall surely sit in ambush for them on Your straight path. Satan replied:

Arrogance is a severe antidote for those who falter, but Satan remains a vivid illustration for those who desire penance. Pride is challenging for those who view free will as Satan's domain, for angels epitomize purity without free will.

Quran: In Surah Al-Araf: 12, Al Hijr: 26-27, and Ar-Rahman: 14-19, stated that man was created out of clay and jinn out of fire.

Quran: Surah Araf:7:11. WE initiated your creation,then WE initiated your creation, then WE gave you each a shape, and then WE said to the angels: 'Prostrate before Adam.' They all prostrated except Iblis: he was not one of those who fell Prostrate.

Quran: Surah Taha: 20:124. And whoever turns away from My remembrance - indeed, he will have a depressed life, and we will gather him on the Day of Resurrection blind."

Through prayer and supplication, a person can ask for Allah's guidance, mercy, and guidance, mercy, and protection. Allah's love and mercy are greater than any other force and can vanquish any darkness. Allah has knowledge of the humanity that he created. If they sin, they can return ten fold better. Those who seek him will find forgiveness from him. Satan expresses his hatred for believers and righteousness.

One who deceives others is not fit to be in a position of leadership. On the other hand, the Bible presents a distinct perspective on him. When examining the narratives, it becomes evident that they are comparable but have distinct differences

The Satan in question is not merely a dark angel; rather, he is a Jinn. By elucidating his unique characteristics and the nature of his people, their purpose is to transform humanity for the worst.

Bible:John 12:31 — What Kind of Authority Does Satan Exercise? Jesus referred to him as "the ruler of this world"

Quran: Surah Nisa: 4:76.Those who believe fight in the way of Allah, and those who disbelieve fight in the way of the Shaitan. Fight therefore against the friends of the Shaitan; surely the strategy of the Shaitan is weak.

Who granted him the authority to rule when he is weaker than a fly in Islam? It doesn't make sense that Allah, who owns both this world and the next, would allow the Jinn, who were expelled from heaven, to rule this world. His army is weak, and those who recognize his provocations choose to leave instead of staying in the chaotic outbursts that offer no peace.

The Quran highlights multiple instances where Satan's weakness is exposed as he flees when caught. Those who pray and believe see him as powerless, persistent, and taunting, but those who understand his mischief stand against him, not for him.

The exiled has no power, but finds respite as Allah is fair, rewarding his devotion before his evil. He believes that humans are weak, but Allah created them with knowledge of their strengths and weaknesses. Can a human's soul not clarify words for those who seek? The search for truth satisfies those seeking answers.

Before he departed from the heavens to the earth, he started with Adam and Eve and introduced them to disobedience. Together, they fell into his trap and ate from a tree. Allah forbade them from eating from it.

Despite a history of disobedience since creation, humans repented to Allah and received amnesty. It was Satan who lured Adam and Eve into eating from the forbidden tree. Having both been equally at fault, Allah sent them from heaven to earth to make up for their sins.It was Satan who made their private parts visible to them. They continued to cover themselves with leaves. Nowadays,in corrupt societies influencing the world, he does the same thing.

The nudity and pornography industry is booming, readily available, and highly compensated. Allah created the Jinns and humans to worship him. Every living thing worships Allah, except the Jinns, and humans are free-willed. Satan would have received repentance like Adam and Eve did from Allah. It was his arrogance that framed his demeanor. In contrast, he requested respite. Until the day of reckoning. Lead those who respond to his calls.They can pick their faith, believe, or disbelieve. They have choices.There are many beliefs and stories between Islam and Christianity.

This makes collaboration easy. The moral code of all faiths is similar ; however, their stories and beginnings differ dramatically. Their belief holds that Lucifer is the fallen angel, also known as the dark angel, who rebelled against God. Allah cast him out of heaven after creating humans. His expulsion was from Eden.

The major difference is that Islam does not call him an angel, as angels in Islam do as Allah tells them. With no free choice. But Satan had a choice as he was from the Jinn family, as he is a Jinn. Even though the devil is the personification of evil. They accuse him of trying to become equal to God. False statements as he worshiped Allah and was an obedient Jinn.

He had no issue with Allah, but arrogance toward humanity.

That is blasphemous in Islam. He was arrogant, and prideful, as per Islam. He never sought to equal himself. The serpent tempted Eve into sin and tempted Adam, according to the Bible. She first ate the forbidden fruit. God gave Adam the choice between Eden and Eve.

Bible: John 5:18 This was why the Jews were seeking all the more to kill him, because not only was he breaking the Sabbath, but he was even calling God his own Father, making himself equal with God.

Conjugated interpretations are hard to accept from scriptures that have been notably compromised. Per Islam Satan knew who Allah was, he never sought to be equal, except to sway humanity. Jesus did not try to be equal to God nor did Satan.

That is the reason the uninformed communicate all scriptures have interpretations and corrections therefore they assign the ability to keep an open mind which is another dissolution applicable to other scripts not Quran. Satan creates for the weak as the Quran is the only book unchanged and all Salat is performed in one language Arabic for a unified approach to truth all Muslims know the Quran who practice and learn from believers.

Bible:2 Corinthians 4:4 The devil who rules this world has blinded the minds of those who do not believe. They cannot see the light of the Good News -- the Good

In Islam, Allah is the only ruler of the world, not a jinn Satan. The Devil is seen as a weak enemy, he is a distractor and lures those who fall into his traps, sometimes temporal, and sadly for some permanent. There is only one ruler in this world, Allah, and Satan has respite to distract mankind. Those who fall short may listen, but believers will return to the same place they started with Allah, as a Muslim reminds you of Allah.

The distinctions become evident and repetition provides clarity for those who inquire about the nature and principles of Islam.

In the Bible and its epic scriptures, women, beginning with Eve, were held responsible for temptation, not Adam. In this world, women find no place without blame. Throughout its existence, Islam has refrained from targeting women.

300

According to biblical concepts, Adam made the decision to select Eve and consume the forbidden fruit. Consequently, women are depicted as the initial transgressors and instigators of men. Unfounded accusations have been present throughout history.

However, according to the Quran, it is stated that both parties bear equal responsibility and will face consequences. Islamic beliefs attribute this occurrence to Satan's personal motivations, which were fueled by arrogance and jealousy. God, in accordance with the Bible, created humanity to reflect his own image. The Islamic faith holds the belief that God is not human and that humans were not created in his image. The force that binds the universe is the light known as "Nur," rather than any individual human.

Their interpretation of their belief system represents God created man for fellowship, gardening, and multiplying. Stewardship of this world. What about those humans without offspring? Are they not obeying the law? Allah created humans and jinns to worship him not just to multiply.

As per the teachings of the Bible, humanity is inherently burdened with original sin, and baptism serves as a means of purification. In the Islamic faith, it is believed that all human beings are born as Muslims, without any sins, and with a belief in Allah. In accordance with Islamic teachings, sin is not transferable.

The accumulation of sins serves as a testament to the personal dissatisfaction experienced by each human being who, after nurturing their faith, must make the conscious choice to denounce all wrongdoing and seek refuge. Certain individuals deviate from numerous paths, while others discover Islam in the most unexpected manner, when destiny intervenes rather than human agency.

The purpose of Allah creating darkness and light was to serve as a means of measuring time for humans, rather than for Himself. Consequently, Allah is not reliant on darkness or light for the purpose of timekeeping. Conversely, he employs both to ensure the organization of mankind. Because angels of light cannot transform into angels of darkness. The idea of Satan being a dark angel is dissolved. Angels are light not darkness.

Opposition to Islamic belief. Satan even tempts Jesus, whom they claim to be God. Christendom's history does not collaborate with Islam, though some stories may be comparable. Muslims can only believe the altered text if it agrees with the Qur'an.

Jesus of Islam ascended to Allah while still alive, not dead. The Islamic Jesus will experience life and death like all humans upon his return. If he were a God, he wouldn't experience birth or death. The question of who is right in this discovery arises in the minds of those whose beliefs are not strong.

Can humans distinguish the truth when the Quran's preservation is guaranteed by Allah and the Bible verses clearly state that Jesus will answer and distance himself from liars? If the world rejects liars, shouldn't the Prophet of Allah be able to see the distinctions?

Muslims cannot include the Prophet Muhammad to make amends for our wrongdoings.

The consequences of our actions belong to us alone. Likewise, Satan will also say, "Punish them, they knew who I was, and Allah will give justice to every human on this earth." Islam is bold." Only one Quran exists in Islam, not versions of books. The association with this faith is solely with consequences, not force.

Allah destroyed multiple lands after warning both jinns and humans repeatedly. Humans being flooded, drowned, and killed exemplify the destruction of earth. The extent of Allah's mercy is unfathomable. Allah can decide to terminate his creation if he finds it unacceptable for malevolent beings to seize control.

Why would Allah allow evil to occupy his earth when people of belief can bring bliss to this world? Do not fear those who leave in defiance, nor the believers who depart alongside them; time is of the essence. Those who remain on this earth have no exit, as it is planned. Fear not death, but rather fear the deeds that are carried away by the deceased.

Quran: Surah Nisa;4:133. If He wills, He can take you away, O people, and bring others. And is Allah over that All-Powerful.

There are many shades of creation humans cannot fathom, but deceit has a price for those who ignore the truth. Therefore, it is imperative to take heed of Allah's warnings and live life under His commands. Muslims must strive to be righteous in their actions and remember that Allah is All-Seeing and All-Knowing. Those who repent and turn to Him will find His mercy and grace.

The Bible has many versions. These include the English standard version, the King James version, New American Standard Bible, New English Bible, The revised international version.New King James version, New Living translationTranslation, and New revised standard version. If these versions existed in Islam. Muslims would have renounced Islam. The mind could not comprehend changes. As a result, they do not match these interpretations with Islam. The stories and beliefs of these institutions show a lack of compatibility in many aspects.

Allah purified Prophet Muhammad for this task only through the consequences of preparation and not force.This understanding is not for those who put academia over the Quran. Academia has been enlightened by the Quran, providing explanations for what was previously misunderstood by humans. Explaining is reserved for the intelligent and mindful with pure hearts.

Despite that, he was known for his listening skills. Those who don't believe can only argue here; this understanding is not intended for them.

Those who seek a measure and closeness to the Quran who will find the answers to learn and apply. They will accept the allowance Allah gives to worship him.

Without understanding Islam, humanity cannot worship Him. It requires reflection and pondering.

Today's theologians and academics will put a fair amount of doubt in Muslims' minds about why Allah did not reveal all answers from the beginning of creation.

All questions have been answered in a timely manner. Allah's timing differs from human timing because clocks differ. The concept of right and wrong has never been foreign to man, and Islam is no exception except for its clarity .Some humans are so afraid of human acceptance that they are afraid to say what is true and hesitate to express their differences.

Islamic law cannot be exchanged; it is irrevocable. Human historians can sabotage history. Humanity is not flawless, but Allah is. It is possible to rectify and correct false claims years after the fact. Historians' understanding of history and research accuracy can influence humanity's future.The original research results were not accurate,in some instances but updated information eventually came to light decades later.There were many ideas corrupted by false information.

Some history is delivered correctly, but never precisely. Individuals cannot even accurately narrate a story word for word, let alone the Quran. Allah, who gave the penetration and strength for it, enabled him to endure it precisely and conclude it prior to his departure on earth. "Prophet Muhammad".

A pseudo-society that seeks to find flaws in Allah's message delivery cannot stand up against humanity's history versus the Quranic unaltered delivery. The Quran is the only book under Muhammad's scrutiny. He was not a writer; he was not a reader. This was Allah's mercy.

The disbelievers' accusation makers didn't accuse him of writing his own texts or copying previous texts sent to Israel. As he said things unknown to humanity, they believed he was a magician, a madman, or a poet. But to some, he was a visionary who could see the future. They couldn't fathom how he knew. He did not deliver his own words. It was Allah's words.

Quran: Surah Najm: 53:1-18 "He does not speak of his own desire; It is not but a revelation that is revealed."

Human beings are unique. Humanity cannot hold Satan responsible for all purposeful defiance. The Jinn that enters a human bloodstream commits intentional acts, while some humans do unintentional acts.They stop themselves as soon as they realize the unwarranted direction that invites disobedience to Allah.

Such beings repent and ask for forgiveness. Allah's mercy is limitless.Because Allah gave understanding and the ability to make choices.

Christianity's protocol differs significantly from Islam's. Where a Prophet takes on the sins of people he doesn't know and dies for worthless beings who commit sin every day. As long as he has a ticket and knows, he is dead for them. But sadly, he will say he does not know them.

Bible; The New King James Version: 15:9. *And in vain they worship Me.Teaching as doctrines the commandments of men."*

Quran: Surah Ibrahim: 14:22. Satan will say when the matter is decided: "It was Allah Who gave you a promise of Truth: I, too, promised, but I failed in my promise to you. I had no authority over you except to call you, but ye listened to me: then reproach not me, but reproach your own souls. I can't hear your cries, nor can you hear mine. Associating me with Allah is an act I reject. For wrong-doers, there must be a severe penalty." says Jesus.

In contrast to history, the Quran prohibits alterations. For Muslims, this is the most comprehensive and precise text, and many study it for information that humans lack.

Since the Quran cannot change, Muslims will believe the Quran over history. Muslims cannot learn the Quran and Islam from non-Muslims. In order to create reasonable doubt in young and confused Muslims, these societies make laws and regulations and explain Islam from their point of view.

Islam has indoctrinated the truth, softening with lies to suit the whims of this adulterated regime is not possible. This will ensure that Muslims learn the true teachings of Islam and protect them from misguided information.

A pure strategy for learning the meaning of an Oracle in Islam is to read, reflect, and ponder. We must examine the Quran and not history, through non-Muslims. While human historians can change as time progresses while Islam remains at the forefront.

Muslims must use logic, reason, and understanding to interpret the Quran. The mercy and justice of Allah and the Prophets and messengers of Allah.

The knowledge gained from the Quran is not only spiritual but also practical, as it helps humanity to live a life of peace and harmony. Satan cannot censor the human mind from comprehending and understanding if he so chooses. *He is not a powerful force at all. Islam says he is weak. But mindful and consistent.*

Abu Hurairah handled food during Ramadan. A man came and took the food. He warned the man he would report him to Prophet Muhammad. The person replied by reading the verse of the throne (Aytal Kursi), saying Allah will appoint a protector over you, and no devil will come near you. When he relayed this incident, Prophet Muhammad said Satan told the truth, but otherwise, he was a liar.

If a disbeliever tells you something, do not believe him unless you verify it for yourself. Satan speaks the truth, sometimes to lure a believer. But he is a liar. Believers need further caution that Satan's lies are more dangerous than his truth. Satan's lies can be more attractive than his truth, leading a confused Muslim to decide against his own well-being and interests.

The Jinns and their families can shield themselves from humans and make themselves visible to whomever they wish. They can also take different shapes.

The Quran: Surah Araf: 7: 27 Verily Satan and his soldiers from his tribe or the Jinn. See you there. W where you cannot see them.

Quran: Surah Jinn. 72:1 Say, (O Prophet), Allah revealed it to me that a band of jinn attentively listened to the recitation of the Qur'an) and then (came back to their people) and said:

Quran: Surah Jinn. 72:2. We have indeed heard a wonderful Qur'an which guides us to the Right Way; , so we believe in it, and we will not associate anything with Our Lord in His Divinity.

The term Jinni encompasses diverse categories of jinns. Some spirits torment humans, while others latch onto the souls of children and adults. Inflicting harm upon individuals, jinns possess the ability to either soar through the air or remain stationary. According to Hadith, dogs and donkeys possess the ability to perceive the Jinn.

They can also assume various shapes and forms, such as animals or individuals. They have the ability to metamorphose. Jinns also have the capacity to inhabit humans and compel them to engage in unconventional actions. Allah bestows upon the Jinns a degree of control over humans. Jinns exert their influence on humans through whispering or sowing seeds of confusion and doubt in their minds. The Surahs of the Quran provide a safeguard against malevolence for humanity. Evil cannot shield evil, yet the Quran supersedes it.

Throughout the ages, humans have been enthralled by the mysterious realm of the supernatural. Allah dispatched the Prophet Muhammad to not only the Muslim community but also to all of humanity and the Jinns. Allah enumerates 25 Prophets in the Quran, excluding the vast numbers who preceded them. Allah has unveiled Prophets who had encounters with supernatural beings known as jinns. Prophet Solomon had dominion over the jinns.

In response to the revelations bestowed upon them by Allah, a collective of Jinns embraced the Islamic faith subsequent to their attentive hearing of the Quran. The recitation of the Prophet Muhammad resonated. They exhibited their unwavering belief in the power and truth of Allah, as disclosed by His messenger. Both humans and jinns possess the capacity to exercise free will, regardless of moral outcomes.

Hearts quiver with compassion upon grasping the meaning of the Quranic verses. The purity of the soul purifies seekers. Jinns have the ability to undergo transformations. Allah bestowed upon them the capacity, whereas humans cannot manifest the Jinn form.In the contemporary world, individuals have the ability to alter their physical appearance via plastic surgery, although it can be both daunting and costly. Jinns possess the capability to do this at their discretion.

The example of modern society highlights the yearning to alter their physical appearance due to aging or dissatisfaction, leading them to seek plastic surgery. However, the Jinn possess the ability to transform into any appearance through Allah's permission and blessings. An older lady after being pleased with her plastic surgery, the woman proudly proclaimed to her friends about her newfound beauty, while the parrot persistently echoed that she was unattractive, leading the store owner to admonish the parrot for insulting her appearance.

He ceased as he was aware it would harm the sustenance of his master. Animals have the capacity to perceive things that are invisible to humans, whereas humans possess the ability to comprehend things that animals cannot. As the woman entered the store, the parrot ceased its insults and, upon catching her gaze, muttered "you know." Frustrated by the parrot's persistence, she realized that even after multiple plastic surgeries, he still believed she was unattractive. This incident highlights how humans can alter their appearance through surgery, while Jinns can transform their looks without such procedures, showcasing the creative power of Allah, who bestows His gifts as He pleases.

Quran: Surah Nisa: 4:119.I will order them, and they will change the creation of Allah." Whoever takes Satan as a guardian besides Allah, certainly has suffered a clear suffering.

Although a significant number of Jinns have corrupted humanity, there are also many other Jinns who live peacefully. Although there are a few distinctions, the behavior is quite akin to that of humans. Both the impure Jinns and the impure humans have a common desire to seek filth.

The disobedient Jinns reside in homes that are deteriorating and filled with garbage and waste. The corners that are filled with dirt and darkness. Strikes have no effect on those who have strong beliefs. Jinns who are considered to be pure and clean engage in practices such as performing Salat and reading the Quran. Additionally, they tend to lead a secluded lifestyle, much like humans who have been bestowed with Allah's favor, and choose to distance themselves from those who do not possess such favor.

Those who have faith in Allah can expect to live a life that is both prosperous and fulfilling. Satan, who is known for his disdain towards happy believers, holds a negative sentiment towards them. He positions himself in the midst of relationships that pose a threat to him, thereby fortifying the foundations of Islam.

The intention behind his plot was to undermine the faith of believers. It was within the capabilities of the Jinn to fly. Within a matter of seconds, he swiftly brought the throne, which had originally belonged to the Queen of Sheba, to Solomon. With the permission of Allah, Solomon had the power to control the Jinns. The explanation of the unseen world of jinns has the potential to provide insight into the meaning of the Quran or its direct relevance to humanity.

According to belief, reciting (Surah Baqarah Ayatul Kursi) is said to prevent Jinn from entering a person's home or harming them. In a state of panic and fear, he quickly flees from the scene. In order to protect themselves from evil, the majority of Muslims choose to memorize verses from the Quran and make a daily practice of reciting them. According to belief, it is said that every human being is born with two jinns and two angels specifically assigned to them. The concept of goodness and evil has been debated throughout history.

The righteous jinns pray to Allah. Not a leaf falls without Allah's permission. Cleanliness of the heart, soul, and prayer to Allah with the recitation of the Quran keeps demons away from attending to the righteous.

Quran: Surah Anam. 6:59 And with him are the keys of the unseen: none knows them except Allah. He knows what avails in land and sea. Not a leaf falls, but he knows it. No grain is there within the darknesses of earth, no moist or dry written in a clear record.

Quran: Surah Jinn 72:1 Say [O' Muhammad]: We have revealed it

That a group of Jinn listened [to the Quran].

Quran: Surah Jinn 72:1 Say [O' Muhammad]: We have revealed it

That a group of Jinn listened [to the Quran

Quran: Surah Fatir 35:6 Indeed, Satan is an enemy to you; , so take him as an enemy. He invites his party only as blaze companions.

In the Quran, it is mentioned that understanding and being aware of the enemy is crucial. The main purpose he has is to bring you to the fire, and once you are there, he will make his way back. The Quran, as highlighted in (Surah Al-Jinn), stands alone as the sole book that provides a comprehensive and detailed explanation of it. As the Prophet Muhammad recited the sacred Quran, the Jinns eagerly listened to his recitation, and a significant number of them embraced the faith of Islam. The Jinns, like humans, are also capable of deciding their own beliefs.

Satan's unwavering determination bolsters him, as he believes, yet he reigns supreme amidst those who are feeble and deceitful. He commands a formidable army. They willingly trail behind him. An individual who defies the decrees of Allah is a primordial Jinn. Excuses were nullified and obliterated, as Allah's Book unveiled the answers for those in pursuit of truth. Man has the ability to challenge and adhere to authority.

Humanity includes those who remain steadfast in their belief in Allah's messages. It is simple to manifest defiance towards the person who redirects you from unfavorable, familiar locations to fruitful ones. Allah can guide a person, if he so desires. The individual who has faith in Allah perceives the weakness of Satan and his army.

Quran: Surah Fatir 35:25 If they deny you, so did those before them. Their messengers came to them with obvious proofs, divine books, and enlightening scriptures.

The stagnant waters of a disbeliever or a pleaser of disbelievers can contaminate the clean waters of a believer, as they serve as breeding grounds for bugs. Humans sprint from mosquitoes, termites, cockroaches, and other pests. An example of a contaminated environment is a soiled homeland, contaminated water, or polluted air. Or the evil company Islam focuses on is the human environment impacts human character. Allah gives the example of a tiny mosquito in the Quran. Spiders, ants, stories, and examples are for understanders.

Quran: Surah Fatir 2;26, He misleads many and guides many. And he misleads not to accept the defiantly disobedient.

Life depicts changes. Man can comprehend the beauty of friendship presented by Allah.

We can draw no distinction between obedience to Allah and worldly affairs, which are acceptable in today's society but disrupt the alternative.

Bad friendships can hold back goodness given to a believer. Sometimes self-realization offered by Allah is necessary. Certain subjects may be thorny to entangle in life, but unravel the evil, and Allah guides man to good. Follow the cursed defiant people from Allah, and harm will follow. All good is from Allah.

Satan lost a world of wealth, beauty, and worship of Allah with angels to concentrate on destroying humanity. This left him empty-handed in the darkness of illusion and respite. His team is people who focus on others and have nothing to show.

A human has not seen what he has seen. (Jannah) heaven is a beautiful place that humans have only heard about. Having lived there, he knows what it is like. Satan does not want humans living in this paradise. Despite his arrogance and pride, he was stupid enough to get out of it. Allah created humanity and Jinns to worship him, not defy him. His followers show lack of,.

Quran: Surah Rahman verse 15. And created a Jinn from a ˈsmokelessˈ flame of fire.

Quran: Surah Araf verse 12. You made me from fire and created him from clay.

Quran: Surah Anam: 6:130."O ye assembly of Jinns and men! came there not unto you messengers from amongst you, setting forth unto you My signs, and warning you of the meeting of this day.

When one does not recognize the jewel as a gift from God, it will also slip away in neglect. **Muslims ask Allah to give them a heart that can understand eyes that can see ears that can hear right from wrong.**

Satan has dark characteristics. He sends humans in altered disguises as friends or confidantes. Sometimes using, families who hold disbelief or (shirk) adding partners

the darker souls, doubtful and disoriented. In some cases, a spouse of a significant other or someone who meets your sexual needs and desires.

Without faith, is a foreplay of evil from Satan. His ways are many. The call is, however, rebuffed by weak associates. **Poison can be transmitted from family members, friends, or partners. Evil breeds poison in many ways.**

The stories of the grandsons of the Prophet Muhammad provide examples of life along with many others for those seeking answers. It was Hasan's wife who became his poison. It was his wife Ja'dah, daughter of Al- Ash'ath, the promise he made to her with Muawiyah, and their involvement in a conspiracy.That poisoned Hasan, the grandson of the Prophet Muhammad. She offered him a yogurt drink, and he drank it.

After feeding it to a freedwoman and to Hasan, Prophet Muhammad's grandson, and her husband, the freedwoman vomited poison. However, her husband kept it, but couldn't extract it once it entered his insides, killing him.

He was martyred per Islam. When someone kills a Muslim,upon his death. Muslims are considered martyrs when they die at the hands of others.

Are non-believers who are killed also considered martyrs, or is that exclusive to Muslims and believers of one God? Martyred refers to dying as a believer, not as a non-believer. Who is the belief

in? In the creator who created Adam and Eve Allah. Use any name to refer to him, but Allah has been the only God since before the world existed.

His death reminds us of his family's struggles to uphold Islam. Prophet Muhammad's grandsons were both martyred. Sometimes, the spouse's children's parents' false friendships serve as trials..

And completion of the faith in Allah serves as the final destitute of servitude to Allah. People in one's own family can be enemies or friends. There are many reasons for such divisions, but examples are plentiful for those who seek them. Even dating back to the Abrahamic Prophets.

The act of feeding on the fervor of a non-Muslim or bartering with evil by a Muslim. Lack of faith, greed, self desires, and power lead to the destitute.

Believers are sometimes unaware of this motive. Throughout history, Allah has made visible to humanity everything from kindness to evil, trust to belief, through the example of Prophet Muhammad.

The readings of this Prophet and his family show those who understand quality and character. Allah has placed humans as an example at every threshold. It is not inconceivable to exploit human nature when the story reminds viewers that the wife's desire for power over another man led her to poison her husband, Hasan.

Because of her greed for dinar money and the promise to marry Yazid's son that Mu'awiya made to her, she took to poisoning him. In spite of her greed, marriage, and power, none of these events took place after she committed the act.

Mu'awiya saw her temperament was ruthless, her character was weak, and she could not be trusted. In addition to poisoning her husband, the grandson of Prophet Muhammad, she did not receive anything she was promised by the enemy. Most disbelievers cannot be trusted, and a believer cannot be questioned as to the integrity of the one to believe in Allah. Morality of ethics exists in most humans.

The connection between kindness, belief and trust is seamless for those who believe and those who hope to find solace, regardless of their differences. Rather, it serves as evidence that moral principles are cultivated and nurtured primarily through solidarity in a belief system.

This is done with coherence and an understanding of why one has faith in Allah. Although evil exists, Muslims cannot hold Satan responsible. It is unfathomable, and it is up to each person to decide whether to help or neglect. Death is not a punishment, but a gift. The intentional taking of another's life is martyrdom for a Muslim.

The deceased receive a reward, but suicide is a penalty. Per Islam, martyrdom is for Muslims, not for disbelievers. It's exclusive to believers who submit to Allah alone. The deceased would have been unaware of such an unintentional act before his death.

Disbelievers may draw different conclusions from these facts or even be confused..In the family and among the devout followers of Prophet Muhammad, we see both sad and happy examples. They did not abandon worldly life, instead leaving paradigm-archetype examples of life behind, surrendering their lives to Allah in submission.

Because Allah provided a human life to enjoy and prepare for the next, it can achieve both. **Islam does not blame all these mishaps on Satan. It's part of life and Allah's plan. Martyred Muslims are alive in paradise, says Allah.**

Hussain was the younger son of Ali, grandson of Prophet Muhammad, who was killed by the enemy. In a combination of greed, rebellion, and revenge, they removed his head from his body and presented it to Yazid.

The hardships they faced led them to put Islam at the forefront and stand up for their rights. If Muslims could fathom the true stories, they wouldn't rebel against their own faith. Faith is a process by which someone without faith becomes faithful.

It's part of life and Allah's plan. Examples of Abrahamic Prophets help believers maintain equilibrium. In contrast to Bible stories that can put Prophets to shame, they were also Muslims who faced trial as they submitted to Allah. They accuse these Prophets in the Bible of dishonestly concocting stories to suit their worldview.These trials, and stories are eye-openers for those who see the truth.

By their stories in the Bible.Noah exposed himself shamefully while drunk. The ten commandments were also given to Moses, the murderer. According to the Bible, Satan tempted Jesus, not per Quran.

Every Prophet sent by Allah never claimed to be divine. Many people find it difficult for their subconscious mind to accept the transformation of a singular consistent message into a triune message.The concept emphasizes atonement forgiveness, making it easy to commit sins since love is the primary focus, not laws.

The Bible and the story of the people of Lot have contrasting narratives. This leads to him committing a more serious offense by impregnating both of his daughters. The Bible's intricate narratives are incomprehensible to most people, making it challenging for Muslims to adhere to. The divine message has been tampered with by human interference.

A pure justification of the creator does not support engaging in unrewarded and impermissible acts.

In the Bible, a father interacts closely with his two daughters and condemns same-gender relationships. Why is there no repercussion for impregnating two daughters? Free from penalties.

According to the Bible, he treats the Prophets who came to set examples, leaving behind worse examples. How can humans learn from a Prophet when the justice system is appalled by such events? The collision of human hands with the Divine is clear in prior scriptures. Where can we find a moral character if it sends mixed messages? Consistency is present in all messages of the Quran.

All faiths demand to listen to their script or punishment awaits. As christendom falls in Abrahamic faith becomes imperative to compare the narrative of entrance to heaven which is not easy.

Nevertheless, this faith is founded on the principle of embracing Jesus as the savior who paid the price for their sins, granting them access to heaven. The refusal to accept him as a savior results in the entirety of humanity being subjected to hell. While the deeds themselves are not being questioned, it is the acceptance of a mortal as a savior that grants entrance.

The idea of worshiping deities and seeking entrance to their presence is not a recent development; numerous cultures throughout history have held beliefs in divine beings and their existence on Earth. However, with the advent of Islam and its teachings, the concept of being accountable for one's own actions became more apparent and logical. In a world where payment for deeds is possible, it is difficult to understand how the creator cannot be just.

What is heaven called in Judaism? Shifting ideologies led to changes in previous scripts. Is there a belief in heaven within Judaism? Yes. The term "heaven" mentioned in previous scriptures refers to (Shamayim).

Does (Gehinnom), also known as hell, actually exist? Yes, in Judaism. Hell, known as Jahannam, is a component of the Muslim belief system. The Torah recognizes the afterlife for knowledge seekers, with Allah as the creator God. The Quran explicitly conveys this message.

Resurrection linked to (Sheol). Bones are preserved in the burial ground for judgment day. Cremation is not approved in Judaism or Islam. Christendom is a modified form of Judaism that emerged after Jesus' ascension, incorporating elements of Roman paganism and new script adjustments.

Who fulfills the necessary requirements to be granted access to heaven? Were the individuals who decided to replace Allah with other deities distinct from those who remained steadfast in their singular faith? The issue at hand may be complicated, but Jesus will bring clarity and justification to any misconceptions that arise in due time.

To whom did the first creation offer their prayers? To whom did the father of all Prophets offer prayers? Do you have the answer? Didn't they pray to just one God, Allah? Yes, the books came later. Nevertheless, the worship was all-encompassing for Allah. The answer to who will occupy the earth should be clear.

As the religion of Islam continued to expand and gain followers, the Quran played a crucial role in rectifying any inaccuracies or alterations that may have been present in earlier written texts created by humans. Muslims were advised to alter the direction of prayers, attire, and the grooming of men's beards. In accordance with the religious guidelines, Muslim men had the permission to shave the hair above their lip, while still being obligated to keep a beard.

Islam distinguishes itself from other faiths with its exclusive practice of fasting for a continuous 30 days during (Ramadan) month of fasting for Muslims. The implementation of strict rules created an environment where Muslims could organize themselves effectively and prosper, developing a more refined understanding of life on earth.

The Quran took control of the laws instead of human desires. Dislodging the laws of Allah was not the intention of free will. Humans who equate their desires with free will end up creating self-imposed laws instead of following divine laws. This imbalance causes harm in the long run, contrary to Allah's intention of balancing humanity.

The stories in the Bible make it difficult for humans to grasp cause and effect. Allah is divine, not a fictional character created by laws or defaming stories.

Psalm 19:10, Song of Songs 5:1 NIV5 I have come into my garden, my sister, my bride; ... I have gathered my myrrh and my spice. I have eaten my honeycomb and honey; I have drunk my wine and milk.

Both incestuous relationships and the use of certain words are considered impermissible in Islam. The context of the Bible is not appropriate for all age groups, making it unsuitable for discussions with children.

Many scripts, including those found in the bible, are not considered to have a divine origin. These stories or examples, being sources of negativity in terms of morality, will not be embraced by Muslims.

The nature of Allah is inherently positive, as everything he sends is intended to bring about positive outcomes.

If the previous book and stories do not adhere to the moral code that is addressed to Prophets, it is just as likely that ordinary humans, who are not Prophets, may also partake in such actions or, even more regrettably, engage in even more atrocious behavior. This particular quality is exhibited by the stories found in the Bible.

The books of belief serve as the fundamental basis for everything that exists. Restoring faith in books of previous scriptures can be challenging when ordinary people find the messages in them objectionable, unless one embraces the long-standing belief that there is only one God, a belief that has been prevalent in this society for many decades. Ultimately, individuals may find themselves in a position where they have to establish their own guidelines that are in line with their own moral beliefs.

Exposing the story of Lot suggests it is a pattern acceptable to the Bible.Then he was forgiven, and why should a common man be held accountable when Bible Prophets have horrible stories as well?

While these re-arranged texts differ, they have very few similarities, as they are not simple distinctions that can be resolved. The Bible stories are so different from those of the Quran that some of them are not suitable content and cannot be read by a child.

After society tolerates such ludicrous acts, what is the credibility of believing such Prophets from the Bible? That Allah sends these ill-doings and tells humanity to follow them is incomprehensible in terms of cherry-picking. Islam gives them respect and deems these Prophets Allah sent as examples for humanity.

Their knowledge of what the church exposes keeps changing as time progresses. Knowledge is not hidden; it is readily available to those who pursue it. That is why the conversion rate from Christianity to Islam is increasing in numbers. In contrast, hypocrisy is beyond repair and continues to corrupt the world through unwarranted events.

Clearly, these stories point to right and wrong. They have no implications of corrosion between kindness and sharing truth towards humanity. Many atheists convert to Islam after extensive research and spiritual awakening. It is intended for believers to see the differences, especially new converts and unaware Muslims.

Muslims and uneducated Muslims need lessons from both faiths to understand the major differences.The accusations against these Bible prophets' wrongful behaviors and concocting stories to suit their worldviews are adapted to modern life.

Social media and falsifiers turn events into untrue versions and depictions that do not happen. **Ethics and morality are not always related to faith. The moral compass of right and wrong can also apply to those who don't follow faith. Many people engage in ethical behaviors and conduct business and daily life ethically. As an alternative to religion, belief is portrayed with major differences affecting society.**

Many people leaving other denominations claim that the stories they were exposed to do not sit well with those who have done intense research. The differences are only to depict faith and transformations for those who seek peace in Allah and truth.

The distinctions do not imply that humanity cannot be friends regardless of faith. It is Satan who indulges in behaviors causing diseases of the heart. He is a weak enemy. The Jinn family and humans who disobey Allah are in the same category.

Blaming Satan for ills is not justified. Understanding your enemy is a requirement in Islam. Satan appears in 78 verses of the Quran, mentioned 88 times. Enemies have the ability to hide and attack under the guise of friends or even family. Satan is openly revealed from creation to respite.

Consequently, all excuses given by Muslims or converts to Islam hold no weight. This faith is not based on blind belief. Islam involves a deep exploration for believers to discover truth and grow. As in any academic or business setting, winners don't follow losers. Believers do not adhere to disbelievers. Islam did not conspire with Satan to manipulate the truth through modified scriptures. Human platforms cannot conform to the truth.

They offer the worst advice. The repeated mention of love feels insignificant in these situations. When the meaning is unknown, this country uses the word love.

Jesus explicitly cursed his people in the Bible when he told them to love everyone. Muhammad was the only one who refrained from cursing his people. The allegations and stories of other scriptures contradict the texts in the Quran. The Quran clarified doubts and discrepancies from the Bible to reflect Allah's consistency. Consistency is a trait of people with character. If Allah created humanity, why wouldn't he ensure consistency in his message?

Gospel of Matthew 21:18–22 Here, the fig tree withers immediately after the curse is pronounced. This drives the narrative forward to Jesus' encounter with the Jewish priesthood and his curse against them and the temple.

Those who pursue knowledge can readily access it. It's ironic that the country is so invested in capitalistic moves while flaunting faith with adjustments. Where survival depends on credit cards backed by interest in every move they make. The nation survives by earning interest.

Bible: John 2:15-17 Jesus made a whip, Jesus put together a whip out of strips of leather and chased them out of the Temple, stampeding the sheep and cattle, upending the tables of the loan.

Quran: Surah Imran: 12:132." O believers, do not take doubled and redoubled interest, and fear God so that you may prosper". ." Receiving or paying interest is a major sin in Islam.

Jesus whipping the Jews for taking an interest. Christianity portrays him as loving and forgiving human sins, as he himself asked Allah for forgiveness, just like all the other Prophets did. Islam forbids interest.

Allah's Prophets are consistent. Jesus the Messiah was sent to the Jews of Israel in order to correct their disobedience, not the entire world. Although Prophet Muhammad from the Arabian peninsula was sent as a Prophet of mankind, jinns, and all that exists. Jesus clearly stated that he must go away to send the comforter the truth. Jesus has a job to complete, and he will return to tell defiant people he is not a god. He worships Allah.

Similar to the Jews during that time, they also showed disobedience and dishonesty. Zionism represents a contemporary act of rebellion, as humans consistently seek to defy Allah. The finality sets the tone for the winners, despite humanity's chances. Shirk, making a partner to Allah, is the unforgivable sin for humanity. Allah is watching the human discourse, and the oppression of the weak is leading one to unforeseen consequences.

The journey for learners has just begun. Christians in New York City, USA have the highest number of conversions to Islam. Nations are embracing Islam, not just states. Those who oppose Islam and Muslims are the supporters of tomorrow. Only Allah knows who will be invited to embrace his faith.

King James Bible: 16:7.Nevertheless I tell you the truth; It is expedient for you that I go away: for if I leave not away, the Comforter will not come unto you; but if I depart, I will send him unto you.

King James Bible: Deuteronomy:18:18.I will raise them up a Prophet from among their brethren, like unto thee, and will put my words in his mouth; and he shall speak unto them all that I shall command him.

Prophet Muhammad brought the same message as Allah's other Prophets. The state remained the same. The Jews were taken aback by his arrival from the Arabian Peninsula, but Allah was all-powerful.

Prophet Muhammad will be the only Prophet to testify as the seal of all Prophets on the day of judgment. When humanity is held accountable for every action in this world.

They defied Jesus. Despite Satan's inability to affect individuals, many escape these evils.***As a final testament, Muhammad was sent to seal the seal of Prophets, aakhir us zuma.*** Paul and the apostles who wrote the first testament never met Jesus. They were Jews.

Satan's defiance needs extensive study to comprehend his evil. He mixes truth with lies to keep the collusion from abiding with the truth. Christianity did not exist in Jesus' time. It arrived after his ascension. Islam has been present since Allah created man destined to worship one God.

Many people are leaving organized faiths, especially Islamophobes, claiming that they just believe in God. Their stories clash with the common mind. The Quran explicitly instructs followers to follow Prophet Muhammad. However, this does not mean that people of different faiths cannot be friends. Believers of the same faith are better suited for sharing beliefs.

Jinns eat excrement, live on darkness's borders, and fear light. Their homes are dark, and their hearts are at risk.Humans who like darkness and dislike light resemble jinns. Darkness prefers darkness. Easily influenced individuals are weak and susceptible to being manipulated and betrayed in a failing market by the deceitful ones who enticed them.

Quran: Surah Ibrahim 14;22 But I had no authority over you except that I invited you. Say when judgment takes place. Verily, Allah's word was the truth.

Quran: Surah Maidah 5:8. O you who have believed, be persistent in standing up for God's witnesses in justice. Do not let the hatred of a people prevent you from being just. Be just; that is the way to righteousness. And fear God; he is familiar with what you do.

Quran: Surah Maidah 5:8. O you who have believed, be persistently standing firm for God's witnesses in justice, and do not let the hatred of a people prevent you from being just. Be just; that is nearer to righteousness. And fear God; indeed, God is familiar with what you do.

Quran: Surah Anam: 6:67 For every happening is a finality: and you are going to know..

Just like how one person's behavior can have positive or negative impacts on another, the disbelief in the Council can also leave unexpected consequences.

Islam is characterized by kindness and reciprocity. Pay attention to how nihilists behave. To combat ignorance, believers should choose kindness as the solution.

Believers are haunted by skeptics with ghostly encounters. The cases demonstrate attitudes characterized by negative imbalance. Their evil whispers and advice stem from negative sources. Doubtful believers are easily deceived as Satan manifests in countless ways. Through a human's bloodstream, he has already flowed in and out of Allah's first creation.

An inflated ego often indicates a poor heart. A generous heart is characterized by knowing one's own value. Allah references multiple creatures, including birds, mosquitoes, flies, ants, and insects. Why does Allah mention such small creatures in the Surah? The cave's spider web protects the children from their enemies.

Despite the benefits small creatures bring, why do humans still entertain shallow personalities? The decision of discretion lies with the person aware of the moral conflict. The birds, by carrying stones in their beaks and defeating the elephants, demonstrated the power of small creatures, particularly when they unite in large numbers.

Quran; Surah Fil describes the full story.

It is clear in the Quran. Allah owns all powers. Allah created no one equal, and neither is their demeanor equal. He gives to whoever he wills as he sees fit. To some, he gives without an account.

Quran: Surah Anbiya 21:33, and it is he who created the night and the day, the sun and the moon; all [heavenly bodies] in an orbit are swimming.

Quran: Surah Baqarah 2:28,How can you disbelieve in Allah when you were lifeless, and He brought you to life? Then He will cause you to die. Then He will bring you back to life, and then to Him ; you will return.

Quran: Surah Fussilat 41:34(Good and evil cannot be equal.

Respond to evil with the strengths where feuds become victories. Breaking faulty memories, bad companies and inappropriate habits. It is best suited for a believer. Return to beginnings that brought peace in heart Islam and a believer.

Touching something that had been lying dormant for some time is a better effort than sleeping life away. Life has a randomness that appears when least expected. Introducing a fusional relationship between Allah and humans, giving the seeker completion.

The unity of believers exemplifies Allah's ordained beauty. Man possesses no complexity other than the urgency to change circumstances and gain momentum.

It's the benevolent mercy that he extends to his favored servants in life.Not one of their Lord's signs comes to them, but they turn away from it.Music is another way Satan has invited humanity into the most undesirable places.

Lonely, sad places, nightclubs, and strip clubs where women and men willingly strip to make a buck. Dancing in the most inappropriate rhythms and dancing to the beat of Satan. Alcohol is devoured, and mind-altering drugs are created and composed for entertainment. It's a jungle of mishaps, not an advent of entertainment or success.

It's the saddest of stories when you hear I spent my youth in nightclubs. I remember those days such comments bring an array of regrets for those who hear it as brags, Evil needs to be buried not reinstated as reminders.

It is a sorrowful loss of a splendid period, as youth is among the most valuable times granted to a human being. All originated from localities where malevolence was well-known, from bustling metropolises.

The emphasis lies not on compliments, but rather on a contemporary form of destruction—an alternate reality with a distinct rhythm. <u>The legislation on nudity imposes significant restrictions.</u>

Sketchy outfits that raise suspicion and an appearance that exudes villainy identify evil. Minds that possess a carnivorous nature dabble in all sorts of evil within their reach. The fashion industry, known for its ruthlessness, is responsible for these dilemmas, enticing vulnerable minds to indulge in the unknown.

Music has gained a distinct power and excitement. Their concerts, record sales, and tours all made revenue, and many lost their morals to the beat. Clubbing at a young age and spending youth in places that did not complement later life. Music became addictive and hearts lost the ability to sync with reality for those who answered to it.

Music had a profound effect on our sounds and bodies, which led to social and cultural change. Rock came about as a rejection of old music and attitudes that bridged cultural and religious divides. Society was barely adjusting to the idea and new acceptance of things not acceptable in a society undergoing transformation. Another wave of change followed, even bigger than before the arrival of rap.

Soon the world rocked with satanic beats, and less clothing became acceptable because of the newly adapted culture.The deliberate entrance of Satan and the sound of music echoed throughout New York streets.

In 1971, it played its first unfamiliar sounds. It was an influential year for rock music.

David Bowie, Led Zeppelin, Al Green, John Lennon and more took center stage rocking the sounds of music.

Rap culture broke boundaries and words never heard before first played on the radio in 1979. Rap culture and its influence on music have negatively affected youth and deviants. They showcase undesirable lifestyles, increasing profanity, sexual arousal, demeaning women, and drug use, all catering to evil.

A number of them either committed violent homicides or took their own lives. Evil can also leave reminders that it has a price to pay. Islam has also been embraced by many of these fringe rappers. The discovery of Islam made them realize how obscure and painful their previous life was, with rap music playing a key role.

Hip-hop, heavy metal, Funk, Soul, Jazz, and Disco. The sound appealed to many people, and the words liberated those who wanted to break all the rules of society.

As a first step, jazz was called evil because it stimulated promiscuous sexuality and drugs based on adrenaline and vile words in music got increasingly extreme as time passed.

A display of algorithms and performers has reached the Middle East, and these countries are inviting this barrage against Islamic principles. For instance, Dubai is a popular expat hotspot.

Why did music become a subject we must discuss and how its entering homes and words and sounds affect society. Is this affair innocent or danger lurks as the heart answers to the beats. What will be the profound effect of finality of these beats?

Who is (Dajjal)? A deceiver:

The Dajjal is called (al-Masih ad-Dajjal) in Islam. (Al-Masih) means 'savior' and ad-Dajjal means 'liar'. In simple terms, it refers to the false savior or fake savior.

Islam is the only faith that delves into the depths and safeguards against Dajjal. His arrival is imminent, but the exact timing remains unknown. Islam outlines the stages of this event, ensuring nothing occurs without the prescribed progression.

Is he an evil figure he appears to represent a human did a woman birth him no he is a creation of Allah why did he create evil. It's a test (Kafir) is the word disbeliever scribed on his forehead the believers will be able to read it. He will be able to do magical things; those who follow him will invite fitna. What is fitna?

The term "fitna" in Islam originates from an Arabic verb that denotes the act of enticing or seducing evil. Evil is seducing the world, disguising success as danger lurks in every home. Temptations are closer than imagined. The Jinn family of Satan aids this cause. In the end, who will prevail, the Muslims or the evil forces? Those who disobey and deceive, falsely claiming what is not theirs, and adding mortals in worship all conform to the end times.

Muslims in the Middle East are facing significant challenges, particularly where it all began. All Prophets came to the people of Israel, but Prophet Muhammad emerged uniquely from Saudi Arabia. Islam stands as a distinct belief, offering a sense of closure for all. Allah does not force anyone, and neither do Muslims, but the impact of worship and Islamic laws will soon be clear in establishing law and order.

 Poor people lack land, so why isn't the world giving them any? Israel's destiny is to rise and fall, regardless of the deeds' actions. The lands of Allah will be owned by the righteous, as Allah has made clear. It is not the deceivers and disobedient who are supporting the issue; rather, it is not those who have passed on their burden of sins to someone else. Muslims face challenges, but we are responsible for our own sins. One God, one worship.

The music is intricately linked to the indications of the hour. With one eye impaired, he will bring music to the place where the majority of individuals conform to the rhythm. The deceit within his words will consist of a combination of truth and falsehood.

The music industry has had a major impact on society, both positively and negatively. The lyrics of the rhythm mix truth and falsehood, effortlessly evoking belief in songs that resonate with joy or sorrow. They seek to undermine societal morals and eliminate law, order, and religiosity, while also introducing their own religious beliefs. Human laws prioritize deception and self-interest over divine laws.

Muhammad the Prophet extensively discusses the Dajjal to prepare the Muslim community. Reciting ten verses from Surah Kahf on Fridays safeguards Muslims from the deceiver, Dajjal.

The desire for truth about countries that sow chaos is shared by both believers and non-believers; it is correct to say that Christianity disbands women or denies them the right to rule. Standing for truth is a core belief of Muslims.

Men and women both share false stories about venues without knowing the truth or what they believe is true. Muslims will recount the story and discover that we are right once more. Islam invites believers, not those who regress. The prophet predicted that if Jerusalem thrives, Yathrib will crumble. The war will occur within the religious sects of, Islam, Judaism, and Christendom.

Constantinople in Turkey will witness the conquest and the arrival of the Dajjal antichrist. Constantinople's region has had a significant role in shaping its people, who are known for their big hearts. However, many have been influenced by the negative aspects of Western modernity.

Wasn't it foretold by the Prophet that Muslims would conquer Constantinople? It has come to pass, and now we witness the start of victory, with Constantinople having a role again? Do you see the Turkish people boldly defending Muslim conquests and declaring Turkey as the hub of the Muslim world? The youth's understanding of Islam has been compromised in Turkey during a period of misguided modernity, which coincided with Western influence and resulted in a lack of comprehension among young people, who play a vital role in false glamor.

The formative years are crucial for success; don't let them go to wasteThe presence of evil is an ongoing intrusion. People of all ages are embracing Islam and coming back stronger in this region and globally.

It's a global epidemic, but knowledge is the path to victory. Walking in darkness is acceptable. If a Muslim's inner light knows the truth, we can face trials and challenges and maintain our momentum. Stand up for truth as a Muslim, even if it means standing alone.

Hadith: Abu Dawud: 4294. He (the Prophet) struck his thigh or his shoulder with his hand and said: This is as true as you are here or as you are sitting. (meaning Mu'adh ibn Jabal).

Hadith: Sahih Muslim: 'They [the Muslims] will then fight and a third of the army will run away, whom Allah will never forgive. A third, which would be made up of excellent martyrs in Allah's eye, would be killed, and the third, who would never be put to trial, would win and they would be conquerors of Constantinople.

Hadith: Abu Dawud: 4296. The Prophet (ﷺ) stated that there would be a six-year gap between the great war and the conquest of Constantinople, and the Dajjal (Antichrist) would arise in the seventh year.

The curious minds keep asking questions with not enough time to fully delve in every subject and clarity Islam has sent but the basis of subjects and clarity is enough to feed the curiosity.

(Kuffar la aitbaar) means not trusting those who don't believe in Allah as the one God.

Those who possess belief will discover truth, while those who are adrift can be found across all faiths. Knowing the truth is preferable to ignorance. It is necessary for a Muslim to have theological knowledge. The presence of faith associations does not impact the structural truth.

The Quran has remained unaltered, preserving the teachings of Prophet Muhammad in hadith and practices for seekers of knowledge. The Quran warns against learning from non-Muslims, as they are the same people responsible for chaos and now spreading teachings on social media about the end times.

Muslims need to speak up the truth and invest in channels of truth. Verbally in writings and voiced through every avenue available. Encouraging and teaching our youth about Islam is fair to all of humanity.

Non-Muslims cannot teach about the end times; the Quran and hadiths hold the answers. A knowledgeable Muslim who can provide information about Islam, not biased by current events.

In their corrupt society, speaking the truth is seen as rude and hateful, while false lies are embraced as truth. If it is clear why learn from them, teach them even if it means angering them, its diamond era for Muslims shine now with truth. They engage in acts forbidden by Allah even in matters of sexuality, and any criticism is labeled as hate speech. Those who see truth continue to witness warnings of the end times.

Muslims who are acclimating to academia and wealth have achieved remarkable accomplishments. Numerous countries play a significant role in staging them collectively as Muslims if they bear to step out. If Muslims deviate from Islamic terms, haters will portray them positively.

The faith that everyone is talking about is spreading like wildfire, without discrediting those who try. Despite joining the evil forces and living in discontent as the beats of this rhythm darken their soul, a human still yearns for peace as part of their platform.The inclusion of sexual content in these words led to distress and sadness in many households, resulting in singers and listeners resorting to drug and alcohol overdose.

The cosmic era divided people into those who did evil and those who sculpted their bodies through exercise. Appearance has an impact. The vulnerable and unsettled individuals who mimicked the crowd violated Islamic teachings by tattooing their bodies. This became a global phenomenon for those who chose to mark their bodies forbidden in Islam.

There are marks on their bodies from those heavy times in their lives inscriptions forbidden by Islam for the times they believed were significant in their lives.The pain and the emptiness conveyed a sense of longing for peace, and many sought happiness.

There were many who converted to Islam in this time of sadness; some remained, investing their whole lives in betterment.And some were content with a bit of Islam and living in discontentment. This is a religion from the creator that requires full acceptance, not just a statement saying I am Muslim.

These are just a few examples of how corrupt ventures keep influencing humanity.

Those who are Muslims must compete within themselves to be the most competitive. Being around the brightest or most knowledgeable people is a learning curve.

A company that distorts the mind is not an excuse for evil, since it allows the darkness of the mind to grow. It is only through the alignment of the mind and heart that one can see a belief that does not call out the unbeliever.

In the past, there were no lyrics that aroused the mind and demoralized the moral compass, but music and deception do so now.

The master of exploitation and the believing believers have no tolerance for such oratory. A person who elaborates on the Quran. Continuous music is not something one can handle. One or two songs can be a satisfying indulgence, yet for some, it becomes forbidden.

Even though these sounds can calm some people, they can actually make others more depressed. Azan signifies contentment and happiness for Muslims, unlike music. The melodic Quran has evoked tears of peace and contentment from Muslims and Non-Muslims alike.

Quran: Surah ISRA verse 38 'Verily the ears, the eyes, and the heart, all of them will have questions.

Quran: Surah Nisa 4:81 Allah records what they plan by night. So leave them alone and rely upon Allah. And He is sufficient as the disposer of affairs.

The Muslim world has always adhered to one another's needs. When society sets boundaries for how fast they want to move, society can examine our underlying structure based on Islam.

Quran: Surah Imran 3:134 who spend in the way of Allah both in plenty and hardship, who restrain their anger, and forgive others. Allah loves such a good-doer,

Solitude and surviving alone are among the most powerful resources. Solitude cannot be sustained for long periods; learning and sharing are essential to humanity. Prophet Muhammad spent hours praying alone and in the company of others.

The magnificence of comprehension. Reminding someone of Allah is a task for believers only. While humanity is connected in care, a believer stands apart as a unique entity.

Humanity's resurgence is crucial for survival. Humanity cannot be separated by contrasts, but theology reveals the inquisitive nature of those seeking answers. One response might have cleared up the purpose of confusion. Peace could have been achieved with just one smile or word. Nothing surpasses a single Sujood.

The complexity of faith is intricate. Islam marks the end of the relationship between Allah and humanity. Muslims worship Allah by accepting every Prophet sent by Him, in the Quran.The belief that what Allah gives is the truth, and what humans reject after receiving is doubts.

Similarly, Jews reject Jesus as the final Messiah, while Christians consider him both human and divine. Muslims, however, adhere to the belief that he is the Messiah, and await his arrival when he will speak the truth. The Quran is the ultimate source for truth seekers.

Explanations hold truth regardless of beliefs or theologies. To avoid any hostility, clarifications foster a shared understanding of Islam. Islam ensures all humans are treated equally in matters of justice and receive their due. Upholding the principle of kindness and sharing with humanity, as dictated by Islamic law, results in an increase, not a decrease.

The strength to resist lies and accept others is reinforced by remembering the laws and regulations that shape humanity's path. Showing immunity and acceptance to laws of humanity exposes a weakness. Allah's laws take precedence over any human-made laws. Humanity will answer to Allah, not to humans, as he reigns supreme forever. Brace yourself for the answers. The alignment of preparedness and opportunity completes a person.

CHAPTER 15

IS JEALOUSY FORBIDDEN IN ISLAM? FACT OR FABRICATION.

Is there a way to effectively prohibit emotions? In Islam, is punishment given priority or does it rely more on common sense and factual evidence? Given that Allah is believed to be the creator of primal emotions between individuals, it raises the question of why He would classify it as a sin. While jealousy is not encouraged in Islam, it is not considered a sinful act. Is it deemed sinful for Prophets to display sentiments of jealousy and possessiveness? It is categorically impossible for that to occur.

The act of crossing boundaries and following one's instincts is something that occurs frequently. Jealousy should not be confused with impulsive behavior as they are distinct concepts. Repentance becomes a necessary action in order to correct the ongoing battles with evil. Seeking forgiveness from Allah (Astaghfar) is a necessary step towards spiritual growth and repentance.

Accusations of jealousy towards others are a common response from individuals who have been corrected. The classified accusations serve as a tenuous link for individuals who are not privy to the truth. Jealousy, which is strongly discouraged in Islam, has the potential to escalate situations by causing individuals to engage in sinful behaviors such as backbiting. This, in turn, can lead to the propagation of extended gossip and ultimately result in various sinful outcomes.

Envious individuals commonly engage in the behavior of provoking others, which tends to elicit responses that are influenced by their prior remarks. Allah advises individuals to seek repentance when they unknowingly cause unintended consequences. As an alternative choice, you can choose to engage in reading the (surahs) that are specifically assigned for these actions. It is crucial to understand that each situation is different and, therefore, warrants further discussion.

Quran:Surah Al-Isra; 62. Jealousy also gives birth to so many other sins, like "back backbiting (Gibat) and accusation (Tohmat)". If a jealous person cannot do anything to harm that person with whom he is jealous, then he tries to talk about him at the back, usually with the intention to spoil his image.

While Islam acknowledges unjustified sins, uncontrollable emotions such as jealousy are not considered sinful. Since impulse cannot be held accountable, one can argue that jealousy is not idolatry. Lust may drive fornication, but jealousy is motivated by desire.

Bible:3:3-5 Jealousy is linked to coveting, which is a form of idolatry. Idolatry of the heart is when we make Gods out of our desires. So, when our desire for something takes the place of God, then it is a sin.

By implementing effective approaches, how can people conquer the obstacles that life presents and achieve their maximum capabilities? Embrace the opportunity to uncover and harness the immense inner strength that resides within you, enabling you to overcome any obstacles that come your way in life. Even in the face of seemingly insurmountable challenges, it is crucial to remain faithful. Interchangeably, challenges and obstacles are synonymous, and life would be dull without them. The individuals who find life intriguing make it a point to emphasize positive mindset outcomes and stay away from stagnation.

In this world, the true winners are those who make it their mission to educate others about the value of learning and development, as opposed to those who choose to sow seeds of discord through spreading false rumors. Winners are not determined by feelings of envy. Their primary focus is on their own lives, which leads them to not seek validation from others, indicating that their thinking is not lacking. Envy, insecurity, and fear of losing something are the defining characteristics of this emotion. When jealousy is not properly managed or controlled, it has the ability to morph into a destructive emotion that can cause significant harm.

However, if effectively harnessed, it has the capacity to act as a formidable catalyst in enabling the achievement of your goals. The act of accusing someone close to being jealous is a manifestation of one's own emotional insecurity. Jealousy does not thrive in an environment of happiness and competence.

The misunderstanding of someone's envy towards others' appearance, belongings, or achievements can often be attributed to shallow thinking. As a believer, it is essential to prioritize meaningful discussions and refrain from engaging in trivial gossip. Humans no longer experience envy when their hearts are filled with the presence of Allah. Accusers frequently assert that individuals who lack Allah in their hearts are driven by feelings of jealousy towards believers.

What factors contribute to a Muslim experiencing envy towards individuals who do not adhere to their religious beliefs? Those who follow Islam typically do not feel an inclination towards individuals who live in a manner that goes against its teachings. In an attempt to compensate for their own insecurities, a jealous Muslim resorts to criticizing the flaws of another Muslim.

There are several crucial elements that contribute to the success of this endeavor, such as finding inner peace, eliminating wasteful companies, and making progress on a daily basis. The inner voice, which can manifest as the desire for good or evil, has the potential to appear to both believers and non-believers.Accusations of blame often have a deep connection to the heart, either stemming from genuine emotions or envy.

When it comes to perceiving humanity, individuals often project their emotions and beliefs onto others, viewing the world through their own personal lens. The act of bringing peace to others and oneself is of utmost importance for a believer.

Envy, which can be a toxic poison, becomes particularly detrimental when it starts to impact the lives of individuals who strive for inner peace through their devotion to Allah. Similar to a soldier safeguarding their post, the believer protects their present circumstances. The battle that we are facing is the challenge of understanding the wicked undercurrents. The allure of surface-level accomplishments can cause those who are seeking success to be attracted to a satirical representation that exists on the margins of life.

For individuals who value meaningful relationships and genuine companionship, focusing on superficial decorations is considered unattractive. If you want to win battles that are winnable, you must have faith as the key ingredient. Wealth is a privilege that some individuals are born into, whereas others choose to pursue financial freedom as a means of attaining personal liberty. Trials and efforts are an inevitable part of life, continuously presenting us with challenges and opportunities for growth.

Faith is established upon the grounds of comprehension, rather than being reliant on one's financial status. Faithful individuals can be discovered in various spheres of life. Those who have a strong belief in their faith have chosen to employ their wealth in order to help individuals who are in need. The accumulation of wealth does not have a negative impact on one's faith in Islam.Education is of paramount importance and deserves constant emphasis due to its transformative impact on individuals and society. Formal education and life experiences are two ways in which individuals can acquire knowledge.

Comprehending critical thinking and learning concepts is of utmost importance. Humans tend to give more importance to understanding and following human laws rather than the laws set by Allah, and this is evident in various spheres of life such as education, business, and sports.Allah's blessings were bestowed upon the Muslims, who in turn became the world's educators, sharing their knowledge with others. Learning, as well as being a gift, is something that should be cherished, while wasting time can only impede progress, and pursuing one's dreams can sometimes lead to losing oneself amidst the crowd.

Similar to countless other elements, social media possesses the ability to generate both positive and negative repercussions. A crucial step towards accomplishing your dreams and goals is to devote your energy to improving your skills and deepening your knowledge. The governing authority in the realm of Islam. Those who have never dared to venture outside the confines of their own country or had the chance to explore the enchanting Middle East. Any nation, without exception, would work. Delivering news and presenting opinions as if they are unquestionable truths.

Falsifiers are those who disseminate empty rhetoric without demonstrating any personal achievements. The act of comparing ineffective material with others allows for a clear assessment of their relative strengths and weaknesses. It is through the will of Allah that the recipient is granted and receives. There is absolutely no possibility for anything to be taken away from you. That life and its gifts are rightfully yours to claim. It is important to recognize that this gift is not from people, but rather from Allah.

Success is attainable through perseverance and trying, as humans tend to overlook their own potential. The mask of deceit has been removed, revealing the truth. This is a great opportunity for individuals who are looking to improve their life and deepen their faith. The utilization of this advanced technology, in conjunction with human effort, plays a crucial role. Travel is undoubtedly the greatest teacher one can have.

Those individuals who choose not to visit a country tend to have a heightened sense of curiosity about it. In the Quran, there is a strong encouragement for humans to embark on journeys and discover the wonders of the world. Despite the extensive publicity that Islam has received, there are still many individuals who lack an understanding of its true essence.

The deliverance of Allah is exclusively for those whom He intends it for. Those who are currently opponents may one day transform into worshippers, despite their knowledge and lack of regard for it. The most profound knowledge is possessed by Allah, and individuals who adhere to laws that modify texts will not value the true meaning they interpret. The pursuit of truth and the desire for contentment in one's heart are universal aspirations shared by all individuals. Those who seek solace in their surroundings rarely feel the need to return to familiar places that did not complement their lives.

322

Muslim countries are primarily the ones that have the highest wealth. Envy is the underlying cause of the fear surrounding the potential dominance of Islam. Each and every day, countless souls suffer the tragic loss caused by the regulations and norms of human society, with the gravest consequence being the demise of their spiritual essence. There are numerous countries that actively pursue the possessions that hold great value for Muslims, seeing them as significant symbols of accomplishment.

The healing waters of (Zam-Zam) and the oil and gas pipelines both suffer from the destructive influence of greed.

Saudi Arabia, situated on the Arabian Peninsula, boasts the most abundant mineral deposits on the planet, making it a truly enriched nation. Among the most frequently encountered precious metals, we can find gold, silver, copper, zinc, chromium, manganese, tungsten, lead, tin, aluminum, and iron. Gold, a precious metal, is widely utilized in Saudi Arabia. When comparing Muslims to the general population, it becomes evident that they have been granted more by Allah.

The key to success lies in understanding and correctly utilizing resources, which is half the battle. In order to foster stronger bonds between Muslims and Muslim countries, it is important to address and eliminate animosity that is caused by external factors. During the Golden Age of Islam, Muslims played a pivotal role as the world's educators. The final chapter is still pending and all of this is yet to conclude.

The resolution of problems faced by Muslim countries in turmoil can be achieved by encouraging Muslims to learn and teach, following the example set by Muslims throughout history. Quarrels and fights driven by envy are often instigated by individuals who are ignorant.

Muslims can make a significant impact on the world by coming together and joining forces. Muslims engage in voluntary giving, which is not mandated known as (Sadaqa), particularly during times of catastrophe. A society lacking knowledge perpetuates misconceptions about Islam, resulting in this perilous predicament.

Given the existence of various misconceptions surrounding religion, there arises a pressing need to establish educational programs that can enlighten individuals about the authentic truths and values of Islam. By choosing to take this specific action, it opens up the opportunity to reduce prejudice and cultivate a stronger sense of understanding. Those who embrace faith as their foundation typically have a strong inclination to hold onto it without letting go.

Whether it's day or night, in Islam, time is considered invaluable and should not be squandered. Time remains constant and unaffected by one's financial status. In spite of the peaceful teachings of Islam, the persistent feeling of jealousy drives people to repeatedly return to the same place.

Among the plethora of colors available, it is the one that exudes strength and character that serves as a testament to the enduring nature of Islam.

Many faiths will be washed out in the process. As time goes on, the religion of Islam will continue to grow stronger, and we will inch closer to the day of reckoning. The source of envy is not having what Muslims have.There is no issue with getting along with all humans, nor with beliefs or concepts indoctrinated or preserved in the Quran. What matters is understanding differences.

The combination of effort, work, and dedication is what will allow individuals to achieve this goal. It is crucial to understand that success should not be measured solely by material possessions.

The measurement of an individual's well-being should take into account both their treatment of themselves and their contributions to the well-being of society.

Through the proper utilization of technology, driven by the right motivation and intentions, we have the ability to enhance the world and shape a more prosperous future. Having faith isn't dependent on one's financial status, but rather on their willingness to trust and have belief in a higher power or purpose.

Faith is a quality that can be accessible to anyone, irrespective of their financial status. The inherent power and inspiration within this message have the ability to transcend backgrounds and offer hope to anyone who encounters it.

Quran: Surah Baqarah:2:9.*They desire to deceive Allah and those who believe, and they deceive only themselves, and they do not perceive.*

Quran: Surah Baqarah:2:6.*Surely those who disbelieve, it being alike alike to them whether you warn them, or do not warn them, will not believe.*

Quran: Surah Imran: 3:85 .And whoever desires other than Islam as religion - never will it be accepted from him, and he, in the Hereafter, will be among the losers.

Individuals who are perplexed and harbor feelings of resentment may seek clarification regarding the unique interpretations found within the Muslim community and why they are confined to this specific group. The end of time is predicted by prophecies, which state that Islam will be the only belief system that survives. The worship of only one God presents no challenge that originates from God rather than humans, as "HE" did not create the world with the intention of worshiping mortals.

The beginning of it all can be traced back to humans worshiping Allah, and it is destined to conclude in the same manner. Just as it started, it will conclude in the same manner. The most crucial aspect of life lies in recognizing the importance of God's mercy and devoting oneself to serving Him. While all other religions are destined to disappear, Islam will be the one that endures. In the final analysis, their ultimate allegiance will be towards Allah alone, and no one else. In spite of its seeming absurdity, the human mind simply cannot process or comply with any command that is not under the authority of Muslims.

The ownership of the world, both in the present and for all time to come, belongs solely to Allah. Although the finish line is known for its honesty, it is also capable of tolerating ignorance. Muslims, unlike the world which can establish its own rules and pray, do not depend on deities and mishaps for their well-being. The freedom of those who do not believe will eventually have negative consequences.

The majority of individuals have a grasp of and show admiration for genuineness. The resolute nature of the rhetoric of falsehoods is deeply disconcerting and subject to dispute.

Muslims believe that speaking the truth is a fundamental aspect of their faith. The one law of worshiping Allah alone has been demonstrated by all Prophets throughout history. The current state of chaos is often underestimated by certain individuals. Is their longing for material wealth stronger than the internal struggles they experience? People who have faith in Allah and are followers of Islam comprehend that destiny has already been decided. The ceaseless endeavor for universal solace is demonstrated by individuals undertaking spiritual retreats in pursuit of tranquility.

In Islam, it is believed that the truth should never be feared, and it is important to remain steadfast in upholding it. Moreover, it is paramount to refrain from seeking validation from individuals who flourish in disorder and instead concentrate on what is morally correct.

Among all the truths, there is one that stands above all others, and that is the truth of Allah. Those who uphold this belief will be the ones to vocalize it.

Regrettably, the truth is being subjected to rudeness and malevolence. In the face of evil and injustice, Muslims have risen to the occasion and some have courageously taken action.

Despite the efforts of those who prefer to deceive, the truth has remained spoken for centuries. Is there any point in stopping now? Spreading evil is not rude, but calling someone an extremist who follows Islam is acceptable. Someone who isn't indulgent with their adulterated thoughts. This is the way society works. Only Allah knows the truth, and He will prevail in the end. Despite their attempts to break divine laws and live by their own laws, they still envy believers who live in peace.

The crazed behavior proves responsible for continuing mishaps as the richest beings on earth are believers. The forces of lies and evil are conspiring to unite. Muslims stand up for what is right and believe in strong faith. Only then will Muslims be able to live a righteous life in the midst of chaos. They have the ability to make mistakes, just like anyone else. Muslims still acknowledge the truth despite that being said.

The laws that govern us, which have been delivered by Allah, are not exclusive to Muslims, but rather, they are universal laws that belong to Allah. The act of speaking the truth and then not adhering to it is a matter that lies solely between Allah and the individual, and it is not open for discussion. However, it is important to note that knowledge plays a crucial role in this matter.

Given the facts of exposure and signs of the hour, it becomes quite challenging to negotiate with disbelievers and their entourages. The mention of this can be found in the Scriptures. When a believer experiences suffering in this world, it is seen as an act of mercy from Allah.

The consequences for those who do not have faith are twofold; they will endure suffering in this life and in the hereafter. In the perspective of Muslims, sins that are absolved in this world are considered more deserving of torment than in the afterlife. There is a limit to every human's life in this world.

In the next life, life continues infinitely, never coming to an end. Testing life at various stages is a wiser approach in this world. A crucial element for making judgments in this world is having a clear exit as the fundamental criteria.

The reason why jealousy has no place in performance is because every individual is focused on managing their own life out of loyalty to themselves. Those who possess an understanding of the voyage to this world also make ready for the forthcoming one. Life is filled with beauty and tranquility. When a person gains an understanding of Prophet Muhammad, they also come to appreciate the remarkable achievements of a Prophet who was only human. This is a winning solution.

The soul, despite its inherent peace, remains elusive to the world's understanding, as it cannot be fully comprehended by those who view it from an external perspective. The laws that govern society are created by humans, whereas believers are expected to follow the laws that Allah has ordained. The rules are set by Allah, but he does not enforce them himself. Humans have the ability to establish rules, and it is their responsibility to ensure compliance with those rules.

While human laws have immediate consequences, Allah's laws will also face consequences, but there is a time allotment for those who value time. Whenever a believer goes against the laws set by Allah, they experience regret and seek repentance. Only those who are influenced by peer pressure and seeking approval from a society that fails without Allah's laws are included, not all.

The power to educate society about its flaws and strengths and encourage them to choose the righteous path lies in the hands of those who possess strength. The grains of the world are yearning for peace. With unwavering trust in Allah, individuals can accomplish their goals regardless of the challenges they face. Strength lies within those who can maintain a clear vision of the future, all the while remaining grounded in their roots.

The act of pulling the winners out of the competition is an insidious tactic employed by malevolent companies, as they seek to corrupt and transform these individuals from virtuous to malevolent. The effects of this upheaval will only be felt by those who lack mental strength. Without the support of believers and without Allah's guidance, a believer's life becomes meaningless and devoid of true succession.

The severe failures experienced by certain individuals can be linked to various factors such as a disadvantaged upbringing, impoverished economic conditions, or a turbulent home life. The desire for self-improvement often compels certain individuals to actively search for opportunities within more prestigious families and companies. Those with weak minds are often the ones who find the evil they are actively seeking.

Islam empowers its adherents to withstand external pressures and uphold their moral values. In adversity, and with limited resources, believers uphold moral character through informed decisions. Humanity is unfortunate to be exposed to a distorted view of the world and moral compass through facets.

While some remain true to their beliefs, others are young and mature Muslims seeking acceptance who may sometimes be corrupted. The decline of moral values is causing new societies to stray from morality and put themselves at risk.

For decades, this has been a complete failure. In any setting, acquiring frills and fancies at the cost of losing faith will lead to their downfall. In Islam, there is an emphasis on learning, education, and travel. Some people come back with a formal education and are likely to have a well-rounded character.

While learning about infiltration, one should know the righteous company. Success in Islam heavily relies on faith and belief in statutory laws. Education is crucial, but so is respect for parents, supportive peers, and religious values in life.

The most effective method is aiding lost individuals of Islamic faith, as Islam emphasizes the importance of sharing the wealth of Islam. It is imperative to remember that learning comes not only from an academic formatted setting. But also from experience and guidance.

Education is only meaningful when applied, and it is key to exercising discernment when deciding. Without faith and respect, education is incomplete. But also from life experiences. Both hold immense value and are essential.

The only time to disobey parental requests is toward paganism. Even then, no disrespect. Exit is better to show the truth and dismantle pagan values, leading to upheavals and no progress in the long run.

Defying Allah's laws has a later consequence. He did not create hell for no reason. Everything created has a reason. Heaven has a price, while hell has a price to entice you.

Each awaits the welcome of humans, but Allah has already decided upon the destination. He is Allah, and he knows humans' actions before they happen. Therefore, destiny is pre-written according to what humans do with free choice.

Quran: Surah Baqarah:3:12. *Say to those who disbelieve: You shall be vanquished, and driven together to hell; and evil is the resting-place.*

In a court of law, punishment by humans is deemed acceptable. The day of reckoning is eagerly anticipated by the man. The last rule in every government remains consistent until the next regime assumes control. The analysis and study of Islam includes understanding why one is a Muslim and the laws of any country. Benefits and royalties are entitled to the followers of Islam. Islam is familiar to every household, but its interpretation varies from person to person.

As the world rotates, its occurrence has already been witnessed by people all over the globe. Similar to any government, Allah observes and evaluates the judgment that occurs after implementing the law that has been sent down from above. Those who are unwilling to acknowledge it will have to endure their own personal challenges and face the resulting consequences.

The law of Islam operates in this world as a system of consequences rather than being contingent on behavior. Laws are present in every country, as well as in every city, and it is the responsibility of residents to follow and abide by them.

The purpose of Allah sending messengers and the Quran was to combat ignorance, yet one must be cautious of the consequences that come with arrogance. It may be difficult to fathom, but the truth stands firm, impervious to the influence of humans and Jinns.

The imminent possibility of self-destruction is a threat that looms over both humans and the country. In the absence of spiritual fulfillment, individuals persistently explore various means to accumulate wealth. The world operates on a consistent schedule, but reminders can provide employment by emphasizing the importance of embracing change.

In the event that the introduction of Allah did not have a significant impact, the search can proceed further. The beauty of Allah is prominently displayed and easily noticeable. The search persists, even among those who are ignorant.

Muslims as a whole should not be judged based on the actions of a few wayward individuals. It is within their capacity to modify their behavior and conform to the corrupt times. The notion of regarding a society as successful solely based on material possessions or self-interest, while neglecting the importance of fruitful endeavors, is a perspective that warrants consideration.

When individuals actively engage in the act of believing, they open themselves up to a world of possibilities and increase their chances of acquiring everything they desire. The power of belief is where the greatest wealth can truly be found. Having embraced Islam, a recent convert sought advice from a fellow Muslim. He said " Make me rich" and the Muslim replied "I invited you to my faith. With the permission of Allah, I believed that I had already made you wealthy.

The brief incident serves as a stark reminder of the repercussions that arise from a lack of comprehension regarding the true value of Islam and its abundant spiritual treasures. This lack of understanding drives individuals to relentlessly seek material wealth, only to discover that it is incapable of offering the same comfort and satisfaction as Islam does.

A Muslim woman living in today's Western society chose to embrace modernity, rejecting the outdated Islamic laws that she believes no longer align with her values and experiences. She went against Islamic principles by marrying a man who is not a Muslim. The options for her marriage were restricted to either a Muslim man or someone who converted to Islam.

The rules were irrelevant. Although she was raised Muslim, she did not practice Islam. She would always go back to the mosque to give voluntary charity (Sadaqah) on behalf of her newly married husband. It turned into a routine. Eventually, the Imam asked to meet her spouse. Her response was that he was not a Muslim.

Despite everything, he still insists. She brought him to the mosque one day. The Imam explained that although she continuously gave (Sadaqah) voluntary charity for him, being married to him is not permissible in Islam. When he asked about defying Islam's laws, the Imam responded that there are consequences for breaking any law and she will face them.

The man was unsettled by her preference for her faith over him, evident in her frequent visits to the mosque to give (Sadaqah) voluntary charity. He mentioned he would embrace her faith if he wanted to be with her, thus making their (Sadaqah) the contribution of two Muslims.

If Allah desires, souls who have faith in Him can be guided through a person, a feeling, or a gut instinct. Those who have an affection for you don't challenge your faith, but confront the inner demon that separates you from the worship of Allah.

In the event that the ditch contains a deep hole, it is advisable to refrain from looking at it and instead opt to jump over it. The depth of the ditch will have the power to engulf you entirely, but the jump that follows will serve to elevate you to new heights. Those who have deep faith in their hearts and trust in the existence of Allah are the ones who manage to survive the treacherous ditch, thereby safeguarding their souls.

This distorted nature of some represents the ultimate truth, a truth that serves as a dividing line between a world desperate for answers and a world that actively seeks truth. However, if a man is determined to seek the deepest desires of his heart regarding faith, no one can hinder him, as it is only Allah who has the power to facilitate his journey.

The success of this world may be eagerly pursued by those who believe, but it is the convergence of faith and worldly success that truly defines genuine success. The absence of one can cause the other to lose both balance and momentum.

The purpose of this event is not to engage in a showdown between the discourse surrounding the training of individuals to become minions of a corrupt society. In society, there is a prevailing sense of distrust towards individuals who, out of fear and societal pressure, choose not to accept themselves. They are in a situation where they find themselves caught in between two worlds that they feel like outsiders in.

The fact that they cannot fully articulate their distinct attributes and thoughts acts as a barrier, preventing them from unlocking their full potential and reaching their goals.

The admiration for someone who values their beliefs is nearly universal, as it is hard to find someone who wouldn't appreciate such a person. A common struggle for numerous people is the conflict between conforming to societal norms and maintaining their individuality. The devout followers of Islam exhibit unwavering self-assurance and fully embrace their faith, as it has been revealed to them by Allah.

The aim is to avoid manipulating behavior for personal or societal gain. And time lost can serve as a valuable lesson learned. Positive perspectives on life experiences yield fruitful results in all aspects.

There are humans who have a fear of humans. When humans devour deceit or detain them, they have the capacity to transcend and accept. The believer is aware that Allah saves the unit humans belong to. Allah assures that those who fear Him have no fear of humans.

Those who are not afraid of Allah. As fear becomes the essence of humanity, led by doubts. Evil can hold a disbeliever hostage, while a believer can fight the world alone with Allah's support. Satan and his followers lack strength. Even a fly shows more gumption than disbelievers.

Believers are strong, and have faith that Allah will help them in the end. They trust Allah and are not intimidated by external forces. Satan's power lies only in his ability to deceive and spread fear.

Quran: Surah Ahzab: 33:39. Those who deliver Allah's messages and fear Him, and do not fear anyone but Allah; and Allah is sufficient to account.

Coming to terms with their own identity and accepting who they are is the truth for Muslims. This will enable them to express their qualities without fear of judgment.

By freeing themselves from others' expectations, they can build confidence and unlock their true potential. It's a formal deception that keeps alluded to society bound to the system, even when they seem independent.The consensus of the corrupt norms and the spread of slow poison throughout the world is not independence.

It's a cultic behavior disguised as independence, but controlled by human corruption. Islam is the first democracy and independence but not at a loss of morality and deceit or alterations of laws.

There are particular settings in certain regions with prevalence of Islamophobia that have been deliberately programmed to cause widespread destruction, much like a wildfire that quickly engulfs the entire world.

The harm they inflict, aimed at dismantling families and imposing a web of lies, becomes increasingly suffocating and distorted, resulting in a rise in depression and a desperate quest for inner tranquility. In the quest for answers, some individuals turn to professional psychiatrists, while others find solace in embracing Islam once again.

The disbelievers employ a strategy of mocking and manipulating Muslim parents who have provided their children with a solid foundation to serve their system. In turn, these children are coerced into reciprocating this evil. Including both young adults and easily influenced Muslims.

In societies opposing Islam, individuals who diligently seek their spiritual path either through personal inquiry or with the guidance of a Muslim influence their transition towards embracing Islam. Subsequent to being accepted by nefarious corporations,or companies they are not only reluctant to delete their presence but are also deceived and influenced by foes of Islam, who assert that their selection of faith and name change was misguided.

The malevolence towards Islam manifests in various forms, however, comprehending and amending one's conduct is the internal conquest, aided by those who guide one back to Islam. Muslims have a responsibility to assist the vulnerable rather than resent them, as their actions may be a result of corrupt companies aiming to hinder their progress out of envy.

Individuals across different age brackets who harbor doubts about their chosen belief system are prone to yielding to malevolence and actively participating in its manifestation. Only those who have encountered diverse beliefs can find their way back to Islam as true believers. Nonetheless, it should be emphasized that acquiring knowledge about Islam and treating the world justly are essential components of this deeply ingrained faith known as Islam.

Quran: Surah Anaam :6:147.But if they deny you ˈO Prophetˈ, say, "Your Lord is infinite in mercy, yet His punishment will not be averted from the wicked people.".

When a Muslim shows defiance towards Islam. Satan's missionaries come forward to propagate more evil. It's definitely Satan's team. There is no righteous human who will not see the shift in demeanor once on the right path. Allah's dominance can change the course or keep one stagnant, as only Allah sees the human heart.

Quran: Surah Fatir: 35:6. Indeed, Satan is an enemy to you; , so take him as an enemy. He only invites his party to be among the companions of the Blaze.

An attitude of self-sabotage is not conducive but attractive, for the easily swayed. Or seeking independence to gain self-esteem, but falling deeper into the traps of Satan, as it is a false sense of independence. That overlooks the truth and accepts lies as part of a false notion of independence. This leads to a lack of understanding of the purpose of life and an unclear understanding of the reality of the world.

It can also lead to feelings of powerlessness and a lack of control over the situation. Ultimately, this can impact a person's mental and emotional well-being. The Quran specifies all bills and righteous deeds, all a foreplay of current life and preparation for the future.

The Quran provides clear guidance and direction that can help people lead a life of purpose and meaning. It can help people develop a sense of control over their lives and the world around them. This can lead to increased self-esteem and improved mental and emotional well-being. Laws appear strict from the book followed in societies showing independence.

Bible: Deuteronomy 21:18-21:For anyone who curses his father or his mother shall surely be put to death; he has cursed his father or his mother; his blood is upon him.

The youth, who are impressionable and easily swayed, are being corrupted by a society that completely ignores the valuable guidance found in biblical scripts. The pseudo society forcefully infiltrates and corrupts the world with their presence. The belief that hypocrisy is a superpower has led to its widespread dissemination and eventual extinction. The corrections and notions brought to the table are filled with lies, but there is no need to fear expressing truthful opinions.

Through this process, individuals can cultivate open-mindedness and expand their thinking by acknowledging and understanding differences. The words and actions that showcase independence seem to be at a standstill, surrounded by a plateau of familiarity rather than novelty. It feels like a repetition of past decades, even in the midst of technological advancements and changing fashion trends.

Muslims throughout history have played a significant role in teaching literacy and introducing previously unknown knowledge to the world. While every society possesses its unique narratives, acquiring knowledge about the origins of Islam serves to fortify the foundation. Islam, being the cornerstone of Muslims' success and core beliefs, plays a pivotal role in shaping their lives. The members of this group are strongly influenced to believe that they are an independent entity, but their thinking and behavior are often hindered by the collective mentality. The epidemic's potential impact on Muslims is especially significant and requires attention.

The predominant cultures exert control by limiting independence and ensnaring the vulnerable into believing in the illusion of freedom of speech. Many individuals frequently misuse it as a means to undermine others. Those who aspire to liberate themselves from cultural constraints often find themselves confronted with a formidable obstacle when trying to embrace the concept of freedom of expression. This often leads to them feeling trapped, as they are unable to fully connect with either culture and are constantly torn between the two.

Limitations are present in both academic and business environments, and it is important to recognize them. In the context of a family, it is common for words to be intentionally undermined within a personal environment. Furthermore, this tactic can also be utilized to exert control over Muslim nations and topple governments while pretending to champion freedom of expression. While free speech is a cherished right, it is essential to recognize that it is not without its limitations. Saying disrespectful things about your boss, such as calling them stupid or worse, can result in termination from your position. Disrespecting Islam is deemed as an exercise of free speech in these hypocritical environments.

But bringing truth to the variance of acceptance and the plateau of reminiscing about what the Muslims taught for decades can open many minds. Islam promotes literacy in all spheres of life. An unlettered Prophet, Muhammad, left a thriving legacy for the world to witness.

Therefore, the principles of stature and discipline are at the forefront of Islam. And it's a belief system that well rounds out an individual who seeks success. They are joining Islam in droves but converts need Islamic education, not just entrance. Helping them is Muslims' duty.

A faulty attitude and derailment from Islam will eventually cause ill effects. Since Islam establishes balance and independence in the mind and spirit. Not an upheaval as false modernizations. It is a slow poisoning encased in the deceit of a false sense of independence.

What is (Hassad)? Sometimes, "envy" is used as an accusation rather than the truth.

Envy can manifest silently through envious glances, sarcastic remarks, or even through fabricated lies communicated either verbally or in written form. The evil that resides within individuals can also lead disbelievers to spread malevolence towards believers out of jealousy and a lack of respect. This,

331

in turn, tempts believers to engage in evil acts by promoting obscene indecency and other forms of harmful behavior. It would be unfortunate if a Muslim were to do so. Out of all the evils in the world, nudity is considered to be the most dangerous.

If a country were to have nudity and illicit activities, they would not find the need for firearms. The self-destruction of not just an individual, but an entire nation, is now within reach. It is crucial to reassess the countries where shame is considered a taboo and the values of human decency are severely lacking. Ignorance is the root cause of contempt. Would you opt to preserve friendships that have the capacity to ruin your character, attract insincere friends, and create a life filled with restless behavior that brings about excruciating suffering? Due to their illusionary independence, it is common to feel envious of them, but it is crucial to understand that personal displays of character should not be associated with jealousy.

Those who spread evil, known as "Fitna," cannot be considered innocent. The reason they invite believers to lower levels is because they are under the impression that it is Satan's clever scheme. Unless there is a transformation within such individuals, Islam does not show mercy towards them; however, this situation can be completely prevented by sincerely prioritizing Salat, which serves as both a mercy and a blessing for believers. The significance of incorporating Allah's presence in a Muslim's daily schedule cannot be overstated. The laws that Allah has prescribed are not just rules, but they have a profound impact on the virtue and quality of life.

Hadith: Bukhari: 64:64.Narrated `Aisha: Allah's Messenger (ﷺ) said, "Do good deeds properly, sincerely and moderately and know that your deeds will not make you enter Paradise.

Muslim believers cannot trust disbelievers. Will a Muslim argue as rules can't change to suit the modern facade?

Quran: Surah Imran: 3:28.(3:28) The believers may not take the unbelievers for their allies in preference to those who believe.

Quran: Surah Mumtahanah: 60:1.O believers! Do not take My enemies and yours as trusted allies, showing them affection even though they deny what has come to you of the truth.

Quran: Surah Mumtahnah: 60:2. If they gain the upper hand over you, they would be your open enemies, unleashing their hands and tongues to harm you, and wishing that you would abandon faith.

Quran: Surah Mumtahanah 60:5.Our Lord! Do not subject us to the persecution of disbelievers. Forgive us, Lord! You ˹alone˺ are truly the Almighty, All-Wise."

Quran: Surah Mumtahanah 60:7. Allah may bring goodwill between you and those you ˹now˺ hold as enemies. Allah is most capable. Allah is All-Forgiving, Merciful.

It is important to note that these particular verses of the Quran or Islamic laws should not be interpreted as advocating for a division from humanity. In Islam, it is obligatory to uphold and respect the values of humanity. Trust is a delicate thing that cannot be easily bestowed upon those who doubt, as they have a tendency to reveal secrets at the most unexpected moments. Allah knows hearts. It is a regrettable reality that in today's world, finding someone who can be trusted, especially when it comes to matters of the heart, is a challenge. It is regrettable to say that trustworthiness is a rare quality to find in today's world, even among those who have faith.

In the event that Allah intended for Islam to become the universal faith of mankind. What is the significance of Islam? Throughout history, humanity has embraced the monotheistic belief in Allah, who, in His infinite wisdom, recognized that mankind was ready to receive the ultimate testament of faith and justice. This divine message was delivered by the Prophet Muhammad. He is not solely a Prophet for Muslims, but rather a Prophet for all of humanity, jinns, and every living being in existence.

Quran: Surah Mumtahanah; 60:3. Neither your relatives nor children will benefit you on Judgment Day—He will decide between you ˹all˺. For Allah is All-Seeing of what you do.

How useful is the excuse that they don't know anymore? Research is up to the individual in Islam, as it has opened up every door. Allah sent one person as a guide. Acceptance or rejection is up to the individual. Human beings are enriched by righteous deeds. Change is possible, but it takes time and involves avoiding unethical companies.

Deceiving Allah can also extend to deceiving humanity. The distinction between the two may be unknown to humans. However, Allah is aware of one's innermost feelings. Eventually, evil annihilates humans. Humans may be blind to a person's evils, but animals like dogs and other animals can see right through them. They sometimes witness death, illness, evil, happiness, expected or unexpected visitors, or an intruder.

Jealousy can be displayed by dogs, cats, and other pets. Allah did not make their emotions sinful, similarly. Islam corrects other scripts by appealing to human common sense. Islam provides clarity for human comprehension and progress, not stasis.

Quran: Surah Nur:24:19 Verily those who love that indecency should spread among the believers deserve a painful chastisement in the world and the Hereafter.[16] Allah knows, but you do not know.[

Quran: Surah Isra: 17;62 He then continued: "Look! This is he whom You have exalted above me! If you will grant me respite till the Day of resurrection. I shall uproot the whole of his progeny[75] except only a few."

Quran: Surah Ibrahim: 14:22."Surely whatever Allah promised you was true; as for me, I turned my back on my promise to you. I had no power over you except to call you, and you responded to me. So, do not blame me but blame yourselves.

The most devastating form of poverty is when hearts are impoverished. The act of regularly deceiving Allah cannot be cured by many medical visits to the doctor. Individuals of this nature are not worth being envied or being in the company of. The strong odor emitted by individuals of this kind has a profound impact on those who have faith. The power of belief is such that it can bring about change in believers, particularly when they hold steadfast to their convictions. The beauty of Islam lies in its inclusivity, as it welcomes individuals of all backgrounds and religions to embrace the faith, including non-Muslims. The expression "I envy you" originates from someone who is dissatisfied and genuinely filled with envy. The mouth is incapable of denying the feelings that are expressed by the heart. Such is their insignificance that even Satan himself claims to be unaware of their existence, rendering him incapable of feeling any form of jealousy towards them. There is no room for jealousy in the hearts of believers when it comes to these evils.

The evil eye can manifest in various ways, both silently and loudly, with numerous manifestations. The religion of Islam has sent surahs to serve as a defense mechanism for Muslims when confronted with evil. The believers prioritize expanding their knowledge of the creator's message in their minds.

When individuals witness the success of others, they often find themselves inadvertently comparing their own lives and tallying up their perceived losses. Such events have the ability to reveal either the positive or negative aspects of an individual's character. The person who possesses hypocrisy or malicious intent envies others, lacking any admiration but instead harboring ill-will towards them and constantly undermining their achievements.

The ideology being expressed here is not in alignment with the principles and teachings of Islam. Allah has a deep understanding and insight into human emotions. The intention here is not to misuse, but rather to strive for the betterment of oneself and others. The concept of the evil eye involves looking at someone with envy and wishing they possessed the same knowledge, beauty, wealth, and health. This malicious gaze can arise from various sources and is often intertwined with feelings of jealousy. However, the evil eye is best understood as a manifestation of internal dissatisfaction when one looks upon others with discontent. Devoting time to introspection and reflecting on one's own thoughts and actions is a worthwhile endeavor.

The range of episodes that can be analyzed and learned from is extensive. By consistently reading the assigned (surahs) related to this evil, a believer can effectively protect themselves. The map for Muslims' ethics was drawn by Islam, and it is through the moral code of character that a Muslim can truly understand and embody the faith of Islam. The most impactful way to learn is from a knowledgeable Muslim who not only has a deep understanding of their faith, but also studies the Quran and imparts their knowledge to others, as guided by the teachings of the Prophet Muhammad

Hadith: Bukhari: 5027. The Prophet (ﷺ) said, "The best among you (Muslims) are those who learn the Qur'an and teach it."

By repeating certain concepts, Muslims are reminded of the crucial role that Islam's laws play in promoting growth and grandeur. The implementation of ethical and moral codes is witnessing a fluctuation in different locations around the globe. The practice of wearing amulets was common among the Ancient Greeks and this tradition eventually spread to the Muslim community. Islam prohibits this. To protect from evil, the Quranic (Surahs) and (Sadaqah) suggest the voluntary distribution of resources to the needy.

Within the Bible, there are numerous proverbs that specifically make mention of the concept of the evil eye. In Islam, it is believed that the Quran's protection is necessary to guard against evil, and this protection can be obtained by reciting specific "Surahs". There should be a reduction in the sharing of gains or losses with humanity.

Bible: Matthew 20:15 Is it not lawful for me to do what I wish with what is my own? Or is your eye envious because I am generous?'

Quran: Surah Qalam: 51:52.The disbelievers would almost cut you down with their eyes when they hear ˹you recite˺ the Reminder,1 and say, "He is certainly a madman."They referred to Prophet Muhammad as a madman because they envied his knowledge with evil eyes.

Quran: Surah Dhariyat:51:52 Similarly, there came not to those before them any messenger except that they said, "A magician or a madman."

As they knew what he delivered was true, envy transformed into belief for many.

When it comes to desirability, some people may be attracted to others because of their beauty, humor, knowledge, health, physique, and wealth. The interplay between cultural background, religious conviction, and individual happiness is complex and fascinating.

The presence of time is a constant reminder of the passing moments. Engaging a crowd can be achieved by skillfully utilizing language and setting the perfect atmosphere. Laughing, being happy, and possessing inner beauty are three qualities that contribute to a person's overall well-being. The relationship between Allah and the discipline He expects from His followers. The ability to speak various languages fluently. The desire to achieve what others have can often lead to the development of an evil eye.

Quran: Surah Imran:3:19.Allah's only way is *Islam*. Those who *were* given *the Scripture did not* dispute ˹among themselves˼˹among themselves˼

out of mutual *envy until* knowledge came to *them*.

Bible: Exodus 34:14"For you shall worship no other God, for the Lord, whose name is Jealous, is a jealous God.

The accusations have spread far and wide, to the point where even the Bible implicates God of jealousy. Is there anyone who can fully understand the allegations that have been made against the creator? These allegations are truly astonishing and perplexing, especially for someone who identifies as a Muslim. If even God, who is not exempt from the consequences of this flawed society and is referred to as a jealous God, is held accountable, then how can we expect a human to be exempt?

Allah's nature does not allow for any form of envy towards humans, thus contradicting the notion of Him being a jealous God. The act of relating human traits to Allah is forbidden in Islam as His qualities surpass those of humans. In the Islamic faith, it is believed that Allah dispatched Jesus as the Messiah, and interestingly, he is mentioned alongside Allah in the Bible. Labeling Allah as jealous, which is an act of blasphemy, goes against the belief in Him as the one true God.

Muslims find it challenging to comprehend these concepts because they entail alterations made by humans to previous scriptures. The conscious mind is often dominated by one concept, which is overshadowed by truth rather than stories that do not promote common sense to the mind.. Islam invalidates the majority of beliefs that fail to adapt to its logically simple nature

It is important to clarify that the stories do not pertain to mythology, but instead belong to an Abrahamic faith characterized by monotheism, and they revolve around the concept of Jesus as a divine messenger. The intention is not to create divisions through contradiction, but rather to highlight the significant consequence of associating God with a human and ultimately accusing Him of jealousy, which exceeds any comprehensible theory.

The theory discussed in this case lacks the potential to evolve into a law, as it dismisses the accusations within the Abrahamic faith and highlights the ultimate authority of Allah. Additionally, it underscores the significance of repentance as a means to address the various troubles and deceit that human minds can exhibit. There is no denying that theological differences have a unique quality that distinguishes them from one another.

Quran: Surah Maidah: 5:77:80.Say: "O people of the Book! Come to common terms between us and you: that we worship none but Allah; that we associate no partners with Him; …

Therefore, it's impossible to replicate previous scriptures. The Old Testament was changed, while the Quran is the Last Testament remained unchanged. If jealousy is a sin punishable by death according to Christianity, why is God jealous? Given that he created humans, shouldn't we follow his example?

Bible: ESV: Deuteronomy 4:24. For the LORD your God is a consuming fire, a jealous God.

The human mind isn't resolved by Bible interpretation. It is a legitimate concern and question to ask why God made jealousy a sin in the Bible. The Bible permits jealousy for God, but not for humans. No such statements are found in the Quran. Allah cannot feel envy as he is not human and lacks human emotions. His image is not associated with humanity in Islam. He is impartial, showing mercy to both believers and non-believers. Repentance is crucial, not accusing God of jealousy, as humans cannot fully comprehend Allah's divinity.

The Bible declares that contradicting examples and feeling jealousy is a sin. Allah uses Prophets as examples, not himself, as he is not human. He is a merciful God, not jealous.

How can someone with common sense be persuaded by such teachings? It's impossible, as the human mind cannot discern. As a result, some completely abandon faith while others search for truth. This logic resonates for those who seek it.Will locate truth in Quran.

He created a human. The eyes of a person who hasn't yet realized the light as he or she has seen the darkness of humans' lies. Allah is the light of the world. Muslims will not entertain such blasphemous ideologies. Allah's comparison to a human is inappropriate in Islamic doctrine.

The Almighty has mercy. He still feeds those who lie and alter their beliefs. Success comes to Muslims who learn and teach the Quran's unaltered truth. Islam doesn't imply conveyance according to the Bible and the Quran in the same way.

Islam covers an infinite range of topics. Faith touches everything. What is jealousy in Islam, especially if it's true love in a (halal) permissible relationship? Genuine emotion, which is mostly territorial. As a dog marks his territory, so does a human to an extent, not harming the premises yet showing concern and care. One's decisions affect oneself and others. Love, sharing, and caring are marks of territory.

These grounds are not to be tested. Islam focuses on the security part of a marriage commitment solidified by a contract. And the family who holds Allah's values steadfastly. It is possible for jealousy to exist in a bond. Particularly if it is from Allah. Evil people resent such unions.Satan desires to disrupt any relationship that develops as a result of faith in Allah.

Quran: Surah Falaq" 113.1 Say I seek refuge in the Lord of daybreak

Quran: Surah Falaq 113:.5 And from the evil of an envier when he envies.

Red and green lights are modes of operation in this world. Allah also sends Muslims to Muslims to clarify dilemmas that may lead to some ill behaviors. Having an empowered woman who believes in Allah is a blessing as Khadija to Prophet Muhammad.

Quran: Surah Taubah: 9:71.The believing men and believing women are allies of one another. They enjoin what is right and forbid what is wrong and establish prayer and give zakāh.

Islam's ideologies keep the human soul at peace and at rest.The engagement process in Islam occurs after both parties accept and agree to enter a (halal) permissible relationship. Islam is conscious of human emotions, appears to have an internal mechanism, and is tired of the sluggish current group.

The ability to enjoy rightful surroundings is a breeding ground for happiness in Islam. The thronged society of ignorant and bystanders relishes when a believer falls out of play. In a business-driven society where men and women conduct business, business meetings are understandable. A Muslim woman knows her business dealings. Most meetings and illicit relationships begin at work or in academia.

Sometimes the accuser is guilty ; therefore, there are different issues to deal with for human rights.Freedom, the corrupt world of the progressive pre-dated era, and imitation of pagan ways offers no rule.

Bible:1 Corinthians 3:3 "For you are still of the flesh. For while there is jealousy and strife among you, are you not of the flesh and behaving only in a human way.

Making graphic examples may shatter some and open the eyes of others. The choice is human. For a clearer picture of the differences, it is imperative to know these facts. Someone who has accomplished little in life can also devour envy.

A lack of balance in the moral code of ethics hurts their inner and outer health, and one can waste most of their time. Returns and invites are, according to Allah, who knows the hearts of everyone. Allah's limitless mercy is available to everyone.

Quran: Surah Nisa: 4:144:O you who have believed, do not take the disbelievers as allies instead of the believers. Do you wish to give Allah against yourselves a clear case?

However, it's more prudent to trust in Allah. Moneyed people may be jealous of peasants who show peace instead of material possessions. But material wealth is from Allah, and so is peace. It is possible for a human to have both, of course. That is a follower of the book Quran.

Islam refuses to travel back in time and follow the protocol of the backward society, which has already taken place in the pre-dated days of paganism. Islam is a progressive society, following Allah's law and orders. No room for jealousy and tenuous contentment, as Islam also forbids illicit glances, gazes of the opposite gender, and unwarranted compliments for cheapening, not flattering.

Quran: Surah Nur 24:30 Say to the believing men, lower your gaze and guard their modesty: that will increase purity for them: And Allah is well aware.

The weakness of some men can overshadow their insecurities with resentment of a secure woman. The Islamic faith finesses the other scriptures. Allah sent. As humans altered the other texts. Islamic law has zero tolerance for human oppression.

Certain humans with social and economic status, or sometimes scarcity, have stumbled into the infrastructure, feeling responsible for the oppressed because of current survival conditions.

A human's strength is complex and not limited. The only time subdued is in front of Allah.If one lives in a controlled environment, it is not Islam. It's the structure of an oppressive culture.People may envy others' lives. And make sarcastic comments to inflate their empty egos. This has no place in Islam. Destiny is pre-written.

Humans have to help themselves. Make the change for the better things to come into their lives. Allah recognizes all the acts of humans.

Son-in-law of the Prophet Muhammad Ali. Said, "The man who oppresses a woman, and she sheds tears because of his cruelty". Allah curses every step he takes. Islam respects women. They are fragile. But strong. Allah sent a surah for women. "Surah Nisa" Muslim women excel in business in contemporary society and have achieved success in past societies. Prophet Muhammad's wife, Khadija, was an accomplished businesswoman.

Muslims ran businesses, owned real estate and traded during Islam's early days. Islam does not stop growth, except decline. Aisha was Prophet Muhammad's youngest wife. She was the daughter of his friend Abu Bakr. Marriage gifts strengthened relationships in those days. Islamic kindness exchange is an exchange of gifts. Humans are bound by food, gifts, and marriage.

In "Hindustan times," the age of Aisha was 19, not 9. The only authentication we have is calculations based on what they said. The Quran does not specify her age. She wrote many hadiths after the Prophet's death. She had a high intelligence level. Because she missed the Prophet so much after he passed away, she also asked Allah to show him to her in her dream.

Before he passed away, she chewed on the miswak. The taste of her saliva was the last thing he experienced, a testament to their strong love. Prophet Muhammad's first wife was Khadija. He remained married to her until her passing. Throughout their marriage, she remained his sole wife. She was a clever and astute businesswoman. The woman who was the first to accept Islam.

Khadija was Prophet Muhammad's first wife and only wife until she passed away:

Khadija's exceptional qualities set her apart in any society, and she proposed to marry him. He believed she was the loyal wife who had supported him since the beginning of time and his path to Islam. It brought him wealth and salvation, which meant a lot to him. She had complete faith in the deep love the Prophet felt for her. His wife, Aisha, said. Despite her passing. She felt envy towards her. Did it violate any ethical standards? Absolutely not.

Quran Surah Nisa 4:32. And do not wish for that by which Allah has made some of you exceed others. For men is a share of what they have earned, and for women, a share of what they have earned.

Following Khadija's passing, his life underwent a significant transformation as he became destined to have multiple wives, allowing for the expansion of relations among tribes and providing necessary assistance in safeguarding certain aspects of life. He adored his wife Aisha. He savored every moment spent with her. As a sign of their respect and love, the two of them even shared water from the same mug. He sipped water from the same side as she did; such was his love for her. He was a prophet, but he made time for her. He engaged in playful acts of humor and support and renewed devotion to Allah with her. Devotion to Allah jointly is the most intimate form of intimacy. Islam prohibits ruthless societies, where insecurities become an epidemic of low self-esteem, insults, and envy.

This world instead of expressing kindness finds Insulting names with insults and superficial jokes is a method used to gain undue influence and stoke artificial self-esteem. Decades will come and go. Islam will not adjust to appease people. Islam does not need people. To achieve peace within oneself and live a mannerism lifestyle, people can embrace Islam.

Quran has mentioned that disbelievers cannot be happy for a believer. Nevertheless, today even a believer lacking steadfast belief may show envy through their words and actions. Silent jealousy can contaminate a believer with comments and advice that destabilize weak believers. What kind of jealousy can a believer have over a disbeliever? Compared to an ignorant believer? Both need help.

It is evident from the incident between Prophet Muhammad and Aisha that intimacy and care are not labeled as envy. But it's an emotion aroused by an unplanned action.

Short Story of Prophet Muhammed and Aisha, his wife:

The Prophet of Islam displayed emotional concern for Aisha during a long caravan journey they took together. Inside the caravan, she discovered her necklace was missing. Hoping she would find it, she walked out and kept searching in the desert sand. The sky appeared to be losing light, so she hurried back to the caravan.

Assuming she was behind the curtain in the caravan, they had already left. Frightened, she stood outside, hoping they would realize she was gone. They didn't notice until she returned with a young man and explained that she had been left behind, and he had rescued her in his caravan.

Her story was dismissed by everyone, including the Prophet. Without speaking a word, he stayed silent for several days. Her parents didn't defend her as her tears morphed into anger. Despite that, Allah knew she was speaking the truth. She asserted that Allah would provide for her, making human assistance unnecessary.

Prophet Muhammad, following the imminent emotional trial between himself and his wife Aisha, found himself bewildered. His initial resistance and resistance towards her innocence eventually led her to anger, causing her to leave the judgment to Allah. However, he received a divine message confirming her innocence.

Allah's revelation serves as proof that Aisha's prayer to Him was enough, showcasing her innocence. Powerful emotions were stirred within Prophet Muhammad by the intimacy and closeness. Without a doubt, he possessed emotions. Whether you call it jealousy or something else, it was emotional and ended with Allah answering Aisha's prayers.

The incident exemplifies how human emotions and possessions become clear when the purity of the heart is shared between two believers, and how Satan can disrupt that purity. Allah has utilized Prophet Muhammad as a paradigm for handling doubts, emotions, and possessiveness in relation to his wife Aisha. The example asserts that Satan targets believers and not disbelievers or those under his control, as he has no motive to disrupt relationships with those who defy Allah. He believes he has fulfilled his mission of teaching defiance and does not harbor envy.

Allah displayed this narrative through the Prophet and his wife Aisha, two devout believers whom he highlighted as a model of a harmonious family. The revelation put an end to all doubts, yet modern humans can still be mired in misunderstandings if they both believe.

The reason for seeking repentance is to comprehend the source that divides the two believers. Allah has employed Prophet Muhammad from birth to present a consistent succession of victories and trials, serving as a catalyst for reflection when a circumstance arises that separates two believers, leading them to ascertain the source. However, every episode of a human life, particularly that of a believer, departs after imparting a valuable lesson, as nothing occurs without the will of Allah. The aspiration is to grasp the wisdom conveyed through the dreams, insights, admonitions, and narratives of the Abrahamic Prophets found in the Quran and hadiths.

It is preferable to seek clarification and avoid doubts, as there will be no new revelations for believers. Working with truth and avoiding misunderstandings is the lesson for Muslims regarding belief.

Allah has employed his Prophets as vehicles to depict various human emotions such as tribulations, joy, and sorrow. The divine entity responsible for humanity's inception also furnished tales that correspond to every period and dimension of existence.

The portrayal of Prophet Muhammad's personal life serves as a reminder for humans to deeply understand this event. It conveys various emotions, which some may interpret as jealousy. However, there is no question that Prophet Muhammad was a human and never professed to be partially divine.

Instead, he was a servant of Allah chosen to deliver the final message of the Quran, maintaining purity in his delivery while still experiencing human emotions. Allah's revelation proved her innocence, but humans cannot receive such revelations to prove someone else's innocence. Similarly, the Quran is closed, and the stories and hadiths of Prophet Muhammad have ended. However, those who study Islam, the Quran, and hadiths will find relatable stories that resonate with their personal lives.

The proximity and bond evoked intense sentiments in Prophet Muhammad. He undeniably possessed emotions. Irrespective of the term used, be it jealousy or otherwise, it culminated in Allah responding to Aisha's supplications.

If this narrative can establish connections between numerous believers who have been estranged due to malicious schemes orchestrated by Satan, they can rekindle their faith and gain insight into the complexities of human emotions, misunderstandings, and the insidious influence of Satan's minions, all of which are integral aspects of life.

Understanding the integrity in the caliber of two believers and seeking Allah's forgiveness and guidance is the ultimate supplication. The relationship between Prophet Muhammad and his wife Aisha grew stronger than ever, as his Prophetic insight confirmed the remarkable qualities that Allah had revealed about her.**The only factor in this incident was strong emotions towards his wife.**

Quran: Surah Nur 24:11. Indeed, those who came up with that ˹outrageous˺ slandering group of you. Do not think this is bad for you. Rather, it is good for you.Punishment awaits each, according to their share of the sin. As for their mastermind, he will suffer a tremendous punishment.

Quran: Surah Nur 24:12. If only the believing men and women had thought well of one another,, when you heard this ˹rumor˺, and said, "This is clearly ˹an outrageous˺ slander!"

Quran: Surah Nur 24:13. Why did they not produce four witnesses? Now, since they have failed to produce witnesses, they are ˹truly˺ liars in the sight of Allah.

Quran: Surah Isra: 17:32. Do not commit adultery. The act is truly shameful and evil.

If a Muslim encounters a fellow Muslim or a convert to Islam they deem compatible for a lifelong commitment, they will readily enter into marriage. Should an individual prioritize their personal desires over the laws of Allah in this society they make different decisions. If one is a Muslim, in contemporary trends, they feel obliged to believe that they are breaking laws of Allah and doing a favor by assisting others in assessing compatibility before committing. The disruption applies solely to believers who have strayed from their devotion to Allah due to sexual desires and unlawful actions.

Satan uses fear as the motivating factor, casting doubts on the authority of Allah's laws.Who has the authority to dictate how to live except for the laws of Allah which prescribe terms for a Muslim. If the fear stems from prioritizing the laws of Allah over the laws of humanity, undoubtedly Satan, the adversary, is manipulating the mind, rendering it incapable of grasping the truth except through resentment towards those who serve as reminders of Allah. It is within the purview of a believer to decide, however, actions continue to accrue both virtuous and detrimental outcomes.

These attitudes are more prevalent in regions with Islamophobes and those who resent Islam and perceive its laws as outdated. No region is exempt from laws that violate the principles of Islam, but these laws can be rectified without punishment, as Islam emphasizes redemption over penalties. If something remains unpaid, it can be resolved in daily life by settling the outstanding payments and accrued penalties. Islam is the faith that forgives those who repent and return without punishment and bestows wisdom upon them.

The society promotes relationships by adopting new trends to revive pagan eras. From 1850 to 1910, New York City became the epicenter of commercial sex in the USA. People's passion and buried beliefs developed in brothels and dance halls. Dating hacks and free sex, once stigmatized, are now widely accepted by most societies.

The Mann Act, also known as the white slave traffic act, was enacted by the federal government in 1910. The act criminalized the transportation of females across state or national borders for prostitution.

Politico: The Mann Act criminalized the "transport of any woman or girl" across state lines "for any immoral purpose."

The new act created new relationships and titles for couples, enabling sexual exchange. Replacing the new with the old is a tendency of evil. Tainted ideas and shifts cannot hinder the Islamic belief system. Envy towards such communities is impossible.Constricted by narrow passages, the heart and airways. Wide spaces and open airways enhance breathing. Individuals who have experienced heart failures and shortness of breath are sought after by the human for answers on the sensation of being constricted. Time is the only thing that can reveal the truth. The predetermined destiny of a Muslim determines their chosen path. He will follow the unknown path, unaware of what lies ahead.

The story of the mother and the son.:

Once upon a time, there lived a boy and his mother in a small shack. He helped his mother and felt obligated to provide for her. Their economic situation was poor. She took care of him. As he grew up, he saw others had more than he did, so he started stealing to have more. He continued as he brought home grains, crops, and vegetables.

The mother was cognizant of their financial insufficiency. Evidently, he offered items that were beyond their means. She came to the realization that he had a direct avenue to fulfill the household requirements, even if it meant resorting to theft, notwithstanding her comprehension. She approved of the goods he brought home. Every malicious act carries eventual repercussions.

Despite having a strong suspicion that the goods were stolen, Mother remained apathetic towards the method of acquisition, as it improved her quality of life, prompting her to willingly accept them. She had the knowledge that they had been stolen. In a gentle manner, she cautioned him against thievery, as she derived pleasure from the life he bestowed upon her. At some point, a gentleman made a knocking sound on their door. He cautioned them that his hand would be amputated if he steals again. The Arabian Peninsula was a land where thieves were met with zero tolerance. They admonished him while he cohabitated with his elderly mother.

She fell short as a mother due to her self-centeredness. In addition to her lack of discipline and failure to facilitate his growth, she was also an opportunist. Derived pleasure from the pilfered merchandise. She understood their inability to afford many things. He refrained from marrying, as he believed it was his obligation to provide for her. It is the responsibility of a parent to enforce discipline and instill faith in Islam in their child.

They cannot permit them unrestricted freedom. Islam will undertake investigations into parents and mothers, specifically focusing on those who lack the ability to educate their children about their faith. In particular, mothers who allow their children to steal and profit must answer to their creators.

She warned him against theft, but her delivery lacked severity. She didn't want him to stop, as it would jeopardize her comfortable existence. His sole intention was to appease her, and she willingly embraced the items he transported and brought back. The circumstances became more dire. He became convinced that engaging in misconduct was lucrative, whereas maintaining integrity did not ensure his desired outcomes.

He was veering down the incorrect path with a mother who was vigilant about her self-centered behavior. She was taken aback to uncover her son in handcuffs, apprehended by a man who had knocked on her door. It was a severe transgression he perpetrated. At this time, death was the consequence. Deciding against the act of cutting off his hand due to his theft this crime perpetrated was sizable.

She was in a state of emotional distress. My son is not the one who committed this crime, she asserted confidently. She insisted to the man who brought him home You must be mistaken. The son replied, "I did it. "Allow me the opportunity to bid farewell," as moments of remorse for his parenting and appeasing a self-centered mother brought about the realization that he was the victim of her desire and sheltered his happiness. He wished he had acknowledged his own shortcomings and had someone to confide in who believed in him. Despite his constant efforts to please her, a sense of dissatisfaction always lingered, and now it was too late. He knew he had to submit.

He expressed to his mother moments before parting ways as she wept, fully cognizant that her supplies were running out, even though she had looked after him with her own ulterior motives. "Grant me the honor of your hand," he said, she entreated as she gave him her hand as a symbol of affection. He sank his teeth into her hand forcefully. The probability of her using it again was exceedingly low.

She cried, "Why did you do this?I loved you and single-handedly raised you. In response, he remarked that your failure to enforce discipline has led to the charges he now confronts. The resilience of a mother is demonstrated through her inclination to correct rather than accept.He remorsefully commented and pleaded for forgiveness from Allah, acknowledging his wrongdoing. He longed for a mother who would correct his behavior rather than tolerate his ignorance and the harm he caused others by stealing from them without their knowledge for her benefit.

He fervently implored his Lord to guide him towards rectifying his actions and to enlighten her about the true essence of Allah's mercy, which is founded upon honesty rather than deception. Although he had no intention of accusing her, he ultimately conveyed with sadness that if she had only taught him about Allah, the faith that promotes truthfulness and loyalty, he would have possessed the discernment to distinguish between right and wrong, rather than being devoid of the essential moral compass.

He continuously expressed remorse and offered her guidance to amend her behavior, demonstrating his concern for her well-being. He was even prepared to accept any consequences if she gained insight from the experience, as he believed he had accomplished something meaningful in his life.

He was not granted mercy, instead he met his demise as the crime sought to bring about retribution. The narrative is lucid; the conscious mind cannot hold a parent responsible. It is the duty of parents to instruct children on distinguishing right from wrong. However, beyond a certain age, the parent cannot be held accountable for the individual's actions. The person has the right to modify and improve their own behavior. In Islam, the perpetrator of a crime is punished, not someone else.

The mother was spared, yet each time she glanced at her wounded hand, she comprehended her role in his afflictions. Those who support the rights of others are the true friends in faith. The mother lacked friendship with herself as her soul's alignment with truth prevented her from serving as a role model.

Nevertheless, with the passage of time, life bestowed upon her invaluable lessons that led to personal growth, even in the face of her son's untimely demise. Her son sought repentance from Allah and underwent human justice in the form of punishment, yet the Divine Justice of Allah acknowledged his payment and accepted his repentance as genuine. Such stories serve as examples in countless lives, fostering appreciation for those who guide others towards truth; any individual can provide invaluable assistance in recognizing it.

Quran: Surah Imran: 3:18.(Indeed, the religion in the sight of Allah is Islam.

And those who were given the Scripture did not differ except after knowledge had come to them - out of jealous animosity between themselves. And whoever disbelieves in the verses of Allah, indeed, Allah is quick to take account.

The road is exceedingly treacherous, to the extent that footwear is dispensable unless one wishes to articulate the imperative for Islamic citizenship reform to unveil the veracity. Truth knows no boundaries on slippery roads. Unlike other doctrines, Islamic laws do not rely on human agency. Within the realm of Islam, a perpetual motion and safeguarding of the identical speech and dialect occur. Is there a cause for concern in adhering to the rightful laws and contracts? Is there a parallel between business and the concept of a contract in life? Why shouldn't it be the same in personal relationships? The laws were authored by Allah, not by mortals.

Quran: Surah Nur 24:30 Tell the believing men to lower their gaze and be modest. That is purer for them. Lo! Allah is aware of what they do.

Using examples and stories from the wives of the Prophets, Allah sent them as an example of humanity and human beings. This is to illustrate that every action has a result. Comprehension and cognition of knowledge are astronomical feats. Knowledge is its own power. A person cannot steal the wealth of knowledge or other spoken languages of (Ilm).The Quran repeats itself many times. Life's success can be attributed to continuous repetition in a person's life. Negative behavior adversely affects health and soul. Everything in life, whether favorable or bad, reaps its own results.

Story of Prophet Yusuf:

The story of Prophet Yusuf is packed with strong traits, life's ups and downs, tragedies, and challenges that ultimately result in success. His father had a deep love for him. Yusuf's brothers threw him into a well and deceived the family by claiming he was eaten by a wolf.

Yusuf fell victim to his brothers' malicious envy. As they ripped his shirt to display it to his father, he fought to retain his garment. They alleged that he was devoured by the wolf as a cover-up. Allah had a distinctive and individual plan for Yusuf. He faced a situation where they outnumbered him. The brothers conspired to kill him. Eventually, one of the brothers proposed not killing him, but instead throwing him into the well.

Quran: Surah Yusuf 12:9 Joseph or cast him out to some ˹distant˺ land so that our father's attention will be only ours. Then after that, you may ˹repent and˺ become righteous people!

The caravan paused at the well to fetch water. The bucket was lowered into the well to draw water. Yusuf emerged, holding the bucket. To the surprise of everyone, Yusuf was rescued and sold to the Egyptian Palace of Al Aziz. Instead of treating him as a slave, they raised him as one of their own.

Yusuf's father became blind from crying for him. From a young age, the brothers grew jealous of Yusuf. Evil can be implanted at any age. Envy arose from their father's favoritism towards him. He protected him because he was younger, not because of favoritism.

Believers have relied on dreams as a significant means of communication for centuries. Dreams are regarded as truth by Muslims and should be kept secret from disbelievers and the envious.

Yusuf told his father about a dream he had, in which eleven stars, the sun, and the moon were bowing down to him. His father instructed him to keep the dream a secret. This dream will make the brothers envious. Ignoring their father's warning, Yusuf excitedly shared his dream with his brothers. Just as the father foresaw, jealousy grew among the brothers. Allah sends glimpses of the future through true dreams.

Quran: Surah Yusuf 12:4 of these stories mention) when Joseph (yusufYusuf) said to his father, "o my father indeed I have seen in a dream eleven stars and the sun and the moon; i I saw them prostrating to me.'

Quran: Surah Yusuf 12;5 He said, "O my son, do not relate your vision to your brothers, or they will contrive against you a plan. Indeed, Satan to man is a manifest enemy.'

The evil act was intentionally committed by Yusuf's brothers as a result of their deep-seated feelings of hatred and envy. The presence of wickedness and rage are essential in this intricate web of emotional deceit. This kind of wickedness poses a threat and causes harm to everyone involved. The consequences and wisdom that come from every occurrence in a person's life are significant.

Every soul is known by Allah, as He is aware of all. With great care and precision, Allah distributed the captivating beauty of Yusuf among all of humanity, fragment by fragment, ensuring that everyone could partake in its splendor. As the world becomes more unforgiving, the scarcity of this beauty is becoming more pronounced. The story of Yusuf is overflowing with an abundance of irresistible beauty, intense jealousy, majestic kingship, deep-seated hatred, fiery passion, and an unwavering faith in Allah and his boundless mercy.

These instances are meant to inspire those who possess faith and engage in deep reflection across all aspects of life. Yusuf's attractiveness emanates from a place of love and allure, while Zulekha beseeched Allah to protect her own beauty. Contrary to popular belief, the attraction that occurs between a man and a woman is not inherently sinful. In Islam, marriage is considered a natural phenomenon, contrasting with illicit relationships.

Is it possible for emotions and beauty to have an impact on human behavior? Isn't it Allah, the creator of all things, who has bestowed upon us the power of attraction? Contrary to expectations, Zulekha was not his biological mother. No. Even though she was responsible for taking care of him, it is improbable that she had any secret intentions. Nevertheless, attraction is unpredictable and her sentiments have now altered.

Both of them experienced a deep emotional connection and were strongly attracted to each other. Her beauty was truly exceptional and admired by many. The stunning beauty that he possessed was absolutely breathtaking. The strong attraction that existed between the two individuals compelled him to turn to Allah in prayer, seeking guidance on how to navigate their relationship without causing any displeasure to Him. After some investigation, the king was able to discover the truth that it was the ladies who had made accusations against Zulekha. Can she really be blamed if the attraction was present? Attraction is a force that cannot be overridden by any rules.

According to their testimony, if she were to tear the shirt from the front, he would be held accountable. If the shirt happened to get torn from the back, the responsibility for it lies with her. She openly acknowledged that she lacked the willpower to resist his alluring attractiveness. She extended an invitation to women, encouraging them to join her at the palace and participate in the task of slicing lemons. Moreover, she specifically asked him to be part of the gathering in the room, where the women were gathered with lemons and sharp knives.

Quran: Surah Yusuf: 12:26:27. And a witness from her own household testified, "If his shirt is torn from the front, then she speaks the truth and he is the liar. And if his shirt is torn from behind, then she lies and he is of the truthful ones.

Unable to resist his enchanting appearance, the ladies clumsily sliced their fingers while attempting to get a grip on the elusive lemon. Yusuf was imprisoned by the king.

Zulekha, despite facing punishment and trials, persistently prayed to Allah, asking for the preservation of her beauty and the ability to stay attractive to Yusuf. Her sincere dedication did not go unnoticed by Allah, who granted her prayer. When someone asks with genuine intent, what is the thing that Allah refuses to bestow upon them? He is known for his generous nature; he always gives willingly.

The mercy of Allah was clearly seen when he granted her wish to remain beautiful and marry Yusuf. In this story, the belief in clarity has the power to make anything possible. Believers should not hesitate to ask for their needs, as Allah's generosity in giving is always abundant. The beggar's plea to their creator carries such authenticity that it holds the answers to any question you may have.

Allah granted him the ability to interpret dreams. He offered support to incarcerated individuals. He prayed to Allah for guidance. His talent for interpreting dreams became known during his time in prison. In one man's dream, he offered wine to the king while another balanced bread on his head and two birds feasted on it."Oh two prison companions, as for one of you, he will give drink to his master of wine; but as for the other, he will be crucified, and the birds will eat from his head. The matter has been decreed about which you both inquire." he interpreted the dream.

The story in question also appears in the Bible, although it may not be interpreted in the exact same way, there are undeniable similarities between the two in this incident.

Bible: Genesis 41:17-31 Then Pharaoh said to Joseph, "In my dream I was standing on the bank of the Nile.

Seven cows, shimmering with health, came up out of the river and grazed on He reminded him to include him when talking to his master. Satan diverted his attention until Allah determined the right moment. The king had a dream one day. He is positioned by the banks of the Nile River. The transformation of water into mud occurs. He witnessed seven plump cows trailed by seven skinny cows.The king called out the sorcerers, unhappy with their interpretation. He was told that Yusuf, in prison, could interpret dreams from released people. In order to interpret his dream, the king released him and summoned him.

He interpreted his dream. He said there would be seven years of famine and seven years of harvest. Heavy rains will flourish crops and grapes. The king, so pleased with him, appointed him as a minister for all rations of his storehouse throughout the land. Per Yusuf's request. He wanted to oversee rations and giving.

Quran: Surah Yusuf: 12:54,55. The king ordered his men to bring Yusuf before him; he wanted to grant him a high office. The king said to him, "From now on you will be an honored and trusted person amongst us." Yusuf said, "Put me in charge of the treasuries of the land, I know how to manage them."

Years later, he was confronted by the siblings who had thrown him in the well. His generous nature allowed him to provide abundant provisions for his family. He disclosed his true identity to his brother through a clever act his people placed a gold cup in the rations, ensuring their parents' invitation to the palace and safeguarding the children from any allegations. He summoned his parents to the palace dispelling any accusations.

Despite the theft accusations, he had to bring the parents to the palace. His father cried for his lost son, losing his eyesight in the process. He covered his eyes with Yusuf's shirt as the first thing he did. Yusuf sent his shirt with his younger brother, aware of his future as a Prophet. Smelling his son's shirt confirmed his prayers were answered. Allah's slaves receive His mercy. He recovered his ability to see.

Yusuf's dream from years ago became a reality, reminding us that time is unpredictable, but a believer's dreams are truthful. Yusuf was both a Prophet and a king who ruled Egypt. During his distress, Prophet Muhammad received the (Surah Yusuf) from Allah. This is the only surah among the Quranic surahs that presents a complete narrative.

It explores themes of betrayal, jealousy, imprisonment, kingship, and the fulfillment of dreams. Reading the Arabic Quran enhances the taste and beauty of these stories.

Prophet Muhammad advised the man:

When visiting Prophet Muhammad, the Shepard failed to secure his camel. He neglected his responsibilities towards his own pet. His first recommendation was to secure his camel. He responded while I'm with the Prophet, he never goes astray.

The Prophet in Islam emphasized the importance of fulfilling obligations without offering excuses. Following the camel being tied, the Prophet had a conversation with him. How is it possible for someone to disregard their obligations? Survival is a shared responsibility between (Salat) ritual prayer and daily life, especially for a Muslim.

Quran: Surah ISRA 62. Do you see this one whom you honor above me? If you delay me until the resurrection day, I will surely destroy his descendants, except for believers

The story revolves around a Yehudi woman who was known for her practice of evil magic and her encounter with Prophet Muhammad.

Allah has demonstrated through Prophet Muhammad and his ordeal the jealousy of the Yahudi women towards the Prophet, fueled by intense animosity. She harnesses her malevolent abilities in the realm of sorcery. Islam explicitly demonstrates the efficacy of magic, as evidenced by its temporary impact on the Prophet and the abnormal uneasiness he experienced. As Allah planned to send him assistance, he initiated help through angel Gabriel. However, it is important to note that jealousy caused harm and led to the use of magic. The cure was also sent to remind Muslims to recite the protective surahs in their prayers.

If Muslims possess the ability to comprehend and value the exemplary life of the Prophet of humanity, Prophet Muhammad, they will recognize that he endured both hardships and triumphs in order to guide Muslims and the world in distinguishing between malevolence and virtue. And portray the lengths to which malevolent individuals may go, turning to dark forces like magic to fulfill the depths of envy within their sinister souls. Driven by envy towards Islam's forward momentum, she resorted to performing sinister incantations in an attempt to impede its progress.

Nonetheless, Islam remains impervious, for its veracity originates from Allah. Allah may permit evil to persist to demonstrate the potency of the remedy. Evil is feeble in the face of the potent "surahs" Allah has revealed in the Quran, which possess the capability to ensnare the Jinn and his malevolence. The story is worth lending the ear to in a conscious effort to continue to pray the 'surahs of protection. The malevolent intent. The wicked will employ any means to obtain their desires, while the faithful will humble themselves as supplicants, unlike the Jinn who does not recognize the worth of prayers, but the virtuous Jinn's do as human believers recognize its worth not deception.

The Yahuhi women, known for their mystical powers, performed a ritualistic ceremony in which they cast a powerful and enchanting spell on a single strand of hair taken from the sacred comb of the Prophet Muhammad. With great skill, she intricately knotted the hair and performed a solemn ceremony as she cast it into the well, thereby setting in motion the dark magic spell and its subsequent influence.

Gabriel, the angel renowned for his divine messages, made his grand arrival in order to convey the news of the events that had transpired. After she had tied knots on the hair and threw it into the well, her evil spell started to take effect.

The Muslims were able to register the workings of magic through the divine intervention of Allah, in this story it was the Prophet Muhammad upon whom the magic was attempted. As a means of safeguarding the believers, Allah sent down (surahs) for their protection. The Quran, being a divine source of guidance, offers us valuable insights on safeguarding ourselves. In fact, Allah has emphasized this through the inclusion of two specific surahs: "Falaq and Naas". These (surahs) not only served as a means of protection for the Prophet Muhammad, who was chosen by Allah, but they also serve as a reminder for all believers to seek protection from evil. and recite those surahs daily, It is important to note that every aspect of Islam has a reasoning and purpose behind it.

Quran: Surah Falaq 113:1-5. Say I seek refuge in the Lord of Daybreak from the evil of that which he created, and from the evil of darkness when it settles, and from the evil of blowers in knots, and from the evil of an envier when he envies.

'Masha Allah' Allah has willed it expresses immediate gratitude and protection from evil. Knowledge is the antidote to ignorance; finding a like-minded partner in Islam leads to increased knowledge and blessings.The truth will always be revealed through time. Time efficiency is a non-refundable component. Wise time utilization is a priority for believers.

Engaging in the act of shopping in the market involves participating alongside others who are also on a shopping venture. Furthermore, the act of shopping for knowledge serves to not only transform words into mere expressions but also to intensify your curiosity in my world, thereby establishing an indisputable truth and equilibrium that cannot be undermined.

The invitation to experience the same peace that Muslims have found is open to all. The invitations for this journey are open to anyone who seeks peace, as it is meant to be shared. If we unite and work together, we possess the ability to build a world that is abundant in both understanding and harmony. The moment I crossed into the realm of familiarity, I observed that the words had a familiar quality rather than being foreign, and I have no doubt that they had a significant impact on you.

Visibility is the key to availability, so I must make Islam accessible to you.

CHAPTER 16

TRIALS EVOLVE INTO TRIUMPHS.

By changing our perspective and reevaluating every step, challenges have the potential to transform into triumphs. The quietness that surrounds us not only masks surface troubles but also reveals a deeper understanding. The presence of Prophet Muhammad in history and the teachings of the Quran provided Muslims and the world with a significant and compelling example.

When we delve into the depths of life, we are able to uncover precious pearls that remain hidden. The profundity of life uncovers truths that go beyond the confines of our materialistic world. It is often said that going on a journey can result in gaining profound wisdom and a peaceful state of mind. The adventure that lies ahead has the incredible ability to completely transform and revolutionize your entire life. Intelligence is not determined by brute force, but rather by one's capacity for common sense and understanding.

A vital aspect of practicing Islam involves the careful examination of the Qur'an and the Prophet Muhammad's practices (Sunnah) through the lens of both intellect and sincerity. Strive to gain a deep understanding of the teachings of Islam and how they can be practically implemented in your everyday life. The path to faith and success is opened through the acquisition of knowledge. Knowledge, understanding, and common sense are essential components for both fulfilling Islamic obligations and achieving success.

When words are spoken in faith and learning, their power is capable of transforming trials into remarkable accomplishments. Once words have been spoken, it is impossible to take them back. It is advisable to exercise caution and be mindful when utilizing them. It is surprising how rudeness can sometimes stem from within us, catching us off guard. The presence of faith can greatly contribute to the understanding and admiration of Islamic teachings among others. When faced with challenging circumstances, it can provide solace and serve as a compass when feeling lost.

Even though trials are not initially seen as blessings, one eventually understands that they have a purpose in bringing them closer to Allah. The branches of a tree that is fully covered in leaves provide a wide range of shade options. By visualizing success with a tree full of branches, individuals can find the motivation and determination to reach new heights. The challenges and hardships that people face in life often serve to deepen their faith.

From plea to accomplishment: a story unfolds;

Despite his reputation as the most physically powerful man of this era, he made the choice to place his trust in Allah and dedicated himself fully, always seeking improvement in every facet of his existence. His demeanor reflected that attitude. Due to a significant fall, he found himself in a position where walking was no longer possible. The presence of wheels on his wheelchair became a limiting factor as he maneuvered through his daily life. There was a complete absence of any inner spark within him;

The feeling of dependency on others was so overwhelming that it resembled death rather than simply suffering in solitude. Despite exerting his utmost efforts, he was aware that eventually, he

would have no choice but to seek assistance from humans, a prospect he found undesirable. He expressed a desire for his trials to be kept private and not used as lessons for others.

As the (muezzin) called the call to prayer (azan), he made his way to the mosque in his wheelchair. His legs shook, prompting him to sit down and pray on his wheelchair. The question of why it happened never crossed his mind, considering his good life. He had to address Allah directly, without seeking sympathy or complaining to others. Following the prayer, the crowd began to disperse.

However, he decided to stay and informed the (muezzin) that he would close the door. Being left all alone he genuinely prayed to Allah he said (Ya Allah) you are the benefactor you are the giver you have given me so much I cannot ask for more. I am grateful for the experiences and freedom that enabled me to go to the mosque.

The thought of not being able to prostrate on the ground, which I loved so much, is unbearable to me. Please give me my legs back or bring me back so I can cherish my (sujood) without watching others take my spot. Enable my legs to either show submission or depart. Unsure of how to please Allah, he asked for repentance. In solitude, tears streamed down his stylishly trimmed beard as he wept.

His clothes were soaked with tears, as if angels were pleading with him. Just before the dawn prayer, he drifted off to sleep. You are still here, as confirmed by the voices. When he saw the people, he observed them walking in to pray.

Paying no mind to his inability to walk, he suddenly stood up and declared himself, eliciting exclamations from the crowd about his ability to walk. Despite being unable to walk before, he now appeared completely fine, leaving the crowd amazed. What occurred?

In (sujood), he fell to the ground, praying two (rakat) and expressing his gratitude to Allah, tears of joy flowing. Hearing the (muezzin's) call of the azan, he stood up and went into (sujood), acknowledging the incomprehensible mercy of Allah. Faith and genuine questioning have the power to make anything possible.

This story benefits both Muslims and non-Muslims by emphasizing the value of sujood and belief. Anything is possible with true belief; nothing is too big for Allah.The inspiring story of a young Muslim man who provided stability and assistance to his family. Faith served as his guide:

In this story, a young man is regarded as being more capable than adults:

The intelligent, witty, and intuitive young man was raised by a Muslim mother. With him being the most relied upon, the family had very few members. His responsibility was to be a role model for his sibling and aid his mother. The young man believed he had grown up because of unforeseen duties. Despite his young age, he exceeded expectations that not even adults could meet.

Over time, his mother taught him how to drive. He was incredibly independent and capable of anything. He came from a Muslim family, which imposed numerous restrictions on him.

Despite being protected and supported by rules and regulations, he never failed to assist the small family he felt accountable for. Yes, he did have a father. He didn't dwell with him. However, his mother served as his role model, and her limited knowledge of the world made him feel capable of assisting in areas where she lacked understanding.

Upon gaining independence, he started driving himself to the mosque for Friday prayer during his vacations. His habits improved, and he shined like the stars, but only he knows what he asked Allah for. As he set an example, his sibling thrived. He became the protector and helper the family counted on. He never failed to meet his mother's expectations.

He took his non-Muslim friends to the mosque, where he introduced them to (sujood), letting them experience the beauty of bowing down humbly to Allah. Despite a busy schedule, he worked on prioritizing attending Friday prayers.

As he made his way to the mosque, they started joining him, and it became a habit. Throughout time, he advanced while setting examples for others to learn from. Responsibility plays a significant role. The one responsibility that cannot be abandoned is sujood prayer to Allah. Unexpected achievements arrive as blessings for good deeds. The impact of stories on the mind depends on how they are delivered and received.

It's crucial to acknowledge the revenue generated over the years. What is it? (sujood) is prioritized by Allah over any other revenue. Dividends may accumulate slowly in the human world, but one (sujood) can make a difference in Allah's domain.

The aspiration of a Muslim to go back into (sujood) is beyond mere conversations with fellow humans. The grounding, once taught to a Muslim, cannot be forgotten. The mother, who imparted the knowledge of (sujood) to him, will be leaving this world. The sibling who received his help will get the chance to witness his demeanor and share in the journey of life and personal growth together, fostering unity between them.

In contrast, the days in which he attended the mosque will be etched in our minds for a lifetime. The arrival of angels was witnessed as he came, and on some occasions, he would bring non-Muslims with him, while at other times, he would arrive alone. The responsibility for the continuous return is solely in the hands of Allah and his invitations. The power of a mother's prayer is capable of reaching the sky, whereas the extent of sujood's reach is known only by Allah.

The stories of (sujood) prostration to Allah are plentiful; only those who join this alliance truly understand what they miss if they are absent. Faith cannot be taught; it is the inner dimension of seeking peace that cannot be acquired through anything except (sujood). Muslims are certain; ask those who know its beauty.

In retrospect, it becomes evident that atheists have morals. Faith is not something you can buy. There are individuals who pursue. There are only a few trees that can thrive without human watering, and those trees are robust. Those with inner strength are the ones who can't be derailed but rather mend the tracks for those who stumble.

These provisions are the result of success as they offer both tangible resources and emotional support. Muslims are held accountable by Allah for their actions without hesitation. The entire human race is obligated in this world. While some have faith in Islam and other religions, disbelievers without faith or religion assert themselves as authorities. Only a few books or documentaries showcase a learner, not a faith connoisseur. Learning is not found in conversation or in the advice of nonbelievers. Or individuals who are not Muslim.

Generally, those who excessively engage in talkative rhetoric tend to lack their own sense of faith. Faced with a challenge, their consistent response is to divert the course of the subject. Religion does not play a major role in their lives. Understanding the intricate ways in which lies spread through liars is always fascinating. People who engage in deceitful behavior are ultimately practicing hypocrisy. The Islamic faith holds the belief that hypocrites are specifically assigned to the lowest level of hell.

Quran: Surah Nisa: 4;145.Indeed, the hypocrites will be in the lowest depths of the Fire - and you will never be able to find a helper for them.

The person who dedicates years to studying Islam spends their time in a time-bound learning clinic. In any formal setting, a degree or diploma cannot be obtained without putting in hours of effort.The principle holds true for Islam as well. A tall, timeless boundary separates believers from disbelievers. Learning and comprehending the Quranic text and delivery require time.

The Quran is read first for contemplation, then for faith. Lack of understanding allows the propagation of news from social media without exclusive knowledge.

However, it is vital to remember the importance of cultural diversity and personal choices within the company. Building a successful and productive team relies on finding the right balance between accountability and respect.

Two Muslims who never lost contact:

Recent incidents in this era exemplify that belief is eternal for genuine believers. Two Muslims engaged in lengthy dialogue and laughter. "Allah" was the closing statement that spiritually held them together for many hours.Verbal and written communication endured despite the other Muslim's perplexity.For those unfamiliar with Islam, fear and confusion often cut conversations short, or absence fueled by ignorance, miscommunication, and misunderstandings.

On a particular day, a Muslim individual sends a picture of an underground mosque. The silenced absentee finally responds after prolonged silence but consistently pays attention to messages directed at him. "Let's stay in touch." Says the lost Muslim as he stops, unsure of how to continue. He glances at the picture before responding. "I never lost touch with you," replied the other Muslim. He apologizes and sends one last message before ending the exchange.

The story demonstrates the unbroken connection between two Muslims - one who listened and the other who delivered Allah's word. This exemplifies the beauty of their faith, which transcends individual attitudes and encompasses Islam's essence. If one's faith is true, it remains steadfast amidst chaos, guided solely by Allah's teachings. The presence of a mosque and a fellow Muslim can ignite a believer's heart.

Throughout history, Allah's guidance has been expressed. Islam endures through all eras. Friendships that begin with Islam are pure, and the bonds between families and individuals who share the faith are unforgettable for true believers.

Establishing a climate of understanding and acceptance. When it's not a medical condition, a lack of spirituality can throw a person off balance.It's worse than any medical condition.

Strength and resilience are needed to navigate difficult periods. Only Allah has knowledge of the heart. Dissatisfied individuals struggling with their present circumstances and internal turmoil. Their dissatisfaction with their faith and disagreement with their lifestyle lead them to seek Islam.

Sometimes, they choose a temporal path and find comfort in material possessions or aimlessly travel through time. The company they were running from could once again be the main source of destruction.

They are anchored to evil because of their shifts and turmoil. Also, there are those who don't believe in the company. However, Islam provides a pathway to inner peace through prayer and introspection.

Embrace the fresh and vital wind, leaving behind your reservations. In the end, it's all about discovering and understanding oneself. Low self-esteem can often be attributed to insufficient positive attention, negative upbringing, or a lack of spiritual guidance. Is this a violation of the deception in this illusory world?

Those who decide to follow Allah's path will discover greater rewards. Every person embarks on a journey to discover their purpose and find Allah. Grasping the concept enables individuals to embark on the journey of peace, love, and lawfulness.

Finding a balance between our external environment and our spiritual being is crucial. Technology plays a crucial role in amplifying those traits, particularly in influencing countries. Spreading uncontrollably worldwide, damaging overall health.

For those who easily fall prey to the deception of independence. The recall of damaged equipment is more difficult than adjusting to false sirens.

The severity experienced by an individual, both internally and externally, is often mirrored by their age. This severity can be traced back to the allure of certain habits, which can either propel them towards resounding success or entangle them in a series of mishaps and wasted time. The harsh look that it leaves is something that an observant believer will quickly notice. Regardless of their geographical location, people worldwide who face internal obstacles are able to navigate their way towards solutions.

Deceit can be discovered by humans in various settings, including both well-lit areas and dark corners. Whether someone is looking for evil or good, their efforts will lead them to their desired outcome. Engaging in illicit relationships can have far-reaching consequences, as they not only intensify internal wounds but also increase an individual's vulnerability to unforeseen hardships. While some may argue that comments on this matter are outdated in today's world, it is important to note that Islam has never proclaimed itself to be outdated.

Addiction and self-imposed freedom have a high cost for Muslims, outweighing the pleasures of adapting to a new environment. The restrictions in Islam are meant to preserve the inner health of individuals, not to harm them.

Repentance is seen as essential for salvation in Islam. Muslims who have deviated from the teachings of the Quran, but desire to repent and abandon their wrongdoings. A new beginning and the pursuit of forgiveness. Anyone who desires Allah has the same chance.

Tangible commitments have varying effects on oneself and others. It's not a fleeting fad, but a captivating calmness that those who grasp its purpose encounter. Achieving revenue discipline and preparing for the next journey is crucial for both peace and consolidation of doubts.

Those who have the capacity to comprehend and overcome trials possess the potential to transform them into victories rather than setbacks. In this society, there seems to be a norm of observing negative attributes and rebelling against those who try to correct them, and it is important to establish clear boundaries around this behavior. Individuals who harbor doubts and engage in deceit perceive this particular situation as a direct assault aimed at them.

"Learn the Quran and teach it," Prophet Muhammad advised.

Only someone who is against them would observe a Muslim go off track, choose wrongly, watch from the sidelines, and withhold the truth. Remaining silent is not a Muslim trait, but it risks the derailleur not accepting advice. It's not about making assessments; A simple nudge can alter the path for a few.

Quran: Surah Maidah: 5:54.Believers! If any of you should ever turn away from your faith.Remember that Allah will raise up people whom He loves, and who love Him. The people are humble towards the believers, and firm towards the unbelievers; who will strive hard in the way of Allah and will not fear the reproach of the reproacher.

Quran: Surah Imran: 3;141.And that Allah may purify the believers [through trials] and destroy the disbelievers.

Quran: Surah Raad: 13:28. It is only in His remembrance that our spiritual hearts will find peace and tranquility.

Helplessness and marginalization can be the result. Individuals who don't fit in are frequently marginalized, resulting in feelings of disconnection and powerlessness. In Islam, self-awareness and individuality are encouraged, along with the promotion of spirituality and inner/outer strengths. To achieve a harmonious and all-encompassing approach to life.

The feeling of powerlessness and apathy can prevent goal achievement and personal growth. Since man's creation by Allah, Islam has been their faith. Belief in one God, Allah, is abandoned due to humanity's rejection of belief in mortals and adoption of diluted ideas.

Quran: Surah Taubah: 9:33. It is He who has sent His Messenger with guidance and the religion of truth. To manifest it over all religions, although they who associate others with Allah dislike it.

People of all backgrounds and beliefs are given an opportunity to make a difference and be heard. The mission of Islam is to create an inclusive society where everyone is respected and valued, aiming for clarity and unity among all of humanity.

Islam and other religions differ in various ways, such as the exclusive worship of Allah. Prophets sent by Allah are acknowledged, but none are affiliated with Him.

Creating a safe space for dialogue and mutual understanding is also necessary. Particularly relevant for those residing in a diverse society. Islam cannot be compromised or appeased; it stands alone without altering its truth. Islam, unlike others, resists altering to please humanity.

It emphasizes the importance of faith, charity, and good deeds. It also emphasizes the importance of knowledge and wisdom and encourages its followers to pursue the truth. It's a balance and propagation of serenity through personal enlightenment and goals. Islam's laws are as applicable to Muslims as any law in any country.

Even atheists have to follow the laws of the land. Human laws have no distinction but are universally accepted by humans.However, humans are mesmerized by the dogma of false independence.

Despite following human laws, they believe they are independent of religious laws. Islam gives independence through spirituality and allows humans to make their own decisions with morality and responsibility.Islam is the religion that gives true independence by allowing humans to make their own decisions.

It also teaches us to accept the consequences of actions and accountability for decisions.In this way, the awareness of this existence in this world becomes complete. Instead of transferring blame and codependency to Jesus and claiming Jesus died for their sins.

These differences are crucial in understanding, but humanity stands with all. The spiritual evolution of humanity is in understanding that we are all connected and part of the same divine source. We are all responsible for our own actions, but destiny awaits and pre-planned as Allah knows the soul.

The need to look within to find the true purpose and connect with the divine.The final laws and regulations sent by Allah were designed to improve the quality of human life.

Islam may appear to be restrictive to some. It is designed to guide us toward a life of freedom, to fulfill our true potential as human beings.Muslims' negligence and defiance are not traits of independence, but traits that Satan implanted in the weak.This can lead to furthering negative traits which prevent them from achieving their full potential.

It is imperative to balance accepting constructive criticism and maintaining self-esteem.Similar to a car that needs a jump when the battery dies, human beings cannot be mismatched. This is because their core cannot survive in a soiled atmosphere for an extended period.

It is necessary to check and match the wires that connect the human internal system. A body that survives faulty wiring cannot function. The body, too, has electricity. Find the right balance between criticism and self-esteem to ensure the body functions at its optimal level.

When criticism is excessive, it can erode self-belief, and when self-ego is excessive, it can impede progress and motivation. The secret is discovering the perfect balance.

The balance is preserved. The Quran and the (sunnah) of Muhammad the Prophet inspire humans to succeed by emphasizing endurance, strength, and discipline. As a manual of life for Muslims. A manual is essential for business operations.

Allah ensures that the Quran's closing statement remains constant, providing a life manual for His beloved servants. Those who refuse to be hindered by Satan's negative thinking and doubt can think creatively.

It produces favorable outcomes for the knowledgeable and not for the easily influenced.

The benefits of this undertaking are substantial, whereas those without discipline and seeking advice from the wrong sources will suffer due to their lack of guidance.

When someone embraces evil, their sensitivity to sin diminishes, making it harder to recognize. Consequently, it becomes easier to commit additional sins. Moral degradation can result from this, leading to a cycle.

How is sin defined in a world consumed by self-centered ideas and the desire for societal approval? When Muslims in corrupt societies face such situations, they have the choice to either transform the status quo or become complicit in it. Altering Islam's moral code to meet their specific needs.

There is a danger of losing Islam's laws, discipline, and morals in this situation. And the negative impact they can have on themselves and others. It's a tough reality to accept, especially for Muslim individuals and their families.

Choosing to overlook believers' advice and prioritizing accusations over self-approval. As time passes, evil gradually becomes normalized, making people more prone to participate in it.

Consequently, their inclination to accept accountability diminishes while their tendency to attribute blame to others for their own errors increases. Over time, sin loses its perception as wrongdoing, allowing people to feel justified in their actions.

It's disheartening when a person, especially a Muslim, feels no remorse while committing a sin. The soul loses sensitivity. Whenever he commits sin. His desire is not for repentance, but for arrogance.

Muslims can experience temporary derailment. Separation from authority and Islam is the only hope, repentance. It can take various forms, including prayer and charity.

It's better to feel shame than to lose it.Restoring faith and preventing desensitization require repentance. It relieves the weight of sin and guilt, allowing individuals to reconnect with their faith.

Become aware of the consequences of your actions. In Islam, redemption is achieved through personal corrections. Understanding the consequences of our actions prevents repeating mistakes. Accountability for one's actions is crucial.

Taking ownership of one's mistakes is the first step in redemption and reflects faith in Islam. The dilemma lies with those who do not believe. Why me? Why not you? This is the inquiry.

Quran: Surah Baqarah: 2:39."But those who reject Faith and belie Our Signs, they shall be companions of the Fire; they shall abide therein."

Smiling and laughing are traits of positive people. In a state of bliss, he finds solutions to the problems. Muslim mathematics outshines the proficiency of any math student, as it was invented by Muslims.

Intelligence and knowledge are shared among Muslims. Success for Muslims is impossible without Allah. Muslims still take great pride in these achievements, using them as motivation for continued success.

Muslims have a rich academic heritage and are recognized for their influential contributions to mathematics and beyond. Upholding and building upon this legacy of achievement is a goal for Muslims. To utilize rich knowledge and intelligence to advance in today's society.

In Islam, it is believed that sharing beauty is a Muslim trait, and Muslims utilize their knowledge and intelligence to assist others and challenge societal norms. They are also working towards a more equitable and just society.

Muslims view knowledge as a powerful tool for a better world. Gain knowledge and spread it. The emphasis for Muslims should remain on education and teaching. Guaranteeing that their legacy of accomplishments and knowledge is shared, not kept secret, with the world.

Education is an essential tool for creating a more fair and democratic society, and it should be accessible to all. Through travel and extensive self-research.The Quran emphasizes travel in six surahs. Increasing its importance.

Quran: Surah Ankabut:29;20. See how Allah created the world? Allah will produce the last creation. Indeed, Allah on everything (is) All-Powerful."

Traveling to different places allows individuals to experience different cultures and gain knowledge that formal education cannot.

This can broaden one's perspective and understanding of the world. It can also help to develop skills such as problem-solving, decision-making, communication, and creativity. Islam encourages one to travel to distant lands and see the achievements of many. Travels foster tolerance, and respect. Broaden history knowledge. They can also help build resilience and self-confidence. It can lead to a greater understanding of our place in the world and a better appreciation of our own culture and faith in Islam. This faith of Islam will open many's eyes, as it is the fastest-growing religion in the world.

Islam will finally take over as the pagan world declines. However, when arrogance meets resilience, which will lead to the end of this world, as it all has an end. The judgment day. Self-research involves reading books, exploring technological freedom, and engaging in conversations with knowledgeable people. For Muslims, the Quran is the best source of learning. It is a priceless book of life that has not changed over time.

Since the dawn of Islam, Muslims have learned and expanded their minds to help others and themselves. Travel is the most effective teacher. Most people don't travel, but spread a lot of rhetoric without stepping foot on foreign land. The declaration of the complete book of directions for humanity, especially Muslims. Allah protects the Quran. Rather than a literal signature, this is a declaration from the highest.

Observation and research unveiled a tendency towards introversion when it comes to substantiating the absence of God, as opposed to the evolutionary development of civilization. Despite Darwin's resistance, he couldn't refute the existence of God or higher power, gradually adopting theories that left believers skeptical due to their lack of common sense. He was identified as a theist, not an atheist. However, his transformation took a negative turn as he persistently attempted to persuade the world that all humans evolved from apes.

He published numerous books to convince humans of the nonexistence of God, but perhaps he should consider exploring Hinduism, which upholds the belief in reincarnation. However, he persistently delves into the realm of the unfamiliar solely as an experimental method to vindicate himself from the bitterness he harbors towards the Christian faith, striving to persuade non-Christians or even those who identify as Christians with his absurd ideologies, which lack persuasiveness to the average person and hold no sway over believers.This philosophy persistently engages the minds of the youth who strive to challenge the religious beliefs, indicating his disbelief in the Christian ideology and growing resentment towards the existence of a higher power.

There exists an entity unseen who is not mortal, but distinct from a mortal that is Allah the creator. Darwin, who is also from the USA, comes from the same region where the church of Satan, inspired by Anton LaVey, originated. There is a discernible pattern in the rise of these evils from this particular area.

These malevolent forces are infiltrating educational institutions and introducing new ideologies, necessitating the battle against Islamophobia. Defeating this deceitful evil is not difficult, as it is inherently weak. Understanding is crucial, as even insects like spiders, flies, and mosquitoes can provoke those who deceive, diverting their attention from the true threat. These insects, armed with

357

knowledge and understanding of one God, Allah, can inflict a sting upon those lacking knowledge and understanding.

Afterwards, he proceeded to make alterations to his beliefs and consistently presented his concepts with a sense of constant evolution. The concept of Trinity's laws governing the universe did not hold any belief for him. Taking into account his beliefs and perspectives, it would be fitting to classify him as a deist but gradually evolved to an atheist. Following his previous adherence to Christianity, he later denied the existence of any superpowers attributed to either God or man.

Instead, he explained the concept of evolution, asserting that humans evolved from animals. Although he never managed to convince himself or anyone else that a higher power did not exist, he still classified himself as an atheist. It requires a significant amount of time for him to formulate theories, as opposed to laws. The false theory that is being taught in schools is having a corrupting effect on the younger generation. He lacks faith in the notion and ideology of superintendence and the governance of God. However, he bases his beliefs and allocation of theory on subjective judgment rather than relying on factual evidence.

Quran: Ayah al-Baqarah (The Cow) 2:65. for you are well aware of those from among you who profaned the Sabbath, whereupon We said unto them, "Be as apes despicable!" You are already aware of those of you who broke the Sabbath. We said to them, "Be disgraced apes!"

There is absolute consistency in the Quran regarding the punishment for those who have violated the sabbath, leaving no room for ambiguity. Not only were they admonished, but they were also forced to transform into apes and monkeys, as stated in the Quran as a form of punishment.

The Jews of that era, who chose to defy Allah, were subsequently punished. The entire race, including both Jews and their descendants, did not undergo evolution from apes. The Jews who were defiant were specifically punished to become apes, as their defiance was not inherent. Ultimately, Allah cursed those who disobeyed to become Apes. Darwin potentially juxtaposed this specific verse in the Quran, challenging the validity of the assumption that humans descended from apes.

The punishment only applied to those who disobeyed Allah, not the entire race. Islam does not believe in original sin and does not punish those who have not committed sins. The punishment of being cursed to become apes was specific to a certain group of Jews and it does not imply evolution from apes to humans.

They remained as apes, thus refuting the theory of evolution that humans descended from apes. The battle he initiated is not worth elaborating on as his arguments lack coherence, but the explanation of a single Muslim can effectively dismantle his nonsensical debates. There is no consensus on the idea of human evolution from apes, as the initial humans created by Allah were a man and a woman.

Allah had the ability to effortlessly transform animals into humans, but he deliberately chose not to do so. According to the Quran, it is evident that humans were the primary beings created by Allah. Before humans, other creatures had preexisted, but Allah chose to create humans instead of allowing them to evolve from animals. The Darwinian theory and its opponents promote a futile combination of irrational beliefs in an effort to cater to minds that lack understanding of the truth that Allah is the sole creator.

Humans may struggle alongside Satan, but it is a battle they cannot win. Even Satan himself can acknowledge the malevolent origins he mocks in the scheme he has devised, and Satan too recognizes the presence of a singular entity, Allah. It is Allah who granted him reprieve; he did not attain respite independently.

However, it is important to note that this punishment was specific to the individuals who were punished, rather than being a collective punishment inflicted upon the entire Jewish race. The punishment that was administered to them is intricately linked to the concept of evolution; nevertheless, the Quran presents it as a form of punishment rather than a gradual evolutionary progression.

The Quran states that mankind did not originate from monkeys, contradicting the notion of evolution. The Quran provides a perspective on creation that opposes the concept of evolution. It is worth noting that the punishment mentioned in the Quran is solely intended for those individuals who demonstrated aggression and disobedience during that particular era.

The question that arises as a result of this situation is whether Darwin is essentially implementing the same punishment that is mentioned in the Quran. There has been a suggestion made that questions the concept of humans originating from the evolutionary process. The verse, which is taken from the Quran, is being accused of being dressed in lies, but its clarity leaves no room for doubt about the truth of the Quran.

According to Islamic teachings, human beings are regarded as a distinct life form that was specifically created by Allah, in a manner that sets them apart from any other species. They possess exceptional qualities and capabilities, such as a soul and conscience, knowledge, and the ability to exercise free will. To summarize, Muslims firmly reject the notion that humans simply evolved from apes through random processes.

In resolving their dilemma, Darwin and others turned to Trinitarian beliefs and enterprising theories in order to prove their wrongs. He stated there was no God in his theory, and it was a fight within him to reject the Father, Son, and holy ghost. Later, he accused all faiths of falsification. The exact same concept is applied in today's colluded society. This places all faiths in one but Islam stands alone as a monotheistic faith accepting all Prophets and not turning them into God's or sons.

Despite engaging in debates with Muslim theologians, he failed to provide a convincing argument for his theory. His rhetoric does not support the law. Regardless of his beliefs, Muslims still reject him. Deliberate theories undermine Islamic morality. Deliberate disobedience to Allah is more detrimental than unintentional disobedience. Muslims converting or seeking a path of neglect of Islam facing poverty. Poor hearts are impoverished.

It is possible for anyone to come back. Islam rejecters face bleak outcomes. There are no commas or full stops in Islam, making it a simple faith. Same speed and regulations. The purpose of humanity is not to worship itself, as Allah did not create us for that. Those who deny Christianity merge all religions into one and claim to represent them all, same but Islam won't tolerate arrogance.

Arrogance is not synonymous with ignorance. The soul is a dark place for those who reject light. How can a theory like Darwin's be taught in schools when laws aren't fully established? Islam is a system of law, not just a theory. Watered down societies teach a watered down version of Islam.

Despite the rapid changes in the world, the light bulb throws a bright light before it dies. In a falsified setting. It looks bright before it dies, just like a light bulb. The root of disbelief was not accepting Trinitarianism, which stems from paganism. Falsifying most of the teachings and concepts after Jesus' ascension. Adapting all pagan holidays.

Darwin rejected everything, yet couldn't find Islam either; he only lived in ignorance and perpetuated evil. The distinction between theory and law is that theory is a potential phenomenon. The law is factual. Darwin's theory was never universally accepted as the ultimate truth or fact. Young developing minds are corrupted by schools teaching his unresolved collisions.

First his beliefs as a theist, he recognized the existence of a creator who governs everything, but rejected the Trinity and divine revelation. Additionally, he demonstrated deistic qualities by creating a higher power that did not intervene in the universe. His theory, which aimed to persuade those desiring independence that they held power instead of the creator, failed to resonate with those who had faith or a reasonable doubt and were still searching for answers amidst a barrage of deceit.

While he briefly delved into evolution, the centuries-old belief in reincarnation in Hinduism stands firm - new ideas won't sway a true believer. Darwin's astute observations and ever-changing predictions defied no specific ideology, except for his theory in the end. His research findings did not align with Islam because of the constantly changing ideas. The Quran served as an unalterable final decree, distinct from any other. Islam is unequivocal and leaves no room for doubt regarding Allah's authoritative disciplinary command.

The theory of nihilism is reasonably recent. In the so-hailed pre-archaic times. Humanity celebrated objects either to the pagan Gods they created or the Trinitarian Gods, but there was no such concept as no faith in the formulation.Christianity's holidays hold a close reverence for paganism.

Through their constant research, the intelligent and curious minds eventually distanced themselves from Christianity, as they accused all faiths as one without any concrete evidence to disprove them. The understanding of this ongoing dilemma is rooted in our exploration of pagan ideologies, which some individuals found to be incompatible, resulting in a growing resentment and the pursuit of alternative paths that do not adhere to Islamic principles.

The holidays celebrated in Christendom have pagan roots. The enthusiasm for gift-giving diminishes as children grow older during the celebration of Christmas. December 25th is the day when the Indian pantheon Shiva, was born a symbol copied by Christendom, is reborn.

On this day the cultists celebrated their annual winter solstice. The sun God and illuminated trees celebrated this solstice. An Indian cult that also existed was Mithraism. Expanded to other regions of the Latin and Western world. She was worshiped by Indians as the Goddess of friendship, oaths, and the morning sun. Jesus' birthday was also merged with the sun God Mitra. The Roman army celebrated this day as Jesus' birthday, even though it had no similarities to Jesus except for its pagan origins.

The cult's yearly celebration, Natalis Solis Invicti, took place on the winter solstice. Mitra's birth was celebrated as a cult holiday. Celebrations have been enticed by glitter and bling, with origins tracing back to paganism. This originates from the ancient Indian culture of Hinduism. Westerners were captivated by Hinduism.

Buddhism is modified by numerous practices. Making Buddha's stance mainstream as a spiritual approach serves to attract and entice upcoming societies. They treated Christendom in the same way. The cultures full of glitter have fascinated Westerners.

The teachings of Buddha makeup Buddhism. Karma, rebirth, and impermanence form the basis of this belief. In Islam, none of these concepts apply because life is not about suffering, but about enjoying this world and the next through trial and test. Original sin and salvation through Jesus Christ are not part of Islamic teachings. The differences provide clear comparisons in comprehending Islam as pure monotheism.

Yoga originated from Indian rituals. Indian rituals were integrated into Christianity. Pagan cults are honored during their major holidays. Over 5,000 years ago, yoga originated in Northern India. The Rig Veda was known as ancient Sanskrit texts. There are four Vedas in Sanskrit. Greek and Indian mythology is ancient. Christendom is fascinated by these philosophies. Monotheism is a central aspect of Islamic ideologies.

The color of Islam remains unfading. It's robust and will endure. Upcoming Muslim converts must be aware of the key distinctions and similarities between cultic practices resembling Christendom and behaviors that derail Muslim youth.

Jesus neither celebrated Christmas nor encouraged Jews to adopt a celebration combining pagan rituals for his birth. Can a faith survive if it creates its own rules or borrows from cultic practices, despite the allure of glitter and lights, while not adhering to the beliefs of Jesus, the son of Mary? He wouldn't approve of being honored alongside pagan deities because he believed in one God

Time is crucial, and we must share the truth. The Muslim calendar has two holidays. Muslims have been practicing it since the time of the Prophet Muhammad. The main priorities are giving to the needy, upholding spirituality, fasting and seeking repentance and worship from Allah

The majority of Muslims engage in studying, reading the Quran, and performing Salat, but some are only Muslims in name. This information is especially relevant for those who have recently converted to Islam. (Eid UL Fitr) follows a month of fasting during Ramadan. Muslims celebrate (Eid UL Adha) by paying homage to Allah in Mecca and participating in ((Qurbani) sacrifice of animals to eat, share and celebrate. Abraham underwent a test from Allah.

Allah does not require human sacrifices. He is not a God associated with cults. His name is Allah. Despite this, the sun was never conquered, while Mitra was worshiped as a sun God. Christianity and Hinduism have numerous similarities, but they belong to different faith traditions. Jesus was a monotheist, and the Quran mentions the Prophets from the Bible, even though their stories vary. A person who believes in Jesus as a Prophet and worships only God would identify as a Muslim.

The purpose of Jesus' arrival was directed towards the people of Israel. Muhammad, the Prophet, came to the world as a mercy to humanity and all existence, not to just one hot desert. This statement was made by Allah in the Quran. Unlike his first coming, Jesus will address the world differently in his second coming.

Most of the belief system relies on inserted rhetoric. Jesus will reveal the truth and uncover the lies, despite the many false demonstrations and accompanying true stories.

Easter is also associated with Estre, the Goddess of the spring equinox. Easter incorporated the pagan rituals that followed Jesus' resurrection. Muslims view it as ascension to Allah, not resurrection, which is a significant distinction between the two faiths. Despite.

Hence, certain Easter customs like Easter eggs and Easter bunnies have roots in pagan rituals. Paganism is not linked to the Muslim faith. Jesus did not submit to the paganism exploited by his followers, but instead the people turned him into a Godhead. The same message was sent by Allah to the defiant Israelites through him. The Christian religion further strengthens the defiance.

Jesus was sent by Allah to remind the Israelites about the oneness of God, a key principle of the ten commandments. Associating Jesus with paganism is unacceptable to the Muslim faith, as it rejects all forms of idolatry. The Muslim faith believes in the oneness of God and opposes idol worship. Considering Jesus as a Godhead is not a belief in Islam.

In Islam, it is seen as a grave unforgivable sin to worship Jesus or refer to him as the son of God. These distinctions provide an explanation for theology and learning. Consequently, the Easter bunny, known as a pagan fertility symbol, is tied to the holiday. Eggs, representing new life, are also commonly used as symbols of fertility.

Modern celebrations feature chocolate eggs. The inclusion of paganistic rituals in the modern world's glamor is not well-received by the Islamic world. There is no glamorization or hype in Islam that entices children and is later discarded as they mature. Muslims are increasingly embracing these rituals and acceptance, making it crucial to explain their origins.

It focuses solely on the death of a mortal and the concepts of forgiveness and salvation through him, not on your own actions and responsibility. The notion of someone dying for others' sins is ludicrous in Islam. How is it disrespectful to explore the truth for Allah, who is just, to let another person be blamed for the sins of others. If a fair justice system prohibits blaming others, why is this concept not addressed after finding out the roots of truth. Everyone has the right to their beliefs, but explaining differences won't alter those beliefs.

Jesus had a mother, but no father. Due to not having a father, he cannot be assigned one. Some people disagree with God's design because it does not conform to their minds.Eventually, they decided that Joseph would be Mary's husband, and then they went on to make God the father of Jesus, a sequence of events that might be confusing to most people. The Quran does not state that Joseph was married to Mary.

Bible:Matthew 13: 55-56 states "Is not this the carpenter's son? Isn't his mother called Mary? And are not his brethren James and Joseph and Simon and Jude?

There is a plethora of verses containing allegations towards the family of Jesus' mother, who was deemed pure and gifted with a miraculous virgin birth by Allah. However, owing to their own lack of confidence, they claimed she was wedded to Joseph. Later, she bore additional offspring with a man, despite the belief that Jesus, the son of Mary, was the son of God. Then God elected to bestow upon her a male counterpart for the purpose of conception, rendering this an unfavorable narrative that would be unsuccessful in contemporary cinema, hence the evident cause for individuals disengaging from Christianity, as much of it fails to align with mainstream thinking.

If the God described in the Bible is indeed jealous, he would have fathered a human and subsequently taken away his only son from being Mary's sole child, only to provide her with another human to conceive additional children.Adhering to their unique interpretation of the Bible, he would abstain from introducing a man to a woman with whom he fathered a child, and he bestowed his only begotten son as Jesus.Then he presents Joseph as the father of her other children, which is incredibly illogical and defies common sense. Even someone without theological knowledge would find this analogy untenable.

Bible: John 3:16.For God so loved the world, that he gave his only begotten Son, that whosoever believeth in him should not perish, but have everlasting life. God loves all ...

All of this is a context of confusion, which Islam does not confirm. Mary, the mother of Jesus, was not married and did not have any more children. It would defy common sense to claim a virgin birth for her, only to allow a man to touch her and father more children later, while she conceives and gives birth through male sperm.

Bible: Matthew 1:20.However, after Joseph decides to divorce Mary because of her unexpected pregnancy, an angel warns him in a dream not to do so. The angel advises him to "take Mary as his wife"

Bible:1:24 Matthew When Joseph woke up, he did what the angel commanded him: He took Mary as his wife.

These verses have the power to shatter a common mind into fragments and lead one to forsake faith in Christendom, embracing all religions as one.

It is evident that atheists who have immersed themselves in these narratives have developed a disdain for perplexing human minds with fabrications and have forsaken all beliefs or lumped them together and abandoned them entirely.

Mary's reputation is marred by these verses, leading the Jews to label her a character tainted according to this definition. This raises the question of whether she was married to Joseph while being pregnant by him, and if God impregnated her claiming the child as His own, then God, who prohibits adultery according to the Bible, engages in adultery with a married woman, Mary.

According to the biblical verses mentioned above, Joseph becomes upset when his wife is impregnated by God, assuming the role of the father. He patiently waits for her to have a child before proceeding to impregnate her with more children.

Despite his contemplation of divorcing her because of her character flaws, the angel intervenes. He urges him not to divorce his wife. Islam emphasizes Mary's immaculate character and Jesus' sinlessness, refuting all allegations against this virtuous family.

Pure character of Mary seems to have inherent flaws, per Bible and the deity they invoke lacks the attributes of Allah. The God of Abraham is devoid of human characteristics and does not procreate.

The narratives lack coherence, causing those who seek true faith to relinquish belief in the Bible's tales. All these allegations, the Quran rejects the distorted Bible stories, advocating only for its own narratives if they align precisely.

The Quran portrays Mary and Jesus as pure, refuting baseless allegations against their family. It emphasizes the need to explore the truth, have faith in monotheism, and recognize Jesus as the Messiah. Mary, as she was an unmarried believer, and pure.

None of the evil acts mentioned support the negative claims against this virtuous family of (Imran) Joachim. There is a Surah solely devoted to Mary in the Quran called Surah Maryam, which demonstrates her unparalleled virtue. The portrayal of Mary in the Bible diminishes her, thus Muslims should emphasize the comparisons to honor Mary, who is among the esteemed women of paradise, along with her purified son.

Quran: Surah Maryam: 23:26.Your Lord has provided a stream at your feet. And shake the trunk of this palm tree towards you, it will drop fresh, ripe dates upon you. So eat and drink, and put your heart at ease. But if you see any of the people, say, 'I have vowed silence [1] to the Most Compassionate, so I am not talking to anyone today.'"

Mary did not have to utter a word the day she brought Jesus home. Jesus spoke immediately upon birth. She was given dates, which Muslims in this decade use to break their fast during Ramadan. The respect for Mary, Jesus, and the family of Joachim (Imran) is immense. These disparities create a distinct divergence among Abrahamic faiths. Islam, as a whole, is different, even though the Prophets are shared. The stories and approach of Islam differ, but its pure nature appeals to the masses.

The history can be traced back to the Ephesus Council in 431. Recognizing Mary as the mother of God. During the 13th century, January 1st was observed as a celebration of Jesus' birth through the blessed Mary, and the Hail Mary was recited to honor her. In times of distress and happiness, they compelled the mother and sun Gods to pray to them. Such is the nature of paganism. Contradictory messages and esoteric rituals convey a distinct ideology that diverges from monotheism. Jesus' mission to uphold the same law as Moses clashes with these practices and narratives.

If Jesus adhered to Jewish laws and underwent circumcision, wouldn't it imply that God, who is Jesus or the son of God, engaged in a mortal act? It is sacrilegious to suggest that God or his son possess human traits, such as being circumcised by humans.

It seems that, in this context, humans are deemed more powerful than God or his sons. There is a series of stories that consistently align with weakness. Additionally, he lacks certainty regarding the presence of knowledge of doomsday according to biblical teachings. If he truly is the son of God or a deity himself, he should possess omniscience, an inherent attribute of the God of Abraham.

Bible: Matthew 24:36 states, "Of that day and hour knoweth no one, not even the angels of heaven, neither the Son, but the Father only," while Matthew …

Bible: Luke 2:21-39.And when eight days were completed for the circumcision of the Child, His name was called Jesus, the name given by the angel before He was conceived in the womb.

Muslim males at a young age undergo circumcision in accordance with the Abrahamic faith. Jesus, being a follower of the Abrahamic faith, also adhered to this practice. Islam refutes any allegations against Jesus and his family, leaving the responsibility of answering those claims solely to him. Allah, being just, will ensure that those who fostered evil against Jesus will be held accountable. Muslim males are also obligated to undergo circumcision in accordance with their monotheistic faith.

Humanity has long been cognizant of the myriad cultures and religions, with individuals being attracted to particular hues and tones, while others have assimilated their religious convictions and cultural practices alongside their own. Hindus and Muslims have engaged in cultural exchange, yet their religious beliefs have never collided.Christianity has assimilated a diverse range of cultic practices that sharply hold resemblance to Hinduism.

Christendom, which incorporated pagan roots, Jesus came from Abrahamic roots. Sikhism integrated aspects of Islam and Hinduism to create a doctrine known as Sikhism. The indoctrination of faiths has been a human ideology, but Islam stands apart with unchangeable revelations that concluded with Muhammad and the Quran, which is closed and not subject to corrections.

Prophet Muhammad did not have direct communication with Allah. Except for Moses, Gabriel the angel served as the intermediary for all Prophets. Muhammad's heart was purified to deliver the Quran word for word, and no revelations or Prophets came after his passing. The only Prophet who will come is Jesus.

For some, the clear distinctions do not fit well with human conceptions and beliefs, and they walk away from such faiths.Many others also oppose duality with the concepts of pagan cultures and the premixing of one God's message. There is a deficit of confusion in attendance at the core values of the human born with a soul to worship one God.

Even though many continue to worship pagan Gods and believe in pagan religions, Allah is the only one who answers every human. Those who worship him or those who don't. His judgment rests with him.

The obvious differences are clear differences in view of the current climate. There is no shaking the premise that humanity is kind and friendly.

As consequences and fixations of self-desire that are not fully aligned with spiritual interest.Their attempts to gain acceptance from the confused, while claiming lesser importance, to their own beliefs, corrupt the Muslim faith. It is not uncommon for Muslims who have exposure to corrupt societies accuse a Muslim of being an extremist.

Societal corruption has compared recreational drugs and psychedelics to the state of mind one experiences during prayer. Interestingly, they have even said that prayer releases serotonin just like drugs do. Prayer, (Salat), is neither an ecstasy nor an arousal, but a submission to Allah.Scientists from USA explore some striking similarities between these two experiences, despite their differences.

It is crucial to understand that only scientists from this world can come up with such ideas or compare them to drugs and prayer. Depression, remorse, misery, doubts, and loss of time are the negative effects of drugs.The disorderly orientation that is unpermissible by Islamic concepts has repercussions that society cannot ignore.

To enjoy any moment contrary to Islam's core values, some people need a colorful experience. It can lead to mental health problems as well as physical problems. Despite the trend for today's society, it can disrupt many lifestyles. Neither the biblical text nor any other faith deals with today's colorful societies.

In some cases, it can also pose a threat to financial stability. There is no fear of Islam in explaining things, but it is clear to distinguish between explanations without discriminating against anyone. Regardless of sexual orientation, faith, or religion.

Muslims to Islam, which secures success in this life and stability in the next. Are the followers of Islam. They can only exploit such ideas in corrupt societies since they are incompatible with Islam. The omnipotence of Allah eliminates the need for any additional force for humans to pursue the truth.

If a Muslim had the focus, he would achieve peace, contentment, and faith, not an eschatological high.Sexual stimulation revives these drug addicts, who drink alcohol and take various colorful drugs to achieve a high.They find filth, or do soul-searching through the epidemic of this experience.The Qur'an did not say to take psychedelics to find Allah. Instead, it calls for the submission of the form. Salat in cleanliness (tahara) and a non-intoxicated appearance before Allah.

Through psychology, these confused societies are trying to convince confused Muslims that drug users and addicts possess the same mentality as those who pray.Their gibberish tongues made them believe God was inside of them, and they could only understand him.Islam totally atomizes cultic behavior and explains how worship has no relevance to evil.

They believe they are hearing God's voice while engaging in drug use or speaking in incomprehensible languages. This dilemma is deemed incorrect in Islam. Understanding revelations relies on comprehension of the Prophets' spoken language, which was sent for understanding, not exclusive to them.

Islam takes great prevalence in words and delivery. Speaking in tongues, as per Christian doctrine, is considered biblical. Allah sends languages to comprehend, not to cloud minds, making deceitful to others. The theological differences are highlighted because Jesus is revered as an Abrahamic Prophet.

If no one understood, this would be satanic. Speaking in tongues is often regarded as a spiritual gift given to believers by the Holy Spirit.Islam rejects Christendom's paradox of cultic practices that enable them to communicate in a language they do not know. These differences exist, and they can understand theology to see the prescription ventures do not match on many levels.

By understanding the differences between both religions, one can see that they cannot reconcile the two approaches. Therefore, the two religions cannot be reconciled, as they are different in beliefs. Islam does not accept the concept of a divine mediator between God and humanity and believes in direct access to God through prayer and devotion. Christianity relies on Jesus as a mediator and savior.

Though friendship cannot change belief systems, humanity exists in all faiths, and concepts cannot erase differences in approach. Only becomes an issue if the two are in a union which later ends in disparity.Comparing the ecstasy of drugs and prayer is a decrypting attitude and dogma of Western scientists. Islam rejects the human method as incomparable to submission to Allah.

If this were true, the Quran would be the first to disclose it, the Quran was the first to express embryology. Not scientists, it was Allah. This is because, in Islam, prayer is an act of worship and submission to Allah. In contrast, drugs are substances that humans abuse and damage the brain. Brain cells are permanently damaged. Prayer is a purifying spiritual experience, while drugs can harm health and well-being. Therefore, the two cannot be compared.

Since prayer does not confine human beings to depression, drugs do, but their aura can be repulsive, so it can't have the same effect as prayer.In the frontal cortex, the ability to lie, speak the truth, and have motivation exists. In this area of the cerebrum, many acts can reform or destroy a human.

Quran: Surah Alaq: 96:16.A lying, sinning forelock.

Attraction to another increases dopamine and serotonin. Working out releases happy endorphins and serotonin and helps the body work out and excel. With the release of feel-good hormones, exercise can further amplify attraction feelings and boost mental well-being.The euphoria of responsibility and change may lead to men releasing less serotonin, whereas women experience different contentment and happiness.We cannot compare any of these effects on the body and behavior to a Muslim in Salat or reading the Quran.

Contrary to drug experiences, which destroy the soul, submission to Allah requires contentment within. A drug addict's brain is incompatible with that of a Muslim.Prayer does not involve arousal or addiction; it is a state of submission to Allah. Humans will submit to something. It's ridiculous that this society has even compared this to drugs. Only diluted Muslims or non-Muslims can bargain with this ideology, which is not for Muslims or Islam.

Muslims can dispel the nuisance and disturbance wrought by corrupt ideologists in opposition to Islam by comparing the purpose of prayer to that of those drugs. Similarly, Islam cannot equate drugs and prayer in their personified understanding of corrupt observance. Examples like these are necessary in an non-unauthoritative world where nuisances continue to proclaim their ideas as gospel truth. There is a great deal of difference between Islam and other ideologies.

Muslims follow set laws that cannot be amended, and Salat is number one for a Muslims unless they are mentally incapable of understanding it. It is not possible to teach intelligence in a classroom, either if one already has it or learns to adapt the teachings of a classroom. An intelligent mind can evaluate rhetoric despite gathering knowledge from corrupt societies through academia.

Muslims have advanced the world, but sadly they learn from people who need to be taught, those drifting in a non-disciplinary society, Those addicted to materialism and self-love, and are now corrupting the Muslim world.A corrupt society cannot enjoy outings, travels to places or weddings, and celebrations of sexual unions without stimulants such as alcohol or drugs.

It is this monotony and an epidemic of weakness that plague this society. Islam is fulfilling and does not depend on artificial stimulants to enjoy its beauty. Therefore, it is impossible for Muslims to be part of the upheaval and its barricaded thinking.In order to win the battle against deceit, Muslims must understand the game of deceit. Rather than joining the crowd of mishaps, a Muslim should teach the crowd and guide them to the waters of purity.

The learning is a benefit in every classroom, but it's what an individual takes with it.There is no aspect of Islam that softens the heart of a Muslim more than attendance to mandated Salat.Muslims refrained from disrespecting other believers' faiths. As a longing or self-corrective behavior for Muslims.

The Prophets have laid out all stories and all examples for Muslims to attest to their faith.When a Muslim reveals to Western society loath to compromise Islam and attests, their faith is as significant as Islam, the situation spirals into chaos. A Muslim cannot compromise with non-Muslims. Allah's laws trump the laws of humanity.

A Muslim has no room for debate since Islam's rules, regulations, and submission are incompatible with idol worship or additions to Allah.The instigation towards Islam and Muslims is a continuous effort from these societies.They view Islam as a threat to weak society, which relentlessly displays its weaknesses and ills. There is no limit to what one can say about Islam, such as insulting it, inciting Muslims, or showing disrespect for it.

When teaching free speech, a teacher won't allow countries to say poverty and taxation, school debts, and illiteracy are contributing factors.

Islam was their target. All of their ills only strengthened Islam, and they inspired curious minds to learn more about Muslims and Islam. Allah empowers every Satan attack. An anti-Islam activist burned the Quran in Copenhagen, Sweden, in 2023. The excuse is that he is mentally incapacitated but still capable of hating Muslims. Almost all organizations affiliated with altered regimes and doctrines want to contaminate Islam.

BBC:Jul 27, 2023 — Only this week a far-right group called "Danish Patriots" burned the Quran outside the Iraqi embassy in Copenhagen.

Those who misbehave, disturb peace, threaten Muslims, harm Muslims, or burn the Quran. In this dynamic society, they receive assistance and are placed in mental facilities that support their mental disabilities. Cunning enough to cause damage. When Muslims take action, the blame falls on their race and they are labeled as terrorists. This society is so flawed that it compels Muslims to recognize the need for further progress. We must challenge this society to reveal our true identity as teachers, achievers, and not as losers who shift blame onto others.

This lack of accountability only perpetuates a cycle of intolerance, furthering the divide between cultures and religions.

Fairness in Islam is a principle that must be followed, even if it's against yourself. It is a belief that justice is paramount and that no one should be treated with impunity. This is why justice must be served to those who commit injustices, regardless of their race, religion, or background. This would help to end the cycle of violence and restore trust between cultures and religions.

The recent earthquakes in Muslim countries serve as a warning for Muslims to reflect on their identity and purpose in this world and the imminent end of the world. The earthquake in Turkey in 2023 fostered enhanced collaboration and bolstered ties between Muslim and NonMuslim nations through humanitarian aid.

The reasons behind such events are beyond human comprehension, only Allah knows. However, we should take warnings as reminders to improve ourselves.

Each warning can be amplified as a blessing because it is a mercy, as all lives belong to Allah. Muslims are martyred in disasters.

The complexity of the belief system based on mortals or deities is challenging to examine and swallow as belief with solidarity. It is simply a fallacy of following the ancestors. Whereas faith in Islam is based on an unseen God, Allah. Judaism also believes in one God. Jesus called him (Allah-ha).Therefore, killings, especially those of humans, would be cultic regardless of the theme.

It is also a Christian belief that the Ten Commandments of God include the command not to kill. Muslims gave animals as voluntary gifts for Islamic charity rather than being sacrificed for a cult. The only sin that is costly is shirk, and Allah forgives if He wishes. (Shirk) adding partners to Allah is not forgivable in Islamic doctrine.

Human sacrifices were usually performed to attract good luck and appease the Gods, such as during the dedication of a finished structure like a temple or bridge. Fertility was a recurring theme in ancient religious sacrifices, including those dedicated to the Aztec God of agriculture Xipe Totec.

World History Encyclopedia: Aztec Sacrifice:n Mesoamerican culture human sacrifices were viewed as a repayment for the sacrifices the Gods had themselves made in creating the world and the sun. This idea ...Definition · Origins & Purpose · Preparing The Victims

BBC: Peru child sacrifice discovery may be the largest in history; Apr 28, 2018 — Archaeologists have uncovered what may be the largest single mass child sacrifice event in human history. More than 140 children were sacrificed.

Federal Bureau of Investigation:Feb 5, 2013 —Santa Muerte Inspired Ritualistic killings. Over five centuries ago, worshipers offered the skins of human sacrifices to the Aztec Gods.

The examples are many to understand the human killings rituals killing children for their Gods has been a practice performed for decades. Skulls and

CNN: 2020, archaeologists unearthed a tower of more than 600 skulls while excavating Huey Tzompantli, in the heart of what is now Mexico City. Many of the skulls have perforations thought to have been made so they could be easily hung at the ritual sacrifice site.

The evidence suggests that they bowed down to rituals performed by their ancestors, incorporating lies to make themselves believe someone was sacrificed for them. If things start to make sense, Islamic concepts will bring clarity. Allah is not a God who requires rituals, He is the light, the Nur. Jesus is alive and will return to reveal allegations against him.

These practices are not in accordance with Islam. Many more examples are needed to understand that Jesus was ascended to Allah, not sacrificed for human salvation, in this civilized faith of progression, not regression.

Cults have historical evidence of human sacrifices dating back. Cultic acts of human sacrifice were practiced by the Hebrews, Greeks, Mesoamerica, and European civilizations. What sets Abraham's God Allah apart from cults despite their similar practices? Those hoping for a cultic practice of history repeating will discover that Allah did not make a human sacrifice.

It won't be long before Muslims are proven right once again. Muslims' behaviors are showcased in documentaries that highlight the existence of Islamophobia. Islam didn't support, but stopped barbaric behavior. Does Islam allow justice? Indeed, humanity has benefited greatly from Islam. If the injustice is evident, why do the numbers keep increasing daily, to conversion to Islam especially from countries that oppose Islam and mistreat humans for greed, while still engaging in barbaric rituals in various locations?

Material blitz and available jobs may show success in countries, but homes face doom when defiance persists against Allah. The course of everything is governed by Allah through scripts, with the Quran, as the unaltered one, inviting those interested and called to Islam by the creator, not humans. No one can invite someone to Islam without Allah's will.

There is no permissible way of incorporating partners into Allah's divinity.However, when Allah murders his own son, the complexity of Christian doctrine raises the question of how one can follow this belief. He himself does not keep his promise.

Subsequent to the revelation of the ten commandments, specific individuals deem the "thou shall not kill" doctrine absurd, considering the contradiction it poses to the principles of Abrahamic faith and the Bible beliefs in opposition of "thou shall not kill". In the Christian doctrine, God's act of sacrificing his own son serves as a recompense for the sins of others, akin to ancient cults benefiting from human sacrifice. Some vehemently refuse to accept this idea and completely forsake their faith. Others strive to find Islam, which leads them to an unseen entity, the enlightening power of the universe, known as Allah.

Muslims view this episode in a different light, showing that Allah is merciful, since he took Jesus to himself, and someone else took his place.Although they rejoiced over the death, "WE" took Jesus back,, to tell the truth of the incident to those who don't didn't understand. He will return.

To understand this theory logically, killing the son of any human would be a toxic infrastructure.The suggestive notion that God would take his son and allow murder to forgive humanity's sins is beyond comprehension. For many who doubt theology, faith based on the death of a man may seem incoherent and a struggle to deepen belief.

This is the fact that Allah revealed another revelation after Injil the gospel, the Quran to Prophet Muhammad.It does not mention the other New Testament biblical authors in any text who rose without revelation from Allah.

The apostle Paul of the apostolic testament never met Jesus; he was a Jew, so this section of Christianity is associated with Pauline Christianity. Followed by unknown authors and scribes without divine revelation.

If Paul was the successor of the scribes, Jesus would have talked about him instead of mentioning Muhammad. He said I must go away to send the comforter, who will teach the same as he did, that we should worship Allah. Jesus did not say; instead, worship him. He also worshiped Allah. In the Torah, the Jews also mention Muhammad by name. My expression can only inspire the research of many who search for truth.

Bible: King James Version: *Deuteronomy 18:18* ... "I will raise them up a Prophet from among their brethren, like unto thee, and will put my words in his mouth; and he shall speak unto them.

According to tradition, Paul, who never met Jesus, wrote the New Testament. The four authors are Paul, Mark, Luke, and John. More versions are forthcoming. Before Prophet Muhammad passed away, Allah revealed the Quran to an unlettered Prophet.

Allah has given him the ability to verbalize the Quran word for word. Scribes wrote in his presence.Human beings become subservient to something that they worship. They worship even things unknown.Humanity still feels deeply moved by hearing about the money, beauty, and knowledge of unknown people.

Humanity made such pleas and imaginative efforts to see Allah, the creator, but those endeavors were entirely futile. Allah has made human beings weak and incapable of seeing Allah in this lifetime.The rational explanation is that God is not visible to a human. Having seen a human, one can conclude that he does not walk in the image of God.

God is not a human, and he would not transform himself into a human body. Incomprehensible concepts such as these lead many to disbelief, as idol worship cannot satisfy a person's heart.They merely pacify those who break the law. Such contamination cannot contaminate Islam. In this lifetime, no human will see Allah.

Moses (Musa) expressed a desire to see his creator, could not endure the light, and fainted. In the next life, during judgment and after death, the human will face his creator.

Quran is the word of Allah transcribed verbally to scribes by Prophet Muhammad upon receiving revelations from Angel Gabriel Quran excelled and transcended, from Allah not as a rewrite by Prophet Muhammad, he was an unlettered Prophet.

He did not read or write. All accusations of copying any other book don't conspire with legitimate allegations by disbelievers or competitors.The companions of Prophet Muhammad served as scribes, recording the revelations, comparing notes, and re-reading to him. Allah transcribed his seraphic sublime, divine words, and they made no changes. Allah has revealed this book. He will preserve his book until eternity.

Quran: Surah Hijr: 15:9. "We have without doubt sent down the message, and we will assuredly guard it (from corruption)."

Allah delivered the Quran when the Arab world thrived on literacy and poetry. Arabs excelled in oral poetry competitions held in marketplaces.

The recitation of the Quran stunned many listeners. Many converted to Islam by listening to acoustic rhythms. Concepts delivered by this Prophet. The message of the Quran is quite direct. It clearly transcends the differences and upholds the eternal message it sends to humanity. The continuity of previous books of Abrahamic faith persists in the same delivery. There is only one Allah, the eternal, the merciful, and the beneficent.

In the Arab world, the Quran superseded all literature, making it a milestone to reach.

Allah challenged their poetic literacy. And they questioned themselves. It was impossible for them to argue against this literature from Allah.The Quran challenges humanity to bring a surah man still could not produce.

The smallest Surah in the Quran is no match to the literacy of a human.

Quran: Surah Baqarah 2:23 and if you are in doubt concerning that which we reveal unto our slave (Muhammad), then produce a surah (chapter) of the like thereof and call your witnesses besides Allah if you are truthful.

The Quran was revealed by Allah to Prophet Muhammad over a span of 23 years prior to his death. Both Muslims and non-Muslims acknowledge him as the most trustworthy and honest, (Al Amin, Sadiq). Allah's word triumphed over historical challenges despite Islam's struggles. Muslims faced shunning, stoning, killing, and torture in their efforts to spread Islam. If Muslims could recall and understand the historical struggles of the Prophet and his people, they would see triumph and achievements instead of resistance.

Along with affirming faith, one worships Allah alone. The consequence of disobedience to Allah must be paid in full. He appointed him for the task and carried out trials. Each surah of the Quran was sent by Allah in time as it was assembled and furnished. Allah chose Angel Gabriel to transport the Quran to Prophet Muhammad. Non-believers will be astonished by the paradox in the delivery.

He spoke the truth, except for those battling their inner demons, entangled in a sinister chaos of uncertainty and doubt. Today's confused society promotes fake tabloid stories about Islam through social media, instead of exposing the truth by Islamophobes. The main focus is either to portray Islam as backward or to bombard the media with negative portrayals of individuals with Muslim names.

In Islamic culture, a person's name holds significance and shapes their life, particularly in Islam. The Prophet Muhammad was approached by a man who was worried about his disobedient son. He stated that he would have a conversation with him.

Upon hearing the boy, he was informed by the boy. He didn't make the effort to give me a pleasant name. The father was advised by him to give his son a good name and respect his rights. In Islam, it is crucial to educate about the rights of children and parents.

In Islam, faith is contractual and governed by laws with consequences. Some may question if faith should be about salvation, forgiveness, and love. Islam imposes accountability for actions and rewards good deeds tenfold. Islam offers the fairest justice in the world, making it a path to global peace. This peace has not been granted by Allah to all nations, nor has he bestowed Islam upon all humans. It is predetermined that Muslims will discover their path towards Islam.

Prophet Muhammad was an austere example. He came from the tribe of Quraish. The pursuit of worldly gains was not on his agenda.The delivery of the Quran and the lifestyles of his (sunnah) habits and practices are a living legacy of riding and dictating the lifestyles of the Muslim world.

His kingship held no crown as a prince of many hearts, bearing comfort for humanity.

He walked the streets without a bodyguard or trumpets, and no one wooed his presence. The simplicity he carried was his richness, Islam was his wealth, and his dignity was his passion.The character was flawless. How can a Muslim who follows this Prophet not focus on inner strengths through the example he left behind?

He constantly referred to himself as a slave of Allah, and he warned the Muslim (Ummah) followers of Islam. Follow the eternal Allah, not a human.He did not refer to himself as coming from the Noble tribe of Quraish and a proud Arab.

Pride of any kind is not for a Muslim. It is common in today's society to refer to yourself as proud to be of certain countries that cause chaos even though no heritage or nobility exists.

The fallacy of unsound argument illustrates ignorance, not pride. For a Muslim, this behavior and wordings are unacceptable, and only Allah carries pride. We can present many examples. They choreographed several songs of pride. It is taboo in Islam to display such sketchy lyme.

Those who are confronted with lies versus truth are obligated to tell the truth. Is the next world a real place? Is life a tangible reality? Is death a real phenomenon? Is it fleeting or everlasting? Allah, the creator of life, also spoke of a judgment, suggesting that there will be questioning in the next phase of existence. Believers will be reunited there by Allah, restoring their unity. Disbelievers will meet in the place assigned for them.

In contrast, the Quran makes it clear that a believer's wealth, children, and property serve as a test. The blessing serves the dual purpose of testing behavior and acceptance.

Enemies of Prophet Muhammad tempted him with wealth, kingship, women, entertainment, food, and land.In exchange for Muslims following their faith for half the time, they pledged to follow Islam for the same duration. The propositions did not materialize and Islam refused the council's invitation to paganism.

Despite all the efforts made by the enemy, they achieved no results. There would be no change in Islam for anyone.There was a (surah) Allah sent "for you, your religion for me, my religion". There were no negotiations in matters of faith.

The Muslims foster the monotheistic belief and practices of Prophet Muhammad. Islam is not a representation of Muslims. Islam is a representation of its own.

Quran: Surah Kafirun: 109:06. For you is your religion, and for me is my religion.

Quran: Surah Ankabut 29:48 You O Muhammad were not a reader of any scripture before it nor did you write such a scripture with your right hand for then those who follow falsehood might have a right to doubt it.

For a polytheist, victory is the ultimate end, and triumph concludes in this world. A believer possesses both this world and the next. What if humans fight for this world without believing in the next, or believe in reincarnation? The answers lie in the findings, believe what you will.

Quran: Surah Nisa: 4:82.Then do they not reflect upon the Qur'an? if It had been from [any] other than Allah, they would have found within it much contradiction.

Quran: Al Hijr:15:9 Absolutely, we have revealed the reminder, and absolutely we will preserve it.

Can a Muslim reject their faith today, considering that history contradicts Islamic beliefs and society has progressed? Are they inviting Muslims in unions to follow their faith for half the time and observe the doctrine of Islam for the other half? It didn't work then and it will not work now.

Unions of religions with opposing beliefs are impossible, but friendships can flourish regardless of faith. Despite seeking balance eventually, humans are cordial to all humans, as Islam prioritizes humanity over faith. Humanity always comes before faith in any human's actions. When beliefs become contradictory, making the belief system the subject can lead to a likely disagreement. Having passion for one's own faith is universal. Thrown into the fire, Abraham was punished by his father for his belief in idols.

Faith goes beyond and is manifested in those who believe. The pseudo-culture that lacks belief still submits to something, making humans subservient. How can someone be unaware that Islam stands alone in its faith? Islam extends a kind hand to all humanity but doesn't compromise faith. Muslims will follow the (Sunnah) of Prophet Muhammad, and history will bear witness to that.

Muslims would have followed suit in compromising their faith and engaging in human sacrifice for rewards, if he had done so. Consequently, a Muslim cannot negotiate their religious beliefs for a non-Muslim. Muslims did not honor the eclipse of the Moon when the young boy son of Prophet Muhammad passed away.

Paganistic beliefs contradict Islam, which rejects anything resembling them. Sadness arises when humans leave, but no one is here permanently, which is both a weakness and a guarantee humans must confront. The tabloid effect of a person's actions in life reveals their true relationship with the creator.

There are several examples of stories in the Quran. Each individual is responsible for building the knowledge they need to explore and learn daily. The testing process begins when they gain the senses to understand. Islam provides guidance. It is ultimately up to each individual to be responsible for his own conduct. Trials and achievements are tailored to each individual.

In theology, there is a difference and contrast and pure observation of societal trends. This does not separate friendship and care from humanity regardless of faith. The Quran is the only inscription in this world that is not partially divine and partially human.

Altered scripts lack authenticity as humans can't even correct a simple comma, so how can any script survive with changes by human hands? The Quran's finality triumphs over all achievements and learning, offering limitless rewards to those who make sincere efforts with an open mind. It benefits those with curious minds and promotes friendships and humanity across continents and time zones. Humanity perceives kindness, not religion, but faith is essential for the soul.

CHAPTER 17

THE SIGNIFICANCE OF LAWS, CONTRACTS, AND TRUTH IN ISLAM

The questionnaire raised the query of whether it is mandatory for a follower of Islam to adhere to the laws of their religion, and the quest for an answer is underway. Islam does not enforce obligatory submission to Allah, but rather advocates and incentivizes a voluntary submission.

Regardless of the circumstances, the repercussions of this situation are destined to guarantee distinct results. The laws have their origins in the Quran, establishing it as their foundational basis. The decision rests with Muslims; nonetheless, the rules of this jurisdiction will remain unaltered with regard to Islam.

Quran: Surah Ghafir:16:16. the Day when they will emerge and nothing of them shall be hidden from Allah. (On that Day they will be asked): "Whose is the kingdom today?

Through the divine mercy of Allah, humanity is bestowed with numerous favors, which can be truly enjoyed by adhering to conduct, mannerism, and discipline in every aspect. Islam encompasses a range of aspects, like practical expression, conviction, and behavior, each of which plays a significant role in one's existence. Allah's presence is apparent in every aspect for the observant. Like someone who only sees the vibrant amidst the mundane, they can delve into the optimistic facets of their character.

The captivating allure of green, never fading, is akin to a woman gracefully aging and evoking memories of an eternal green forest. Society is unable to effectively function without the presence of crucial laws and regulations, as disorder would otherwise reign. Laws and regulations establish a structure that facilitates peaceful coexistence. Allah's laws are immutable and immune to any alterations. These laws, deeply ingrained in the Islamic faith, serve as a cornerstone for ensuring justice and fairness in all aspects of life.

These individuals or groups exploit the existing fears and prejudices against Muslims to further their own agendas. They manipulate the uneducated masses by spreading misinformation, stereotypes, and promoting a sense of insecurity. This fear mongering not only perpetuates division and discrimination but also hinders social progress and cohesion.

However, it is important to recognize that this perception is not based on truth, but on a distorted narrative. Muslims, like any other religious or ethnic group, are diverse and multifaceted, comprising individuals with a range of beliefs, values, and contributions to society. Overcoming Islamophobia requires education, dialogue, and a willingness to challenge these unfounded fears and prejudices. As people become more informed and engaged, they will realize that the truth triumphs over lies and fear, leading to a more inclusive and harmonious society.

The act of being cautious and aware ensures that truth triumphs over falsehood. Many times, Muslims are deliberately placed in prominent roles, posing a threat with the purpose of effectively managing the general population and ensuring the protection of their respective countries against perceived threats.

It's worth mentioning that Muslims, just like individuals of various religious backgrounds, migrate to different countries for reasons that are sanctioned by Allah. Until Allah wills it, no human being has the ability to move beyond the boundaries set by their jurisdiction. False leaders are leading their nations to destruction, impacting their citizens' living conditions. The teachings of Islam state that individuals who display traits of being tyrants, deceitful, and hypocritical are destined to rule over the hypocrites.

Conversely, those who are oppressed possess the inherent right to garner support and courageously defend themselves in the face of their oppressors. Muslims have had a significant impact throughout history by not only rescuing people from slavery but also by establishing democratic systems that prioritize the rights of every individual. However, hypocrites resort to shedding insincere tears and utilize social media as a tool to manipulate individuals who are easily swayed by societal trends.

Actively involving educated and skilled Muslims in the system is vital, as it prevents them from being lured into deceptive roles. It is important for individuals to recognize the importance of standing up for their rights, utilizing their skills to advocate for humanity, and highlighting the positive contributions that Muslims can bring to society.

Putting an end to this tyranny is imperative, and the ultimate solution lies in the establishment of Muslim rule, which will bring about a one-world order centered on the principles of Islam rather than paganism. Muslims, when governing, prioritize the preservation and safeguarding of the rights of others, rather than engaging in actions that would harm or dismantle those rights. Ultimately, Jesus will reconcile with Islamic principles in order to proclaim his arrival, not as a Prophet solely for Israel, but as a Prophet of Islam who has always submitted to Allah since the beginning of existence.

These comments serve as a testament to the extensive reign of Muslims throughout history and their invaluable contributions to the world, particularly in the realm of knowledge and enlightenment.

Those who underestimate the power of the Quran as a supreme teacher cannot grasp the significance of not aligning with evil. True humanity lies in resisting the temptations of evil, as it can lead no one towards righteousness.

Only those who wholeheartedly submit to Allah can avoid deception and guide others towards the right path. It is not possible for someone to claim to pray Salat sincerely while their actions contradict their treatment of others, because Salat is intended to soften the heart.

Muslims have delved into areas of knowledge that were previously unknown to humanity, and the next generation of Muslims is making remarkable progress in various fields. The intention behind this trap is to tempt Muslims by offering them independence.

Nevertheless, it is at this very moment that Muslims residing in Islamophobic regions must rise up, regardless of whether they find themselves as the last surviving Muslim on Earth, and fight for their rights and the truth.

The power of sujood, an act performed by a single Muslim, is so great that it has the potential to receive Allah's forgiveness and bring blessings to the land where it is performed. Regrettably, the haters fail to grasp the importance of Muslims' sujood in preserving harmony worldwide, as this concept eludes them.

The Islamic coverage encompasses a broad range of topics, such as economics, politics, and morality. Divine instructions demand attentiveness, not neglect. Laws in the world can be changed and negotiated. Quantum physics explains the laws of attraction, a theory that resonates with many. It's either negative or positive thinking. Thoughts impact the mind, driving individuals to connect with similar thinkers or those who desire a vibrant existence.

Allah magnifies and harmonizes all simplicity laws for success. The allure of seeking discipline draws Muslims towards finding contentment with Allah's laws. Designed by the creator of the universe, not by humans.

Human rights, established by laws, cannot be compromised as no jurisdiction functions by breaking laws. Allah's laws are both simple and easily comprehensible, but yield powerful results. True contentment and inner peace result from following them. These laws can bring blessings and prosperity to both this world and the next.

Satan, an envious Jinns, does not abide by any laws except negotiating with weak victims to follow the ways that are conducive to growth of humanity he aims for destruction and harbors hatred towards believers. His exit from heaven carries malevolence towards those who abide by the laws.

Deceit and greed find empowerment in the laws of most countries. There is a growing global trend where borrowing with interest is employed as a method to establish credibility and worth. The society will face repercussions if they fail to fulfill their debts.

Debts can be quantified in monetary units, with the value of trust in the transaction of borrowing and repaying the debt leading to interest in societies that engage in interest-based lending, resulting in the borrower accruing more losses than assistance, creating a battle against a remorseless adversary who shows no compassion for the disadvantaged. Earth, being a habitat for humans, bears unsettled debts owed to the creator. In relation to actions, not interest.

Judgment can be perceived as unsettled obligations for the ultimate existence on earth, where individuals have unrestrictedly exploited resources such as the atmosphere, dwellings, crops, grains, atmosphere, and water. The payment for this usage was not a transaction between two individuals. Islam is a faith that emphasizes logic and reason over illusions.

Quran: Surah Baqarah: 2:275. Those *who devour usury will not stand* on the same platform as those driven to madness. That is because they say: "Trade is like usury."

Bible:The Old Testament authority - Exodus 22:25, Leviticus 25:35, and Deuteronomy 20:19 - does not constitute a blanket ban on interest-taking, but condemns taking interest from the poor, and within the Jewish community. The taking of interest was forbidden to clerics from AD 314.

Jesus did not show mercy to interest chargers. He opted to whip them. Jews and Christians belonging to Abrahamic faith do not avoid interest accumulation on loans. They live in an exploitative society, financially draining individuals and forcing them to sacrifice their living conditions to cover endless interest payments.

In certain regions, home ownership is pride but difficult due to unchanging principal borrowed for elongated periods. The amount of principal resolutes stationary despite years of interest payments. Taking someone's hard-earned money is against the law of humanity. The credit card usage and raise interest rates to showcase borrowing strength, but it becomes burdensome for borrowers necessities.

Allah, in His infinite wisdom, was able to foresee the immense potential within humanity. As a result, He explicitly prohibited the practice of charging interest. However, it is unfortunate that humans tend to resist and deviate from compliance with this divine guidance. Consequently, the subsequent events unfold in a manner that ultimately leads to the failure of these laws that are meant to safeguard and protect society.

A prevailing trend is emerging, where individuals prioritize their own laws and show defiance. Taking interest along with the principal of funds borrowed is strictly prohibited in Islam, therefore, it is improbable that any Muslim country would involve itself in such practices. Muslims are told to avoid interest and instead prioritize engaging in trade that offers greater benefits. Yet, in many circumstances, residing in countries and making use of the system's access is unavoidable.

Humanity is afraid to break human laws but never flinches before breaking Allah's laws. When his own arrogance causes him to be expelled from heaven, Satan instinctively blames humans. He had complete confidence in his own understanding, and his arrogance compelled him to strike a deal that would bring temporary contentment.

Therefore, his followers face the same discontentment when everything appears glamorous without the laws. The consequences include spiritual emptiness and inner depression, particularly for believers. This secret is known only to the person who defies Allah. Compliance and quality control are aspects of human life regulated by human laws. Allah's hierarchy ensures compliance without causing injustice to anyone.

The laws are clear, there's no room for ambiguity. Every human in the world will ultimately proclaim the truth when answering. Islam recognizes and addresses the truth that individuals will come to know at least once. The decision to follow or not is up to you. Islam will be presented to everyone by Allah. Satan's society claims false independence by resisting laws. Humanity was not exempt from Allah's laws upon creation. Believers can also fall prey to deceitful temptations. Repeated behavior is of ills is concerning as believers are aware of right and wrong. Repentance is always essential for resolving any dilemma.

Blame has a long history that dates back centuries. Throughout history, humans have consistently placed blame on others. Christendom assigned the burden of blame to Jesus by calling it resurrection and viewing it as the solution to their sins through salvation.

Instead of shouldering blame, Islam responded by labeling it as hypocrisy and creating an unwelcoming place for hypocrites. Is it possible for a hypocrite to change? Absolutely, as long as time allows it.

The council used paganism to manipulate people's minds and establish regimes that served their own criteria, making humans into Gods. Primal instincts drove humans, who were still adjusting to the idea of an unseen God, to seek a tangible deity for worship.

The manipulator soon establishes their own council, creating a legacy of deceit. The Council of Nicaea established in Constantinople known as modern day Turkey the Trinity and voted within the Christian church, despite it not being based on the Bible.

Turkey, formerly known as Constantinople, is the land where a myriad of captivating transformations, conflicts, and triumphs occurred. The historical milestones of the Byzantine empire being conquered by the Ottoman empire illuminated the Muslim world with its radiant splendor, as predicted by Prophet Muhammad.

Muslims have shown disinterest and refrain from exploiting those who are unable to repay their debts. Borrowing entails evaluating creditworthiness, while depriving individuals of nonexistent resources is cruel. The Bible underwent modifications by Constantine in Constantinople. That marked the commencement but not the conclusion.

Without research, repeated lies can be mistaken for truth, especially in indoctrination of substance. Doubt arises when truth and lies are intertwined, confusing indecisive individuals, until lies are repeated enough to be accepted as truth over time, fueled by power, deceit, and greed. However, over time, many people walk away and no longer align with their conscious thoughts.

CBS news: Sep 14, 2022 — Christianity in the U.S. is quickly shrinking and may no longer be the majority religion within just a few decades, research finds.

The Guardian:Jan 23, 2023 — As the US adjusts to an increasingly non-religious population, thousands of churches are closing each year

Pew Research Center: Why Muslims are the world's fastest -growing religious group.

The truth is unstoppable. The only religion of the world will be Islam before the end of the world. People who don't recognize its capacity to establish truth and instead depend only on instinct and leave. Occasionally, people come across Islam. Despite this, churches persist in following indoctrinated doctrines instead of Jesus' ideologies, altering the methodology and concepts to align with their own desires. Although Islam acknowledges him, it is essential to explain the variations, since he has a contrasting position and identity in Islam.

The Gospel, sent by Allah (Ingel), was altered by them to differentiate between the divine and human aspects. A color-coding system applied to the Bible. The humanized gospel. It eventually became a widely accepted doctrine among various sects. Some refer to him as the son of God, while others describe him as three in one or even as God himself. The manipulation prepared centuries ago makes the indoctrination of paganism concrete and obvious for those who see it. Finally, they stated he walked on earth as God in human form.

Humans can walk, but light can be transmitted by injection of truth. Islam rejects the idea of humans created in the image of Allah, since humanity is incapable of fully understanding him. For centuries, people in these cultures have been practicing paganism and idol worship, which has been influencing the human mind.Pagan statues in the Kabba were eliminated when Islam emerged. The people with pagan ancestry wanted to keep the statues to honor their ancestors and remember their worship. Islam expected that this would cause humans to forget the purpose of those statues and begin worshiping them.

Islam rejects all negotiations, except for the acceptance of revelations from Prophets and the worship of an unseen God. A battle has been waged by pagan worshippers. The Kabba is exclusively accessible to Muslims in Islam. The rationale behind prioritizing complete devotion to one God, instead of integrating paganism into a monotheistic belief is apparent. It is clear to a believer that this makes sense. Monotheism is the faith of all Prophets, and Muslims have followed the same path since the beginning of creation. The name of Islam was given as a final statement when humanity was prepared.

The Messiah had a task to fulfill, but the Jews resisted and the Christians were nonexistent. After Jesus' ascension, they began identifying as Christians and professing to follow his teachings. There was a rise of a new religion called Christianity. Jesus didn't call his followers Christians; they were Jews. Pauline Christianity emerged in later years, shaped by individuals who were influenced by Paul's teachings, even though he was initially Jewish.

Theology and comparative study help in acquiring knowledge.Despite the Jews' rejection of Jesus, Allah plans to send him back to fulfill his incomplete mission. The emergence of Christianity further challenges their beliefs. Replacing God with a mortal or defying both has a deceptive nature.Both pieces of evidence are compelling and cannot be ignored. The world is going through tough times, and there are pagan worshippers who claim Jesus is God returning to Earth.

These theological answers may surprise some and be harsh for others. Muslims who fear humans are disconnected from Islam because the truth is fearless.Islam is governed by Allah and the Quran, which remains unaltered, allows believers to provide explanations for those who seek understanding. Inviting people to Islam is not useful if they don't seek truth or remain in ignorance. Muslims who lack comprehension need guidance and questions from knowledgeable individuals who read the Quran.

Jesus won't identify as a Christian when he arrives. Instead, he will declare himself Muslim and pray dawn prayers. Islam is a personal belief, but more people are converting worldwide, leading Muslims to share their faith. Muhammad, who is known as a historical figure and also as the Prophet of Islam and humanity, dedicated his life to practicing the Islamic faith. Jesus, in his teachings, did not promote Christianity and did not instruct the Jewish community to adopt Christian beliefs.

Jesus was sent to the people of Israel with the purpose of carrying on the laws of Moses, just as Muhammad followed the teachings of Jesus and the fundamental principle of worshiping one God. Moses did not worship Jesus, nor did he mention God was coming to walk on earth as a human because of his inability to bear to see God's light, and likewise, Jesus never declared that he should be worshiped.

This is in line with the message that Jesus was sent to deliver, the consistent message and any deviation from it would result in punishment for not following. The primary reason Jews reject him as a Prophet is because they argue that the punishment imposed on him could not have occurred if he truly was a Prophet. The fact that the Quran clarified the punishment did not occur, and that he was taken up alive, not dead, serves as a continual reminder.

Neither did he claim that he would die for their sins, nor did he instruct them to worship him or anticipate the emergence of his followers who would utilize him for the atonement of their sins. This is evident in the subsequent development of new implications and doctrine by Paul and other authors in what is now known as Pauline Christianity.

The facts that are being presented in this context are specifically targeted towards individuals who are actively seeking answers and information pertaining to theology and the practical. distinctions within it. It is worth noting that the speaker Jesus also made reference to the arrival of a voice of truth who would share the same teachings as him, namely Muhammad, the Prophet who preached a consistent message that aligned with the teachings of Moses, Jesus, and all the other Prophets.

In the scenario where all the answers are evident and comprehensible, if a human being still denies that it is Allah who is the driving force behind everything, no other human can persuade someone who has veered off the right path.

Since the previous scriptures have undergone notable changes, it is difficult to argue that those books are authentic. This leaves us with only one book, the Quran, if one is seeking the truth in solidarity and a cohesive belief system that supports previous scriptures and Prophets. However, it is important to note that the validity of other scripts is contingent upon their alignment with the Quran.

` Although Christians were not specifically mentioned in the Bible, they are indeed referenced in the Quran. The acceptance of the truth that Jesus delivered was a straightforward and uncomplicated understanding, as a series of consistent instructions fell into place.

As the request is being deliberated, modifications are being made to both the books and scripts. The relentless pursuit of truth within the teachings of Islam is the genuine path to follow, with the Quran serving as the sole text that has endured without any modifications.

Quran: Surah Imran:come to common terms as between us and you: That we worship none but Allah; that we associate no partners with him; that we erect not from among ourselves ...

Jesus was not a Christian, he was Jewish, but his beliefs were monotheistic, not pagan. A mortal's worship is called paganism, and Prophets throughout history have submitted to Allah's will.The Creator abstains from excreting personal waste, eating, following Satan, getting circumcised, and being killed.

Only those who make a distinction understand that an Abrahamic Prophet cannot represent paganism. But Islam thrives on the same belief, and no man was born to change it. One God is Allah alone, free of any human.This comparison is not against faith, but about clarity in understanding that some clarification episodes haven't been dusted off with truth. But corroded by concepts that require attendance of any kind.

People have a choice of expressing responsibility for their actions and work to make amends for their mistakes. This is the only way to foster understanding, growth, and forgiveness. Muslims have stood tall explaining truth concepts for those with no disregard for humanity, but truth has a platform of its own and no fear. It's not racist prejudice or any other words found in the dictionary. Instead, it's the word of truth that has no fear and only offers salvation to those who correct within. God's Prophets did not focus on survival rather than on the kingdom.

The kingdom belongs to Allah. Moses' law passed down the same message to other Prophets as well.The same way that Jesus established the same law of one worship from the beginning of time.All Prophets focused on the same deliverance without exception.

Islam continues with the same laws and belief in one God under the new name and mark of Islam. And those who follow one God and accept Muhammad as the last Prophet of Allah are Muslims. For the Jewish people of Israel, Jesus was sent to mark disorder and disobedience and lead them to righteousness.

Being born of a virgin named Mary, he faced difficulty in succeeding with them, as they were not inclined to obey his laws. The disorder in question was ultimately attributed to individuals with wicked intentions, who firmly held the belief that the concept of a virgin birth was an impossibility.

Consequently, they unfoundedly accused Mary of engaging in secretive affairs to explain the birth of her child. Their defiance was clear as they expressed their disbelief at the capabilities of Allah. The purpose of his mission was not to save the world, but rather to fulfill a different objective.

Prophet Muhammad, who is revered as the Prophet of humanity globally, Jesus was specifically sent to the Jewish community in Israel (Yahudi). His next course of action will be to address the world, acknowledging the false accusations made against him and disclaiming any knowledge of the individuals who accused him.

Jesus's survival in this life, which consists of birth and death, also depends on Allah as he is not God but created by God. Islamic concepts are so simple, even a child can comprehend them. It is possible to have a flawed belief system if the understanding is beyond human comprehension.

Certain Muslims persist in not following Islamic principles, while numerous individuals willingly seek to convert to Islam. Many converts to Islam come from countries that are against it but end up embracing it. Islam received rebuke and attack. Truth continues to grow despite false accusations on social media.

Many give up faith completely and believe in the universe. Islam has no place for degenerative societies.Allah designed it to cover all human understandings without limiting them. Except for those who seek blame and defiance, Islam does not allow decryption.Thus allowing one to continue and regress against oneself and blame notions continue.

By recognizing Jesus as their savior, people can experience the liberation from their sins. Contrary to other religions, Islam does not have a figure considered as a savior. Time management in this world requires a holistic approach, encompassing spiritual, physical, and mental aspects of life.

One of the principles in Islam is the prohibition of placing blame on others, which is rooted in the denial of original sin. The distinctions between the Abrahamic faith and Christianity are so vast that comparisons can only serve to expand one's understanding, as individuals apply these thoughts and practices to their daily lives. Although the two may seem similar at a glance, a deeper exploration reveals the profound differences that shape these belief systems.

The concept of worshiping a mortal, as opposed to worshiping an unseen light and substance that one has not encountered can be difficult for certain individuals. The separation of belief systems will not be revealed until the end of time, regardless of whether. In Islam, the belief is centered around an unseen God who is not portrayed as a feeble human or insinuated as anything other than a radiant light called Nur, which remains unseen by anyone.

Essentially, the ultimate responder to every human being is Allah alone. There are instances where combining different religions can cause individuals to distance themselves from their own faith, as it is important for religions to be in sync.

The blending of these religious backgrounds can either dilute the laws of Islam or integrate them if both parties have a mutual respect for them. In any circumstance, Islam will not engage in negotiations or make concessions on terms or laws to please the other party.

The intention behind Islam's laws, which were meticulously crafted by Allah, is to promote the growth and progress of mankind, irrespective of the final outcome. Observing that humanity was ready to receive, he proceeded to deliver the final laws. The giver is aware of the readiness of humanity to accept, as the instinctual urge towards openness naturally seeks beliefs and practices that are aligned.

The heart, when adorned with the matter that perfectly matches the truth molecules, possesses the ability to embrace unbiased truth and unequivocally reject falsehoods. The system that Allah created was designed for the purpose of obedience to him. The struggle to extend invitations to additional deities or emblems is indicative of a message that lacks coherence from the depths of one's subconscious.

The obviousness of being distracted and deviating from the path of serenity can become quite apparent. The truthfulness of the delivery of the former can be understood by the latter only if there is a recognition of one God.

Many individuals partake in the period's celebration associated with fertility. The event in question actually occurred before Easter, and it is interesting to note that Easter itself has its roots in pagan traditions. The fertility of both the heart and mind is the fundamental basis for human contentment. When there is emotional distance, the significance of fertility and reproduction diminishes.

The foundation of environmental consciousness is rooted in one's own system. Repentance is sought by both our mental and physical selves as we address our internal systems. Medical visits alone do not address the core issue. Certain individuals are provided with warnings, whereas others are not granted the same privilege. The ultimate responsibility for taking care of one's health and well-being lies with the individual.

Making thoughtful and sustainable decisions has the potential to create a better future, not only for oneself but also for the world. Perhaps the most unfavorable outcome occurs when an individual, already burdened with health issues, is provided with a second chance to seek the right path. instead some cause havoc not only in their own life but also in the world around them.

This serves as a prime example of deceit within a broader context, emphasizing the fact that some individuals never seem to learn from their mistakes and are given chances, while others quickly comprehend the lesson. In the end, this situation shows the mercy of Allah. Taking on the. responsibility of preparing for the eternal journey falls upon the believer, as they comprehend the necessity of surpassing the present world.

Only a believer can contain it, as the path to disbelievers is unpredictable. Glitz and glamor offer no solace in the inner soul. A disbeliever and a believer cannot survive together in the long run. The purpose of human creation by Allah is not to delegate responsibility for life and deeds to another.

The conscious mind is the one that holds the knowledge of the truth. Every human soul was recorded in the same catalog, which was under the constant surveillance of Allah.Mother carries a child in this world to deliver on earth except the first creation that was created. To succeed in a crash course on Islam, one must prioritize attendance. Satan designates another God to be worshiped.

Allah always grants something within a specific timeframe. Islam will persist in upholding the previous scriptures. Alterations or mismatches of other scripts with the Quran can lead to dismissal per Islamic doctrine.

There has been tampering with the core of the root. All Prophets of the Abrahamic faith, including Jesus, are united as brothers. The Quran is recited worldwide daily. Throughout the world, it echoes loudly the call to Muslim prayer around the world. This is an emblem of Islam that will not die, but the world will die. Allah's word lives forever.

Do the stories in the Quran serve as lessons from the Prophets and impactful stories? Do the Bible stories that mock Prophets and use love as a passive aggressive tool fall under the category of love?

The hypocrisy lies within the system of some humans, where love is used as a replacement for laws, perpetuating a cycle of deception. In these societies, love is frequently mentioned, often without a complete comprehension of its true significance. The word love cannot exist without the presence of respect and alliance towards the things that a human loves.

The love and admiration one has for Allah is the foundation for developing a sincere reverence for His laws. When a person has a deep love for humanity, they are given the ability to express their devotion to Allah, as love cannot coexist with falsehoods. The statement that "Allah loves everybody" is not accurate because he has created hell specifically for those who are defiant.

There are individuals who choose to selectively embrace certain aspects of the all-encompassing knowledge about human beings that resonate with their inherent characteristics. The fundamental principle is to prioritize and respect Islamic laws above all, for Muslims and love will subsequently manifest itself.

Comparing the Bible and Quran is necessary, and Muslims live in a society that values forgiveness and love. However, the stories in the Bible do not align with the belief in a merciful God who tested Abraham and wouldn't send his people with such negative habits.

For instance, there are biblical accounts of Prophet Lot having sexual relations with his daughters, and Prophet Noah being intoxicated. According to the Bible, Prophet Solomon had one hundred wives. Satan tempted Jesus, the Messiah, for forty days. Moses, despite being presented as a murderer, is given the ten commandments.

Was the intention of Allah to send Prophets for the purpose of establishing laws and serving as examples, or was it for the purpose of violating laws, the difference between the two is so noticeable that it cannot be ignored.

Ordinary humans tend to hesitate when it comes to breaking laws, and if they do, their conscience does bother them. However, believers find it troubling when they break laws, but the Prophets of the Bible had no issues with it, as they were specifically chosen to deliver the word of Allah. The transcriptions in the Bible may not be easily recognizable unless one actively pursues the truth.

Despite attributing divinity to Mary's son, their portrayal of a God named Jesus or identified as the son of God, according to the Bible, suggests that he was easily influenced by Satan, thereby undermining his worth. If we consider the notion that Satan, a jinn, has the ability to deceive God, a question arises regarding the power dynamics between the creation and the creator.

384

This raises the question of who holds more power. However, it is important to note that Satan, being a jinn, cannot lead astray the one who created him or the creator's son. Therefore, upon thorough understanding, the entire narrative not only dismisses any reasonable doubt but also completely refutes the idea. It is worth emphasizing multiple times that Jesus in Islam is pure and beyond any measure.

Recognizing that Jesus had to depart until the times changed, Allah, therefore, sent Prophet Muhammad. Jesus mentioned this matter, however, their understanding and interpretation aligned more closely with that of the Holy Spirit.

The Holy Spirit's resonance after Jesus' departure is a concept that many fail to comprehend, which in turn makes the advocacy of imagination seem incomprehensible to them.. Despite his limited time on earth, being only 33 years old which is half the age of Prophet Muhammad, the defiant Jews refused to listen to him.

The duration of his second coming, and how long he will be on earth during that time, remains unknown. However, it is certain that this staged world will eventually come to an end, leading to the judgment of all humanity.

While Muhammad fulfilled the prophecy and was regarded as the spirit of truth, it is certain that Jesus will make a return to unveil the truth and confront the accusations made against him.

Bible: John 14:16-17 And I will ask the Father, and he will give you another advocate to help you and be with you forever - the Spirit of truth.

Bible NIV: Mark 1:7.And this was his message: "After me comes the one more powerful than I, the straps of whose sandals I am not worthy to stoop down and untie.

They could not bear the truth as the continuous alterations by others continued to mesmerize the lies created by Satan. Jesus clearly cursed the defiant Jews. Then came Paul from the Jewish clan, who inaugurated the New Testament when indeed, he never met Jesus. Neither was he foretold that he would be the Prophet of Allah. The only Prophet told by name, even in the Torah, is the Prophet Muhammad.

Bible: Deuteronomy 18:18.I will raise them up a Prophet from among their brethren, like unto thee, and will put my words in his mouth; and he shall speak unto them all that I.

The Prophet was raised from among the people to be Prophet Muhammad. It is impossible to believe any script that human hands have adjusted to their liking. Such as encrypted laws which are color-coded to distinguish between what is from God and what is from humans in the Bible. The Quran contains all the words spoken by Allah to an unlettered Prophet who delivered word to word.

Before he drew away, the Quran chapters ended. Making laws the order of the Islamic world. Jews rejected Jesus, and Christians turned him into a triune God or son of God. Muslims understood he was a Prophet, a Messiah. Despite efforts from evil forces, Islam is gaining popularity among the masses. It's unfortunate that some Muslims who do not research their faith. The goal is to not to follow or add pagan ways to please the pagans but to learn Islam at its best.

Regardless of the Christian denomination, in certain regions the focal point of faith is Jesus in the Bible. The meeting in Nicea, present-day Turkey, completely transformed the concept of Christendom. The decision to choose Christianity was political, not divine. The Trinity was formed by combining the three main Gods of the Roman Empire into a single, all-powerful deity.

The Roman Empire used religion to control its people. The emperor Constantine, who declared Christianity the official religion of the Roman Empire, also decided this concept would work as the pagans were enchanted by deities. This helped to unify the empire under one faith and ensured the emperor had control over the people. The Bible has proven to be a source of both divine and human implications time and time again. The churches continued to preach the same as Constantine's agreement. Which resembles the truth implicated with lies. Therefore, Western culture still adapts human desires to the divine, and the method is the same.

Bible: NIV: The Disciples' grief will turn to joy: Jesus went on to say, In a little while you will see me no more and then after a little while you will see me.

Jesus warned the disciples and also told them the voice of truth will come who will talk about me the brethren Prophet Muhammad. The Jews did not listen to him despite all his miracles. Allah sent the Prophet Muhammad. Jesus did not talk about Paul and the New Testament. This has no correlation to the book as Paul was not a Prophet nor mentioned by Jesus or Muhammad. This Quran has not undergone any changes and will not undergo any changes in the future.

Quran: Surah Baqarah: 2:79. So woe to those who write the "scripture" with their own hands, then say, "This is from Allah ," in order to exchange it for a small price.

Bible: Isaiah 29:15. Woe to those who go to great depths to hide their plans from the LORD, who do their work in darkness and think, "Who sees us?

Bible: KJV: 16:12:14. Howbeit when he, the Spirit of truth, is come, he will guide you into all truth: for he shall not speak of himself : but whatsoever he shall hear that shall he speak: and he will shew you things to come.

Bible: Timothy 1:15, apostle Paul claims to have been "the foremost" of sinners

Prophet Muhammad completed the Prophethood by delivering revelations as told he was coming. There are still people who see visions today, but that doesn't make them Prophets. Therefore the only Prophets are the ones who receive revelations from Allah, not visionaries. Paul was an apostle, not a Prophet, with no revelations from Allah. Jesus did not mention Pauline Christianity or the authors of the Gospels. Ingel is the sole Gospel from Allah to Jesus.

There was a 400-year gap between the Old and New Testaments. If a book was introduced after the Prophet Muhammad's passing, it would not qualify as the Quran. The customs and practices he left behind are his (Sunnah) and practices. No one can add or subtract from the Quran, as it is the sole testament of Allah. The book contains clarifications, but solely for the perceptive. While people have the freedom to worship any belief, it's important to clarify that the Bible belongs to the Abrahamic faith with pagan customs and modifications.

Some people have rejected this doctrine; others follow blindly without questioning the source. Allowing lies to intermix with divine words. Regardless of whether the source is true, Islam has no issue asking questions to understand and proclaim the truth. Similarly, the Quran is clear to be the first source to clarify, read, ponder, and believe. Or understand what it means to reciprocate to others. Understanding nothing about delivery would become impossible to thrive.

Therefore, it is essential to ask questions when faced with doubts. It is also imperative to recognize the source of the information and ensure it is reliable. The Quran is the most valuable source of learning. Ultimately, recognizing Islam's core beliefs can contribute to the spread of the true message of Islam.It is crucial for truth-seekers to research the history and roots of truth.

Those who waver come back, but those who stay firm find purpose in their true beliefs. How can a Muslim not acknowledge the truth and the dire reality of Abrahamic faiths, which aim to worship one God? Christians saw Jesus' hanging as a means of washing away their sins, while Jews saw it as a curse. Hanging someone on a tree was considered the most degrading act. In Jewish belief if he was from God, he could not experience such things. Despite their gloating, he was not killed, according to Islam.

Quran: Surah Nisa: 4:157: And for their saying, "Indeed, we have killed the Messiah, Jesus, the son of Mary, the messenger of Allah." And they did not kill him, nor did they crucify him; , but another was made to resemble him to them. And indeed, those who differ over it are in doubt about it. They have no knowledge of it except the following assumption. And they did not kill him, for certain.

This narrative became a cornerstone of Christian beliefs and formed the basis of redemption in Christianity. Islam declined all of it and said it was blasphemous to think of God sacrificing his son. Islam instead believes that God is all-powerful and does not need human sacrifice.Thus, redemption in Islam is achieved through repentance, charity, and faith. Beliefs have no barriers, despite contrasting differences.

Muslims, per the Quran, believe he was raised up to God and not killed. The Quran says that someone else took his place. That is a major distinction between the three Abrahamic faiths. Jews and Christians reject the Islamic belief of Jesus' ascension. The prevailing biblical insistence is that Jesus was crucified and later rose from the dead after three days.

The Quran clarifies Jesus was saved from the cross and raised up to God.When a cross is accepted, what is known as a cultic barrage of untrue accusations becomes a premeditated collusion among the populace. Wooden crosses made of gold and silver with decorative and altered designs remind us of Allah's injustices. Islam sees no paradox in allegations except the nuance of clear explanations. However, Jesus himself is coming to tell the tale of his second visit to this world. Muslims see the picturesque truth revealed in the Quran. If this does not sit well with humans it is meant to clarify not stir up events of increasing ignorance without understanding. This is the dilemma of prideful humans.

Islamic theology describes how Muslims perceive the faith of Islam and respect for each and every Prophet sent by Allah. Muslims believe that Jesus will return to Earth near the end of time to bring justice and peace. They also believe in the coming of the Mahdi, a messianic figure who will bring justice and peace to the world. Muslims are taught to have faith and trust in the will of Allah and to follow the teachings of the Prophets. Finally, the four books sent to the Prophets are believed to bring together the final teachings of Allah when the Mahdi arrives.

These books are the Torah, the Bible, the Qur'an, and the Psalms. Then Jesus will come; he is the Messiah, the closing statement of all Prophets. It is believed that prior to Jesus' return, the Mahdi will bring about the coming era of peace and justice. The world will be filled with prosperity and joy. Muslims are encouraged to live their lives in preparation for this time and strive to be worthy of it. As time passes, Allah's laws will reestablish the unified force of Islam will again prevail. Why? Because Islam is a monotheistic faith and never fails.

It's the final content of humanity that saves the soul without the interference of any deity or human. The Mehdi first, then the truth will be revealed through Jesus, son of Mary, not the son of God. This is a path of light and truth that will lead humanity to a righteous end, a world filled with justice and mercy. The true nature of the universe will be revealed, and all of humanity will be unified in a single faith. With this, peace will come, and the righteous will be saved. The laws of Islam will never shift as humanity evolves. The correction will be made towards humanity, not to Islam.

There is no change to this faith, and its doctrine is complete as it came from Allah. It is a way of life that is timeless and can be practiced by all without prejudice. Allah created these rules to be followed by all of mankind to establish a more just and equitable society. They are meant to benefit everyone, regardless of race, religion, or creed, and bring people closer to true salvation and peace.

They represent Allah's mercy and kindness, and humans can or cannot strive to fulfill the divine plan. It's up to the individual's soul. A challenging quest for clarification can be eye-opening in theology and lead to a long pursuit of the truth through long-term research. There are many who have fought Islam and surrendered after reading the Quran. And became the most effective converts. Those who have undertaken such a quest can find themselves exposed to a wealth of knowledge that can bring them closer to the truth.

This journey can be instrumental in changing lives and bringing people closer to their Creator. Islam has no adjustments, laws and rules are implications of justice and endurance of this life and clarity. Islam draws no such possibility of man-made words as the previous scriptures, except Allah will protect his last and final scripture Quran.

The journey of truth involves shedding light on reality, not just tolerating and accepting lies in society. It is the duty of a Muslim to stand for truth and deliver it. Those who recognize Allah's blessings of capabilities and knowledge understand that withholding truth would be hypocritical to please others. It is best to seek truth in order to please Allah and entrust everything to Him.

Human cruelty is watching another Muslim's soul darkened by corruption and saying nothing about it. Muslims are responsible for upholding Islamic laws, not defying them. Not following or not listening is a personal choice.

Islam notes reminders from sources unknown, but guidance can only come from Allah for those he calls back. Allah needs no one but those closest to him who can benefit from him and pray. Prayer too is an allowance. Allah's throne needs no humans, but humans depend on him.

Humanity cannot change certain laws. Not following government laws and regulations has punishments. The consequences of not adhering to Allah's laws are concrete and eternal. Allah's laws need to be followed, not avoided or ignored, or negotiated. "He" is the true source of justice and fairness.

The Quran is the book of laws that govern the state and the human believer who wishes to follow them. It attends to all aspects of human life and everything that holds life. Along with stories affecting humanity and examples from everyday life.

Allah sent four books to the Prophets for that time. The Quran is a timeless capsule sent to everyone seeking guidance from Allah throughout history. Despite its simplicity, Allah has given it to humanity as a guide without alteration, and Allah will erase it when Allah sees fit. Regarding the Kabba, there will come a time when people will walk by and say Muslims used to worship here.

There will be no evidence left after but the name of Allah. Now is the time to make the absolute most of it.It has all been leading toward the written prophecies and the end of times. Many signs of the hour have come true, and they continue. Although the gospel of Isa (Ingel) has altered. Those remnants of truth in Ingel (Gospel) will convey the truth that Allah is the one true God.

Bible Gateway: John 14;28. "You heard me say, 'I am going away, and I am coming back to you.' If you loved me, you would be glad that I am going to the Father, for the Father is greater than I.

Bible: Nkjv: 15:30. I can do nothing. As I hear, I judge; and my judgment is righteous because I do not seek. My own will but the will of the Father who sent me.

He would not claim his weakness if he were God. Submission to Allah is clear.In the early days of Jesus being born to Mary, he was an infant, just like any other. As an infant, he could not care for himself. God does not need a mother or human to nurture and care for him. Jesus' human qualities are clear: He is mortal. He cannot evolve around as a God. But Satan can mesmerize humans and make them believe in humans instead of Allah.The concept is so bizarre that three become one. So Jesus evolved, according to Christianity, from a human to a God. It can apply the same concept to atheists who claim humans are descended from primates.

The concept was officially adopted by the Council of Nicea in 325 A.D. and has been the official doctrine of the Christian Church ever since. In the Quran, there is no altering of the divine text by human hands or by councils implementing their concepts. Theology and history do not stifle religions but only become an issue if these unions are tied to two faiths. People need to understand that truth has no religion. Allah's law is to revere him alone, not his creation.

Finally, humans revolt and worship nothing or continue to worship another human, which is Satan's tactic to mislead the masses. The deceitful tactics of the evil employer need to be studied and analyzed rather than followed blindly as gospel truth.

But many are running away from mortal worship in Christendom and declaring no religious beliefs. Except for their own way of worship, which is accepting the hierarchy and naming it the universe.

It has risen from this epidemic since the pagan era before the Quran, the closing statement. Islam was not given a name until Prophet Muhammad's rise. The faith of Adam and Eve is Islam. How so? Islam is based on the worship of one god, Allah. There is no argument. From the beginning, 'We' created man ; it has been his faith. As a final statement, it was exposed to the world. Closing statement is the Quran.

There have been decades of disobedience for those who don't believe.

They filled the Egypt museum with mummies, kings, and Pharaohs, and the Pharaoh who once ruled became an example of what can be from disobedience. Rulers and deceivers are displayed, and Egypt is a Muslim country. Those who have traveled can tell what they have seen.

If examples don't suit the disobedient, ears and eyes are shut. There is a misalignment of human hearts that will continue until Allah sees fit. He is The Most High and All-Knowing, and His plan is perfect.

Intricate differences in theology can become a concept of learning and choices. These choices can shape beliefs, values, and actions. Theology is a powerful tool for understanding the world and our place in it. It can also help us find meaning and purpose in life.There is no drama, non fiction that can commit a sane Muslim to believe he is a triune God. No matter what congregation of belief they join, from Catholic to Born Again Christians. The concept never changes, he remains the triune God.Their fights were disagreements between their sects. Later, they used the same ideology; they also committed Muslims to fighting each other based on the same concept.

Conquer by division. Understanding is clarity, which is Satan's trick to confuse minds and place himself as the arrogant and the doubtful who do not seek the truth.

It is the dark concept of Satan and his partisans.The key is to understand and leave contaminated surroundings. Throughout human history, faith has been embedded within all humans without interruption.Sharing truth becomes more important as a Muslim, especially in a world of collisions. e

The Islamic youth and newly converted need education that does not collide and ricochet from wall to wall. As a result, the inner health is eventually damaged.

Allah's will is his will.Practicing (Shirk), including the worship of other Gods, or association and attachment to Allah. (Shirk) in Islam has zero tolerance. If one dies without repentance. This is an unforgivable sin.

Bible: Matthew 12:31:32. I say to you, any sin and blasphemy shall be forgiven by men, but blasphemy against the Spirit shall not be forgiven.

Quran: Surah As Shura: 42:51. It is not fitting for a man that *Allah* speaks to him except by inspiration, or from behind a veil. By sending an official emissary to reveal.

Quran: Surah Isra: 17;23.Thy Lord hath decreed, that ye worship none save Him, and (that ye show) kindness to parents. If one of them or both of them attain old age with thee, say not "uff.

New king King James Version:7:21:33.I Never Knew You - "Not everyone who says to Me, 'Lord, Lord,' shall enter the kingdom of heaven, but he who does the will of My Father in heaven.

In his teachings, Jesus makes it clear that he does not associate himself with kingship or Godship, emphasizing that Allah is the true Lord and not him. The commandments of Allah must be followed in order to properly observe and abide by the ten commandments of Allah. It is explicitly stated in the ten commandments that worshiping any God other than me is prohibited, without any mention of Allah transforming into a triune God.

This information holds special relevance for young Muslims who have deviated from their path and for those who have recently embraced Islam. The writer's words serve as explanations, but it is the creator's bliss that truly brings about understanding. The human being that He created is inherently weak and lacks the ability to witness His divine light within the span of their lifetime.

The human graph Allah created is explicit from birth when a baby is born helpless,naked without clothing, with no baggage straight from the mother's entrails.The absence of clothing at birth symbolizes the profound fragility and unadulterated nature of the birth process. Following the arrival, he is immediately dressed, while the infant is swiftly adorned with the word of Allah.

When a Muslim is born, they are commonly exposed to the Azan call to prayer, as it is seen by many Muslims as a responsibility, symbolizing the immersion of the child in truth from the very start. The future does not depend on the parent or the mother, but rather on Allah, who reveals it as life unfolds. From being dependent to becoming independent, a human grows.

Sometimes respectful and sometimes disrespectful to those who assisted during life stages. The only time a human walks out of this episode of life is when a parent or caregiver tells them to let go of Allah and continue paganism. After the truth becomes clear. Even then, Muslims can fulfill their responsibilities or not.

Helplessness during infancy returns into old age. Some may have difficulty caring for the elderly, while others might fear helping them, and others may abuse them.

Old age is a blessing for those who leave examples and for some cleaning the soul in this world with illnesses if it is a Muslim. A Muslim will say I wish I had paid for my sins in this world than in the other.Some become a burden as the freshness of a newborn is not the same as it is at an older age. Such are the stages of life that the graph bends and never stops. Jesus also went through growing stages from birth to adulthood. He certainly didn't raise himself. God does not have to be raised

Some are born with diseases, and others invite them disrespectfully.Jesus showed the same capabilities of hunger and thirst as attending to personal needs, which disqualifies him. In all aspects as a God. Or the son of God. God is not mortal. Not just by observation, but also by his own words. Islam is clear.Allah has sent Prophets for deliveries and directions. They, too, have not seen him.

All messages came to Prophets through the angel Gabriel. He talked to Moses directly. Angel Gabriel does not visit the earth as the revelations end. Only on (lailatul qadr) night of decree in Ramadan angel Gabriel appears on earth. Along with thousands of angels. This night will tell the tale of the next year. Each year it's documented.

It is clarity of understanding with placed contracts, not a visionary drama that is incomprehensible to the human mind. These concepts presented by Christianity are not aligning with Islam. There is so much difference between them until they agree on the same terms. There will always be a collision between belief presentations.

Quran: Surah Imran: 3:64. Say, "O People of the Scripture, come to a word that is equitable between us and you - That we will not worship except Allah and not associate anything with Him and not take one another as lords instead of Allah."

But if they turn away, then say, "Bear witness that we are Muslims submitting to Him."

There are many friendships. But societal beliefs do not match. The only consistent alignment is Allah's belief. (Alloheim) Not Jesus. There is a risk of epidemic outbreaks if such unions occur without counter-settling beliefs. Common sense prevents non-comprehensible drama fiction from being adopted.

Quranic laws and contracts are eternal. With the passing of time, there are no modifications or alterations. Allah is not the subject of the examination.

Upon sending coherent messages from the creator, Allah will evaluate and test the human based on the individual's position. Excuses will not absolve the creator.The passion for hunger, want, and desire can weigh up to many examples. There is something that sits with the human mind. Such is the Quran, so even a child can comprehend what it says. Muslims are exposed to Islam at four years old and follow this path as life progresses.

The start with a clean slate, is for those who convert to Islam wholeheartedly embrace the religion. The extent to which they contribute to evil and portray Islam as limiting is contingent upon their determination. Witnessing the constraints of life from a different perspective may lead one to appreciate the liberating aspects of Islam, if they comprehend the benefits over restrictions.

Whether someone is brought up in the Islamic faith or decides to embrace it later on, both scenarios lead to a significant shift in one's life. The embodiment of faith in someone who converts to Islam is highly regarded and carries great prestige. The new reform has effectively cleansed his past deeds, leaving him with a fresh start.

In society, all males and females are grouped together. Islam acknowledges that males and females have distinct identities and mentalities. The intermingling and changing concepts of beliefs, along with unions that do not prioritize Islam.

They combined all genders into one file and falsely claimed they are all the same, then did the same with faiths. The idea is deceptive; it doesn't allow for individualism in thinking.

The separate identity of Islam is fully outlined, compromising Abrahamic faith texts. Islam is the only faith that remains unchanged. It's a singular identifier, not plural.They create vigilance and contrasting beliefs with Abrahamic faiths, leading to a curse on future generations who engage in pagan adaptations. Friendships or associations don't imply a lack of theological education; they can enlighten the faithful.

Some individuals were raised as Muslims or converted to Islam in order to appreciate its beauty. The contrast between beauty and ugliness is striking today, particularly in a society that values superficial modernization. They always return to the same evil ground. In the context of certain souls. The glow that comes from serving Allah is so bright that even strangers can feel its beauty within.

Those who are mindful and intelligent know that nothing is achievable without Allah.Those who persevere experience enduring beauty. Those who have knowledge of Allah stay within these limits. Fake freedom seems like a form of confinement. Islam provides a breath of fresh air, protection, and numerous benefits for seekers.

Uncovering hidden strengths is a part of the hungry person's development. There are various manifestations of hunger. The purpose could be to satisfy both the soul and the stomach. Topics include social economics, power entrepreneurship, sports, academia, social status, and travel. The feeling of hunger has no limits. Allah is the most fulfilling hunger. Knowing Allah simplifies all powers and makes tasks easier for humanity. Life moves forward.

People are curious about how someone accomplishes so much. Identify the creator who filled hunger. Such is the admission and entrance of a believer. It is difficult to leave Allah's land after quenching thirst and hunger. Laws and contracts are part of the Islamic faith and enforced by the highest Allah's court. Islam does not punish until Allah sends the message.

Islamic law governs all aspects of life and lays out actions. Allah did not impose life on humans without direction in the world he created. Self-discipline is not an imposition, it's a mandated act for healthy survival. Despite the fact that Islam acknowledges mercy, no human has been left to wander without guidance. The fine threads of life. It is necessary to uphold Allah's rules and discipline for survival.

Detailed official documents and contracts, including marriages. Islam summons two witnesses. Notarization and witnesses hold true in humanity. Allah had the laws planned when humans had no plans. The Real Estate power of attorney is not valid until notarized and witnessed. Human laws are bound by discipline. Muslims cannot ignore Allah's laws.

Islamic law requires a scribe or notary, as well as two witnesses, to verify the testimony. This was an official ruling in the Quran over 1400 years ago. All aspects of life are completed through Islam. Once you receive a loan from another Quran, let the scribe witness and record the transaction.

Quran: Surah Baqarah: 282. O you who have believed, when you contract a debt for a specified term, write it down. And let a scribe write [it] between you in justice.

It is not up to the party assuming liability to dictate the contract terms. Liability assumption requires sound judgment. If it is a minor, a guardian is necessary. The person giving the loan must dictate the loan term. If both parties agree, the scribe cannot refuse to put this transaction in writing, along with the witnesses.

Power of attorney or a scribe, notaries administered in contemporary society, copying Islam. Disbelievers have paved the way to control the masses with lies. Gender equality is one issue critics have repeatedly raised. To exploit the narrative that Islam discriminates against and oppresses women, many critics bring up testimony. Alleging that a woman's testimony is half that of a man.

Quran: Surah Baqarah 283. If two men are not available, then one man and two women, such as you, as witnesses. So that if either of the two slides overlooks the other, it may refresh her memory. And the witnesses should not refuse to testify when they are called upon to do so.

Many uninformed people find it challenging to understand. All contractual laws stem from Islam. It imposed security deposits on transactions. The willful giving and ensuring of the collateral security is a trust (Amaanah) in Real Estate transactions. In today's world, it is applied just as it was done by Islam 1400 years ago.

Willful or negligent behavior can invalidate a transaction. The security deposit would cover some damages. Real estate laws are an essential part of all transactions between two or more parties, as prescribed by Islam and the Quran.

Any exchange or liability should be contracted on paper with time limitations except for marriage. Due to its nature, we cannot read until death separates us as this commitment is false.Sometimes, it works until one ceases to exist in this world for some time on a limited duration. As marriage is also a contract in Islam, time is not limited to this contractual transaction.

Islam does not interpret illusions except facts. They must handle items entrusted to them in a willful transaction without negligence. It is crucial that all parties involved in a transaction witness the proceeds of a money or real estate transaction. And pertaining to all transactions involving money or goods. A person who spends money without the consent of the person who left it with them and invests the money in gains must compensate the person for the gains. Interest is not part of Islamic transactions.

Quran: Surah Baqarah 2:283. The piece of gold that you took is collateral for a security deposit. And there is nothing wrong with stipulating collateral when giving a loan, because Allah, the Exalted, says, "Then a security deposit should be taken."

All collateral or security held must be secure and governed by policies agreed upon by all parties involved. Any inadvertent handling requires restitution by remittance, and such are the regulations of Islam.

As Allah further enters the realm of Real Estate, it leaves no room for a man to be inconsistent. Security insurance for the landlord or owner. Prescription of Islam.

Because of the formal purposes of the Quran, the laws of life cannot be reversed. When chosen correctly, they simply improve the scene. A deposit is a security to be collected in the process of lease or purchase.

Quran: Surah Baqarah: 2:283.And if you are on a journey and cannot find a scribe, then a security deposit [should be] taken. And if one of you entrusts another,

The Quran first mentions the need for a guarantee of security to be collected from occupants, and this principle is then adopted by countries worldwide. Furthermore, when buying a home, an initial deposit is a standard requirement. The law, which has been adopted from the principles of Islam, has had a significant impact on contemporary society. Furthermore, the Quran emphasizes the importance of drafting a will and ensuring that assets and possessions are distributed in accordance with Islamic law.

Quran: Surah Baqarah:2:180.Prescribed for you when death approaches [any] one of you if he leaves wealth [is that he should make] a bequest for the family. (will mandated)

It also explained the deduction of bequests and debts of the deceased.

Islam covers all aspects of human life for a Muslim.It is common in some incidents for the deceased to leave no will or instructions. These properties enter probate, and the court system can become very costly and have attorney costs.

In Islamic law, they avoid all of this because Muslims must write a will and execute it.

Many people have sought living trusts. There is something fascinating about Islam 1400 years ago, when it made laws regarding the intricacies of life. No drama, no fantasies, and no unproven lies exist in Islam. Direct order with no setbacks or changes.

It's a factual book, the Quran, with laws and regulations guiding humanity's principles.

It is a far cry for a Muslim who compromises Islam's laws to comprise the laws of disbelievers. It also seems to collide with previous scriptures' altered beliefs.

This epidemic is ongoing, and those who are mentally weak are adjusting to their pagan roots.

Bible Hub: Matthew 12:40.For as Jonah was in the belly of the huge fish three days and three nights, so the Son of Man will be in the heart of the earth three days and three nights.

Jesus cited Jonah as an example. To illustrate a point, he selected Jonah, who was alive in the fish's stomach. This indicated that Jesus was informing people about his imminent departure, emphasizing that he would be alive, similar to Jonah.Jesus' choice of Jonah as a point of reference indicates his existence, as Jonah's well-known survival in the belly of a fish suggests he was alive. Before his departure, Jesus set an example to show his future ascension to Allah.

According to the Quran, Satan cannot tempt Jesus, as he was born sinless.The claims against him are groundless and unsubstantiated. If Jesus was tempted by Satan, why can't those who defied and wanted to crucify him be forgiven? Wasn't Jesus forgiven after being tempted by Satan? Why didn't Allah control the evil of people and prevent the crucifixion?

It wasn't Jesus who died, but rather someone who was made to resemble him. Allah's protection would have been with the son of Mary if he wasn't sent as a sacrificial escape code for sinners. The notion of lies becoming more pervasive has been an implicated doctrine for centuries, and it's not surprising after examining its historical roots. Certain people are unable to completely rid themselves of their cultic instincts.

Did he have to die for the sins of ruthless falsifiers? The Quran anticipated the birth of Jesus and recognized its significance by dedicating a full surah to Mary. A new faith emerged in its entirety after the crucifixion.

During Muhammad's time, Islam was present, and he followed it, while Jesus did not follow Christianity but adhered to the laws of Allah, referred to as Aloheim. Those who have blinders on will never be able to understand strayed Muslims or non-Muslims, no matter how clearly it is explained.

Claiming Satan tempted him for 40 days contradicts worshiping him as God. Jesus has a strong faith and is near to Allah. His preaching was backed by Allah's teachings, and he propagated the same message. He was chosen by Allah to spread His word.

All believers should strive to follow his example of faith and piety, as it serves as a valuable model to emulate. The modified Bible text is specifically designed to control masses. The Quran's dominance is attributed to its unchangeable nature, which strengthens its influence.

Quran: Surah NIsa: 4:157. and their statement that they murdered Jesus, son of Mary, the Messenger of God, when, in fact, they could not have murdered him nor crucified him.

The irony that is deeply embedded in Jesus' explanations has had a significant impact for centuries. Nonetheless, those who comprehend the Muslim analogy will acknowledge that the core of their faith is not based on the principles of crucifixion and salvation. If one were to uncover the fact that Muslims have played a significant role in the field of education throughout history.

Ignoring the needs of one's body can result in a multitude of health difficulties. There is a growing desire for wealth among people. The loss of wealth is not something that should be considered a significant loss. This can be obtained repeatedly, without any limitations. Losing one's health means losing something vital. There is no denying the fact that good health is undeniably one of the most precious blessings one can have. The maintenance of good health is crucial for one's survival. The temporary nature of wealth highlights the importance of good health, which is the true source of happiness.

Deceitful shades obscure daily life with false allegations. The Islamic faith does not include the use of pacifiers. Boldly spoken, it reveals the truth. Every soul will be questioned by Allah. Blaming outside interference is not justified. Muslims have a responsibility to aid injured people, particularly those with soul-related illnesses.

Quran: Surah An'am: 6:164. No interference from outside sources can be blamed.

Say: Shall I seek other than Allah for Lord, when He is Lord of all things? Each soul earned only on its own account, nor did any laden bear another's load.

The world is in chaos due to the concept of a free pass, which is distorting morals to align with personal choices. Islam's laws for individuals lack an enforcer. Allah cannot be reformatted, and the

Quran achieved its ultimate reform without human involvement. At a critical moment, specific civilizations intersect with the world.

These evildoers target Muslim families and associates, aiming to alter their beliefs and promote a false sense of collectivism disguised as individualism. Islam is a faith that values individualism and collective strength, but it is resistant to reformists who seek to change regimes and corrupt its principles. If someone has haters of Islam, it implies that knowing is a battle for a believer and that Islam is seen as a threat to weak minds. The observation is obvious and ongoing while these gossipers continue to spread evil.

The invitation to explore new ways of thinking is limitless. Despite the irony, we must respect the laws of human courts even though they are failing. While laws around the world have changed over the years, Islam has remained steadfast.

The Hare Krishna movement experienced rapid growth, attracting followers of pagan worship and seeing migration, with Indian cults joining the ashrams. The majority of pagans originated from cults. What does pagan worship in a cult entail? Islam is not a religion that suppresses people with lies, but it grows for those who seek truth.

For centuries, the Eastern philosophical approach has been enlightening Westerners with its profound wisdom and insights. However, what remains perplexing is the absence of the mythological contrast to the worship of deities as a common factor. They find Hinduism appealing due to its acceptance of deities and climate. Society has been impacted by the persistent actions of cults, which involve the troubling practices of worshiping humans and engaging in sexual abuse of altar boys. Consequently, the Catholic Church, with its false deities and distorted confessional beliefs, is often perceived as a prominent force of evil.

The victims of evil were many. Is there a belief that Jesus' death was meant to cover the sins of those who commit heinous crimes and engage in incestuous relationships within their families? Jesus, who symbolizes truth, is not sent to endorse the falsehoods that are spread about him.

Times of India:Jun 21, 2023 — "Twelve orphans were housed at the ashram, including four girls. We will interact with the inmates in connection with the case," police added.

Nbc: May 23-2023: Catholic clergy sexually abused nearly 2000 kids in Illinois.

Al Jazeera:Oct 5, 2021 — A series of abuse scandals, often involving children, have rocked the Catholic Church in recent decades.

India faith:Sep 13, 2022 — On average, about 80 clerics are accused of sexually abusing children each year, and an average of 200 children are victimized each year.

If faith comes from Allah, it is seamless, just like in Islam. There are no dark abysses that require filling. There's no way to fix it once human hands get involved. Despite variations in scripts, the underlying belief remains the same: the worship of one Allah, one God. On the other hand, those who reject human intervention either accept it or settle for one deity. Islam does not promote a belief system where humans create interchangeable laws based on faith.

Quran: Surah Maidah 5:82.You will surely find the most intense of the people in animosity toward the believers [to be] the Jews and those who associate others with Allāh; and you will find the nearest of them in affection to the believers those who say, "We are Christians." That is because among them are priests and monks and because they are not arrogant.

Quran: Surah Rahman: 55:19:21. He recorded the two sea's meeting side by side. Between them is a barrier neither of them can transgress. Then which of the favors of Allah that ye deny?

Many friendships have existed between all faiths as time passed.

Islam will not compromise its regulations and laws expounded by Allah.

As with all prophecies, Jesus represents Islamic beliefs. In contrast, Islam and Christianity give their titles differently, just as Allah separated the two seas.

Hindus went a step ahead and brought back Jesus through reincarnation, labeling him as an avatar reincarnation of Krishna. Jesus supposedly practiced yoga, which brought him closer to Indian philosophies, and he traveled to India.

Except for the beginning and ending having the same pronunciation truth, the Quran doesn't mention any of this. Various versions of Jesus' pictures are created despite the absence of any living witnesses, perpetuating the falsehood.

The soul of a Muslim is the spirit that resides in their body, leaving when Allah takes it. It is also believed that the soul exits the body during sleep at night. The spirit living inside a human is not holy. Common sense lacks spiritual logic in a human awaiting mortal redemption.

If you believe in the Bible, it teaches that your body becomes God's temple and His spirit resides within you. What happens to people with evil spirits inside them? In Islam, the soul (Nafs) is believed to be the spirit, and only the one who possesses it has the ability to pursue virtue or goodness.

God, as a light, would not regard himself or inhabit a frail human. Humans are unable to withstand his radiance, but he bestows mercy upon all who cry out to him, perceiving the silence and the loudness of their hearts. His proximity is closer than the jugular vein, but he does not reside within a weak human.

Bible :kJV: 16:19;20: Do you not know that your bodies are temples of the Holy Spirit, who is in you, whom you have received from God? You are not your own; you were bought at a price. Therefore, honor God with your bodies.

Upon uncovering the truth, they either embrace God's oneness or influence others negatively with their limited mindset. The paradox of belief lies in the distinction between communes and cults, but understanding the truth is key. Allah is the sole creator, not created by anyone else. He is completely unique and there is no one else like him. Allah is his name. (Surah Al-Ikhlas)

Some individuals lose interest and exhibit self-destructive behavior, such as continuing to smoke or consume drugs and alcohol, despite being aware of the detrimental effects on their health. Having good health is a blessing. You will be questioned by Allah about how you took care of it. A human's biggest asset is their health, along with Allah's presence.

They replicated Islamic laws across the globe. The Quran was the first to establish laws on subjects previously unfamiliar to mankind. They have been orbiting the doctrine for decades, and we must enlighten the world to perceive that rules and regulations are the descendants of Islam. Muslim women thrived and excelled because of Islamic laws. However, it is true in marginalized societies in the Muslim world suffering because of socioeconomic status, who take a back seat because of economics, not because of faith, Islam is progressive.

Islam granted Muslim women ownership and property rights, rather than engaging in conflict. The right to divorce is recognized in Islamic laws. In these Western societies, women faced an arduous struggle for validation and tirelessly fought for their rights.

The United States assumed the forefront in divorces in 1916. States are obligated to respect divorces based on the faith in credit clause of the U.S. due to the U.S. Supreme Court's ruling in Williams v. North Carolina. Constitution. Islam did not require human intervention in court proceedings in subsequent years. Divorce was legalized under Islamic law well in advance of the West. The prevalence of divorce rates has positioned the Western world as the foremost nation.

Islam is the sole Abrahamic doctrine that recognizes this concession within marriages. Women are not considered property to be owned by men in Islam. The Quran uses the metaphor of garments to illustrate the mutual support and protection between spouses. A divine union cannot be easily interchanged with any other accepted statute. Islam cannot be adorned with trivial plastic scenarios. Unless it conforms to the tenets of Islamic legislation. The contract possesses equivalent rights to any other beneficiary contract.

If the agency lacks courtesy, reliability, trust, and clarity, the couple can terminate the contract. Islam intersects with humanity in a reasonable way at every point. Allah grants time to those who cannot live a fulfilling life without their ovules. The most powerful alliance is spiritual, guided by Allah. We cannot disregard these unions, as Allah values integrity greatly.

Marriage is part of living in harmony and provides security for both in Islam. Conflicts or external influences that threaten unions. Alternatively, unplanned internal conflicts occur. In Islam, things can work out amicably. Some separations are necessary for destiny to work, and sometimes it's necessary to return for it to do its work. Allah has a unique plan.Nothing happens without the permission of Allah.

Islam blames no one. It has given solutions to the problems of laws and contracts.

It's clear that the blame belongs to those who do not understand that life is based on discipline and laws, regulations, and contracts. Islamic teachings apply to daily life and unions, and Islam focuses on solutions, not blame.

A person may use destiny as a weapon of blame unless the individual takes action to progress. Once we have taken all necessary measures, humans can cite destiny.

Here is an example of how one might have a calling. The practice of this faith can only produce the passionate zing Islam encouraged the marriage of Muslim men to women who converted to Islam, including those who were divorced, widowed, or single.

It also prompted Muslim women to enter into marriages with men who converted to Islam. Marriage is both a (Sunnah) and held in high regard in Islam.

The interference and advice of disbelievers and gossipers can be extremely harmful. The room becomes dusty when unforeseen forces, such as wind, intervene. Life is like dust in the face of the unexpected wind.

Is it logical to share incompatible issues with a non-believer? Islam has established its own governing principles. Allah alone would hold the position of judge, with the final decision and outcome in any such matters. Respect the request to leave without criticizing the other person's choices. If correction as a Muslim doesn't work, facing judgment from Allah is the planned outcome.

In three days, believers will come together for reconciliation, turning conflicts into fueled ego for those who refuse reconciliation.The lack of resolution in most disputes is caused by stubbornness and individuals' insistence on a specific format, ignoring Quranic principles and displaying totalitarian behavior. It's better to maintain your personal attitude than to not conform to theirs.

The one who prioritizes evil over the well-being of the faithful is the one who is misguided. Kindness in life has been emphasized by Allah. Allah's mercy is overwhelmingly abundant, with ninety-nine portions, in contrast to only one portion of anger. Devout individuals are afraid of Allah's wrath and seek His forgiveness for their shortcomings.

Quran: Surah Luqman 31:18. Do not (contemptuously) turn your face away from people, nor tread haughtily upon the earth. Allah does not love the arrogant and the vainglorious.

Forgiveness is an essential indication that demonstrates human growth through life's challenges. It aids in humanity's progress. Quarreling souls fought within for many years. Muslims must incorporate spirituality into a tangible aspect of life based on strong beliefs. By helping themselves, one can also share their beauty with others.

There's no greater example than Prophet Muhammad, with Islam leaving nothing to our imagination. It encompasses all laws and contracts, ranging from business to matters of the heart, as well as imposing regulations on the family of the deceased.

Funeral arrangements must be made immediately following the death of a loved one. The wishes of the deceased must be communicated before they pass away. It is important to inform newly converted Muslims that cremation is not practiced in Islam. Others perform the last prayer of (Janazah) before the burial of the deceased. Another possibility is to discard the deceased in the ocean.

Non-Muslims' funerals are sometimes delayed for weeks in certain countries due to uncontrollable factors or lack of funds for burial. The family seeks funds on social media or other platforms. In Islam, waiting over others or cremation is not permitted.Spreading ashes of the dead is prohibited by Islamic principles. Late human research finds that human ashes are not environmentally friendly.

Islam is a contractual faith with regulations covering human life.Rights include birth to death. A contract to be clothed, sheltered, and educated about Islam and Allah. A contract exists between the children and their parents In the (Deen) faith of Allah, divorce, marriage, friendship, plants, animals, reconciliation, revolving revenue, and "Zakat" mandated giving on those who can afford 2.5% as circulation of the portion of wealth do not take leave. In Allah's presence, nothing can hold its course in the wildest situations. One's future is the continuation of the present.

Per Islamic law, lenders are empowered to dictate the terms and time of the contract to the borrower. The adaptation of this law can be traced back to the Quran. The rest of the world has copied and is now following the same guidelines. The Lord of the worlds entrusted the Quran to humanity without imposing any contractual obligations on Muslims. Whether by birth or conversion, embracing Islam is seen as a personal agreement with the faith.

Continuously breaking the contract comes with a certain cost. Contracts, whether they are personal or business-related, remain valid as long as they are written and agreed upon by both parties. The only exception to this rule is marriage, which does not have a time limit and is not subject to the enforcement of a contractual time frame.

The parameters of examples stifle the understanding that a human is on borrowed time and contracted by death. Islam disallows interest on funds borrowed as lenders are citing,in certain regions penalties follow if a borrower breaks a contract of paying interest. Islam was the first to dictate how a borrower and a lender entered into an agreement, later the entire world followed, but 1400 years ago the Quran set the rules.The laws of Islam were borrowed but altered by concepts of greed.

Quran: Surah Baqarah 2:283. And if you are on a journey and cannot find a scribe, then a security deposit should be taken. If one of you entrusts another, then let the entrusted discharge his trust faithfully with fear of Allah. Do not conceal testimony, for whoever conceals it in his heart is indeed sinful, and Allah is Knowing he Knows of what you do.

Islam is contractual and beneficial to humans. It leaves nothing to your imagination, and it flies against all the norms of society if they understand it.

Allah provided avenues and people who would quench the thirst with the proper answers. Truth has accompanied such unity. It upheld balance in society, relationships, and bonds.The laws of responsibility for a man do not change in the faith of Islam. The man must clothe and shelter his offspring should he have any during this marriage.Subsidizing financially for a full year prior to exit and helping until she remarries or receives alimony, as agreed upon.

There are no comparable situations since Islam does not place a burden on women who are married .By doing this, they prevent women from being placed in situations that might become compromising. Islam places great importance on safety and is well-informed about worldly matters. Educating women is crucial for their preparedness during times of distress or unexpected events. In Islam, women have achieved victories and left remarkable legacies, showcasing their astounding strength and promising support.

In the context of marital separations, the management of financial matters and responsibility assumes great importance, particularly when children are involved. In a society that purports to uphold liberal values, it is not uncommon for one parent to neglect their duties, thereby burdening the other parent with the entire responsibility. Multiple factors significantly impact the various episodes of people's lives.

Certain individuals prioritize loyalty in their speech, yet fail to provide any aid to their nation beyond empty rhetoric, all the while lacking the confidence to support their own family. Within this society, the emphasis is placed on culture rather than religion, leading to the victimization of numerous foreigners.

There are occurrences where local contexts prioritize the status quo over Islamic laws.Failing to adhere to Islamic laws can lead to unfavorable situations for individuals. Islam provides solutions to issues that require education academically and mindfully for many Muslims to resolve. This is exemplified in numerous cases. Islam, functioning as an autonomous entity within a larger political structure, has established regulations governing various aspects of life.The burden of non-compliance with both secular and religious laws falls on the personification and ability to manipulate or be justful in this society. Belief in Allah makes difficult circumstances easier and leads to a better life.

The mother nurtures the child and teaches the fundamentals of faith, morality, and discipline, and she is the first teacher who teaches a child about Allah. Mothers and children are also contractually responsible for each other. Islam has always stressed the importance of a mother teaching a child the faith because she is the child's first educator, not the school.A mother who nurses her child and spends time with her child usually has successful offspring.

In certain societies, individuals are constrained by their employment and financial obligations, which limits their capacity to devote full-time attention to their children. Consequently, they face the risk of their children acquiring the practices taught at childcare institutions during their formative years.

In specific situations, grandparents assume the responsibility of caring for their grandchildren. When a mother requires assistance during her child's developmental years, it falls upon the extended family to provide support. If the father is incapable of providing for the family or his death.

In accordance with Islamic law, it is expected that children provide support to their parents as they age, without sacrificing their own livelihoods. Nevertheless, in the Islamic faith, there is a fundamental principle of upholding the welfare of parents, where the dynamics shift as time progresses, and the responsibility of caring for the young transitions into a duty to support the elderly.

Even in cases of divorce or illegitimate relationships, fathers are still legally bound by responsibility. Islamic law grants the contract of marriage the right to be dissolved, considering its reasons and circumstances. In accordance with the teachings of the Christian religion, divorce is not permitted. According to biblical teachings, divorce is only deemed acceptable in cases of sexual immorality, making it an exceptional circumstance.Despite the efforts made to address this issue, the number of individuals seeking divorce as a result of marital misconduct continues to remain at a high level. Some women, who are unable to provide for their own well-being and that of their children, often turn to sources or actions that impede the progress of moral growth.

Within the dynamics of a family, it is common for roles to be interchangeable, meaning that either the father or the mother can take on the role of the breadwinner to support the family, or both parents can collectively contribute to this aspect. Sometimes, women endure stress as they choose between personal growth and keeping their family intact.

In pre-archaic societies, which are considered to be modern in a misleading manner, it is frequently observed that men tend to abandon women. On the other hand, although less prevalent, there are instances where women also abandon their families, leaving them to shoulder the burden of family responsibilities on their own. In a place where people consider themselves modern, but are actually backward, this occurrence is most prevalent, especially when compared to previous generations who displayed more responsibility.

It is only the almighty who knows the results that fate holds, yet the question still lingers: only has dominion over destiny. Allah, in whom humans believe, is reputed to have determined destiny and possesses knowledge of both the visible and the hidden. (Elm e ghaib) He wrote extensively about the inevitable fate of humans, having full knowledge of the choices they would ultimately make. Within the pages of the book of life lies the predetermined destiny that awaits us all.

Quran: Surah Isra: 17:13. We have bound every human's destiny to their neck.On the day of judgment. WE We will bring forth to each person a record which they will find laid open.

Most stress people experience is in their necks. Destiny of each individual is written behind his neck.

Quran: Surah Isra: 17:13. We have tied every person's destiny about his neck and, on the Day of Judgment We will bring out a book for him, which he will find spread open in front of him.

Quran: Surah Qiyamah: 75;4. Yes ˹indeed˺! We are ˹most˺ capable of restoring ˹even˺ their very fingertips.

The Quran provides detailed references to various aspects of human anatomy, including the development laws and contractual agreements that encompass the entire body. Despite the advancements in our technology-driven society, notaries still rely on the traditional method of using ink to capture fingerprints and witness signatures on important documents. It is worth noting that during the fourth month, the mother's entrails were instrumental in observing the development of fingertips.

The Quran uses the word "Banan" in Surah Qiyamah to describe all the fingers. During his time as a British officer in India, William Herschel made notable observations regarding unique characteristics present in his fingertips. It was in the year 1858 when he first began utilizing fingerprints for scientific agreements.

The Quran holds the distinction of being the first written work to make reference to fingerprints, recognizing their individuality and importance. The unique and distinctive characteristics of each fingerprint set them apart from one another. The distinguishing factor between physical fingers, like a thumb or finger, and images of fingers is their ability to unlock phone doors. Can the Quran be unlocked by the fingers, which are used to unlock the facets of life in high tech society? This is a question that pertains to Muslims. (Insha Allah) God willing.

This matter is mentioned in the Quran, which is the sacred text of the Islamic faith. It was on the day of resurrection that Allah made this truth evident to the entirety of humanity. In accordance with Islamic teachings, it is believed that Allah will recreate humans in a manner that allows for the clear visibility and accessibility of all details, even down to the fingertips. In the Quran, there are references made by Allah to the fingertips of human beings.Allah has not overlooked anything. Allah, being divine, possesses the attribute of omniscience and does not possess any human qualities such as forgetfulness. Individuals who actively seek truth will ultimately find it.

Quran: Surah Qiyamah 75:4. Not to speak of building up your skeleton once again by gathering together the major bones? We can make the most delicate parts of your body, even your fingertips, as they used to be before.

There are certain individuals among the human population who have never had the opportunity to experience the institution of marriage. By engaging in a lifestyle of fornication, they missed out on the beautiful and rewarding experience of being married and sharing a life together. Allah stated that he created humanity in pairs, which raises the question of whether every human has the opportunity to find their perfect match, something that has always intrigued mankind. The reason why all things were created in pairs is because as some trees die, some pairs break and some never meet.

Quran: Surah Dhariyat 51:39 And we created pairs of all things, so perhaps you would be mindful. Certain restrictions apply in the sacrament of marriage. When life progresses, the deen's way of life becomes the strength of character that holds one's relationship together for Muslims.

Quran: Surah Fussilat: 31:53.Soon will we show them our signs in the furthest horizons and in their own souls until it becomes manifest to them that this is the truth"

The beauty of a selfless connection bestowed by Allah is most joyous when expressed through laughter or conversation centered around the mention of Allah's word or stories. It is Allah, the one who governs all affairs, who bestows upon him a clear and unmistakable signal.There are moments when humanity ventures towards the sail. In the absence of rough tides, the sail finds itself in calm waters, creating a serene environment. For those who have faith in Allah they possess the ability to navigate jagged waves effortlessly and experience a smooth sailing journey devoid of any tides. The waves, which were once turbulent, can subside, resulting in calmer waters.

Once Prophet Muhammad received the answers he was seeking, he decided to discontinue his visits to the cave of Hira. Once an individual comes to the realization that their prayer has been answered, they can apply the same analogy to courses that did not bring them peace. The most challenging aspect is the lack of knowledge regarding when prayers have been answered.The multitude of roles that humans assume in life is truly infinite, going beyond the boundaries of available room for classification. In the eyes of a Muslim, the one who leads others to Allah is greatly admired. Within the realm of possibility, is there a chance to negotiate for a space that holds such immeasurable value? The belief of Muslims is firm in the notion that even the small space required for sujood, the act of prostration, has the potential to bring about victory in battles.

CHAPTER 18

EXEMPLARY PARADIGMS OF PROPHETS IN THE QURAN.

Valuable allies are control and vitality. The religions, including Islam and the Abrahamic faiths, all uphold proper conduct and respect for jurisdiction. In Islam, the issue is not whether one has legitimate desires or the precarious lifestyle caused by codependent environments due to negligence or failure to eliminate conflicting beliefs.

Acknowledging errors and redirecting promptly are the essence of faith and belief. No one is exempt from error. Muslims can exceed expectations. Angels questioned why Allah created humans with free will to destroy his universe, as they themselves had no free will.

They saw the Jinns' downfall and disrespect towards the earth with free will. They preferred no will over free will, fearing the chaos it brought. Allah reminded the angels of their limited understanding of humans. He expects humans to surpass all other creatures on earth, despite giving them free will. Muslims have a responsibility to uphold the eternal truth and beliefs that humanity was born with.

Allah acknowledges human progress and neglect. Sharing knowledge, practicing kindness, and submitting to Him are our responsibilities as earth's representatives. To recognize the lures, it becomes necessary to understand Satan's tactics and his supporters who disrupt successful societies. The believer recognizes the unhappiness in embracing evil. Allah grants everyone the ability to thrive, but Salat differentiates good from evil and protects from deception. The deceiver alienates believers, but Allah protects those who remain steadfast in Salat. The absence of Islam's main tenet signifies a lack of understanding.

A person with a clean lifestyle won't be motivated to befriend someone with questionable desires and evil attached to them. Demonstrating flawless habits despite life's unexpected turns shows the possibility of straying but also the beauty of rectification.

Scrutinizing a character's embrace of evil and virtue is not inherent in belief. The transformation of demeanor empowers words to reflect changes and embrace truth, visible to the world. The world sees the serenity one brings to climate change, making it unnecessary to voice one's character. Embracing imperfections is repentance's essence and a lesson of humility to Allah.

Achievers distinguish themselves from non-achievers through their use of time. Time travel distinguishes wanderers from those who stay put. Feeling lost and mesmerized as others prioritize their lives and misuse technology, while life slips away unnoticed, as time waits for no one who fails to recognize its importance. Humanity's hope for goodness lies in Allah, not humans. The location of one's heart alignment is a secret they alone can alter.

Quran: Surah Baqarah 2:30. Just think when your Lord said to the angels: "Lo! I am about to place a vicegerent on earth," they said: "Will You place on it one who will spread mischief and shed blood while we celebrate Your glory and extol Your holiness?" He said: "Surely I know what you do not know."

Believers actively choose to cultivate a stable and peaceful environment, walking away from danger towards the sustaining light with faith.Peace, kindness, and justice are emphasized in Islam.

It is an effective approach for preserving believers' mental health and maintaining overall societal health. Islam promotes moderation and avoiding extremes. Believers and disbelievers have access to Allah for support in managing their unwanted desires.

The Prophets in the Quran demonstrate the challenges faced by humanity across different eras. They become the ultimate source of guidance for those who seek it. A given situation or idea can be understood in various unique ways, known as interpretations. Their basis is formed by personal experiences, perspectives, and biases.

How people interpret things affects their responses and interactions with the world. Ambiguity isn't a universal aspect of explanations. Islam provides happiness and contentment to its followers through its laws, not limitations.

Prioritizing peaceful resolutions and being mindful of decisions is paramount. Ultimately, we have the power to opt for peace and oppose violence and destruction. Inappropriate behavior leads to a dysfunctional company. Prophets are sent by the Quran as examples to establish critical thinking and balance.

Believers lose out when they fall through life as disbelievers dictate. It leads to time, energy, and fulfillment being wasted. Prioritizing personal growth and spiritual journey involves taking a step back. It's not just a step back from progress, but also from a company that negatively affects the minds of those who offer no spiritual growth but harbor resentment.

The role of guidance and Islam in the early years for Muslim parents cannot be emphasized enough. Society's influence leads many individuals to become correctional officers in order to discipline parents who disciplined them using Islam.

Society has become a crowd that portrays Islam as outdated, encouraging them to demonstrate their brutal power and independence in contrast to Islam, which encourages such behavior.

Those who cannot develop their own values force their beliefs onto society, fostering individualism and rebellion against Allah. Nevertheless, this is an obsolete front of malevolence camouflaged as contemporary, effortlessly exploited.

Allah determines family, while humans determine friends. Throughout history, both harsh and pleasant times have been seen as trials, particularly when examining the lives of Prophets.

Poisons one inflicts upon oneself are not trials, but evil manifestations from within. Allah, the origin of all goodness, ensures that not everyone will confront identical obstacles.

Despite not having a kind father, Abraham, the Prophet, became the most ideal human and father of all Prophets. Numerous examples illustrate how certain incidents can build personal resilience.

Trials have persisted consistently throughout history, some chosen willingly and others dictated by destiny. Some turned challenges into valuable lessons, while others fell into self-pity and loneliness without solving the issue. Successful winners perceive every challenge as a chance to display their abilities.

Quran: Surah Baqarah: 2:137.So if they believe in what you believe, then they will indeed be ˹rightly˺ guided. But if they turn away, they are simply opposed ˹to the truth˺

Quran: Surah Anfal:8:30. And remember , O Prophet Muhammad. When those who disbelieved plotted against you to restrain, kill or evict you from Makkah.

The faith of those who don't consider faith important can be severely tested in difficult situations, particularly for practicing Muslims or new converts. Faith and breathing are equally important.

This holds particular significance during challenging times. Uncertainty makes it difficult to distinguish the truth. Abraham's example serves as a reminder to remain strong and unwavering in our beliefs. It can also assist us in understanding the value of truth, regardless of the situation. Choosing Islam as a faith may not receive support from a parent practicing pagan worship.

Respect for a strong belief system will prevent the embargo of Satanic whispers after the change. Those who oppose Islam and lack faith will not succeed when their beliefs clash. If it enters the dwellings of those who lack knowledge about Islam's beliefs and principles. There is a chance that opposition to faith can turn into enemies, as if it is influenced by Satan. Allah's knowledge encompasses the hearts of humans, concealed by destiny. He has the power to direct anyone he desires.

Exhibiting premature independence by setting boundaries and reacting aggressively. In the majority of cases, the parent's nurturing is necessary for the child to become independent. Society is grappling with the spread of evil, alarming even conservatives. Harshness is used to counteract the spread of evil and resentment towards independent homes and parents.

Islam upholds human rights and places significant value on recompense for this perspective. The destructive army knows no national boundaries. His relentless pursuit of prey and interference with prayer motivates him. Satan flees when the (azan) call to prayer is sounded and (Surah Al-Baqarah) is recited.

Quran: Surah Isra: 17;53. Satan sows dissension among them; he is the sworn enemy of human beings.

The teacher possesses a wealth of knowledge. An example showcasing moral and ethical behavior. This allows students to replicate the teacher and encourage self-improvement. In this era of false modernity and low wages.

In modernized settings, teachers are losing respect and focusing more on salary than student welfare, making them worse than students. Societies that are prey to individualism with collective thoughts implanted from a manipulative system lack thorough documentation of this application of mistrust. Finding a teacher for Islamic values becomes difficult if the home is negligent, unless one seeks their own education.

As a child, Prophet Muhammad experienced the loss of his parents. Those who took care of him had a big impact on his life. Abu Talib, his uncle, worked as a merchant. Muhammad peace be upon him frequently joined him during his journeys. Consequently, Prophet Muhammad developed a profound comprehension of the world and its inhabitants. This later proved beneficial in his leadership position.

Islam, despite mankind worshiping one God since the beginning, was introduced as the ultimate and conclusive chapter. Khadija's faith in her husband grew stronger in their faith-based relationship. Allah sent Salams through the angel Gabriel to only one woman, and that was Khadija, first wife of Prophet Muhammad. She held the distinction of being the first Muslim woman. Throughout her husband's Prophetic career, she remained steadfast and supportive. She set an example for all Muslim women with her strong character.

The Prophet Muhammad peace be upon him found strength in her courage and loyalty. The trials of this Prophet are relatable to people growing up in any decade. Those who follow this prophet can use their preparation for Prophethood as a character reference. Although he was raised in a nurturing atmosphere, he experienced several hardships as a child. Attributes he cherished were honesty and integrity.

His reputation also included acts of generosity and kindness towards those in his vicinity. As he grew older, Muhammad excelled as a merchant and gained widespread respect. There was widespread recognition of his exceptional truthfulness. His humility and compassion were qualities that garnered admiration. He was renowned for both his wisdom and willingness to assist others.

He was a leader and an example for many. His life stories are well-documented and relevant for those who seek the truth. To mold a character from events that benefit their own interests. He inspired those around him, and his legacy continues to impact the world today. His teachings and life are still embraced by many and provide guidance to those who seek it.

His kindness and generosity are seen as a foundation to imitate. The initial step in Islam is self-improvement, which enables one to assist others. He exemplified faith and compassion.

He demonstrates how positive role models can transform someone's life. He demonstrated the power of making a difference. Moreover, he asserted that amidst treachery and hate, humans will develop a fondness for the four-legged animal.

His reference to animals was based on the belief that humans would lose trust and seek love and passion in animals' genuine nature and forgiveness. In today's world, dogs have become valued companions, particularly in societies that prioritize modernity over humans. He demonstrated the potential for a more compassionate world to exist.

He believed in the power of people coming together to create a world filled with generosity, kindness, love, peace, and justice. He symbolized hope and faith. Writing about this Prophet contributes to academic and moral ethics. His teachings and spirit will endure eternally, even in his absence. The demonstration of his faith and goodwill is a legacy for those who are impacted.

He was ultimately selected to convey the Quran, and his (Sunnah) actions and traditions served as a lasting model for seekers of guidance. He demonstrated the beauty of a world brimming with love and compassion. He had no formal education; His character and interactions with Muslims and non-Muslims are beyond words. Thus, the Quran is more than a book; it is a living guide for all generations. It serves as a reminder that faith and righteousness pave the way to a brighter future.

Muslim mothers bear a significant burden as per Islamic teachings, and this fact cannot be emphasized or reiterated too much. It is her privilege and duty as a believing woman to shape the character of her unborn child after he reaches a certain age and teach Islam. The surviving parent assumes responsibility if she is deceased. If both parents are no longer alive, relatives will be brought in.

In order to embrace the peace of Islam, Muslims adopt this formula as a legacy of viral diplomacy. Sensibility and functionality govern every aspect of life. In any circumstance, faith is always the priority. Allah sent the Quran as a closing statement because it is significant. We aspire to be excellent role models and create a nurturing environment for growth and development.Coherence and duality are intentionally implemented. Society's brainwashing promotes independence, but it has consequences for Islam and other faiths.

Respect is an inherent Islamic value that forms the basis for other values. Each person has the responsibility to interpret and act accordingly, but it should never be underestimated. If a Muslim grows up with truth, they may fight for falsified rhetoric due to the influence of deceit. The Prophets sent by Allah were meant to advise the misguided, not make false claims.

Prophets in the Bible are shown as poor examples, promoting mischief to rationalize their evil acts, leading to severe punishments in human courts. Allah's justice is paramount; he cannot allow them to continue as Prophets, spreading negative acts and teachings. The examples set by Islamic Prophets are meant to bring serenity, not to shame them. We cannot overlook the vast examples of Jesus, Moses, Noah, Lot, and many others. The Jews claimed Mary, Jesus' mother, was an adulteress. This would shock Muslims, but the truth cannot be hidden. Defaming Muslims, including the Prophets and Mary, is something the practice has no qualms about.

 Kissing is a form of intimacy that can lead to sexual arousal between a man and a woman. In the Bible, there is a story about Jesus, the Prophet, kissing his disciple Mary Magdalene on the lips in front of people. However, this story is considered absurd to Muslims, as it goes against their beliefs and values. In Islam, Prophets were sent by Allah to set examples for normal humans to follow, but engaging in physical relationships or having affairs outside of marriage is not permitted. Therefore, the idea of Jesus having an affair with Mary Magdalene is inconceivable in Islam. The stories and teachings of the Prophets hold great importance in shaping moral conduct for Muslims. These stories contrast with the Bible and Quran, emphasizing human fallibility and the importance of repentance. Islam prohibits the expression of sexual behavior by Prophets, including Jesus, whom they consider to be either God or the son of God in a triune form.

Bible: 63:33:36. Mary Magdalene.He loved her more than all the disciples, and used to kiss her often on her mouth"

Bible: ESV: Luke 8:2.So were some women who had been healed of evil spirits and sicknesses. One was Mary Magdalene. Seven demons had come out of her.

Mary Magdalene, associated with demons and promiscuity, was involved with Jesus, who kissed her which contradicts Abrahamic faith. Mary Magdalene addressed Jesus as Lord and received kisses from him when he was on earth. Conflicting stories greatly affect Muslim and Christian theology. The Bible depicts a Prophet acting promiscuously, raising questions about the behavior of teachers and their influence on students. Christian lands see forbidden acts as prejudice and racism. Humans make mistakes, repentance is available, not through Prophets or Jesus, who is sinless as per Islam.

The repetition of curtailed truth can turn into a web of lies. Islam sends Prophets to set examples and promote learning, not to lead astray. If Prophets can create such vast problems, a normal person can do worse. Christendom believes Jesus bore others' sins as a forgiver. But the Lord of the Universe, Allah, is just. For each individual, justice is justified. Allah cannot send Prophets who undermine their character. He sent Prophets to show their exemplary character during life's trials.

Therefore, it is essential to uphold the Abrahamic Prophets' legacy and teachings. Islamic concepts and Quranic proceedings. Striving to emulate the Prophets' morality and character and working together to build a better future. Respect is the foundation for positive growth and transformation. Education and awareness are critical to understanding this legacy.

The story of a young Muslim man in this era:

A young Muslim man, hailing from the Middle East, migrated to a new land. Raised in a devout Muslim family, he abided by the laws and regulations of Islam diligently. Upon arriving in the Western world, he was unaware of the ease of accessing adult content websites. His eyes beheld unfamiliar sights, igniting a curiosity that compelled him to subscribe to the service. Despite his guilt, he seldom perused the content, mindful of adhering to Islamic principles. In his fervor for newfound freedom, he extended the subscription to both Muslim and non-Muslim acquaintances.

Each time he conversed with his Muslim mother, a wave of guilt washed over him for the newfound indulgences he never thought he would engage in. On a particular day, plagued by hunger, he set off in his vehicle to procure nourishment for his domicile, unaware of the calamitous accident that awaited him, ultimately leading to his demise. The family was notified and promptly arranged the Janazah funeral. Friends and family gathered to attend the somber burial of the young Muslim man. The subscription had been activated.

Those who were added to his subscription were displeased by what he had left behind and made earnest efforts to delete it, but it was conveyed that only he could terminate his subscription. He was absent, but in a brief period of acclimation to a different environment, he engaged in actions he typically wouldn't. No one took it upon themselves to caution him or dissuade him, as nobody expressed concern by saying "don't do it."

They discussed his transformation, but refrained from advising against it from a religious standpoint as a Muslim. In the event that one Muslim is incapable of admonishing another Muslim, it may be a critical juncture for both the observer and the participant; it is incumbent upon a Muslim to assist their fellow. The legacy left behind by a Muslim or believer should align harmoniously with the guidelines established by their creator. It is an illustration to ensure that our methods align with approved lifestyles as virtuous deeds bring about joy. There is no need to actively seek wrongdoing, particularly when Allah provides cautionary reminders. It is a blessing from Allah to correct the path of a faithful believer and Muslim.

Individuals possess the agency to determine the trajectory they will pursue. Allah had prior knowledge of what would occur. Those who find comfort in Allah, triumph by comprehending triumphs and expressing gratitude for hardships. The conceited triumphs are evanescent. The character of Prophet Muhammad in the Quran exemplifies remarkable morality, endurance, and truthfulness.

He embodied righteousness, compassion, mercy, and kindness. His life served as an inspiration to millions of people across the globe. His teachings have had a profound impact on the world.

Those who comprehend his delivery of Islam's message continue to endeavor to practice it in the present.

His teachings continue to hold relevance in the modern world and serve as inspiration to those who adhere to them. He serves as a wellspring of hope and fortitude for many. His legacy is characterized by a commitment to peace and justice, spanning both secular and religious spheres, and he serves as an ongoing source of motivation for many. Nevertheless, all of Allah's Prophets are regarded as credible. The epitome of their examples. Islam acknowledges the sanctity of each Prophet appointed by Allah.

Quran: Surah Ahzab 33:21 There has certainly been the Messenger of Allah. This is an excellent pattern for anyone whose hope is in Allah and the Last Prophet.

Bible: Isaiah 30:26.- The light of the moon shall be as the light of the sun. "The promise now rises higher and higher, and passes from earth to heaven"

Quran: Surah Furqan: 25:61.Blessed is He Who has placed stars in heaven and has set in it the glowing sun (that produces light) and the glittering moon (that reflects light).

Individuals are provided with a calendar that depicts their daily life, excluding time they used up. Life and actions are intertwined. Mankind is bestowed with a calendar by Allah, which is predicated on the celestial movements of the sun and moon. He generates both sunlight and moonlight and monitors their cycles. The reckoning could commence at any given moment, devoid of any means to anticipate the passage of time.

Islam, as a religion, offers a unique and fresh perspective on understanding and comprehending the truth. Just as the moon reflects the sunlight, Islamic concepts reflect the divine wisdom and guidance that are essential for a fulfilling and purposeful life. Those who possess a deep understanding of Islam can connect to this invitation to truth in a profound way. Islam, in its pure form, remains unaltered and unaffected by human interpretations or manipulations. It is neither injured nor repaired, as it encompasses timeless principles and teachings that are relevant to all eras and societies. The truth presented by Islamic concepts is comprehensive, covering all aspects of life, including spirituality, morality, social justice, and personal development.

To fully comprehend Islam, one must approach it with an open mind and a willingness to explore its teachings without preconceived notions or biases. This requires seeking knowledge from authentic sources, such as the Quran and the teachings of the Prophet Muhammad (peace be upon him), as well as engaging in thoughtful reflection and contemplation. By embracing Islamic concepts with sincerity and humility, individuals can embark on a transformative journey of self-discovery and spiritual growth. They can gain a deeper understanding of the purpose of life, the nature of God, and the importance of compassion, justice, and unity. Through this understanding, they can develop a strong connection with their Creator and navigate the challenges of the world with wisdom and resilience.

In essence, Islam offers a connective response to those who possess a unique and fresh perspective, inviting them to explore and comprehend the truth it presents. It is a religion that remains unchanged and unharmed, providing a comprehensive framework for living a fulfilling and purposeful life.

Sunlight is reflected by the moon, generating moonlight. The moon does not generate its own light. It was later revealed by scientists and predicted by the Quran.In contrast, the moon refracts the radiance of the sun's light. Here's the rationale for the moon's glowing presence in the darkness of the sky. The fluctuating angle of sunlight results in the different phases of the moon.

Various lunar phases arise from the shifting sunlight angle during the moon's orbit around Earth. The reason for the heightened luminosity of a full moon in contrast to the first moon. Greek philosophers arrived at the conclusion that the moon did not emit its own light through extensive research and observation. The Quran informed Muslims that those who read it were educated even before scientists educated the world.

The Quran corrects the Bible instead of copying it, since numerous human hands have touched it, making it impossible to mix the divine word with human touch. The sun doesn't provide the moon's light, doesn't the Bible contradict human observations? Scientific findings were foretold by the Quran. Altering someone's writings is challenging, let alone changing a divine text, which is blasphemous. The only time a Muslim can trust its literal meaning is when it aligns with the Quran. The truth in previous scriptures is blended with human influences.

The Earth is spherical, not round. The Quran documents miracles like Prophet Muhammad splitting the moon to demonstrate Allah's wonders. Allah is the omnipotent creator of the universe. The universe's wonders support this belief.

KJV: Isaiah: 40;22. It is he that sitteth upon the circle of the earth, and the inhabitants thereof are as grasshoppers; that stretcheth out the heavens as a curtain.

Quran: Surah Naziat: 79:30."And the earth, moreover, Hath He made egg shaped."

Translations cannot fully convey the meaning of the Quran, but language is a powerful tool that should be explored. The Quran covers all aspects of science, law, contracts, personal relationships, and family matters. Allah sent a precise and unchanging manual for humanity.

The shape of the earth is not circular. The Quran states that the Earth is spherical and flattened for standing. Despite the vast amount of earth, it remains passive when shaped for walking but retaliates when intruded upon after death for those who defy Allah. Consider the difficulty of traversing it without the ability to walk. The manner in which Allah facilitates human existence is truly astonishing. To how many blessings can one show gratitude to Allah?

Quran: Surah Nuh: 71;16."[Can't you see that He] made the moon a light in their midst and made the sun as a lamp?

Quran: Surah Nuh: 71;16.Allah has created the seven heavens in tiers and has made the moon a light therein,, and made the sun a lamp. He made a distinction between them.

Quran: Surah Yunus 10:49 Tell them: 'I have no power to harm or benefit even myself except what Allah may will. There is an appointed term for every person; and when the end of their term comes, neither can they put it off for an hour, nor can they bring it an hour before.

The decision to end it lies with Allah. Many communities have experienced notable enhancements. Many communities have experienced multiple collapses. The decline was more severe for most people compared to the high point. Spiritual death can be more devastating than physical death. The peak of the Egyptian king Firon is one of the most impressive examples. He was ruined by his pride, arrogance, and ego.

Egypt is predominantly Muslim. This is the mercy of Allah. It's a place where paganistic idols and sorcerers made important decisions. Allah's law and order are unmatched. Egypt was destined to become a Muslim country according to Allah's plan. Just as wretched humans can transform into devoted Muslims. One who believes can turn into a nonbeliever. Even someone who doesn't believe can come to believe.

Humans are predestined by Allah. He understands the hearts of everyone. Each soul is compensated accordingly by Allah. He is aware of their actions and non-actions. The book of records notes that he already knows the consequences of their actions. Prophet Muhammad persevered without losing hope.

Changes and revelations were caused by a dramatic order from Allah.Allah used the angel Gabriel to awaken his subconscious knowledge and truth, which he then shared with the world. This deeply spiritual journey has given purpose and meaning to the Muslim world during both happy and troubled times.

The power of kindness, a smile, and a helping hand. In the face of challenges, he was always prepared to engage. By meditating for hours, Allah granted him the power to conquer any obstacle. Islam underwent significant changes during its metamorphosis. It went through a transition over a 23-year period. His only assertion was that he served Allah.

Just like in the story of Prophet Yusuf, parents would bow to the king before humans started bowing to higher authorities. Subsequently, Allah only granted this privilege to him. Such is the mercy of Allah. He consistently aligns his wants and preferences with the necessity for change.

The application of humanity's passion grows with each passing day. Everything is within our grasp. With Allah as the guide of contentment and ease, no storm is too difficult to overcome. The synopsis and paradox of confusion are useful for those who avoid understanding Islam. Deceit comes in various shades. Particularly for Muslims or believers who need to distinguish Satan's evil whispers from the truth.

Overcoming obstacles is not the only aspect of healthy living. It's a passionate example of perseverance, faith, tenacity, and hope for believers. No matter where a believer lives, their belief system remains unchanged. The clueless will argue. Depart from my country or land. Does one's birthright disregard another's entrance? Ignorant individuals blend weakness, illiteracy, and anger.

The people in question lack moral integrity and do not contribute anything to anyone, not even themselves. They have no entitlement to any land. He returns to nothing but the dust. Certain individuals crave acknowledgement for their achievements and strive for respect regarding their desires.

Insecurities divide the subconscious, showing evil and independence. The costly risk of independence is deceit without an alliance with Allah. Respect, humility, kindness - his rules require them, not arrogance. Behavior is the source of respect and dignity. Humility, not arrogance, is what earns gratitude. The main source of responsibility-personified coherence comes from having a strong understanding of Islam's faith and values. Defiant individuals find the deliberate disregard for Islamic values less relevant, regardless of the source.

Deceit and bad company will remain until self-correction takes over. The inner self is under attack. Allah's laws are always superior to others.The metaphor of the womb taking a back seat explains the mother's role in upholding Allah's laws and rules. When faced with irrational evil words, the best course of action is to leave rather than engage in heated conversation. Prophet Muhammad changed the world without seeking attention or recognition.

He simply focused on the task at hand and followed Allah's teachings. Others' opinions did not distract him. Despite facing adversity, he remained patient and forgiving. The Quran is clearly stated by Allah as easy to understand. Those who search for truth in the Quran and Muhammad's Sunnah will discover it.

Quran: Surah Qamar: 54:17.: We have made the Quran easy to understand, but is there anyone who would pay attention?

Quran: Surah Araf: 7:26.We have provided for you clothing to cover your nakedness and as an adornment. However, the best clothing is righteousness. This is one of Allah's bounties.

Many sources exist, and Allah stills performs miracles in our world today. The truth about Allah can be found by those who seek guidance from the Quran and the (Sunnah) his ways and practices. The occupation of land by humans is always accompanied by restrictions. Higher authorities establish human rights and regulations.

It provides guidelines for all areas of life, such as politics, ethics, and social behavior. Prohibiting alterations, the Quran is the only book that governs any decade. Other scriptures have manipulated the text to fit political circumstances and greed. In any situation, the Quran remains eternally relevant and serves as a source of guidance.

Islam addresses a wide range of topics, from literacy to contract laws to morality to family relationships. The recipient is not deceptive. Believers are not held hostage by Satan. Tempting is part of his job requirement. Believers will witness blissful and magnificent permissible acts, while defiance and disdainful behavior seek instant gratification. A lifetime is how long reliance and alliance with Allah endure.

They are facing the threat of being devoured by their enemies. Occasionally, they sabotage themselves. Those who don't adhere to Islam's protocol are deceived by falsehoods and influenced by corrupt individuals or nonbelievers. The spider exemplifies those who are deceived by falsehoods and captivated by manipulators. Muslims require more than just academic pursuits alone. Female spiders consume male spiders before, during, or after mating. It is possible for females to be eaten, although it is not common.

Such is the home of a Muslim where women with no faith eat up a male's home. The house is fragile, just as a spider's home is weak, says the Quran. In a home where female and male residents do not thank Allah to break in peace and sanctuary of a home, an individual lives in the weak environment of a spider. If a male does not follow the Muslim religion, the woman who acts as the spawner can eat him.

Allah uses small creatures like spiders, ants, and flies to illustrate the impact a tiny creature can have on humans. A fly constantly buzzing around a person teaches the need for self-protection. These examples demonstrate how humans can guard against the evident harm even the tiny fly can cause disturbance. Surely Satan can tempt but finality of decision lies within the human.

Quran: Surah Hajj:22:73.O humanity! A lesson is set forth, so listen to it ˹carefully˺: those ˹idols˺ you invoke besides Allah can never create ˹so much as˺ a fly, even if they ˹all˺ were to come together for that. And if a fly were to snatch anything away from them, they cannot ˹even˺ retrieve it from the fly. How powerless are those who invoke and those invoked!

Glitz, bling, academics, travel, and entrepreneurial pursuits are not enough for a strong Muslim house without Allah and (Salat) ritual prayer. The spider's dwelling is fragile. This parable is best suited for the faithless. Female spiders can be harmful. Particularly non-believers. Spiders that trap or assist Muslims are good examples. Allah illustrates with a parable.

Quran: Surah Ankaboot: 29:41.The parable of those who take [beings or forces] other than God for their protectors is that of the spider which builds itself a house:

For, behold, the frailest of all houses is the spider's house. Could they understand this.

It doesn't take long for those who pay attention to parables to see them. People who pass by as strangers to their own beliefs leave behind no trails or remnants of their own selves. There are examples and concepts for spiders that are not only for females. A male without faith in Islam in a Muslim's home is a dead home.

A weak male can be devoured by the female spider with lack of belief. By cross-referencing society, a male may accept actions outside of Islam. In Allah's judgments, males and females will be judged equally. A believer always learns from any example, even if it's unconventional. Regardless of who resides within, faith serves as the bedrock of any household.

In Islam, it is hypocritical to break Allah's laws while upholding humans' laws. A continuous effort to defy Allah is not a mistake, but an act of defiance. There's an expense tied to it. Destiny is in the hands of Allah. The most important thing you have is your health. The beginning of destruction occurs when spiritual health is lost, unless it is repaired. It's the heart that counts. If Allah desires, all things are within reach.

Quran: Surah Ankaboot: 29:2 DO MEN THINK that on their [mere] saying, "We have attained faith" they will be left to themselves, and will not be put to a test?

Quran: Surah Rahman 55:41 By their marks on their forelocks and feet, Allah will identify the guilty.

The Quran provides examples that explain why Allah chose fragile creatures to illustrate strength and weakness. Women and men raised in Islam or recently converted to Islam. To understand Islam, proper education is necessary.

Practicing Muslims educate numerous converts. Omar, who had converted to Islam, became both a teacher and second caliph of Islam. He embodied Islam, famous for his strength, integrity, morals, and names. These attributes alone do not fully capture his submissive nature to Allah. He held himself responsible for his pagan worship, but in the end, he embraced Allah and his dedication was evident to all.

Both the Quran and Salat possess a rhythmic quality. The movement is continuous and repetitive, similar to the recitation of the Quran in Salat. The actions and sound work together, creating a continuous and flowing experience. The repentant Muslim's actions aim to improve and spread the beauty and knowledge of Islam.

Jesus and his small family:

Mary, the mother of Jesus. In addition to her mother, she has an uncle named Zakariyah.Despite Hannah's age, she couldn't resist the strong urge to become a mother. The blessed event of birth cannot be discounted. It was in Allah's name that she prayed for a child and promised to dedicate it to the temple. Hannah was expecting a child.

Although her husband did not live long enough to witness the birth of his child, Imran was filled with immense joy. Hannah gave birth to a girl.Allah blessed her with a daughter she named her Maryam. Being barren can be challenging for many women.

Men who desire to leave a legacy are no different. With time, others begin having children. Some see them as blessings, while others see them as trials. Whoever Allah chooses, he gives progeny they can call their own. Death and life are beyond the control of humans.

Hannah pledged to offer her child to the temple in exchange for Allah's blessing.She entrusted her infant daughter Mary to the temple, dedicating her to God. She was named Mary. Zakirayah was Mary's guardian. The story's empowering pattern involves Hannah keeping her promise to God by giving her daughter to the temple. God fulfilled her wish for a daughter at an older age.

Despite being an elderly mother, her heart remained unchanged, solidifying her character. Lack of integrity is a character flaw that can be corrected through repentance. However, Hannah was a woman of character.The world has changed, and honor is no longer valued; strength of character lies in keeping one's word.

Every time Zakirayah visited Mary, she always had food trays. He inquired where she received the food trays. According to her, it was sent by her Lord. Her unwavering faith in her Lord inspired him to believe he could also ask for anything he desired. Because of his old age, he prayed for a son and was blessed with John the Baptist. The creator is Allah; ask him and you will receive.

Mary's documented purity aligns with her and her mother's character. The angel Gabriel knew of her purity and informed her that Allah chose her to bear a son. That is a miracle among all the other miracles of Allah that does not employ him as the father of the child.Gabriel the angel informed Mary of her impending motherhood. She said no man has touched me. He assured her of Allah's unlimited capabilities. She neither questioned Allah's powers nor claimed Allah as the father.

It's evident that she was chosen to bring Jesus as the ultimate conclusion to this world. The significance of sharing the explanation of this episode is crucial due to the differing story it holds compared to other Prophets in previous scriptures.

Quran: Surah Imran 3:47.She said: "O my Lord! How shall I have a son when no man hath touched me?" He said: "Even so: Allah createth what He willeth: When He hath decreed a plan, He wills .

Quran: Surah Tahrim: 66:12. And the example of Mary, the daughter of 'Imran, who guarded her chastity, so We blew into her garment through Our angel.

Male sperm did not play a role in the conception of Jesus. By Allah's command, an angel blew the spirit into her garment. Is it challenging for certain humans to grasp what Allah is capable of? After enduring the pains of childbirth, she returned with the baby. His birthplace is not specifically mentioned in the Quran, but it is described as a distant location. Instead of fleeing to a new place, she returned despite her fear of her chastity and she held no fear of the Jews.The baby spoke of the future and will speak of the truth again in the second coming.He defended his mother's dignity, leaving the Jews dismayed. She feared Allah, not humans.

Many miracles exist - Moses divided the sea, Muhammad cleaved the moon, Noah built an ark, Jonah resided within a fish's belly. Hence, it's puzzling why Mary gives birth without a father.In its entirety, it is questioned. Were the first humans created by Allah without parents? Did he serve as their father? No.

Allah blessed Mary with motherhood, and her son became the Messiah, a Prophet. Grasping it is straightforward. Humans give gifts to their loved ones, so why can't Allah give gifts to humans? Only the ungrateful reject gifts and fail to understand their delivery, while pure hearts accept with sincerity. Satan rejected his gift in heaven, and his followers reject gifts, too. Believers accept gifts from Allah and fellow believers. Hypocrites who can't accept gifts from Allah or believers have tainted hearts in need of repentance.

To safeguard the mother's honor, Allah, understanding human nature, made Jesus speak at birth, an event not recorded in the Bible but mentioned in the Quran. It's not unimaginable for them to grasp that a child can speak and bear witness for his mother. Days like those are a thing of the past, and women like that era no longer exist. The chastity and demeanor of the women are not alike. Yet, the mind can conceive of the existence of women like these.

People who doubted Allah's power turned Mary's gift into a web of lies. He performed numerous miracles for the people of that era, but none of those who witnessed them are alive today. Allah knew that humans would doubt the existence of miracles and beliefs.Islam prioritized the Quran as a guide, incorporating its laws and stories for the benefit of humanity, rather than focusing on miracles.

The truth can only be revealed by Jesus. Allah will reveal his presence to humans during the time of judgment, not in this world. When humans possess the truth, they can either defy or not defy justice. Some may find answers through the analogy of Muslim beliefs, while others may persist in their belief in the cleansing power of mortal blood.

These ceremonies resemble paganistic error. No one can stop an individual who harnesses the power of belief, be it a person, animal, or nature. Allah is the sole authority in controlling humans; Jesus cannot exert control without Allah's consent. In Allah's domain of permanence, discord is not meant to be a force if answers don't align with thinking. The search for knowledge has led humanity to seek clear contrasts in theological sense.

Bible Esv: Leviticus 17:11. For the life of the flesh is in the blood, and I have given it for you on the altar. To make atonement for your souls, for it is the blood that makes atonement by life.

Al-Bukhaari (6472) and Muslim (220) narrated from Ibn 'Abbas (may Allah be pleased with him) that the Messenger of Allah (blessings and peace of Allah be upon him) said: "Seventy thousand of my ummah will enter Paradise without being brought to account; they are the ones who did not ask for Ruqyah or believe in omens or use cautery and they put their trust in their Lord."

Jews and Muslims, who are cousins, still have numerous disagreements. This ongoing history includes exile from Israel which was a consequence of disobedience from Allah, not Muslims. Muslims supported and formed numerous friendships with them. Both Jews and Muslims believed in one God, Allah, as part of their monotheistic faith.The Jews or the Muslims didn't adhere to the Christian practice of human worship. Muhammad prayed in the same direction as the Jews because Moses prayed to Allah and brought ten commandments.

Over time, Allah separated Islam from other scriptures due to discrepancies in interpretations and alterations that did not align with true belief. Jesus is not considered a God or son of God by Jews or Muslims. Cultic inventions led to the rise of this pagan belief at a later time. The faith originated from a human, not from Allah. However, it still falls under the Abrahamic faith because Jesus is descended from Abraham and was given the gospel (Ingel). Not Pauline Christianity.

The search for belief in humanity has remained steady as pagans and believers turn to nature to find deep spiritual significance in the cycles of growth, death, and warnings. Humans, just like Abraham, have wondered if the moon and the sun are Gods. When they both come and go, he recognizes the unwavering presence of Allah; Allah neither rests nor vanishes.

Trusting your instincts and seeking answers in solitude is the key to finding personal fulfillment in matters of the heart. The Quran is always a reliable source for answers, as is the guidance of someone placed in your life by Allah.

The bleeding of another human's blood doesn't contain the answers. Does a just God allow one human to bleed for another? In Islam, purity takes precedence over doubt, offering explanations for conjectures and promoting self-correction instead of seeking to ruin others. Although hope exists, no one is responsible for the salvation or redemption of another's soul. Not knowing the unknown, breathing, and getting hungry are not attributes of Allah.

Humans are guided by faith and love, going to extreme measures to strengthen their beliefs, even at the cost of sacrificing their own son. They do it to please the God who created blood sacrifice through vision and occult practices. Discussing ongoing theological disparities to highlight their harmful impact on society rather than uplifting it. Islam is an ongoing journey of personal development and lasting commitment, not dependent on another person. The practices of Muhammad are left behind to endure, but he is not the Prophet who will absolve the sins of his people; Allah will judge accordingly.

Their sacrifices will also be carried out. Allah understands human mentality and would not require human blood sacrifice like in Abraham's faith. It's definitely not a cult. Occult practices persist today, allowing for the possibility of blood sacrifices that haunt believers.

The Hill: On Easter some Christians become targets for persecution. Apr 9, 2023 — Sadly, for many Christians around the world, Holy Week and Easter Sunday become a time of fear and violence.

Los Angeles Times:Apr 7, 2023 — Eight Filipinos were nailed to crosses to reenact Jesus Christ's suffering in a gory Good Friday tradition that draws thousands of devotees.

Theology is not a topic of controversy because the laws of the Quran were written by Allah, not humans. Many were misguided by human hands despite the divine nature of the revelations of other Abrahamic scriptures he sent. The Quranic delivery and statements are completely truthful, eliminating any possibility of controversy.

The controversy surrounding the delivery of Islam is animosity. Public disputes involve controversial accusations and political disagreements, while religion is not typically controversial as it follows laws written by Allah. However, it can become an argument when individuals are fully aware that these laws are adapted to suit human lives on a daily basis. As truth is disregarded, lies lead to arguments, claiming politeness.

Bible: Galatians 1:4. The Lord Jesus Christ "who gave Himself for our sins so He might rescue us from this present evil age, according to the will of our God and Father. He gave Himself for our sins; He paid the penalty and provided atonement.

Quran: Surah Nisa 4:157 And for their saying, "Indeed, we have killed the Messiah, Jesus, the son of Mary, the messenger of Allah". ." And they did not kill him, nor did they crucify him.

It may leave many to question, but Islam does not negate the authority and power of Allah. He can do anything. All he has to do is say "Be," and it is. Islam also rejects any human addressed as God or son of God, as Allah is not mortal and requires no companionship or attachments.

Quran: Surah Muminoon 23:91 Allah has taken no son, nor has there ever been. Any deity with him. [If there had been], then each deity would have taken what it created, and some of them,

Islam fully refutes any attachments to Allah through a human. Understanding Islam is clear that Jesus of Islam is not the same as Jesus of Christianity. Its beliefs and writings do not match.Judaism does not see Jesus as fulfilling the messianic prophecies, and also, the virgin birth is not accepted by them to complete the prophecy of the Messiah.

Christian theology contradicts Jewish theology and the Islamic concept of Jesus.The only commonality is that he is the Messiah for Muslims, but if he is anything more than the Messiah, Muslims do not accept him as proclaimed by other texts.A return to the Abrahamic faith is only a return to monotheistic belief and to believe in the Prophets Allah has sent.

This puts Islam at the forefront of belief in the concepts of monotheism and belief in the Quran's consistent message. Allah is one, and the Messiah is Jesus.These differences characterize belief systems. Many stories of the prior scriptures do not match the Quran; the presentation is entirely different in many aspects. Alterations and revisions to the previous text have been assembled and fashioned to keep up with the times. Islam will not adapt to the times, but the times will adjust to Islam. As time belongs to Allah, not humans.

The Prophets presented in Islam hold dignity throughout the Quran and trials. Clearly, Allah has sent Prophets to live by their example. If Abraham had to sacrifice his son for Allah, then by default, humans would have to sacrifice their oldest for Allah

Allah assigned Jesus a job which was not completed. He is alive in Islamic belief, and another soul replaced him.

Only truth and comparisons are available to anyone who wants to know the differences. Theology and contrast are not for human satisfaction. A softening or addition of lies does not displace the truth except for the intended truth that the highest power preserves. Those who change the text may find the truth controversial. For a Muslim, truth comes first, not controversy. Allah always keeps his promises. He is not a human and no human who talks about Allah restricts themselves to please a human. Allah first, then humans.

Life challenges have given believers hope and triumph. This hope gives us the strength to endure hardships and find joy amid suffering. Faith can bring peace and assurance amid chaos and despair. Through this hope, humanity can trust in God's sovereignty and plan for their lives.

The mild comparisons between Christianity and Islam are thought-provoking. Allah is seen as One in both Judaism and Islam. Jesus was rejected by the Jews as the Messiah. It is accepted by Muslims. In anticipation of the expected Messiah from David's descendants, the third temple was constructed in Israel. Jesus Isa Ibn Maryam is acknowledged as the Messiah by Muslims. Christendom shares that commonality, but belief differs.

He is not a triune God, the son of God, or God himself evolved in Islamic belief. These distinctions cannot be repaired, only completely discarded, and studying is necessary for converts to Islam. Understanding the accepted truth necessitates departing from current conditions.The Quran and

Muhammad serve as a divine guide for all of humanity, not just Muslims. The fairness of Allah is reflected in the Prophets he sent.

The burial of Pharaohs was practiced by Egyptians, and ritual killings have been present in numerous cultures for many years. The survival of faith in Islam depends on leading by example. Human sacrifice is rejected. If Allah uses his Prophets to promote something,such as human sacrifice Muslims will make sacrifices for him.

Thus, Islam refutes these acts. In Islam, everything is a contract between God and humans, so people are not faced with this dilemma by Allah. Judged based on the evaluations of every soul. Sacrificial animals like lambs and sheep are feasted upon during the Hajj season, specifically during the celebration of Eid Al Adha.

Allah's intention for humans on earth is not to be sacrificed. The Islamic faith acknowledges that sacrificing humans serves no purpose, as individuals are solely responsible for their own conduct. It's unfair to appropriate someone else's righteous acts, exploit them for human pleasure, or absolve others of their wrongdoings. This can't possibly be the justice system of a human court of law.

Allah is the highest-ranking judge. According to Islamic beliefs, one cannot be held responsible for the sins of others. Every individual is responsible for their actions in Islam. Allah states that saving one life is equal to saving all of humanity. Islam rejects the idea of sacrificing humans on earth, be it through virtuous or evil deeds. Blood sacrifice is not a part of Islamic faith. Muslims follow the example of Abraham, the father of all Abrahamic Prophets. Muslims who are unfamiliar with their own faith may find answers that also help them navigate the dilemma of cultural influence on their beliefs.

Quran: Surah Maryam 19:88:92 And they say, "The Most Merciful has taken [for Himself] a son." You have done an atrocious thing. The heavens almost rupture.

Thus, Allah makes an oath of his own. In the end, humans will not alter the last scripture.Abraham's example is clearly apparent. Allah communicated to Abraham through a vision and dream, commanding him to make a sacrifice of his son. He fervently followed his dream. Allah bestowed upon him a lamb, illustrating the unnecessary nature of human sacrifice. Allah puts those he loves the most to the test, and Abraham demonstrated his worth by earning the name khareen. He poses a challenge to their faith and belief in him.

The believer consistently holds onto hope in Allah. It is inconceivable to defy the will of Allah. No words can truly encapsulate the boundless kindness of Allah, which is unequivocally just. Given that this episode merely provides a pretext for individuals to act freely, disregarding the suffering of others, he would never prioritize one person over another. Islam holds the ultimate decree. Until the ultimate pronouncement, neither heavenly sanctuary nor infernal abyss is revisited. The justice system is in anticipation of the findings, regardless of personal inclinations.

Quran: Surah Hijr 15:9. Verily we: It is we who have sent down the Quran. And surely we will guard it from corruption.

Bible: John 12:31, 14:30, 16:11 Jesus called Satan the "prince [ruler] of this world. Paul called him "the prince of the power of the air

Bible : New king King James Version: Matthew 4:1;11. Satan Tempts Jesus - Then Jesus was led up by the Spirit into the wilderness to be tempted by the devil. And when He had fasted forty days.

Contribution through loyalty, kindness, or exemplary behavior would protect someone from disparagement or dishonor. Peace prizes are awarded to deserving individuals. Every Prophet's trial ends in triumph and victory. Allah does not punish Prophets for others' sins. The Quran remains unchanged, no errors.The legacy of Abraham sheds light on all those connected to his lineage, particularly the Abrahamic Prophets, who will not deviate from his belief and embrace pagan practices.

The act of sacrificing a lamb is a joyous occasion of communal sharing and generosity for Muslims. The manifestation of Allah's mercy is apparent in the permissibility of consuming animals as sustenance. Similar to humans, animals and trees possess an inherent understanding of their purpose. It could be beneficial to take note of Allah's mercy, as the answers may lie within the Quran and the practices of Prophet Muhammad.

The meat is divided and exulted. Upon completion of the hajj, men adhere to the Sunnah of Prophet Muhammad by shaving their heads. There is no requirement to completely shave the head except to trim a section of it for men. It is obligatory to shave or trim a minimum of one-quarter of the hair following the completion of pilgrimage rites (hajj/'umra).

Allah has the power to bring rain during a drought and to bring wind on a calm day. He can also cause earthquakes, floods, and the sinking of cities. He can raise water levels on beaches and seas, part the seas, and create a human through the Virgin Mary.

When Jesus arrives, Mehdi the descendent from the family of Prophet Muhammad will assume the role of leading the Salat, with Jesus following in prayer. Mehdi's task will be completed, and Jesus will persist in his mission to unveil the truth. He made no alterations to the belief structure, instead conveying the identical message as every Prophet dispatched by Allah with the identical purpose.

In today's society, successful businesses exhibit a high level of consistency. Allah surpasses all businesses in infiniteness and delivers humans an identical message. Praise and revere the one God, Allah is for monotheistic faiths. According to Islam, the crucifixion is denied and Jesus is replaced with the Quranic text stating that he ascended to Allah while still alive.

Mother Mary did not deny that she conceived without a man or that Jesus' crucifixion was not her son. She knew it was not her son. Allah does not inflict punishment upon a family or individual for virtuous actions. Trials metamorphose into accomplishments and examples for those who inhabit this planet.

The harsh truth wipes out any religion that doesn't worship Allah, while new faiths spring up daily. Allah knows that the Abrahamic faith is monotheistic, not polytheistic. The rise of new faiths and adjustments to Abrahamic scriptures cannot be halted; respecting beliefs is essential in Islam. Differences in theology don't diminish respect for humanity, but understanding the concepts provides clarity rather than a mandate to follow Islam.

A word persists in a universe of thriving falsehood and dissolved handwritten obligations. Those who inhabit a realm of uncertainty labor to grasp the dialogue between Allah and followers. Those who possess a profound comprehension of the principles and veracity of delivery yearn to acquire further knowledge, rather than isolating themselves from adherents.

Story of Prophet Soloman (Suleiman):

Solomon is renowned for his presence in both the Bible and the Quran. In Islam, he is perceived as an epitome of conviction, fortitude, ardor, equity, and limitless empowerment. Let's delve into the exquisite allure and fervor of this Prophet within an Islamic framework.

The presence of material wealth does not impede a genuine believer's worship in the narrative of Prophet Solomon. His plea determines the manner in which Allah responds to his request.

Solomon attained all his aspirations from Allah. He held the belief that with his unwavering faith, all things were achievable and that every supplication in Allah could be granted. Solomon possessed grandeur in this mortal domain. He accomplished Prophethood and assumed the role of a king. Allah showered him with boundless gifts. Soloman fervently implored Allah for distinctive blessings. He possessed the extraordinary power to engage in dialogue with animals and interpret their language. As a regal figure and a seer, he wielded control over the jinns.

He had the skill to alter the magnitude of the breeze. Those who are recipients of Allah's blessings are bestowed with countless favors. Why would humanity plead to fellow humans when the creator answers genuine, open-hearted (dua) prayers?

Solomon had a run-in with ants, the minuscule creatures. Upon arriving at the valley of ants, an ant cautioned its comrades to retreat to their dwellings. The group of ants stated that we will be overcome by Solomon's formidable army. He conversed in the language of all creatures, including animals and jinns. A smile emerged on Solomon's countenance.

Quran: Surah Naml 27:18. Until, when they came upon the valley of the ants, an ant said, "O ants, enter your dwellings so that Solomon will not crush you."

He instructed his army to shift to the side. Allah's divine power granted him unparalleled command of language. In this society that has wholeheartedly embraced modernization. Scientists have dedicated decades to the study of ants and discovered their communication abilities and shared traits with humans. The Quran was the first to reveal that they communicate, have colonies, and possess provisions similar to human life. Frequently, they fall short of conforming to the foretold narratives of past scriptures.

Bible: Problem: First Kings 11:3 says Solomon had 700 wives and 300 concubines.

The Quran does not discuss large numbers of marriages of Solomon like the Bible does. There is no advantage to marrying 700 wives. Allah has demonstrated his power through Prophets for the benefit of humanity. Similarly, killing one person for another does not bring any benefit to the one who was killed. Therefore, Islam emphasizes examples that benefit humanity. All the stories in the Quran hold immense significance in serving as examples for learning at any stage of life.

These implication stories create a disparity with the teachings of the Quran since Prophets are meant to serve as role models, and contaminated stories offer no advantages. The stories of the Islamic faith are readily comprehensible to all individuals owing to their straightforwardness. The concept of a human having 700 wives is unimaginable.To genuinely believe, comprehension is necessary to apprehend the supremacy of faith. The stories of Prophets in the Quran stand apart due to their unadulterated nature, unlike other religious texts.

Quran: Surah Naml 27:20 Solomon inspected the birds and said: "Why do I not see the hoopoe? Is he among the absentees?

Quran: Surah Naml 27:20 Solomon inspected the birds and said: Why do I not see the hoopoe? Is he among the absentees?

Quran: Surah Naml 27:21 I will surely punish him with a severe punishment. Unless he brings me clear authorization.

In the course of Solomon's existence, his animals and avian companions roamed without restraint, possessing the innate knowledge of when to return to their abodes. In contrast to contemporary zoos, they refrained from confining the animals in cages. It was Solomon's routine to instruct animals to stay in their habitat for the duration of the night. His gift of comprehending animals' language enabled him to communicate with and exert control over them. As the sun descended, they made their way back home.

In the fading light of evening, Solomon conducted a meticulous count of his animals and discerned the absence of Hoopoe. As a ruler characterized by discipline and Prophetic foresight. He did not discern between creatures and beasts. In order to obey Allah's rules, he had to adhere to regulations. As a consequence, he enforced discipline on the bird.

Hoopoe elaborated on her absence and tardiness, attributing it to her journey to a distant land. She informed Solomon that she had witnessed a woman of great influence engaged in prayer to someone other than Allah. The Queen of Sheba was extended an invitation from Solomon via the bird Hoopoe. He did not administer punishment to her. Hoopoe the bird had furnished him with invaluable information.

The bird Hoopoe returned, bearing an invitation from Soloman to the Queen of Sheba. The invitation was to visit Solomon's palace in the name of Allah. She graciously accepted the invitation. She sought advice from her superiors. They informed her that the burden of responsibility for this matter lay upon her. Given that this was her inaugural independent decision, she was uncertain of what course of action to take. Humans cannot meddle with the affairs of Allah.

Quran: Surah Naml 27;22. But the hoopoe stayed not long and said, "I have encompassed [in knowledge] that which you have not encompassed, and I have come to you from Sheba with certain news.

Quran: Surah Naml 27:38. Solomon asked his people, "Who among you can bring her throne before (she, the queen of Sheba) comes to me submissively?"

Upon graciously accepting his invitation, he was bestowed with lavish gifts from the Queen of Sheba. Gift giving is seen as an expression of friendship and gratitude by Muslims and the departed Prophets. The act of bestowing and exchanging cultivates friendships. This practice persists among Muslims even in contemporary society, where showering with gifts is a customary tradition. No one has ever declined a gift, as it symbolizes friendship and warmth, and he was delighted to accept her gifts and her acceptance of his invitation.

He deeply moved the heart of a woman who ruled and sought solace from anyone except Allah. Allah was beckoning her to embrace his faith through the Prophet Solomon.He will provide you with opportunities to practice righteousness within his faith. In Islam, color, race, or stature holds no importance, regardless of being a king, Queen, Prophet, or Peasant. Islam embodies status, rather than an individual. Serving Allah with unwavering devotion.

Upon reaching her destination, the Queen of Sheba was engulfed with emotions as she traveled to meet him, as the invitation was specifically sent by him. Upon laying eyes on his palace, she was captivated by its enchanting beauty. He exhibited a demeanor of kindness towards her and experienced great joy upon her acceptance of his invitation. The narrative was on the verge of commencing. Regardless of one's material wealth, believers are deeply influenced by love stories, but nothing compares to the significance of faith.

The meeting with Solomon instilled in her the notion that his God wielded greater power than pagan ideologies. Her eyes expanded in surprise as she beheld her throne adorned in an altered fashion. Her confidence fluctuated. She was unsure of whether the throne belonged to her. Ifrit, the supernatural being, the Jinn delivered Solomon her throne. He possessed the capacity to soar at a velocity surpassing that of light. Solomon exerted control over animals, wind, and jinns. He had a mastery of their language.

Solonom resided in a glass house atop water, an enchanting sight where he could observe fish and indulge his passion for animals. These creatures swam beneath the house, prompting her to lift her dress cautiously, overwhelmed with emotion. The mansion was constructed using glass slabs that were transparent. The glass flooring offered a vantage point to observe the aquatic creatures in motion. Solomon provided her with reassurance that she would remain dry as she observed the fish and lifted the dress that was long.

The palace he possessed was truly breathtaking. He conveyed to her that Allah had bestowed upon him a multitude of blessings. His fate was predestined by Allah. Life and the blessings bestowed by Allah were intended for him to distribute. Islam was the most profound gift she was bestowed. She accepted Islam with Solomon and became a believer.He asked for her hand in marriage and she agreed. She was a faithful adherent, affirming her belief in his God and embracing his monotheistic faith, which serves as the fundamental principle of Islam. The Quran contains the narrative of this story.Solomon conferred upon her a new name as a committed believer. Prior to embracing Islam, she was referred to as Makeda. Bilquis became her new moniker.

The absence of understanding hinders one's capacity to transcend the binary opposition and embrace faith. The most significant aspects of life are one's name and faith. It was a predestined revolution of companionship by Allah for her. The aim was to demonstrate a woman's relinquishment to the supremacy of Allah, as she embraced the faith of Solomon and modified her name. With his companionship. She was prepared to undergo any alteration to revolutionize her faith, demeanor, and belief in Allah. Desiring assistance, she longed to communicate the magnificence of understanding that the blessings of Allah are not only solitary, but rather a divine gift.

Islam entails surrendering to the divine will of Allah. Each Prophet sent by Allah received the identical message and submission. Islam is a divine mercy bestowed by the Creator, containing explicit narratives in the Quran for those who grasp its significance. The Sabians originate from Sheba. She held the title of a princess, famously referred to as the Queen of Sheba. Princesses and princes, like the peasant, are bound by their servitude to Allah.

The core of Islam is the act of submitting to the will of Allah. The message and submission bestowed upon each Prophet sent by Allah were indistinguishable. Islam, bestowed by the Creator as a form of mercy, presents explicit narratives in the Quran for those who grasp its significance. Sabians trace their roots back to Sheba.She was referred to as the Queen of Sheba, she initially held the title of princess. Similar to commoners, princesses and princes have the ability to transform, as they are all subservient to Allah, which includes the Prophets.

By the permission of Allah, faith has the power to elevate one's social status, as exemplified in this narrative. Bilquis held not only the title of a queen, but also the title of a believer and was married to a Prophet.It reinforces the notion of equality under Allah's boundless mercy. Through their prayers to Allah, they both discovered happiness in their shared life. She maintained steadfast beliefs. Despite her abundant wealth, she reciprocates the peace bestowed upon her as a believer, aligning with her newfound faith. In Islam, adherents believe that material wealth holds little significance and can be attained in conjunction with spiritual fulfillment. She was a woman of unwavering beliefs.

Quran: Surah Naml 27:44 She said, "My Lord! Surely I have been unjust to myself. I submit with Suleiman to Allah, the Lord of the worlds."

Solomon 's gifts were exclusively granted to him by Allah, unattainable by any other Prophet or individuals. He possessed unwavering faith and was confident that Allah would grant his requests. Just as gifts and miracles bestowed by Allah cannot be transferred to a human, animal, or jinn. The same logic and paradox of simplicity are not hard to understand. Sins cannot be passed from one person to another. The logic of Islam remains steadfast. Islam symbolizes the victory of the ultimate creator and the concluding proclamation of the Quran.

Any form of faith that emerges not subsequent to the Quran's final declaration is deemed unacceptable by Muslims. There is no Prophet other than Prophet Muhammad, who is regarded as the final Prophet. Solomon's miracles were intricately detailed. The pattern of Allah remains consistent in every aspect. This is exclusive only to those chosen by God. The sole unvarying proclamation each Prophet reaffirmed was a belief structure and subservient devotion to a singular Allah that remained unchanged.

Solomon had an intense ardor for horses as they utterly entranced his admiration. Solomon neglected his prayer while amusing himself with the horse, instructing his servants to bring the horse to him as he tenderly caressed it.He beseeched Allah to refrain from granting him anything that would divert him from his devotions, such was his immeasurable faith.

The breed of horses with the highest superiority ran at greater speed, but Allah granted him control of the wind, which made their journeys faster. Solomon had the ability to control the wind by Allah's consent. It was one of the presents he received. It is regrettable that the Bible portrays Soloman in a disparate manner compared to the Quran. In the Quran, Solomon is portrayed as a sagacious and equitable leader who perpetually maintained his modesty. He utilized his talents to serve Allah and his community.

Conversely, the Bible presents a contrasting image of him, depicting him as an egocentric king. The discrepancy in Solomon's representations underscores the discrepancy in ideologies. It functions as a reminder that both faiths have separate understandings of the same stories, which can vary significantly.

Bible: King James Version:11: But king Solomon loved many strange women, together with the daughter of Pharaoh, women of the Moabites, Ammonites, Edomites, Zidonians, and Hittites:

Isn't it due to this reason that these corroded ideologies promote independence by disguising it as love? If God dispatches Prophets with deception, what is the moral? However, the Quran does not have any affiliations with Prophets who should be disgraced, as seen in the Bible. This exemplifies hypocrisy, advocating one thing while engaging in contradictory behavior.

The lesson is that our deeds carry more weight than our speech. In contrast, Islam instructs that Prophets deserve respect and obedience. Prophets were chosen as paragons of compliance to Allah amidst challenges, not deception. While the Bible portrays Solomon as immoral, the Quran offers an alternative depiction of him.

This illustrates the strength of faith and its capability to transcend human rationality. It is also a reminder that our words and actions should be congruent. Aim to embody the principles we espouse. These differences are so extreme that it's implausible for a man to possess 700 wives in addition to concubines, as stated in the Bible.

Making him a Prophet in the Bible has no benefit. The Quran is a logical study, not devoid of logic.Interpreting the differences in the Bible literally, cannot comprehend its authentic message.Living by the Quran's values after understanding its clear messages and examples becomes clear.

The Quran only shares beneficial commands, rules, and regulations. These commands, rules, or regulations are understandable to the common mind. Comprehending the deeds of those Prophets is unfathomable.

Quran: Surah Anbiya 21:81 and to Solomon we subjected the raging winds blowing by his command to the land we had showered with blessings. It is we who know everything.

Allah granted him power over Jinns. He comprehended bird and animal languages. He had legendary control over the wind. Allah gave Soloman exclusive rights to his gifts. He requested exclusive gifts to remain with him during and after his lifetime. Allah granted his wish.

Quran: Surah Saad 35;39 He prayed, "My Lord! Forgive me, and grant me an authority that will never be matched by anyone after me. You are indeed the Giver ˈof all bountiesˈ

The angel of death came to Solomon. Greeting his Lord was sufficient for him. He leaned on the pedestal. No one dared disturb him as an angel of death seized his soul. He stood motionless. Some questioned his worthiness of veneration.

Some believed he served his Lord. The Quran doesn't mention his duration of standing. Jinn persisted in working. The unknown is known only by Allah. Few suspected the use of magic to remain motionless. He abstained from eating and drinking. His death went unnoticed. He obeyed Allah's command as insects devoured his staff. This is how people learned he was dead; such is Allah's beauty. Solomon (Suleiman) fell to the ground as they ate the staff from the bottom, and the kingdom shouted he had died

Quran: Surah Saba 34;14 When we executed our decree of death on Solomon, nothing showed to the jinn that he was dead except a worm eating away his staff.

Because of its organized structure, the Palace... The Jinn couldn't comprehend what lay beyond a realm. They wouldn't have accepted continuous chastisement and tedious work. Solomon's kingdom enforced laws rigorously. Violations faced severe punishment due to strict law enforcement. Solomon's rule encouraged diligence and productivity. This helped him build a successful empire. He left behind admirable qualities as a king and a Prophet. The animals in his kingdom lived happily in the palace with him.

His devotion to Allah tells a story of a princess converting to King Solomon's faith.Despite their combined wealth, they still prioritized the worship of Allah. They experienced greater bliss worshiping Allah together and thanked Allah for their surroundings. His efforts and blessings from Allah improved his devotion, never neglecting it. Faith provided him with everything he owned, enduring the test of time and leaving a story for all to read. He converted and married a queen, and his empire thrived with the power of faith and Allah's gifts. Faith + daily effort = limitless possibilities.

Story of Jonah:

The Prophets surely experience frustration due to disobedient people. Constantly reminding them with no results can be exasperating for any human. Only Allah can perceive the repetition of good and evil behavior and foresee the consequences. Humans are unsure how to react when faced with someone who never listens or responds in kind, but relentlessly Prophets are compelled to continue delivering the message.

Jonah (Yunus) acted without thinking about the consequences of leaving his assignment without Allah's permission. He neglected to think. Despite his human instincts, he failed to remember his Prophetic duty.

Nonetheless, Jonah decided to walk away from the situation that brought him no success, regardless of his repeated efforts to aid the disobedient. Despite continuous warnings, they persisted in their evil ways, and no matter how much he informed them about the mercy of Allah, nothing was fruitful. He felt sad and hopeless, unable to change the situation. Finally, he made a sudden, unplanned decision after losing hope.

Jonah did not intentionally disobey Allah by leaving without permission. He reached a breaking point and couldn't continue. Allah appointed him for a job. Allah's duties are a gift, not a calamity. The people of Nineveh are engaging in wickedness at the start of the story. Allah selected Jonah to convey the principles of change and the worship of God. Despite his efforts, they refused. There was a dark storm about to take place, the clouds were dark, and Jonah took leave of his people.

When the weather was stormy, he courageously embarked on a ship filled with unfamiliar faces, and together they sailed away as the sea unpredictably shifted its course. Jonah, along with the other people on the ship, shared the same experience. Due to their knowledge of the pagan roots and their strong belief in superstition, they found themselves filled with terror. The ship's fair weather was believed to have been compromised as a result of the presence of an unknown individual on board.

Jonah boarded a ship amidst a growing storm, the violent wind shaking the ship's magnitude. Initially, they believed that the ship's weight was causing it to pitch and sway due to heavy luggage. Hoping the ship would stabilize, they decided to throw the luggage into the ocean.

There was no shift in their direction. In their frustration, they turned to Jonah the Prophet and opted to draw names to determine the outcome. Prophet Jonah was chosen, and they quickly recognized him, causing them to throw him into the water. They lifted him and tossed him into the ocean.In the cold depths of the ocean, he fought against the harsh, violent waves. He shouted and prayed to Allah for assistance.Jonah was swallowed alive by a fish sent by Allah.

In this unexpected turn of events, he found himself spending three days and three nights inside the fish's stomach, an unfamiliar environment that filled him with terror but also became his temporary shelter. Amidst the turbulent waters, he raised his voice in a shout and fought against the fish's movements as it carried him within its belly.The unexpected force caused him to move vigorously from side to side.

Allah is capable of handling any challenge, and no miracle is too difficult for Him. There is nothing that Allah cannot handle; His power is limitless. While some people are able to endure the harshest conditions with his assistance, others sadly perish without anyone noticing. Jonah, who had an unfinished task, still had to complete it.

Despite facing a new challenge, he yearned to be with those who had ignored him, yet his determination was consumed by overwhelming despair. He lamented to his maker about regretting his departure from his people. Despite his genuine cries, Allah's mercy exceeded his request. If Jonah hadn't begged for repentance, he would have remained in the stomach of the fish. The merciful Lord forgave him. Jesus gave the reference to Jonah.

Quran: Surah Anbiya 21:87 He cried through the depths of darkness (saying): "there There is no God, but you glorified be you! Truly, I have been the wrongdoer.

When faced with challenging circumstances, a significant number of individuals who practice Islam often find solace in reciting the prayer of Jonah as mentioned in the Arabic Quran. Deep within the belly, shrouded in darkness, Jonah fervently offered his prayers. Filled with fear, he repented and earnestly sought forgiveness and mercy from his Lord.

From within the stomach of the fish, he cried out in anguish in the dark depths of the sea. After being swallowed by the Fish, Jonah miraculously emerged alive, shivering from the cold and his body covered in scales. The evidence of the creator's mercy is undeniable. The execution of his plan can involve the utilization of a range of objects, including plants, fish, people, or any other thing.

Quran: Surah Saffat 143:144 "Had he not been of them who glorify Allah, he would have indeed remained inside its belly (the fish) till the day of resurrection."

Many people expressed their sadness at having missed Jonah when he left. It is truly remarkable how impossible it is for us to forget the person who not only guides us and helps us find our path, but also leaves an indelible mark on our subconscious mind, demonstrating humanity towards one another and spreading the word of Allah. Unable to resist, they made a conscious decision to alter their behavior, hoping that one day Jonah would be informed of their transformation and decide to return.

By acknowledging and appreciating the presence of the person who guides us, we can ensure that we don't miss their valuable influence in our lives. By expressing our gratitude to Allah for sending guidance and support, we acknowledge and appreciate the profound influence they have on our individual development and overall happiness. Actively listening to and internalizing the advice and teachings they provide is crucial, as it allows us to incorporate and embed them deep within our subconscious mind.

Despite facing his own trials and going through experiences of disobedience and repentance, he didn't hesitate to make his way to the people of Nineveh as soon as he regained his strength. The immeasurable joy he experienced upon sighting his people whom he had left behind was indescribable. It is truly a remarkable feeling to see someone you have shared the word of Allah with undergo such a profound transformation. The meaningful exchange between the two of them brought explicit joy to both of their hearts.

Having reformed and changed their ways, the people were longing for him. The timing and plans that Allah has are known only to Him. The primary focus of this story is to highlight the significance of belief, perseverance, and repentance.

Given that Jesus drew a parallel between his time on earth and Jonah's time in the sea, it is natural to question why the people of Nineveh did not worship Jonah as a deity, considering they recognized him as a Prophet and were unaware of his fate inside the fish. It is highly unlikely that an ordinary person would be able to survive inside the stomach of a fish and still maintain their life.

Just as Jonah's mission unfolded and he eventually returned to his people, it is believed that Jesus will also return to deliver the truth about the events of this life. This truth emphasizes that neither Jonah nor Jesus should be worshiped, as they are both messengers and mortal beings. While these distinctions are present, it is important to note that people have the liberty to worship whomever they desire.

When faced with challenges, believers often achieve outcomes that exceed their expectations. Despite his faith, Jonah lacked patience. The paradoxes of man can yield unforeseen outcomes, contingent on the strength of one's faith in Allah. Angry disbelievers lash out, while remorseful believers apologize. Such is the fate of a believer. Enduring life's trials and demands leads to a happy and prosperous life.

The principle works both ways - just as sweetness and genuineness are met with kindness, evil is also met with evil. Overwhelmed and filled with gratitude to Allah, upon his return, the disbelievers transformed into believers, and he cried tears of joy and continuous repentance to Allah. Allah, in his infinite wisdom, chooses to guide those whom he wishes to his (deen). He has complete control over every single event that takes place. City dwellers may have the illusion of control, but in reality, they are powerless. The ultimate authority and power lies solely in the hands of Allah.

Humanity is nothing without Allah's will. If it is Allah's will, faith can fulfill desires. Sadness can arise from a heavy heart. Hope is found in a light heart. While trapped in the fish's belly, Jonah gives us hope. Through prayer, he shows us light and hope in darkness where there seems to be none. To progress positively, avoid reciprocating evil deeds as negativity cannot lead to positivity.

In a believer's home, there is a different passion and peace than in a disbelever's home. The reason is that glitter is less tangible compared to bliss or living space. The mansion is where faith is strong, the mansion is the heart of a believer and passion for belief is stronger than any worldly pursuit. Belief remains with humans while the world is temporary

Additionally, it is crucial to mention that the miracles performed by the Prophets were consistently witnessed by the people of that era; however, these stories continue to be relevant and resonate in contemporary times. It is essential to acknowledge that no miracle is beyond the capabilities of Allah, thereby implying that attributing divinity to his messengers would cast doubt upon the authenticity of their miracles and transfer divine power to the human beings chosen as messengers.

Given the vastness of historical records, it would be possible for the human mind to fully comprehend. The reason why Allah proclaimed the Quran as a living miracle is because the Prophets have passed away and Islam, along with any faith referring to themselves as an Abrahamic faith, does not worship any deities. While the distinctions are clear, it is the responsibility of the human will to choose the path that is destined, and it is essential to recognize that Islam is not for everyone.

Explanations serve as a means to provide clarity to those who seek answers and encounter uncertainties while delving into the nuances and differences found within the Abrahamic faiths.

Quran: Surah Naziat 79:30."Take on only as much as you can do of good deeds, for the best of deeds is that which is done consistently, even if it is little."

In order to display a contrast of daily life, encounters are important.Think of this tablet as a person who dances for exercise and to maintain their physique, not in nightclubs. The vigorous workouts in intense aerobics can be compared to other aerobic exercises in terms of their impact on the physique.

In today's society, the act of dancing in exercise is often frowned upon, as it is seen as a provocative and potentially harmful activity in dance clubs. The association of dance with sexual mixing and arousal has led to the belief that these comparisons are crucial in understanding its impact on our society. The purpose of using it in life is primarily for individuals who aim to enhance their overall health and aerobic fitness, rather than for the purpose of sexual arousal.

The influence of movements on humans can differ significantly, just as faith can shape the monotone voice that individuals seek in their quest for soulful inspiration. Through the use of illustrations and comparisons, the examples briefly pique the reader's interest by showcasing the societal emphasis on physical attractiveness and less attention to spiritual advancement.

The act of dancing within a society to exercise only in gyms or classes only suited for aerobics can be likened to possessing faith even in the absence of complete understanding. The act of having faith without comprehension can be likened to dancing in a club rather than harnessing it for personal physical betterment. Dance is widely recognized and acknowledged as an effective preventive health measure, as it seamlessly integrates aerobic exercise into daily routines.

The brain releases dopamine, which acts as a natural mood enhancer, and endorphins, which serve as natural pain relievers. Despite the fact that prayer and dance are distinct activities, they share common characteristics such as the need for stationary positions and balance. These similarities can contribute to the learning process by promoting repetition and improvement.The workout begins with stretching and synchronizes the body's rhythms to the beat, adapting to the heart's palpitations. By incorporating intense stretching exercises into your daily workout routine, you will be able to achieve the pinnacle of physical fitness and overall well-being. Those individuals who are involved in weightlifting or individuals who work towards achieving a sculpted physique experience a similar outcome, beginning and concluding at the same point.

The importance of physical health is particularly significant for individuals who devote their lives to nurturing their bodies. Those who understand the demands of physical work recognize that it requires intensity, dedication, and time. However, it is equally important to prioritize spiritual well-being. Many people incorporate practices such as meditation and yoga into their routine to seek internal peace while also focusing on their physical health. By engaging in the constant movements of Salat, which serve as repetitions of peace and devotion to Allah, Islam promotes a balanced and disciplined life, fostering alignment in both physical and mental aspects. Furthermore, it encourages individuals to make continuous efforts towards improving their body, mind, and spirit alignment.

The importance of wholeness in completing a person can be grasped by examining various examples that life offers.To fully grasp the intricacies of Islam, one must undertake a comparative study and thoroughly examine the Abrahamic faiths, all of which share the belief in monotheism.

Regardless of one's faith, achieving tranquility can have a profound impact on everyday life, as it can turn the lows into the highs.

Those individuals who have experienced the highs of life have, without a doubt, also experienced the lows. The steady pursuit and integration of spiritual and physical growth are essential. To maintain a balance, it is necessary to pay attention to both aspects. It's not just about the physical aspect of burning calories, but also about achieving a harmonious equilibrium that suits your individual needs. The promotion of continuous progress is a fundamental aspect of Islam.

When it comes to certain individuals, gyms are considered the optimal environments for both physical strength building and confidence boosting. There are numerous aspects to working out, however, the ethic of (Salat) ritual prayer stands out as a unique practice that requires consistency every day without any breaks, and it entails attending at various intervals five times a day.

By maintaining this daily discipline, one can achieve balance in all aspects of life. It's important to note that the church, mosque, or temple of humans is not a physical structure, but rather a spiritual concept. The pursuit of truth and the endeavor to bring meaning to the human soul can be likened to a gymnasium that exercises and strengthens the heart. Similar to how the body needs physical exercise, the soul also craves spiritual nourishment.

Muslims find solace in performing (Salat),ritual prayer as it serves as a source of comfort for them, while those who are seeking knowledge can draw inspiration from countless examples. It is solely Allah who possesses the knowledge of what truly brings peace to one's heart, as He graciously communicates through (Salat)ritual prayer with those who diligently pursue the truth. Health and exercise contribute to physical, spiritual well-being and life balance.

Writing with genuine truth is preferable, while speaking with genuine heart is transcendent; the fear of expressing the truth is hypocritical and should be adequately punished. If there were penalties for deceit, manipulation would cease, but the world has become so accustomed to deception that the truth is seen as burdensome. Devoid of a predetermined structure, I communicate from the depths of my heart, as it is the sole avenue to touch your heart. The purpose of delivery is to facilitate unimpeded reading of the truth for those who comprehend.

There is indisputably a shared belief per Islam that souls coexisted 50,000 years prior to Allah's earthly creation of humanity. Each soul possessed innate knowledge of the truth and the creator, serving as a perpetual reminder for those who seek truth. Those who recall the truth will ultimately realize that falsehoods offer no solace, whereas truth can unlock unforeseen triumphs. Balance is a place of serenity, a tranquil haven that provides an atmosphere conducive to finding peace for both the body and the soul, nurturing the tranquility of one's heart.The key to achieving the best and most effective deeds lies in consistency.

CHAPTER 19

UNCOVER TRUTH BY REVISITING THE PAST.

Stories from the past have an impact, but the Quran is timeless.

Throughout history, humanity has placed its trust and reliance on Allah. Learning is subjective because it is perceived differently by different individuals. Truth, in its various forms, can often manifest in abstract ways across different genres such as science fiction, drama, comedy, tragedy, or even in the form of rewritten scripts. The Quran, being an all-encompassing and independent source of knowledge, covers a wide range of subjects and stands alone as a comprehensive source of wisdom.

Truth seekers will see perfect alignment. Motion is more beneficial than stillness. Observing silently helps one learn from the conversation, ignoring skeptics. Excessive silence does not encourage learning. Provisions are granted to seekers by Allah. The Almighty does not weigh down humans. The Quran offers guidance through examples, prophets, and dignitaries.

Arrogance and self-sabotage are the principal causes of stagnation. Insubordination towards Allah is highly dissatisfying. It's possible to give treasures to someone who doesn't value or accept them. Despite the echoing narrative, he remains clueless about its meaning. Piety in Islam is a divine blessing that covers both spiritual and material prosperity.

Engaging in the act of prostration, also known as "Sujood", has the potential to contribute to the accumulation of inner peace and even wealth. The gift of recognition is something that cannot be measured and holds immense value. When hunger is not acknowledged, it can lead to a decrease in appetite. The appetite, which used to be satisfied, no longer has any concerns. A clear demonstration of arrogance and ingratitude is when someone ignores the hunger that accompanies contentment. It is of utmost importance to recognize the mercy and blessings of Allah. The outcome varies greatly for different individuals; some are able to make a strong comeback, while others, consumed by their losses and lacking faith, have a sorrowful exit.

It is essential to keep in mind the importance of gratitude and appreciation for gifts. Blessings and talents are present, and improving oneself and sharing benefits with those nearby or distanced. Humans hold onto this format, regardless of the situation. Thriving on self-confidence. Those self-reliant don't rely on others. Arrogance is not welcomed in Islam, but evil leads to self-destructive behavior.

Humans do not possess the ability to create themselves, determine the course of their own mortality, or control the intricacies of life and death, as these matters rest solely in the hands of Allah. The undeniable necessity for oxygen in order to breathe, which humans cannot survive without, serves as a clear indication of their perpetual reliance and inability to be entirely free from needs.

Allah does not rely on anything or anyone as He is self-sufficient. The focus of human deeds serves as a constant reminder that life is not guaranteed, and those who have the opportunity to experience it must understand the importance of cherishing every moment, as it can be taken away at any time. The focus of both words and actions has a significant impact on human survival and character, and it is worth noting that the word "Bismillah" holds great importance. The word symbolizes the beginning, and for Muslims, "Bismillah" represents a positive start.

The Quran opens each surah with "bismillah hir rahman nir Rahim," in the name of God most gracious and merciful except for (Surah Taubah). Reconciling the conflict between good and evil brings rewards. Comparisons in religious texts highlight wisdom and discernment. Being vigilant is crucial for success and distinguishing between the righteous and the wicked. Ultimately, God is the judge.

Satan used to prostrate to Allah, arrogance surpassed his humility. His story serves as an example for those who draw lessons from the past and apply them to the present.

Quran: Surah Araf: 7:12. Allah asked, what prevented you from prostrating when I commanded you? He replied I am better than he is. You created me from fire and him from clay.

Quran: Surah Araf: 7:13. Allah said, Then get down from Paradise. It is not for you to be arrogant here. So leave. You are truly one of the ones disgraced.

Quran: Surah Araf; 7:14.He appealed then delayed my end until the day of resurrection.

Quran: Surah Araf: 7:15. Allah said you are delayed until the appointed day. The mercy of Allah is comprehensible. He still allows the arrogant to walk on his earth.

Humility and greetings have played a crucial role in history. Greeting a guest is crucial in every culture. Displaying humility and tenderness when hosting a guest shows piety. Non-compliers are strongly influenced by the evil army. Satan refused to welcome his guests with humility and kindness, opting for evil and deceit.Hatred and envy replaced gratitude for the guest. Witnessing non-angelic individuals entering heaven's door. He displayed anger. Chaos was his intention, but he got upset when two humans Allah created entered his pavilion. The ignorant are part of his evil, weak army.

Allah warned Satan due to his chaotic actions. His challenge is balancing disorder and non-peace. He and his people are weak adversaries of believers. He received respite on earth as a mercy from his creator. Without Allah's respite, humans wouldn't have an enemy; they have the capacity to differentiate between right and wrong. This demonstrates the importance of hospitality as a virtue in most cultures. Satan declined to greet his guests more warmly.

The internal amplifier can be a form of perception, similar to how "Salat" can become a habit. Attendees who are sublime and attentive are desired. In some cases, the motion carries on even without concentration. The attendee's heart is observed by Allah. Continuous efforts make achieving life balance possible.

Human understanding cannot grasp the mercy of Allah. The word "Bismillah" brings happiness. Exterminate malevolence and engagement. Allah is the ontological source of a servant's existence. Similarly, disobedience is displayed by someone who turns away. Islamic rules are not forced on Muslims. Paybacks cannot be negotiated, regardless of how the rules are applied. They will serve according to Allah "Ar Rahman's" justice. The most compassionate.

"Bismillah" marks the start of a Muslim's journey. At the beginning of each day, upon waking up, getting dressed, eating, traveling, studying, working, and praying, we recite the word. The importance of this world is endless, as is the beginning and the end of it. Sometimes, Muslims recite it countless times repetitively.

A tale about a woman who recognized the strength of "Bismillah":

In the early days of Islam, a Muslim woman worked for the Jewish community. Her favorite phrase was "Bismillah". Hearing "Bismillah" in Allah's name all day is not what they intended to hear. As a result, they orchestrated her release.

It was reported to her that a ring had gone missing. The ring she had never seen led to her indirect accusation and blame. In her panic, the woman repeatedly said "Bismillah", trusting Allah to protect her. Her employers conspired against her and disposed of the ring in the ocean. While searching everywhere and saying "bismillah," she never gave up.

They requested that she vacate the premises. She believed they no longer wanted her services due to their allegations against her. Once more, she uttered "Bismillah". Sadness welled up in her eyes because stealing went against her nature. The purity of the heart is often misunderstood, leading to cruelty from humans. Humans can make decisions without understanding their own chaotic patterns.

They were convinced she wouldn't locate it. Allah's mercy knows no bounds. They hoped that the ring, which would eliminate her, would remain undiscovered. She said, "Please let me prepare a meal for you before I leave".

She had a strong desire to ensure that they had enough food and did not go hungry. The men granted her permission to prepare and cook the meal. While tears were flowing down her face, she pleaded and cried out to Allah, desperately seeking to protect her honor, as she swore with utmost sincerity that she had never taken the ring. Her utterances of "Bismillah" persisted without interruption. After successfully apprehending the fish, they presented it to her with the intention of her preparing a meal with it. With a powerful shout of "Bismillah," she skillfully opened up the fish, revealing the precious ring that had been concealed inside. The power of "Bismillah" astonished the men.

By the permission of Allah, a fish was able to swallow the ring that had been caught by the men. The accusation quickly turned into remorse as they shared looks of dismay and distress, and invoked the power of "Bismillah".They quickly accepted Islam ". There is no worry or happiness that is too insignificant. Any action or endeavor that begins with the phrase "Bismillah" is inherently positive. Anything that starts with "Bismillah" is destined for success. If it is, it will happen by God's design. (Insha Allah)

Muslims commonly use the phrase "Insha Allah" in their conversations. The phrase "if Allah wills it" is frequently used by Muslims when discussing events that are yet to happen or are uncertain. When asked about their availability, Muslims often respond with "Insha Allah" after discussing an upcoming event. There have been jokes circulating among comedians who have humorously suggested that it might be best not to seek the opinions of Muslims when it comes to important events. "Insha Allah", God willing he will respond.

The reason Muslims use the phrase 'InshaAllah' is because they believe that everything is in Allah's control and will, so they say it to acknowledge that their plans are subject to Allah's decree.

The presence of InshaAllah in a Muslim's life can determine if a meeting will undergo any changes. Since the unseen is solely determined and attributed by Allah, it renders tomorrow's events unpredictable for us humans. The phrase "Insha Allah" holds great importance for Muslims and is frequently emphasized. Muslims are known for their diligent work ethic, yet they understand that ultimately, it is Allah who has the final say.

Quran: Surah Kahf 18:23 *And never say anything like: I will certainly do this tomorrow.*

Quran: Surah Anfal: 8:28 Know that your wealth and your children are only a test and with Allah is a great reward. Your worldly possessions and your children are only a test and temptations, tremendous reward is with Allah.

Bible Psalms: 127;3. Children are a blessing and a gift from the Lord.

Muslims often use the phrase "Masha Allah" as a way to express their admiration towards something that is considered precious, beautiful, and kind. This act symbolizes our appreciation for the beauty and abundance bestowed upon us by Allah. "Masha Allah" serves not only as an expression of praise to God, but it is also utilized to recognize and celebrate achievements.

The story of the garden's demise is found in Surah Kahf. He had nothing left in his possession. Overwhelmed with tears and unexpected turmoil, he sincerely conveyed his heartfelt apologies to Allah for the regrettable oversight of neglecting to recite Masha Allah, acknowledging that pride had overshadowed his gratitude. The small words used in Arabic carry immense significance and have a great impact. The origin of all goodness can be attributed to Allah. Despite putting forth their utmost efforts, humans are completely incapable of matching the immense power possessed by Allah. The fleeting nature of pride and self-indulgence proves to be harmful. Loss is the consequence of pride, as it is only Allah who possesses the authority to grant and revoke.

Quran: Surah Kahf: 18:29.And why did you, when you entered your garden, not say, 'What Allah willed [has occurred]; there is no power except in Allah '?

According to the Quran, both children and wealth are seen as trials and examinations that we undergo in our journey on this earth. Every parent can attest to the fact that they have encountered various challenges, whether significant or trivial, and only they truly comprehend the profound extent of adversity.

No one who has experienced the same stages of life can truly compare the experiences and difficulties of another individual. Each and every individual, with a particular emphasis on parents, has to face their own set of unique challenges. If parents provide a home filled with bliss during their children's formative years, and if the children turn out better than expected upon exiting, then the parent can consider themselves victorious in the war of parenting. The ones who choose to disregard Allah find themselves defeated in the ongoing struggle against the formidable Satan, whereas those who consistently acknowledge their roots understand that the vitality of the foundation directly influences the overall growth and prosperity of the tree.

Over time, this expression has become increasingly unspoken and undervalued, as people struggle to grasp its true significance. Despite the hardships that humanity encounters, they demonstrate resilience and come out on top, attaining not just the predicted consequences but also some unforeseen ones. The inclusion of the beautiful words "Masha Allah, Alhamdulillah, and Insha Allah" in every episode serves as a powerful reminder to Muslims of the blessings and guidance that come with reciting these words.

The Bible views children as blessings, whereas the Quran considers them trials. The Quran makes sense to every parent who has raised children, children become trials for some parents and blessings for others. The Quran becomes clearer and more direct with simple logical explanations.

Children can be taught everything, but their decisions remain beyond control. Noah surely taught his child about Allah. He defied his father and Allah by following his mind. The child who brings joy is a blessing to both parent and child. The loss of faith after being taught is a test, not a benefit. Muslims aspire for tranquility, not tribulations. Allah has control over the rest.

Bible: Psalms: 123:3-5. Behold, children are a heritage from the Lord, the fruit of the womb a reward. Like arrows in the hand of a warrior are the children of one's youth. Blessed is the man who fills his quiver with them!

Bible gateway: Psalms 127:3.Children are a blessing and a gift from the Lord.

Quran: Surah Al Anfal: 8:28. And know that your wealth and your children are only a test and that with Allah is a great reward. and know that your worldly possessions and your children are only a test and a temptation and that there is a tremendous reward with God.

Understanding the Quran is the truth, a blessing from Allah. Raising children who constantly challenge their parents is a trial, not a blessing. The mother who enjoys raising her children also blesses her family and sets examples of worship. One parent follows Allah's laws, while the other does not. The home needs stability and understanding. The Bible sees wealth and children as blessings, while the Quran corrects this and views them as trials. However, by turning these trials into achievements, they can become blessings. Practicing with faith. Masha Allah is often said by Muslims when they see children raised with appreciation for others.

(Astaghfar) is the word that is repeated the most, surpassing all others. I beseech Allah for His forgiveness. Seeking forgiveness from Allah (Astaghfar) is a powerful way to tap into an abundant source of power. The profound significance of this word greatly influences an individual's decision-making process when it comes to distinguishing between good and evil, as well as their capacity to decline.

When Muslims come across news of evil succumbing misfortunes or when faced with trials that serve as a source of learning, they often utter the word "Astaghfar" as a way of seeking forgiveness and finding solace. This recitation is done on a constant basis. We implore Allah to bestow his forgiveness upon us.

Muslims engage in sustainable and beneficial repetitive practices, such as Astaghfar, which greatly contribute to their overall well-being.

Prophet Muhammad sought forgiveness from Allah by reciting Astaghfar frequently and standing for hours. Despite being the last messenger of Allah to humanity, he remained humble and obedient to Allah. Islam incorporated countless parables into the word Astaghfar.

Hasan Al Basri was visited by a man. To disclose to him the information about his hardships. He instructed him to seek forgiveness from Allah through prayer. He advised a person complaining about poverty to seek forgiveness from Allah. A man expressed his desire for a child but could not have one. He advised praying to Allah for forgiveness. (Astaghfar)

When a man mentioned his garden was in drought, he requested him to pray for forgiveness to Allah (Astaghfar). Abundant power lives in this word Astaghfar. The foundation of spirituality lies in accepting and forgiving Allah's creation and making efforts in life. Prophet Muhammad did not tell humans to do anything he didn't do. He sought forgiveness from Allah and recommended others to do the same.

In Islam, the Quran provides the basis for stories and examples, showcasing the prophets' actions as models to follow. Parables are filled with extraordinary stories that humans can learn from and understand. They are universally understood. Repeating small words in Arabic has a profound effect on the heart.

Prophet Muhammad's calling was to spread Islam as soon as Allah told him. For years, he prayed for truth in solitude, yearning for truth in an era of paganism. It was only the beginning of his adventure. Khadija was a believing woman who strengthened her own belief. She understood the revelations he was receiving were the answer to his daily worship seeking answers that already belonged to him. Were delivered when Allah saw fit. He had been prepared for the journey since birth. Prophet Muhammad was born into a noble Quraish family, but his trials were not associated with nobility. Since he was an infant, trials have worked together. His constant trial process ultimately led him to prophethood, so there is no mismatch between these endeavors.

He was the most ideal husband. They had a unit of happiness. When Allah is the principal source of bliss, life is unbelievably fulfilling. The world talks about Muhammad and Khadijah's love story. There is no more interesting love story than a couple who fall in love with Allah and their faith and share the same beliefs. Ultimately, such a story will outweigh all love stories, so this plantation proves succession, as Allah is the primary source.

The world is filled with countless love stories. I'll share a few narratives. The story revolves around Laila Majnu. The story originates from the Arabian Peninsula. They were separated because of circumstances and external sources. She felt an overpowering longing for him. The emptiness felt in love stories, like this one where separation defines the relationship and desire replaces love, stems from the realization that love often originates from self-desires, the beautiful connection one feels towards the other. True love is only experienced by those who love Allah together.

It is said that her cause of death was heart failure, he wrote poems on her grave. They desired a meeting to take place after her death. Majnu longed to meet her in the next life. In the aftermath of her passing, the two drifted apart, and their love story never prospered. There are various forms in which different types of stories exist. All of these stories, except for faith and integrity, are impossible to fully imagine in succession. The love story of Muhammad and Khadija is a narrative of success.

Romeo and Juliet's love story came to an end. When Romeo dies from poison, Juliet cannot survive without him and stabs herself. These love stories are not meant to be a guide for life. The increasing influence of humans has made these stories something to be feared. Suicide is deemed an unforgivable sin in Islam. According to Islamic beliefs, Satan, not God, influences this love. Although they may sound like tragedies, they are ultimately love stories. Allah's love and harmony enrich the true love story.

At the age of 14, the Mughal Emperor Shah Jehan fell in love with his bride. Shah Jehan commemorated his wife by building the Taj Mahal after she passed away while giving birth. This is one of the world's seven wonders. This world is filled with love stories. Tragedy is a common theme in these movies or stories, often evoking tears from women.

Love respect care faith all expounded in one was the strength of marriage most Muslims would love to have and experience. The marriage was lengthy and strong. It strengthened faith in the togetherness that could never break those who know the value the marriages strengthen they don't diminish.

The love story of Muhammad and Khadija set an example of worship, care, and love for men and women. This privilege belongs only to her. After twenty-five years of blissful union, she passed away, leaving dearly missed. She remained by his side throughout every life venture, and they believed nothing was impossible together since their marriage. After getting married, he became a prophet, and she had married an honest man who worked for her before marriage. However, she was the wife of a prophet when she passed away. She remained constant in her demeanor, being both his friend and his wife. What could a man desire beyond this? When marriage freedom is united by faith.

Unity of faith and kindness kept this love story going, regardless of any trials. When nobody believed in him, Khadija did. She knew him. The long-awaited prayer and desire for answers were fulfilled in prophethood. As their love for Allah grew, most prophets neglected their families. Prophet Muhammad gave attention to all aspects of his prophethood and family. He stated that marriage should be determined by lineage, beauty, wealth, and belief. Marry with faith in Allah as a last resort if the first three fail. According to the Quran, a believing slave is superior to a polytheist who distorts your faith.

Quran: Surah Baqarah: 2:221. Do not marry polytheistic women until they believe; for a believing slave-woman is better than a free polytheist, even though she may look pleasant to you. There was undeniable trust between them, reciprocated with deep faith which is the strongest bond between believers. A woman who believes in God is the strength of a household, just as a believing man is the source of wealth. Prophet Muhammad is an example of a Muslim.

The most notable women who will make it to heaven are Khadija, Khuwaylid's daughter, and Muhammad's daughter Fatima. The pharaoh's wife and Muzahim's daughter Asiya; and Mary, Imran's daughter. Islam has powerful women who serve as examples. Some Muslim women still show academic influence and keep faith alive as a source of strength. Excluding women who advocate for rights on social media through falsehoods for personal gain. Contrasting with today's new world, the demeanor of these women who left a legacy of success and peace offers hope for Muslim women. Having integrity, morals, and unwavering faith in Allah.

These societal ills are fueled by accepting greed. Muslims who embrace regressive modernization face the consequences of oppressive laws. In this recently established country, followers view social media news as family and spread false rhetoric as absolute truth. Without conversations, minds stagnate, and using technology as a companion hinders growth instead of fostering it.

Doubt fades as a believer encounters truth, feeling both trepidation and restlessness. This ceases to exist when the divine takes over. Those seeking solace find tranquility in surrendering past prophets, books, and Dhikr conversations to Allah. To enter the door, aligning yourself with believers, not disbelievers is peace restored. Joining the best company and searching for the truth. Only then can the believer find solace in the divine and experience truth. The start of a comeback comes from repentance and regret. Only Allah has control over the outcome. Despite its ancient origins, Islam remains an innovative and progressive faith.

The ongoing Middle East war has resulted in the displacement of many families from their homes. During Omar's rule in Israel, peace and friendships flourished between Jews, Muslims, and Christians. Eventually, their greed, alliances, and hope in Jesus drive them to organize help to the promised land in anticipation of Jesus coming to rescue them.

Quran: Surah Hajj: 22:39. Permission to fight back is hereby granted to those being fought, for they have been wronged.

Quran: Surah Hajj: 22:40. Those who were unjustly expelled from their homes for no other reason than their saying: " Allah is our Lord".

Quran: Surah Nisa. 4:75. And what is [the matter] with you that you fight not in the cause of Allah and [for] the oppressed among men, women,

KJB: Bible: Deuteronomy 20:1-4 - When thou goest out to battle against thine enemies, and seest horses, and chariots, and a people more than thou, be not afraid of them:

Evangelicals expect Armageddon, hoping for Jesus to save them. Treacherous times call for a different focus than rescuing souls. The ones who will be saved are the ones who know Allah for who he is, the owner of the two worlds, not his prophets; they are also his servants. Islam encourages active resistance against invaders.

The signs of the final hour can be divided into two groups.

1) Minor signs

are events of a normal nature prophesied by Prophet Muhammad to take place before (Qiyamah) doomsday. These events include alcohol consumption, knowledge lifting, prevalence of ignorance and immorality, and signs of this nature. Minor signs continue.

2) Major signs

All the events that the Prophet prophesied to take place before (Qiyamah) doomsday are major signs as outlined in Hadiths. The Prophet said, 'The last hour will not be until you have seen ten signs'.The first sign to man was the death of the Prophet Muhammad. Muslims were told to prepare for the creator's meeting before he left. Some of the major signs include. Coming of (Yajuj and Majuj) Gog and Magog Mehdi from the prophet's family descent of (Isa) Jesus son of Maryam. Sun will rise from the West. Arrival of the beast with a mark (Dajjal). Smoke landslides and fires will erupt. The pilgrimage of Muslims visiting Kabbah will not exist. The brief study is only the beginning of researching the Quran and Sunnah. A Muslim belief is a paradox for knowledge seekers to find a partner in search of Islam's truth.

Emerging as a progressive faith, Islam received its name as the last testament consistently delivered by the closure, signifying its significance. The teachings and traditions of Hadiths have consistently been a source of revival.Aisha, grieving the loss of her husband, embarked on a journey of authoring countless hadiths. In a meticulous effort, Hafsa took on the task of arranging all the verses of the Quran in their proper order. Following the passing of the prophet, Islam has continued to thrive and be revived throughout the passage of time. It has been continuously reminded and upheld as a legacy by his wives, the Muslims of those eras, and through the continuous delivery of reminders in every timeline by Muslims.

Prophet Muhammad gave Hafsa his wife the Quranic parchments and writings. She also acted as a guardian for safekeeping. In the aftermath of his passing, she bestowed them upon her father, Omar. The entire Quran was memorized by her. The first woman to become a hafiz of the Quran was Hafsa. The revelations ended with his passing.

She was recognized for her exceptional organizational skills and intelligence. Omar arranged them in order and burned those that were in any disorderly fashion. Omar transformed parchments into a book by compiling the Quran. The Quran was organized based on the order of revelations received. As her husband, he entrusted them to her, she kept them intact. The Quran contains no versions or authors, just one book sent by Allah, read in the same order worldwide in the Islamic world.

Humanity used to write on leaves before progressing to paper books, and computers and technology keep improving, but the Quran will remain the same. It can withstand any change in time since Allah created time. Technology will change but the Quran will not change.

Spoken words cannot be retracted, while written words remain unaltered. The chapter of the Quran has concluded. Those who surrender to Allah will find that their decisions and choices shape their lives, reflecting the purity in their hearts. Islam's foundation rests on moral values and principles that transcend the physical world. It highlights the spiritual bond shared by committed individuals. This kind of commitment holds more value and lasts longer compared to one solely based on physical attraction or societal approval. This is valid in a world that changes at lightning speed.

In a society where having one wife is burdensome, particularly in Western society, how can a man have four wives? Muslims must be mindful of the restrictions that come with permissibility in Islam. Rather than engaging in extravagance or passing down the heirloom, they made this decision for multiple reasons.

Zina is the term for illicit sexual intercourse between a man and a woman. Sex outside of marriage is considered zina. In Islam, fornication refers to a man entering a woman's privacy. Defying Allah persistently by performing this event illicitly leads to unease and discontentment.The unions of married couples after holy matrimony sexual acts become permissible. Acts in accordance with Allah's laws bring bliss and contentment.

A rapist's proposal of marriage to an unwilling woman is supported by the Bible. Sexual violence and outdated attitudes towards women are examples of harmful attitudes. It is contested in any period, especially today, whether the Bible provides moral guidance regarding women's rights.

Bible: New king James Version: Deuteronomy: 22:29 the man who lay with her shall give the young woman's father fifty silver shekels and she will be his wife because he has violated her. He may not divorce her as long as he lives.

In Islam, the concept of justice is central to its teachings. However, the scenario of marrying a rapist described in the bible does not align with the principles of justice and fairness that Islam promotes. In Islamic law, consent is a fundamental aspect of any marriage. Forced marriage is strictly prohibited, and a woman cannot be forced to marry her rapist. Islam places great emphasis on the protection of women's rights and dignity. The misconception mentioned may arise from a misunderstanding or misinterpretation of certain cultural practices that have unfortunately been associated with Islam. It is important to distinguish between cultural practices and the true teachings of the religion.

In cases of rape, Islam advocates for severe punishments for the perpetrator. The punishment for rape in Islamic law is not marriage to the victim, but rather severe penalties such as lashes or stoning, depending on the circumstances and the jurisdiction. The aim is to ensure justice for the victim and deter such heinous acts.

Islamic laws and contracts are meant to be based on faith and consent, not force. They are designed to protect the rights and well-being of individuals, including women. It is crucial to approach the study of any religion with a comprehensive understanding of its teachings, rather than drawing conclusions based on isolated incidents or cultural practices that may contradict its principles.

In Islam, the concept of Zina, which refers to sexual intercourse outside of marriage, including rape, is considered a severe offense and is punishable under Islamic law. Contrary to the Bible, where marrying the rapist is mentioned as a potential resolution, Islam does not enforce such a practice. Instead, Islam emphasizes the importance of protecting the rights and dignity of women. The laws of the Quran may be deemed harsh by some, but they are designed to ensure justice and maintain a moral society.

The experience of receiving mixed signals can be deeply traumatizing, especially considering the contradictory messages conveyed in the Bible where women are instructed to marry their rapists. The woman's invasion of privacy will not be condoned by God; it's impossible. The questions and answers provided in this discussion serve as the basis for understanding the issue of cruelty towards women. Throughout various stages, these women have consistently fought for independence, whereas Islam inherently grants women independence from birth.

Some people gossip about Muslims but would a rapist not be killed, to justify honor. Islam would not subjugate a woman to marry her rapist. There are stifling questions and answers, but daily softness is revealed through hypocrisy and harsh truths are hidden in this two-faced society. Comprehension is better for the uninformed.

Bible: Deuteronomy: 22:28:29 Does command a rape victim to marry her rapist? Why would God command a woman to marry the man who just raped her?

Quran 5:5, You shall maintain CHASTITY, not committing adultery, nor taking secret lovers. Anyone who rejects faith, all his work will be in vain, and in the Hereafter he will be with the losers.

Quran 24:30 Tell the believing men that they shall subdue their eyes (and not stare at the women), and to maintain their CHASTITY. This is purer for them. God is fully Cognizant of everything they do.

Quran 24:31 And tell the believing women to subdue their eyes, and maintain their CHASTITY.

Quran 24:33,You shall not force your girls to commit prostitution, seeking the materials of this world, if they wish to be chaste. If anyone forces them, then God, seeing that they are forced, is Forgiver, Merciful.

It is essential to understand that these laws should be applied in the appropriate context. The notion of sin in Islam is not made public unless there are four credible witnesses who have witnessed the act. This stringent requirement aims to protect individuals from false accusations and preserve their reputation. Muslims are encouraged to seek repentance and forgiveness from Allah, as sincerity in repentance is considered paramount. It is important to differentiate between the teachings of Islam and the actions of individuals who may misinterpret or misapply these teachings.

The notion of Islam being labeled as savage or barbaric due to these laws is a misconception, as Islam promotes justice, compassion, and equality for all. Islam emphasizes not sharing consensual sins but repenting in private. Rape, being non-consensual, should be severely punished. Consensual acts should be kept secret and repented privately in Islam.

The occurrence of forced acts on women has resulted in a rise in crime, with the biblical text suggesting that the victim should marry the rapist as a form of support. In the Middle East, severe punishments are imposed if these crimes are witnessed, however, women are free to walk alone in Muslim countries at all hours, and interestingly, the night is just as safe as the day. Despite the false publicity coming from those places that fail to ensure safety for women within their borders.

The Business Standard: The United States has a rape rate of 27.3. As in many other countries with 84,767 reported rape incidents.

Wikipedia: Rapes in India: Violence against women. Of the total 31,677 rape cases, 28,147(nearly 89%) of the rapes were committed by persons known to the victim. The share of victims who were minors or below 18.

Quora: Saudi Arabia has the minimum rape crime rate in the world because of its sharia law. ..

NIV Bible:1 Corinthians: 7:28.But if you do marry, you have not sinned; and if a virgin marries, she has not sinned. But those who marry will face many troubles in this life, and I want to spare you this

In verses, the Bible discourages the act of marriage and cautions about the potential troubles it may cause. By emphasizing illogicality, it brings attention to the fact that entering into a union without peace is not rational. Conversely, according to Islamic teachings, marriage is considered the completion of one's faith, also referred to as the "deen" way of life. According to the Bible verse, Jesus came to disrupt family dynamics, as the man worship causes turmoil within families. These conflicting messages seem contradictory and lack coherence. On the other hand, the Quran emphasizes the importance of maintaining strong familial bonds, stating that doing so not only enhances overall well-being but also increases provisions and blessings (rizq).

The act of promoting oppression and causing the separation of families is undoubtedly the most egregious action one can take. Furthermore, the messages being conveyed lack coherence, as Jesus himself issues a clear warning about the nature of marriage - that it is destined to be disrupted. The lack of motivation for individuals to enter into this sacred union stems from the Bible's prophecy of an inherent lack of unity within it. If there are already divisions being predicted by the prophet, with individuals associating themselves as the offspring of god or gods, it would be difficult to remain oblivious to the possibility that the end could be closer than expected. In contrast, Islam does not view marriage as a trial; instead, it sees it as enhancing one's faith, considering it a joyous union between a man and a woman.

The Quran instructs believers to maintain strong connections with both their family members and their relatives. In cases where either relationship becomes strained or distant, individuals are encouraged to actively seek reconciliation. If these attempts at reconciliation are unsuccessful, it is important to remember that Allah is just and will ensure justice for those who oppress others.

Oppression is not limited to family relations, but rather extends to people, nations, and countries who oppress others, and in turn, they will face oppression themselves. Allah's purpose in sending Prophet Muhammad, the prophet of humanity, was not to sever ties or discourage marriage, but rather to promote strong bonds with family and all of humanity, regardless of their religious beliefs.

Quran 2:19, OPPRESSION is worse than murder.

Hatemongers falsely blamed Muslims for crimes they didn't commit. Exposing a healthy environment requires adherence to Islam's laws and avoiding gossip about those influenced by fake news, while also recognizing the similarities and contrasts between Eastern and Western cultures and biblical approaches.

For those who have traveled to the Middle East, specifically Saudi Arabia, Dubai, Qatar, Aman, Riyadh, and more. The lands are constantly illuminated with a bright and radiant light. Those who are familiar with the Middle East and those who have had the opportunity to witness the newfound safety in Muslim cities, where both men and women can freely walk at any hour, can confirm this statement.

While women have the privilege of unrestricted movement and round-the-clock shopping, social media often falsely portrays Muslim regions as hazardous for women during nighttime. Despite the fact that certain countries are spreading dangerous lies, many expats still opt to move here because of the safe and protected environment enjoyed by residents. The negative influence affects individuals who lack the ability to distinguish between truth and falsehood, causing them to unknowingly spread false information about these countries. Unlike those who criticize this rhetoric, women in the Middle East actually have the privilege of accessing safe spaces where they can walk alone at night without fear.

The lands where rhetoric is prevalent have a concerning lack of safety, which poses a significant danger to both women and men. This is especially true when these incidents happen at inappropriate hours and in unsuitable locations. The assertions made about these regions can be supported by both the news coverage and the local residents. Given the increasing global awareness of unsafe areas, it is becoming less crucial to mention specific names, as most individuals prioritize their safety while operating a vehicle.

The distinctions, although they do not impact friendships, are still worth noting and can be compared to the contrasts found in various aspects, particularly within biblical contexts and environments.

The difference or contrast between thought reporting and biblical elements is incredibly vast. Distinguishing between the Bible and the Quran is important because they have differing views on the concept of marriage. While some individuals may have apprehensions about marriage, Zina illicit sex is not condoned.

In the Islamic faith, marriage plays a significant role in symbolizing the joy that comes from the union of two individuals, particularly when they share the same faith.

Khadija Prophet Muhammad's wife helped him with every mission, and they had one path to follow together, Allah. After she died, he married more women. Islam allows up to four wives for men but suggests only one. Other books have countless wives.

Many of his marriages were to build friendships or help widows, divorced women, and the helpless. If he wanted wealth, he could have had that too. It was a powerful prophet whose opponents offered everything to stop Islam's spread. Islam has no alternatives or compensation for compromises in matters of faith.

Islam condoned marriage as a completion of faith and halal affairs in life to learn responsibility and share the emotional and physical state with each other. During wartime, many women were left alone and unable to take care of themselves. The prophet of Islam married divorced and widowed women which later became a "Sunnah" customs and practices. And to marry converts.

His path was one, and his rights were from Allah, not his own. As part of the emergence of Islam and the "sunnah" customs and practices of the prophet Muhammad, respect for the Muslim world vastly differs from other societies. Women of any status in society did not debase themselves for men's adoration by exposing themselves. Instead, men who liked women married them in the Islamic world. Prophet Muhammad respected humanity.

Jesus per the Biblical script came to break families apart, not indicated in the Quran. The identity and personification of Islam's Jesus are entirely different and Islam is for marriage and not breaking families apart. Your ability to maintain close ties with the family will enable you to sustain yourself as the family can sometimes be challenging. Allah blesses those with blessed families. But sending a prophet to destroy families is beyond comprehension for Muslims.

NLT Bible: Luke 12:49-56.No, I have come to divide people against each other! 52 From now on families will be split apart, three in favor of me, and two against—or two in favor ...

442

Islam prefers men to have one wife. Men who can afford more than one wife can choose up to four wives. This assumes that they divide and share their time equally, as well as material goods and gifts. It's not about adding numbers and saying you have more than one wife. Instead, it comes with responsibility which is hardly practiced with one wife. When men contemplate marrying one, they encounter a war within themselves. They can marry four in certain circumstances. It's not a harem, it's a responsibility and duty that comes with marital affairs in Islam.

If these countries wanted to respect the females they had to fight for decades for independence. The same holds for those in this society who claim equal rights. It is essential to clarify these misunderstandings and dilemmas by focusing on differences. While the Prophet Muhammad loved his daughter, she helped her father.

Fatima was greeted with kindness, love, and respect as her father stood up and offered her a seat upon entering the room. Back in the days when paganism was prevalent, women were not granted a position in the realm of personal or political rights. Before the advent of Islam and the demonstration of respect for women, the idea of wives being treated equally was not even entertained in households.

In Islam, the birth of a daughter is seen as a blessing and a cause for celebration. Prophet Muhammad himself emphasized the importance of treating daughters with love and respect. He said, "Whoever has one or three daughters or sisters, and he treats them kindly and fears Allah regarding them, then Paradise is certainly guaranteed for him." This teaching highlights the significance of daughters in a family and the rewards associated with raising them. Islam encourages equal treatment and opportunities for both sons and daughters, rejecting the notion that boys are more important for continuing the family lineage. This shift in mindset has helped combat the historical practice of gender-based infanticide and has elevated the status of women in Muslim societies.

In a Muslim family, the daughter is considered to be the shining light that brightens up the entire household. Through generations, traditions and faith were passed down to the boy.Many cultures consider the birth of a boy as the eldest child to be a significant cause for celebration. In Muslim cultures, the belief that the eldest sibling is a protector and serves as a role model for their siblings still prevails. However, if the child happens to be a girl, Allah blesses her with the strength required for her to be placed first. All beliefs are centered on Allah.

Despite getting married, the girl remains steadfast in her attachment to the place she calls home. In Muslim households, daughters hold a special place and are considered valuable possessions. The boy, with his strength, serves as the pillar of support for the entire family. Each individual, whether they are a boy or a girl, possesses their own inherent worth that cannot be substituted by another.

The struggles that individuals face are often filled with complications. A positive attitude is the only way to align the heart and mind. Keeping the alignment of the heart and mind is essential for maintaining the integrity of a believer's core. In order to foster belief comprehension and dialogue, education and learning are indispensable. Given that life is a relentless struggle for many individuals, it is through unwavering perseverance that one can ultimately overcome any obstacles that come their way. There is nothing that can fail when it comes from Allah.

It is possible that humans may perceive his problems as insurmountable. The ultimate objective is to extract valuable lessons from this particular experience and utilize them to persevere and achieve further success. Throughout history, the Islamic faith has encountered significant opposition and resistance from numerous individuals and groups. Prophet Muhammad's unique characteristic was that he never complained about his followers to Allah, unlike other prophets. In contrast, all of the other prophets expressed their disapproval towards their disobedient people by cursing them, and as a result, a few even abandoned them. Muhammad, may peace be upon him, is regarded as the prophet who brought guidance and wisdom to all of humanity.

The prophet, in his unwavering character, never complained even when he was in dire need of help; rather, he beseeched Allah for assistance. If we take into consideration how Prophet Muhammad would view his people and their demeanor towards Islam, we can infer that he would expect them to embody the principles and teachings of Islam in their actions, speech, and interactions.

Prophet Muhammad was known for his humility, compassion, and justice, and he emphasized the importance of treating others with kindness and respect. As ambassadors of Islam, he would likely expect his followers to be exemplars of these qualities, promoting peace, harmony, and justice in their communities. He would want them to be honest, trustworthy, and to fulfill their responsibilities towards their families, neighbors, and society as a whole. Prophet Muhammad encouraged learning, seeking knowledge, and spreading wisdom, so he would expect his followers to be knowledgeable about Islam and to share its teachings with others in a gentle and persuasive manner. Additionally, he would emphasize the importance of unity among Muslims and working towards the betterment of society, promoting social justice, and helping those in need.His desire is for the Muslim community to actively engage in the pursuit of justice, standing firm against the oppressors and ensuring that the weak are not subjected to further oppression. Overall, Prophet Muhammad would view his people as representatives of Islam and would expect them to embody its values, principles, and teachings in every aspect of their lives.

If he were to hear what is being said about him, in my words he would certainly not be displeased. Those who reject the truth are simply ignorant. If the Prophet of Islam were alive today, he would have resolved the dilemma without the need for social media. Muslims would have taken a different position, and both Muslims and non-Muslims hold great admiration for this prophet. Numerous educated non-Muslims have even left comments praising him.

Reverend Bosworth Smith. A fellow of Trinity College, Oxford, said, "He was Caesar and Pope in one." John William Draper, an American scientist, and philosopher, wrote: "Muhammad was the man who availed the greatest influence on humans." Annie Besant, President of the Indian National Congress, said: I re-read and find a new sense of reverence for the almighty Arabian teacher. Edward Gibbon wrote: "Muhammad's memory is capacious, his imagination vivid, and his judgment quick. He possessed courage in thought and action.

Prof. Michael Hart, an astronomer, physicist, and historian of science, said Muhammad may surprise some as the only person in history who has succeeded both religiously and secularly. Gandhi, a nationalist leader from India, wrote: "I became more convinced that it was not the sword that brought Islam, it was the simplicity and utter effacement of the prophet. His scrupulous regard for his promises, followers, and humanity. When I turn the pages, I wish there was more to read about this prophet."

Despite all the challenges, he achieved peace in the Arabian Peninsula. The practice and way of life were non-negotiable for them. Islam was a message to the world about Allah's intolerance for compromise to Islam and the Quran. Islam did not compel disbelievers to adopt its practices. One cannot ignore the laws, regulations, and nuances of this prophet when reading about him as a Muslim.

Immaturity in humans can often lead to misguided actions. The internal upheavals are distractions, assisted by the devil. The conflict remains near to someone like this.

Misguided individuals may experience doubt, confusion, and anger. We seek Allah's protection from evil and guidance towards goodness. The goal of Islam is to explain the prophet's experiences, including the rules, laws, and challenges he underwent, for the improvement of mankind.

Disregarding words and actions while claiming to be Muslim is a cruel act. Some demeanors are unfixable even by a tornado. Perhaps it's a slow walk in the rain. Experiencing the sensation of water and thunder. Quranic narratives stand out from other religious texts. Allah sent the Quran to correct the changes made by humans to his other sacred texts, rather than duplicating them.

Quran: Surah Yaseen 36:69 And we did not give Prophet Muhammad knowledge of poetry, nor is it befitting for him. It is not but a message and a clear Qur'an.

Quran: Surah Qasas 28:56 Surely you cannot guide whom you love, but Allah guides whom He pleases, and He knows best the followers of the right way.

The question of whether destiny is determined by human choice or if it is predetermined is one query that frequently arises in the minds of individuals, and it often leads to contemplation of Allah's role in this matter. The power inherent in pre-written documents is their capacity to dispel any uncertainties within the human population pertaining to intangible matters, irrespective of whether they lean towards positivity or negativity. The source of virtuous behavior can be traced back to Allah, while harmful behavior tends to stem from within oneself. The outcome of a human's performance, which is known only by Allah, determines their destiny.

There are numerous pathways that surround us. Instead of conforming to societal norms, the best path for a person can be discovered by wholeheartedly following their own heart. The undermining of faith occurs when individuals who do not believe are granted the freedom to make choices that pertain to matters of faith. The act of continuously learning is crucial in order to ensure that progress continues to be made. Learning is given priority by Islam and its followers are required to prioritize it.

The essence of this journey lies in the continuous process of learning and the exchange of ideas and different perspectives. The discovery of one's destiny is an inevitable journey that every individual is bound to embark upon, as they are guided towards it.

CHAPTER 20

FAITH ATTRACTS STABILITY AND PEACE IS SOUGHT.

Laws govern the concepts of control and vitality, and distractions hinder human beings from abiding by these contractual laws. Islam, as a religion, establishes a contractual agreement between Allah and its followers, known as Muslims. Whether someone is born into Islam or converts to it, it is essential to have a comprehensive understanding that Islam operates on the basis of a contract with its own set of statutory laws that are applicable to all its adherents. This faith is widely accepted and does not show any signs of retracting its support for the current laws that have been implemented and are already established.

The laws enacted in the State of Islam can be incredibly mesmerizing, captivating both newcomers to Islam and individuals who have grown up in a society that embraces a progressive lifestyle rooted in Islam. There is a common misconception that it is backward, but this is often misrepresented.

It is not possible for someone who has only gained knowledge through breaking laws, without any cultural foundation, to become a teacher, common sense rejects the notion. The residents of this council Islam are urging for the adoption of laws and are determined to set an example by adhering to them with utmost integrity.

 Muslims have the ability to withdraw without any ill intentions, from contractual laws of Islam but it is important to note that negligence cannot be used as an excuse. No Muslim undermines their own performance; our objective is to win, not to lose. At every turn, the Muslims demonstrate their winning spirit, asserting their individuality and resisting the suppression of personal beliefs.

Through the clever use of humor and wit, a young Muslim man vividly portrays the stark contrast between Islam and the temptation to renounce it, effectively showcasing the unwavering hold the faith has on people. "Hotel California," which is a well-known song, was performed by the rock band known as the Eagles. The comparison becomes even more intriguing when we include the young, humorous, educated, and thriving Muslim man. In addition, it is important to highlight that the song is unquestionably remarkable.

While there is no direct association with Islam, Muslims do have an understanding and are receptive to various forms of humor. By exploring relations, correlations, comparisons, and the appreciation of humor, one can gain a submissive truth that leads to a deeper understanding. In many instances, Muslims may find themselves drifting away from Islam.This is particularly relevant for individuals who have been exposed to Western civilization and are living in a society that does not align with Islamic beliefs. There are two dimensions to this exposure, and one can choose to delve deeper into the search for understanding Islam, or alternatively, explore the societal code that opposes Islam placing self-made laws above any biblical law.

However, individuals who go through various life experiences often find themselves returning to their faith with a deep sense of reverence. Their assurance of coming back is founded on the knowledge they have acquired.

"Last thing I remember

I was running for the door

I had to find the passage back

To the place I was before

"Relax, " said the night man

"We are programmed to receive

You can check out any time you like

But you can never leave!"

In the memory, the final scene he can vividly remember involves him frantically making his way towards the exit, desperately searching for the route that would take him back to the place he had previously been. However, once you enter, there is no possibility of leaving. The young Muslim man made a comparison that resonated with those who understand, finding profound truth in the connection, infused with humor and dialect. Evidently, he, along with many others, attempted to explore life outside of Islam while residing in Western societies, enticed by the allure of freedom over the constraints imposed by Islam. However, ultimately, they returned to the familiar laws and regulations.

The parallel can also be drawn with a young Muslim woman who was raised in the faith but did not actively practice it, finding herself torn between the expectations of Western society for independence and progress, and the adherence to all the laws of Islam. Nevertheless, she maintained a strong adherence to the core values and principles of Islam.

Moreover, she consistently displayed her intelligence, entrepreneurial spirit, and resilience in every aspect of her life. In her pursuit of success, she faced numerous challenges and obstacles, yet she remained steadfast and fought against them to achieve her goals. Once she finally managed to break free from her dependency on others and fully embraced her newfound independence.

In her pursuit of independence, she refused to let the constraints of Islam hinder her progress, and she persistently pushed forward. The liberation grants Western society the freedom to combat Islam in all forms, without being bound by the limitations imposed by Allah.

Nevertheless, falling victim to the system devised by humans and becoming enslaved to it. In her quest to establish herself as an independent business owner, she was determined to break free from the system that forced her to spend countless hours catering to the needs of others in order to generate income.

By valuing time and recognizing the strength within herself, she fought fiercely to maintain her independence, understanding that this was not only important for her, but also a crucial stepping stone towards ventures that surpass the limits of human imagination.

With triumphant determination, she excelled in every aspect of this society, while we marvel at her achievements in this world. She accomplished them through countless hours of hard work, unwavering perseverance, and a resolute mindset that conquers all challenges.

As time continues to pass, the inherent nature within us instinctively seeks peace and the accomplishments that we believe are rightfully ours. Eventually, this inner longing for peace leads us to Islam, where we find solace and fulfillment. In doing so, we also rediscover the source that we had previously neglected and left unchecked for a period of time. The delivery of the song is valid and holds significance. She decides to return to Islam, bringing along all her achievements that she acquired during her absence from the faith.

The existence of Islam was a crucial factor in completing the sense of liberation and liberty she felt, particularly due to her awareness of the humor and success of a young man. Despite his attempts to distance himself from Islam, he ultimately found himself returning to the same familiar place, driven by his accomplishments and the longing for peace within the religion.

His ability to incorporate humor in his expressions served as a remarkable contrast, particularly in relation to the societal norms of today. By explaining complex concepts with a touch of humor, he not only entertained but also imparted practical theories and truths. Moreover, he highlighted the inescapable return to Islam, akin to the difficulty of checking out from this hotel.

The young lady had a close relationship with a young man who happened to be her brother. She greatly admired him and he was always there to support and assist her in every way possible. Not only did he provide assistance to her, but he also used his sense of humor and ability to draw comparisons to positively impact the world. In particular, he focused on helping young and old Muslims who had strayed from their path but eventually found their way back.

As he unintentionally drew comparisons to the song, he came to understand the exciting and authentic nature of this match, resulting in his invitation of many to Islam. Surprisingly, these individuals found his unintended humor to be reminiscent of their past experiences. With exhaustion setting in, they found their way back to the same hotel, Islam, and prepared to rest in familiar quarters.

With the passage of time, she also began to comprehend the literal meaning behind his words, leading them both to return to Islam as anticipated, after a considerable amount of time had elapsed. As the song suggests, it is deemed more favorable to return rather than not returning, as stated a believer can check out but cannot leave. The complexity lies in the understanding that the rules apply equally to both genders, as they both strive to find solace within themselves, despite all their worldly accomplishments.

Ultimately, they are all in search of the primary solace - inner peace. These examples, which cannot be divorced from daily life, highlight the humorous nature of Muslims and their appreciation for the contrasts that stimulate the human mind. His mother was aware of his exceptional qualities, as he lived up to the expectations associated with his name, embodying integrity.

Similarly, his sister was recognized as a beacon of light, choosing to depart from her familiar world while still radiating the divine light bestowed upon them by Allah, which even shone during her pregnancy. It is a rare feat for mothers to claim such an experience, but these two luminous souls not only shone alongside her but also continued to illuminate the world beyond.

Prophet Muhammads mother said the light shined in her stomach. There are not many mothers who can express positive experiences of their offspring in this trying climate of this world. There is no comparison with the prophet of Islam but point stated is every mother knows her child if she can leave this world by saying she has hope in them she is the winner the world envies "mashallah" please remember to look up the meaning of lyrics of "hotel California".

This journey will be similar to understanding the lyrics of a song, such as "Hotel California" sung by the rock band Eagles, where both the young and the old can interpret and appreciate the meaning.

Despite enduring decades of trials, the Muslim community has persistently sought to learn about the historical facts and ardently embrace the examples that are crucial in understanding Islam. The Quran and hadiths house a plethora of examples that Muslims frequently use to guide others towards the truth and educate those interested in the Islamic world.

The Battle of Karbala serves as yet another illustration of how mistrust can lead to devastating wars. The enemy's invitations for alliance ended up leading to wars. Women endured unspeakable acts of torture while the innocent children suffered immensely. The Prophet Muhammad's family serves as a living example, as they have courageously faced not only victories but also wars against strong opposition.

It is impossible for Muslims to deny the occurrence and ongoing significance of this event, as those who disregard their creator are likened to water that is stagnant.

The event, which occurred on the 10th of Muharram in 680 AD, was a confrontation near the Euphrates River in present-day Iraq involving Imam Hussain. He was against the people of Yazid, who were known as enemies of Islam. Despite being outnumbered by the opposition and deceived during the reconciliation meeting, he ended up in a war. Throughout history, Muslims have consistently advocated for the protection and promotion of human rights.

In his pursuit of righteousness, he dedicated himself to learning and embracing the teachings of his grandfather, Prophet Muhammad. Even in the face of martyrdom, bestowed upon him by Allah, he remained resolute in upholding the principles of Islam, ensuring that its rights were never compromised for himself, his family, or his people.

Many individuals withdrew from the situation due to their apprehension of Yazid, who was a human tyrant;only a few stood alongside a small army of Imam Hussain. However, the significance of this event for Muslims does not lie in their defeat by a non-believer, but rather in the act of relinquishing everything one possesses in order to preserve their rights as a Muslim.

According to Muslim beliefs, martyrdom is considered the ultimate honor, surpassing any other experience, as it is believed that those who die as martyrs not only receive justice for the injustices they suffered in this life, but also experience eternal happiness in the next life, as defined by Allah. On the day of judgment, every single human being that has ever lived will come to know the truth.

The example that applies to Palestine is that those who have died as martyrs are still alive, while those who have oppressed the weak will face torment in both this world and the hereafter. Zain al-Abidin, who was the son of Imam Hussain, unfortunately, couldn't participate in the war of Karbala due to his severe illness. However, he later became renowned for delivering numerous sermons and playing a significant role in the aftermath of Karbala.

Despite the tragic martyrdom of his father, Zain al-Abidin continued to actively engage with Islam, showcasing his exceptional intelligence and remarkable oratory skills. Zain, a name commonly associated with Muslim individuals, is often linked to high levels of intelligence and a strong sense of spirituality. Zainab, the grand-daughter of the Prophet Muhammad, made substantial contributions to the education of Islam. Her efforts to bring light to people and ensure the preservation of her grandfather's legacy were commendable. Fatima and Ali were the parents of this intelligent daughter.

Fatima was regarded as the beloved daughter of Prophet Muhammad. The unchangeable nature of Isam's history highlights the importance of trials in strengthening one's faith. In this ever-changing world, those who are unwavering in their efforts to convey the truth of Islam are akin to soldiers of Allah, preserving the heritage of their predecessors who have done so much under all conditions.

In their relentless pursuit of truth, educated Muslim men and women strive to propagate and promote the teachings of Islam. The significance of this legacy is not determined by the advancements in today's society or the progress of humanity. Muslim women have shown exceptional achievements and progress ever since the inception of Islam.

Women in Islam will strive to excel alongside men. The unstoppable progression of Islam is dependent on educating Muslims and attracting converts who require education and acceptance from the Muslim community. It is through this education and acceptance that Muslims can effectively teach others about Islam, ultimately leading to the masses discovering the ultimate truth.

The martyrdom of the Prophets' family serves as a lasting legacy, reminding Muslims that even during times of hardship, it is crucial to have a goal of learning and teaching the truth of Islam in this world, which is undeniably evident. The trials that one person experiences do not align with those of the other.

It is the duty of a Muslim to provide assistance to the oppressors, as it is an opportunity granted by Allah to demonstrate true dignity through tangible help, rather than engaging in empty rhetoric and futile arguments on social media that often lead to insults instead of assistance. Every Muslim should prioritize knowledge of the history of Islam as a fundamental requirement. Every Muslim who possesses knowledge about Islam has the potential to serve as a vocal advocate for the faith, providing guidance and information to those seeking to understand it.

The outcome of this event was the tragic massacre of a significantly outnumbered Alid team, led by Husayn ibn Ali, against the army of the Umayyad Dynasty who supported Yazid. The historical significance of this event remains recognized by both Shia and Sunni Muslims, as it commemorates the martyrdom of the prophets' grandsons, making it an important and tragic incident in their history.

However, there is a difference in the way the two sects approach attendance at this tragic event. The practice of "matam," which involves self-flagellation, is not part of the customs followed by Sunni Muslims. It is important to note that self-flagellation is not limited only to Shia Muslims.

Even though Sunnis may experience grief, it is crucial to highlight that this grief does not manifest in any form of physical self-harm. It should be acknowledged that not all Shia Muslims take part in the event of ceremonies and self tortures; however, there are individuals who do so in order to commemorate the tragic incident.

The intentions of the Shia Muslims was not to elevate Imam Hussain prophet's grandson to the status of a god or to supplant a human deity with him as god. Despite the practices not being in accordance with Islamic concepts, it is important to note that Allah is the only god in Islam.

Even if certain emerging sects incorporate practices not sanctioned by Islam, the fundamental truth remains unaltered. The matter of the relationship between Allah and them is solely their concern, however, Islam strictly prohibits any additions or partners to Allah, demonstrating a zero tolerance policy.

The divide that exists today among Muslims can be traced back to a disagreement over who should succeed Prophet Muhammad after his death. The division within Islam arises from the elderly population's desire for the successor of Prophet Muhammad to be Ali, who was his son-in-law and a member of his family. The person who took the Caliphate at that time was Abu Bakr, his father in law. Later on, Omar Bin Khattab, who was also a companion of the Prophet.

The prophet was married to his daughter Hafsa and became the second Caliph. Uthman, a member of the Umayyad family in the Quraysh clan, became the third Caliph and was also a close companion of the Prophet. Not only was he the son-in-law of Prophet Muhammad, but he was also counted among the first individuals to convert to Islam. In separate instances, he entered into marriage with two of the prophet's daughters, beginning with Rukayya and subsequently Umm Kalthum.

The prophet himself read the nikah for his daughters. He stated if he had more daughters he would prefer a man like him to be the husband for his daughters. That is an honor when the prophet validates his character.

The Caliphate was bestowed upon him by Omar the second caliph known as Prince of believers and held the title as "Amir ul Mumineen" the leader of believers before his passing. The caliphate should have been granted to Ali, insisted a small faction of Muslims who remained loyal to Ali, since it was not Ali himself who provoked conflicts with the other caliphs, but rather the people who caused turmoil and divisions.

The third caliph Uthman his personality hails from the mighty Umayyad clan, known for their prominence. Despite facing opposition from his family, Uthman still became one of the first converts

Islam has effectively captivated the masses by emphasizing the importance of marriage and alliances, which promote unity and acceptance. This is achieved through various practices, including gift giving, visiting lands, and welcoming unions and friendships. While numerous lands have witnessed the horrors of war, they have also been the birthplaces of countless friendships and the beginning of joyful unions.

It remains a tragic reality that Muslims are still being martyred by their opposition, prompting us to recall the martyrdom of the prophets' grandsons at the hands of their enemies. Iman Hussain not only endured torture, but it was also taken to the extreme of separating his head from his body.

Muslims come together to share their victories instead of dwelling on the tragedy of being oppressed by the enemy, which is just one example of their ongoing efforts to honor and remember the Prophet's family. In the context of Islam, victory is epitomized through the courageous act of a Muslim who lays down their life for the sake of truth, demonstrating resilience in the face of human laws and pledging their allegiance to the divine laws set forth by Allah. The celebration of a Muslim who stood for truth, gained martyrdom, and believed in not negotiating with disbelievers is a testament to the notion that martyrdom is preferable to hypocrisy.

It is crucial for every practicing Muslim to explain Islam in the appropriate context, without prejudice or ill intentions towards fellow Muslims. In order to combat the efforts of the enemy to divide Muslims, it is crucial that we prioritize unity rather than divisions.

The companions of Prophet Muhammad in Saudi Arabia underwent a significant conversion to Islam, and their commitment to the faith was marked by their unwavering integrity and honor. As a result, they became shining examples of thriving legacies that will be remembered for generations to come. In the life of a Muslim, the concepts of honor, dignity, and character all intertwine and have a significant influence.

The fourth and final caliph of the Rashidun Caliphate, which was the successor to the Islamic state of Prophet Muhammad, was Alī ibn Talib. Notably, he was also the father of Hassan and Hussain, who were the grandsons of Prophet Muhammad. Despite the fact that he eventually became the fourth caliph, the resentment of not being the first continued to divide Muslims into Sunni and Shia factions.

While getting along in any culture may not be the issue, it is important to address how these prolonged separations can create divisions among the "ummah" people.These separations stem from misunderstandings, and if all Muslims unite as one body, they will become the strongest of all armies. It is important for Muslims to safeguard the overall harmony of Islam by avoiding divisions that can be exploited by opposition forces, in order to preserve the serenity of the entire Muslim community. Despite the existence of many divisions, one thing remains constant - the Quran. It is the unifying force that binds all Muslims together, as we all read from the same Quran. This serves as a powerful testament to our unity as one body of Muslims.

The society, which relies on collective speech, imposes an embargo on sharing the events with the unified system of humanity. This embargo leaves no room for persistently teaching the society about the roots and strength of Islam, which are embedded in the inherent nature of truth and individualism.

The path towards a united society starts with individuals gaining perspective and embracing truth. It requires personal growth, expressing one's character, pursuing individual interests, and seeking repentance, all without blaming others or burdening them. Islam is a strength, not a weakness.

The use of the collective pronoun "we" serves as a symbol of their unity and their shared struggle for independence within a society that promotes false rhetoric, where individuals support each other in shouldering their burdens.

The process of personal growth and improvement leads to the development of positive attitudes and perspectives towards life. By following this path, individuals can make better decisions that will not only enhance their current lives but also prepare them for the next phase.

Quran: Surah Maidah: (5:67) O Messenger! Deliver what has been revealed to you from your Lord, for if you fail to do that, you have not fulfilled the task of His messengers.

To please this dimmed society, some behave as this society has structured their minds and expect the unexpected if one agrees with the mindset of the human. They have used false words to describe what has caused society to act in such a way in countries and settings that are epitomes of chaos rather than progress.

Since ancient times, humans have used animals for work and pleasure. Those who seek revenue to meet ends in this society that demands existence in demand of an exterior outlook or an interior need are abusing humans as shifts of work never end for those seeking revenue to meet ends. Regardless of how you view this venue, time is the essence of monetary gains. Those who value time also pray at allotted times of Salat. The countries that show the glitz also sacrifice the hours to serve the humans.

Humans can become fascinated by pleasure and material possessions to the point of being consumed by society's dictates. Routines may be tiresome to some and continuous to others. A believer views contentment as spiritual and worldly achievements. An intelligent and softened heart sees a connection to belief systems as more valuable than humans' ideas.

It is imperative to remember that one should not be too strict with oneself; rather, one should seek balance and harmony in their life. Compassion and understanding are key to living a life in line with religious teachings and beliefs. Eating should be a joyous experience shared with others. A humble spirit is essential for understanding the importance of belief systems and the power of faith.

This understanding helps to build a stronger connection between an individual and their faith, creating a sense of peace and connection to the divine. Hope is a benefit to those who believe, and disbelievers are a blockade to those who only have their own foundations. The gift of Allah and hope are the best gifts a believer can receive. Salat is the biggest gift for a Muslim and a believer who shares it. Those conversations are priceless.

Allah's miracles are abundant even in this day and age where revelations ceased with the prophet Muhammad. Miracles of life are endless for those who know the purity of gifts, for those who don't understand doubts rule the blessings and for those who understand blessings rule the gravity of sublime belief not in time but in the surety of delivery as it comes from Allah.

In today's world, people hold multiple jobs or more. However, where is the strength in their core for those who see mistakes as comebacks? Mistakes are duly noted by Allah and reason for getting closer to Allah in repentance. To keep their belief in Allah in check, they need a balance of inner resistance.

Islam would not exist if the Prophet Muhammad tailored his speech to appease the people. The text would be watered down and reorganized to appease humans instead of Allah. Believers will never fear another human when delivering Allah's word. A mere attempt to show the signs leading one to the right path and progress in delving into the Arabic Quran can never justify its words or interpretations.

A story or an example can change a life. Taking risks and striving when things get tough are attributes of this type of commitment. It provides security and a platform for building a better future. Success in relationships is built on values and understanding. It's crucial to commit to something as skin deep.

Belief cannot be forced or deliberated. It's the inner soul that feeds the truth to a believer. Finding the meaning of life takes more than superficiality. Peace is a component and manifestation of truth. Despite this, they cannot achieve real meaning or satisfaction in their lives. They remain trapped in a cycle of searching for something they will never find. This is the cost of superficial wants.

Serving humans and fighting Islam's organized faith is a dilemma for some. It's challenging for some to battle human impositions, but for those of faith, thriving isn't difficult. In particular, it is not a promising game for a Muslim who neglects Islam. They are completely oblivious to Allah's divine laws and guidance, and instead, they prefer society's trends. This attitude of worshiping humans instead of Allah will never succeed, as Allah's will prevails. Although humans are given a free choice, their choice exerts their will and destiny, but Allah's will supersedes human will.

As Allah knows each individual's heart, human actions are determined by their own choices; however, Allah is the ultimate and final authority in all matters. He knows the consequences of our actions before we experience them. He is merciful and forgiving, yet also just. Allah controls our lives and destinies.

Being a servant of society may seem like a win. While pleasing humans versus Allah results in damage at a slower pace, sometimes faster than a tornado, in the long run, it does result in destruction. The most effective way to serve Allah is to leave behind a legacy that benefits humanity. This could be done by leaving behind a positive example, a legacy of knowledge, or a way of life that can be followed.

In the end, life is for those who strive for the highest. They don't give up on their dreams or beliefs for others. This is a commitment that stands the test of time and brings out the best in each other. It is a relationship that nurtures and encourages growth, understanding, and acceptance. It is a bond worth cherishing and protecting. Allah's tests and trials are unique to each individual. Though trials are not recounted for decades, everyone knows that each trial provided a closer relationship with God to the individual. For some unfortunates, it separated them from Allah.

Despite this, having faith and relying on Allah's guidance can help individuals see the positive in every trial. It doesn't matter how challenging or seemingly insurmountable they are. **The weakest of humans are those who say it's not suitable for someone else, so I will change my course. Even in the face of adversity, those with strong relationships can weather the storm and come out stronger than ever.**

A commitment based on mutual respect, understanding, and shared values is an investment that pays dividends for a lifetime. Those who prioritize pleasing others and disbelievers, even when their beliefs are proven true, will face dire consequences.

True inner strength is demonstrated by perseverance despite opposition and difficulty. Faith relationships are truly tested in these challenging moments. A strong foundation for a lasting bond is built on compromise and sacrifice for relationship success. But not at the risk of sacrificing Islam.

In particular, if this bond is the beginning of a shared belief system, it's a win. This commitment is the foundation of any successful relationship; if it is cultivated and nurtured, it is the source of spiritual blessings and (barakah). It can bring two people closer to Allah and each other, and this is the greatest blessing of all. It is when there are two or more followers.

If faith isn't present, the shaky ground can crumble. To build a successful foundation, faith is at the core. The same faith for a Muslim and the same faith for any belief system is the semantics of success. Faith gives us the ability to understand one another, share a connection, and find comfort. It's the glue that binds us together and the rock that keeps us standing.

It's not the ability to seek people's approval, it's the ability to transform oneself and ensure correction. Faith's core requires resolving matters within it. No religion demands evil or

transcendence, nor is it connected to an evil society composed of deceit. Faith shields against doubt and evil.

Quran: Surah Luqman: 31;18. And do not turn your nose up to people, norwalk pridefully upon the earth. Surely Allah does not like whoever is arrogant, or boastful.

The major upheaval of this transformation is the refusal to let go of poor company. Loyalty to time and evil is entrapment, not progression. Believers need not be distracted by distractions or put on pedestals. This type of behavior can harm believers' faith, as it makes them depend on external validation instead of their own beliefs. This can weaken their faith and make them vulnerable to criticism and manipulation.

Disbelievers' pedestal is short-lived. The most effective example is (Firon) the Pharaoh of Egypt. Despite his power and wealth, Firon's commitment to his people was short-lived. His lack of commitment, arrogance, and greed ultimately led to his downfall. Respect, understanding, and shared values are the foundations of genuine commitment. Allah's power can overthrow any dynasty.

Leadership must be unwavering and not oppressive. Allah's power will ultimately overthrow or keep any leader in power. The rule of tyrants in countries is often a result of changing discourse among the people and a lack of values and commitment from leaders. An oppressed country is placed under the reign of a tyrant due to his demeanor reflecting the people's behavior. It is impossible for a nation or a person to weather disobedience.

Muslim countries face trials, and each trial strengthens when Allah backs them. No believer has ever lost to a disbeliever. Even impossible trials will become pleasantries.

Many dynasties collapsed when commitment became superficial. Any regime cannot sustain long-term disobedience. He can rain and bring drought. Allah is all-powerful. Allah is the only powerful and almighty ruler, and any leader who does not follow His commands will be overthrown.

A nation's strength and success are based on its commitment to Allah. Allah chooses nation rulers. As the nation's attitude changes, the best leaders can be removed and the worst represents the country. Allah's will determines the fate of a nation, and only through His grace are people blessed with success and prosperity. Ultimately, a nation's strength lies in its devotion to Allah. It is the nation that makes them deserving or undeserving of Allah's wrath.

Nations that follow Allah's commands will be blessed, while those who do not will be punished. Ultimately, Allah controls and decides any nation's fate. While the earth's personnel and demeanor change, Allah's plan remains.

Allah will question tyrants, rich people, and oppressors. A just crowd oppressed by an oppressor will suffer and be punished by Allah as well. Allah's time, not people's time. However, sometimes tyrants mislead the innocent and seek evil. In the same vein, many countries collapsed because of Allah's disobedience. The Pharaoh's wealth dwarfed Western society's economy, and he drowned from his disobedience to Allah. In His superb justice system, there are no cracks. This example shows Allah's command prevails.

The disobedience of people personifies evil during prophets' reigns throughout history. However, Muhammad (pbuh) is said to be the last prophet and had the most followers. What does that say? It clarifies that those who believe in one Allah will reign as the majority, not the minority.

The Aqsa Mosque, located in the Old City of Jerusalem, holds immense religious significance to Muslims around the world. According to Islamic tradition, it is believed to be the second holiest site in Islam, after the Kaaba in Mecca. The Prophet Muhammad's journey, known as the Night Journey of" Isra and Mi'raj", is a pivotal event in Islamic history. It is believed that the Prophet was transported from the Kaaba to the Aqsa Mosque on the miraculous creature known as Buraq. Once at the Aqsa Mosque, Muhammad (pbuh) ascended to heaven, where he encountered various prophets and led them in prayer. This event not only solidified the importance of the Aqsa Mosque in Islamic belief but also established the connection between the Abrahamic faiths, as it brought together revered figures such as Abraham, Jesus, and Moses among others. As a result, the Aqsa Mosque remains a symbol of unity, spirituality, and historical significance for Muslims worldwide.

Quran: Surah Isra: 17:1. It is he who carried his servant by night from the mosque in Makkah to the mosque in Jerusalem (Aqsa) whose surroundings we have blessed that we might show him some of our signs. Indeed he alone is hearing all-seeing.

The night of Isra "wal Mi'raj", also known as the Night Journey and Ascension, is a significant event in Islamic history. During this miraculous journey, the Prophet was bestowed with numerous blessings and gifts, one of which was the gift of "Salat" prayer. Initially, Allah commanded the Prophet to instruct his followers to pray fifty times a day. However, upon witnessing the Prophet's concern for the difficulty his "Ummah" his people would face in fulfilling this obligation, he implored Allah to reduce the number of prayers.

After several pleas, Allah graciously reduced the daily prayers to five times a day while still maintaining the reward of fifty times. This divine mandate made it obligatory for all Muslims to perform Salat five times a day. Muslims believe that through the regular observance of Salat, they can cleanse themselves of sins and seek forgiveness from Allah. While mistakes or sins may occur in one's daily life, Muslims can rectify them through sincere repentance and voluntary acts of charity, known as "sadaqah". The Night of "Isra wal Miraj" took place in the month of Rajab, specifically on the 27th day of the Hijri calendar, marking it as a significant and spiritually significant occasion for Muslims worldwide.

On the night of Miraj, Prophet Muhammad received another gift, which was forgiveness for those who do not associate partners with Allah. This gift emphasized the importance of monotheism and unity in faith. Allah has commanded believers to maintain faith in one God and to come together in belief, particularly within the Abrahamic faiths. Prophet Abraham (peace be upon him) is considered the father of the Abrahamic faiths, as he was a devout follower of monotheism and played a significant role in establishing this belief. Therefore, the gift of forgiveness on the night of Miraj served as a reminder of the unity among believers and the importance of following the path of monotheism, as exemplified by Prophet Abraham.

Quran: Surah Maidah 5:68, Say O People of the Scripture! Ye have naught (of guidance) till ye observe the Torah and the Gospel and that which was revealed unto you from your Lord.

Quran: Surah Baqarah :2:286. Allah does not lay a responsibility on anyone beyond his capacity. In his favor shall be whatever good each one does, and against him whatever evil he does. (Believers!

Quran: Surah Ghafir:40:5. Before them, Noah's people denied the truth, as did other enemy forces afterward. Every community plotted against its prophet to seize him, and argued in falsehood, ˹hoping˺ to discredit the truth with it. So I seized them. And how ˹horrible˺ was my punishment? **Prophets, teachers, leaders, parents, children,** spouses, and families are all justified by Allah's justice. Islam places no burden on another soul. Individual actions will be judged according to their merits.

Just as the Islamic calendar varies, so do the practices of Muslims, showcasing their unique traditions for those who adhere to the principles of Islam. For those who are in pursuit of a well-structured life, the contagious event of peace serves as a formative experience.

The Islamic calendar is based on the lunar cycles, with each month beginning and ending with the sighting of the new moon. This calendar system has been followed by Muslims since the time of Omar bin Khattab, who contributed to the" Hijri calendar". It is used to determine the dates of religious observances and events. The lunar calendar consists of 12 months, which can be either 29 or 30 days long, depending on the sighting of the moon. This results in a total of either 354 or 355 days in a year. In contrast, the calendar used in the business world and by most countries is the Gregorian calendar, which is a solar calendar based on the Earth's orbit around the sun.

It consists of 365 days, with an extra day added every four years in a leap year. This calendar was introduced by Pope Gregory XIII in 1582 and is now widely adopted worldwide.The difference in calendars reflects the distinct approach of Muslims towards time and religious practices. The Islamic calendar emphasizes the importance of lunar cycles and the observance of religious events based on the sighting of the moon.

This adherence to the lunar calendar serves as a reminder of the Islamic faith and its connection to the divine guidance provided by Allah.While the use of different calendars can sometimes lead to practical challenges, such as coordinating schedules and planning events, it also highlights the unique cultural and religious practices of the Muslim community. The Islamic calendar serves as a symbol of unity and devotion among Muslims worldwide, reinforcing their commitment to the principles of monotheism and the teachings of the Quran

Living on infertile ground has both benefits and hazards. Rotted wood is a favorite food source for termites. Humans spray poison on them, and they eventually die. Disbelievers are examples of such behavior. Working in an unfiltered company is not the best environment for Muslims. Allah separates such individuals from believers.

Stagnation and disobedience to Allah's laws are silent deaths for Muslims. Islam's log of life displays chronicles of mannerisms, etiquette, and food habits. There is no room for change or contemplation in Islam's finest refinement. There are no changes to vocabulary terms, scripts, or rules. Discipline and allowances were established for animals, food, and water. Creators know what their creations need. The defiance extends to swine consumption, which is prohibited by previous Scriptures.

A humanely raised animal eating a natural diet and raised in an ethical environment will yield the highest quality of taste and nutrition. As Halal meat is tasty when Allah's name is mentioned, it

should be consumed, but not excessively. Furthermore, humane slaughter methods make meat healthier than other types of meat. In addition, it promotes animal welfare and sustainability. Our bodies and minds are directly affected by what we consume. Moderate and within the law, eating is permissible in moderation. Spiritual harmony and peace are achieved by staying true to beliefs and following religious teachings. Human nature is defiant, suffers, and eats unhealthy things, especially pigs.

For those who belong to the Abrahamic faith, it is considered evil and a defiance to consume pork, as Jesus himself did not consume this animal and did not encourage its consumption. Eating pork would be seen as a violation of the Mosaic law, and the remainder of this principle is consistently emphasized. Jesus came to fulfill the law, not to disregard or go against it.

Bible: Deuteronomy: 14:8. And don't eat pork, since pigs have divided hoofs, but they do not chew their cud. Don't even touch a dead pig! ... You can eat any fish that has fins and scales.

Quran: Surah Maidah 5:3. Forbidden to you are carrion, blood, and swine; what is slaughtered in the name of any other than Allah; what is killed by strangling, beating, or fall.

As a test, Allah sent this prohibited animal to earth. Laws govern right and wrong, and people can obey them or not. There are numerous instances of defiance in every religious sect. Muslims are not excluded since humans are defiant.

During the intense competition for food, pigs engage in a unique behavior where they not only invite their mates but also offer them to other pigs. Once he completes the mating process, he proceeds to observe the other animals engaging in mating activities with his partner. His nature encompasses shamelessness as a defining characteristic. Humanity was presented with a test as a way to gauge their abilities.

In this defiant world, it is considered acceptable for wives to engage in partner swapping and have multiple sexual partners. While not universally applicable, these applications are highly acceptable in corroded defiant settings for most individuals. By using a pig as an example, it becomes evident that humans can possess immoral qualities similar to that of a pig. Furthermore, consuming such an animal is detrimental to one's health, and the knowledge of the pig's character would likely cause disgust in a typical person due to its filthy demeanor. Consequently, when individuals deviate from the path of morality, they are often likened to pigs. Eating this animal is prohibited in Islam, and it also serves as a test of defiance for those who go against the laws of the Abrahamic faiths.

A nuance of negligence is considered acceptable in this society by analogy, rather than morality. The world, like all societies, still holds conservative values. Observations and statements cannot describe a collective society. Some people may have adapted to evil's effects.

By drawing several contrasts, it is possible to illustrate the cost of defying Allah. The number of cases of African swine fever had increased. The number of pigs that perished reached into the millions, causing numerous individuals to fall ill. While it is challenging to provide a complete description of the pig's character, it is interesting to observe that societies consuming pigs and embracing liberal ideologies tend to display resemblances.

Those who choose to consume venom, which is forbidden by Allah, put themselves in danger of contracting swine viruses. There are four specific verses in the Quran that explicitly prohibit the consumption of swine. The consumption of swine as part of the diet in certain countries leads to the occurrence of diseases caused by swine viruses. When Allah prohibits these actions, some people may argue that Islam is overly strict even in matters that seem trivial. This has led to the need for clarification on various questions that have been answered sufficiently.

Four books were bestowed upon humanity by Allah, all of them carrying the same crucial message of worshiping Him. Christendom, in its pursuit of following its desires rather than the laws, has shifted its focus towards Jesus. The consumption of pigs has become common practice in religious celebrations as well as in daily meals. The current state of affairs is such that not only have pagan rituals infiltrated, but the Mosaic laws, which were once intertwined with the Bible, are no longer fully observed, except in the Quran, which remains unchanged.

Monotheism generally overpowers polytheism in most cases. Monotheistic doctrine and obedience impact adjustments. Moses, Jesus, and Mohammed all demonstrated their devoti's laws and commands.

The simultaneous enforcement of all laws requires a consistent and unwavering commitment to following them. They have tailored everything to fit their own preferences. If Muslims choose to adhere to man-made rituals in order to satisfy their whims, it can be seen as a loud cry. The act of demonstrating defiance in Muslim society should not be seen as an expression of ignorance, but rather as an opportunity to address grievances and reinforce one's beliefs.

The distinction, which serves as a parable, is characterized by its stark contrast and defiance. When an individual devotes decades to the pursuit of truth instead of succumbing to deception, the truth not only unifies humanity but also fortifies it. The faithful individuals will not cause any disruptions to humanity; instead, they will provide assistance in the appropriate direction. Instead of misdirection, the lost are in need of guidance. Living by this motto is something that Clarity prioritizes.

The Gospel of Jesus the Ingel provides a clear explanation about Jesus' purpose, stating that he came to fulfill Moses' law rather than altering it. In accordance with the teachings of the Quran, the law is in harmony with the belief in a single god. Nevertheless, the commandments remain the same. The question of how Christendom reached a consensus on Pauline Christianity is one that deserves examination. Paul was not mentioned by Jesus in his discourse. The two individuals did not come together and meet. Prophet Muhammad, according to belief and proof, accomplished the fulfillment of the prophecies.

Bible ESV:5:17-20."Do not think that I have come to abolish the Law or the Prophets; I have not come to abolish them but to fulfill them.

These obvious distinctions alone are not enough to explain the adaptations, as there is no logical conclusion that can be drawn from them. It is important for Muslims to avoid falling into this trap, as they are aware of the consequences and historical context. Contrasting information serves as educational material to make informed decisions for all individuals.

The allegations made suggest that Jesus was ridiculed in his acts of worship and claimed to possess divinity by deviants. In his address, he made it clear that his intention was to fulfill the law of Moses. It is evident that his aim is to modify the existing legislation and transform himself into a divine being. The project aligns with the principles outlined in the Bible. The discordant message can be a source of trouble for someone who desires clarity. According to the Quran, he is referred to as the Messiah, and it is this designation that ensures his honor remains intact.

The majority of individuals who identify as evangelicals have a strong desire to propagate their faith by publicly demonstrating their commitment to their newfound belief through the act of baptism. It is often observed that people are quick to impose rules on others, without adhering to those rules themselves, but rather modifying them to suit their own needs.

If their demands are not met, these individuals will employ religion as a tool to condemn Muslims and assert forgiveness through Jesus the prophet and Messiah. The initial statement that greets your ears is, "I identify as a devout Christian with strong moral values." The same pattern of deceptive tactics persists with the proclamation, "I am a person of integrity." If there is any validity to these assertions, they should not require vocalization, as individuals are capable of forming their own judgments based on actions, which often speak louder than mere words.

Prophet Muhammad never asserted his own greatness or claimed to be the ultimate Muslim. Instead, he personified the values of Islam, which is a religion based on logic and evidence. It is important to note that there is no trace of hypocrisy present here. Instead of engaging in gossip, we choose to repent when we make mistakes. When someone remains honest and keeps silent, the passage of time will ultimately expose their genuine intentions. Just as Satan tries to divert attention, he inadvertently exposes his wrongdoing. Additionally, his inclination to propagate false information and the presence of his network of manipulators necessitates a sense of caution when lending an ear to his whispers.

The company of a believer is far superior to that of a thousand disbelievers. The difference between evangelicals and other sects of Christendom continues to persist. Their stance is in support of Israel. Their conviction that Jesus will come to save them is the reason behind their actions.

The engagement in an act that simultaneously showcases both kindness and hypocrisy by relaying the message to others, claiming that Jesus himself is urging them to implore you to accept him as your savior. Unfounded accusations have been made against him, insinuating that he is instructing people to worship him. It is astonishing to note that a few individuals take it to the extreme of asserting that the very words they utter are actually being spoken by Jesus himself, as he communicates his profound affection and care for them.

It is only through Allah that the prophets can confirm the authenticity of their messages and visions in dreams, as it is impossible to receive such messages or view prophets in person unless it is a dream during sleep. Witnessing the presence of a prophet, particularly the esteemed Prophet Muhammad, is a divine blessing and a manifestation of Allah's mercy.

If anyone has had the privilege of seeing Prophet Muhammad in a dream, they would surely remember it upon waking, for Satan is incapable of imitating him and no one can assume his likeness. A person who is fortunate enough to see him in a dream is considered a great mercy bestowed by Allah. Dreams hold a significant amount of value for a Muslim individual. Some individuals might find it impossible to believe that Jesus can appear in front of them and communicate with them, as they argue that if this were true, the Quran would have explicitly mentioned that prophets can manifest themselves after their passing.

Any claim of a human form taken by Satan, other than in a dream, lacks authenticity. There have been instances where individuals have witnessed Prophet Muhammad in their dreams, leading them to convert to Islam. After witnessing him in a dream, certain Muslims hold steadfast to their dreams, being cautious not to disclose them to disbelievers or believers who may harbor envy. As the times are constantly evolving, it is becoming increasingly difficult for a believer to trust anyone. However, it is important to remember that Allah is the ultimate jurist, listener, and the one who holds all the secrets and dreams of a believer.

In the Muslim faith, there is a deep respect for an individual's freedom of choice, and it is not the intention to impose Islam on anyone. The freedom is yours to either select Islam as your faith or opt for a different path. However, Allah does not rely on numerical values.

He is aware of the individuals who will worship him. The truth is, these monotonous invitations are not only insincere, but they also highlight the hypocrisy in our society, where everyday life goes on while laws are being violated constantly. However, Muslims are fully cognizant of the teachings of Islam and they do not enforce their religious beliefs onto others, recognizing that faith is a divine invitation from Allah, rather than a mandate from any individual.

In the Quran, it is stated that human prophets, sent with guidance, and revelations, are acknowledged as prophets of Allah, yet they are not regarded as being on the same level as Allah.

The Quran, with the intention of benefiting and enriching humanity, prohibits the consumption of swine and alcohol, engaging in adultery and fornication, stealing, and spreading gossip. It is a common occurrence for believers in Islam to stumble and give in to their temptations and desires, yet they can find solace in the fact that Allah is ever-forgiving.

Prophet Muhammad's law was essentially identical to the previous law, but with the added aspect of Allah tailoring it to suit the specific needs of humanity and incorporating the invaluable practice of "Salat" mandated prayer. While all prophets worshiped one god, the Quran introduced a wealth of knowledge that addressed various aspects of humanity's curiosity. It provided insights into topics such as the Big Bang theory, science, embryology, the uniqueness of fingerprints, relationships, marriage, fornication, stealing, punishments, miracles, and much more. The depth and elegance of the Arabic Quran go beyond what can be conveyed in a mere paragraph, making it a text unparalleled in its sophistication and availability to humans.

When it comes to believers, gossip can have a devastating impact, as it has the ability to shatter both the speaker and the listener, and can also expose pretentious information about them or anyone else for that matter. The significance of contrasts and differences is growing, especially in specific countries. The subject matter of this is heavily influenced by the way humanity speaks and communicates. Ultimately, it is humanity that unravels and elucidates the truth. Allah, in His infinite wisdom and mercy, grants us the permission and ability to both understand and provide for the needs of our bodies, minds, and souls.

Allah provides for every human being, regardless of whether or not they worship him. The followers of his faith are well aware of the advantages and benefits that come from adhering to rules, laws, and regulations. In order to ensure the safety of their pets, dog owners have the option to place various items such as collars, stamps, chips, and inks on their bodies to aid in locating lost dogs.

What happens to those individuals who are unable to find God and feel lost in their search? There is no tracking system in place, and individuals who go astray will face penalization. The decision to have faith is ultimately a personal choice. People who claim to have happiness but either consider it unattainable or have never truly experienced it. What if there was someone who engages in impermissible actions on a daily basis and boldly proclaims their happiness? Going against the will of Allah, it brings negative consequences rather than happiness.

People tend to show a willingness to adhere to societal rules, but they often display a defiance towards the rules set by Allah. When a Muslim has the intention to disobey Allah's laws, what sort of license do they possess? There are certain incidents where the dog may never return to join them due to the fact that he symbolizes the appearance of a stray dog. The choice available to a believer who is seeking truth in a safe environment is comparable to the choice made by a dog who selected stray dogs to join in a pack.

Those who are easily stirred and strayed by disbelievers tend to lose sight of their own beliefs easily. Returning is the most effective option. Muslims are advised to carefully select their companions and ensure they are of good character. Those who have faith in something are typically honest and do not deceive others. Individuals who have the ability to grasp clarity through the use of examples have the potential to personify their difficulties and successfully navigate towards the correct course of action. Another example that showcases his remarkable ability is his capacity to smell and find his way back home, the very place that provided him with nourishment and support. Muslims will continuously abide by the path that is familiar to them in order to attain the utmost peace.

It is possible for a dog to find and take on a new owner. Just like non-believers, believers also have the ability to do the same. With just a single word, it is possible to bring believers back to Allah and reconnect them with his people. It puzzles individuals how the master, who bestowed souls upon humanity, could depart from the human world and leave us in a state of wonder. Those who are on a quest for deeper thinking and understanding succeed along with learning.

For those who pass by and leave a message about how not to be like them, all it takes is a simple example of how not to live. The pursuit of excellence is a fundamental aspect of Islam, as Muslims firmly believe that Allah supports and aids those who actively seek self-improvement. The loyalty shown by a dog to its master can be compared to the loyalty displayed by humans. Comparing humans and dogs is not a valid or accurate comparison to make. Humans have no master except for Allah, who holds complete dominion over them. There is a chance that the dog may be owned by multiple people.

Dogs have been trained by Muslims for centuries. Many of these animals have been trained and rescued by Muslims. In order to keep the animals trained, it is important to first train yourself as a Muslim, as this is the best path for a believer. By choosing to ignore rules or openly opposing Islam, individuals inadvertently have become the epitome of devout Muslims, as their psyche can be triggered by anything, propelling them to embody the essence of the faith.

Balbir Singh, an individual from India, took part in the demolition of a mosque. Later on in his life, he embraced the Islamic faith and took it upon himself to construct more than 90 mosques. Despite being the one who initially destroyed the Babri mosque, he took it upon himself to fix the damages and went on to build a staggering 90 more. After adopting the name Muhammed Amir, he made sure to live by it.

Arnoud Van Doorn, similar to many others, harbored negative sentiments towards Islam. He was a member of the right-wing political party PVV and he gained notoriety for creating films that were seen as disrespectful to Islam, particularly those involving Muhammad peace be upon him. During the latter part of 2013, he shared a tweet on his Twitter account, displaying the Muslim Shahada in Arabic. Twitter played a significant role in helping him embrace his shahada as a Muslim. Utilizing the popular social media platform, he shared his thoughts by tweeting on Twitter. That he was a Muslim to the world. Social media has the power to drastically transform the lives of certain individuals, while simultaneously serving as a platform for mischief and malevolence for others. People who possess such qualities often leave behind traces that serve as examples.

Twitter played a significant role in the acceptance of Islam for many people, including Arnoud Van Doorn. Those aware of the threshold will appreciate and refrain from abusing it. Social media is a continuous stream of good and bad. Muslims implore using it for good. Examples are magnificent, not counting flaws of Muslims later the son of Arnoud Van Doorn accepted Islam. Converts can inspire families who disapprove of their choices.

The platform he and many have discovered and utilized to express and assert his beliefs on social media gained significance. Many individuals who are in search of Islam have discovered it in the most unexpected of ways, and have managed to sustain their faith by utilizing the resources that have recognized and supported their values. Those who harbored hatred towards Islam were the ones who left behind a considerable amount of wealth, and it is within the capacity of a Muslim to discuss the riches they left behind. Once they discovered Islam, they experienced a complete transformation of faith and were able to preserve their belief, which serves as a valuable lesson for Muslims who were born into this faith. These are just a few examples of individuals who truly believe in their cause.

In order to safeguard the memories of the start of Islam from the impact of evil, he turned to Twitter as a way to maintain a constant state of happiness. The manner in which something is utilized gains significance, particularly when the truth becomes known to a human being. After accepting Islam, he traveled to Mecca, the sacred land, where he paid homage and expressed his intention to create another movie that would honor Prophet Muhammad and the Islamic faith.

All Muslims have received his apology for his actions, marking a significant moment of reconciliation. When someone offers an apology, it signifies their intention to avoid making the same error in the future. In addition to rectifying his derogatory actions, he underwent a complete transformation in his attitude and began to show deep respect and admiration towards Islam and the Muslim community as a whole. It is difficult to comprehend how anyone could possibly forget such remarkable performances. In this current era, characterized by strong contemplation and doubts overshadowing belief, these individuals managed to shine.

Not only was Joram Van Klaveren a fierce critic of Islam, but he also served as an unexpected muse for cartoonists. While writing anti-Islamic books Allah caused a change in his heart, resulting in his book having a different impact.

He wrote about his journey, detailing his transformation and conversion to Islam, ultimately embracing the faith and becoming a devoted Muslim. Individuals who possess an understanding of the truth should embark on an exploration of the intricacies encompassed within this particular chapter of life, alongside fellow believers, while placing utmost reliance on Allah. However, it is important to note that this research merely signifies the commencement of a much larger journey. Paul Kennedy, originally from Africa, was a devoted priest who received support from the Vatican with the purpose of spreading Christianity.

Following the rise of anti-Islam sentiments, he made the life-changing decision to convert to Islam, which resulted in him losing all of his wealth. Despite this setback, he dedicated himself to spreading Islam throughout the entire country. It is incredible to see how people from various backgrounds and walks of life are united in their pursuit of truth. I could dedicate an entire book to showcasing these stories. For those who are in search of it, Islam represents a sublime truth. The search for truth is a straight and uncomplicated path, devoid of any obstacles or challenges to overcome. Islam has witnessed a remarkable shift as its staunchest adversaries have now become its biggest advocates.

Muslims generally hold the belief that within the principles and teachings of Islam, there are no gray areas.

There are two possibilities - either he is bound by the rules or he is governed by his own set of rules. Muslims follow Allah's rules and guidance. The rules and guidance provided by life are evident in every episode we encounter. The multitude of experiences that make up the episodes of our lives serve as constant reminders of the boundless power that Allah possesses. The sound of gratitude is like a sweet melody to a believer, whereas to a disbeliever, the sound of hatred echoes with pride and arrogance.

Those who truly recognize the significance and joy of connecting with Allah are encouraged to observe salat-mandated prayer at the designated times. Living in accordance with one's beliefs is considered a way of life for those who are devout. It is truly unfortunate for those individuals who possess knowledge about Islam but choose not to delve deeper and comprehend the essence of their own faith. Conversely, some individuals make an effort to acquire knowledge about everything they decide to follow. The hearts of those who seek the path are opened by Allah, whereas those who waste time are left to navigate a narrow path. A feeling of tightness surrounds the heart, causing it to constrict.

Quran: Surah An'am 6:125.So whoever Allāh wants to guide - He expands his breasts intending to contain Islam. Whenever He wants to send astray. He makes his breasts tight and constricted as though he were climbing into the sky. Allah defiles those who do not believe.

Islam has a profound impact on every facet of life. The path of Islam is characterized by its straightness, devoid of any holes or ridges. For centuries, Muslims have adhered to the practice of cleanliness before prayers, as mandated by the Islamic rules that emphasize the importance of cleanliness prior to engaging in prayer. When it comes to cleaning, water is the ultimate method, not limited to just paper.

The affordability of bidets is limited to the wealthy, whereas the poorest Muslims have relied on water for personal hygiene for centuries. The directive to follow this comes from Islam, not from any human authority. The act of washing hands after using the restroom and engaging in dry cleaning is a prevalent practice among Westerners.

The absence of water in disease-vulnerable regions, which are highly susceptible to filth-related illnesses, results in the occurrence of diseases. In the Islamic faith, it is obligatory for a Muslim to relieve themselves whenever needed, and cleanse with water afterwards. They will eventually come to the understanding that water is the solitary source for cleaning.

Muslims are obligated to adhere to specific laws in Islam, laws that are commonly recognized and followed by Muslims. The adjustment to the Muslim mandates is a complex task that will demand their efforts for centuries. The teachings of Islam encompass comprehensive descriptions of survival, addressing the well-being of both the soul and the body in great detail. In the Middle East, public restrooms are equipped with personal cleaning water for hygiene purposes. When Westerners travel to the Middle East, it is common for them to be curious about the object water that Muslims use for their prayers.

Personal hygiene backwardness is observable in so many other areas that need to be corrected if a collective society that claims individuality needs to be educated properly. If Muslims join their ways instead of keeping their ways, the weak-minded are always affected, since they do not realize the polarity of this venture: Islam is progressive. Will not delve into reverse ideologies.

There is no room for stagnation, and it promotes health, vitality, healthy food, and soul searching. Prayer is crucial for humanity's survival. Muslims don't even bury the dead before cleansing the body with water to prepare for meeting Allah. Allah knows all rhetorical and written statements. He cites all rhetorical declarations.

The current system accepts contracts by drafting them. Islam has a script that never changes with the times. The soul of a believer bears witness. Throughout history, stories reinforce and legitimize belief, and examples endure truth in hearts. Prophet Muhammad's sayings and sunnah could save many Muslims. Islam teaches humanity the right to survive.

The regulations and laws are clearly outlined in the Islamic curriculum. The repetition of these laws can cause frustration among those who don't believe, but it is important to note that Allah did not intend these laws for them. These laws are specifically designed for individuals who comprehend that the theatrical performance of Allah is advantageous to humanity as a whole, rather than benefiting Allah on an individual level. The rules we follow are based on the Quran, not created by humans. It is Allah who knows the reasons for imposing these rules in the Quran. Ponder the Quran.

Quran: Surah Baqarah:2:221.A believing slave is better than an associating woman, no matter how attractive she may seem to you. Do not let [your daughters] marry men who associate others with Allah.

The Quran emphasizes Islam's importance. Wrong decisions can cause unexpected things. Some may find repetition tiresome, but truth and restrictions always clear confused minds. The corrupt world embraces egocentric desires, calling Quranic laws restrictive. They would think twice if Allah restricted their (Rizq) sustenance.

By masking the deceivers with these darkening ideologies, they attempt to blindfold those who have been deceived. For some, it's obvious, but some weak-minded Muslims are caught in strands of illusion and deceit from Satan and his people. The righteous will always be laughed at in a society discolored by deceit and false depictions of pleasing disbelievers. But for believers, faith does not bleed, as it is stronger than any other color available.

Story of Barsisa the righteous monk who finally faces penalty:

The narrative of Barsisa, the monk, is an emblematic case. An elegant monk, he was faithful to his architect, his Lord. Barsisa, the monk, had an impressive demeanor and was devoted to his creator. His character impresses many as his devotion to his creator defines his nature. His actions established trust in him.

The brothers saw Barsisa as a model of truth and faith because of his beliefs and actions. The brothers entrusted Barsisa with looking after their sister and ensuring her well-being. She persisted in her devotion to Allah. She was both beautiful and righteous.

Barisa initially refused to take on the responsibility of caring for their sister, but after much insistence and expressing the need, he eventually agreed to help out as a considerate and compassionate monk. He was a young, handsome man who trusted easily. He opted to stay away from temptation. The brothers claimed they perceived him as law-abiding, and their dedication to Allah led them to ensure his honor.

They expressed their intention to influence Barsisa and hold him accountable for their sister's safety. Despite initial resistance, he eventually came around and accepted the job with restrictions. The handsome young monk structured his life around laws that aligned with the rules of the god.

Their residence was located within a shared compound, with their houses conveniently situated right next to each other. The two of them were practically next-door neighbors. A proposal was put forward, suggesting that she possesses the capability to sustain herself. His duties include giving her at least one meal. She went to the market by herself, showcasing her capabilities as a young woman. However, her brothers, who had never left her alone before, were concerned about her safety. They couldn't think of anyone more trustworthy than Barsisa.

Although the sister had a strong independent nature, the brothers decided to assign Barsisa the responsibility of checking up on her and ensuring her safety. They gave him a small task of providing her with one meal as a way to maintain contact and ensure she was doing well.

Despite encountering resistance and persuasion, he agreed to assume the responsibilities and carry on with his duties, assuming he was doing a good deed. Barsisa consistently delivered her meal to her door at a specific time, and she always got it. Satan, being the hindrance, obstructs all the positives. He solely focuses on individuals who engage in righteous and accountable deeds according to Allah. He has no inclination to visit his own people since they reside under his authority.

He closely followed Barsisa's endeavors with interest. His soft-spoken words appeared genuine and muted. He questioned Barsisa about his habit of dropping the meal in front of her door.He whispered the question of dining with her. Barsisa didn't view it as mischievous.

Satan returned to his murmurs, further. He asked, "Why do you speak to her through the door?" She is lonely. She has no brothers. Barsisa acknowledged he did nothing wrong. Taking note of her gentle tone, he appreciated her visit through the door. Indeed, it was for a few minutes. Satan retreated to murmur further to Barsisa. He suggested you know her. Why don't you eat supper with her?

Barsisa considered this a moment of hospitality to have supper with her. He asked if he could eat with her. She complied, realizing her brothers had entrusted him. Satan returned to his murmurs as Barsisa ate dinner with her every day. The pure meeting turned into interest, as they were both attractive and appealing.

They became familiar with each other through daily contact and spending time together. (Zina) fornication earned a place between them. Despite their attraction to each other, the most unexpected act took place that neither of them would have planned. Comfortable with each other, his kindness earned a place in her heart. His charm attracted her, his kind words and voice changed her into the softness she held for him, which she did not expect. She was attractive and intelligent, as well as possessing the demeanor of a young woman who believed in God, which enchanted him.

He was also a god-fearing man, so she trusted him. Nevertheless, emotions come when least expected. Some can control them, while others regretfully settle into actions that are unapproved by God. All this could have been resolved. He could have married her instead of taking a different path. It is what Satan drove to, and he diverted two followers into actions not permitted by Allah. He was told that she was expecting a child. It shocked him to find himself in a situation he did not prepare for, since he was a devotee. His steps unnerved him, and he smothered her.

After she passed away he buried her. His problems were over, and he planned to tell the brothers that she had passed away. Satan made many calls to Barsisa. As the brothers returned, he wept. Your sister died of illness. The brothers were deeply grateful to Barsisa and suffered a fall. They failed their sister, and they weren't there to facilitate. The brothers got up with the same dream: they shouted the sister did not die of natural causes. They ran to the grave and learned he suffocated her.

They encountered Barsisa. He could not deceive for too long. His inner traits were not bad. He was a victim of circumstances he did not know how to handle. He was a monk derailed by Satan's murmurs.

The brothers presented the case of Barsisa and their deceased sister to the presiding Sultan, seeking his judgment. The fear of the accord consumed Barsisa, who was burdened by guilt and felt trapped with no alternatives, as both parties nervously awaited the verdict from the judge and the jury. Barsisa's actions would be determined by the Sultan's decision. He was summoned by the Sultan to appear before him. Barsisa, feeling both frightened and apologetic, had a firsthand experience of adversity. The verdict rendered was a death sentence, as the individual was found guilty of the heinous crime of murdering a young woman.

Barsisa, who was known as a monk, unexpectedly found himself involved in something he never anticipated. Despite facing adversity, he never entertained the idea of engaging in ill deeds or allowing immoral thoughts to enter his mind. The thought constantly plagued him that he could have proposed marriage to her, as their attraction had brought about unforeseen consequences that he had never anticipated.

However, he came to the realization that it was too late to act on these desires. Both of them were believers, and she would have felt deeply honored to be his wife. He sat in dismay, understanding the course of time could not be changed.Satan returned to him, once again and he added, "You have nobody after you dedicated your soul to Allah." You are today facing death. Prostrate to me, I can save you. If you prostrate yourself before me, I have the ability to save you. Feeling disheartened and desperate, Barsisa ultimately succumbed to Satan's final request. He answered, "You fool, I cannot save myself, and certainly, I cannot rescue you." The king judged. Barsisa, upon realizing the futility of the situation, surrendered. In the end, Barsisa chose to give up and surrender. Unfortunately, he met his demise and lost his life. It is unfortunate that he passed away without being a believer, which adds to the sorrow.

Quran: Surah Hashr: 16:17 Their allies deceived them, like Shaitan, when he said to the man: "Disbelieve in Allah." But when humans disbelieve in Allah, Shaitan says: "I am free of you, I fear Allah, the Lord of the 'Alamin (humanity, jinn, and all that exists)!"

So the end of both will be that they will be in the fire, abiding. Such is the recompense of the Zalimun (i.e., polytheists, wrong-doers, disbelievers in Allah and in His Oneness.

The presentation focuses on the moralistic tragedy of Barsisa. Satan, who is accursed, accepts his task with great earnestness. The only people he shows up to are those who are the strongest in their worship. He specifically distracts those who pray to Allah, which disrupts the regulation of the believers. Barsisa had the ability to fulfill the marriage and attraction he felt towards the young woman. Islam encourages lawful relationships and permits marriages that are in accordance with the principles of Halal. However, he chose to become confused and acted impulsively, following the whispered suggestions of Satan.

Satan's intention was to not only seize two followers from their devotion to Allah but also to burden them with the weight of his own existence. An adherent would find no utility or advantage in involving themselves with Satan. He is urging for a large number of individuals to be present in the fire, as it is his ultimate destination. In his perception, disrupting the good offers him a reprieve. As the human takes the course, they have the option to either focus on following the successive route or become distracted by the curves, resulting in driving in the wrong direction.

The act of forbidding specific rules and regulations of Islam is causing discomfort to this society, just as it has for numerous generations before this one. Throughout history, there has been a longstanding presence of disobedience to Allah within society. Even if they choose to disobey, Allah still provides for them and allows them to persist in their belief that they do not need Him, as they believe they can achieve everything on their own.

Sharing these examples and stories is of utmost importance as they have the power to greatly impact the lives of believers. Once they are read, they can serve as a transformative tool, guided by the help of Allah, to turn lives around in a profound way.

It is important to be mindful of Satan's whispers while also being receptive to the invitations of a believer, as this can guide one towards a righteous path. Despite any mistakes made by a believer, those who possess knowledge of Allah can lead themselves and others back to the familiar grounds of belief. Providing material for Allah is not a laborious task; it is easy. Allah forbids liquor in Islam. There is no means of working around it. Veto takes no alterations in Islam.

It appeared not to have regulations until afterward. But progressively, Allah expressed all the procedures to Muslims through the Quran and Sunnah policies and operations of Prophet Muhammad. Quran defines wager and liquor may have some benefits, but impairment is greater next to the benefit. Allah created humanity. He identifies the benefits and losses for humans.

The amazing story of Malik Ibn Dinar:

Malik Ibn Dinar narrated his own story, which makes it conducive to learning:

In his roles as a civil servant, police officer, and traveler, he described a carefree life captivated by liquor, which he turned to in both happy and difficult times. He bought a slave girl and later married her. He fathered a daughter with her and gave her the name Fatima. His eyes were filled with coolness.

His love for her surpassed his love for liquor, yet he still clung to his habits. His explanation didn't attribute it to a faulty habit. He indulged in liquor without any self-imposed restrictions. He savored a sip of liquor one evening. Using her fist, Fatima struck him. The jug hit the ground. If anyone else had achieved that, he would be angry. Since Fatima was a baby, she could not face the consequences of her actions.

He saw it as a warning and decided to quit drinking alcohol. To satisfy this exceptional daughter, he would sacrifice everything. Allah has tests and plans in store for believers. Death visited and took Fatima back when she was five years old. He felt sadness and emptiness.

In order to cope with his pain, he turned to alcohol as a means of escape. His willpower was no match for the temptation, leaving him unable to resist. Fatima was the reason why he made the decision to stop drinking. Sadly, she had departed from this world, leaving behind a void that can never be filled. Every day, he asked himself who could be the person capable of making him quit drinking, but nothing compared to the love he felt for this beautiful girl.

Despite her passing at a young age, his daughter continued to hold a piece of his heart, which was completely unexpected. He was fully aware that death had no possibility of reversing itself, thus leaving him with nothing. The individual who had been responsible for instigating change was no longer present in the midst of his existence. He frequently found himself questioning whether life was cruel or if he was undeserving of happiness, which in turn led him to drink more in an attempt to alleviate the emptiness he felt inside.

To carry on in this world, he had to remain sedated; the pain was unbearable whenever he longed for his young daughter. He longed to be numb and free from the pain. He drank continuously day and night to numb his pain. During his unrestricted stroll, he came upon a five-year-old girl who had a profound impact on him.

As he recalled his own daughter, he developed a fondness for this young girl who was of a similar age. It had been a while since he had smiled, but as he interacted with her, he discovered a spark of joy and a restrained smile appeared on his face. The continuous numbness he felt made him question his own actions and wonder if he would ever be able to experience life again. Despite this inner struggle, he chose to keep his pain to himself, only revealing it through deep reflection.

After his heart underwent a transformation, he sensed that another transition was occurring. In the end, he came to the realization that the path he had been following did not have the power to determine his ultimate destiny. At that moment, he was on the verge of a transformative change. His sadness was so profound that it could not be alleviated by anything.

During his slumber, he had an experience of a dream. The commencement of the long-awaited judgment day had finally arrived and people were filled with a mix of emotions. The unfolding of a chaotic scene resulted in people frantically fleeing. The only person who realized that he was being followed was him, and the one following him was a black snake. In order to escape from the serpent, he continued running until he finally reached the highest point of the ridge. The presence of an attractive elderly man caught attention as he stood by himself. With a desperate plea, he implored the elderly man for assistance. I am in need of your help, as I am currently being trailed by a black snake.Please help me for the sake of Allah.

The elderly man responded, stating his age and weakness. I am not capable of saving you. Seek out another individual. He reached the mountain's peak, terrified and full of fear, as he ran. He witnessed children playing. In their midst was a girl who bore a striking resemblance to Fatima. Fatima's vividness matched that of her silhouette. "Oh, it's you!" he shouted when he saw Fatima. There's a snake right behind me.

Fatima replied, "Oh, Father, the black snake represents your evil deeds, while the serene, elderly man represents your good deeds." She sat on his lap and played with his beard as she did when she was with him. She pushed the snake with one hand and looked kindly at the elderly man. With so many evil deeds on your record, you would sink without help. The snake is behind you because your righteous deeds are so few. She said it was time to change your ways.

She recited a verse from the Quran. The dream was over. It was the time of prayer after sunset for Muslims. He rushed to the mosque for prayer. He heard the "muezzin" reciting the same verse Fatima

469

had recited from the Quran in his dream. "Has Allah not moved the hearts of believers? Has the time not come?"

His eyes were wet with the truth and reality of his dream. A broad smile spread across his face as he ran to the mosque. In belief and desire to run to admission and presence and devotion to Allah. He knew Allah sent Fatima as a warning to change his ways. He knew how thankful he was to the creator. Allah sends whom he wishes to his servant in person or in a dream. The mercy of Allah knows no bounds, as it arrives in both expected and unexpected times, leaving no room for doubt in this world or the next.

Quran: Surah Hadid: 57:16. (Has the time not yet come for believers' hearts to be humbled at the remembrance of Allah? What has been revealed of the truth, and not be like those given the Scripture before—those who were spoiled for so long that their hearts became hardened. And many of them are still rebellious.

It filled his eyes with tears and filled his heart with passion. As he heard the verse the muezzin was reciting, he dreamed of the verse. Allah sent Fatima to him in a dream to help him. There is a turning point in each human's life who seeks Allah. He seeks his path, and Allah shows him the way. If a person chooses evil, Satan leads the way.

Someone could not sway him for too long, because his heart was soft. Allah would show him the way. His passion for travel continued, as did his passion for faith. He wanted to tell everyone about his beliefs and faith.

Because of his learning, he has many stories to tell and examples to leave behind. He traveled from Saudi Arabia to India. The scholar continued to spread Islam as part of his mission. His mission was to invite people to something so precious to him.

His appreciation for Islam was indescribable. He had been on the other side of the fence. In evil discourse, he had no place anymore. He had found his God, which he would share. The stories he tells are emblematic of learning that extends beyond one's expression or episode. Those who truly learned Islam never strayed from the course.Many of his adventures serve as examples for humanity to draw inspiration from. He was a leader in his time.

While some individuals choose to abandon the habit of consuming alcohol, others turn it into a lifelong series of events, refusing to let go of the detrimental impact it has on their overall well-being. When a person is summoned by Allah, they run because they are familiar with the caller's identity. The believer's response to Allah remains the same, no matter who he sends.

There are individuals who consciously subject themselves to injustice, possessing a complete understanding of the advantages and disadvantages not associated with Islam. The primary source of joy for this society lies in engaging in social activities and embracing the consumption of alcoholic beverages. Wine is often associated with elegance, as it symbolizes refinement and sophistication. Islam does not discriminate based on how something is wrapped or aged.

The commencement of weddings and other celebratory occasions frequently involves a hint of defiance and the active encouragement of alcoholic beverages. This statement goes against the teachings of Islam in every way. It's interesting to ponder why Allah doesn't consider something that appears insignificant and irrelevant to be of any significance.

The main objective of the proposed measure is to address the problem of intoxication by introducing legislation that would enforce a complete ban on the consumption of alcohol. Although it may sound restrictive, it is important to note that alcohol consumption is widely recognized as the primary factor contributing to societal discord. The understanding of Islamic statutory laws affirms that the consumption of alcohol is already banned for believers, as Allah has declared so.

If Muslim countries continue this ban it may appear boring for those who find excitement through intoxication experiencing life in its true form could be a nature of revival taught by the Quran.

In society, individuals have the freedom to act as they choose, while Islam does not impose restrictions on anyone. The suggestive comments provided are only meant to clarify the discussion and highlight the potential harm and affliction caused by alcohol. It is important to note that Allah would not prohibit something as simple as a beverage made from fermented fruits. While humans typically avoid consuming rotted fruits, it is quite contradictory that they willingly consume rotten drinks in search of intoxication, thereby engaging in a deceptive act.

Humanity was created by Allah and throughout history, he has always provided proper guidance to his people. No human has the authority to claim or override Allah's laws. Any attempt to do so is not a matter of legislation but an act of defiance against his divine authority.

The pressure to conform to societal standards, particularly in diverse settings, can be overwhelming for those who lack inner strength, often leading to their downfall. Peer pressure has a detrimental impact on Muslim identities. The presence of wine and alcohol can serve as a catalyst for starting off vacations and business meetings.

This society can only find pleasure when operating on a different frequency, like Satan with his temptations. Depending on the person you ask, one drink is acceptable. The effects are not as bad as expected. They believe that alcohol has a calming effect on the mind. Muslims find peace in their minds without needing disobedience to fuel joy.

Islam's script does not include partially performed acts. Laws, which are embargoed and empowered by compromises, are not influenced by human desires. Omar Bin Khattab, a convert to Islam, leaves a lasting legacy. He refrained from consuming alcohol after accepting Islam. While he found pleasure in drinking, he gave it up after converting to Islam.

Such are those who value their faith not a fad but never underestimate the one who repents is stronger than one who doesn't. It is characterized by falsehood and irrationality. Behavior characterized by falsehood and irrationality. Partaking in alcohol at a party may be perceived as a cure for malevolence.

Praying Salat in front of disbelievers is embarrassing for some hypocrites, but indulging in prohibited activities like drinking is effortless. Brain development is hindered and functions are impaired by alcohol. Additionally, it impairs judgment and decision-making, resulting in higher risk-taking and potential danger.

Furthermore, alcohol consumption is connected to a range of health problems, including liver disease, heart disease, and certain types of cancer. The venue is being glamorized by a Satanic plot involving alcohol.

Drunks can tell you about the mishaps and tragedies that fill bars. Due to the stories they shared, they were left with the unhappy terrain of time loss. The temptations differ based on the people you surround yourself with. It is believed that humans are shaped by the people they associate with. Choosing the right company and environment is of utmost importance.

If Allah deems something negative, why would a human believer oppose it? Repentance can fix mistakes, but persistently defying Allah is not just a mistake, it is a deliberate choice to embrace evil and rebellion. Pleasing society and desires, not Allah's laws. They are considered outdated by some. Lack of comprehension of paganism and its era is a prominent issue in modernization.

Prophet Muhammad before he gained prophethood was invited as a young man to celebrations he agreed to attend twice. Both times Allah made him sleepy and he could not attend the functions. When Allah wants to protect a human he makes provisions.

Prophet Muhammad's life serves as a constant reminder to Muslims, from birth to his passing. Every mother recalls pregnancy and the moment she holds her unborn child. His mother recounted the light she witnessed radiating from her womb to Busra.

Some children disrupt the balance in families and society. Problem-solving and setting examples occur in families, society, and religion. The womb is the safest environment for a child. Muhammad, the prophet, was safeguarded by Allah in this world and the hereafter. Prophet Muhammad's mother, Amina, was widowed before his birth.

Her economic situation was poor after losing her husband. Milk bottles were not an option at that time. If the mother couldn't breastfeed, they would seek a wet nurse. The bond between mother and child cannot be compared to anything else, just like the maximum nutrients found in mother's milk.

Furthermore, her milk surpasses that of a wet nurse. Amina couldn't produce sufficient milk, so she opted to seek a wet nurse. Halima and her husband faced financial difficulties, especially after Halima gave birth. This gathering was attended by them. The location where mothers bring their infants to hire a wet nurse. She was a youthful mother in search of a wet nurse position. Amina's baby was chosen as the final selection. Accompanying him was a mother who, as the sole caregiver, was raising her child alone. She knew that the families who came with their husbands had a greater quantity of possessions than she did. Halima had no choice but to accept him, as he was the sole remaining infant.

The arrival of this precious baby completely transformed her house, filling it with a brilliant light that illuminated every room and filled her heart with joy. The long period of dryness and water scarcity has finally come to an end as the drought has turned around. The cattle she owned had plenty of food and were able to produce an abundance of milk after they came back home. As soon as he arrived, a complete transformation took place and everything changed.

The udders of the goats and sheep were full. Their observation of the change in agriculture was immediate. Allah's blessings filled her home without limit. The love she felt for the newest member of her family surpassed even the love she had for her own child. The family members were filled with love and affection, which flourished and grew stronger over time. Mohammad had a great time playing with her son throughout his childhood, as he was constantly surrounded by love.

Amina, who lived alone, dedicated herself to providing her son with a nurturing and supportive family environment in which he could thrive and grow. Despite being a widow, she preferred him to have a family rather than being alone with her. When he visited his biological mother, Halima was by his side as his companion. Amina noticed the sadness in Halima's eyes and decided to let him stay longer, fearing the child's separation.

Some of his life stories and episodes may surprise many, and some may even doubt them. Islam is meant for believers, not doubters. Prophet Muhammad played with a boy who grew up alongside him. Angel Gabriel arrived as the boys played together, laid him down, opened his heart, and cleansed it with Zam Zam water. Witnessing the scene, the boy became flustered and rushed to inform his mother.

Despite facing multiple challenges, each obstacle only served to strengthen Muhammad (pbuh). Every human being is subjected to tests by Allah, and they must endure them. Halima, upon hearing this, made the decision to bring him to live with his mother. Above all else, her greatest desire was for his safety.

Jibril, an angel renowned for faithfully executing divine commands and adhering to his role, went beyond expectations by conducting not only one but two open-heart surgeries on Prophet Muhammad. The purpose behind these procedures was to purify the Prophet's heart from any lingering presence of malevolence. On his chest, there was a visible mark, and on his back, he carried the distinguished seal of the prophets. Prophet Muhammad, in his teachings, emphasized that a dark spot can be found in the heart of every person. The act of carving it out and purifying him for a task was accomplished by Allah, who then sent angel Gabriel to extract it. The assertion made by him was that Allah had specifically commanded his jinns to live a righteous life.

Considering that Allah purified Prophet Muhammad's heart, it raises the question as to why this purification was not granted to all individuals. Tests and evaluations to establish the existence of different phenomena are carried out by Jinn the Satan and his followers. The magnitude and efficiency were completely extinguished.

The task at hand required him to ensure the delivery of the Quran in its authentic, unaltered state. From the very instant of his birth, he was endowed with the necessary tools and faced challenges that were unparalleled in comparison to those encountered by anyone else. When he was a child, it was only his heart that had the strength to endure the trials that Allah had destined for him. Allah's purification of him was so profound that the tests of time and challenges that arose were insurmountable for both children and adults.

The childhood and adulthood of Prophet Muhammad could have an impact on many individuals, and some may doubt the histories and prophets of Islam. The purpose of such records is not to convince skeptics. At the age of six, his mother fell ill. Barakah, the young midwife, was entrusted with her son at birth. Barakah, I'm leaving, so I'm entrusting Muhammad to you.

At a young age, she had a strong bond with his mother. He held her in high regard. They shared jokes and laughter. Muhammad (pbuh) resided with his birth mother for 1 year. They journeyed together traditionally in a caravan just the two of them. He was a child when she passed away on this trip and he had to wait for the caravans to see him. His mother's death was the first he witnessed and his first funeral.

Throughout the different stages of his life, Muhammad peace be upon him faced numerous challenges that tested his character and resilience. With each test he took, he was being prepared for success from a very young age. Trials have the potential to be a source of strength, rather than a source of weakness, for humans. The stability of everything is maintained through the strength and mercy of Allah. At the young age of six, he experienced the devastating loss of his mother, and tragically, two years later, his grandpa also passed away. Although he had to change guardians occasionally, he was always able to adapt to any situation that Allah presented him with.When his uncle Abu Talib, who had recently been appointed as the clan head, took charge of him. At the age of 25, Muhammad (pbuh) entered into a marriage with a widowed woman who was both older than him and possessed considerable wealth.

Prophet Muhammad's moral character was reinforced and made resilient through the trials he faced during his lifetime. In the present time, there exists a wide range of psychiatric treatments and medications available to assist men who are facing drug addiction or experiencing paranoia as a result of life challenges. While these may offer a cure for a select few, they can also contribute to confusion and dependence in a society that prioritizes the use of drugs. When trust is absent, it induces a sense of panic in individuals, leading them to doubt both themselves and those around them.

Trusting long-term friendships that are unhealthy and do not prioritize the well-being of believers or reverts who turn to Islam during times of hardships or depression. In the context of Islam, independent embrace of the religion is not commonly observed; rather, it is typically embraced within a collective or communal framework. Although an individual may extend help, it is crucial to remember that all invitations to this faith come exclusively from Allah.

The challenges were persistent. The Quraish factions did everything in their power to disrupt the escalation of Islam. Muhammad (pbuh) held a job that was empowering. The assignment lacked a specified end date. There's no voting ballot or throne.

Allah appointed him to deliver the message given by Allah. The transmission of the Quran was believed to frighten many, leading to the overthrow of Islam. Only one person was assigned to complete the task. Without title or fame, he was the most successful executive, fully prepared for the job. When Allah decrees, doubts vanish and accomplishments remain.

Quran: Surah Baqarah 2:212. And Allah gives provision to whom he wills without account.

Story of the lady who wanted to leave town to escape Prophet Muhammad:

The panicked lady of revolutionary reform and dogma in the society she lived in. The new prophet did not appeal to her when she found out that the prophet was changing course and many were turning to him.

She ventured out of town in distress and needed help; she complained to Prophet Muhammad. He was a shining example of humor, patience, and understanding. In distress and worry, she asked, "I must leave now.". She believed that geo-political force was spreading. Have you seen or heard about the man spreading Islam?

She continued before he could answer. It was said that he was a terrible person. I have to leave this city before encountering him. Her luggage weighed her down as she carried a lot. Upon hearing her concern and distress, he extended an offer to help her reach her destination.

They covered a great distance together on foot. He assisted with her luggage. The duration was extended because of her advanced age. During their journey, she had a conversation with him. She valued his acts of kindness towards her. After a lengthy journey, she said, I have finally arrived at my destination, so please drop my luggage"

She expressed gratitude. "Who are you?" she questioned." What is your name? You're quite a handsome, young man. Joking and smiling were his greatest pleasures. In response, he stated that his name was Muhammad, the prophet of Allah, and that you are running away from me. The lady was taken aback. She, too, found it amusing. Together, they burst into laughter.

She stated that I ran from you. The story is unmistakably clear, leaving no room to escape from what you don't comprehend. She stated her fondness for her home. Knowing you, there's no need for me to run. I wish to be taken back. He wasn't bothered. He was thrilled to spend time with her and bring her home. Seekers of truth frequently discover instances from previous eras. In addition to the present. Finding it is within reach.

His mannerisms and humor captured her heart. Her acceptance of Islam came with the belief that a compassionate individual would never spread falsehoods. We can learn many lessons from this prophet's story. He offered his help with the household chores. Even with numerous responsibilities, he still found time to fix his clothes and shoes.

His daily hours were filled with productive activities. Despite his sublime devotion to Allah, he always made time for his family and worldly obligations. How was he able to have such a large amount of time? He held many roles: prophet, leader, husband, father, teacher, friend, and guardian of humanity.

To fulfill his duty of worship and repentance for himself and his people, he opted to reduce his sleep and spend more time in devotion. Out of all the prophets, he stands out as the only one who, when facing judgment, openly acknowledges his people as his own (Ummati) and earnestly appeals to Allah for their forgiveness. Hadith says everyone else will respond (nafsi nafsi).Me,me! Paying attention to the actions of the self-centered world reveals its true nature, and in light of this, having faith as a believer becomes the sole source of friendship one truly needs.

Except for Muhammad (pbuh), every prophet has implored Allah to punish and curse those who defied them. He didn't complain about his people to Allah, not even once. How can anyone not adhere to the sunnah of this prophet, considering his immense contributions to his ummah and people is his living legacy.

Islam brought forth concepts of freedom, justice, humanity, respect, and ownership. The relevance of the Prophets' stories endures for believers. Prophet Ibrahim's trials assess his commitment to monotheism, the fundamental belief of Islam.

Humanity fails to recognize the tests and strength of believers, like Hajar, wife of Prophet Ibrahim, who had her faith tested along with concern for her child. Those who have departed leave behind a legacy, while the legacy of a woman in Mecca has been providing the Zam Zam water for decades. The wells would have dried up, but this water has provided healing and health to many pilgrims.

No scriptures were released by Allah during Abraham's time. As a monotheistic believer in Allah, he stood firmly on pure faith. One morning, Ibrahim woke up and told his wife Hajar to get ready because they were going on a journey.

In the Arabian peninsula's scorching heat, Hagar (Hajar) prepared herself and her infant son with provisions for a few days. Following that, she went on a road trip with her husband and infant son. A barren land devoid of fruits, trees, or water, absent of people, only the faint whisper of her heart and her young son.

On occasion, birds would take flight in search of water sources. In the midst of this scorching heat, Allah commanded Abraham to leave his family behind, as he had his own reasons for every trial. It is through the trials of one individual that the world can reap benefits, while the evil actions of others reveal a different side. These examples serve as compelling evidence, but only those who truly comprehend can grasp their significance.

She directed a question towards her husband. Was it at the behest of Allah that you decided to leave us behind? The answer that he gave was positive and in the affirmative. He is tasked with the responsibility of looking after us and ensuring our well-being. The commands of Allah are always based on a purpose or rationale, ensuring their grounding and significance. The lack of concern that I feel is a result of my belief in Allah's plan, which remains unknown to me. When her husband bid farewell, neither of them questioned Allah's decree. He is dedicated to prioritizing our well-being and will take all the steps required to ensure that we are well taken care of. The faith that believers have left behind is so immense and profound that if people persevere in holding onto it, they can experience just a fraction of the bliss that is attained by a heart that believes.

She sprinted between Safa and Marwa. In search of food and water for her and the baby. She witnessed an angel using his heel to dig into the ground. Using her hands, she formed a basin and water gushed out from the ground. She quickly nourished her infant and consumed some of it. Prophet Muhammad claimed that without her making a basin, with her hands the world would have been flooded with this water. This water was named Zam Zam by her.

Zam Zam is what she called the water. There are various healing properties and nutrients found in the water. Billions of Muslims in Mecca rely on the well. Muslims who visit Mecca follow Hagar's ritual and run from Safa to Marwa.

Hagar's story is a powerful example of how believers in Islam are encouraged to actively pursue their goals and make use of the resources granted to them by Allah. By immersing themselves in the inspiring narratives of Allah, believers can gain wisdom and guidance for their existence. Hagar, instead of succumbing to fear and helplessness, took initiative and actively sought a solution to her and her baby's thirst. She recognized her rights as the sole owner of the well granted to her by Allah and traded with the people who came to settle in the area.

This not only fulfilled her own needs but also allowed her to contribute to the community. The intelligent Muslim women in Saudi Arabia, and throughout the Muslim world are inspired by Hagar's example, have also recognized their rights and responsibilities in society. They have utilized their intelligence and skills to make significant contributions to their communities. Through their appreciation and cherishing of the gifts believers in Islam can lead fulfilling lives and strive to make a positive impact on the world around them. She was not idle; she relentlessly ran in search of water until she was blessed by Allah with it. She refused to stay put; instead, she tirelessly sought what she needed. In Islam, one must search to find; there is no finding without searching.

The circumstances were challenging. They arrived in droves to make their home there. Her water became a feast for the birds and animals. The birds' chirping brought joy to her and humans alike. Hajar made her rights and usage clear on her terms. If she hadn't done that, she might have forfeited her rights and gift. With unwavering faith, she stood strong, knowing Allah was by her side. She asserted her ownership of the water and its terms of use.

Despite numerous clans arriving for water, Allah granted her access to water that she would only have by asserting her riparian rights. The spread of water in Mecca brought celebration among birds. Man cannot survive in any climate, especially Saudi Arabia's scorching heat, without water. She passed on her knowledge of Allah to her son. When Allah called her back, she left behind her son and the Zamzam water well for all Muslims to enjoy.

Ismail and Ibrahim hadn't crossed paths in years. Hagar was his single parent. That path was destined for this family by Allah. His mother instilled in him the belief in Allah and his commands, and the reason behind his father's abandonment. The water they received was proof of faith and Allah's mercy. Zamzam water, the most beneficial water in the world, became accessible to the Muslim world through her trials.

Being a single mother is often described as difficult by many women in this society. Learning is plausible for Muslim women, it's easy. If Allah selected single parenthood for a believing woman, it was intentional. He will provide the help required for survival and encourage progress rather than regression.

The master will ensure the well-being of both the parent and the child. Single mothers who are believers will prosper. The heart's affairs are not destined for success when a woman brags about material success and achievements but lacks faith. A person who instills belief in their children is not a failure. She was chosen by Allah for the job because He knew she had the strength to do it. This story showcases a dutiful woman's strength, finding it in Allah and leading by example in society.

It has been claimed by skeptics that Abraham never embarked on a journey to Mecca. The healing waters of ZamZam, which are still shared by all Muslim pilgrims and Saudi Arabia, were provided to Hagar through her pleading. Throughout the story, Abraham's unwavering role as the father of all Abrahamic prophets is evident, both in the beginning and consistent belief in one god, Allah. The importance of his role lies in his ability to establish the worship of one god, which he accomplished by faithfully acting upon his dreams, showcasing the unwavering strength of his belief. Hagar, a believing woman, faced many trials, but her perseverance led to providing water for all pilgrims. Without her struggles, the needs of the pilgrims and Muslims in Saudi Arabia would not be met. These stories of trials and victories serve as divine commands from Allah that believers understand and follow.

No one can justify why things happen in life, but for a believer, the outcomes are blissful. Single mothers in Islam and believers under stress have no excuses as both possess the strength to fulfill their duties through faith. For a believer, teaching their children about faith is the most important thing.

Many nations have proposed and endorsed the idea of installing pipelines to access this water. Many ridicule Islam, yet seek its advantages. Despite tearing a family apart, the same water now provides for millions of Muslims. Her life has surpassed all expectations. Her ability to find water stems from the hardships she's experienced. Every mother hopes for a son and a daughter. Faith binds them to their mother if they remain faithful to their creator.

Some may disagree and argue that all mothers desire to instill faith in their children. Muslim families who forsake Islam for other faiths do not receive mercy from the religion, demonstrating equilibrium. Only Islam acknowledges Allah as a whole, worships one God, and recognizes every prophet sent by Allah as a prophet.

The compass for human minds is set without negating or cherry-picking. Allah accepts only monotheism. His prophets brought forth monotheism. Christians do not recognize Muhammad the prophet of humanity and view Jesus as the son of God or God Himself who walked on earth. Similarly, most Jews do not recognize Jesus and Prophet Muhammad. Muslims acknowledge every prophet as a servant of Allah and believe in one god. Islam is the only accepted faith and will eventually rule the world before the end of time. The world has that fear, and it's justified.

Quran: Surah Imran: 3;19.Indeed, the religion in the sight of Allah is Islam

Quran: Surah Imran 3;85.And whoever desires other than Islam as religion - never will be accepted from him, and he, in the Hereafter, will be among the losers.

The story of Abraham and Hagar's son is an interesting example:

Today's society cannot be appeased by Islam when faith is at stake. They have been rebelling for centuries and subscribe to pagan ideologies. Satan's plan involves inviting and confusing Muslims. All things are permissible, with restrictions and laws that cannot be interchanged to accommodate other cultures or beliefs. Ismail was the son of Ibrahim and Hagar. He was dutiful to Allah. So were both his parents. Abraham's family forms the foundation for trials and achievements.

Quran: Surah Baqarah:2:133. Or did you witness when death came to Jacob? He asked his children.

Jacob, in his final moments before death, summoned his sons and family. Whom will you worship once I'm gone? They responded, affirming their commitment to worship one god, Allah. One God is the same God worshiped by your forefathers- Abraham, Ishmael, and Isaac. We all surrender to his authority. Worshiping Allah is believed to protect the soul.

The significance of belief in Allah, the one God, has been shown by prophets. The pollution started when Christendom as an Abrahamic faith bestowed godhood upon the prophet Jesus. The start of chaos had arrived. The purification of a believer's soul can rectify disobedience to Allah. Islamic law forbids the addition or partnership with Allah.

Muslims must forsake ideologies, yet Islam remains unwavering in certain evil or pagan practices and rituals. Consequently, it is impracticable to uphold two faiths within a home. Regulations and laws exist in Islam. If humans' laws cannot be broken by the human court system, why would Allah's laws be any different? The laws maintain the justified nature of the Quran. Islam's uncompromising laws remain unaffected by friendship and differences.

Human courts are governed by laws, and judges operate within those courts. In the human court, no human argues with the presiding judge, but Muslims advocate breaking Allah's laws. Appeasing opposition to Islam relies on ignorance, not knowledge. Instead of deceiving, true believers will demonstrate the truth and simplicity of Islam.

These are the warriors of Islam and the soldiers of Allah. No society can influence them enough to compromise their faith. Who taught whom, that is the question. During the Dark Ages, they offered assistance to the European continent but eventually neglected and negatively impacted the Muslim population. This does not align with the values of true Muslims. Muslims are choosing to teach and assist those who need help, rather than appeasing misguided directions.

Islam is the fastest-growing religion, but simply converting is insufficient. To appreciate and nurture the growth of the human soul, we must learn Islam. Living in certain countries may falsely depict Islam as backward and extremist, distorting its true essence.

Worship is non-negotiable in Islam, regardless of others' opinions. It's only Allah. Their worship is unique to them. Dogs and sandstone deities are also worshiped by some.

Prophet Yaqub is an example of parents expressing concern for faith on their deathbeds. Deliberate disobedience of parents is observed among some offspring in today's corrupt society. Show independence to appease disbelievers.

The purpose of humans as believers is to demonstrate what not to do and avoid selling their souls for worldly gains. Islam advises against associating with underminers. The Quran states Prophet Muhammad said, "I have perfected your religion for you" on this day. When delivering the message, he made Allah and his people his witnesses.

The skeptics would question why, if Allah and his religion are perfect, this message wasn't delivered from the beginning of time. Since the dawn of humanity, worship has been a practice that has endured through the ages. Allah, in His acknowledgement, affirms that the Quran is the sole religion that holds His favor, owing to its inherent qualities of being unchangeable and protected by Allah.

The way that statement was expressed seems to come across as harsh. What should be considered is the perspective of others and their faiths, who may feel excluded by such a forceful approach that seems to restrict all forms of worship. The worship ceremony commenced by acknowledging the existence of a singular god, Allah. It is important to note that there are no valid justifications to dilute or distort this truth, and whether or not to follow this belief lies solely within the discretion of each individual.

Even though they were fully aware of the consequences, they still made the decision to tamper with their scriptural documents. The Torah, which serves as the sacred text of Judaism, and the Gospel of Jesus, which Christianity adopted as its central religious scripture, hold significant importance. It is worth noting that the Gospel came to the Jews even though Christianity did not exist during the time of Jesus.

After Jesus ascended, a new branch emerged, known as Christianly. The religion of Islam came into existence and gained prominence during the time of Prophet Muhammad. Despite the fact that Allah possesses infinite knowledge, humans have chosen to reject the opportunities and stages bestowed upon them. The rejection that Jesus experienced came from them. Muhammad's (pbuh) ability to handle all of humanity, despite facing rejection and trials, was truly remarkable. At the height of Islam's success, he passed away after successfully fulfilling his assigned task. Islam's goal is to preserve its distinctiveness and individuality, rather than assimilating into other cultures. Since the beginning of creation, Islam has existed, and worship is merely one facet of this enduring religion. The understanding of the Quran is not only the final statement but also the conclusive and definitive one.

Quran: Surah Maidah 5:3. Today, I have perfected your religion for you, and I have completed My blessing upon you, and I have approved Islam for your religion.

Lack of responsibility or personal conflicts can cause parents to leave. Ibrahim obeyed Allah and left his wife and infant. Zamzam water is a global story, although this example pertains to Saudi Arabia and Muslims. Upon hearing of Hagar's death, he journeyed to visit Ismail. He knocked on his son's door. After a young woman opened the door, he inquired about their well-being.

In distress, she complained about their economic condition and her husband's long hours with no change in sight. He sent his greetings to Ismail without revealing his identity. After a strenuous day, Ismail came home to discover that someone had visited in his absence. Who was present? She responded. Someone conveyed greetings to you and suggested replacing your house's door.

The stories of the past prophets, when encountered in the present day environment, have the potential to serve as obstacles and interference in the lives of others. Showcasing the importance of belief, as well as a wife's commitment to upholding privacy within her home and supporting her husband, plays a pivotal role in this example. When it comes to managing a household, a woman who gives priority to baseless foundations and excludes Allah would struggle, as for a believer, Allah should always come first.

Ismail felt the need to tell his wife that he was, in fact, my father. His request was for me to divorce you. The prophet Abraham perceived a lack of integrity in the women who chose to disclose the secrets of her home and challenges, viewing her act of sharing with a stranger as a form of exploitation that violates the sanctity of one's household. In Islam, privacy is highly valued and considered a test of one's character, thus revealing one's personal matters to others is seen as degrading and was the reason why Abraham, the father of all prophets, did not view her as a suitable wife, based on his faith in Allah.

A fundamental aspect of practicing Islam is ensuring that every Muslim home is equipped with a door that is seen as a welcoming gesture for Allah. In terms of the role of women, they are often referred to as a blessing and are seen as the gateway to the home, due to their unwavering beliefs and capability to preserve the sanctity of the household while abiding by the laws of Allah.The establishment of the ambiance in the house is primarily attributed to the lady, particularly in the absence of belief in Allah and a lack of religious commitment. The home does not receive any benefits or advantages from this situation.

Abraham understood the significance of having a virtuous and faithful woman as an essential element in establishing a joyful and harmonious household. It presents a unique challenge in our society to try and understand how a parent can interfere in their son's life, even if they never played a role in raising him or not. As Allah had a different plan for Ismail, his father, who was serving as the mediator, complied with the message delivered during the dissolution of marriage. Life, in its pure and untarnished state, exhibited a sense of perfection and beauty. Faith is regarded with reverence by those who believe.

Believers lead broad paths. Pleasing Allah is a believer's priority over pleasing humans. The believer's path is beyond the corrupted world's understanding. These examples are only for believers.

In Islam, private matters are to be shared between two people only. The examples are clear and without grievances or challenges. Two parties and Allah share the responsibility. Limited to individuals with strong beliefs. Ibrahim distanced himself from Ismail temporarily. He finally returned to visit Ismail.

On his second visit, he was greeted by a different woman. He repeated the same questions, asking about their well-being and her husband's whereabouts. Dates and water were her sole provisions. The attitude was that of a believer depending on Allah. Allah shows mercy when a believer knocks the door. Gratitude was expressed differently, but the economic conditions remained unchanged.

Abraham asked about their meat consumption, she responded yes he raised his hands, and prayed for abundance and good health. Daily meat consumption is not advised unless in Saudi Arabia, where the power of Abraham's prayer makes it safe.

He recommended informing your spouse. It has enough strength to endure the door's threshold. Ismail arrived home after a long day at work and asked about a visitor. Being the prophet's son, he was aware that someone had come to visit. He was aware that it was his father. She responded by saying it was an older man and she explained the message. Abraham suggested maintaining the sturdy threshold of this front door and refraining from changing it.

He hugged his wife and expressed gratitude. My father is overjoyed by you. Just as Allah is pleased with a believer, a human who believes is also elated. Women are the key to maintaining steadfast faith in a home. Faith is rendered ineffective without this threshold. In a home where material wealth rises and faith collapses, believers have no place.

The contrast between Ismail's story and Abraham's actions hits a seeker within seconds of meeting. It's remarkable to observe the varying demeanor and gratitude towards Allah as I paraphrase the narratives. Contrasting acts of faith between believers and disbelievers. As a society, we make comparisons between episodes. Success always follows those who believe.

Abraham was an exceptional host. He always looked forward to having company for meals. Upon arrival, he requested his wife to cook for the guests although they had no desire to eat.

The deliverers were angels. In his later years. They brought news of Allah's blessing - he would become a father. Despite her infertility, Sarah would soon become a mother. Abraham was tested and blessed by the Almighty. Everything is possible if Allah will. Sarah pondered whether I could conceive a child. My husband and I are older, but Allah's decree remains. Articulating Allah's actions is not something anyone can do.

Quran: Surah Hud 11:72. She said: 'Woe is me! Shall I bear a child now that I am an old woman and my husband is well advanced in years? This is indeed strange!'

Abraham always shared his meals with guests. When he didn't have anyone joining him, he was restless. After some time, some guests joined him, and he became upset when they did not say Bismillah in Allah's name upon starting the meal. Despite this, Allah has revealed that He provides food for believers and disbelievers, so you need not worry. As Allah and his power over everything exists, he has corrected his prophets to prove his divinity exceeds all human desires and rules.

In Islam, the prophets left stories and examples to learn from that showcase their extravagant character. Allah ensures that regardless of faith, humanity can obtain possessions such as shelter, food, education, and material needs.

Ultimately, a person's deeds determine what they bring along, recognizing that their time on earth is temporary. Belief is the primary success for a Muslim in Islam, not worldly success and accomplishments. Success in both this world and the next is achieved by recognizing that both worlds belong to Allah.

The lives of Abraham and all of Allah's prophets serve as many examples. Narrating every story would be impossible. While it's impossible to address every story, we can still share the most relevant examples to learn from. Allah possesses the power to accomplish anything instantaneously. Islam provides strength to believers during their weakest moments. Those who believe in Allah the Creator have been given unwavering strength. My focus remains on sharing relatable stories from this world and the past.

Those who are consumed by their desire for pleasure and material possessions often find themselves overpowered by the societal norms that dictate their behavior. The experience of routines varies from person to person, with some finding them exhausting and others finding them ongoing.

For those who believe, contentment involves finding satisfaction in both spiritual and worldly achievements. Belief systems hold more significance for an intelligent and empathetic heart than human ideas do.

It is crucial to consistently remind oneself about the need to maintain flexibility and avoid rigidity. Crucially, compassion and understanding play a vital role in aligning our lives with religious teachings and beliefs. Sharing a meal with others is a delightful experience that brings joy and happiness. Only those who possess a humble spirit can truly grasp the significance of belief systems and the immense power of faith.

The bond between an individual and their faith is deepened and enriched when they grasp the comprehension of this concept, leading to a heightened feeling of serenity and a stronger connection to the divine. Hope functions as a valuable advantage for individuals who believe, whereas those who do not believe create obstacles for those who have only established the basics. The ultimate gifts for a believer are the gift of Allah and the gift of hope. Salat, when practiced by a Muslim and a believer, is regarded as the ultimate gift. The value of those conversations cannot be measured.

Even without new revelations, the miracles of Allah continue to manifest themselves in this day and age. Those who appreciate the purity of gifts understand that blessings are governed by the power of unwavering belief, not limited by time but by the certainty of divine providence, while those who lack understanding allow doubts to hinder their blessings. The eyes act as a conduit to the soul, granting insight to those capable of perceiving the unadulterated truth. The eyes can interpret the truth when the soul is present and attuned to its true essence. Excluding the truth from the world leads to a disadvantage, while courageously delivering the truth is better as the eyes can see, but the soul understands the truth.

CHAPTER 21

ALLAH'S MIRACLES KNOW NO BOUNDS.

Allah's shade transcends all boundaries. Allah's directions and believer's light can guide those who strive for self-improvement. Trust, loyalty, and honesty are the foundation of this bond.

Faith promotes unity and growth among its members. Accepting things without Allah's permission and making excuses showcases neglect. The persistence of humanity lies in the search for ways to defy or adapt. Allah possesses mercy and knowledge of the human heart.

Quran: Surah Baqarah:2:48. Fear the Day when no one shall avail another when no intercession will be accepted, when no one will be ransomed, and no criminal will receive any help.

Continuous depictions aimed at understanding defiance offer no rewards. The lack of quick comprehension in human beings conceals the irreversible expenditure of time, which seems to pass more swiftly for those who interpret resistance as triumphs. The examples of altered scripts that pre-date the Quran serve as a valuable lesson in what not to do. The continuous breaking of rules acts as an impediment to progress. Neither of them is supporting this world, nor are they making any preparations for the next. Allah bestowed his favor upon Israel. Being favored by Allah is a tremendous privilege that we cherish.

Leading to harsh punishment and exile. Allah does not reward disobedience and misuse of authority. Allah provides opportunities, but Justice reveals consequences."Surah Isra" states Jews will rise and cause corruption twice. The downfall is imminent, regardless of how the rise occurs. As the righteous will finally own and dwell in the promised land. The validation of Aqsa belongs to the oppressed and patient. By studying the Quran daily, it becomes part of one's routine. The Quran provides answers to questions. My writings are like dribbles of the Holy Quran. Aqsa mosque is exclusive to Muslims, but the complex is open to everyone. Mecca is a mosque that excludes non-Muslims.

Quran: Surah Isra: 17;4 And We conveyed to the Children of Israel in the Scripture that, "You will surely cause corruption on the earth twice, and you will surely reach haughtiness in the end.

Disbelievers share traits with Satan - pride and ego. Muslims rely on Allah as their superpower. Muslims have won wars despite being outnumbered, so today will be no different.

Despite the increasing number of Muslims, their unity does not reflect numerical growth. If Muslims were to come together in unity and align their numerical numbers, they would have the power to make a significant impact on the world. By unifying with truth and embodying the principles of a common source, they would have the privilege to assist all of humanity, regardless of their religion or color. Islam, being a faith that upholds democratic values, is often sought by many minorities who have experienced rejection. The history of Islam will serve as evidence for its remarkable expansion. The driving force behind Muslims embracing this faith was not the sword, but rather the clarity, unity, and the belief in one God that encompasses the peace that every individual strives to find within their faith.

Our time and Allah's time are not synchronized.Those who walk on earth must be aware that it belongs to Allah. It can swallow humans too. Walking arrogantly is wasteful as humans own nothing. Quran cautions against arrogance in walking on earth.

When it comes to tearing up the earth, humans are powerless, but the earth has the ability to tear apart every part of the body when it forcefully squeezes the defiant. One might argue, particularly, that it is impossible for a deceased body to experience pain. In the faith of Islam, the pain of the grave is mentioned because the victims are seen paying the price for the way they used this earth.

Quran: Surah ISRA" 17:37. Do not strut about arrogantly. You cannot cut through the earth, nor reach the mountains' heights.

Quran: Surah Baqarah:2:47. O children of Israel! Remember those blessings of Mine with which I graced you, and how I favored you above all other people ·

Quran: Surah Baqarah> 2:113."The Christians have naught (to stand) upon; and the Christians say: "The Jews have naught (To stand) upon." Yet they (Profess to) study the (same) Book. Like unto their word is what those who say who know not, but Allah will judge between them in their quarrel on the Day of Judgment.

Jesus was initially sent to Israel's Jewish people before Christians adopted him as their savior. Despite past tensions, these groups intermarry and have interfaith relationships. Muslims oppose altered belief systems. The God of this world and the next cannot be compared to mortals, he sent as co-equals. Disagreement is evident and not overshadowed. Muslims solely worship Allah and acknowledge Muhammad as the last prophet.

If someone were to commit the act of killing a God, it could potentially have adverse effects on their friendships, and society considers it unacceptable to enter into marriage with an individual or ancestral background of those who have been accused of such a deed.

The incident of calling a human a God and then stating that the human killed him is something that defies common sense, no matter how you try to rationalize it. Forgiving an individual for committing evil against another is relatively simple, but when it involves questioning the existence of God, it becomes impossible to coexist with anyone from that particular race. Any slight disagreement would serve as a reminder to the other person that they killed the person they regarded as divine, even if the ancestral connection was directly responsible decades ago. This alone would be enough to discourage any kind of ties between them. The allegation is not something that can be easily dismissed or treated lightly, so comprehending the gravity of the allegation becomes a challenge for someone who hears the story for the first time.

Throughout centuries, pagan worship has demanded human sacrifices from Gods, yet there has never been a recorded instance in the entirety of human history where humans have sacrificed a God on behalf of humans. Regardless of how one examines the concept, the story fails to engage the average person's mind. The logic behind it does not persuade the mind to concur, as the theological disparities are immense.

To comprehend it, one must explain it in simple terms that the common person can grasp. When it comes to theological matters, the common individual cannot find agreement. Christendom presents a stark contrast to Eastern cultures, as well as a striking contrast to Hinduism. The practice of sacrificing humans and animals for Gods was observed by various civilizations, including the

Hindus, Greeks, Romans,Egyptians before Islam, Aztecs, and Mayans, however, it is important to note that Gods were not sacrificed for humans. Our goal is to ensure that both those who can ponder and those who disagree are able to understand and clearly see this contrast and explanation.

Despite the fact that there have been instances of human sacrifices for Satanic operations among practitioners of magic, it is crucial to highlight that the main jinn, Satan, was not among those sacrificed. The complexity of this concept necessitates the presence of individuals in order to provide a simple contrast that can be easily understood by the human mind.

The notion that a mortal killing a God demonstrates weakness rather than strength is utterly blasphemous and absurd. One of the reasons why Jews initially rejected him is because they couldn't accept the idea of the virgin birth, just like Christians who also came up with their own interpretations. However, Muslims remained steadfast in their belief in the divine delivery of the Quran, recognizing it as one of Allah's numerous miracles.

Individuals who follow Hinduism and hold belief in many Gods and in mythology place great significance on the preservation and reverence of their statues. They would not tolerate any form of destruction or form friendships with those who disrespect their religious symbols. It is crucial to recognize that worship practices and personal beliefs can vary. One important point to note is that individuals avoid befriending those who cause harm to their deities.

The strong support of the Jewish community by Christendom and Christian philosophy supporters is evident, making accusations of killing Jesus nonsensical. Karma in Hinduism is the link between actions and their consequences. The concept of Karma's purity is universal in all faiths. Jesus' truth clarifies allegations, serving as karma. The Quran states that Jews cannot gloat because they did not kill the Messiah. Christians will discover the truth upon his arrival and refer to the history of Christendom's roots.

The strength of Allah surpasses any weakness or false boasting from Jews, as Allah elevated his prophet to himself and ensured that no human hands could touch the son of Mary, preventing him from being used as a blood sacrifice in a pagan ritual.

Despite their own struggles, it is astonishing to witness individuals supporting the perpetrators of Jesus and those accused of his murder. Especially supporting the land of crucifixion per Christian doctrine.

It is challenging to fully grasp the concept of providing help to oppress the weak while simultaneously expressing condemnation, as it involves navigating through the inherent hypocrisy and illogical nature of such behavior. The decline of the regions, which sends assistance from nations they believe were involved in the crucifixion of their lord, is highly hypocritical as they provide aid to those who they perceive as responsible for his demise, based on their own interpretations rather than the teachings of the Quran.

The region that provides support to them is just one of many sources that support the unjust, which, when combined with the high prevalence of illness, has resulted in a higher demand for psychiatric assistance. This demand is especially evident among the population living in oppressed areas who shelter the support for the truly oppressed in the Middle East.

They employ falsehoods to mask their true intentions, all the while exposing the weaknesses and oppression faced by other nations. Paradoxically, they actively contribute to the problems they claim to oppose, particularly when it comes to their involvement in anti-Islamic initiatives, conveniently deflecting blame and supporting onto the very enemy they associate with the crucifixion of Jesus.

Those who consistently struggle to honor their commitments, including their own personal integrity, find it exceptionally difficult to maintain relationships, which becomes an arduous task.Accusing someone of deicide creates chaos, not unity. Races and generations would be banned if that were true. False allegations spread through anti-Islamic rhetoric in this society. History shows their habit of blame and allegations for centuries.

Jesus is not a target for Muslims. Jesus' killing is not connected to Muslims. The accusation of Jews killing Jesus is baseless and divisive. Supporting Jews and Israel contradicts the claim that they murdered him. Crimes are punished, not rewarded.

Throughout history, countless Muslims have not feared their lives in the name of upholding the honor of truth and their faith, Islam. In the context of Islamic belief, it is believed that Jesus was not killed, thereby highlighting the distinction between Judaism and Islam, the two Abrahamic faiths continue with belief in one God but different theologies.

The existence of Christianity is contingent upon Jesus being accused of dying, assuming the burden of others' sins, and undertaking the task of salvation.Furthermore, according to the belief, Jesus will return and reveal the truth to all those who worship him. The entire foundation of the faith rests upon the killing and crucifixion of the Messiah, as well as the belief that through his death, the salvation of others' sins can be attained. Despite the Jews gloating over his death, Islam holds the belief that they were not responsible.

However, if Christians maintain the belief that they killed him, it would be illogical for them to form alliances with Jews and Israel. This statement holds true for everyone, including the Jews. The majority of Jewish individuals do not find him significant, therefore, it is illogical to support Israel solely based on the fact that he was from there. Every prophet throughout history emerged from the lands of the Middle East, with Saudi Arabia being the sole holder of the prophet Muhammad. The validity of the point for discussion of theology is difficult to ignore, considering that Imam Hussain, the grandson of the Prophet, was martyred. Despite this, Muslims remained steadfast in their faith in Islam and did not elevate him to the status of a deity. Instead, they stayed true to their belief in the oneness of God.

The question arises when Jesus, unequivocally, reveals to the world that he is a prophet who follows the Abrahamic faith and identifies as a Muslim. It is evident that all prophets pray to and submit to a single God , which, by definition,is not a human and all prophets worshiping him makes them Muslim.

Through the use of examples in theology, it becomes evident that the Muslims are correct, as the Quran has remained unaltered and will forever remain that way. In this world, it is common sense to believe that someone who keeps their word is honorable, while someone who alters their word, blames others, and shows hypocrisy cannot be trusted. The reason Christianity is considered an Abrahamic faith is solely because the faith of Jesus aligns with the principles of Abraham.

The gospel, known as the Ingel, was given to him by Allah. The contrast between the two faiths is crucial, as both hold Jesus in high regard; however, the Islamic perspective portrays Jesus as pure, free of sin, and holds the title of the Messiah, without any proximity to God or being His co-equal.

In recent times, there has been a noticeable trend where many churches are closing their doors, while on the other hand, mosques are opening up. While friendships can exist between faiths, it becomes a controversy when truth is suppressed and lies are prevalent.

Islam denies humans the power of Godhood, highlighting their weakness to forgive. Forgiveness is a priority for Muslims, who also reject human divinity. Islam stresses forgiveness and no human worship. This consistent stance highlights the contrast between Abrahamic faith and paganistic divinity. Islam does not consider Jesus divine or blame anyone for his death. He ascended alive to Allah and will return to reveal the truth.

Israel is recognized as God's slave. Allah gave Jacob (Ya'qub) the title. (Yaqub) Jacob was called "Israel" which means the "servant of God". This was Abraham's family. There is only one God, and that did not change for the Jews, nor for the Muslims. Christianity was only incorporated by Christians as a deity through the creation of a human prophet. Jews and Muslims both denied it. But Christians who support Israel in Jesus' wake believe he will return to save their souls. It's a picture explanation.

Israel's current state of chaos is becoming increasingly evident. Those who consider themselves as God's slaves firmly adhere to His will and do not defy Him. However, it is important to note that evil has been exiled twice, indicating a pattern of wrongdoing. Some individuals claim that they do not have land, asserting their claim on the land they were exiled from. The Earth is vast and no land truly belongs to a human, except in death. However, the truth is that these individuals attempt to justify their actions by stealing the property of others and accumulating wealth through foreign assistance. They back the unjust as they falsely believe that their salvation will come from the land where Jesus once walked, but they are mistaken. The true path to salvation lies in deeds. Jesus will be descending from Damascus, Syria, a land associated with Muslims, not Israel. Israel will only flourish when they defy all odds and claim lands that are historically shared by all faiths, with the support of foreign allies who also see Jesus as their savior. It is important to emphasize that it is the righteous, not the defiant, who will ultimately reclaim the land. Many immigrants have shown that people living in Muslim lands do not wish to change their homes.

Hence, the question arises: why were Muslims, who already had a home in the holy land, forced to leave or face eradication? This unjust treatment is reminiscent of the thin line between justice and oppression. Those who aid in seizing lands without considering the consequences are oblivious to the fact that their souls are being snatched away in darkness. They may live in a world lit by man-made light, but their souls remain in darkness, unable to perceive the true light. Darkness cannot coexist with light, but light can illuminate darkness. Muslims, who fearlessly speak the truth without hesitation or fear, possess a light within them that originates from their unwavering devotion to Allah.

There are individuals who assert that they treat others well and never commit any wrongdoing. However, this perception of their niceness contradicts the teachings of Allah. The judgment of whether they truly avoid doing wrong lies between them and their creator.

In the past, Allah showed favoritism towards the children of Israel, but this favoritism came to an end when they defied Him, as is the case in any society. The justice of Allah surpasses the strength of any court system. Their defiance led to the loss of their status as the chosen people. The prophet who emerged from Saudi Arabia, not Israel, was both the final and last prophet, and as a result, even the map of (Sujood) prostration (Qibla) direction was altered.

The Prophet Muhammad, who hailed from Saudi Arabia, was the sole prophet from that region. The designation of Jews (Yahudis) as the chosen people is still upheld in both the Torah and the Bible. However, according to the Quran, being favored does not imply defiance, as it rejects this notion. Due to defiance, it transformed into the past tense. Those who were exiled had no chance of returning unless they were invited by believers, just as the Muslims had invited them during the reign of Omar bin Khattab.

The history and stories of the Quran are known for their unwavering commitment to presenting the truth in its unaltered form.

Christians who eagerly anticipate the second coming of Jesus. When it comes to defining the individuals who created him in a false light, he adamantly refuses to acknowledge those who made him a God and a son of God. The rules of the Quran, which are consistent, are the ones that have an impact on us in a restrictive society, as not opposed to the rules of the society itself.

The concept of Zionism, which is supported by those who await Jesus to forgive and carry the burden of sins, holds no significance in the morality of humanity. For those who support Zionism.It is believed that Jesus will bring about forgiveness and liberation, and therefore, supporting this ideology is crucial. Any prophet would never support the oppression of any human being, as it goes against the principles of compassion and justice.

The cruelty of oppression is so severe that anyone who condones or supports it cannot be forgiven. In fact, Allah does not forgive oppressors, as oppression is considered worse than murder. While murder may result in death, oppression leads to daily suffering, which is unbearable. No one can claim to uphold humanity while participating in the endorsement of Zionism. Muslims, in general, oppose Zionism on all fronts, and those who engage in fair negotiations and provide land for the oppressed are seen as righteous. Allah will punish those who collaborate with evil tenfold, and even the land itself will seek revenge against those who mistreated it. One of the unique aspects of Islam is that power can shift unexpectedly. Today, someone may hold power, but tomorrow it may rest with the least expected. Muslims are aware of the concept of Jesus' second coming, but there are variations in its depiction across different scriptures. Islam only accepts stories from previous scriptures if they align with the teachings of the Quran, as the Quran is considered the final testament and supersedes all previous laws.

While there is a common misconception that Zionism and Judaism are the same, they are entirely different. Zionism is an ideology that seeks to establish a Jewish state in the Middle East.

Zionism emerged in the late 19th century as a response to rising anti-Semitism and the desire for a homeland for the Jewish people. The movement gained momentum after the atrocities of the Holocaust, leading to the establishment of the state of Israel in 1948. While the original intent of Zionism was to provide a haven for Jews, the implementation of this ideology has resulted in the displacement, marginalization, and oppression of Palestinian communities backed by foreign revenue and all provisions.

Zionism has been used as a cover to justify the expansion of Israeli settlements, the construction of separation walls, and the denial of basic rights to Palestinians. These actions have led to a deepening humanitarian crisis, with Palestinians facing restrictions on their movement, limited access to resources, and ongoing violence. It has been used to justify acts of discrimination and violence against Palestinians and other minority groups in the region. Zionism is a very dangerous and destructive force and must be strongly opposed.

The ongoing conflict between Israel and Palestine is a direct consequence of the Zionist ideology.Another approach is through history backed by humans not theology. Jesus' crucifixion was a historical event that occurred under Roman rule, and blaming an entire group of people for his death is both unjust and unfounded. The act of separating religion from political ideologies and objectively addressing the issues at hand allows for the emergence of different perspectives.

Given the current circumstances, it is crucial for the Muslim community to step forward and assume responsibility for leading the way. They are strong advocates for justice, equality, and the recognition of the rights of all individuals who live in the region. In Palestine, the rights of individuals are being stripped away, leaving them with a difficult choice: either make a compromise with evil or continue to endure the ongoing discourse. While Allah has a plan, it is important to acknowledge that helping the oppressed is a fundamental duty of Muslims.

The evil oppressors, who claim to be the chosen, are backed by evangelicals. Mecca which is rightfully Muslims according to the law of Allah, has been gifted to Muslims. No one is permitted to enter except Muslims. If something rightfully belongs to someone, there is no need to engage in a struggle for it; it automatically becomes their possession, as it is meant for them and comes effortlessly. This gift, which is a matter of common sense, does not involve the oppression of others. It was given to Muslims by Allah, with the condition that only Muslims are allowed to visit Kabba. This gift has attracted millions of visitors. The land of Israel was initially given to the Jewish people, but it was later taken back. It raises the question of whether it is justifiable to fight for a land that Allah had exiled one from in a theological context.

The incident of Sabbath breakers is a tangible contrast to the revival of breaking laws. The number of Jews fighting for rightful causes and standing firm on beliefs in courtship and togetherness is relatively small, as they are aware of history and intend not to repeat its mistakes to serve as truth.

Since detours only bring us back to the same destination, wouldn't it be more logical to adhere to the laws of the Quran without as it consists of no alterations. The Sabbath-breakers, who were specifically instructed not to engage in fishing activities on Saturdays, demonstrated their determination by strengthening their resolve. Instead of using fishing rods, they discovered a fish net and opted to catch fish using it. However, their strategic placement of the net was intended to entice the fish to swim into it, ensuring their successful capture. The minds and hearts of those who believe in Allah are gifted with obedience, leaving no possibility to deceive him. Despite the fact that believers had done nothing wrong, they were unable to find ways to defy him and satisfy themselves. The defiance from the past was not met with generous compensation, and the same can be expected for the defiance and greed that exist today. In addition, those who lend their support to the forces of evil will also face appropriate consequences.

Quran: Surah Araf: 7:163.And ask them about the town by the sea - when they transgressed in [the matter of] the sabbath - when their fish came to them openly on their sabbath day, and the day they had no sabbath they did not come to them. Due to their disobedience, We set them up for trial.

489

They still caught it, but in a roundabout manner, they found defiance's allegiance. Allah punished them, as nothing was hidden. The same error repeats as people seek methods to confront their woes and break laws, expecting no repercussions.

Quran: Surah Araf: 7;166. So when they were insolent about what they had been forbidden, We said to them, "Be apes, despised."

Quran: Surah Nisa: 4:16. Punish both of those among you who are guilty of this sin, then if they repent and mend their ways, leave them alone. For Allah is always ready to forgive.

Quran: Surah Nisa: 4:161, And [for] their taking of usury while they had been forbidden from it, and their consuming of the people's wealth unjustly. And We have prepared for the disbelievers among them a painful punishment.

Another factor that contributes to defiance is usury:

Bible: Deuteronomy: 23:20. Unto a stranger thou mayest lend upon usury; but unto thy brother thou shalt not lend upon usury: that the LORD thy God may bless thee in all that thou settest thine hand to in the land whither thou goest to possess it.

The verse is so clear that it provokes doubts about potential alterations made to serve the interests of the source, leaving one with no option but to question the underlying motives. It is inconceivable that Allah would ever issue a command to forgive the interest on loans within one's family while charging others in need.

These verses shed light on the inclination towards unfair lending and exploitation of the weak, presenting a case for Allah for the unfairness. To ensure the welfare of all individuals, it becomes imperative to refer to the Quran and identify laws that prioritize the well-being of humanity as a whole, rather than catering solely to a particular belief system.

The sheer number of conjugated verses is astounding, and what is even more fascinating is how they all align perfectly with the concept of faith. When the faith of Islam is brought up, it often triggers feelings of resentment among those who hold the belief that other faiths do not possess the same grounding that can be found in many verses of previous scriptures.

It is important to recognize that Islam is firmly rooted in principles of humility, justice, fairness, and the prohibition of usury, all of which are applicable to the entire human race, not just limited to Muslims and their families. This serves as the true justification for the preservation of the unaltered Quran.

With the time limitations in place, it becomes a daunting task to consistently furnish evidence for each event and verse.

Quran: Surah Imran; 13-132. "O believers, take not doubled and redoubled interest, and fear God so that you may prosper". Receiving or paying interest is deemed to be a major sin in Islam.

Usury, the practice of charging interest on loans, is incorporated into the daily lives of both Jews and Christians, and they often make excuses for engaging in it. Usury is a concept that is not utilized by Muslims, making them unique among nations. Despite their abundance of wealth, it is not increasing or multiplying. Individuals who practice usury may have countries that gleam with opulence, but they should recognize that their downfall is getting nearer.

The outcome of defying is known by Allah. This is not just a temporary event, but rather a deliberate and enduring state. Despite the challenges posed by the harsh waters, humans persistently walk through them, demonstrating their resilience and determination. Those who have a deep understanding of trials and have the ability to turn them into virtues of solidifying their beliefs will find that their navigation becomes stable, and they can reap the benefits by exercising patience.

Navigating through the vast seas can often be seen as a humble prayer to Allah, seeking guidance to explore the depths of shores and finding anchors specifically designed for a particular individual. In countries where the presence of moral values is scarce, Muslims often find themselves facing tyranny. This evil not only affects those countries but also spreads across the world through relationships that prioritize fulfilling desires over faith.

Allah extends an invitation for others to embrace his faith by creating favorable circumstances. The purpose of endurance in any relationship does not serve those who battle faith from the beginning, since, for a Muslim, Allah comes first.

It is Allah's divine plan that determines whether someone will continue to follow this faith or not. Allah knows each heart. Every faith in every region faces the same dilemma. The belief systems of different faiths cannot be intertwined or merged.

Bible: Matthew 23;25. The Pharisees and scribes *used law details as a coverup for their sin. Rather than practicing it with humility, they sought to reject their sinful way of doing things.*

The Pharisees purposely displayed their righteousness through their outward attention and actions, rather than it being accidental, it was deliberate hypocrisy. Jesus called them hypocrites. Referencing their adulterated nature. The example of these incidents can lay the foundations for practicing Muslims.

While licenses are legally required for unions in certain countries, Allah's law demands strict adherence to his rules. Rather than abiding by the laws of Allah, it is objective when a practicing Muslim, decides to adhere to the laws of disbelievers. While society's laws and regulations are in a constant state of flux, Islam remains dynamic and continues to experience growth. Organizing events that promote defiance while identifying as a practicing Muslim is contradictory to this society. Islam and the other faiths, despite their shared roots in Abraham, have conflicting ideologies that lead to clashes.

Adages and faith are often perceived as tiresome and burdensome by most individuals. On the other hand, if Allah decides to impose additional burdens on an individual, it becomes even more important for those who have faith to adhere to the laws to the best of their capabilities. The Quran states that every person is only given trials and difficulties that they have the strength and ability to overcome. While mistakes are expected to persist, they will occur in predetermined locations.

In spite of acknowledging and respecting the faith of other religions, Islam stands firm without making concessions. During the pagan era, there was a significant event where pagans challenged Muhammad peace be upon him, and this is where it originated from.

They proposed that he should practice their faith with only half the frequency as they do. The reason Allah sent the revelation is because Islam strictly adheres to the belief in worshiping only Allah and does not compromise with other religions or worship any other deities.

Quran: Surah Kafirun: 108:6. *For you, it* is *your religion*, and for *me, it* is *my religion*."

This surah is clear: it draws the line between Muslims who will not compromise for the sake of pleasing a mortal and sabotage or change course. Only worship is Allah. As a compromise, Islam does not bend the rules to accommodate changes in society and times. For those seeking an understanding of Islamic concepts and principles, these clarifications clarify many curiosities.

As with other scripts, Islam does not preoccupy humanity with changing laws. This faith withholds time, but time will not change Islam's faith. Instead, this faith encourages individuals to understand, learn, and appreciate the law.

It emphasizes the importance of following God's rules and staying true to your faith. Laws can be violated or followed, but Allah's favor or deceit is reflected in them.

Living in many countries, with backward views many face the same parity, which hits more Muslim homes than one can imagine. Therefore, it is essential to educate people on Allah's laws. To prevent them from falling into any form of sin or mistake that would lead them away from His path.

Islam allows interfaith marriages to take place based on its conditions, not the discourse of man-made laws. The acceptance of human laws reflects society, not Allah. Among all faiths, Islam is the only one that allows Muslim men to marry chaste and faithful women. Restrictions and conditions apply. Where terms aren't dictated and Islam isn't compromised.

Marriage between a Christian woman and a non-Christian man requires baptism in Christendom. Re-baptizing her if she has been living in a wedlock that disqualifies her from being Catholic.

Non-Christian men must also agree to raise their children as Catholics. He enters the realm of baptism. Christendom's plasma wears many colors, but the branding remains the same. In retrospect, Jesus appears to be God, the son of God, or the triune God.

This viewpoint is completely contradictory to the principles of Islam. Another important aspect is that Jews, similar to other religions, have a requirement for conversion prior to marriage, with a particular emphasis on the maternal lineage for transmitting their beliefs. Even though Christian women do not change the fundamentals of Islam, these variations provide valuable insights for Muslims.

When it comes to marriage, the restriction is placed upon women as they are limited to marrying Muslim men, whereas Muslim men are granted the privilege to marry individuals from the people of the book. These laws have been implemented with a firm approach and carry significant restrictions. Choosing "Nikka" is not optional, it is a requirement.

For instance, a hypothetical situation where a man is on the verge of starving to death and has no other choice but to eat pork in order to survive, even though he doesn't have any personal preference for it. By taking into account exceptions and providing honest answers, the acceptability of the situation increases. However, in a modern society, where technology and practicing Muslims are within a hand span of each other.

It is absolutely unacceptable to provide any excuses. Defiance serves no other purpose than to defy. The focus for individuals who adhere to Islam should be on finding a venue or environment that is in accordance with the teachings and principles of Allah, rather than aiming to please other people.

Mistakes are not planned. They occur spontaneously, and repentance is readily available. Planned ventures are not mistakes. They are subordinate to defiance if it does not meet Allah's guidelines.

In today's archaic world, there is no need for compromises and adjustments. By adhering to the law, Muslims can play a significant role in shaping a brighter future. It is impossible to argue that compromising Islam and respecting their beliefs means joining them. It is crucial to actively work towards the betterment of their communities and inspire others through their actions.

The essence of being a true Muslim lies in emphasizing the positive aspects of life and working towards a brighter tomorrow. The only way to guarantee true peace and harmony is by following this approach. The subjects in question have a habit of frequently taking flights that are closer to their place of residence.

This is specifically targeted towards Muslim families who are living abroad. Within this illusion, Muslims are presented as being more elusive or as being more dependable and appealing in contrast to individuals of alternative faiths. Within the framework of the Islamic faith, individuals are able to cultivate strong family values, experience a profound sense of belonging, and find solace in the assurance that an ideal life can indeed be attained.

The essential element in comprehending and embracing our mistakes lies in practicing humility. In the event that pride and arrogance serve as the governing forces that lead Satan to prey upon those who lack mental strength, how can an individual identify the error? Time holds greater significance in Allah's prayer compared to seeking solace in pride.

In Islam, the importance of humility cannot be overstated, as it enables believers to acknowledge their errors, learn from them, and ultimately grow in their faith. By embracing humility, individuals can effectively navigate the delicate balance between pursuing a deeper faith and savoring the joys of life.

Hadith: Prophet Muhammad said: The shade of Allah its rulings. A just ruler. A youth who grows up in the worship of Allah. A man whose heart is attached to the mosques. Two people who love one another for the sake of Allah, two believers.

It's the smile and coherence with Allah's generous allowance. In Allah's shade, the heat is maintained at a sublime level. A breeze in the heat brings waves of coolness in this shade, which is meant for those who understand their dilemmas.

Striving to be an example of a positive lifestyle and reflection is not amiss for oneself or others. When one is around such an inspiring soul, it's almost impossible not to emulate it. With kindness and patience, one should support and guide oneself first before guiding others.

To be kind to ourselves and to seek guidance from Allah in all our endeavors. Employment of oneself while motivating others to follow suit. A dilemma for educated and nonliterate Muslims in Islamic theology. Literature and ideologies of knowledge can be helpful or detrimental.

If Muslims or disbelievers point fingers at educated people in Islamic theology who take the opposite path, they are renamed hypocrites. In contrast to pointing fingers, bouncers who bounce in life without knowing have little to say about Islam. When they have a limited understanding of Islam. Hypocrisy causes this paradox. Instead, it is a consequence of self-desire and a lack of control over life's thesis that drives it.

This society, as an example, actively encourages and supports illicit acts and promotes the idea of dating in order to find comprehensive compatibilities.Throughout history Muslims have found solace and togetherness in the sacred bond of marriage, with faith serving as the ultimate foundation of compatibility. By superseding the laws of Allah, their own laws fail to improve the quality of life. The venues of the land, which are occupied by individuals who consistently shift blame onto others for their actions, continues. If the situation doesn't unfold as planned, they shoulder the blame on others for acts of defiance just like their sins. In Islam, it is emphasized that engaging in actions like defying Allah, involving oneself in illicit activities, practicing usury, spreading lies and deceit, unlawfully taking lands, altering one's sexuality, and condoning forbidden activities are all considered to be part of Satan's deceptive strategies, preying on those who become vulnerable. The examples can become the range of pondering.

A human soul seeks peace without faith, but gains are not sources of ultimate happiness. The only thing that can fill this void is faith in Allah. Believers must be on guard against the enemy and remain steadfast in their faith. This is the only way to achieve true peace and contentment.

While it is more challenging to see a believer fall apart, it is to cross the line and delve deep into darkness after he gains knowledge. Watching him fall, plummeting to the dark side of modernity and evil influence, is more pleasurable for Satan and his people. Therefore, it is essential to find someone who shares your core beliefs and values

Since deeds hold reverence for good or bad and both have a daily record produced for each individual. Before entering the heavens, Allah is fair with His dealings. The slopes are always easy, but the hills are more challenging for the climbers in life. Diving into hell is easy, but climbing into heaven is challenging. Prophets repent to Allah, as examples.

The impression that humans are weak and need Allah's assistance at all costs is accurate. Helping Muslims has become a duty, not a choice. Use the truth to shift the mind. Sometimes they listen or lash out. There is no need for the corrector to worry about whether the correction can be made; it is up to Allah.

Among the prophets, none asked to see Allah except Moses, who fainted before he could handle the light. No human can see Allah's light in the weak form. He was created whether he was a prophet or an ordinary person.

It is impossible to claim that Jesus walked on earth as a God in a human body is blasphemous. If Moses could not bear to see him by logic, he cannot re-appear in human form and man can bear to see him. There are no lies in the sense of a human. The love portraying that Jesus loves you is also a wrong statement as he cursed the people who defied him and so did Moses. Those who defied Allah were not loved by prophets. Accepting Islam did not result in Prophet Muhammad being rejected by his people. Jesus didn't identify as Christian, but Muhammad did as Muslim. Jesus, like Muslims, believes in one God, Allah.

Bible: Galatians 3:13, but Christ rescues us from the law's curse. When he was hung on the cross, he received the curse for our wrongdoing. For it is written in the Scriptures, "Cursed is everyone who hangs on a tree."

First, he cursed them, then took the curse upon him and died for them. Is this logical? Yet the Jews believe anyone hung on a tree is cursed. While Muslims hold ground, he was raised up to Allah alive, not dead. Muslims who are unaware of the truth and reasons should also be informed about this subject. Cannot be emphasized enough.

They finally walk out of fabricated stories as most don't follow common sense and say god cares for us all. It is untrue that he does not love those who might defy him and who allegedly violate the scriptures. Would a human say I love someone who lies against another? God is just, he is not unfair, and he does not treat lies to love. Islamic justice is not based on salvation but on deeds.

These individuals are not inclined to understand their own beliefs, let alone comment on faith they have no clue about. Disasters and redress stories are used to serve different interests than those that align with faith. Anti Islamic rhetoric threatens most countries, especially those who hide behind deceit. This view is used to create fear and hatred towards the religion and its followers. It has led to Islamophobic sentiments around the world, with far-reaching consequences.

The negative portrayal of Islam in the media has only exacerbated the problem. Most people are focused on negativity and curiosity about the restrictions and pre-dated era imposed on modern society. Upon questioning their own beliefs and further research, they learn Islam is today, tomorrow, and yesterday. This is not changing, as it was designed to suit any time. It's the truth and reality of life and structure for humanity and all that exists, not looking back to the paganistic era.

Therefore, the most effective approach is to use Islam's teachings to promote self-improvement and inspire others. This will help to create a positive image of Islam and show its true values of peace and tolerance. To eliminate the fact that all faiths aren't the same, it is imperative to outline their differences. Islam stands out as the only faith that isn't changing.

Additionally, it will help create bridges between different faiths and cultures. Muslims are not threatened by any faith, as alterations don't excite Muslims. The book they hold is unchanged. The oath is from Allah, not humans.

This can lead to alienation and negative judgment. The same is true for people who make choices unpalatable to society, such as conservatives or Muslims. The only way to change is within, not to appease others, but Islam requires nurturing from the Muslim community. Most Muslims who have strayed from the path and return to it, like new converts, make deliberate changes that are noticed by the world.

The amazing story of a pious man and a young lad:

The story of a young lad can affect the adults of this time as faith and piety have no age, time, or decade. The mercy of Allah is granted to those who seek him sometimes unintentionally and sometimes in an intensive search. Either way, who says man won't find the path he seeks? It will meet him at every crossroads as life events put people or persons on the path one least expects. In life, some stay while others leave, but time tells why and who enters.

Sharing beliefs is vital for those with a strong sense of faith. In the depths of the jungle, there was a true worshiper who prayed to Allah. A young boy approached him as he called out wholeheartedly. Who does not appreciate strength in the young? They are impressionable and need the right guidance.

People try to correct their insecurities, often without acknowledging them. Many use faith to overcome the dilemma of weaknesses and insecurities. The elderly man's purity and faith astound the young boy, who is in awe of the believer's strength.

The young lad's interest intrigued the pious man, and the young lad said, please teach me how to pray and cry out to Allah. The pious man told him, Say Alef, "It means the first letter of the alphabet in Arabic" But he did not tell him he only taught him the first letter of the alphabet. He wanted to test the young lad to see if he was attentive.

The young lad believed he was reaching out to his creator. His innocence and desire to know the creator did not question his mind regarding what he was taught. He was thankful for being taught how to call his creator.

The pleading young lad asked his creator to answer him. As he called out he felt peace and knew the answer was on its way. Many hours he attended to his creator. It was when his heart was empty that the call to his creator filled everything with joy. He cried out to his creator loudly in the jungle as he grazed his animals.

Walking alone at all hours to the same jungle to greet his creator alone had become a habit. He noticed the answer was closer than he expected. There was a change in the wind, the earth felt different, the heart was full of contentment and his "Alef" was answered. It was not what he called his creator, rather how he called with hope and belief was his conviction of his faith.

His faith brought him unprecedented convictions. After months of practice, he learned Alef. He ran to the pious man. Would you like to hear me call the creator? The pious man replied yes, say it. The lad replied, no, I have to take you to the jungle. I cannot say it here.

The pious man followed the young lad as he recited "Alef" the first word of the Arabic alphabet loudly with a tremor in his heart, his eyes filled with tears. He repeated three times as the wind blew, and the trees swayed, the thunder in the sky, the earth seemed to move. Rain poured in joyous showers. The pious man could not believe his call to Allah. He answered him. The pious man did not know what to say. Tears rolled down his cheeks. He said the creator had answered you. When I called "Alef", he replied, "This is what I experienced." said the young lad.

The young lad said teach me another word. The pious man replied, "You have exceeded me." There is nothing I can teach you, but you have taught me. Such faith is unwavering. Nothing or no one can change a believer's course. The person who has found his faith does not let it go for anyone, because they have found Allah. Only a believer can complete that faith, not a nonbeliever.

Metamorphosis cannot be respected if nothing changes, since stagnation is not Islam. In Islam, faith and an individual are inextricably linked. The Prophet Abraham is the most exemplary example. His father was his enemy. He remained devoted to Allah. His father, along with the clan, threatened to stone and kill him, followed by more torture.

This shows that faith in Allah is stronger than anything else. It can even break through the toughest of barriers. This can lead to a breakdown in communication between people who don't take faith seriously.

Boundaries or intricacies do not hinder those who learn about Allah and life. Every time, the soul's search is fulfilled. Calling out one's soul is something anyone can hear. Why wouldn't Allah respond to a soul that longs to know about him? Stories of those who have departed are just a brief glimpse into life, urging us not to neglect the search for the creator. If the creator is on your side, the world is in your hands.

Some become scholars and leaders and teach the world. The most compelling example is Omar E Farooq. His voice resonates in the hearts of those who know the strength and arrogance of his fight against Islam that ended with his conversion to Islam. His heart softened, the words became softer, and he was made the second caliph of Islam because of his power to rule in the name of Islam.

Tall handsome-looking man with all the power of strength did not misuse it except to justify his actions and be fair to those he was responsible for. How can one not talk about this convert who followed and shadowed prophet Muhammad? He was taught by the finest. When Allah favors a person, he can send whomever he wishes to help.

Doubts take a shift when Allah wants the truth to come forward and lies buried. Humanity's doubts and dilemmas were closed by the Quran. Many man-made faiths can rise, but for a Muslim, an unaltered Quran will not change. Allah will send a human to be a guide and part of Islam's journey.

Allah's message remains unchanged. No matter who he sends as a guide, parent, relative stranger, friend confidant rules don't change in Islam. There is no superintendent for another. Individuals are accountable for their actions. Islamic belief is that no one dies for another's sins. The act of shifting blame and shouldering deceit to latch on to and purify someone else's sins doesn't exist.

Bible ESV: Galatians 2:20. I have been crucified in Christ. It is no longer I who live, but Christ who dwells in me. And the life I now experience in the flesh. I live by faith in the Son of God, who loved me and gave himself up for me.

The passage states that God has been crucified in Christ. At this place, three become one. Islam prohibits such thoughts. In the infinite universe, Allah will never be born or die, for he is all-powerful. Who took care of the world when this God was crucified and died for humans? Will the world survive without God?

It is impossible for God to exhibit any human qualities. He is not a human being. The relevance of these differences in belief systems cannot be underestimated. While Christendom's God was selflessly sacrificing himself to absolve their sins, who was entrusted with the task of overseeing the world?

A God, or even a person in charge, is essential for the proper functioning of the world, as well as businesses, households, and corporations. Taking that logic into account, it leads us to wonder about the entity or entities that had authority over the world in God's absence during the convergence of the three. His death was an act of atonement for their sins, and he subsequently emerged as the Godhead.

The concept of the Trinity in Christianity asserts that the Father, Son, and holy ghost are unified as a single being. The description suggests that the story has elements of both science and fiction, making it difficult to categorize into a single genre. The human mind is incapable of comprehending such a concept. Consequently, these civilizations create their own regulations and profess that Jesus has love for every person. Regardless of the specific religious denomination one adheres to, it is widely accepted that the father, son, and holy ghost are integral components of Christianity. In Islam, all three are rejected. Given that Islam is a monotheistic faith, its theological principles are not subject to negotiation.

Christianity as a whole, as well as evangelicals, are repeated phrases to say Jesus loves us and forgives us. Their belief is exclusive to them, imposed on others by a constant memorandum of force. People are flocking to Islam without any force, but faith is not learned, but the name is Muslim. Any school is not for wasting time. The doctrine of Islam is for learning and applying to live in the company of a believer who has no clue about Islam. The believer is not sheltered from disbelievers' opposition.

It is still imperative to understand the dilemmas and the clarity of theology. The Bible's words clarify that Jesus is God's servant, which is ignored in most cases. Allah possesses no human qualities. He does not sleep, eat, or need rest, and he is not weary as humans. Similarly, if he rested on the seventh day, who ran the kingdom? The concept of Allah having human qualities makes no sense, except for Godliness, followed by crucifixion to resolve the insolvency of being an individual and dying for other humans which is blasphemous.

According to the Quran, Allah has no human qualities, and Jesus is not found to be a God, so Muslims completely reject the accusations against him. The Quran clarifies proofs. It will surprise some that Islam rejects humans as Gods. Muslims fear Allah, not humans. Was Jesus afraid of Allah or humans? Was he going to come back and agree with them in the future? No, the truth is closer than expected to proving Muslims are right again. In the presence of Allah, he is alive and living.

Bible: New King James Version: Genesis 2:2:-3. And on the seventh day, God ended His work, and He rested on the seventh day from all His work He had done.

Quran: Surah Ghafir: 40:61. It is Allah who has made the night for you to rest in and the day bright. Surely Allah is ever bountiful to humanity, but most people are ungrateful.

Ironically, the whole faith of Christendom rests and hinges on Jesus' resurrection. If truth is declared then will the faith be abolished completely as it only survives on the crucifixion of a mortal a Prophet the Messiah sent to Jews who did not succeed as they overthrew him and their defiance continued even after all the miracles his people did not waver. It was time for the prophet Muhammad to come from an unknown destination which shocked the Jews as all others came from Israel, not Saudi Arabia. Can Allah shock the nerves of human expectation? Why not who created the nerves?

The "Sahaba" people who were with the prophet Muhammad were Abu Bakr and Omar bin Khattab. Did they write their own Quran on the sidelines? No it didn't happen. A new book after Jesus was sent who wrote the New Testament, Jesus didn't tell anyone that a new book would follow. Continuous changes do not sit well with the mind of one searching for truth. The book Bible is divine and human therefore it is not authentic but some truth still exists, but for a Muslim coherency and belief, we need truth, not falsified truth and those who seek truth can explore.

The conjugated rearranged ideologies are destroying the epic core of human beings, so when such invitations turn into unions without settling ideology and faith, they can destroy countries. It is easy for those unaware of their own beliefs to destroy a home, and it can corrode a Muslim who is unaware of his own beliefs.

Matthew, Mark, Luke, and John the canonical Bibles were all produced during the Roman Empire seeking to gain control over people. This was not a told or executed plan delivered by Jesus. None of these were eyewitnesses to Jesus' ministry. They did not receive any revelations from Allah. In this case, the reader has been guided to Islam since Islam does not have any loopholes. Because the

Quran does not exist as a divine and human writings, it remains unchanged from Allah. If Muslims didn't like what it said in certain verses, it was beyond the scope of a Muslim to change.

That is one of the biggest reasons why religion is shifting without full knowledge which also applies to Islam. There is a need for education among Muslims, but those who fall short follow nothing but two basic statements: We believe in Allah and the last prophet. Islam has more to fill in, and this is just the beginning.

As a Muslim of this organized faith, learning is mandated so is "Salat". There can be no organization without rules, and Islam has its own set of rules to align humanity. A Muslim needs education not distraction from sources lacking Islamic knowledge. A mistake cannot be blamed for knowledge, but repentance with knowledge is the best antidote to mistakes.

"I am a spiritualist" according to the latest dogma. In other words, I follow my own rules and reject organized religion, but Muslims cannot become spiritualists in a society that accepts everything. The rules of Allah prevail over human spirituality and examples can only serve to open minds to seek the doctrine of Islam not implications and rearrangements from human hands. The only way to discover knowledge is with a knowledgeable believer.

Throughout history, Jews have read and interpreted the Torah in different ways. God's hand was also called tight and stingy according to them as defiance crept upon many. God's hand is stingy, but he still feeds them. When Muslims falter, they lack words but seek logic, since Islam is factual and not fiction.

Quran: Surah Maidah: 5;64.The Jews say: "Allah's hand is tied up." Be their hands tied up and be accursed for the (blasphemy) they utter. Nay, both His hands are wide.

Those who possess a strong belief are the ones who are motivated to seek and discover the truth. The impact of comparisons can vary greatly, with some finding them enchanting and others experiencing rejection.

The presence of different theologies should not detract from our ability to treat each other with kindness and respect. Allah designed the cycle of days and nights to provide humans with rest and rejuvenation, not for His own rest. Rest is not something he requires. It should be noted that he is not weak. The entire universe is owned by him. The world would collapse in an instant if he were not present, even for a single second.

The fact that humans were able to use him as a means to manipulate lies in previous texts, in order to navigate a multitude of wrongdoings and deceitful calculations, is absolutely mind-blowing. It is impossible to assign blame and pay for another's deceit in a human tribunal, let alone Allah's justice system. The justice system that exists within humanity is inadequate. The act of worshiping humanity is not within humanity's capabilities. The difficulty arises from the fact that humans were not meant to be in a position of authority over humanity in worship.

More than 30,000 alterations were made in the New Testament alone, with over 5,000 of them being derived from improved Greek manuscripts. This is a reminder that is specifically intended for those individuals who claim to possess the absolute truth of the gospel. The notion that humanity does not make an effort is unfounded and should never be assumed. The purpose of these theological differences is solely to shift the mindset of those who seek truth, as opposed to being mere human adjustments. It is undeniable that this is the only surviving text of the Quran.

The character of those who seek integrity is never clouded in this diverse society, as we always acknowledge the existence of humanity and decent perceptions and attitudes. Observers of a coward's behavior are compelled to retaliate and attack him. Among those who fear Allah, there is no fear of humans.

Theological explications and distinctions serve as clarifications, helping to shed light on complex concepts. However, it is important to note that despite our differences, humanity as a whole remains united. The only exception to this unity is found in individuals, driven by their own fears, exploit the vulnerability of others and perceive fellow humans as threats. Those who project strength can attribute it to either their unyielding faith or profound fear; in either case, the strength they exhibit stems from the faith or fear they harbor.

Those are the ones who only harbor apprehension deep within their hearts. It should be emphasized that Prophet Muhammad did not conceal himself. The collective pursuit of truth unites humanity, encompassing both those who believe and those who do not.

Egypt's downfall, which was caused by a combination of factors such as the reign of the Pharaoh and the prevalence of idol worship, serves as a perfect example of the consequences of these practices. In Egypt, a predominantly Muslim nation, it is customary to observe prayer five times daily. The decision of who attends is solely up to each individual. Regardless of the past idol worship, the call to "Salat" is loud and it encourages Muslims in this country to participate. This serves as concrete evidence supporting the idea that paganism does not have a long-lasting existence.

The Adhan, which is the Muslim Call to Prayer, has been broadcast from mosques in the USA since 1970. Dearborn, Michigan is the birthplace of the American Muslim Society, which was established in 1938. Among all the mosques, this particular one was the first to use a loudspeaker to transmit all five prayer calls.

In April 2023, Minneapolis Metropolis became the first city to pass a resolution that allows the Adhan to be broadcasted five times a day, year-round. It is expected that most cities will soon accept this call. The rhythmic cadence of the Quran, bestowed by Allah, has the power to completely transform the essence of truth. The call to Muslim prayer, known as Adhan, is a universal practice observed across the globe. The rotation of Muslim prayers occurs daily, throughout the entire day and night. The mercy that is bestowed upon us is from Allah.

As Islam fulfills its promise and enters every home, the need for clarity has become crucial. Regardless of whether it's through social media platforms or any other means, one will inevitably become aware of it sooner rather than later. The actions of the world are adjusted by covering the eyes of those individuals who are unable to perceive the truth. Those who are in search of understanding and clarity of differences are guided by Allah. Within the corrupt civilizations, this community is recognized for disregarding respect for parents and instead viewing the age of graduation as a point where individuals attain equal status to their parents.

Bible: Mathew 15:4.For God said, 'Honor your father and mother,' and, 'He who speaks evil of father or mother is to be put to death.'

Bible: NIV: Exodus: 20:12."Honor your father and your mother, so that you may live long in the land the Lord your God is giving you.

Quran: Surah Baqarah;2:141.That was a community that had already gone before. For them is what they earned, and for you is what you have earned. And you will not be accountable for what they have done.

Those individuals who have strayed from Allah's path are the ones who will experience the silent death. Especially in light of the knowledge of the truth. The cure for spiritual death, defiance, and arrogance is attainable. The act of repentance serves as the sole means to gauge the inner well-being of one's heart, particularly for individuals who identify as Muslims or believers.

The widening of the road to the heart was made possible through its extension. It is Allah who abundantly provides. Allah is aware of the hearts of individuals who are in search of truth. The impact of my writings can be instrumental in guiding humanity towards the truth it is searching for. While theology itself may not alter one's kindness towards humanity, it is through recognizing and embracing our differences that we can gain a deeper understanding and appreciation for worship.

Islam, in contrast to common practices, upholds its principles with unwavering commitment, emphasizing the importance of truth and sincerity over duplicity and diplomacy. The stories and examples that have been passed down from hundreds of years ago continue to resonate with humanity, offering valuable life lessons and relatable experiences for every stage of life. The relevance of history hinges upon the relevance of these stories to life. The subject of history is included in the curriculum and it is taught by them in schools.

Historians and theologians in the Western world are consistently finding and presenting newly discovered information. The Quran has preserved its information in its original form. These stories, which have deep and resourceful meaning in life, can provide valuable lessons for believers to learn from.

Using examples and stories from the prophets, one can better understand Islam's faith. The Quran provides numerous examples that serve as valuable lessons. One of the valuable aspects of the Quran is its provision of various examples for us to reflect upon. Although the characters may be the same, the narratives diverge completely when one reads the stories in the other text.

The mind cannot comprehend how Abraham's god would help humans pick prophets with less demeanor than convicts in today's world. In Islam, there are no mimicking prophets like those in the Bible who display derogatory demeanors, unlike Quranic prophets. Quranic prophets display character, beauty, patience, and durability in their demeanor to mimic Allah's prophets. They endured hardships but kept their character intact.

The prophets of the Bible, including Lot, were able to continue prophesying despite their involvement in incestuous relationships, particularly with his own daughters. According to the Bible, it is mentioned that he, being a prophet, impregnated both of his daughters. The prophet of Islam would not be able to continue living if he engaged in incestuous relationships or claimed to have prophetic abilities.

While a human court would typically impose punishment for such an offense, according to the Bible, it is evident that he was granted forgiveness. The Quranic law mandates that, in the Muslim world, he would be subjected to public lashing if this were to happen.

The Quran holds immense importance for Muslims, serving as a fundamental source of strength and guidance, thus making it crucial for individuals to dedicate themselves to understanding its teachings which emphasizes the importance of learning its teachings. Within the Bible, there are multiple accounts that make references to prophets. Engaging in acts that demonstrate both demeaning and disrespectful behavior. What factors might hinder an individual, who does not proclaim themselves as a prophet, from committing demeaning acts that are influenced by the Bible? Those who possess a moral code of ethics find it distasteful to involve themselves in rhetoric and mishaps.

Throughout history, there have been instances where high-rise performers and prophets, despite committing horrific acts, sought forgiveness and ultimately found their stories included in the pages of the Bible. The portrayal of these prophets in the Quran is quite distinct and offers a different perspective on their lives. If Lot's example has the power to send a shiver down the spine of any parent, it is Allah's mercy that keeps him alive and refrains from punishing him. However, it would be absolutely absurd to reward him by punishing the entire population of Lot.

In the Bible, while enduring the punishment inflicted upon Lot's people, he not only falls prey to the temptation of alcohol but also engages in the unthinkable act of impregnating his own daughters. In retrospect, Allah punished the people of Lot for engaging in intimate relationships with other men, yet interestingly, Lot himself was spared from this punishment, despite the fact that he impregnated two of his daughters. The scriptures categorize them as part of the people of Lot adding in numbers.

What is particularly disturbing in the eyes of humans today is two men together, which is the norm in society today. Or a father impregnating his daughters. If this isn't enough to understand, lies and allegations about prophets are on the rise. Muslims who are not educated in rhetoric will suffer the consequences.

There will be no differences or guidelines for truth among Muslims unless Muslims show differences. Believers struggle to understand the belief system because it is rooted in a tyrannical and incomprehensible display of defiance that is constant in nature.

Because most believers walk away from this faith and paint all faiths as the same, they do not discard what they hear from this episode and presentation.

Lot's story is completely different in the Quran as opposed to the Bible. According to the Bible Lot's daughters both conceived a child by sleeping with their father. There are no prophets in the Quran who commit such inappropriate acts. Does this give free rein to predators? If the Bible prophets can do this, why can't others who do the same be forgiven while someone else is punished for them?

These implications make no sense for a believer to think this script can be dissected and believed as it is color-coded. If the Quran had a mix of people and divine ideas, the Quran would lose authenticity it does not have any interpretations mixed with human hands, some Muslims still do not follow the Quran, as reading these stories should serve as a signal that what they hold in their hand is truth and what they follow is falsified if it comes from disbelievers. Match with a believer to do (dhikr) dialogue about Allah daily to expand Islamic knowledge.

Hiding illegitimate children and parents due to shame was a burden in the past, particularly in a society with certain moral standards, but nowadays, such practices are widely seen as normal criticism is called outdated. In society, prophets from the Bible, like Lot, are accepted and respected, as people understand that they can attain success despite their morally questionable actions, and therefore, they refrain from criticizing them.

By delving into the contributions made by the prophets mentioned in the Bible, you can gain a deeper understanding of their accomplishments. It is worth noting, however, that despite their remarkable deeds, these prophets also committed acts that are considered worse than what is prevalent in today's society.

This realization highlights the current societal predicament, where there is a lack of proper laws and a focus solely on generating revenue. Muslims who diligently uphold the laws and strive for accomplishments are driven individuals in all aspects of life. Furthermore, as if that wasn't enough, they choose to attack individuals with differing opinions and falsely claim that it is an act of love. The principles and ideologies of Islam can be clearly explained and demonstrated by the mere existence of this society.

Conversely, within the Bible, there exists a combination of rules that often contradict one another, making it challenging for Muslims to engage in meaningful religious discussions. Believers view the "deen" way of life as a powerful source of guidance, inspiring and empowering Muslims to pursue excellence rather than regress.

The altered biblical text acknowledges the differentiation and clings to the errors of Muslims in order to suppress them. Despite faltering in your understanding of Islam, do not let your shortcomings diminish the truth of Islam. It is Allah who forgives sins, not humans. According to Allah, seeking forgiveness from the person you have wronged is necessary, but sins should not be publicly broadcasted like in Islamophobic countries. They expose the person's flaws and sins, which even ancient cultures did not do.

This society is becoming literate in recent generations but is influenced by those who promote ignorance, despite the teachings of Muslims throughout history. The teachings emphasized a methodology that promotes learning and sharing, rather than self-destruction. From culinary traditions to intellectual pursuits, everything is meant to be shared by all of humanity, not just Muslims, as Islam teaches equality and inclusivity. These malevolent forces must be thwarted through wisdom and understanding to benefit humanity. The brilliance remains untapped, but profundity is vital for survival. Do not fear, but disseminate knowledge of Islam, even if society exposes your imperfections. Allah grants forgiveness while Satan reveals imperfections; Allah will ultimately reveal the truth.

Bible NIV: Genesis: 19:36.So both of Lot's daughters became pregnant by their father. ... The older daughter had a son, and she named him Moab; he is the father of the Moabites of today.

Bible NIV: Genesis: 19;36:38.Genesis 19:36-38 In-Context · 34 The next day, the older daughter

said to the younger, "Last night I slept with my father. · 35 So they got their father to drink.

Bible NIV: 17:29:32, But the day Lot left Sodom, fire and sulfur rained down from heaven and destroyed them.. ...

Individuals who are guided by Allah have the opportunity to come to terms with various situations and acquire knowledge. However, there are some individuals who return to a society that is covered in cobwebs, struggling with the demands of Islam because the rules they are accustomed to do not align with the teachings of Islam. By embracing this, humanity is essentially limited to one singular belief system. The concept of permissibility encompasses all actions, even those that are normally considered impermissible, even when it comes to involving your child.

Ludicrous. The fact that someone can believe this as truth is not only painful but also incorrect. Islam is distinguished from other religions by several magnetic differences, although it is crucial to acknowledge that believers perceive God as a singular entity. To provide an illustration, consider the situation where a prophet is capable of committing treacherous acts and still receiving forgiveness. In such a case, it can be concluded that impregnating one's offspring, along with other evil acts, is not penalized except for the condition of prophethood. Moreover, while homosexual men are punished for engaging in acts that are not permissible, Lot does not face any punishment despite his involvement in similar actions. The sick ideologies that are being promoted need to be expanded upon and brought to light rather than being hidden. Muslims do not consider the story of Lot in the Bible to be meaningful or comprehensive.

When engaging in inappropriate acts with your own daughters, there is a moral dilemma: ethical bankruptcy surrounding the concept of forgiveness is questionable. In Islam, engaging in lewd acts is considered a serious offense and the punishment for such acts is death. Not only would individuals without faith can see variances even a prophet of Allah would strongly disagree. Unlike those stories, the Quran takes a different approach by using examples and preaching about the virtues of prophets sent by Allah, intending for people to learn from them. By repeatedly emphasizing the concept of salvation and minimizing the significance of these stories, the idea of this faith being Abrahamic, like Islam, is negated, as Islam places the responsibility of salvation on one's own deeds.

In this decade, an emerging movement within the pseudo society is championing for the legalization of incest among immediate family members, and it is poised to become a tangible outcome. Although permitted in Islam, the longstanding practice of cousin marriage has played a significant role in preserving familial wealth and success. While these regions were initially reluctant to violate Biblical laws, they eventually embraced opposition against Islamophobic countries, exposing the contradiction of protecting lands that endorse oppression.

The magnitude of hypocrisy is so immense according to Islamic laws that the hypocrites are destined for the lowest depths of hell. The defiant and hypocrites are distinct; comprehending this disparity is substantial. The defiant possess the capacity to evolve, whereas hypocrites advance non-biblical ideologies and advocate for legislation safeguarding abortion, contradicting biblical principles in these areas. The oppressive nature of publicly displaying hypocrisy and manipulating the masses with a façade of independence is a seductive evil for those ensnared by it.

LGBT is frequently employed as an exemplification of acknowledging and embracing various genders and relationships. Islam, in contrast to other legal systems, remains unchanging in its laws. However, Islam does not impose its laws forcefully nor disregard human flaws and desires. Instead, it encourages repentance over open defiance, as judgment awaits in the end. Only after establishing the laws of Islam as absolute.

Muslim countries adhering to Islamic law are not involved in voicing their opinions on changing laws in other regimes, but corrupt regimes feel compelled to interfere and express their distress of laws of Muslim countries even when their laws lack moral authenticity. However, the depiction of independence is gradually diminishing, with the primary emphasis remaining on sexuality and personal lives, which detracts from the intrigue surrounding their self-destructive behavior and its potential impact on both themselves and the world, within the realm of deceit and confrontations,

504

reshaping them as mere facades of independence. Deceiving the masses and intricately meddling in personal matters such as sexuality and abortions - you name it.

The goal is to make them believe they are gaining independence, while in reality, they are surrendering the innate independence humanity is born with and devoting all their time to serving those who exploit others' time. It is the duty of Muslims to utilize their knowledge and employ the youth in the fields, sharing the truth and aiding the recovery of the masses from deceitful ventures, for the benefit of the world and not just a few. There are two distinct sectors within the divisions of this region. One embraces Christianity, while the other embraces a pseudo culture, both lacking public interest except for their own.

The hypocrisy is prevalent and easily discernible, as even a Muslim with minimal education can perceive that the timeline is regressive, with remnants of a prehistoric era intertwined in this society. The house of Pharaoh underwent a gradual deterioration rather than an abrupt collapse, just as deceitful regimes may experience a rise before an inevitable downfall. The Muslims need to steadfastly contribute to the enlightenment and education of the world, rather than impeding the progress of Islam. It is an undeniable fact that Muslims will ultimately govern, as Allah restores lands to the righteous. While waiting passively is not the solution, educating the masses with truth and aiding humanity is the essence of Islamic justice, irrespective of their beliefs. The Muslim rule has contributed to global progress, reviving rather than altering remnants of history through those who possess the true knowledge.

In this society, there is a decline in moral values where the agreed-upon age for engaging in heinous predatory acts is deemed acceptable against Islamic principles. The political influence in Islamophobic regions is significant, as they are paving the way for their own downfall through gradual but impending divine punishment. They are repeating the forbidden practices of the pagan era and displaying ignorance. These regions are manipulating the mind, promoting independence, but impacting mental health and ethical standards in an effort to demonstrate equality where democracy is absent. It is a contamination and an agenda fueled by falsehoods and deception, often aimed at perpetuating Islamophobia. It is the responsibility of every Muslim to activate their senses and contribute to the world's literacy and compatibility, especially in times of regressed society that defies the laws of Allah.

The stories and reputation that do not uphold moral values or integrity have been subject to questioning by a significant number of intellectuals who follow this faith. Due to alterations made to previous scripture. The consequence of this was that certain followers of these books made the decision to completely abandon their faith.

Their lack of integrity stemmed from the fact that their morality and scrupulousness were not in line with ethical standards it posed. The act of merging all faiths together is an unattainable goal, unless one possesses an understanding of the truth. Taking into account the vast number of stories available, it becomes an impossible task to analyze them all. Nevertheless, we strive to maintain equilibrium in our analysis by primarily examining Islam's presentation, while also incorporating a few comparisons with previously altered scriptures.

As the only book human hands have not altered, the Quran will preserve its last revelation. Allah also revealed previous revelations. And seeing what humans had done, he took the oath to guard the Quran. Some placed Islam in the same basket as their spirituality and voiced their beliefs. All because of inconsistencies in belief systems and inaccuracies known to them. Despite this, the

Quran and its consistent delivery remained unaffected. The Islamic faith is firm and holds no contradiction, and it holds firm to its laws. Following or not following is a human virtue, but Islam will not change or falter.

Rather than leaving behind demoralizing instances, the prophets of Islam left behind inspiring legacies for future generations. This statement holds true when discussing the beliefs and practices of Islam. Rather than engaging in ludicrous acts, Islam promotes a simple belief system centered around morals and ethics. Instead of adhering to a belief system that imposes contradictory rules, one can find inspiration and guidance by studying the examples set by prophets as role models.

A noticeable divergence can be observed between the stories presented in these texts and the corresponding belief systems. Throughout centuries, both the old and revised testaments have been subject to continuous changes. There is no denying the fact that both references and history are completely incorrect. The Quran has remained intact throughout the years. Regardless of the ever-changing whims and fancies of people, it will remain unchanged.

The dissemination of reference and clarity, although not pleasing to hear or read, has been a well-known fact for decades, only becoming apparent when contrasted with other information. The faith of individuals is not influenced by their social skills. Throughout history, humans have held the unwavering belief that if they actively search, they will ultimately discover the entity responsible for their creation. Regardless of an individual's religious beliefs, he is available and accessible to everyone.

The situation only becomes problematic when two different faiths coexist within the same household, as their contrasting beliefs and their coexistence create a contradiction. In certain cases, even when two individuals share the same faith, their relationship may struggle to endure within the same household if one person holds strong beliefs while the other regards faith as a relatively insignificant aspect of their life. The straightforwardness of the Quran may not resonate with all individuals. Nevertheless, the Quran remains unyielding in its refusal to conform or adjust to the ever-changing world. Humans will never be able to override the Quran, regardless of the era.

In the era of the Lot of Islam, there was a prevailing preference among men for other men, which was not in alignment with the principles of Islamic faith. Seeking divine intervention, he prayed to Allah, imploring Him to punish those who had not followed His commandments. His prayer was honored by Allah. It would be illogical and contradictory for him to pray to Allah, asking for punishment for their actions, only to engage in even more harmful actions himself. There is no resemblance whatsoever between the belief system found in certain texts and stories of this religion and that of the Muslim belief system.

In contrast to numerous stories that lack coherence. While these differences and straightforward explanations may not be appealing to everyone, it is important to consider them. The relationship between them and their followers is not characterized by truth, but rather by conflict and a lack of clarity due to sensationalized media coverage.

Quran: Surah Hud 11:77. When our messenger angels came to Lut, he was distressed and worried by their arrival.

Quran: Surah Hud 11:78.He said, "This is a terrible day."And the men of his people—who were used to shameful deeds—came to him rushing. He pleaded, "O my people! Here are my daughters for marriage'—they are pure for you. So fear Allah, and do not humiliate me by disrespecting my guests. Is there not even a single right-minded man among you?"

Quran: Surah Araf 7:80:81. Indeed, you approach men with desire, instead of women. Rather, you are transgressing people contrast to that account

Islam presents a different narrative in which the prophet Lot departed the city under the cover of darkness, accompanied by his two daughters, and spent the entire night engaged in prayer. Despite the fact that he attended to leaving quietly, his wife chose not to accompany him. In the evening, following the events of that day, Allah's wrath was unleashed upon the city due to the disobedience shown towards Allah, resulting in the complete destruction of the city. The Quran deals with individuals who go against its teachings, as dictated by its will.

Countries that follow Islamic law as their governing system have their own set of rules and regulations. Providing a concise explanation of the variances should not cause any agitation, however, having knowledge of the legislations, regulations, and the art of storytelling is always advantageous and never poses a challenge. While it is true that humanity is aware of all the laws, it is crucial to understand that Allah's laws are not subject to criticism, as they are not enforced upon believers or disbelievers. Consequences are guaranteed.

In Islam, a husband cannot refer to his wife as a mother or sister. Or if he is interested in marrying her. Compared to a wife, a mother, daughter, or sister is not treated the same. When a woman marries a man, her boundaries differ from those of his mother and sister. Islam emphasizes mahram and non-mahram. There are permissible and non-permissible relations. The "surah" addresses the complaint made by a woman to the Prophet about her husband using his mother to contrast with her.

Respecting the wife as a wife, and not condoning disrespect in the relationship, was the message. To defame her, she cannot be called a mother or sister. The Islamic faith holds these names in high regard and sees them as barriers not to be crossed. The "Surah Mujadila", which affirms women's rights along with the "Surah Nisa".

Quran: Surah Mujadila 58:1. Indeed Allah has heard her say she disputes with you concerning her husband and complains to Allah.

Society claims modernity is backward, and its language is odd for accountability, with wives often called mothers.As a crude joke, defaming words are not permissible.These relations are pure and serious in Islam. This faith takes nothing for granted. Islam is based on respect. In Islam, humor is not taboo, but insults are not considered humor. A simple concept is equally significant. Islam emphasizes words and actions.

Without respect, nothing can thrive. Love cannot come without respect. It violates Islamic teaching about such relationships. These connotations make no sense in Muslim contexts. To free a slave or fast for deceitful acts, giving voluntary (Sadaqah) alms is required. Islam pays back every act of good and deceit.

Following faith is not the problem. It's understanding and delivering it. One can ponder a Quranic explanation before believing. It is impossible to cultivate faith if its understanding is inadequate. Divine knowledge exists. Each human bears responsibility for what he does with his knowledge. It is up to each individual to make their own choices in life.

The story of Moses (Musa) holds truth to the belief of a mother:

A wide variety of choices are available. Time has a limited supply, just as it was for the people before us. For one to win their battle within themselves, one must understand the stories and formats within the leeway of their understanding. This is to engage in the truth.

The process of interpreting and comparing examples and stories is a time-consuming mind exercise, so use it wisely. The heart is the most valuable aspect of Islam. It's not uncommon for magicians, astronomers, and people of faith to understand dreams and warnings. People with a darker side seek magic and jinns as consultants.

If the Pharaoh, king of Egypt, had listened to Allah's call sooner rather than later, his life may have been different. When people suffered from Pharaoh's aggressions, Allah revealed the Torah directly to Moses. The ancient Egyptians saw dreams as divine messages from their gods and used magic to receive answers and warnings.

Throughout Moses' history, Pharaoh's dream plays a prominent role in understanding dreams. As believers and prophets understood, certain dreams contained prophetic predictions and warnings. When the prophet Yusuf told his father of his dream, he told him not to tell anyone. He said it would provoke jealousy. In a dream Allah sent to Yusuf as a young lad, he saw eleven stars, the sun and moon prostrating before him. Interpreting the dream, it came into existence years later. His eleven brothers, his mother, and his father bowed to him.

The sorcerers, and kings, understood that these dreams came from a higher source and took precedence over believers. Moses' story began with Pharaoh's dream. Egyptians practiced idolatry and worshiped men along with idols. The house of the Pharaoh was where Moses was raised. They didn't know he would stand up for Egypt one day. There are many lessons to learn. One can look at today's society to understand paganism. This took place when the Egyptian Pharaoh oppressed the Israelites.

Quran: Surah Qasas 28:4. Indeed, Pharaoh transgressed in the land[3] and divided its people into sections. [4] One group of them humiliated and slew their sons and spared their daughters.[5] Truly, he was among the mischief-makers.

Quran: Surah Qasas 28:9. The wife of Pharaoh said: "Here is a delight of the eye to me and to you. Do not kill him. Maybe he will prove useful for us, or we may adopt him as a son."[12] They were unaware of the end of it all.

The playground of Pharaoh is filled with a multitude of practices and symbols throughout history. In the Pharaoh's dream, he saw a vision of a young boy who would bring an end to kingship. Seeking help from magicians during that era, he turned to them. The information regarding the person's identity could not be disclosed by them. His fear of losing control over his kingdom led him to want to eradicate every newborn boy. Dreams have consistently played a central role in the lives of kings, prophets, and believers for countless decades.

Musa's mother, overwhelmed with fear, immediately shielded her newborn son after his birth. The newborn was commanded by Allah to be set adrift on the sea. The hearts of mothers are fragile and require gentle care. The new mother had recently given birth to a beautiful and precious baby boy. Through His divine power, Allah illuminated her heart with the virtue of obedience. Despite the challenges she faced, she held onto her unwavering faith. Taking utmost care, she gently put the baby in a crate, ensuring his comfort by covering him with a soft blanket. Although his mother struggled to send him away, it was the ocean that ultimately carried him away from Pharaoh's massacre. With nothing else to hold onto, all she had left was faith.

With each passing moment, the crate continued to float on the undulating water waves, while the shores gradually transformed into a vivid and profound spectacle, amplifying the serene journey of the baby as it floated atop the water. The intensity of the anxiety experienced by a mother who didn't know what had happened to her child was overwhelming, but all she had was her belief.

Slowly and peacefully, the baby made its way towards the water corner located by the grand mansion. Pharaoh's wife, while observing the gentle waters, caught sight of him. The home of Pharaoh was where the baby eventually found himself. In conversation, Pharaoh's wife mentioned how adorable their baby was. The palace became his residence. Pharaoh had a fondness for Musa. The plan of Allah had been established and was in motion.

The anxiety and fear led the Pharaoh to exterminate all newborn sons as a means of self-preservation. Through his attentive care, he fosters and raises a young boy who will ultimately grow into a courageous protector of the children of Israel, bravely opposing him

Allah alone possesses the understanding of how what you avoid can become your deliverance and what you seek can become your confusion if you turn to Allah. It is through our faith that we are guided towards the right path.

Bible: Exodus 14:13-31 Moses answered the people, "Do not be afraid. Stand firm and you will see the deliverance the LORD will bring you today.

It was Allah who guided his mother back to him. It was her unwavering faith that ultimately led her back to her beloved son. It was Allah who had a plan in motion. Despite their efforts, the individuals at the palace were unsuccessful in getting the baby to drink milk. Allah, in His infinite mercy, made it possible for the mother to feed her newborn with her own milk. The sister made a plea or appeal. It was mentioned by her that there is a possibility my mother might meet the criteria to serve in the palace. After some discussion, they came to an agreement to give her an opportunity. The main objective for them was to ensure the survival of the baby. If he continues to refrain from eating, it is possible that he may become ill, and this situation has made the utmost importance of the baby's survival a major concern.

The palace called upon her to fulfill the role of a wet nurse. This was a common phenomenon during those times. Immediately upon seeing her, the infant grasped onto her without hesitation. Despite the challenging circumstances, Allah's mercy shone through as she sailed the baby into the water as a means of rescue. Allah brought them together, and during his infancy, he solely relied on his mother's milk for sustenance.

Quran: Surah Qasas 28:7 We[9] suggested to the mother of Moses: "Suckle your child, but when you fear for his life, cast him into the river. And be not fearful nor grieve, for We shall restore him to you and make him one of the Messengers.

Quran: Surah Ash-sharh 94:05. Indeed, there is ease with hardship.

Allah had a specific plan for Moses, which involved him taking on the role of leading the believers and separating from the unbelievers. The act of freeing the Egyptians was performed by him. While Moses enjoyed a life of opulence and extravagance in the palace, his true journey and purpose were only just beginning. For him, letting go of disbelievers and embracing Allah in his life was not considered a sacrifice. The path that was destined for him is the one he followed.

From the moment he was born, he faced numerous trials, but he was ultimately saved by Allah. During the initial period, his way of living was akin to that of a prince. Subsequently, he went on to become a prophet. Allah's plans are guided by a predetermined path. The portrayal of Moses in the Quran differs significantly from the depiction found in the Bible. The distinction between stories and presentations becomes evident when considering their differences in practice and delivery. In the Bible, he is depicted as a murderer in the script, however, it is important to note that Allah spoke directly to him and granted him ten commands.

Bible: Exodus 2;12 Moses was a murderer who was changed by the hand of God. He was chosen for God's purpose. Any mistake a person makes, God can recycle and transform.

Bible: Exodus: 2;11;15. Moses Commits Murder and Flees to Midian ... In time Moses grew up. Then he went to ∟ see ⌐ his people and watched them suffering under forced labor.

Two people can deliver the same sentence, but their presentation can change its meaning. A further difference is in the Quran's sound, which is exemplary, factual, soft, and commanding in its own right. This command applies to anyone who seeks to understand and learn.

Moses' story recounts the faith of a mother to save her child and what Allah planned for his present and future. Remarkably, he was patient throughout his life. Floating in the waves as an infant, being raised as a king, then grazing animals and cleaning the surroundings.

As Allah can do the impossible, Moses' patience shines like a diamond, as it was the most intimate quality that held him in faith. Moses prayed: "Give me anything positive that will benefit me." There are many "duas" Moses supplicated and prayed for, and Muslims repeat the same ones in distress and supplication to Allah.

Moses is mentioned by name 136 times in the Quran, which highlights the great reverence given to him for the important duties he was tasked with. These duties included confronting the people of Pharaoh, opposing his rule, and leading the Israelites to freedom. Although the task was not easy, Moses successfully accomplished it. In addition, he adhered to Muslim ideologies, as evidenced by the belief that had Allah intended, Egypt would have been designated for Jews. However, Egypt remains a predominantly Muslim country, underscoring the fact that he implemented the same laws as previous prophets, aligning them with the principles of Islam for Muslims.

The miracles attributed to him are numerous, including the famous act of parting the Red Sea. It is worth mentioning that the miracles performed by all prophets were only witnessed by the people of their respective times. However, the true miracle lies in the message he brought, which remains relevant even in our contemporary society. This message emphasized the worship of one God, a belief consistent with the teachings of Islam.

We cannot negate the differences between the biblical text and the Quran, as Islam emphasizes the Moses of Islam in a different light. In the Bible, he is a murderer and flees to Madyan. Oxidized dignity and a blackened character make it difficult to acknowledge significance. There are vast differences between the Quran and other scriptures.

Moses, in an attempt to resolve the conflict, decides to intervene and actively engages in the dispute. Moses, in a fit of anger, delivers a striking blow to the Egyptian, which ultimately results in the untimely demise of the latter. However, it is important to note that this act was not intentional, but rather a manifestation of his immense strength overpowering his anger.

The Quran does not label Moses as a murderer when he unintentionally struck someone, as it explains that he was not aware of his own strength. However, it was not his intention to cause any harm or take someone's life. The occurrence that substituted the story in the Bible as a murderer for a prophet of Allah is a highly complex and sensitive incident. Moses' emotions were filled with sadness rather than a desire for retaliation.

Quran: Surah Qasas 28;33. He said, "My Lord, I killed someone from among them, and I fear they will kill me."

A revelation from Allah revealed the events that unfolded in the Quran. Recognizing the imminent danger posed by his adversaries, Moses took refuge in Madyan, fully aware that his life was at stake. He provided service to a family that included an older man and multiple daughters. Moses granted them liberation from a plethora of tasks.

Raised as a prince, he received training in archery, strength, and various other skills. They taught Kings' sons many traits. Moses mastered them all. Pharaoh's son resented his father and Moses. He could not bear to think that his father showed more interest in Moses than in him. It is the demeanor of the person who makes others like him.

His intentions were pure, which made the pharaoh favor him. It was not in his nature to cause harm to others, as his mission extended beyond mere conflicts. Allah had a bigger plan for him.Allah orchestrated a series of events in his life, placing him in situations that required him to fulfill duties he was never trained for. As he continued to supplicate to Allah, his true purpose and destiny remained a mystery.

The heart of Moses underwent a profound change after he relocated to Madyan. The fact that he was the son of Israelites was unknown to him. He strongly opposed any form of oppression and actively campaigned for the freedom of the oppressed Israelites. Despite numerous pleas and requests, the Pharaoh remained resolute in his refusal. Nefertari, the Egyptian queen, experienced a deep and profound love that blossomed within her heart for none other than Moses. Even though she found out his true identity, she still maintained her position as the Princess. She not only ensured his safety but also expressed her willingness to spend her life with him. In spite of her love for Moses, she had to marry Ramsey due to circumstances beyond her control. Moses' destiny was in a constant state of flux, always changing. It possessed an enchanting quality.

Moses, known for his prophethood, had a multitude of roles throughout his life. Moses experienced significant transformations in his life, and these transformations were achieved through the virtues of patience and endurance. With the approval of his employer, he married his oldest daughter, which was a significant decision for him. As he gained prophethood, Allah meticulously examined every phase of his life. His fate and future were ultimately determined by Allah.

His existence mirrored that of a prince, until the moment he made the decision to abandon the comforts of the palace in order to safeguard the Israelites. Upon witnessing the torment inflicted upon the Israelites, Moses was compelled to take action in order to shield them from harm. Allah had a divine plan specifically designed for him, which was in place from the very beginning. Moses had a distinct and unique purpose in life. Upon his departure from Egypt, he ventured towards Madyan. Following a lengthy period of eight years spent working tirelessly, he found himself drawn to the idea of marrying the oldest girl. Once he was married, he continued his quest to find Allah's guidance. His increasing devotion to Allah led him to revisit Pharaoh's palace and deliver a warning to the people.

His request was to release the Israelites from captivity. After trying multiple times and facing rejection, they ultimately declined, but Allah was on his side. Despite his warning, the people of Pharaoh chose to ignore him. Their actions and behavior clearly demonstrated that they were evil individuals. Moses was accused of practicing sorcery by Pharaoh, who proceeded to persecute him and the children of Israel. Dealing with the trials faced by the Israelites, Moses had to navigate through delicate circumstances. Moses fervently implored Allah, beseeching Him to open his heart to embrace goodness and liberate him from the impediment that tied his tongue. The act of delivering a speech carries great meaning and importance. In it, sound bites from a person's voice can leave lasting impressions on the listener's mind and heart. Moreover, he made a specific request to his brother Aaron, requesting his presence as his companion.

Quran: Surah Taha 20:25 Fill my heart with the courage that may enable me to perform the obligations connected with the noble mission of a messenger. And give me the confidence for its fulfillment. Prophet Moses prayed for this because he realized the grave responsibilities of the noble mission.

Quran: Surah Taha 20:44 And speak to him with a gentle speech. Perhaps they may be reminded or fear Allah.

The auditory quality of a sentence can be modified merely by employing a contrasting vocal intonation. Islam emphasizes voice as an inscription of one's inner being. The act of imparting one's inner self bears immense significance. The key to success lies in delivering with an exuding voice that reflects the nature of confidence or lack thereof, while maintaining a truthful and confident delivery. At the core, the voice that speaks with passion is rooted in truth.

The course of humanity is significantly molded by a pleasing voice, possessing the power to create a lasting impression, as well as stir unwelcome recollections. The believer or the ordinary individual often neglects and relinquishes the unpleasantness, yet the profoundness of truth reverberates in every human who seeks the voice that spoke the truth. The truth of monotheism is discovered in Islam, and the unaltered Quran serves as the unequivocal voice of truth that reverberates globally, overshadowing those who exploit the truth to propagate Islamophobic rhetoric in nations apprehensive of the growing Muslim population.

The lack of understanding among Pharaoh's people ultimately resulted in the magicians surrendering to the Lord of Moses. Despite being presented with evidence from Allah, some of them stubbornly chose not to believe. Moses made a request to view the presence of Allah. The light, in all its brilliance, engulfed the majestic mountain, leaving nothing but ashes in its wake.

Moses experienced a moment of overwhelming emotion and lost consciousness when he mustered the courage to request a divine encounter with Allah, and in response, Allah graciously unveiled a fraction of His radiant essence to Moses. Throughout the span of our lives, the inherent limitations of the human species prevent us from attaining the ability to visually perceive Allah. In the next life, humans will have to confront their Lord when their deeds are revealed.

Ignorance comes with a steep cost, and it is important to note that Allah never destroyed any land without sending warnings beforehand. It is within the capacity of any human to provide these warnings, and failing to listen to them will have consequences, just like what happened to the land of

Pharaoh, which is the Muslim country Egypt. As visitors tour the museum, they have the unique opportunity to witness Pharaoh lying undisturbed in a box, while numerous individuals observe him.

Nevertheless, there is a steep price to be paid for grasping deliberate disobedience to Allah. As the truth became irrefutable, the Muslims rose to power and began their reign over Egypt, ultimately resulting in the disappearance of pagan worship, sorcerers, and magic. Over time, Egypt has transitioned into a predominantly Muslim country.

Magic was a prevalent phenomenon during the time of Moses. In the era when Jesus lived, the spread of diseases posed significant challenges to communities. In the era of Muhammad, there was a significant abundance of literacy.Due to this outcome, magicians ultimately decided to abandon their attempts to rival Moses, acknowledging him as the greatest magician. Magic has no power compared to the ultimate source of power, which is Allah. The prevalence of leprosy was high during that time, and among the many miracles performed by Jesus, he cured the lepers.

The Quran, brought by Muhammad,peace be upon him contained acoustic sounds and syllables that were unparalleled by the literal Arabs. Throughout history, there have been numerous prophets who were sent in accordance with the prevailing beliefs and needs of their respective eras. Due to their inability to match his Quranic abilities, he was accused of being either a madman or a magician. The capacity of the human mind is facing significant constraints, creating a sense of urgency. Those individuals who have a deep comprehension of the power of Allah are aware that His workings are in accordance with His own time and knowledge, rather than being influenced by our human understanding of time.

The fate of each individual is unique, as it depends on Allah. Paraphrasing the stories from the Quran is possible, however, to obtain a more accurate understanding, we can refer to the Arabic Quran.

Examples and stories derived from the Quran play a pivotal role within the fabric of our society. Curiosity can be sparked by simply changing the timeline of this capsule. The determination of whether humanity is progressing in the correct direction ultimately lies with each individual, however, through the act of sharing ideas and thoughts, there is a potential for inspiration to arise.The ten commandments were given to Moses, and they have held significance for all Abrahamic faiths. When faced with weakness, the human condition can manifest both fragility and strength, albeit to different degrees for different people. The staff of Moses is currently on display in a museum located in Turkiye, serving as a reminder of ancient history.

Quran: Surah Maidah 5:25 Moses said: 'My Lord! I have control over none but myself and my brother; so distinguish between us and the transgressing people.

Quran: Surah Taubah 9:114.And the request of forgiveness of Abraham for his father was only because of a promise he had made to him. But when it became apparent to Abraham that his father was an enemy of Allah.

Quran: Surah An'am 6:59. And with him are the keys of the unseen none knows them except him. He knows what is on land and in the sea. Not a leaf falls, but that he knows it. No grain is there within the darknesses of the earth and no moist or dry thing but that it is written in a clear record.

The prophets prayed for every challenge instead of giving up. Failures are those humans who remember the wrong and persist in the same direction. Winners are humans who remember victory

and follow the right path. When desires crumble, people feel sadness or ill feelings, but Allah's will remains.

Each trial reinforces human patterns, strengthening the believer's faith. The things destined for you arrive unexpectedly, but trust in Allah remains constant even in sadness, and the determination to accept and keep hoping turns life's challenges into triumphs. The Muslim character stands strong with other believers.

The prophet Muhammad's wife, Khadija, introduced him to her uncle Varaqa, who was known for his wisdom. As his initial revelation, he was informed about the incident. "This is the prophet we've been waiting for," he responded.

Eventually, the people surrounding him will exile him from Mecca. He asserted to her that he was the seal of prophets. These valuable reminders serve Muslims living in an environment or family that does not believe in their faith, it can be challenging to maintain a strong and flourishing connection to their beliefs. The faith of a believer can face challenges and doubts when confronted with opposition and skepticism from their own family and supposed friends.

Despite many challenges since birth, he left, increasing the number of Muslims embracing Islam. Why aren't Muslims interested in learning history and the Quran? He wouldn't be surprised by the current state of Muslims.

The majority of Muslims are Sunnis, followers of Prophet Muhammad. He claimed that the number of Muslims would increase rapidly, but their faith would remain fleeting, like foam on water. Muslims and seekers have all options available and everything is clear. The surroundings can have a significant impact on matters of faith.

Believers are not part of a disbelievers' council, as their hearts belong to Allah. He alters his environment based on what his heart tells him to believe. The prophet discovered Islam in the scorching desert of the Arabian Peninsula. Even a cloud followed him, but the tree cried when he didn't lean on it.

Once Muslims know the faith of Islam, nothing can alter their attitude. It's disheartening to halt the conversation about this prophet. However, I have documented numerous stories about this prophet and all the prophets.

Throughout the revelations, Prophet Muhammad's stories are persistent. After prophet Muhammad's, revelations ceased to occur. Upon the death of his mother, Umm Ayman took care of him. After witnessing Muhammad's death, she cried. Tears were shed by her. Her heart was filled with emptiness. She knew one day he would return to his Lord, but she understood that the revelations had ceased to exist.

Those tears of sorrow became stronger as she too loved hearing from God the revelations he had sent through him, but what he left behind was the Quran, which was an eternal testament. After the final law, all laws are abolished.

All the old laws have been replaced by the new law. For all of humanity, the Quran represents the latest and final version of closure. Muhammad was the seal of all Abrahamic prophets. With the finality of the Quran, Abrahamic faith was concluded.

Following a tragedy, he was granted his own river, "Kauthar". Familiarity with tragedies was not uncommon, and familiarity with trials or victories was also not uncommon.

Believers will find their thirst quenched by the flowing river. As Hagar quenched the thirst of many pilgrims through her hardships, Muhammad received the river "Kauthar".This will serve as a refreshing fountain, satisfying the thirst of believers who seek spiritual nourishment. On the day of judgment, believers will exclusively receive this water from Prophet Muhammad.

Following the tragic loss of his son, he was granted the river Kauthar by Allah, symbolizing that even in times of sorrow, there is always something to be shared with others. The smallest "Surah" of the Quran is "Surah Kauthar" which was revealed.

Quran: Surah Nisa:4:79.Whatever good befalls you is from Allah and whatever evil befalls you is from yourself. We have sent you ˹O Prophet˺ as a messenger to ˹all˺ people. And Allah is sufficient as a Witness.

Bible Isaiah:45;7. I form the light, and create darkness: I make peace, and create evil: I the LORD do all these things.

Every good thing that exists originates from Allah, while all evil stems from within ourselves.

A mother who detains her child without any belief can be seen as a toxic presence that affects the child negatively. Being a correctional mother at any age and implementing the laws of Allah is considered a great blessing. The love that Allah has for us surpasses even the love of a mother, as His mercy constitutes 99 percent of His compassion, while His anger comprises merely one percent.

The warnings that follow are an act of mercy, as the continuous disobedience of individuals has led to the rise of tyrannical leaders who have caused devastation to both lands and people. It seems that the leaders of today have a tendency to view the times with a blind eye towards their own greed and a penchant for pointing fingers.

When it comes to individuals who lack belief in their own worthiness to confront the obstacles that come their way, the question arises: should their destiny be determined by Allah or by fellow humans? The ultimate decision lies in the hands of Allah, not the powerless human.

Allah sent Prophet Muhammad to humanity as a mercy, and not exclusively to Muslims. There is a price to pay for defiance, and at this point, making excuses is no longer an option.

In this high-tech society, the only remedy for a diseased heart is through the process of learning. Considering how effortless it is to engage with malevolence, why not put in the same effort to engage with learning and enhance shared knowledge through dialogue? When you choose to partner up with a believer, it is seen as a blessing from Allah for those who are seeking. With a sense of sobriety and profound joy, a married believer has emerged victorious in the battles that were once mere aspirations.

Quran: Surah Imran: 3:31 (O Messenger!) Tell people: 'If you indeed love Allah, follow me, and Allah will love you and will forgive you your sins. Allah is All-Forgiving and all-compassionate.

Quran: Surah Maidah: 5:54. Believers! If any of you should ever turn away from your faith, remember that Allah will raise a people whom He loves, and who love Him; a people humble towards the

The conversion of the strongest of men to Islam during Muhammad's lifetime left no room for doubt about Allah's presence. Muslims who have not fully grasped the teachings of Islam are considered to be the source of evil within the religion, but it is believed that Allah has the ability to alter individuals' hearts if he wishes to do so. The faith of individuals is guided by the will of Allah, not by the will of man, thus enabling anyone to embrace their own beliefs.

The comprehensibility of Allah's straightforward language can be attributed to his summoning you to my designated location through my book. Although the Quran is primarily intended for believers, it's worth mentioning that non-Muslims and atheists can also choose to read and explore its contents.

The task of recording individual records is carried out by angels on a daily basis. The book of records will be presented by Allah at the time of judgment. It is beyond question that the Book of Virtuous Deeds holds greater value for every individual when compared to the Book of Wicked Deeds. It does not matter what you seek because it will eventually come to you. Each chapter of my book contains a message and a hope for humanity.

The influence of referencing Islam is remarkable as it has the ability to shape individuals' demeanor and impart knowledge to society. By being in the company of a devoted believer, one's life can take a different path, especially for Muslims who firmly believe in the consequences of their actions and the importance of being answerable to them. This concept is further elucidated in the book of records.

Education enhances freedom by acknowledging the significance of humanity in contrasting theological perspectives.

The ultimate aim of a believer is to have the weight of good deeds outweigh the bad in the record book of believers, resulting in one of the most exceptional and favorable accounts ever documented in your name, will be waiting for you should it align with God's will.

"Insha Allah" By the will of Allah.

CHAPTER 22

BELIEVERS BELIEVE IN ALL CONDITIONS.

Writing, dialogue discussions help people advance knowledge and reach their peak potential. This applies to any retrospective thinking or action in daily life. Writing and dialogue discussions can generate fresh insights and facilitate meaningful exchanges.

It contributes to understanding, critical thinking, knowledge and development. Ultimately, it empowers individuals to reach their goals and excel in productivity. The act of filtering evil, even in small ways, can touch believers.

During a conversation between two believers (Dhikr), dialogue Allah is often cited as a topic or closing note. The parables and caveats of life bring a human closer to Allah because of the constant hunger to know about the faith one follows. There is no doubt that the mule follows the master without knowing where he is going. Constant and consistent, the road is similar, but the new road always sparkles in the eyes of the mule and the master. Believers cannot find contentment on a bumpy road.

The act of laughing, arguing or sarcasm is a way for disbelievers to demonstrate their discontentment with life without faith. Since they don't share the same values as believers. Humans can hold common morals even without organized faith, but comparing belief systems with such companies means crossing roads that are not to be crossed.

Small gestures hold great importance in Islamic doctrine, urging Muslims to continue teaching and reaching out even to those who have closed themselves off. Loneliness and longing for a good life can lead individuals astray, but those who understand Islam go beyond this, recognizing the duty to share and the impact of actions, for Allah sees all. Some eagerly learn in this society, but spread gossip and falsehoods through social media, especially in regions with Islamophobia, deceiving others with fear.

Muslims need attendance to opportunities to hold your own and engage when someone reaches out. Truth is the dominant force guiding mankind to discover what they seek. Islam shapes lives, going beyond just praying, by banishing doubts and fixing potential. Allah created this world, knowing good and evil. Truth resides in believers' hearts. Nature confirms the truth. Islam purifies society.

Islam promotes self-improvement and balance, not excess. The prophet of Islam had his own life, maintained connections, propagated Islam, and worshiped privately and in congregation.He actively engaged with his surroundings all day. He served as both a commander and a prophet. Praying Salat five times shows balance and progress.

Muslims are aware that Satan's deception and continuous imbalance causes the intruder to attack his prey with whispers and deceitful friendships he places to distract the believers who choose to listen, they can also differentiate the ploy and change course. That is why Islam emphasizes knowing the enemy. Denial is the worst enemy for those who believe they have no enemies. Islam affirms everyone has witnessed light in this world. Without defending against wrong, learning is impossible. Both offense and defense are needed in every game. Muslims encourage their children to learn about other faiths to maintain their connection with Islam.

When times pass, the soul will recall good times. With evil whispers that reach deep into the soul, Satan keeps the weak in anxiety, mishaps, arrogance, and evil thoughts.

Deliberate seclusion or withdrawal is for reflection and solitude to seek forgiveness and answers from Allah. Would it be better if believers chose seclusion and loneliness as those who discard Salat and waste time? It's not practical, as spiritual seclusion differs from depression or loneliness. As social animals, humans learn, teach, and continue the dialogue in leadership and roles. If Muslims don't participate in productive conversations, stagnation is worse than trying hard to achieve goals. No point in neglecting this world because Allah created it. A believer can reach the spiritual side and succeed through limitations and productivity. One believer can uphold a thousand disbelievers.

Evil captures the weak as his prey he keeps close by, his eye on a believer. Knowing the enemy's tactics is the battle of the soul. Sometimes your own shadow becomes your enemy. Or the family member or people you consider your closest confidants can be your most dangerous enemies. Whenever Muslims ask Allah for mercy, they are constantly urging the master to free them from the evil they perceive around them. "Surah Falaq and Aytal Kursi" are "Surahs" of protection from evil.

The Quran is full of blessings, and informative words that make sense, and delivery is precise, the creator speaks with a rhythmic context that is easier to memorize than any human song. The heart will locate its findings. Muslims face the East when praying Salat. But it's the genuine search for the middle ground and stillness of the heart. As the body faces the East, does the heart align with the direction? This is an affair of a believer. One who cannot shelter his peace cannot shelter others. Not being able to escape the shadow of disbelievers within one's family is a weakness in the belief system. Those who cannot nurture their soul cannot nurture others.

The company one keeps in this world will solidify who you are on Doom's Day. If a believer rises with the disbelievers, then what was he seeking? The company will balance judgment as it does in this world. The company benefits the seeker's soul. The weight of darkness lies heavy on the heart, seeking no contentment and dragging it through life.

Believers find contentment in every moment. From a believer's perspective, the grass is always green. Allah's will penetrates the mind, sending contentment waves throughout. Patience can be a challenging trait during tough times for some, but learning is the most rewarding experience for a believer. No one can take Allah's grants from anyone, as Allah is a giver, not a taker. He is a generous and merciful God. He even distributes to non-believers. The believer, however, has trials that give him strength through the belief system.

Allah's favors are numerous, but everything belongs to Allah. He can keep humanity or any living thing for as long as he can. Behaviors have repercussions, and Allah explains their outcomes in the past and the future.

Quran: Al Hadid: 5:54.O you who have believed, whoever of you reverts from his religion. Allāh will bring forth [in place of them] a people. He will love and who will love Him [who are] humble toward the believers, strong against the disbelievers; they strive in the cause of Allāh and do not fear the blame of a critic. That is Allah's favor; He bestows it upon whom He wills. And Allāh is the All-encompassing and Knowing.

Believers learn to trust in Allah's plan and believe whatever happens is for his benefit. They understand that Allah knows everything and never abandons them, even in the darkest of times. This faith gives believers the strength to persevere and find light in any situation. With social media and Satan and his family's corruption, those seeking evil discover corruption within. Why do humans face catastrophes in life? There might be a reason for this, as the person who continues to help is also rewarded by helping the drowning person. How can one question life's complexities when a human being is so weak?

Can one human become the answer to another's prayer? Destiny has no questions, only answers. The solution may be found after the answer arrives. But some still seek answers when the prayer has already been answered. This is as long as the soul is in touch with Allah seeking the balance of this life and gravitating towards preparing for the next.

Questions are for seekers but who learns from them if disbelievers are your teachers? In the end, the substantial gain one seeks is not adequate for survival. One who imposes his laws to rearrange Allah's laws is incomprehensive of collisions with faith. There have been many changes in previous texts that led many to disbelief and others to discover the truth. Revelations in the Quran are the final and ultimate truth. Don't believe Islam is for everyone. If God wanted one nation, he would have done it. Humans will seek what the heart desires. Allah will change anyone's condition

Quran: Surah Raad: 13;11. For each one are angels before and behind him who protect him by the decree of Allāh. Indeed, Allāh will not change the condition of a people until they change what is in themselves. And when Allāh intends for a people ill, there is no repelling it. And there is not for them besides Him any patron.

Only a select few are fortunate enough to receive the gift of time, peace, durability, and the ability to prostrate in prayer to Allah, in addition to worldly contentment. Unfortunately, not everyone possesses the understanding to comprehend what they read, and even fewer individuals recognize and appreciate the blessings they have been bestowed with.

Jews initially hesitated to disobey Jesus, who was sent to them, but they eventually defied him. Now, they await another prophet, but waiting or building temples won't help in receiving someone from David's lineage. The selection of the Messiah is determined by Allah, not humans.

Despite the fact that Christianity and Islam, two of the Abrahamic faiths, share the prophet Jesus, they are unable to completely reconcile their differences through biblical texts and stories.Quran speaks with illustration "less is better," where direct and eloquent words are used without clutter, maintaining a precise and concise cadence. The book is not elongated, as there is no reason for using too many words when the delivery is already precise.

Bible: Mark 11:16, Jesus then put an embargo on people carrying any merchandise through the Temple, a sanction which would have disrupted all commerce.

Bible: Mathew 21:12 Jesus went into the temple and threw out all those buying and selling. He overturned the tables of the money changers and the chairs of those selling doves.

Quran: Surah Maidah: 5;78.Those of the children of Israel who took to unbelief have been cursed by the tongue of David and Jesus, son of Mary, for they rebelled and exceeded the bounds of right.

Quran: Surah Araf:7:38 A nation enters Hill, it will curse the one that went before it, and when all are gathered there, the last of them shall say of the first: 'Our Lord!

Nations disobeying Allah will face a destined outcome. Actions shape one's journey. Disobedience leads nations to curse each other. Every nation who disobeyed Allah will be cursing one another; they will blame each other for misleading them into chaos. The chaos in this world causes conflict between nations and people.The signs are manifesting and truth research is impending. History cannot sway disobedience and has been the foundation for generations .Only Jesus will return to tell the world his place in this world and the defiance of those who did not mind him and continued with new allegations, only more colorful than the next.

The breeze is influenced by a combination of factors, including weather systems, thermal heating, current, clouds, and geography. Character properties influence the human's sail.Trust the process, life has reasons for everything. The current against the discourse can become the guide to a better place. Faith and hope will sustain a believer. Wealthy families and nobles have well-documented histories. Family descendants seek answers and hidden dues in mansions and properties. Occasionally in small shacks.All seek peace in a place where they willingly worship Allah. The obsession with this staged world blinds some and returns some to the truth.

Quran: Surah Maryam: 19:93.Not one of the beings in the heavens and the earth but must come to (Allah) Most Gracious as a servant.

While for some wealth is undeniable, for others poverty is a reality, but both families can have many family secrets passed down through generations. These secrets are often buried in the past, and only recently, for some, have they been revealed.

Uncovering a Muslim family's generational devotion to Islam is their greatest secret. Despite mistakes, worship continued as Prophet Jacob asked his family who they would pray to after his departure - all answered Allah. The legacy of peace lies in resilient Muslim families, not gossip. Being born in Islam is a blessing, but converting and learning late is an achievement. The only way to remember the Muslim families is through their legacy of seeking peace, regardless of wealth, and humbling themselves like peasants. "Salat" in Islam showcases democracy and equality.

Many stories remain untold, concealed with the departed. Learning Islam opens doors for families and converts to excel. Seek stories that deepen faith, not scars of evil acts - Satan's plan is to waste time and not complement life. Allah is not responsible for human faults; Islam is straightforward unless it serves others by sharing stories like the remarkable account of Omar bin Khattab, may Allah be pleased with him, consuming Alcohol was his habit before accepting Islam, yet his narrative illustrates his exceptional conversion.

The lack of Islam in households causes people to fixate on irrelevant issues, making gossip a central focus in their lives. The search for Allah emphasizes the importance of prophet stories in Islam, offering valuable lessons for personal growth. Instead of wasting time on idle gossip, it is more beneficial to dedicate oneself to learning and reciting (Surahs and Duas) verses from the Quran and prayers.

The enticing allure lies in witnessing the unsettling bursts of false rhetoric that undermine one's faith, urging one to make a primal choice to stand with believers and seekers of progress, rather than succumb to chaos.Curiosity leads to questions, but Islam prohibits gossip from spreading, as humans are never precise. The exception is a preliminary hearing for execution, where witnesses can mislead the jury and prosecutor. The final judgment lies with Allah.

Some people can protect their lineage while hiding darkness and exposing light. It's a great quality that remembering bad things is not worth sharing. Good shares are interesting. Lineage and material wealth both have gaps that need to be filled by descendants as the search for this mirage continues.

Many stories remain untold, concealed with the departed. Learning Islam opens doors for families and converts to excel. Seek stories that deepen faith, not scars of evil acts - Satan's plan is to waste time and not complement life. Allah is responsible for human placement; Islam is clear unless it benefits others by sharing the story, don't gossip. Omar (may Allah be pleased with him) drank prior to embracing Islam, but his story shows he was the finest convert.

Muslims learn about lineage to enhance themselves and their background comprehension.Non-Muslims also seek ancestral background knowledge to answer questions about their own backgrounds.

Converts from Islamophobic backgrounds exhibit exemplary behavior as Muslims, despite their pagan lineage. Allah can change the hearts of those he invites to his faith. With the exception of Prophet Muhammad's family, behavior and actions are more significant than lineage in daily life.

Sometimes knowing the truth answers many questions, and sometimes being disdainful of not understanding history is not beneficial. One could say I don't care about my lineage. There is a weakness in the source, and understanding history can answer daily questions. Knowing your true identity can empower you to achieve more. It can provide a sense of belonging and understanding of your strengths and weaknesses.

It can also open the door to new possibilities and help you realize your full potential. Allah grants wealth and lineage. He gives to whom he wills without accounting for distribution.

Wealth and lineage are also gifts. Believers' ultimate ecstasy is spirituality and closeness to Allah. Beat all odds of plastic frills in this temporal world but who says contentment with material bliss is not worthwhile? The one who is content and does not depend on a disbeliever for his livelihood is more blessed than one can imagine.

Muslims pray to Allah not to allow disbelievers to control believers. Sure, life has left examples and traces that the Quran and the hadiths have left behind. The Quran holds value in understanding the complexity of the verses, but some people do not understand no matter what is explained.

Could it be deaf ears and closed hearts with constricted passageways? Hearts that are open to seeing and unseeing the truth are the deeds of the soul when one is alone in private hours. Allah compensates all hearts as he sees fit. Time alters history as generations pass. There is no reason why he wouldn't judge humans in rotation and how they deal with each other. Some people have the upper hand and some don't -- Allah is the final judge.

Some people are ashamed to say they come from wealthy families and become commoners without any connection to their past. There is a strong correlation between lineage wealth and behavior. This can be a blessing in disguise as it forces them to work hard and strive for success. This teaches them independence and perseverance.

Furthermore, it can be an opportunity to start anew, letting go of any stigma associated with inherited wealth. It can also recognize that anything is possible with hard work and dedication. Opportunity in this world sees no lineage, but history only mentions those with this status.

This privilege is only available to royalty, academicians, and national leaders. The prophet Muhammad beat every historian and national leader. The Quraish were nobles, especially the clan of Hashemites which prophet Muhammad held his lineage but he embargoed his trials and served as a primary teacher.

He was an example for his people, having a profound impact on millions around the world. His teachings continue to inspire and guide people today, over 1400 years after his death. He is respected and revered for his integrity and wisdom.

This prophet's history is well documented as people shadowed him, inspired by his knowledge and actions. This includes his companions Abu Bakr and Omar Bin Khattab and many who followed him, known as "Sahaba" are companions in learning. Some who envied him kept a close eye on him. His history is pure, and nothing to hide from. It's a transparent book, and Muslims are told to follow his "sunnah" ways and practices.

No human in any family is worth emulating, except for Prophet Muhammad. Even emulating a fraction of his ways consistently can change the human discourse. Ancestral generations of some left a legacy of high quality, but improvement is necessary for everyone. Humans are interested in knowing historical findings, but learning from reliable sources is crucial.

The prophet's legacy is appreciated by Muslims and non-Muslims, except for the ignorant, who lash out of jealousy. He is not here to protect himself. Muslims love this prophet so much that no disrespect is tolerated. The only thing left to emulate is Prophet Muhammad's "sunnah". His ways and practices.

Emotions influence impulsive decisions; mistakes are irrevocable, but change is possible. He left a teaching emphasizing the importance of correcting mistakes over stagnation.

Satan takes the respite he requested very seriously. He is unwavering and relentless in his perseverance. Persistence pays off, but so does devotion to Islam for Muslims. As an example of an inscription that exemplifies Muslim identity, it embodies integrity, morality, and grandiosity of behavior.

If these traits are missing, carrying this name becomes a hardship for those who don't understand Islam. Muslims at times and in trials may not reflect the balance or traits of the "Ummah" his people he left behind. Demonstrating importance and arrogance while not following their faith, they identify themselves as Muslims. Displaying character defects for the public to see that they are Muslims is not a private sin.

When an identifier declares their identity as a Muslim, inviting others to display inappropriate behavior is not acceptable or productive. If it is a Muslim, there is no reason to blame disbelievers for pointing fingers.

It is their way of downing the Muslims who occasionally slip into actions that are not suitable for Muslim behavior. Continuous mishaps are a habit and delusion. The worst of Muslims not only sin but also invite and spread sin, playing into Satan's hands. Educating Muslims is a duty for Muslims and all humanity.

If two Muslims condone behavior not compatible with Islam, then fixing it to match the faith is most effective with repentance. Hope never leaves a believer, and returning is stronger than ever. What is more concerning is sinning and telling others or displaying another participant's wrongness instead of correcting them.

Islam does not live through Muslims, but Muslims live through Islam for those who practice. Learning is bliss from the right sources.

This journey of faith and knowledge is a never-ending process of learning and growth. Without understanding it is difficult to reach inner wealth. It's the wave and movement of this pendulum that form the basis of human intricacies. Knowledge is the key to self-discovery and personal growth. It is by understanding one's faith that we can gain true wisdom and insight.

Self-discovery is the only way to gain true wisdom and insight. Knowledge is power, but true growth occurs through its application.

To personify that all religions are the same is not true. It comes from conjugated minds exposed to a mingled source of patented script altered by humans. The majority of the Bible's history has been forgotten, and lies told enough times are taken as truth. When the lie is repeated enough times, it becomes plausible to believe. Especially if it is passed down through generations, one can uphold it as truth.

In the end, pretending becomes a presentation of how life happens in the biblical text and personal experience. Until one day, someone discovers the lies they were told wrapped up as truth. Allah promised to never change the Quran format under any circumstance or decade as humanity evolves. Whenever lies do not make sense, humans question what he is fed.

As a result, Islam attracts more converts every day. There are no deities in this belief system, no modified stories, and no one who takes on others' sins. The Quran consists of fewer pages chronologically, but the words are direct and precise. The book is suitable for all ages.

The Quran provides easily accessible and understandable knowledge. It also encourages critical thinking and believers to seek knowledge and truth. Learning to convert is impossible by oneself and "dhikr" talks of Allah. Dialogue sharing is a must in uplifting the understanding of concepts, stories and explanations. One who isolates oneself is not learning but trapped as conversations bring out curiosity, not loneliness.

It is a personal journey to seek knowledge and understanding of the divine. It is a journey to learn to live in harmony and accept the divine will. The journey of self-discovery and ultimate bliss. Socialization, business, and friendships are not affected by theological differences; distinctions clarify reality for many seeking answers.

Islam is pure monotheism. This is a fact. In Islam, adjustment to appease humans is not a sacrifice, but a downfall and deception by Satan that requires watering down faith. Predestination refers to the idea that Allah has decided and that the heart will shift or unshaven whatever the soul seeks.

In this era of survival, where man-made laws take precedence over divine laws, Islam's fascinating laws may be challenging. Despite biblical scripts sharing commonalities, storylines differ within the collision compound, where moral behavior and belief are revealed.

The Ten Commandments are upheld by Muslims, Jews, and Christians.

"Thou shalt have no other Gods before me." Jesus stands as a Godhead, defying the command.

"Thou shalt not make any graven image." Graven images of Jesus surround Christendom.

"Thou shalt not take the name of the Lord thy God in vain." Cursing is a characteristic of the eroded way of living.

As a practice, practicing Jews observe the Sabbath day to keep it holy. Those who contribute to unfairness bear the responsibility. Land exploitation and oppression continue.True Jews advocate for justice, not land.

"Honor thy father and thy mother." The lack of respect children have for their parents turns this world into a forgotten meadow.

"Thou shalt not kill." Senseless killings are joining the epidemic that is engulfing the world.

"Thou shalt not commit adultery." Fornication and adultery are rampant in many countries, spreading like wildfire and becoming widely accepted in modern society.

Belief in Jesus is crucial for Christian salvation. The merging of mirrors and cultic beliefs with a human deity is hard to comprehend. Jesus was a monotheist, emerging from Abrahamic faith. The Bible declares Satan's rule in this land. In Islam, only Allah is recognized as the sole ruler.

Muslims deny Satan the authority to govern his universe and refuse the new roles of bad demeanor assigned to his prophets. Telling the harsh truth takes courage and fearlessness. Fear comes from hiding the truth.

Muslims didn't succeed through lies but through learning, sharing, and telling the truth. Many people find the answer clear and choose not to follow the Bible, instead relying on their good morals.

Disobedience led to the exile of Jews. Many desire to own land, but in this society, some cannot own land by force, which violates human rights. Regions and superpowers supporting Jesus the Messiah seek help in the hope of salvation, but aiding oppressors contradicts common sense. Backing up what doesn't belong is not religiously or ethically essential.

Allah has warranted after trials. The righteous will inherit His lands. Each prophet sent by Allah worships one God and accepts Prophet Muhammad as the last prophet. Unfortunately, speaking the truth can lead to expulsion, as experienced by those who dare to speak up. Be the last to speak truth, even if you stand alone as a Muslim believer.

Bible: 2 Corinthians 4:4 The devil who rules this world has blinded the minds of those who do not believe. They cannot see the light of the Good News -- the Good.

Only Allah, the creator of Jesus, has dominion over this world; Satan cannot possess or rule here.Satan ruling the world would absolve his followers, as the Bible mentions his influence on Jesus. The Quran grants him only respite time by his request. In Islam, Satan is considered weaker than a fly and runs away when confronted. The Quran advises understanding and avoiding false temptations of enemies. Allah owns Satan and he is the owner of two worlds.

Allah, for Muslims, is the owner of this world, while Satan receives no forgiveness, only respite. Jesus, a mortal human, opts to pray to Allah rather than praying to himself. Jesus is a believer he came to deliver truth.

Can anyone have faith in anything? Of course, Christianity associates Jesus with Divine, while Islam recognizes him as a Messiah who follows Allah's laws. When truth is the response, they will leave, claiming they don't involve themselves in controversies. The clarity of Islam is unmistakable; it is not man-made, but owned by Allah. Muslims read and memorize the Quran as humanity and all that exists live on borrowed time.

Jesus' contrasts serve as a reminder of his crucial role in both Islam and Christendom. The contrast in beliefs surrounding a human prophet cannot be muted but instead becomes apparent through the decisions individuals make to believe.

Other faiths, as well as Muslims, have also conspired to defy Allah by allowing the whispering evil to enter their soul to replace good deeds. Muslims understand Islamic jurisdiction, despite occasional deviations. Particularly in countries where human laws are prioritized over divine laws. Drawing conclusions becomes essential for those who are too lazy to explore over time.

"Thou shalt not steal." Stealing others' land and claiming it is like a sealer and a healer telling them they are sending help; the help is to help themselves.

If they steal from their soul after knowing the truth, it's not difficult to steal from others. Defiance makes humans unlikely to believe deception can continue without a curtain.

People conceal their deceit from others, but Allah's vision is unobstructed. If there is no fear of Allah, why fear humans?

A curtain is the best solution to protect against evil and align with Allah's laws and truth. Christianity was the first religion to annul the commandments. They believed Jesus was equal to God. There is a belief that he transformed from a singular God to a triune God.

Very few Christians believe he is only the Messiah and not the son of God or God himself. Defiance in this sphere continues to make fornication and adultery acceptable.

Those who believed in selective scripture intervened; believers were called backward, and the subject was closed. Even if parents correct wrongs after a certain age, the evil company that holds the deceit clan shuts them down.

In today's technological world, the mouth and fingers stand defiant. Those who use technology learn and deliver. Allah's book has not changed, and justice awaits those who violate his laws.

While all faiths do not compel us to follow Allah's quotes, humans still have the choice of resisting or lying. Alternatively, you can abide by divine laws. The payback for defying Allah and elevating humans above him is horrific since Allah did not create humanity for that purpose. Besides the ten commandments Muslims follow, they also have five pillars of Islam.

The Five Pillars of Islam

The profession of faith "Shahada". Islam believes "There is no God but God, and Muhammad is the Messenger of God" is central to Islam. ...

Prayer "Salat". Muslims pray facing Mecca five times a day: at dawn, noon, mid-afternoon, sunset, and after dark. ...

Alms "Zakat".

Fasting "Sawm".

Pilgrimage "Hajj".

The Quran, as the central religious text of Islam, holds a distinct position when compared to previous Biblical texts such as the Torah and the New Testament. While there are shared stories with different themes, the Quran offers a unique perspective and emphasizes different aspects of religious teachings. It presents a comprehensive and final revelation from Allah, addressing the specific needs and challenges of humanity throughout time.

The Quran provides guidance on various aspects of life, including personal conduct, family relationships, social justice, and spirituality. By following its teachings, believers aim to attain inner peace and harmony, as well as establish a just and righteous society. This requires not only faith but also understanding and the application of Allah's divine laws. Through integrating faith and knowledge, individuals strive to align their desires with the principles outlined in the Quran, ultimately finding tranquility and fulfillment in their lives.

Revisions to the human script are imperative prior to the presentation. The written work of human authors necessitates editing and proofreading prior to presentation. Securing meticulous delivery and explanations of information. The mind articulates, while the heart imbues the book with sincerity. Editing persists irrespective of cognitive considerations and the pristine nature of the presentation. The Quran of Allah remains untouched by any editorial changes.

Allah allows for the exploration of my inner perception and the juxtaposition of Christianity and Islam, using suggestive examples and scriptural references in contrast to Islam as an Abrahamic religion, alongside the Abrahamic prophet Jesus, and an audacious truth. In my book, I offer stimulating comparisons between the past and present. The Quran was unveiled in its unaltered and unverified state, in sharp contrast to a human rendering. Therefore, the credibility of the Bible is in doubt, as it is a well-known fact that it has been subject to human modifications throughout its existence.After the ascension of Jesus the Messiah.

The precise delivery of my clarity opens the minds of those who seek to explore the Quran and Islam. This is done by understanding the disengagement with corrupt lifestyles based on delusions that are tempting but empty of soul fulfillment. Whatever one seeks will be provided.

Souls seeking purity and seeking to know Allah receive His blessings. Quoting the Quran and messages from other scripts elongated with examples of estranged society and pseudo-culture world views. Rewrites and corrections are human presentations of clarity and eye-openers for those seeking truth in the Quran and Islam.

The pseudo lifestyle and pagan influence of this society trap those who fall into it. Liberating Muslims who seek truth see both sides of the coin and appreciate Islam's purity. Growth is Islam, not decadence.

As Muslims rose to power during the European era, the world benefited from their learning and spreading achievements. It is those who are uneducated in this arena of learning in Islam who fall short and follow pseudo-pagan lifestyles mesmerized by lies and deceit. This thronged civilization does not count deceit days, for Pharaoh's kingdom was short-lived. Mummies hold the truth to the end of this empire.

The perfection of Allah's revelations lies in their flawless delivery and precision. It is divine revelations and perfectly crafted. The Lord of the world ensures that His message is conveyed with utmost clarity and accuracy. The intricacies of truth have been tapped into by previous scriptures.

Allah's words are inherently perfect. When a revelation is corrected or modified, it loses its original dimension of delivery and may lose its intended impact. Therefore, the final product of Allah's revelations is not only easy to read but also deeply enjoyable and profound, as it remains untouched by human imperfections."The Quran"

The words of Allah are immutable, much less my writings. No one can finish my sentences, therefore, how can mankind reorganize any segment of a biblical text, resulting in the loss of authenticity, causing some to aimlessly wander in search of truth? The coherent explanations are reduced to mere echoes of truth. If one cannot fulfill the thoughts of another human, it becomes impossible to accept any scripture at face value after it has been tampered with.

The Quran left no such questions as words of Allah resonate through a prophet who could not read or write. The syntax of the Quran leaves one in realizing this sound and the syntax can leave a person who does not speak Arabic in awe of learning this precise book.Perhaps my writings have stimulated the conscious mind with divergent perspectives. Monotheism holds a distinct significance that becomes diluted through subsequent additions, eroding its original purpose as the foundation of Abrahamic faith.

A conscious mind seeks enlightenment for those who find a higher power through spirituality, rather than organized religion. The purpose of the search is evident, as it involves the rejection of deities, particularly in relation to individuals brought up in Christianity who have rejected the narrative and modifications of biblical stories, proclaiming the disregard for the scripture and identifying as spiritualists. This transmissible influence originates from the domain of Christian beliefs. Islam remains undisputed and the Quran remains unaltered; however, the resistance among Muslims stems from the constraints and obligations of adhering to the vibrant and lively societal regulations.

The adherence to Islamic principles occasionally conflicts with the interdependence on this society, which is why Muslims deviate from following them. However, they often return and attend Jumuah, the congregational Friday prayers, at the mosque, even if they have not performed the obligatory salat. The rules and regulations are ordained by Allah for all Muslims. Laws can be prescribed, but enforcing their prayer decisions is not possible; they can only be explained. This exemplifies the beauty of Islam - no coercion, only education for the ignorant to make their own choices. Those who engage in prayer and hold beliefs in deities and mythology are not in a state of confusion, unlike India, which has a large population of Hindus who do not identify as spiritualists. It originates from the Western regions where Christian beliefs are rejected, which contradicts many who fail to understand the truth after the Bible underwent modifications.

The Christian faith is comparable to Hinduism in terms of the concept of reincarnation. In Christianity, Jesus is considered to have died and then returned as God through reincarnation. This is in contrast to Abrahamic faiths, wherein Abraham's prayers were directed towards Allah, not Jesus. Furthermore, the differentiation rests on the notion that a human prophet can undergo evolution or reincarnation as a deity. The similarities are unequivocal and cannot be denied. Constantine, who initially professed a belief in one God, eventually adopted Christianity and supported its accompanying changes. However, the lure of control and greed led him and the council, after voting, to alter religions and scripts in order to deceive people. All of this took place in Constantinople, also known as Turkey, which serves as a constant reminder.

The epidemic of greed cannot be monotonous, but the recipient seeking truth requires receptivity to the coherence of understanding the message delivered by a Muslim without hesitation. Those in search of reincarnation and the belief in returning to earth seek solace in retreating to Indian philosophies. Christians who renounce their belief in the singular, unseen God known as Allah have strayed from the Abrahamic faith and embrace Jesus as their divine figure, expecting spiritual metamorphoses akin to Hindu reincarnations, all the while seeking enlightenment within the pages of the Bible.

After engaging in a discussion about clarity, it becomes the duty of every person to discover their own theological path. Differences in beliefs can only enhance understanding and promote the exploration of diverse perspectives in Islam, which values truth, purity, and openness in both belief and practice. The choice to contrast Abrahamic faith theologies, particularly within Christianity, lies with each individual. One area of interest is the Islamic perspective on Jesus, emphasizing his role as an Abrahamic prophet and the Messiah, rather than as a deity or the son of God. It is believed that he did not undergo any evolutionary changes and remains alive, awaiting the timing designated by Allah to reveal the truth. This understanding is emphasized by Muslims.

Westerners are highly attracted to such dogmas, where "ashrams" temples are provided for free by some organizations and utilized by them. Islam declares individuality but does not entertain the possibility of humans returning to earth after living this life except when judged on judgment day.

Not following the rules has no literal meaning, except that Allah ordained the prescription to meet the needs of humans in every aspect, and "Salat" is a mandated affair between Muslims and Allah. A society that doesn't understand Islam as a whole is not to follow in the chaos by relaxing laws implemented in any decade.

A plastic society, however, colludes with colorful dogmas in the name of false rhetoric and independence. Allah is the only one who answers all prayers. It is human nature to bow to someone or something. Allah created humans subservient. Despite his arrogance, he is the servant of something, and this is not an understatement, but rather a statement of truth.

Hunger and chaos drive crimes to the surface, just like poverty in any society. Muslims losing Islam is the source of ultimate poverty.Whether a Muslim is academically educated, well-traveled, materialistically well-off, or outwardly healthy, the poverty no one can see is the poverty of the soul.

The material and physical wealth are obvious to the visionaries but the contentment of the soul with "Salat" for a Muslim is ultimate. Acquiring physical material and success in this world is not limited to Muslims. Material and spiritual wealth have been received by prophets, contributing significantly to human development. Money is not evil for Muslims; it is mandated for giving zakat and helps rotate revenue. Islam promotes continual giving and benefits for Muslims in all aspects of life, with Allah's support leading to desired achievements. Muslims don't emphasize the happiness of disbelievers who defy Allah. A Muslim can ask Allah for desires in line with Islam and find contentment in answered prayers.

As a result, the solar system one bargained for will affect inner and outer well-being. Hope the sun never stops shining and generating electricity.

The acquisition of darkness is a risk in a world of deceit, which bargains at the cost of joining Satan's tribe. Some return and some never see the light. But the glitz and glamor don't satisfy the soul. Muslims cannot be enriched without Islam. To understand Islam's enrichment a Muslim must know its sweetness. The only true friend a Muslim needs is Allah's rope.

Friendship comes with faith, responsibility, trust, and behavior. There is a lot of responsibility to this word "friendship". Prophet Muhammad Abu Bakr and Omar bin Khattab shared a friendship that man could not imagine. Having a friend in faith who still reaches out in all avenues, with reminders of Allah is a friend.

How can one be a friend who deters a Muslim from his or her faith? These implications and arguments convince others that all faiths are the same is a harmful belief. In light of the continuous differences, it is evident that Islam stands apart from other religions. But association with humans and all of humanity cannot be negated but the word friend cannot be assigned so easily.

But friendships survive without faith and humanity can count on each other. In contrast, a Muslim who directs you to Islam is a real friend. A true believer who reminds you of your faith upon witnessing a derailment is also a friend of faith. He reminds one of the balance one needs in all times of happiness and trials. In some cultures, wealth and lineage can mix, but finding a poor friend whose belief stands strong puts a lot more weight than possessions in the material world.

The affluent hold lineage and wealth for generations. Affluence and material goods are accessible along with lavish living. Giving relentlessly and sometimes hoarding as a hobby. Islamic law forbids hoarding. Long-term friendships are wasteful if they result in destruction or wrongdoings. And several invaluable friendships that have no meaning or advancement in spending time with humans as friends who contract the negligence of time and bad advice. **Best to keep quality friendships meaningful that lead people to Allah's way not away from Allah and believers.**

Poison lurks for those who see progression as setbacks when negative words morph into documented jealousy that comes through with unexpected words.

People without religious affiliation or behavior suddenly become advisors and haters in this episode of life. Differentiating virtue from evil becomes a distinction for those who know the difference.

Satan uses this tactic to keep doubtful or fearful people from walking out. But hoarding can also relate to people who don't benefit but add numbers as friends quality is better than quantity in all aspects of survival.

The friendships of genuine friends who see strength in endurance, stability, and communication leave a soul cleansed, not dirty. Those who sided with Prophet Muhammad left legacies buried next to him and became Islam's caliphs. Two genuine friends accompanied Prophet Muhammad in his faith, beliefs, and military pursuits, but Allah was their common goal. These friendships are rare, and when they occur, they are fortuitous if they are based on shared beliefs.

Prophet Muhammad was driven out of Mecca by Prophet Muhammad's people. When he returned, they expected revenge. Kindness was this prophet's hallmark, not vengeance. Most Saudis embraced Islam after he returned with confidence and belief.

Trusted people can become mortal enemies if their faith is lacking. When you need help, your doubts can become your enemy. The envy and insecurity of disbelievers can lead to prejudices about revenge. It takes a believer to walk the path with a calm, collected attitude.

A close companion of the Prophet Muhammad, Abu Bakr was the first to convert to Islam. As he embraced his faith, he became close to the prophet who taught it to him. Immediately, he accepted Islam. His passion for his beliefs led him to teach others. His love for him was greater than his love for himself. Throughout this affair, Islam upheld its values and shared beliefs. The bond between them was unbreakable.

The strongest threads were used to weave together friendship bonds between them because faith overrides everything. Faith friendship with a staunch believer is unbreakable. Even if they tested this union to its limits, the color wouldn't bleed. He married his daughter Aisha to Prophet Muhammad.

Marriage always strengthens bonds, and as a wealthy individual, Abu Bakr was privileged to buy slaves and free them.

Abu Bakr bought and liberated Bilal, a slave. Bilal had unwavering faith. He was unwavering in his loyalty to prophet Muhammad. He became a follower of Islam. Converted to Islam in its early stages.After enduring hardship, Bilal was released from slavery by Allah. He was a devout follower of Islam. Bilal Ibn Rabbah was the inaugural "muezzin", his voice echoing through the serene deserts and mountains of Saudi Arabia. Omar bin Khattab proposed the "Azan" call to Muslim prayer and the Prophet Muhammad instructed Bilal to announce the call to prayer due to his beautiful voice. He was the one who gave the Azan after Prophet Muhammad's passing. Bilal's voice trembled with sadness as he read the Azan, bidding farewell to the prophet.

The crowd performed "Salat" for "Janazah" final prayer with a somber atmosphere and tears, acknowledging Allah's ownership of the world, not humans. Muslims pray throughout their life, but the final "Janazah" prayer is performed by other Muslims.The prayer is attended by every Muslim who is willing to pray and beseech Allah asking for forgiveness for the deceased and also for those who attended. Muslims can request Allah to place the deceased in Jannah, except for Prophet Muhammad and the prophets of Islam who already have a place in heaven. The destination of arrival in 'Jannah' heaven is determined by Allah, not by Muslims. Non-believers who do humanitarian deeds will answer to Allah. Satan lures them with good deeds then leads them astray. Learning about Allah is top priority. Islam's teachings are continuous and everlasting.

Unable to handle the sadness of Mecca after the prophet's departure, Bilal requested Abu Bakr's permission to go to Syria and engage in self-learning. "Jihad" has multiple meanings. Allah elevated him from slavery to becoming a companion of the Prophet Muhammad and calling Muslims to prayer. Islam held his heart, and his faith was faultless.

Converts spent time with Prophet Muhammad. Unlike today, converts of that time didn't stay in their environment. Abu Bakr joined Prophet Muhammad in the migration from Mecca to Medina amidst growing hostility towards Muslims. His shared faith made him a loyal friend. His life was dedicated to Islam and its teachers. Islam was on the rise. Mecca's chief plotted to kill Prophet Muhammad, viewing Islam as a threat to disbelievers.

Allah revealed his intentions, allowing him to flee to Medina, while Abu Bakr fearlessly took his place. While people conspired to kill prophet Muhammad, he slept in the prophet's bed. He had no fear for his life. He supported his friend and prophet. Prophet Muhammad fled to Medina. Instead, they discovered Abu Bakr, renowned for his devotion to Islam and friendship. Humans can compare the bond between two men united by Islam. He was deeply rooted in Islam, with strong commitments and healthy bonds. They embraced Islam despite difficult times.

The faith of believers in those times was unshakeable. Abu Bakr became a devoted follower of Islam and Muhammad peace be upon him through friendship. Islamic women strengthened Islam's men by expelling evil with righteousness. They married and had families. The home is illuminated by women in Islam. The home of Allah's word has eternal light, even when dimmed at night for rest. Allah and his angels guard believers' homes. Disbelievers' homes are guarded by evil and darkness, even with the lights on.

Quran: Surah Zukhruf 43:67. Friends on that day will become enemies to one another except the God-fearing.

Quran: Surah Anfal 8:65.O prophet! rouse the believers to fight. if they are twenty of you who persevere, they shall vanquish two hundred; and if there be of you a hundred, they shall vanquish a thousand of those who disbelieve, for they are a people who lack understanding.

Faith in Allah strengthens friendships. It marked the era of goodwill among believers. Abu Bakr joined the prophet in battles. Some Muslims were weak in the battle of Uhud, but Abu Bakr remained steadfast in his faith. Amid the peace talks of Hudaibiya with Prophet Muhammad, Abu Bakr witnessed the Quraish touching the prophets' beard. Enraged, he drew his sword to warn him.

People held great respect for the Prophet Muhammad. Love and respect were his desired reciprocation. There is no room for wavering in exchanges like that for believers. The religion was spread with believers' assistance. Companies with unreliable sources, past activities, and evil individuals cannot be retained. They cut ties with anyone who didn't follow their rules. Islam was the driving force for these Muslims not exit.The stampede's fairness varies, but it decides one's destiny. They fought for an unjust cause, sparing the children, trees, and women. Animals in Allah-sanctioned wars have the right to justice.

The Quran states that believers are superior to disbelievers. Believers have unwavering faith in Allah. He is significantly stronger. The Quran repeatedly demonstrates disbelievers' lostness. Muslims can conquer disbelievers with small armies. Allah ensures believers have no doubts. Islam promotes learning and sharing, not isolation from teaching others.

Once they embraced Islam, they eagerly learned about this Islamic jewel. They formed strong bonds and ties between Islam's followers and the prophet through marriage. It wasn't a game for them. Faith frequently shifts lifestyle perspectives. The believers set aside prejudices for upcoming Muslims in honor of Allah and the learner. Islam comes first.

Abu Bakr's generosity was evident in the Battle of Badr. He relinquished all his belongings, including household items. He left nothing for his family. When the prophet asked him if he had left anything behind for his family, he said Allah would provide.

Abu Bakr stated his faith in Allah, mirroring his belief in the prophet. Satan couldn't overcome him. He appreciated the one who taught him about Islam and Allah. Believers' conversion speaks volumes today. Islam being at the top requires action, not just words.

Complaints of exclusion and marriage restrictions are common among converts to Islam. Are we reluctant or ashamed to embrace converts from the Muslim community? They refuse Islam's clear path, embracing diverse perspectives. Muslims accept and embrace converts, uniting through the acceptance of one God and the last prophet Muhammad. Allegations of non-acceptance are unfounded; some choose not to leave the dark threads behind.

Prophet Muhammad loved Abu Bakr, and many believed he was the chosen caliph after his death. He led the last prayer before the Prophet's death. When the prophet drew the curtain, he witnessed Abu Bakr leading the "Jumuah" Friday Salat congregation. He was prepared to go back to his creator. His family knew he was ready to go back. His daughter cried, then grinned.

Aisha, his wife, was puzzled by her tears and subsequent smile when her father returned to Allah. She responded. My father told me I'll join him soon. She died shortly after her father's death. The Muslim world was in chaos and indecisive. Losing the prophet was intense for Muslims, but Islam stood strong.

Prophet Muhammad did not announce the Islamic Caliph before his death. Omar, a prominent figure in the Muslim community, reacted with shock and anger upon hearing the news. He angrily paced with a sword. He threatened to kill anyone who says the prophet is dead. The Muslim community accepted his passing, leaving behind the Quran and the Sunnah. Islam fosters unity and love. The Muslim world was stable. Islam is invincible. It was a lasting presence. Sources that don't pertain don't weaken Islam.The Quran is a valuable investment for followers. Our shared strength and unity rely on respecting and dignifying this religion. Abu Bakr emphasized worshiping Allah, not Muhammad.

The attendees remembered those strong words. Muhammad is a beloved messenger, yet Islam, from Allah, encompasses all. Why would a Muslim abandon Islam and its teachings? Allah's word is everlasting. The crowd grew more attentive. His meaningful words moved many. The crowd needed action to grab their attention.

Omar extended his hand in a gesture of greeting and identified him as the inaugural Caliph of Islam. He ascended to the role of the inaugural caliph after being warmly embraced by him. The crowd collectively chanted "Takbir" as an expression of their approval, proclaiming "Allah Hu Akbar" God is supreme. With a formidable intellect and deep comprehension, he predicted the pandemonium that would arise due to delays in choosing the Caliph.

As soon as he stood up on the podium, he assumed an aura of prestige and unwavering commitment to truth, positioning himself as the esteemed leader preceding a Caliphate, distinct from the prophethood of Islam. The stability and adherence to the laws of the Quran and the teachings of Prophet Muhammad endured. The laws of the Quran governed Islam alongside the sunnah, emphasizing the importance of spreading the truth and ruling with justice, as exemplified by the prophet Muhammad. The world would forever change for those familiar with his absence, yet his words resonate with those who never had the chance to meet him.

Muslims who possess knowledge of this faith continue to educate and disseminate its abundance of wisdom, benefiting all of humanity, not solely Muslims. Due to the compassionate nature of Islam, numerous converts who encounter turmoil are drawn to the faith, while others seeking knowledge of monotheistic worship are guided towards the path of Allah, the sole creator, finding solace in their newfound spiritual home. Islam swiftly made its mark as the prophet Muhammad faced challenges in its establishment.

The velocity of truth outpaced its resistance by some. Concealing the truth poses no difficulty, as it was bestowed by Allah, irrespective of the trials. Prophet Muhammad built an empire without relying on familial ties, recognizing only Allah as the ultimate authority. By referring to himself as Allah's servant, he established a profound legacy that even the most powerful ruler or humblest Muslim honors with equal humility. If individuals have observed Muslims performing Salat collectively, they would witness the profound beauty and unity of humility displayed in worship, where one's head rests on the ground and their forehead touches the earth, exemplifying the unparalleled reverence towards Allah that surpasses all deserving. Observing the Muslim Salat in congregation is worthwhile, as the call to prayer Azan has the power to deeply resonate with those who understand the worship of Allah, the one true God.

It perseveres in creating opportunities for those in pursuit of truth to embark on a more enriching existence while spreading its uncomplicated nature to others. Individuals who have experienced anguish in their lives turn to Islam and discover the comfort they were seeking, while those who detach from these revelations require assistance from Muslims, as companionship serves as the most influential educator, alongside self-study and the application of truth.

Abu Bakr possessed honesty, care, and kindness. Equitable and knowledgeable man. He was the first Caliph, known as the Magna Carta. Abu Bakr showcased the legacy of Muhammad's government of the people. Islam, the first respected democracy, was honored by all. Islam granted freedom to follow one's religion, without allowing modification by other faiths. Allah's authority over man is upheld in Islam. Successions of outer influence divide the Muslim "ummah" people. Abu Bakr embodied the teachings of the prophet Muhammad in his rule. The legacy carried on as Omar bin Khattab supported Abu Bakr. Abu Bakr had no despair. His faith was divine, leadership fair, and governed by the Quran and Sunnah.

Islam is organized in its state and government. No modifications or interference with former legislation can be made to the documented rules. Islam may be flexible with certain clauses in times of dire necessity. It's a document and contract between Allah and humans, encompassing all aspects of life. Islam values integrity, justice, morality, credibility, and more. Omar bin Khattab, an Islam convert, was the second Caliph. He assumed Abu Bakr's position after his passing.

The story of Omar bin Khattab is fascinating;

Omar, a Muslim convert, went from wanting to destroy Islam to becoming a staunch Muslim. It is Allah who influences hearts. He came with the intention to kill prophet Muhammad. Upon learning he was accused of spreading Islam, his rage drove him to take action. Allah had an exceptional plan. Muhammad peace be upon him prayed for a powerful man to embrace Islam. Omar would be the one.

His sister- and brother-in-law embraced Islam. Confronting his sister, he let his emotions and anger take over. His aggressive behavior made him feel ashamed. He requested to read the Quran. The Quran changed his perspective on his previous protest. He apologized regretfully to his sister after being angry at her. He converted to Islam with prophet Muhammad.

He entrusted Prophet Muhammad with reading his "Shahada" testimony of faith. Their bond strengthened. He declared his allegiance to Islam. Omar endured and excelled through Allah's commands. Formerly an opponent of Islam, he converted and became a staunch Muslim. Despite his intimidating appearance, he was kind.

Omar pursued public speaking and literacy. Poetry was his passion, he generated extra income from his talent. His dominant passion for literature was coupled with humility and fear of God. Supported Prophet Muhammad in battle, shared wealth, and helped humanity as a Muslim.

The passing of the prophet Muhammad threw him off balance. Zaid with Omar's request to compile the Quranic texts he worked diligently. He burned out-of-sequence copies. The Quran is read worldwide in the order of revelations. He was Hafsa's father. Omar studied the Quran every day. All Muslims recite the same Quran in a consistent order, without different versions. Hafsa memorized the Quran and wrote many hadiths. Omar was Muhammad's father-in-law.

He succeeded Abu Bakr as the second caliph and ruler. As an arbitrator, he made no assumptions about the characters until confronting them. Omar's acceptance of Islam allowed open practice for Muslims. His strength and devotion were a compliment to the Muslim world.

They called him "Prince of the Believers" for being a staunch Muslim. He remains significant in many hearts and has a profound impact. One of his traits was being principled as a jurist. Believers granted him the title of Farooq for his justice-loving allegiance. Omar's name resonated as the "Prince of Believers" despite not being a prophet. His standout traits include simplicity, tenacity, justice, honesty, and dedication to Islam.

It would be disrespectful to not uphold his values by replicating his name as Omar. Mosques named after him are in Jerusalem, Beirut, Dubai, and Los Angeles. Many others are not listed. Investigating his traits and justice can reveal how Islam molds the world as a living legacy of Allah's laws. Following Islamic laws, he led wars when necessary for justice and spread Islam.

The qualities he possessed were qualities of justice, peace, and honesty. That sets an excellent example for both converts and born Muslims with his moral character that upholds Islam. He stood for truth, not hypocrisy. Omar conquered Alexandria and allegedly burned the library. This might confuse some. The accusations are questionable.

As a second Muslim caliph, he protected churches and synagogues. His actions remain probable to some but taboo to people who know his history. To say "there is no need for any book that disagrees with the Quran" Islam does not prohibit learning. Knowledge does not hinder expression or learning. He is unlikely to decide against others' rights.

If this were true, he would have also ordered churches and synagogues burned. He ensured the safety of expats, residents, and non-Muslims. Belief in everything you hear without witnessing truth is not possible for man. Islam emphasizes the importance of being present to witness before spreading falsehood.

Decision-making is essential for critical thinking. Achievers have enemies and fans. Having no enemies or fans is a sign of accomplishing nothing. Even friends crave substance. Omar possessed powerful character and integrity, with Islam as his guiding teacher and companion. They ceremonially invited him and gave him the keys to Jerusalem. He gave his servant on a horse equal time. He was tall and well-built.

Upon arrival in Jerusalem, his servant rode a horse. He fell into the ditch, soiling his clothes. Muslims were embarrassed by his appearance and the servant was riding the horse. He kept his word, showing strength of character and displaying Islam. His integrity is evident in numerous incidents.

As chief during Muslim rule in Jerusalem, he ensured peace. Jerusalem's inhabitants gave Omar the keys, and he protected their belongings and city walls. He received the surrender of Sophronia's patriarch. In addition, he got keys to the Sepulcher church. This church is still guarded and cared for by Muslims. His integrity made it clear that he couldn't have done anything negative. Honesty was his trait in his transactions.

Resulting from Muslim conquest. Arab dominance in Palestine was solidified. Greed is an incurable affliction. The desire for more. The West's obsession with the Middle East destroyed its historical lands.

Passion and faith are necessary to understand Omar's heart. Emotion and feeling are absent in the frigid heart. His heart was fully committed. Brightly burning passion and faith fought for justice. Loved by Allah, feared by Satan. Satan walked on the other side of the street whenever he walked. His devout beliefs protected him from Satan's evil whispers.

Despite his ability to scare Satan, he feared only Allah. Faith in love and respect originates from the creator and has no boundaries. Fatima the daughter of Prophet Muhammad asked a question, which was answered in the hadiths.

Hadith: Bukhari 3468.I asked my father, who was the most esteemed of people, after the holy prophet, and he answered, "Abu Bakr" I asked him who was the noblest of people after Abu Bakr, and he replied, "Omar"

His commitment fully engaged him to Islam and never turned back. He admired prophet Muhammad the most. He surpassed expectations as a Muslim, reaching new heights in life. Omar, the prince of believers, enriched Muslims' lives as a reminder through his accomplishments. Prophet Muhammad believed he would spread Islam to many countries as a convert. A company embodies business. Believers are most effective with others not alone, and faith is strengthened in the presence of faith. Without any shared interests, he couldn't fit in with them. He was the top performer.

Originally, my sole intention for writing a book was to focus on the second Caliph of Islam, known for his immense fortitude. My zeal redirected towards exploring further and sharing within Allah's boundaries.The man was stern. He joked sparingly, saw himself as ordinary, and avoided risks for himself and his family. He wore simple clothes and patched them himself. Islam would spread and expand the empire, as prophet Muhammad predicted. In the Mediterranean, Omar the Prince of believers maintained Islam and conquered many countries. Under his rule Islam flourished. Non Muslims did not despair; they were given fair rights and independence to follow their faiths. His passion drove him to teach and spread Islam. When asked to pray in a Jerusalem church by a Catholic priest, he declined and prayed outside.

He suspected Muslims might take ownership of the church after he died. He understood the importance of respecting others' faith, yet confidently embraced the purity of Islam. Despite his respect, he refused to compromise his faith or bend the rules for anyone. His ruling with Islam as his legacy led him to pray outside the church. A mosque named Omar was built in Jerusalem by Muslim builders later on.

Quran: Surah Baqarah 2"165. "The believers are stronger in their love for Allah."

The Prophet Muhammad's migration to Madinah led to the creation of the Hijri calendar. Omar conquered multiple regions including Iraq, Egypt, Libya, Tripoli, Persia, Khurasan, and Eastern Anatolia. In South Armenian Sajistan, during his reign... Over two-thirds of the Eastern Roman Empire and beyond. The man was an intelligent spokesperson. He offered jobs and accommodated office needs. He appointed officials and funded the military during his administration. Each state office fulfilled its duties under the administration.

He introduced military record-keeping and established police forces for civil peace. Trade with powerful government officials was prohibited if it was not in line with justice. The Muslim community faced the Plague of Amwas due to conflicts, around 17 years into the Hijri calendar, during Omar bin Khattab's conquest of Jerusalem.

Approximately 20,000 to 25,000 Muslims were affected by the plague outbreak. Caliph Omar discovered a plague in the Levant on his visit. He and his people returned to Medina.

He avoided areas affected by the plague. Abu Ubaydah had a different opinion. Ibn al-Jarrah argued that he fled from Allah's decree upon the country with plague. Regardless of disagreements and provocative comments that did not align with Islam and advice prophet Muhamad left behind he

535

turned around disregarding him. Abu Ubaydah stayed back and eventually succumbed to the plague and faced death. He held significant power. His reasoning was clear - he refused to lead his people into infected regions. Stay away from plague-infected lands. If the plague occurs in your land, do not leave. Muslims have historically taken precautions during plagues.

During the plagues in Kufah and Jarif Iraq, they wore masks and isolated themselves. Uthman ibn Affan was the third Caliph of Islam and a companion of Prophet Muhammad. The fourth Caliph was Ali ibn Talib, Prophet Muhammad's son-in-law. Their legacy continues to be told for generations to come. The three Abrahamic faiths have a strong connection to Jerusalem.

Quran: Surah ISRA 17:1 Exalted is he who took his servant by night from al-Masjid al-Haram to al-masjid al-Aqsa whose surroundings we have blessed to show him of our signs. Indeed, he is the all-hearing and the all-seeing.

With his own hands, Omar bin Khattab cleaned the Aqsa mosque. Romans used this mosque as a dumpster. Limited access for Muslims to the Aqsa Mosque is increasingly painful over the years. Repentance is part of the Muslim faith. Some people opposing Islam are unaware of its history. A glimpse of my book can shed light on aspects of Islam and Muslims.Omar (r.a.) prayed for martyrdom following his hajj in 23 Hijri, as mentioned by Imam Ibn Kathir. As narrated by Zaid bin Aslam, in the land of the Prophet (s.a.w) "ṣallā -llāhu ʿalayhī wa-sallam".

His desire for martyrdom perplexed people. Everything is achievable. Seeking Allah is all humans need to do. He died as a martyr. He questioned if the killer was Muslim. The crowd loudly protested "No" Abu Lulu, a disbelieving tyrant, stabbed him with a two-edged sword during morning prayer. He was attacked by an enslaved Persian Christian named **Abu Luluah. After** facing unexpected death winds. Following some suffering, he died after being stabbed by Abu Lu'lu'ah. Why did this man become the answer to his martyrdom prayers? Destiny is guaranteed and prayers are answered.

He was leading a congregational prayer in the mosque.Only the Muslim would understand the honor of martyrdom while leading Muslims to prayer was he was stabbed his destiny had a calling. The man who had a personal conflict and did not wait for him to help him. Instead he got angry with impatience and took matters into his own hands. He stabbed him with a double-edged sword and mortally wounded him. The crowd ran for the one who raised his hand upon Omar the second Calif. Abu Lulua took his own life.

Before dying, he urged Muslims to continue "Salat" and stressed its importance. Islam demands "Salat", not superficiality. The Islamic faith assigns responsibility to individuals. Associations require adherence to rules, not impulsive actions or violations. The choice to disobey is only possible within Allah's regulations. Allah's rules are prescribed, not forced. Judgment will prevail later and consequences are guaranteed.

The examination of the grave of a person who adhered or not to prescribed but unenforced regulations on this earth is a crucial aspect of Islamic doctrine, serving as a fundamental element in understanding a Muslim's way of life. In Islamic belief, the correctness of a person's answers hinges on their pre-death relevancy, that upheld the life conduct, iman (faith), and deeds such as salat (prayer) and shahadah (Islamic profession of faith).

Gaining knowledge about their faith is an imperative for a Muslim that must not be overlooked, as ignorance can breed arrogance and a mindset misaligned with Islamic principles. The way someone exists in this world will be evident in where they are laid to rest. Overlooking Salat is a nontrivial issue for a Muslim. It may appear inconsequential in the quest for a meaningful life and disregarding Islamic principles, but Salat has no exceptions. If Allah had not considered it of utmost importance as the second pillar of Islam, it would not be mandatory. Praying Salat is not an excuse for uncontrolled conduct. It aids in nurturing the heart of a Muslim, empowering them to become a holistic individual, and fulfill their obligations to oneself and the world, as inhabitants of this planet.

"Quran: Surah Taha: 20;14.*Indeed, I am Allah. There is no deity except Me, so worship Me and* establish prayer for My remembrance.

The dedication is astounding after being stabbed during morning prayers. He asked someone else to take his place and continue leading "Salat"ritual prayer. "Salat" stops for no human; it continues as life and death are in Allah's court. The angry man killed multiple people before taking his own life in this episode. Omar lived by Allah's laws. Due to his devotion to Islam and Allah, "The Prince of Believers" has left behind numerous cherished examples.

He asked Prophet Muhammad's wife, Aisha, if they could place him next to Prophet Muhammad. Aisha, his wife, said yes. He instructed them to place his corpse in front of her door and question her again; if she replied yes, continue. They did as he instructed, and both times she said yes. They buried him next to Muhammad the prophet of humanity. On either side of Prophet Muhammad, they buried both of his friends, Abu Bakr and Omar bin Khattab.

As he knew the end was near, he finished his last sentence saying there is no God but Allah. "Shahada" testimony of faith in Allah and Muhammad is his slave and messenger. He left the world with his beliefs and the beliefs of every Muslim.

These friends were unwavering. Those friendships are irreplaceable. Muhammad peace be upon him passed away at 63. Abu Bakr and Omar Bin Khattab both passed away at 63. They rest on either side of Prophet Muhammad. Their legacy provides lessons on life from devoted Muslims.

Gratitude is emphasized in Islam and most faiths. Certain stories have a lasting impact on someone's life, influencing their behavior long term. Requires strong faith and genuine soul-searching. Muslims historically mentioned the Prince of Believers when discussing Omar. My conversation would be incomplete without mentioning the past Caliphs of Islam.

The story of the king and his assistant, Shukar:

The ancient story shares the tale of Shukar, a servant whose name means grateful. With abundant faith in Allah, he expressed gratitude for all things, continuously uttering "Alhamdulillah" - praise be to God. He was known for his strong belief, and the king never separated from him on hunts and travels.

Their travels strengthened their bond. The king's finger injured during the hunt as he pulled the spear from the deer he hurt himself. Seeing no empathy from Shukar he diminished his appreciation for him. The hurt king expected sympathy and empathy from Shukar. Instead Shukar chose to say "Alhamdulillah" to express gratitude. The king was disappointed by his lack of compassion. To assert his authority, he imprisoned Shukar for not showing respect to the king. Shukar's fear was reserved for Allah alone, not the king. He thanked the king for imprisoning him, saying "Alhamdulillah" praise be to God for sending him to prison. The king was increasingly angry and did not want to see him. In anger, the king rode off to another hunt after wrapping his finger. The king missed Shukar, but he wanted to teach him a lesson by not inviting him. The king had a lesson in store.

Upon landing in a remote area, he encountered a group of people who seemed isolated and unfamiliar. They appeared strange, spoke a different language, and welcomed him as their king. They bowed to him in respect. He was happy to be greeted, especially after feeling hurt by Shukar's gratitude to Allah instead of sympathy. The people provided food and hospitality to the king. They planned to sacrifice the king as a ritual to their Gods. The king attempted to flee, but they were preparing him for a ritual sacrifice to their Gods. The primitive people screamed, saying he is not perfect for our Gods' sacrifice because he is missing a finger, and they released the king. The king rode the horse and exclaimed "Alhamdulillah" praising God. He arrived at the palace, ordered Shukar's release, and recounted the story of the primitives sparing him due to his imperfect finger. Shukar exclaimed "Alhamdulillah" in praise of God.

Shukar said the king's imprisonment saved him from being sacrificed by those people. He was healthy and had all his fingers. Shukar cried tears of joy. He said "Alhamdulillah" praise be to Allah he saved me by imprisoning me.

The king saw his strong belief and admired him. The king and the people learnt from Shukar and every one recited together "Alhamdulillah" praise be to Allah. Believers thank Allah in all situations. Only Allah knows the reasons behind events, which teach us life lessons.

"Alhamdulillah" praise be to Allah…

Story of Abdullah, once impatient walked outpatient:

A long time ago, there lived a man named Abdullah, who visited the camp of an old man with no hands, no feet, and no eyes. In the jungle's quietness, all he could hear was a feeble voice thanking Allah. A small light lit up the tent, and he walked up to see who it was. Abdullah asked the old man why he was so grateful to Allah. He was dependent on another human; he had no ability to take care of himself but he continued to show gratitude.

Allah has given me hearing and preserved my speech. He has provided me with a young lad who helps me. He has been missing for days. Please help me locate him. Abdullah, the stranger, galloped on his horse to search for the boy. It was getting dark. He wanted to help an elderly man. To his dismay, he found the boy lying on the ground. The young boy had passed away. In his arms he held the boy with sadness as he mounted his frail body on the back of his horse. Heartbroken and afraid of how he would deliver the sad news to the old man. He remembered the prophet's Yaqub story. As he walked up to the man, afraid to share the news, the old man said he knew the boy had passed away.

He repeatedly wept, seeking Allah's forgiveness. He emphasized that Allah is our inspiration and destination. He described the young lad's demeanor. He was calm and patient. A young lad faced challenges caring for a crippled man. Abdullah's heart softened as he prayed for patience. Abdullah witnessed the elderly man's final moments, seeking forgiveness from Allah.

Two patient individuals, young and old, taught Abdullah patience. Their possessions were few, but they possessed patience. He spent the entire night digging two graves, burying the believers, and praying for their souls at dawn. The elderly man expressed happiness and gratitude to Abdullah in his dream. Allah teaches lessons from multiple sources. Only Allah knows the stories that teach us patience. Abdullah recalled the journey that taught him patience.

Quran: Surah Baqarah: 2; 156 Inna lillahi wa Inna ilaihi raji'un (from Allah we come to him on our return.

538

Eventually, every Muslim will enter paradise with the belief in one God and Prophet Muhammad as the last prophet of humanity.But judgment will first serve the deeds in this world. Never conclude that being a Muslim doesn't mean committing earthly deeds. The shift and balance is continuous learning. Islam does not give humans the authority to determine who goes to paradise; that is Allah's justice.

Religion demands dedication to learning, whether through personal exploration or from an Islamic follower. Non-believers suffer tragically as their souls are repeatedly killed before death. "Rabbi ul-alameen": Allah is Lord of all worlds. Occurs 42 times in the Quran. Allah transcends description. He hasn't been seen by anyone.

Muhammad peace be upon him warned against turning homes into graveyards. Allah receives the "sujood" of true believers, not of those who don't pray to Him. Those homes are dead without "sujood" especially if it's a home of a Muslim. He grants permission for worshippers to worship him.The Quran is not in chronological order. Every revelation is presented as needed. Understanding Quranic scripts and comparing them with other texts is challenging.

The Abrahamic faiths share prophets not books sent by Allah. Islam is irreplaceable, but respect for other religions remains unchanged. Combining this with Islam violates its principles, as Islam does not compromise its rules. The Quran is the only book Muslims follow but educating in different religions in theology is passion for Muslims.The choice of worship is given, but consequences are non-negotiable; learning theology helps us seek balance and peace in the world. Muslims find peace with an unseen God, unrelated to humanity.

Humanity is improved by learning and teaching. Witnessing my words and faith as symbols of truth and comparisons profoundly impacted me spiritually. It stirred up a sense of familiarity. Honoring Allah is the key to beliefs, and guides dreams and manifestations of a believer. As truth touches the heart of those who seek answers. Human relationships do not influence theological differences. Expressing spirituality and closeness with their creator, gratitude and repentance become companions. Some admire and covet the ability to communicate honestly and openly. Informed Muslims fearlessly express the unaltered Quran.

Writing about Islam can indeed be overwhelming and humbling. It brings a deep sense of responsibility to convey the profound beauty and essence of this faith to Muslims and non-Muslims alike. Understanding the magnitude of the Prophet Muhammad's experience, receiving the divine revelations of the Quran from Allah, is crucial. It was far from a simple task; it required immense patience, endurance, and dedication. The trials and challenges faced by Islam throughout history, as well as the Prophet's efforts in shaping the Arabian Peninsula and spreading Islam globally, are a testament to the strength and resilience of this religion. Every Muslim has a duty to not only embrace and practice Islam but also to deepen their knowledge and understanding of its teachings. By doing so, they can truly comprehend the profound impact and significance of their faith.

Without fear of Allah, people seek validation from others. Truth is the sanctuary for those who know Allah. Islam's discipline is globally admired, with tears shed by believers and nonbelievers during "Azan" the call to Muslim prayer. They see Islam as a threat and combat it, but Islam is fearless. Trials won't lead Muslims to forsake Islam. Evil is weak strength lies in Allah.

The complexity of delivering the truth and balancing words necessitates the need for corrections, editing, proofreading, and concluding. No one can complete another person's thoughts. It's impossible to accept a script that has been biblically altered without a question. If it succeeds in making the mind believe its truth, its falsehood. Authenticity is diminished once the alterations are done. The effects are consistent regardless of whether applied to biblical texts or human writings. Mixing human hands with Allah's words devalues the delivery.

Humans cannot correct each other's thoughts. Allah, as the author, ensured that the Quranic revelations were flawless and did not need any corrections or editing. Precise delivery, not poetry, characterizes Quranic quotations in terms of syntax and melody. Exploring the Quran in my writings allows me to delve deeper. Whomever Allah wills, he will guide and allow them to talk about him is a privilege.

There are no words to convey the essence of pure faith, unhinged and unchanged by humans. Someone who worries about what others think cannot progress. As a Muslim only worries about pleasing Allah, all falls into place as humans are servants of Allah. By sharing my passion and words, Allah has strengthened my belief and curiosity.The path to connect truth with humanity starts with cultivating a mind and heart that perceive similarity. Researchers in search of their distinctive journey. Diving into life in pursuit of self-worth. I confidently share my thoughts and freely express myself. Identifying differences is aided by sharing intimate thoughts and experiences. The straight path to one God, Allah, is present in all belief systems and cultures.

Regardless of one's beliefs, everyone can achieve a connection with Allah. For those who prioritize pleasing Allah and seek to reconcile humanity, it is not a challenge to explain the differences between Islam and other faiths, especially the Abrahamic ones, as truth transcends categorization by no color but transparency. Expressing truth becomes easier without fearing human disapproval; the accurate appraisal should come from Allah, not humans. Therefore, it is simple to distinguish and uphold the truth of Islamic concepts.

It's the venue a Muslim knows: the distinctions bring clarity, not hostility. This is if I was afraid of what people would think of the truth and my presentation. I would refrain from speaking the truth and seek humanity's approval. I seek Allah's approval. Allah's fear is not concerned with human approval and thinking. There will never be a time when a human is pleased with another person. I aim to deliver the truth to please Allah, not humans, in my delivery and approach.

Individuals who actively seek validation from higher authorities frequently fail to acknowledge that those authorities are equally responsible to Allah. During times of trial, it becomes effortless to disobey Allah, who is both invisible to humanity and closer than any human. Appeasing humans becomes an obligatory action for certain individuals. However, those are the moments when believers' faith faces examination.Recognizing that humans are Allah's possessions, the awareness of His presence necessitates unwavering commitment to seeking His approval in every aspect. The conscious mind actively pursues truth even when alone. People will promptly shift direction once they become aware of the contrast. If it is the will of Allah, those who remain steadfast will experience the euphoria of accomplishment, and it will become their guiding route.

Hadith: Bukhari 7405: Abu Huraira narrated: The Prophet said, "Allah says: 'I am just as My slave thinks I am, (i.e., I can do for him what he thinks I can do for him

Allah's due is compensation with no expectation. Your thoughts about him dictate your obligations. Allah brings unexpected blessings when faith is strong. But when hope becomes tired and burdensome, doubts trap the mind, and things stagnate and falter in receiving. Your imagination shapes how you perceive Allah.

Obeying Allah's laws and having knowledge of him brings joy to Muslims. It has empowered me to feel pure happiness. Writing and expressing about Allah, prophets, and life experiences shapes and becomes part of life.

Praying and writing about him are both forms of allowance, ensuring pure thoughts to share his benevolence. It's not about words, but the inner being who comprehends the profound delivery. Making it simpler for those who want to understand. The ultimate source of learning is the Quran, the book of Allah. This world and the next.

As a person walks towards Allah, he quickly runs towards them. As life goes on, I've realized my talents and I'm grateful for non taxable blessings from Allah. Seeing Islam as the ultimate embodiment of my beliefs, I view it as a gift for my expression of truth.

Every Muslim who practices, follows, or hopes for a return to Islam. I have no reservations in stating that Allah provides without limit to those he chooses. I can share my thoughts and knowledge with you. I express gratitude to Allah for his blessings and hope our paths may cross by Allah's will.

Like all Muslims, I seek Allah's forgiveness for unintentional mistakes in delivering theology. Intending to serve Islam and promote knowledge, not hostility.

Allah orchestrated an impromptu gathering for me to meet all of you. In our conversation, I shared my thoughts, reviewed and referred to my scripts, and was subservient to Allah for the allocation of time and my delivery. Islam clarifies that when two or more individuals meet. It is never a coincidence. There's always a reason behind the meeting. The meeting we had was meticulously organized. The world harbors the most valuable treasures: health and time. The supreme delight is experienced by those who have knowledge of Allah.

The title of my book, "Delivery Is Power," signifies my conviction in Allah's supremacy as the ultimate fount of power. The delivery of the Quran exudes a commanding presence. The addition of Quranic references in my writings contributes to the book's title by providing a deeper understanding of the Quran's significance in empowering Muslims. These words reverberate within the title, conveying a profound significance, all while paying homage to Islam and its principles of veracity. Both words delivery and power give the meaning to my book as without the formative and true delivery there is no power with Allah's help the "Delivery is Power"!!!!

Kind Regards!

SALAMWALAIKUM !!! (PEACE BE UNTO YOU)

SUMMARY

My writing provides the framework for my conclusion. There are no limits to the knowledge that relentless seekers can acquire. Those who are blind to the truth cannot guide others who are also blind, highlighting the crucial role of valuable companionship, even if it exists only within one's aura. Your genuine essence manifests in solitude; Muslim assumes utmost importance for a Muslim. "It is an honor to identify as a Muslim". There are no misunderstandings, as all of humanity possesses equal value, but a believer discerns the message being conveyed by others in matters of faith.

The aim was to restore the untainted essence of Islam and awaken dormant truth-seekers through my literary contributions. The pendulum possesses elusive riches for the seeker. Gifts that harmonize with belief hold great worth. Muslims aspire for achievement in material, academic, physical, and spiritual dimensions. Achieving balance requires the expulsion of intruders through faith. A passionate heart understands beauty in physical training, spirituality, travel, and enjoying nature and art. The ability to balance life can be weakened without the other. Consistency is key for balancing daily Salat and Quran reading at dawn.To give to the world, one must first absorb its beauty within.

My writing lacks a predetermined structure; it mirrors the flow of my thoughts. The idea of mapping out how it should be conveyed has been suggested repeatedly, but spontaneity is inherent in my nature. I express myself as thoughts arise, rather than adhering to the prescribed rules of writing. Allah did not dictate how truth should be expressed; it flows naturally. Lies, on the other hand, require manipulation and plotting. My words are an honest reflection of my heart; I speak from a place of sincerity. The Quran is a collection of revelations tailored to the circumstances and requirements of that era. However, the word of a Muslim like myself is the truth derived from a deep understanding of Islam and the ability to express theological concepts with spontaneous thoughts. Immediate transcription of thoughts as they arise is my guiding principle.

Our shared moments are essential to the narrative. Individuals perceive words differently. The human mind is intricate and contradictory. Perception is a decision. Devotion to Allah doesn't bestow mind-reading capabilities. Regardless of beliefs, seeking solace within and finding peace is humanity's destiny after considering all perspectives is key to the road of success.

My comparisons of Islam, Christianity, and Abrahamic faiths provide a Muslim perspective on history and contemporary views. Fear of humans breeds silence, but fear of Allah compels honesty.

Writing and sharing this book improved my self-understanding. Open-minded readers facilitate open learning flows. Humanity prays to Allah for solace and seeks companionship to discuss Him. The truth is that the search for peace exists in every human, although all faiths are not the same. Islam is the only monotheistic faith with an unaltered Quran, making it authentic.

I believe Allah enabled me to speak my mind with strength and honesty." Alhamdulillah".praise be to God. His justice is unmatched by its pristine nature. Solidarity ensures justice, regardless of belief. Humanity has prayed to Allah since creation. Insha Allah, I will end strongly with you as I close the book.

Kind regards!

"We have without doubt sent a message, and we will certainly protect it (from corruption)."
[Quran 15:9]